Spyhunter

The Secret History of German Intelligence

Michael Shrimpton LLB

Spyhunter

The Secret History of German Intelligence

Michael Shrimpton LLB

Sometime Chairman of the
Immigration Appeal Tribunal

with a foreword by
Dr Robert Kaplan

authorHOUSE®

AuthorHouse™ UK
1663 Liberty Drive
Bloomington, IN 47403 USA
www.authorhouse.co.uk
Phone: UK TFN: 0800 0148641 (Toll Free inside the UK)
UK Local: (02) 0369 56322 (+44 20 3695 6322 from outside the UK)

Published by AuthorHouse 08/21/2025

ISBN: 979-8-8230-9443-6 (sc)
ISBN: 979-8-8230-9444-3 (hc)
ISBN: 979-8-8230-9442-9 (e)

Library of Congress Control Number: 2025917297

Print information available on the last page.

Dedicated to my parents, Peter Roy and Eithne Shrimpton,
and to my beloved partner Henry.

Contents

Part Three - The DVD

Acknowledgements

This book could not have been written without the strong support of family and friends, to whom I am extremely grateful. I have also had tremendous support from a team of researchers, non-blind peer reviewers, proofreaders, colleagues in the Intelligence Community and fellow authors, who have been generous with their time and comments. Only my learned friend Rafail Veli Esq. in Canada, has been bold enough to agree to be named. This is probably a tribute to the efficiency of the Royal Canadian Mounted Police, who do not tolerate German spies misbehaving on their patch!

I am also most grateful to Dr Robert Kaplan in Jerusalem, for his kind and thoughtful Foreword. He has an instinctive feel for the problems facing both the author and the reader of an intelligence history such as this. I can only respectfully endorse his recommendation that readers use their own eyes and think with their own minds.

If any one feels they have been left out they need only tell me and I shall ensure that they are named in the next edition. This is an intelligence text, and the black agency I have written about, the DVD, are very real, with a long reach. It is quite understandable that people do not want to risk being strafed in the early hours with Schmeissers by a 'Jerry' goon squad. I am sure that I should be grateful to the Cabinet Office, for sanctioning an illegal raid on my home in a desperate effort, *Spycatcher* style, to suppress publication. There is nothing like an illegal raid and book seizure to boost sales. I hope that Thames Valley Police enjoyed the book, even though it was written for the informed and intelligent reader, no offence intended. I am afraid that I am unlikely to get a ticket to this year's Thames Valley Secret Policeman's Ball.

Many thanks are due to Vanessa and the team at AuthorHouse for their excellent work on this new edition.

Any errors are of course my responsibility and mine alone.

Foreword

Michael Shrimpton's *Spyhunter* is an important book, which if its lesson is learned, should change the course of history. Its subject is the conspiratorial means employed by Germany to achieve its goals from its founding in 1870 until the present day.

War has been the non-conspiratorial means employed by Germany: - World War II preceded by World War I, preceded by the Franco-Prussian War, preceded the war with Austria, preceded by war with Denmark. In *Spyhunter*, Shrimpton focuses on Germany's conspiracies - pre-war, wartime, post-war and "peace" time.

In recent decades conspiracy has got a bad name, often confusedly equated with "conspiracy theory". "Conspiracy theory", a term which since the mid-1960s "has acquired a somewhat derogatory meaning, implying a paranoid tendency to see the influence of some malign covert agency in events", serves as a label to be slapped onto an alleged conspiracy in order to discredit it regardless of the evidence for its existence. A respected professor of history at a Boston university demonstrated this when he told me "I don't believe in conspiracies". Clearly this professor did not really mean what he said. As a professor of modern European history he has taught about the Dreyfus Affair, in which French army leaders *conspired* to convict Captain Alfred Dreyfus of treason and *conspired* to prevent proper judicial review of the case, and has taught about the outbreak of World War I in which a small group of German leaders *conspired* to launch a war of aggression while making it appear to be a war of defense.

A conspiracy is a plan of action to do evil concocted in secret by a relatively few individuals. In contrast "conspiracy theory" refers to a supposed conspiracy for which there is no reliable or even plausible evidence. The fact that the subject of *Spyhunter* is conspiracy will lead some, including, of course, those directly or indirectly in the pay of Germany, to dismiss it out of hand as "conspiracy theory".

Mr Shrimpton's book may have difficulty receiving the attention it deserves due to the fact that it is an intelligence history. In contrast with the familiar academic histories, which cite sources that are publicly available such as books, newspapers, archives, letters, diaries as well as interviews of identified sources, intelligence history relies on unidentified or partially unidentified sources who as a condition for communicating with the author, require that their identity not be disclosed.

Intelligence histories are relatively rare. I can recall reading only three - John Loftus's *The Secret War Against the Jews,* Cees Wiebes' *Intelligence in the War in Bosnia, 1992-1995* and now Michael Shrimpton's *Spyhunter.* Wiebe's work is highly respected and I refer to it as a source myself.

Regarding the question of whether the government of today's Germany maintains Germany's goals of the past or has given them up, Shrimpton differs sharply from the common view. It is easily understood that leaders of Germany would want others to believe that its present aims differ from those of the past whether in fact they do or do not. Awareness of this should help those who are interested in the question discerning discrepancies between the impression German leaders would like to convey and the goals which, in fact, they pursue; motives may be discerned if looked for with care.

I myself have written a book strikingly similar to Mr Shrimpton's in overall theme but quite different regarding the events dealt with, the time frames covered and the types of evidence employed. My book (*The Soros Connection: George Soros - An Agent for Germany in its Third Attempt to Rule the World?* with appendices at www.robertekaplan.net) is a standard academic-type history, fully documented with endnote references. When I wrote my book I had never heard of Mr Shrimpton, nor was I aware of most of the specific points he makes in his book (I want to thank JS for introducing the two of us). Yet in both specific points and larger conceptions, our books fit together like pieces of a jigsaw puzzle, each confirming the other.

Shrimpton makes the point that Germany has a high degree of control over non-German media, but does not elaborate on it. In my own work I devote considerable space to the subject. Our books complement each other regarding the time frames focused on. Because of Britain's stringent libel laws, Shrimpton makes sure that the individuals he cites by name as agents of Germany are no longer living. I, operating under the law of the United States, have written mostly about agents of Germany who are alive and active today.

German methods of cultivating agents of influence reveal considerable continuity. One case that Mr Shrimpton might have mentioned but does not is that of the American media mogul William Randolph Hearst (1863- 1951). From his earliest days in the newspaper business, Hearst demonstrated clear signs of being an agent of influence in the employ of Germany.

Confronting a book such as *Spyhunter,* the reader might want an evaluation from an outside, expert authority. As a cautionary tale, I report here my own experience with historians who might be presumed to be expert authorities.

On the way to the final version of my book I asked several historians of my acquaintance to read what I had written and give me feedback. One was the above-mentioned history professor from Boston. In a phone conversation several weeks after he had received my book I asked for his reaction. He told me he could not accept the book's thesis because he "do[es] not believe in conspiracies". At the time I did not have the presence of mind to ask him if he had read the book.

Another was a professor of history living in the Jerusalem neighbourhood where I reside. This professor is a slight acquaintance of mine (I once presented a lecture in a course he was teaching). Several months after giving him a copy of my book, I happened to pass him sitting on a park bench. Taking the opportunity, I asked him if he had read my book. He replied that he had "dipped into it in a couple of places" and that what I had written about German policy was "completely wrong".

A third historian to whom I had given a copy of my book was a person whose own book I have used as a source in my writing. In a phone call several weeks after sending him a copy of my book, I asked for his reaction. In a voice dripping with dubiousness he told me that what I had written about Germany was "completely wrong". Now I did have the presence of mind to ask if he had read the book. He replied that he had not. I suggested that he might read it and that I would call back in a couple of weeks. When I did call back, this historian's words about the thesis of book were about the same as before, but his tone of voice was now less emotion laden. Now I had the impression that he had looked into the book but had not actually read it (because of the poor quality of the phone connection I'm not sure I caught all his words and we were unable to continue to converse).

Even good historians (which I consider the three above-mentioned to be), can say foolish and arrogant things such as claiming not to "believe in conspiracies", or evaluating a book by "dipping into it in a couple of places" or by not reading it all. Particularly in regard to a book so against the ordinary way of thinking about Germany today, as Mr Shrimpton's is, the reader should read with his or her own eyes, think with his or her own mind. Do not shun the opinions of professional historians, but if you do get an opinion from one, inquire if the giver of the opinion has read the book and ask if the giver of the opinion is in any way a recipient of funding or other benefits from German sources.

As every American and British historian of modern Europe should realise, the historical profession has a particularly shameful record regarding its understanding of Germany in the twentieth century. From the immediate post-World War I years to the early 1960s, historians were in large part responsible for massive misunderstanding of the origins of the World War and the aims and intentions of Germany in that conflict, until then, the most lethal in the history of mankind. The failure of the historians to understand German actions and intentions in World War I must be counted as one of, if not the most important, causes of World War II in which Germany continued its enterprise with goals almost identical to the ones it had pursued in its first world war.

It was not until the early 1960s and the work of the German historian Fritz Fischer which described in detail Germany's aggressive aims in World War I that marked a turn to truth regarding the causes of World War I, the aims of Germany in it and the gradual, if halting, progress of discarding of the junk history which had dominated after the Great War.

The false history of the interwar years - that the war was the result of bankers, munitions manufacturers, international anarchy, secret diplomacy etc., or simply mistaken confusion (that Europe had slithered into a war no one really wanted) was largely the result of the work of the German Foreign Office.

The German government has always exercised a strong control of the German press. In Bismarck's day the control was draconian and obvious: wayward publications would be shut down. After Bismarck, control of the press became more sophisticated and largely invisible to the public. An example of this was the years-long campaign in the 1920s and 30s to deny German responsibility for World War I.

In that campaign the government enlisted thousands of journalists, editors and owners to produce a ceaseless flood of hundreds of articles a week over a period of years from virtually all political perspectives all pointing to the same conclusion. The historian Holger Herwig reports that "a random sample of the Weimar press during any given week revealed that it was not at all unusual for about three hundred German papers to publish between 1,600 and 1,700 articles on these themes based on material distributed by the Working Committee of German Associations (*Arbeitsausschuss Deutscher Verbande*, or ADV). The ADV was an organisation founded by the Foreign Ministry in April 1921 without public knowledge or participation...committed to spreading the Foreign Ministry's message to as many [press] agencies and papers as possible".

Both my own and Shrimpton's books point to a fundamental problem confronting democratic governments: the ease with which their politicians and government officials can be suborned by a foreign power. While Shrimpton mentions the role of blackmail in Germany's recruitment and maintenance of agents of influence, to my thinking it is ordinary gifting which generally serves as Germany's method of choice. Both can be seen regarding Ted Heath, the Conservative prime minister who in the 1970s brought Great Britain into the European Economic Community.

According to Shrimpton, Heath was recruited by Germany as a student at Oxford and was subject to blackmail because he was a paedophile who murdered boys he abused. I knew nothing of Heath's Oxford connection, although I was aware of Oxford serving in other cases as a recruiting ground for agents of Germany. Nor was I aware of any connection between Heath and perverse sexual appetites and practices. My own understanding was that the gift Heath received from Germany - a prize for "statesmanship" from the Alfred Toepfer Foundation equivalent to his salary for eight years as a Member of Parliament, and roughly equivalent to the Nobel Peace prize - was what greased the way for Heath. In either case, how to deal with the subornation of their leaders or future leaders stands as a fundamental unsolved problem facing democracies.

To return to the difference between a real conspiracy and a "conspiracy theory", the archetype conspiracy theory, at least in the English speaking world, is the one put forward in *The Protocols of the Elders of Zion* and promoted by German governments for several purposes over the past 100- plus years. *The Protocols of the Elders of Zion* is the quintessential conspiracy theory, the archetype for which the response "I don't believe in conspiracies" was an appropriate response, a response which represented the 'sophisticate's' response to "conspiracy theories" - a response which later spilled over to become a response to any suggestion of the existence of a conspiracy (exemplified by the statement of the Boston professor of history referred to above).

Those who fabricated and promoted the idea of the conspiracy of *The Protocol of the Elders of Zion* used the fact that there was *no* evidence for the existence of such Elders or evidence for their alleged activities as evidence of the infinite cleverness of the Elders of Zion who were able to run a huge conspiracy without leaving a trace of evidence of what they had done.

In contrast to "conspiracy theories", real conspiracies do leave signs of having taken place because they require communication between conspirators and, more importantly, communication between those who direct the conspiracy and those implement it.

The German conspiracies with which I and Shrimpton deal entail communications and actions which leave evidence of their having taken place. The task of researchers is to expose them. With application of a modicum of intelligence and effort, the task is not impossibly difficult.

The history professor from Boston might learn something of interest from *Spyhunter*. One of this professor's agonies, were the students who enter his course on World War I inculcated with pre-Fischer false history regarding it. An oft-repeated part of that false history is the quote from the British Prime Minister David Lloyd George asserting that World War I was unintended; that "Europe had slithered into war". Shrimpton writes that Lloyd George was a German asset. If so, both his "slithering" pronouncement and his pre-war opposition to Britain entering the war are understandable as ordinary work for an agent for Germany.

I have witnessed the continuing efforts of the German government to corrupt the understanding of history. One instance was at a small meeting of non-German students and professors with two German historians – one young, in the early years of his academic career, the other a senior man in the field who often acted as an "ambassador" for Germany at academic meetings and conferences abroad. The conversation was free and flowing, touching on varied topics and questions of interest to historians of modern Europe.... until I asked the younger of two a question: What is contemporary thinking in Germany regarding the causes of World War I. He replied briefly: "I cannot answer that" and abruptly ceased speaking. I witnessed another instance of the German government's exercise of control over German historians at a lecture given by one at the Goethe Institute in Jerusalem. Quite irrelevant to the subject of the talk, the lecturer included a lengthy savaging of Daniel Goldhagen's *Hitler's Willing Executioners* which had been published not long before and which the German professoriate had been unanimous in attacking. Goldhagen's book, the speaker said, had added nothing at all to the understanding of the history it dealt with.

After the talk, in face to face conversation with the speaker, I asked: "Are you saying that Goldhagen's book had nothing new or interesting to tell readers?". Now, out of earshot of others in the audience which would have included members of the German diplomatic staff, the speaker replied words to the effect "No, not at all. Goldhagen revealed the attitudes of ordinary Germans to the killing of the Jews during the Holocaust.... important information which we did not have before".

Both cases reflect the reality that German academics are aware to the threats to their professional advancement for saying the "wrong" thing. With that in mind I suggest that there should be a site where German academics (and others, including journalists, authors and editors) can write openly (if anonymously) without fear of being identified and punished for what they say.

Robert E. Kaplan, 1st September 2013

Preface To The Third Edition

How did a barrister get involved with Intelligence?

My entry into the fascinating world of spooks and spook-shops came about almost accidentally, in 1997-8. Before then I was just a poor, humble barrister (then my day job), lugging my wig and gown to Uxbridge County Court, Snaresbrook Crown Court and other *palais de justice*. I also dispensed my own brand of justice on the old and much-missed Immigration Appeal Tribunal, where we gave everybody a fair hearing before deporting them. I also sat as an immigration judge hearing appeals against refusal of political asylum.

My life was a humdrum, everyday existence of emergency *habeas corpus* applications, battles in the Court of Appeal, standing in general elections, saving railway lines, appearing on TV, hearing political asylum appeals and so on. Like many people, including a lot of historians, I thought that World War II had ended in 1945, which in one sense it had. I even thought that General Eisenhower had been on the side of the Allies in World War II and that Admiral Wilhelm Canaris, wartime head of German Intelligence, had been executed back in 1945.

Then I decided to buy a Bentley - just a small one of course, as I was still only a junior barrister. King's Counsel have a posh silk gown, which is why they are called "silks", whereas we juniors had mixed polyester and cotton affairs. That is why we were called "polyesters". Having invested in a small Turbo R, at a time when my bank manager was still talking to me, I popped along as usual to the Earl's Court Motorfair, an *ersatz* version of the Motor Show, to admire the latest Bentleys, Rolls- Royces, Astons, TVRs, Morgans, Jaguars, and Daimlers. Sadly, there were no Bristols. I glared at the Benzes and other European offerings, of course. As the proud new owner of a pre-owned Bentley, I wandered onto the Rolls-Royce stand and my life changed forever.

I had always been a petrol-head and first visited the Motor Show in 1975. This was a pilgrimage, as I had grown up in Australia. My then mode of transport was a 49 cc Garelli 3-speed moped, on which I had just popped over to Rome to see Pope Paul VI, a good man with respect. This had been courtesy of an invitation kindly arranged by His Excellency the Papal Nuncio in Canberra. Rolls-Royce had just launched their magnificent Camargue, with its shades of Lady Penelope's Royce (never "Rollers"!) from the *Thunderbirds*. Some hated it, but I loved it, even if it didn't have a cannon mounted behind the radiator.

I was treated on the Rolls-Royce stand as though I was a potential customer and resolved that one day I would be. This resolve was strengthened by my first encounter with a Rolls on the road - a very nice Silver Shadow (this was 1975 remember). She was majestically ascending Henley Hill as though it were flat, whilst I was negotiating my way down the hill in my overloaded Garelli, on the way to visit my grandparents. We didn't have many Rolls-Royces in Townsville.

Sadly, by 1997 Rolls had been reversed into Vickers, a decision about as sensible as reversing a Silver Spur into a bollard. They were in the process, as they thought, of selling the company to BMW, another curious decision. Vickers lied to me, denying that they had any intention of selling, in particular to the Germans. Call it a quirk, but I just hate being lied to. Nissan, Fiat, or Volkswagen could get away with lying to their customers, but not Rolls-Royce.

After the auction was announced, sending a shockwave throughout Britain, I came up with a new business concept, on this scale at any rate. It had only been tried once before, with Aston Martin. The idea was to have a Customer Buy-Out, or CBO. Tricky with Volkswagen or Nissan owners, but the investment vehicle (Kingdom Holding Corporation) of the first owner the newly formed, Rolls-Royce Action Committee approached, His Highness Prince al-Waleed bin Talal bin Abdulaziz, was worth more than ten times the size of Vickers.

Whilst the media endlessly patronized the British team, we were busy talking to some of the wealthiest and most powerful Rolls-Royce and Bentley owners in the world. The talks with His Highness, conducted through an intermediary, did not last long, however. Word got back to me that the media had got it wrong and His Highness had only expressed in buying *a* Rolls-Royce, not the factory!

For me it was a new world, as my Phantom VI glided to a halt on the tarmac besides a chartered Lear 35A for an urgent dash to Switzerland, or swept past the Bank of England to yet another appointment in the City. I made new friends, including some at BMW, whose charming CEO, Bernd Pischetsrieder, invited me to lunch on the BMW stand at the Geneva Salon. For the benefit of readers who are not motoring enthusiasts the Geneva Salon is nothing to do with hairdressing.

As I explained to Bernd, the British team had come to appreciate that BMW was not a German company, as many motoring journalists had surmised. It's *Bavarian*. We also appreciated that whilst not all the customers were gents, or ladies, as the case may be (this is a gender-neutral book, written in strict compliance with the Bar Council's Equal Opportunities Policy) the Boards, both supervisory and managerial, and the leading shareholders certainly were. Had Crewe Motors Ltd (the 'newco') successfully taken over Vickers (our real business plan, necessitating *inter alia* a strategy for the tank division and discreet chats with tanker generals over brandies in the back of the Phantom) the intention was to offer a seat on the Board to Bernd. We also hoped to tempt Eberhard von Kunheim, a very serious Bavarian indeed, into joining him.

Aftermath of the battle to save Rolls-Royce Motors

The battle for Rolls was lost, but there were Board level discussions about the trademarks and keeping VW's hands off the sacred Spirit of Ecstasy. VW's Chief Executive, Ferdinand Piech, was forced out. Coincidentally this happened after I ensured that key VW shareholders were briefed, in German, in Frankfurt, by a retired intelligence officer, over the private warnings I delivered to VW re their not getting their hands on the trademarks. Both VW and BMW altered their business models to retain manufacturing in Britain.

It was a tactical victory for Germany, but a strategic defeat. They exposed their main intelligence agency, the *Deutscher Verteidigungsdienst* (DVD), and their offshore Medium Term Note (MTN) high-yield trading programmes. To summarise, the British team made two interesting discoveries:

(1) German Intelligence had not been shut down in 1945 as the world had been told, but renamed and re-organised, with a covert HQ at Dachau near Munich, about a klick from the infamous concentration camp. Since then, Germany had been waging a covert intelligence war against Britain, the United States, Canada, Israel, Australia, New Zealand, Russia, Chile and Taiwan etc., i.e. the Good Guys.

(2) Most bank profits are made offshore, using esoteric, highly leveraged, highly dangerous (not least for the banks, as they found out to their cost in the Global Financial Crisis (GFC)) dollar and euro denominated financial products, which are purportedly controlled by the US Federal Reserve but are in fact controlled from Frankfurt.

For me these were not only life-changing discoveries but nearly life-ending. The DVD tried to assassinate me in 1999, using the highly toxic agent saxitoxin, of which more anon. My life was saved by the NHS, which had failed to diagnose a rather large hiatus hernia. This had the happy result that the poison was largely counteracted by stomach acid in my oesophagus, although my poor old oesophagus was left in a bit of a mess.[1] Court ushers who knew me always put out extra water!

'Jerry' has trapdoor access into most computerised NHS records but of course knew no more about my true medical condition than the NHS. Naturally, nothing was done by the Security Service (MI5). Apparently the episode was officially categorised as a 'spot of food poisoning". Had I been shot it would probably have been put down as 'lead poisoning'.

The episode had its amusing aspects, even if crawling from the bathroom in agony at 3 am to telephone for an ambulance thinking that I was about to snuff it, then collapsing unconscious on the floor, was not one of them. No one will let me listen to the GCHQ and NSA recordings of the intercepted calls between DVD HQ in Dachau, Correa Group in Frankfurt and the German death squad in London, but apparently they are hilarious. I presume they are something along the lines of *"Ja, Schrimpton is kaput, wunderbar"*, then, after the horrible truth dawned, *"nein he is nicht kaput, dumkopf"* and so on. With apologies to Sir Roger Moore (he came up with the line in *Moonraker*) GCHQ really ought to get the recordings into the shops for Christmas.

General Pinochet

Then someone - to be more precise the British and Spanish governments – came up with the bright idea of enticing that nice man General Pinochet, by far the nicest dictator I have ever met, to London. There he was arrested on trumpery torture charges. I was starting to build up my intelligence contacts by now. It seems that word had got around INTELCOM that 'Jerry' had tried to whack me in London. This enhanced my credibility no end. It was further enhanced when the NSA decrypted a fax to Peking out of the Chinese Embassy in London. It asked one Peter F., then head of the Chinese SIS for Western Europe (they have a poor sense of geography in the Middle Kingdom, which indeed is why they call it the "Middle" Kingdom, and think that Britain is in Europe) for authority to assassinate me.

Arrangements were made for a very nice Chilean two-star intelligence general who had scarcely tortured anybody, to visit my then chambers for afternoon tea. This social call illustrated the drawbacks of the traditional barristers' chambers for intelligence law work. There was a moment of awkwardness on the stairs as chambers' resident lefty bumped into the general, who was perfectly charming. My assurance that he was a very nice Chilean general seemed not to have the intended effect of calming her down, but there it was.

For the avoidance of doubt I have only ever tortured syntax. Barristers are not allowed to torture people (there is Bar Standards Board guidance about this). This is one reason, it may be thought, why so many questions go unanswered during cross-examination. Such interrogations as I have undertaken have been entirely unofficial and civilised affairs, conducted over a glass of Scotch, or schnapps, as the case may be.

My informal advice to the Chilean Government (this was just an afternoon tea after all) must of course remain confidential, although it has long been in the public domain that I was consulted. Suffice to say aspects of that advice were contrary to the formal legal advice being tendered to Santiago. I was proved right and others wrong, and I was cleared to visit General Augusto Pinochet Ugarté at Wentworth, where the general was under house arrest. The general, a charming man, and I, got along well. We had a serious discussion during a walk in the lovely garden and it wasn't all about the petunias.

Shortly thereafter I visited Washington, armed with a letter of introduction, to negotiate the general's release with *inter alia* those nice people the CIA. 'All the way with the CIA' is my motto. The CIA was represented, deniably of course, by another nice general, Lieutenant-General Vernon (Dick) Walters, who chanced to have been a long-serving Deputy Director and, for a short while, Acting Director, of Central Intelligence. The Agency sensibly set up a little front company, a travel agency specialising in Morocco. It wasn't likely to generate much footfall in Washington - if they'd chosen Ethiopia they'd have had trouble keeping the lines clear. It took care of business.

There were probably more bugs in my room than bedbugs in a French doss-house. Dick and I had our discussion over afternoon tea, naturally, in the splendid surroundings of the Willard Hotel's magnificent lobby. If you have serious business in Washington, you stay at either the Willard or the Hay Adams. The Willard is nicer and is only a stone's throw from the White House. It's also on the right side of town should you need to pop over to CIA or the Pentagon.

It so happened that a former National Security Adviser to the President, the late Dr Henry Kissinger, had kindly provided me with the direct-dial number for his successor. I knew it was a good number when the nice lady at the other end of the line's first question was "Sir, how did you get this number?". The White House were well aware of the discussions. Dear old Dick Walters was probably reporting back to President Clinton.

After these purely informal talks, which officially never happened, valuable guidance was offered to the British Foreign Secretary, Robin Cook. Sadly, he later fell, or to be more precise was pushed, down a mountain. HMG sounded out the Chileans about them applying to London to have the general returned on medical grounds. After that it was just a question of providing further valuable guidance to the doctors preparing the medical report.

By extraordinary coincidence, I chanced to drop in on the Chilean Military Attaché for a cup of tea as the first draft, in Spanish, of the medical report came off the fax machine. It needed a little work, although for the avoidance of doubt barristers do not draft experts' reports. There is however no rule against pointing out weaknesses in a report, or highlighting any issues which have not been addressed.

My first tangles with *al Qaeda*

I was becoming a 'go-to' man in London for legal problems involving retired dictators or intelligence officers. At around this time the DVD were planning a major terrorist attack on the United States, which the world now knows as 9/11. It was fronted through *al Qaeda*, using one of the DVD's brighter tame Muslims, a man named Osama bin Laden. His DVD handler was code-named Whiskey. Bin Laden had provided considerable intelligence on the *mujahadeen* to the DVD-backed Soviets during their invasion of Afghanistan. Most of the boys who were doing the actual fighting later joined the Northern Alliance.

Bin Laden's involvement in attempting to lift some weapons-grade U-235 from the Philippines had been spotted by me, leading to *inter alia* an airstrike, albeit just a small one, against the Joro Liberation Front, an *al Qaeda* affiliate. You are nobody in the intelligence community until you've given advice which leads to an airstrike, or had a satellite moved. As Dick Walters explained to me the NRO always kick up a fuss whenever you ask them to shift a bird. They rarely fail to mention the cost, or the absence of orbiting petrol stations.

All major *al Qaeda* attacks are preceded by reconnaissance. The recon terrorists are an advance party and are withdrawn before the attack cells move in. All this requires cash - lots of it - and safe houses, which in turn require more cash. Forget the "half a million dollars" estimate knocked out by the 9/11 Commission. Those sorts of figures may be true for a limited period prior to the attack. They bear no relation at all to the overall cost of a major terrorist operation, which might take years of careful planning and forethought, and do not include the costs of the sponsoring state's intelligence service. The pilot training alone for 9/11[2] required writing off a Boeing 767 simulator. Those are big-ticket items.

The cash for 9/11 was laundered through an Arab bank in London, which conveniently also handled the PLO's cash. There was discreet assistance from one of the quieter bits of British Intelligence, which had been trying to shut down said Arab bank for years. No one could suppose that a country as great as Britain relies solely on GCHQ, MI5 and MI6 for her intelligence. An officially 'retired' CIA officer, a brilliant former U- 2 pilot, who preceded Frank (Gary) Powers on the U-2 programme, who shall be referred to only as 'Bill',[3] got inside the bank. He got very close to the accounts being used for the 9/11 reconnaissance but was 'made' by a security camera and shopped to GO2, or General Operations 2, the German operation in London. It shares its headquarters with MI6 at Vauxhall Cross, not that most MI6 officers are aware.

Those very nice people the Mossad, who are great fun to work with, were also tracking these funds. Their man, to whom I shall refer only as 'Moses',[4] who was working with Bill, was also set up. As it happens this was done via Kiev, where *al Qaeda* not only had a purchasing cell but some government backing. Russia's very professional external intelligence service, the SVR, eventually put a stop to that nonsense. 'Bill' and 'Moses' were both arrested. I advised or represented in each case.

One advantage of being known as an intelligence lawyer is that you can cut through a lot of bull-dust when you first get involved in a case and the other side pour scorn, as they often do, on the idea that there is any intelligence angle. It is usually scorn, never a balanced view, very often the 'my cat is a dog syndrome'. "My cat has four legs, my dog has four legs, therefore my cat is a dog; James Bond is a fictional intelligence officer, therefore any reference to intelligence must be fiction."

Back in the late 90s I had to work hard to make the point that there was an intelligence angle. Both cases had their humorous aspects. Whilst the police and Crown Prosecution Service (CPS) were furiously denying any intelligence aspect to 'Bill's' case, their key witness turned out to be an Iraqi spy, who was also talking to the Iranian intelligence service VEVAK, coded material seized from 'Bill' found its way to Teheran and the CIA were busy dragging senior officers off boats at weekends, disrupting fishing trips on the glorious Chesapeake Bay (sorry about that guys).

'Mose's' case was dropped by the CPS like a hot brick after the involvement of the Ukrainian mafia was exposed. Certain illegalities on the part of a key prosecution witness were also spotted by yours truly, who promptly shopped said witness to Kiev, sorry, consulted with the proper Ukrainian authorities over applicable Ukrainian law to certain offshore financial transactions disclosed in the unused material. These are the bits the prosecution don't want to use, often for good reason. In an intelligence case, they tend be to be supplied in vast quantities, usually late, in the hope you'll never get around to reading it. The good stuff is usually at the bottom of the last box.

The cases also had their less humorous aspects. The coded material, which thanks to the complicity of the police and the CPS (which had been penetrated by Iran's VEVAK, one of the dangers of politically correct recruiting) had found its way to Teheran, led to the loss of several CIA assets. One of them was tortured to death in Evin Prison in Teheran. Next time a CPS lawyer tells you that he or she doesn't believe in torture or capital punishment you have my permission to snort derisively. Both 'Bill' and 'Moses' got back home without a stain upon their character, which was more than could be said for the police and the CPS.

You are either 'in' the intelligence community (INTELCOM) or you are not. I was now in. Leaving is usually not as easy as handing in your notice by the way.

Why This Book?

That's how I got involved in the intelligence field. Why this book? As I discovered, the problems with compromised intelligence and state bureaucracies are enormous. There are so many high-level DVD penetration assets in London, Washington, Jerusalem, Canberra, Moscow and elsewhere that by the end of 2010 it was almost impossible to make any significant progress anywhere. I had nothing but contempt for the weak Coalition Government in the UK. The feeling was mutual, by the way.

I had almost no contact with the Obama Administration, whose commitment to the Global War on Terror was lukewarm, to put it mildly. On that issue I found myself in respectful agreement with Secretary Gates, although we might disagree on the amusing 'death of bin Laden' narrative. This was presumably inspired by a hilarious old CIA training video, also released as a motion picture, *Wag the Dog.*[5] They whacked *a* bin Laden, who disappeared after the brilliant SEALs raid, unsurprisingly, since he was buried at sea (they needed a body). They did not take out *the* bin Laden, who as we shall see [6] was taken out by his own side, i.e. the DVD, in July 2009.

After years of fighting brushfires, I came to the conclusion that the problem had to be tackled at source, i.e. Dachau. Indeed I came to that conclusion years ago, but was unable to persuade anybody to take effective action. No politician or intelligence bureaucrat is going to do the right thing without pressure, sadly. There is a dearth of statesmen in the Western world, although in President Trump America may have a statesman of the Thatcher class in the making. There can be no heat on the DVD whilst politicians and bureaucrats rush around frantically trying to hush up its very existence.

The McCann Case

My frustration came to a head with the kidnap and tragic murder of poor little Madeleine McCann. I am not, I hope, naïve, but I really did not believe that Whitehall, Washington, the Vatican, Canberra, Brussels and the rest would play politics with the life of a four-year-old girl in the way that they did. In fairness the Good Guys at the Vatican, of which there are a number (including the late Pope Benedict XVI) did their best to assist. Madeleine's distracted parents were given an almighty run-around, with desperate efforts being made to keep the truth about what had really happened to their daughter away from them.

The case sent a shockwave around INTELCOM, which knew that she had been kidnapped by one of the DVD's brutal paedophile rings. Sickening overheads of tiny, pathetic graves clustered round the DVD's snuff movie facilities (the first one was tracked down near Toledo, Spain – after that the SATINT boys knew what to look for), where abused children were murdered by the bus-load, shocked even hardened intelligence officers. Deep behind the scenes they had a similar impact to the first photographs of Belsen. A picture paints a thousand words.

I have cried all the tears I am going to cry over that case. My rage is now cold. The DVD are going to be dragged out into the light and they will not like it. Nothing could be less relevant at this stage than that others in INTELCOM are unable or unwilling to come forward, or that verification of the DVD for people outside the intelligence community is not easy. Somebody has to be first, although in fact I am following in the footsteps of the murdered journalist Christopher Story FRSA, whom I was proud to call a friend.

Time for a break

Finally, after a dozen years of battling with flinty-hearted DVD assets in official positions in Western governments and intelligence agencies, crass official stupidity, deception, almost casual immorality and heavy pressure, including trumped-up Bar disciplinary charges (which eventually blew up in the other side's face), I was ready for a break. The best way to avoid burn out is to step back from the fray for a while. You cannot stay sharp for twice the length of World War II without a break, or as we lawyers would say, an *interregnum.*

The world never sleeps. With 3 am calls from the CIA, frequent calls to and from most of the world's time zones, some encrypted, and the demands of practice at the Bar, sometimes neither did I. When I stepped off the plane in Brisbane, Queensland, just before Christmas 2010, to start work on the first edition of this book I could have slept for a week.

A snapshot of my life might illustrate why I needed a break. In early 2005, after attending a reception at Heritage[7] and an inaugural ball in Washington the night-before, I had a purely informal breakfast with the Air Intelligence Agency ('he's an Englishman and he likes Froot Loops' [8]), where there was some interest in who had trained the 9/11 pilots. AIA, since renamed, were headquartered at Lackland AFB, Texas, but the good people there rack up a fair amount of frequent flyer mileage between San Antonio and Baltimore. I then picked up a rented Caddy, with the excellent NorthStar 4.5 litre V8, the design consultants on which were friends, from Avis at Baltimore Airport. BWI is the handiest airport for those nice people the NSA. In fact NSA seemed closer to the terminal than the rental car counters (wisely they have since been relocated, to the airport!).

Avis asked me where I was headed with their nice new Cadillac. Since this was the middle of winter, an ice storm was moving in, Baltimore is on the east coast and Los Angeles isn't, they had some conceptual difficulty with the answer "I'm just popping over to LA". Big Caddies have large boots, great for swallowing a hundredweight of luggage (it's always the files which add the weight). Road trips are fun, anyway.

They are also great for informal intelligence liaison, e.g. in gas stations. In America they usually have canopies (i.e. no overheads), somewhere to sit down, coffee and a good cover-story. "Michael, what were you doing at the Kwik Shop gas station in Abilene just off I-70?" "Just getting some gas, boys." "Now how come two Mexican intelligence officers in a Volkswagen, plus a Crown Victoria which we happen to have traced to the DEA were spotted going into the same gas station just before you?" "Guess they must have been short of gas too."

First stop was the charming city of Charleston, West Virginia, one of the prettiest states in the Union, except where Big Coal has chopped the tops off the mountains. I wish they would stop doing that. That was followed by the delightful little town of Bailey, Colorado, high up in the Rockies, on US285. Bailey will be familiar to fans of the wickedly funny *South Park*, the creators of which hail from nearby Conifer, with its friendly shops and banks. Thence to LA, via the scenic route - Wolf Creek Pass and the Grand Canyon. A quick side-trip to Monterey CA, near San Jose, for a chat about some missing nuclear weapons (only small ones - the three 15 kiloton (KT) South African ones which went walkies after the end of the odious *apartheid* regime and ended up in Iraq), then back to Washington to deliver a speech at the inaugural Intelligence Conference (INTELCON).

The trip from LA to Washington was also via the scenic route, that being the one which goes via Tucson (DEA - wonderful people, straight thinkers and shooters, a real tonic for anyone who has ever had to deal with Thames Valley Police), San Antonio TX (a little drinkies with a retired CIA buddy), Houston (courtesy call on the FBI, who had been having a slight problem with the Iranians, who had a crazy plan to smuggle one of the South African nukes into Galveston in a shipping container and detonate it, with a view to knocking out Houston and blaming it on *al Qaeda*), New Orleans LA (a small problem with sabotage at a Shuttle fuel tank plant), Pensacola FL, Fort Lauderdale FL, Jacksonville FL, the great state of Georgia and the Carolinas (a working breakfast with 'Bill' at a Denny's Diner [9]). Then INTELCON a courtesy call on the NSA for afternoon tea (sadly they only had Pepsi), then back to Avis.

I will never forget the look on the face of the nice young man at the Avis counter who took the mileage reading. "7,725 miles, you've only had the car 17 days!" "Well, you did say *unlimited* mileage." A retired CIA friend, who had started his impressive career in Laos, said he got tired just reading my schedule. The CIA didn't know the half of it (that meeting with the Mexicans, e.g., to warn them about DVD control of a drugs cartel down south and that the trouble was headed their way). Aside from an over-long haul in one day from Biloxi Mississippi to Fort Lauderdale (don't, at least not until they get that bridge fixed in Pensacola), it was fun, and a pleasant break from my usual routine.

Ground Rules

There are only a dozen:

(1) This is an intelligence text. It will be read by most major intelligence agencies and hopefully feature on the odd intelligence syllabus. It may be written at times in a light-hearted style but that's because I hate boring my readers and I like to leave my audience with a smile. We are in a crisis, but it's not serious.

(2) It covers a lot of ground. A number of topics, such as the assassinations of President Kennedy, Princess Diana and Dr Kelly, the sabotage of the Comets, the downing of PanAm 103 and TWA 800, and 9/11, deserve fuller treatment. Each of those topics would justify a book on their own. I am not primarily an intelligence author however, but an intelligence specialist. This book has been

written with serious intelligence purposes in mind - closing down the German DVD, moving to a more effective strategy in the Global War on Terror and increasing aviation safety amongst them.

(3) I am not a spy, but an intelligence specialist – an intelligence and national security lawyer, analyst, academic, and author. I may have roared around in Bentleys, flown on Concorde, been catapulted off the deck of an aircraft carrier and dated handsome men, and I probably have a greater familiarity with flying aircraft and firing sidearms and assault rifles than most lawyers, but I am not James Bond and do not pretend to be. This does not mean that I did not enjoy the amusing "Name: James Bond, Organization: Universal Exports" badge at INTELCON (thanks guys).

(4) I am not a conspiracy theorist. Indeed I have little patience with those who work backwards from a desired result, will not let facts stand in the way of their argument and fill their minds with nonsense about the American military-industrial complex, crackpot theories about Jewish plans for world domination, the Iraq War being all about oil, or whatever.

(5) So far to the contrary this book seeks to explode some popular conspiracy theories, put about in some cases by people who should know better (no names, no pack drill, but Sir John Chilcot comes to mind), not that conspiracy theories are a recent phenomenon. Many in the last century fell for the silly conspiracy theory that the USS *Maine* (ACR-1) had not been mined by the Spanish in Havana Harbour on 15th February 1898 and that the United States Navy Board of Inquiry findings[10] were reached in bad faith. The 'Top Ten' Conspiracy Theories of the 21st century appear to be:

   (i) Western governments lied about WMDs being in Iraq (they did not), and their absence, by and large, after the invasion meant they were absent before (a *non sequitur*).

   (ii) President Bush and/or Vice-President Cheney ordered 9/11 (it was planned long before they took office and the first either was aware of the attacks was shortly after the first tower was hit) in order to provide a pretext to invade Afghanistan and Iraq. Curiously both wars are widely held by the Toyota Prius-driving *bien pensant* classes to have been disastrous mistakes.

   (iii) The Twin Towers, were blown up by the CIA or the Mossad, because *inter alia* the melting point of steel is above the flashpoint of kerosene. It is, but steel loses half its structural strength at 600°C, creating the conditions, when allied with heavy damage to the external support columns, for a concertina collapse.

(iv) President Putin ordered the murder of Lt-Col Litvinenko in London. He died of peritonitis, not polonium poisoning, and self-ingested Prussian Blue, the antidote to polonium, which caused his death.

(v) President Putin sanctioned the murder of left-wing journalist Anna Politkovskaya, who had been pushing a conspiracy theory of her own about 'human rights abuses' by Russian security forces in Chechnya. She was murdered, but by a DVD asset in order to embarrass Putin. There have been breaches of discipline in Chechnya, usually associated with alcohol, but on the whole the Russian security forces behaved credibly in difficult circumstances.

(vi) The Americans mistreated detainees in Guantanamo Bay, including the Ethiopian terrorist Binyam Mohammed. They did not. The camp is under the jurisdiction of the United States Marine Corps, strict military discipline was maintained, as anyone who knows the US Marines would expect, and detainees were treated with scrupulous correctness. Binyam's genital injury was old, pre-dating his detention.

(vii) CIA/MI6/MI5 (take your pick) have been torturing Muslims in the War on Terror. Discounting waterboarding - which is used in training by both the British and the Americans - and whilst unpleasant falls short of any sensible definition of torture, neither CIA, MI5 nor MI6 have tortured anybody. In so far as Muslim terrorist suspects have been tortured it has been by their own governments, in accordance with applicable municipal law, and only in a proper case, i.e. with a view to gaining vital information to save lives, or prevent injury or serious damage to property.

(viii) The CIA unlawfully rendited terrorist suspects. Terrorists captured on the battlefield, including Pakistan, were rendited, but to their own countries with the agreement of their own governments. Some were dual nationals but it is axiomatic that the second country of nationality has no *locus standi* as regards treatment by the first. Arrogantly the British Foreign Office and Australian Department of Foreign Affairs and Trade have interfered on behalf of dual nationals but they had no business doing so.

(ix) The 7/7 bombers in London were suicide bombers. They were not and were duped into believing that their IEDs were timed to detonate 10 minutes after arming, hence the backpacks instead of suicide vests.

(x) The Metropolitan Police shot an unarmed, innocent man, Jean Charles de Menezes, at Stockwell Underground Station in London on 22nd July 2005. He was an electronics/explosives expert working for *al Qaeda*. Having rigged the timers used on 7/7 he was in a panic, as the 21/7 terrorists smelt a rat and withdrew the detonators from their IEDs, i.e. they were on the loose. He also designed the cellphone-based timers for Madrid, making him an accessory to at least two incidents of mass murder. So far from being unarmed he was carrying a special version of the Makarov 9mm semi-automatic, with integral silencer, when shot, hence the bulge in his jacket, which was mistaken for a suicide vest. Unlike better-informed forces like the West Midlands, the Met were still pushing the suicide bomber theory.

(6) There are three stages of intelligence, sometimes referred to as 'acquisition, evaluation and distribution'. This book is at the third, i.e. distribution, stage, i.e. what you are reading is finished product. You are NOT obliged to accept it and are free to reject it, sit on it until confirmation comes along or conduct your own evaluation. There is, however, no point asking me to disclose my intelligence sources or evidence, which in turn could not be done without exposing sources, in some cases to physical risk. Sources and evidence must and will remain secret. Different rules apply, some of the time, in courts of law but even in the courts evidence is routinely suppressed. British and American judges have long recognised the principle of suppression of evidence on national security grounds or in order to protect informants, i.e. sources. The Crown Court in England and Wales suppresses evidence at the request of the prosecution on a daily basis, indeed the Crown Court Rules no longer require a judge to inform the defence.

(7) You will not therefore find sources named in this book, unless they have died, and even then not if naming them might expose another source. Intelligence is not a game and loose talk burns up real people, sometime very good people. I am quite determined that no Good Guy is going to die as a result of this book. The Bad Guys will have to take their chance.

(8) Much of what appears herein will be new to readers outside INTELCOM, but that is the whole point of writing it - a revelation cannot be a revelation if it's already out there. The corollary of 'need to know', after all, is 'need to tell'. In the judgment of myself, and others, the electorates of the democracies need to know what is set out in this book. If intelligence is about speaking truth to power than perhaps it's about time we saw some real people power - no informed decision can be made about economic policy e.g. without knowing about what is happening offshore, as the amounts are so large they can affect onshore, i.e. real as opposed to paper, economies.

(9) This book is written in good faith and is not an exercise in deception - save for sanitising intelligence to protect sources I do not do disinformation, despite what might be suggested by trolls on the Internet. Apart from military deception to deceive the enemy in wartime, disinformation is essentially a Bad Guy tactic, or something dodgy politicians do, if that is not a tautology.

(10) As indicated, no one has to believe what I say in this book. That is a judgment each reader has to make for himself or herself, but do not expect secretive governments, banks or intelligence agencies to become forthcoming overnight. They will be aware how reluctant decision-makers are to rely on non-official sources, the principal reason for the success of Iran's deception operation over its phoney enriched-uranium program and why Western governments have acted as if Iran did not already possess nuclear weapons. 'Badge Syndrome' is a very real and dangerous phenomenon, which I have encountered time and again - because I cannot flash a badge[11] the intelligence I provide, may be discounted if contradicted by an agency source, without an objective or professional evaluation of the competing intelligence. A friend of mine suffered so badly from the syndrome he walked straight into a death trap and was murdered by a DVD asset inside a US agency. The Bad Guy had a badge and that was what mattered most to my late friend. If you are swallowing fake intel the one thing the Bad Guys will never, ever do is tell you.

(11) Being a member of the broader intelligence community gives me privileged access to information usually denied historians, judges, politicians and journalists, who generally speaking are in the humiliating position of being dependent upon controlled, i.e. censored, information. With distinguished exceptions like Lord Roberts, historians are mostly confined to published, i.e. open,

sources and do not publish genuinely fresh insights, although few are forced like poor Thomas Carlyle to throw away their entire manuscript and write a fresh one composed mostly of gibberish. He found out that we had bankrolled the French Revolution in revenge for the French bankrolling the American - a synopsis of the real history however found its way into what remained of the Secret Office. Judges are engaged in what is essentially a limited fact-finding exercise based on carefully controlled data, which is why their findings of fact are often suspect, through no fault of theirs. This applies particularly in intelligence cases, where material evidence is routinely withheld. Politicians, especially those in office, rarely think for themselves and are dependent upon received opinions and manipulated data from bureaucrats, including intel-crats, whilst most journalists do as they're told, which is why the global warming hoax has had such traction.

(12) I have signed the Official Secrets Act and my policy is one of strict compliance with it, but the Act only applies to official secrets. Many secrets are unofficial. The facts that Sir Edward Heath was gay, was blackmailed and recruited whilst at Balliol College, Oxford, by the Abwehr and remained a German asset until his demise are secrets but not official secrets, as officially he wasn't. I did not submit the manuscript of the first edition in advance to any intelligence agency for vetting, at least not voluntarily at any rate. My then home in Wendover, Buckinghamshire, was raided by Thames Valley Police (Britain's answer to *Police Squad*) in April 2012 and every electronic copy of the manuscript seized, along with my working notes. The elegant reason I did not submit it in advance is that it would have been not so much vetted as shredded, but it should not be supposed that I do not have unofficial support, not to mention protection, from within INTELCOM.

How can stuff be kept quiet for so long?

To those who say that 'this stuff cannot have been kept secret for so long' I would respond that it is surprising what can be kept quiet if powerful and secretive elites so decree. Consider the following dozen examples, amongst my favourites:

(1) Muslim elites have conspired to keep the origins of Islam and the identity of the authors of the Koran a secret for over 1,300 years. Officially of course the author is God, but we know that can't be

right, as otherwise it would have been written in English! The failure to understand that the key difference between Christianity and Islam is that our Bloke ascended to Heaven whereas theirs didn't, even for a night (admittedly a theologian might put this slightly differently) led directly, with respect, to a major intelligence failure by the CIA. They wrongly assumed that Osama bin Laden was genuinely religious. The contagion spread to the FBI, who asked me what I thought bin Laden was up to in Macau. They had difficulty with respect in grasping the concept that he might have popped into the casino for a flutter and around to his tailors (they weren't very good by the way - there are better tailors in Hong Kong, but HK was a bit too visible) to be measured for a couple of new suits, especially as he had lost a bit of weight at Tora Bora. The jihadi outfits were strictly for the punters. When a friend of mine popped round to the old safe house for lunch the chap was wearing a business suit, probably one of the two he picked up in Macau.

(2) Prince John agreed to be a vassal of King Philip II of France and the kidnap of his just and illustrious brother King Richard the Lionheart was set up by the French. To this day schoolchildren are taught (if Good King Richard, who by the way killed a lot of Muslims in an earlier phase of the Clash of Civilizations (only bad ones, of course) is mentioned at all) that the kidnap was done purely for cash. It's as though someone decided one morning it would be a good idea to nip out and kidnap the King of England. You are advised not to try it at home, but should you decide to organize the kidnap of a king you will find that it is a fairly major undertaking.

(3) The Black Death, which for centuries was blamed on peripatetic rats, or infected people coming down with a touch of Bubonic Plague and deciding to visit their relatives (if you are unfortunate enough to come down with the Bubonic Plague you may find that the last thing you will want to do is travel, let alone in a horse and cart on an unmade road, roads in the Middle Ages being even bumpier than the M1 is today), was in fact spread deliberately. It had far more to do with the Byzantine internal politics, as it were, of the Vatican than the travel requirements of rats or plague victims.

(4) The ill-fated and tragic Children's Crusade was supposed to have struck a series of misfortunes, put down to a lack of planning and really bad luck, but was in fact shopped by the Bad Guys at

the Vatican, the politics of which are complex. You have to know whether you're talking to the Good Guys or the Jesuits. The Bad Guys struck a deal with the Muslims for the unfortunate young people to be sold into slavery, mostly of the very nasty, sexual sort, in order to protect Muslim control of the Holy Land.

(5) King Charles 1, like King John a bad King, was also a vassal of the King of France, as indeed were most Scottish monarchs, including that wretched woman Mary Queen of Scots. Oliver Cromwell, who started out as a Good Guy but went off a bit towards the end, only sanctioned the King's execution (at one point he was willing to restore Him to the Throne) after his intelligence service, run by a nice chap called Hampden, found this out.

(6) Both the Old and Young Pretenders were bankrolled by the French, as a strategic response to the threat posed to France by the Act of Union. The French sponsored the 1798 rebellion in Ireland for much the same reason, in a desperate effort to stop the Union between Britain and Ireland. To this day these rebellions are portrayed by historians and the media as spontaneous uprisings by 'oppressed' Scots or Irishmen, as the case may be.

(7) Lord North was as bent as a three-bob note and worked for the French, who later sponsored the Stamp Act in a cynical and successful attempt to provoke Britain's American colonies into rebellion. President Washington, to his everlasting credit, booted the French out, hence the Quasi-War. To this day American schoolkids are taught that nice old King George III was a nasty tyrant who was in charge of His government's policy. The government were in fact controlled by the elected Prime Minister (albeit with a less than universal franchise), who in turn was controlled by the French.

(8) The Zulus, who are still popularly supposed to have been in charge of their military strategy in the Zulu Wars, were in fact advised by German military advisers and intelligence officers, as part of Germany's drive to control Africa. Over a century later this was thought sufficiently sensitive to have persuaded certain senior South African politicians and intelligence officers, who should have known better, that they were justified in acceding to a German request to assassinate the distinguished British historian of the Zulu Wars, David Rattray. David was working for British Intelligence. He was allegedly murdered in a robbery in which nothing except computer files was stolen - thankfully they missed the back-up flash-drives.

(9) The Imperial General Staff and the brilliant Field Marshal Lord Haig in particular are still blamed for the high cost of victory in the great Somme Offensive. In fact David Lloyd George was a German spy and had tipped off 'the Hun', who had time to deepen and harden his trenches against the expected artillery bombardment, which was designed to save casualties. The Royal Engineers, who know a bit about fortification, appreciated after inspecting captured enemy trenches that 'Harry Hun' must have had foreknowledge of the British offensive and so advised the C-in-C. When these facts were finally appreciated by the Conservative and Unionist Party, who were briefed in at my old club as it happens, they pulled the plug on the Coalition Government, which was about as pointless as the 2010 one. Most histories of the Great War are about as factual as *Blackadder Goes Forth* [12] albeit not as funny. Ironically, the champagne-quaffing men in charge who were too gutless to show their faces at the Front were Liberal Party politicians, not generals, most if not all of whom had seen combat. Lloyd George, who didn't know one end of a rifle from another and had never served in the Forces, let alone seen combat, was no more a military genius than Karl Marx was a Marxist or I am a violinist.

(10) The reason most U-Boat sinkings in World War II are clustered around coasts is because until genuine submarines (i.e. the Type XXI) came along in 1944 'Jerry's' U-Boat fleet was essentially a coastal, not ocean-going, fleet of submersibles. There is a large cluster around Ireland because a large part of the U-Boat fleet was based on Ireland's west coast, with neutral-flagged freighters acting as submarine tenders. MI6, which was run by a German spy for the whole of World War II, were able to suppress this vital intelligence from Churchill and the Admiralty for the duration of the Battle of the Atlantic and long after. The Irish Free State government were fully in the loop and Irish 'neutrality' was a hollow sham.

(11) Even after the passage of 70 years the American people cannot be told, officially at any rate, that the reason the Manhattan Project was called the Manhattan Project is because the target was Manhattan, which would have struck a severe blow at American morale, not to mention her economy. The top German, 'atom spies' were of course Albert Einstein, or as he is known in INTELCOM, 'von' Einstein, and Robert Oppenheimer (ditto). Fuchs and the others all worked for Germany, not Russia, but Russia sounded better.

(12) Large sections of the media, including the amusingly inaccurate (although in fairness the producers gave alert viewers several clues that their version of history was dodgy, like having Ambassador Kennedy running around in 1941 in a 1953 Bentley and B-17Es flying in 1939, nearly three years before that model first flew[13]) Canadian mini-series *The Kennedys* will still have you believe Lee Harvey Oswald assassinated President Kennedy. Oswald never fired a shot - unsurprisingly, since in an oversight he had not taken a rifle to work in the Texas School Book Depository that day (presumably they had a severe policy on returning books late). 'His' rifle was not fired at all that day, which helps explain why there is no ballistics match with the fatal rounds. When handed in to the absurd Warren Commission it did not even have an ammunition clip, without which rapid fire on the Mannlicher-Carcano[14] 6.5mm is impossible, yet photos of it minus clip have been reprinted uncritically in thousands of newspapers and hundreds of books and you will still find people on the Internet pushing a photo in the which the clip makes a mysterious reappearance.

Keeping people in the dark is the job of politicians, narrative historians, judges, bankers and the media. Getting at the truth is the job of INTELCOM. You do not have to accept what is said here, indeed you should always apply your own mind to anything you are told and compare new information to known facts. Either intelligence is accurate or it isn't. If it is it will dovetail with other hard data. Most people know the truth when they see it however and sometimes one source is all you get. You can die waiting for that second source. Sometimes - as with the intelligence in 1916 on Lloyd George working for the Germans – other people die whilst you sit on your bottom waiting for that second source.

If you are as intelligence illiterate as 'Colonel' Crittenden, the RAF Group Captain in the hilarious American television comedy *Hogan's Heroes*,[15] (played superbly by that fine character actor Bernard Fox), whose grasp of intelligence was even weaker than the producers' grasp of RAF ranks,[16] or Lord Justice Scott Baker (no offence intended) then this book is not for you. This is a book for thinking readers, which is why you will not see too many journalists or politicians reading it.

Smart generals want to know what lies over the hill and therefore value both intelligence and reconnaissance. Dumb generals charge up the hill, over it and into an ambush, which is why they usually don't get a second star. In fairness to both the British and American armies the idiots are usually weeded out before they get that second started and started making mistakes which get thousands killed, not hundreds. Sadly, the political selection process is not as sophisticated as the military's and plenty of idiots make it to the top. Even if they are not idiots few politicians are able to handle intelligence. They tend to suffer badly from Badge Syndrome and inflated egos. Some of them can be very hard work indeed.

I have met William Hague, the former British Foreign Secretary, a couple of times over the years. In 1997 I was asked to ring wavering MPs on behalf of his leadership campaign when I was still officially in the Labour Party (I was happy to do so). The man didn't even respond when I offered to brief him in after he was appointed Foreign Secretary.

It probably wouldn't have made much difference anyway, as all it would have taken for my advice to be disregarded would be to have had the Permanent Secretary or Chief of MI6 contradict it. Neither was apparently aware of, or prepared to acknowledge the existence of, the DVD, from which it follows with respect that any British Government they were advising, was going to be pretty easily out-manoeuvered by them.

Thus no one made any effort in 2011 to protect Gaddafi, after his capture, from assassination by the DVD, who took him out, for the blindingly obvious reason that he was a DVD asset, installed by the Germans in 1969. 'Blind Freddy' - if he knew about the DVD that is - could see that 'Jerry' would want to retain control of a major oil- producing state and would manoeuvre to install a replacement client, in this case *al Qaeda*. It was like watching a slow train crash, but there it is. You can only lead a horse to water, you can't make it drink. If you discount the human cost the British, French, Italian and Obama Administration blundering over Libya was quite comical really. There were better-informed Bedouins in tents. I got on with writing the first edition of this book, or since I was Down Under, went down the beach. Syria was a predictable shambles as well.

The disparate episodes described in this book are linked by a common theme, the machinations of the 'Wily Hun'. There is a reason for that - the Germans are the Bad Guys. If they do not wish to be described as the Bad Guys then they have to shut down the DVD, stop sponsoring terrorism and cease their endless political and economic interference in other people's countries.

This does not mean that Allied intelligence agencies are not capable of getting up to mischief of their own accord, that is to say mischief without the intervention of a German penetration asset seeking to embarrass them, but most of what the Good Guys do meets the test laid down by one of GCHQ's better directors with respect, Sir David Omand.[17] We can defend it if it gets out, which it surely will. Assassinations, starting wars, sabotage of ships and aircraft in peacetime, blackmail and bribery of politicians, mass-murder and genocide are basically German things.

I am no more anti-German than dear old Bomber Harris. If I occasionally sound a trifle anti-German it is not because I am opposed to the Germans, but what they, specifically the DVD, have been up to. In most cases this is without the approval of the weak German federal government and is in every case without the knowledge or consent of the German people. In most cases the people of Germany, who are basically quite decent, would be appalled, which is why the DVD takes great care to hide its activities from them. Of course there are nice Germans - I have met at least a dozen, including a Generaloberst,[18] and I am sure there are more. The tragedy of Germany is that the nice Germans have never been in control.

For the avoidance of doubt I do not pretend to have all the answers, nor, contrary to the lies and rumours spread by my competitors[19] am I a know-all, although I may be a 'know-a-lot'. I am not perfect, although I am working hard to correct my major faults - excessive modesty, natural shyness and too great an inclination to hide my lights under a bushel.

There is no point asking me if there is life after death, e.g. You'll have to ask me after I'm dead, when I would be in a position to give a more definitive answer. For the answers to the other great questions - did Gilligan ever leave the island, did Captain Parmenter and Melody ever marry, were Hogan and his heroes ever liberated from LuftStalag XIII, did the Robinson family find their way home (in their own time that is[20]) from space and did Lt-Cdr McHale and his crew make it through World War II without being court-martialled - you will have to look elsewhere.

Unsurprisingly, since the Cabinet Office desperately tried to stop publication by having my manuscript and back-ups seized on the spurious ground that they were evidence of a bomb hoax (the prosecution at my musical comedy trial in 2014 before a blackmailed judge, since murdered, and a tampered with jury fought successfully to stop them seeing the book), the first two editions of this book were rather rushed. The original publisher, in the States, also insisted on American spellings and usage, with the result that entire book had to be translated back into English. My apologies to readers of the first two editions for the typos and odd mix of spellings.

1. If they offer you a sedative when they push the tube with a camera down your throat, take it.
2. See Chapter 28. Having been used to train the pilots the Iraqis needed to lose the simulator fast. They are a bit more expensive than video games.
3. His name wasn't Bill.
4. His or her name wasn't Moses.
5. Baltimore Pictures, 1997, directed by Barry Levinson. CIA officer Charles Young was brilliantly portrayed by the able and underrated American actor William Macy. The reference to it being a 'training video' is ironic by the way, for those who do not do irony.
6. Chapter 30.
7. The Heritage Foundation, a think-tank worthy of the name, in Washington DC, very handy for Congress (and Washington's beautifully restored Union Station), where intellectual rigour is the order of the day. Favoured visitors get to store their bags downstairs (thanks Freda), very useful if you are hauling out of town on AMTRAK.
8. A tasty and nutritious breakfast cereal, made by Kelloggs at Grand Fork Michigan, full of natural goodness. You can't get them in Britain, sadly, not proper ones at any rate. Kelloggs once shipped over a courtesy carton to me, which was nice of them.
9. Great diners - never left one hungry, not sure it's allowed. If you're driving down a freeway and it's chow time, never drive past a Denny's.
10. Reached with great care and deliberation, after a site visit to Havana and inspection of the wreck by divers. The key point of course is that the hull was bent inwards, i.e. the explosion was external not internal - in an internal explosion the hull is bent outwards, NTSB please note.
11. This is not strictly accurate - I have a small collection of semi-official badges and 'challenge coins' which will convey to informed law enforcement (i.e. not Thames Valley Police) or intelligence officers I am dealing with for the first time that I am probably on the inside, not a wannabe on the outside, i.e. it is worth making background checks. DVD assets inside Western agencies and intel-crats with their noses out of joint routinely try the 'he's a wannabe and not with any agency' line and it can work with stupids or people outside INTELCOM. There is not much I can do about that.
12. A wickedly funny BBC series starring the brilliant Rowan Atkinson as Captain Blackadder, a less than archetypal British infantry officer (he couldn't afford a horse). The Haig character, General Melchett, was beautifully played by Stephen Fry. It was however a comedy, not a military history.
13. The E model was developed in response to RAF Bomber Command criticisms, e.g. the lack of protection and, ironically, powered gun-turrets (handheld .50 calibres are almost useless except at short range) after the B- 17C was trialled by the RAF in 1941. Sadly, the performance advantage of the B-17C was not maintained by sufficiently up-rating the engines, one of the problems of having a German spy in the procurement loop. The B-17E entered service just before Pearl Harbor.

14. Pedants will tell you that it should be called a 'Mannlicher' only, or a Carcano only. I think 'Mannlicher-Carcano' is correct and helps to distinguish the Italian Army rifles from the version used by the Imperial Austro- Hungarian Army. The rifle was of ancient pattern even in 1963. Superb work by film director Oliver Stone has shown that the rifles depicted in the staged photo with Oswald and the photo of Lt Day handing one in to Dallas PD are different weapons, of different barrel lengths.
15. CBS, air dates 17th September 1965 to 28th March 1971. Someone on the production team knew their intelligence as they gave the name of the top German spy in the Nixon Administration (it wasn't Nixon) to a German spy in the 6th series, following which the programme was pulled, with the usual bogus excuses. The lead actor Robert Crane who played the eponymous Colonel Hogan (and very well too) is a true hero of television comedy. He was assassinated in Scottsdale Arizona on 29th June 1978 by a probable DVD/COREA Group operative, John Henry Carpenter, who played on one of Crane's few weaknesses - he was over-fond of the ladies - and preceded the murder with a lengthy character assassination. A number of the leading actors in the series had served in the US Armed Forces (Crane was too young for World War II but volunteered for the National Guard) and had either fled German persecution or been interned by the Germans. The 1993 book *The Murder of Bob Crane*: *Who Killed the Star of Hogan's Heroes,* by Robert Graysmith gives the basic facts but with respect misses the intelligence connection. It was turned into a film, *Auto Focus: The Murder of Bob Crane,* in 2002 (Propaganda Film, directed by Paul Schrader). As one of only two American actors to have been assassinated by German intelligence (the other being Marilyn Monroe) it would be fitting for Robert Crane's life and career to be recognized by a special Emmy or Oscar.
16. The RAF hasn't had colonels since 1918. It was the world's first air force and the decision was soon taken to create air ranks, none of which were shared with the other fighting services. Thus the RAF equivalent of Captain was Flight Lieutenant, Major - Squadron Leader, Lieutenant-Colonel - Wing Commander, Colonel - Group Captain and so on. In practice, as aircraft became more complex and crews got larger squadrons would be commanded by Wing Commanders, wings by Group Captains and groups by Air Commodores (RAF 1-stars), or even 2-stars (Air Vice-Marshals). Sadly, thanks to idiotic defence cuts, the RAF is now so small - as in the 1930s it's a very agreeable flying club which occasionally gets to drop bombs on people - it is effectively a group.
17. Director GCHQ July 1996 to December 1997, Permanent Secretary at the Home Office 1997-2002 and Security and Intelligence Co-Ordinator at the Cabinet Office 2002-2005. Nice man and highly intelligent but supported John Scarlett's appointment as 'C'. His was an experimental appointment at Cheltenham, testing out a new theory that the Director of GCHQ should be highly intelligent. With respect to his immediate successors, the experiment was not repeated.
18. Markus Wolf.
19. With apologies to that fine actor Joe Don Baker, whose line this was in *The Living Daylights*. Great film - many spooks enjoy Bond movies, even if they sometimes part company with reality (the biggest fiction being the idea that MI6 is an

effective intelligence agency working in the British interest), in the same way that lawyers enjoy watching *Rumpole of the Bailey*, *LA Law*, or *Boston Legal*, and cops enjoy watching *Softly Softly*, *The Bill* and *Hill Street Blues*. Strangely this rule does not seem to apply to casualty nurses and emergency doctors.

20. Of course they return to Earth in one episode of *Lost in Space*, but in the 1950s. One thing we do know is that time travel is not possible, because if it were the Germans would discover it and the *Bismarck* would never have been sunk. Travelling forward in time, without the possibility of returning to one's own time, poses fewer theoretical *conundrums* and is impossible to disprove by reference to the historical record (so far as we know there is nobody where they shouldn't be - certainly no androids have ever governed California), but seems to me to be wildly improbable.

Note On Sources

This is an intelligence text, not an academic treatise, although it has been peer-reviewed, one of the peer reviewers is familiar with the German DVD and another was present when a German military intelligence officer admitted to Luftwaffe pilots having flown for North Vietnam in the Vietnam War. That is not to say that it does not aim at intellectual rigour, indeed such are the consequences of failure that there is no field of human endeavour, including science, where intellectual rigour is more highly prized than in intelligence work.

Major intelligence mistakes are usually punished with loss of life, either somebody else's or your own. Since getting it right also has its hazards, such as being thrown into prison, it \is not a field for the faint of heart, or for those of a generally nervous disposition. They are usually encouraged to consider accountancy, flower arranging or politics instead.

Historians usually are limited to OSINT (Open Source Intelligence), that is to say other histories, public records, newspapers, journals, the History Channel and Wikipedia. Even where they have access to unpublished diaries, private journals or correspondence these are usually open for inspection by other historians. This is fine from the standpoint of peer review and academic rigour. Having been both a legal and intelligence academic I am not unfamiliar with the demands of academia. There is one major flaw with OSINT however - it means that historians, almost invariably, are limited to what other people choose to tell them, or wish them to know. This book tells you what the Bad Guys do NOT want you to know.

Intelligence history - and this is essentially an intelligence history, concentrating on the influence and activities of the covert German DVD - is about finding out what really happened (WRH) as opposed to what other people want you to think happened (WOPWYTTH). Since WRH is often far removed from WOPWYTTH, i.e. what you can read about in a book available from the well-stocked Barnes and Noble store at Dulles when your plane is delayed by the need to de-ice the wings again, historians, academics and commentators can get a trifle upset when the truth comes out. Apart from anything else it may mean a new edition of their book. This cannot be helped.

To take Tony Robinson's (a.k.a. Baldrick's) rather good *Time Team* programme as an analogy, the academic historian is trying to work out which building went where without getting his or her hands dirty, whilst the intelligence historian is digging a trench, to see what we've really got. The academic historian skates over the surface whilst the intelligence historian digs deep. *Time Team* by the way is a programme where a group of people go around digging up things. Baldrick was Blackadder's dogsbody.

The German nuclear weapons programme is a classic example. For decades historians and politicians blandly and confidently asserted that there was 'no evidence' that Nazi Germany had tested nuclear weapons. Any assertion to the contrary was dismissed as a 'conspiracy theory'. Since most of the evidence, along with some of the scientists, had been deposited into a salt mine near Hannover at the end of the war, and no one had thought to check for radioactivity on the test sites, what they should have said was 'so far we have not been able find any evidence'. Since they hadn't looked for it that wou ld not have been an exceptionable statement.

There are no signs at Dulles saying that the airport is named after a couple of German spies, but it is. For some reason, possibly to do with how the road-signs might look on the Beltway, Washington never adopted my tongue-in-cheek suggestion that Dulles be renamed the "Von Dulles International Flughafen". Even the Germans have never named an airport after one of their intelligence people, which is why Frankfurt-am-Main Airport is not called the "Heinrich Himmler Flughafen". This could be the first book, which helps get an airport renamed. "Richard B. Cheney International" has a nice ring to it.

An intelligence author is *not* limited to published sources, indeed he or she would be turning out pretty dull books if they were. You might as well buy an official history, tune into CNN, or, even worse, the BBC. I have tried to avoid dullness in this book wherever possible.

Historians, usually, do not have the problem that they might get their sources sacked, tortured or shot, or all three (usually in that order) if they blow their identity. I have been involved in operations where some blabbermouth has gotten someone shot, or, in one case, interrogated, hit on the head with a soft weapon (to keep the pathologist guessing) and dumped into a canal in Gloucestershire. That was poor Matthew Johnson, the courageous cleaner at GCHQ Cheltenham, who was reporting to British Intelligence and cleaning up more than GO2 (General Operations 2) wanted him to.

It's no fun being told that another life has been thrown away needlessly because of a security leak. That particular operation was hazardous enough since it involved getting tactical intelligence out of GCHQ, never an easy task, and onto the battlefield before it passed its 'use-by' date. "Hey, Terry Taliban was planning to ambush you last Tuesday." "Yeah, we know."

Lord Roberts or the late, lamented Sir John Keegan do (or did) not have the problem of revising their footnotes for the next edition by changing the status of sources from 'current' to 'ex'. I am quite determined that no Good Guys are going to die as a result of this book. That is non-negotiable. My covert sources are staying that way. Of course OSINT sources are given in the endnotes and the Bibliography, but the 'juicy' stuff tends to come from covert sources, to which only a generic and heavily sanitised guide is given below. Contacts, usually indirect, with Heads of State or former Heads of State have been excluded as a diplomatic courtesy.

Sources sadly no longer with us, for whose friendship, information, support, advice and guidance I shall forever remain grateful include Lieutenant-General Vernon Walters of the CIA, General Augusto Pinochet Ugarté of Chile, Vice-Admiral Sir Louis Le Bailly, a former Director- General of Intelligence in Britain, Generaloberst Markus Wolf of the Stasi and DVD, albeit that he parted only reluctantly with intelligence about the latter, and Norris McWhirter, cofounder of the Guinness Book of Records.

I also knew, or met, or am indebted to, former Prime Ministers Lady Thatcher, Lord Home of the Hirsel and Lord Callaghan, former journalist and Cabinet Minister Lord Deedes, Lieutenant-General Sir Martin Garrod, formerly Commandant General of the Royal Marines, former Lord Chancellor and Nuremberg war crimes prosecutor Lord Elwyn- Jones, Lord Edmund-Davies, the distinguished Law Lord and Great Train Robbery trial judge, former intelligence officer and great Parliamentarian Enoch Powell, Michael Foot, another great Parliamentarian, Lord (Peter) Shore, Lord Harris of High Cross, Winston Spencer Churchill, grandson of Sir Winston, the 10th Duke of Devonshire (Andrew), Baroness Park of Monmouth, a distinguished former MI6 officer, and former Rhodesian Prime Minister Ian Smith.

There is no safe way, for the live sources, of getting around the problem of not being able to identify them. This does *not* mean that readers have to accept what I say, any more than viewers of *Time Team* have to accept that they've found some more Roman pottery, but it does mean that you may have to do your own digging. Either a statement is true or it is not. If it is then confirmation is usually possible, since the truth is objective, i.e. fact, not opinion.

United Kingdom

As you might gather from the acknowledgements above you would have to go back to the Baldwin era (1935-37) to find a British government with not a single member who had not met me at some time. Obviously, many of these meetings were well after the minister in question had left office. Naming only those who have passed away I have had dealings with, or bumped into, *inter alia* William (Bill) Deedes, who covered the Abyssinian Crisis in 1936 for the *Telegraph*, of which he was later Editor, Sir Alec Douglas-Home (who was present at the Munich Conference in 1938 and was Prime Minister 1963-64), Sir Edward Heath (Prime Minister 1970- 74), Peter Walker, Enoch Powell, Lord Shawcross, Lord Elwyn-Jones, Lord Shore, Michael Foot, Lord Callaghan (Prime Minister 1976-9) and the great Lady Thatcher (Prime Minister 1979-1990).

Military contacts run up to 5-star level for all three services, i.e. Admirals of the Fleet, Field-Marshals and Marshals of the Royal Air Force, and include Special Forces. Intelligence and law enforcement contacts include dealings with serving or retired officers of MI5, MI6, GCHQ, the Defence Intelligence Staff (DIS), GO2, Metropolitan Police, provincial and Northern Ireland Special Branches, SO13 (now Counter- Terrorism Command), intelligence officers in each armed service, intelligence specialists at the Cabinet Office, the Joint Air Reconnaissance Intelligence Centre (JARIC), the Joint Terrorism Analysis Centre (JTAC), the old Customs National Intelligence Department, Immigration Service Intelligence Unit and what were the National Criminal Intelligence Service (NCIS), National Crime Squad (NCS) and the Serious and Organised Crime Agency (SOCA).

Government departments with officials of which I have met or dealt with include the Cabinet Office, Ministry of Defence, Treasury, Bank of England, Foreign Office, Home Office, Lord Chancellor's Department, the Attorney-General's office, Department of Health (over Covid) and Department of Trade and Industry. I am not a Freemason but have had a number of congenial working lunches and breakfasts with Masons, and have met senior Masons up to 33°. I am also known to a number of members of the aristocracy, up to and including the rank of Duke.

I have met or spoken with senior judges and Parliamentarians with responsibility for intelligence oversight. I also have extensive defence industry contacts and have met academics specialising in the intelligence field, and fellow intelligence authors. From time to time I have peer- reviewed publications in the field, or advised on draft manuscripts. I also have sources and contacts in the City and amongst bankers, up to Board level.

I was intelligence adviser to BBC TV's *Spooks* (*MI-5* in the US) for part of the 4th and the 5th series and have had extensive dealings with investigative journalists and defence and intelligence commentators in the media. I also have a range of private sources, including aviation, scientific, forensic, computer, weapons and medical specialists. There have also been contacts with think-tanks and research establishments, and extensive diplomatic contacts with representatives to the Court of St. James.

There have been contacts with the Gibraltar and other colonial governments, including with counterintelligence specialists. I have visited, and given a televised speech in, Gibraltar. I was the founding SIGSec of British Mensa's Intelligence and National Security Special Interest Group.

United States

My dealings with the Federal Government generally have been limited to the White House, National Security Council, the Pentagon, the State Department, the Treasury Department, Justice, the Department of Energy, the National Nuclear Security Administration and Centers for Disease Control (off-campus). Military contacts have been to 4-star level, in all four services, i.e. including the excellent US Marine Corps, both serving and retired. I have been flown in a US military aircraft and have visited a US warship at sea.

I have extensive US defence industry and aviation contacts up to Board level and good political contacts in Washington, with conservative think-tanks, Congress and the excellent Jewish Institute for National Security Affairs (JINSA). There have been lower-level contacts with international organisations such as the UN, in New York City, and the Washington- based World Bank, although contacts there are always away from base. I have visited 39 US states including Hawai'i and Alaska. There have been a number of meetings with Washington-based diplomats.

Intelligence and law enforcement contacts have generally been limited to those very nice people the National Security Agency (NSA), the Central Intelligence Agency (CIA), Office of Net Assessment, Federal Bureau of Investigation (FBI), Office of Naval Intelligence (ONI), Air Intelligence Agency (AIA), as was, US Army Intelligence and Security Command, Drug Enforcement Administration (DEA), Director of National Intelligence (DNI) (very limited), Department of Homeland Security (DHS) (again, very limited), New York Police Department (NYPD), Los Angeles Police Department (LAPD), Amtrak Police Department (relating to issues of transportation security), and a number of smaller local law enforcement agencies.

Intelligence officers I have dealt with in the States include the highly capable late Lieutenant-General Vernon (Dick) Walters, Deputy Director of the CIA and briefly Acting Director. I have had the experience of having a working breakfast with one former Director of Central Intelligence at a club in Washington and having another I know walk in the door and come across to say 'hi'. The meeting with a former CIA Director on K Street in 2009 was completely by chance by the way, contrary to rumour.

I have a large number of media sources in the States and have been a member of the Association for the United States Army (AUSA). I was a member of the United States Naval Institute (USNI) for some years. I am in touch with a number of American fellow-authors in the intelligence and national security field and am a columnist on the intelligence website www.VTForeignPolicy.com.

Canada

There have been contacts with the Privy Council Office in Ottawa, with Canadian naval and military officers and Canadian diplomats in London, plus indirect contact with the Canadian Secret Intelligence Service (CSIS) and the Royal Canadian Mounted Police (RCMP). Political contacts go up to former Prime Minister level. I have visited five Canadian provinces and the Yukon Territory.

Mexico

I have not visited the Federated Mexican States but have sources inside CISEN, the principal Mexican external intelligence agency and have met with Mexican intelligence officers in the United States. I have travelled the length of the US/Mexican border.

Chile

Having acted for that nice man General Pinochet, former President of Chile, of course I have senior Chilean military, military intelligence and political contacts.

Latin America

My contacts and sources are generally thinner in the rest of Latin America but I have been in communication with Brazilian military intelligence and the Brazilian government, through cut-outs, Colombian military intelligence and a number of Latin American diplomats up to ambassador level, from South America, Central America and Cuba.

Russia

I have met with intelligence officers from the very professional SVR, FSB, and GRU, former KGB officers up to general rank, members of the Russian federal government and some regional governments, members of the Duma, journalists and oil company executives. I have visited Moscow and Smolensk, and Minsk in neighbouring Byelorussia. Most contacts with the Russian intelligence services have been indirect, i.e. through cut- outs. I have been interviewed by *Russia Today* and appeared on Russian state television.

Rest of Eastern Europe

I have visited each of the Baltic States, Poland, the Czech Republic, and Bulgaria. There have been contacts with MPs, senior government figures, diplomats and intelligence officers. Usually these visits have been low-key, but I have given a speech in Vilnius. My favourite resort on the Baltic is Jurmala, where the KGB used to have a seaside dacha, which has been turned into a comfortable hotel, right on the beach. Contacts with the Ukrainians have tended to be in London.

Scandinavia

There have been discreet contacts with the Norwegians on intelligence matters and I have a number of sources in Norway, with contact via cut-outs. The night sky over northern Norway is being monitored for the Aurora Borealis-like effects noted with Scalar High-Energy transmissions. I have also bumped into Norwegian diplomats, although the drinkies in the interval during the concert at the excellent Tchaikovsky Center in Moscow was purely by chance. There have also been meetings with brave former members of the Norwegian Resistance. I have visited *inter alia* Oslo, Bergen and Geraingerfjiord (this is not a travelogue, but the railway journey between Oslo and Bergen is warmly recommended).

I have also visited Helsinki, Stockholm and Copenhagen, but these have been mostly political visits, or for a memorable sailing holiday in the Stockholm Archipelago. I have been on Danish and Swedish radio and television and met senior politicians, lawyers, diplomats and intelligence officers. I have not been to the Faeroe Islands or Greenland, but there were discreet contacts, some indirect, with Torshavn and Nook over the plans of the Danish Government to exclude them from the referenda relating to the EU.

Central Europe including Germany

I have travelled the length and breadth of Germany, visiting *inter alia* Berlin, Düsseldorf, Essen, Bonn, Cologne, Frankfurt, Wiesbaden, Freidrichshafen and Munich. My contacts have included intelligence and Foreign Ministry officials, diplomats, bankers and industrialists, e.g. a CEO of BMW. There have been direct and indirect contacts with the old German aristocracy, many of whom are appalled by what German Intelligence has been getting up to.

German intelligence officers I have met have include officers from the BfV, BND and the DVD itself, although they may not have introduced themselves as such, and retired officers of the Abwehr, some well into their 90s. The highest ranking was probably the late Generaloberst Markus Wolf, of the Abwehr, HVA (Stasi) and DVD, a nice man - I even had his home telephone number in East Berlin, which I did not obtain by looking up "Spies" in the Berlin Yellow Pages.

There has been no direct contact with former members of the NSDAP, but I have dealt with or met several people who themselves met the party leader, Reichskanzler Adolf Hitler. I have also dealt with retired German intelligence officers who knew or worked for *inter alia* Admiral Wilhelm Canaris, Deputy Führer Rudolf Hess, Reichsmarschall Herman Goering, Reichsführer Heinrich Himmler, Generaloberst Alfred Jodl, ReichsProtektor Reinhard Heydrich (a charming man by all accounts, but no pussycat), SS-Obergruppenführer Kaltenbrunner, SS-Standartanführer Otto Skorzeny and Eva Braun (but only post-war).

From time to time I have bumped into Bundeswehr, Deutsche Marine and Luftwaffe officers, both serving and retired, but contacts with more senior officers tend to be through cut-outs, especially where they have served in an intelligence capacity. I also have sources in the German media. The most sensitive meetings have been held outside Germany, in London, Washington or locations close to the German frontier, e.g. Belgium, Luxembourg and Switzerland. The best European car for a discreet chat on the move, in my humble opinion, is the old Mercedes 600 Pullman, usually complete with curtains, a splendid device.

I have visited Switzerland and Austria and have contacts there as well, including banking contacts in Switzerland, mostly indirect. I have visited *inter alia* the charming cities or towns of Zurich, Geneva, St. Moritz, Basel, Innsbruck, Graz, Salzburg and Vienna.

Western Europe

I have an extensive range of EU contacts and sources, including MEPs and officials or former officials of the European Commission and have visited Luxembourg, Brussels and Strasbourg. I have had direct or indirect dealings with senior French and Italian politicians, military and intelligence officers, and members of the Bourbon family (very nice people). I have only visited

Spain three times but have dealt with the main Spanish internal intelligence service, the CNI, and met with Spanish diplomats.

I have met with serving and retired officers of the excellent AIVD, the Dutch internal intelligence service, who have been at war with the DVD for years (e.g. over their narcotics trafficking through Rotterdam). There have also been contacts with military and naval intelligence officers. I have visited *inter alia* Amsterdam, Rotterdam, The Hague and Utrecht. There have been contacts with Dutch politicians and journalists, but usually indirectly.

In Italy I have visited *inter alia* Genoa, Milan, Turin, Florence, Rome and Venice. My dealings with Italian intelligence officers have tended to be through cut-outs, but I have had conversations with a senior serving admiral and the Italian Ambassador to London once gave me a lift in his official Lancia!

Contacts with those nice people the Vatican have been up to a very senior level. Although I have direct-dial telephone numbers, the Vatican are very professional and tend to prefer discreet, indirect approaches. They also do not like to hurry things, understandably, as they are the world's oldest functioning intelligence bureaucracy (they also do religion). With branches everywhere they have the most wonderful facility to get hard copy documents and photographs moved across frontiers, slowly but securely. The Society of Jesus (the Jesuits), are not big fans of Michael to put it mildly but there has been the odd working breakfast (the Vatican prefer lunch). When dealing with the Vatican it is always best to bear in mind that religion is one of their core functions, whereas with the Jesuits it is purely a cover story.

The Balkans

I have visited Zagreb, Belgrade and Athens. My contacts have included serving military and intelligence officers and I was able to set up an intelligence exchange over the shoot-down of the Lockheed F-117A Stealth Fighter over Serbia (not the fault of the plane or the pilot - the mission was betrayed by the French).

Africa

I had extensive dealings in the old days with the South African ANC and Namibian SWAPO, and limited dealings with Angola's FAPLA and the Zimbabwean ZANLA and ZAPU. Some of those contacts have of course moved into government, but having been active in the Anti-Apartheid Movement counts for little in South Africa these days. There have been contacts with serving and former South African intelligence officers and special forces soldiers, including former members of 32 Battalion and mercenaries (only nice ones of course). My Zimbabwe/Rhodesian contacts included the late Ian Smith, former Prime Minister, a nice man, and retired members of the excellent Selous Scouts and Rhodesian Light Infantry.

Israel

There have of course been dealings with those very nice people the Mossad, but I have also met officers of the efficient Shin Bet/General Security Service and have had pleasant dealings with Aman, the very effective military intelligence service. They were thoughtful enough to ensure that one of my articles was on the display rack of the rather good library at their HQ when I popped in to say hello.

I have political, think-tank and media contacts in Jerusalem, both direct and indirect. I have also seen a number of the scenic highlights including the Golan Heights, the West Bank (where I had my one and only camel ride) and the Lebanese/Israeli frontier.

Turkey and the Middle East

I have contacts inside the proficient MIT intelligence service and with the very disciplined Turkish military. The Turks have always been most courteous in their dealings with me, but intel contact has to be discreet with a pro-German Islamist government in power in Ankara.

The late King Hussein of Jordan, a fine man with respect, was a friend of several friends and there are occasional contacts with Amman. I have not been across the Allenby Bridge however (although friends of mine have, one accompanying the late Mrs Golda Meir, a stateswoman in the Thatcher class with respect, on a discreet visit). There have been contacts with Iraqi government officials and intelligence officers since the 2003 war, but these have been either in London or through cut-outs.

I have several channels into Teheran and a number of Iranian sources, as they well know, and say no more. As explained in the Preface one friend in the CIA had a source blown (by GO2, not his fault) in Teheran, who was promptly picked up, tortured and executed in a horrible fashion by having something acidic poured down his throat. Not a nice way to go. Once again please don't ask me for "the evidence", i.e. the names of my sources, as a refusal may offend.

There has been the odd contact with Kabul and I have bumped into people close to that nice man, with respect, President Karzai. I did not go out to Afghanistan, although friends of mine did.

Far East

I have had indirect contact with sources in Peking and Taipei, including those nice people the Kuomintang. I have had very civil dealings with Taiwanese diplomats. There are some surprisingly old families in the Far East and occasionally messages are passed back and forth, but I am not a Far East specialist and tend to tread warily. There have been contacts with Tokyo of course and my analysis of Fukushima managed to find its way onto a desk in Japanese Intelligence.

I have only visited Bangkok, Kuala Lumpur and Singapore, but have contacts, mostly indirect, in all three, plus Hanoi. The courageous, spirited and one-legged (a bit tricky to impersonate, although you would have to be a fairly lunatic intelligence officer to come up with a plan which involved impersonating Daphne) Baroness Park of Monmouth was British Consul in Hanoi during the Vietnam War. Daphne, sadly, is no longer with us, and is now with Head Office.

Jakarta is a bit thin on the contacts side - only a couple. South Korea is even thinner.

Australasia

I have travelled widely in Australia and New Zealand, and popped into Fiji. I have political, intelligence and military contacts up to a fairly senior level, but they are usually indirect. I have lived in or visited Brisbane, Sydney, Melbourne, Perth, Adelaide, Hobart, Alice Springs, Wellington, Christchurch, Auckland, Bourke and Wagga Wagga.

Glossary

AAM - Anti-Apartheid Movement.

ABIN - *Agencia Brasileira de Inteligencia* - Brazilian Intelligence Agency.

Abwehr - Principal German external intelligence agency in the Nazi period.

ADF - Automatic Direction Finding, an early radio navigation aid giving bearing but not range, unless you turned 90^0 to port or starboard, set the clock and took a further bearing after a timed interval.

AIVD - *Algemene Inlichtingen-en Veiligheidsdienst* - Netherlands General Intelligence and Security Service, the Dutch internal service. Well led, highly professional, loyal to the House of Orange and very nice people.

ANC - African National Congress.

Black - Covert intelligence agency or operation, usually not dependent on official forms of finance such as taxation.

BOI - Bureau of Investigation, forerunner of the FBI and just as useless, no offence.

BOSS - South African Bureau of State Security, effectively German- controlled.

BND - *Bundesnachrichtendienst* – Federal Intelligence Service. The fluffy side of German intelligence, usually very charming, but heavily penetrated by the DVD. Don't ask them about the DVD - it's like asking a German admiral 'how they're getting on in the Kriegsmarine these days' (I did that once, and in the German Embassty too!) and can lead to moments of awkwardness.

BfV - *Bundesamt für Verfassungsschutz* - Federal Office for the Protection of the Constitution. Not to be confused with the British Volkswagen Festival, although they do drive Volkswagens (they prefer Audis). Nice people, but they can get very frustrated - they put in a lot of hard work tracking terrorists like Mohammed Atta then find they're in the pay of the DVD.

CIA - Central Intelligence Agency. After the NSA, the second-largest and second most important US intelligence agency, set up in 1947. Heavily penetrated, its first three directors were all DVD.

COMINT - Communications Intelligence. Some in INTELCOM use it interchangeably with SIGINT, but I tend to reserve that expression for interception of military traffic, especially radio.

CORREA Group - The DVD's principal operation inside the CIA, based near Frankfurt Airport. It's very black. Named after the German spy Mathias F. Correa, a high-ranking Abwehr/DVD penetration asset inside OSS/CIA.

DDI - Deputy Director Intelligence. The analytical side of the CIA can be a bit stand-offish and overly prone to politicising the intelligence, as with the links between the Iraqi *Mukhabarat* and 9/11. Much less fun than the DDO's boys.

DIA - Defense Intelligence Agency. The Pentagon's principal intelligence agency, it did good work in the Global War on Terror. Too many of its people report to CIA however, and this has compromised some counter-terrorist operations, whilst helping others, as false intel has been run through them into CIA and thence onto the Bad Guys. The DIA boys need more plumbers on the strength - too many leaks. Their preliminary battle damage assessment following the 21st June attack on Iran was clearly an attempt to discredit President Trump.

DDO - Deputy Director Operations. The kinetic side of the CIA, usually very nice people. Now known as the National Clandestine Service.

DME - Distance Measuring Equipment. Usually linked to the VOR it gives a pilot the distance to the transmitter. The military version is known as TACAN. In the days before INS and GPS it was a highly valued radio navigation aid and it still has its uses.

DNC - Director of Naval Construction (British Admiralty).

DVD - *Deutscher Verteidigungsdienst* - German Defence Service. The most powerful German intelligence agency, black, and largely in control of the Federal German Republic, it controlled both West and East German overt intelligence agencies in the Cold War. For over 65 years it has been the world's blackest, most ruthless and most powerful intelligence agency, but it suffers from four great weaknesses - it thinks it's invincible, which can lead it to bite off more than it can chew, it tends to suffer from hissy fits, thereby exposing its operations in pointless revenge attacks, it is bitterly internally divided into factions and it is so ruthless that like its predecessors the Gestapo and the SD, it tends to give Germany a bad name. The Gestapo were actually nicer.

ELINT - Electronic Intelligence. Essentially analysis of the opposition's electro-magnetic spectrum, such as the frequencies and bearings of his radar transmitters.

FADEC - Full Authority Digital Engine Control. Computerised control of engines in place of old-fashioned 'steam' throttle linkages. Very effective in increasing reliability and reducing fuel consumption and emissions, it allows for much more sensitive engine control. No modern engine designed for commercial service would be introduced without FADEC, but it introduced a vulnerability spotted by the DVD, in that insertion of additional lines of software code can induce engine failure at a critical time, as with Flights BA038 and AI171. Commercial FADEC systems are too easily tampered with.

FBI - Federal Bureau of Investigation. The principal US internal intelligence service, it is also a law enforcement agency. Thanks partly to its media profile (Efrem Zimbalist Junior etc.) it enjoys an inflated reputation. Its institutional failure to 'get' that terrorism is state- sponsored increased American vulnerability to terrorism prior to 9/11. It also suffers from excessive political interference from Washington and is overly bureaucratic. They also do lousy coffee.

FL - Flight Level. Altitude, expressed by deleting the last two zeroes, thus FL260 is 26,000 ft.

FSB - *Federalnaya Sluzhba Bezopasnosti* – Federal Security Service. The principal Russian internal intelligence service, highly effective, well-informed and very professional, more so than say the FBI or MI5. They are respectful of Russia's modern democracy and a vast improvement on the KGB. Very *kulturny* – much nicer than the FBI or MI5.

GCHQ - Government Communications Headquarters. The UK's answer to the NSA, but less professional, less well-equipped and much more heavily penetrated by the DVD, which has trapdoors into all its systems. Its predecessor was the Government Code and Cypher School, which fondly imagined itself to be unknown to the enemy even though, its main operational base, Bletchley Park, had actually been purchased by a German agent. Has acquired an unfortunate reputation for sitting on tactical intelligence and allowing the military to walk into ambushes. It threw away a lot of good lives in the Global War on Terror.

Gestapo - *Geheime Staatspolizei* – Secret State Police. Principal overt German internal intelligence agency in the Third Reich period, it merged into the DVD in 1945 and is still operational, but with different uniforms and a little more subtlety. Under-estimated, partly thanks to fictional portrayals like Howard Caine's wickedly funny 'Major' Hochstetter in *Hogan's Heroes*, they were in fact somewhat more professional and rather better led than say Thames Valley Police. The faked deaths of senior Gestapo officers like Heinrich Müller in 1945 were very well done, so much so that for decades many in the West thought that the organisation had simply disappeared. Their record of treatment of suspects whilst in custody was patchy and they were responsible for a number of human rights violations. They made the same mistake as MI5 did in the War on Terror and after 1933 expanded too rapidly, going for quantity as the expense of quality. Like MI5 they lowered their average IQ. That can create real problems in an intelligence bureaucracy because people with high IQs tend not to be conformist, as they can think for themselves. This leads to lack of promotion and you end up having smart people reporting to stupid people. MI5 have not been able to find a way round the problem.

GO2 - General Operations 2. The inspiration for Ian Fleming's fictional 'OO' section, GO2 is the covert German operation in London, although the Director, sometimes double-hatted with the Chief (C) of MI6 (e.g. Maurice Oldfield) is always a British double-agent. Very dangerous, it specialises in wet-work and has a good (i.e. bad) reputation for being able to carry out and disguise political assassinations effectively, like Hugh Gaitskell's. It blotted its copybook, however, with the panicked David Kelly assassination, leaving a trail a child could follow, if not a judge or a journalist, with respect. It has always enjoyed a close relationship with German assets in the Cabinet Office, which has been heavily penetrated since it was set up. The Cabinet Office also has a number of useful idiots on the payroll, who think they are reporting to MI6 when they are in fact reporting to GO2.

GPS - Global Positioning System. Highly effective US satellite-based navigation system using positioning satellites in high earth orbit. Aircraft systems can even be programmed to give altitude. The system can be switched off in war or time of emergency and pilots can place too much reliance on it, leading to reduced situational awareness. It is not infallible. **GPWS** - Ground Proximity Warning System. Officially a system designed to prevent controlled flights into terrain by providing pilots with a warning that they are about to impact the ground, in practice it simply tells them that they are about to crash and may even have contributed to accidents by distracting pilots at a critical moment.

GRU - *Glavnoye Razvedyvatel'noye Upravleniye* – Main Intelligence Directorate of the Armed Forces of the Russian Federation. Highly competent, and very nice people, they have long had a handle on the DVD, and took out

Stalin. The boys did good work in Chechnya, paying an appropriate regard to suspects' human rights.

IFR - Instrument Flight Rules. These apply in conditions of limited visibility but in practice most large commercial aircraft fly by them all the time, regardless of visibility.

IMINT - Imagery or Imaging Intelligence. Photographs and other overhead imagery such as infra-red. Modern cameras have very high resolution and can take oblique pictures, i.e. the satellite does not need to be overhead. Even the 48inch focal length cameras on the Lockheed SR-71 could map terrain out to over 1,500 miles from track.

INS - Inertial Navigation System. Gyro-based navigation system. In commercial aircraft they are normally grouped in three, i.e. there are two back-ups. If there were only two it might be difficult to tell which was giving the correct reading. As they are gyro-based they are independent of radio beams or satellite signals but they have two weaknesses: they need to be programmed with the correct ramp or starting co-ordinates and are vulnerable to sabotage, as with the Mull of Kintyre Chinook and KAL007. They are so reliable that as with GPS they can create over-dependence, leading pilots to ignore contrary indications, as happened on KAL, where an old-fashioned radio navigator would probably have picked up that they were drifting out of radio range when they shouldn't, i.e. were way off-course.

INTELCOM - Acronym for Intelligence Community. Informal but handy, although not everybody uses it.

INTELCON - The Intelligence Conference, Washington 2005. The greatest international gathering of spooks and spook shops ever assembled it broke down inter-agency and international barriers and led directly to several major defeats for *al Qaeda*, including the loss of bin Laden. Since that in turn exposed the extent of covert Pakistani support for *al Qaeda* in the long run it has probably doomed Pakistan. The wash-up from INTELCON has not yet concluded. It was such a good idea there was heavy pressure from DVD assets in Washington to shut it down. Unfortunately for the Bad Guys it was effectively moved offshore, literally, and re-invented as the Spy Cruise. These cruises involved lots of spooks drinking and talking well into the night on a very comfortable cruise-ship with distant and very discreet naval and air cover. It's the ship Somali pirates did *not* want to attack, not that they spent much time off Somalia. Apparently, there was usually someone sober enough to shoot back.

ISI - Inter-Services Intelligence Agency, Pakistan. Sponsoring agency of the Taliban it is effectively a sister agency of the Chinese SIS, heavily penetrated by the DVD, whose assets set up Pakistan. Its antics in Afghanistan led to the first armed clash between US and Pakistani armed forces, in 2011, and rightly so - possibly the first of many. It is heavily into narcotics smuggling and has carried out a number of assassinations, including those of Bob Woolmer and Benazir Bhutto. Nice people, I met them both.

KGB - *Komitet Gosudarstvennoy Bezopastnosti* - Committee for State Security. The principal civilian Soviet intelligence agency, set up in 1954 to reflect the loss of DVD control in Moscow after the executions of Stalin and Beria and the subject of numerous conspiracy theories, perhaps half of which are true. It was never able to rid itself of DVD double-agents entirely but was far more reluctant to involve itself in assassinations and covert operations against Russia's former wartime allies than popular fiction or Hollywood would have you believe.

MAC - *Mudiad Amddiffyn Cymru* – Movement for the Defence of Wales. Welsh terrorist organisation set up in the 1960s. They were quite nice terrorists, preferring blowing up things to people, indeed the only people they ever blew up were themselves.

MANPADS - Man-Portable Air Defence Systems. Your basic shoulder-launched, short-range SAM, the sort of SAM Walmart might sell you.

MI5 - The main UK internal intelligence service, whose first director- general was the German spy Vernon Kell, although that's not quite how it's put on the MI5 website. Headquartered at Thames House in London it is now quite large, with over 4,000 personnel, having started life as a two men and a dachshund operation, very effective at protecting its budget. Less effective at protecting the UK, but that's not entirely its fault, as it's badly penetrated by GO2. On the other hand that's a bit like a flu epidemic at the Centers for Disease Control in Atlanta, i.e. deserving of sympathy but suggestive of inefficiency in the discharge of a core function.

MI6 - The main overt UK external intelligence agency, with more plastic rocks than a garden centre. Heavily penetrated by the DVD and the Foreign Office it has never been able to provide adequate warning of events such as the fall of the Shah and the invasion of the Falklands. Shares its headquarters with GO2 at Vauxhall Cross, a.k.a the 'Wedding Cake', a.k.a the 'Palace of Varieties'. The fact that most MI6 officers are unaware of GO2's existence says all we need to know about its intelligence-gathering capabilities, which are better in Kazakhstan than they are in London.

They have some nice kit however and if you ever want to stage a car-crash their catalogue is always worth a look-through.

MI18 - The most covert and powerful of all British intelligence agencies it was also the most informal. It never had a permanent HQ, its directors, who included Admiral Godfrey (who became 'M' in the Bond books) always being double-hatted, preferably double bowler-hatted. It reported directly to Churchill, but never at Downing Street, always at Chequers or Chartwell, and to the King, for part of World War II via the then Duke of Devonshire, a terribly nice man. Ian Fleming was one of its more famous agents and blocking the 1941 Hess/Halifax coup its greatest achievement, although forcing out the German agents Attlee, Macmillan and Wilson were also landmark achievements. It was set up in 1830 by the Duke of Wellington and has gone through various guises, adopting 'MI18' on the reorganisation of intelligence following the discovery that Vernon Kell, Prince Louis von Battenberg and Lloyd George were German spies. Field Marshals Sir Douglas Haig and Sir William Robertson were two of its most effective officers in World War I. Officially disbanded in 1945, it kept going, as an even more informal network. It maintains cordial relations with the United Grand Lodge of England. MI18 typically meets in clubs and country houses, but since the war has been a network rather than an agency. It is very decentralised and almost impossible to penetrate. There is no list of officers, e.g., and extensive use of cut-outs means that even the Boss does not know who is in and who isn't. Some former intelligence chiefs are invited to 'join', others are so dim that they go through their entire intelligence careers thinking that there is no one above them. Strange things can happen when they run interference on an MI18 operation, however. A typical senior MI18 officer would be more John Steed (*Avengers*) than James Bond.

MIT - *Milli Istihbarat Teskilati* - National Intelligence Organization (Turkey). Nice people and very efficient. Good at torture - they rarely lose people, and usually don't leave marks.

MOSSAD - *HaMossad le Modi'in ule Tafkidim Meyuchadim* - the Institute for Intelligence and Special Duties (sometimes translated as 'Operations'), the famed Israeli external intelligence agency. Very nice people, they were the first Western agency after MI18 to pick up on the DVD. There was a lot more to the Eichmann arrest than has been revealed publicly, e.g. They are very professional, but can be a bit difficult to persuade to a different point of view. The other main Israeli agencies are Shin Bet (known as the General Security Service in the Occupied Territories), the internal service, and Aman, military intelligence, again very professional. A lot of nonsense has been talked about Shin Bet/GSS, in particular there has been captious criticism of their treatment of Palestinian detainees. Shin Bet respect the human rights of detainees but don't make a fetish of it.

MTN - Medium Term Note. As described in the text 'offshore' trading of MTNs in Switzerland was one of the more important means by which Germany funded both world wars. It's why the Germans never invaded Switzerland. A typical MTN has a face value of $100,000,000 and might be for 10 years with a 3% coupon.

NCB - National Coal Board. A covert means of transferring control of Britain's coal industry to Germany, played a key role in setting up the Aberfan Disaster.

NKVD - *Narodny Komissariat Vnutrennich Del* – People's Commisariat for Internal Affairs. Soviet intelligence agency, predecessor but one to the KGB, controlled by the Abwehr, e.g. through their agent Lavrentiy Beri. A sort of Soviet answer to Thames Valley Police.

NRO - National Reconnaissance Office. Owns US spy satellites and hates shifting them to a different orbit.

NSA - National Security Agency, the largest and most professional US intelligence agency, with apologies to the CIA. Headquartered at Fort George G. Meade Maryland, it concentrates on COMINT, SIGINT and ELINT. Very nice people, but if you have lunch there don't order the fried chicken steak.

NSC - National Security Council. White House based bureaucracy, dominated by the CIA and designed to keep intelligence from the President, although that is not what it says on the website. From time to time it produces largely pointless national intelligence estimates, although they are a reliable guide to what is unlikely to happen.

ONA - Office of Net Assessment, the smart part of the Pentagon. You won't get offered a job there without a PhD, preferably two. A bit stingy with the coffee, though. You don't just open the door, walk in and say 'hi'. Your escort, who will have a gun, will open the door for you. Very nice people, especially the late Dr Andy Marshall, but they've got to do something about that coffee.

ONI - Office of Naval Intelligence. Been around a long time, very able, very professional and always a pleasure to talk to.

OSINT - Open Source Intelligence, the sort available to historians, i.e. everybody. Often under-valued for that reason, it can in fact be a valuable resource. The trick is to know where to look.

RLM - *Reichsluftfahrtministerium* - Ministry of Aviation, the Third Reich's answer to the Ministry of Defence and just about as effective at procurement.

ROE - Rules of Engagement, limitations on what your side can do.

SAS - Special Air Service. British Army special forces, grew out of the famous Long Range Desert Group in World War II, commanded by a friend of a friend of mine, MI18's Lt-Col David Stirling, who was betrayed from Cairo and captured by the 'Jerries'. Based at Hereford in the West of England, partly to stop MOD from poking their noses in, they are serious people (the SAS that is, not the MOD). The original SAS was the covert agent-dropping operation started during World War I, i.e. Bill Johns's crowd. The name was revived in 1941. A first-rate bunch of chaps. They are very appreciative of people who tip them off about ambushes. You want them on your side. They report to Director Special Forces whose number I have, although it's only for use in emergencies. The last time I rang it required five minutes of explanation as to how I had acquired it. If the DSF is an idiot, or an MOD/Cabinet Office stooge (it can happen) the chain of command can bypass to MI18, but the SAS have to pretend to obey orders. In that event, if there were to be a war, one of their first tasks would be to shoot the Director. Very well-behaved in Iraq and Afghanistan, only shooting terrorists in custody if they tried to escape.

SATINT - Satellite Intelligence. Not a widely used acronym, but useful shorthand for any satellite-sourced intelligence, which could be IMINT, ELINT or COMINT.

SBS - Special Boat Service. The Royal Navy's answer to the SAS, very good, especially at getting their feet wet. They also do nuclear weapons searches in deserts, especially if the Chief of the Defence Staff is an admiral and doesn't trust the 'brown jobs'.

SD - *Sicherheitsdienst* – Security Service. The intelligence arm of the Nazi Party and the SS. Smarter than MI5, and better dressed. Senior SD officers - Heydrich, e.g. - could be quite charming and might even play the piano for you. Of course they might take the wires out afterwards and hang you, but they would probably be quite apologetic about it. They are supposed to have done a good lunch. Not many of the boys left now, but if you bump into them they will offer you coffee and be quite sociable.

SIGINT - Signals Intelligence.

SOE - Special Operations Executive. One of the bits of MI18 which came out into the open in World War II, with Hugh Dalton as director. They did good work, but were penetrated, leading e.g. to the compromising of their Dutch network. 'Jerry' got his revenge on Dalton after the war, when he was set up by the *Economist*, then very much pro-German, and forced out as Chancellor of the Exchequer in favour of Germany's Sir Stafford Cripps. Cripps was in favour of austerity for everyone but himself.

SS - *Shutzstaffel* - Protection Squadron. The notorious Nazi paramilitary outfit headed by Heinrich Himmler. I know or have known only a handful of people who met Himmler, including Sir Edward Heath, but Heinrich seems to have been rather more charming than the man portrayed by Hollywood. He was certainly more charming than Ted Heath, and threw a good drinks party.

SSK - Diesel-electric submarine, nowadays much more tactically useful thanks to Air Independent Propulsion. Britain used to be very good in this area and the Russians and Germans still are.

SSN - Nuclear submarine, non-ballistic, i.e. hunter-killers.

SVR - *Sluzbha Vneshney Razvedki* – Foreign Intelligence Service. Much nicer than its predecessor the KGB, like the FSB it is very professional and respectful of Russia's democracy. Nice people, although they had a slightly grumpy Head of Station in London a few years back, who did not do small talk.

SWAPO - South West Africa People's Organisation. Met their boss once (Sam Nujoma – charming man).

TACAN - Tactical Air Navigation – see DME.

USAAC - US Army Air Corps, predecessor of the US Army Air Forces. The name changed in 1941, although technically the USAAC was not abolished until the following year.

USMC - United States Marine Corps. Very good people, framed by the DVD and *al Qaeda* at al-Haditha.

VEVAK - *Vezarat-e Ettela'at va Amniyat-e Keshvar* - Ministry of Intelligence and National Security, Islamic Republic of Iran, now known as the Ministry of Intelligence and Security. Not very nice people, but at least they will usually offer you something sparkling over lunch.

VOR/VHF - Omnidirectional Radio range. A great improvement over ADF although limited to about 150 miles depending on your altitude, transmitter power, reception conditions and intervening terrain, still very important, despite INS and GPS, essentially a short-range system though.

VFR - Visual Flight Rules, the see and avoid flight rules usually followed by light aircraft pilots. The minima for VFR differ between airspace regulators.

Part One

A POTTED AUTOBIOGRAPHY

1

Early Life

I was born in the RAF hospital at Ely, Cambridgeshire, on 9th March 1957, to Eithne Shrimpton, a former nurse in the Princess Mary's Royal Air Force Nursing Service, and Flying Officer Peter Roy Shrimpton ("Shrimpers"). Dad was then flying that gentleman's aeroplane, the Hawker Hunter, from RAF Waterbeach, near Cambridge. Sadly, both hospital and RAF station have since been shut, in pursuance of government policy to leave Britain undefended as much as possible and have casualties treated as unsympathetically as possible, i.e. in civilian hospitals. It is not accidental that both my parents had an RAF connection. That's how they met, whilst serving in RAF Germany.

Peter Shrimpton came from a Liberal family, his father's Christian names (William Ewart) being a clue. He was born on 23rd September 1930 in Bloxham, Oxfordshire. Our Lady Church has the tallest church spire in Oxfordshire. William Ewart Shrimpton was a teacher and by all accounts a good one, although not the easiest man for my dear grandmother, Ivy Kathleen, to live with. Sensibly, he had a passion for steam engines, traction engines in particular. After he retired he was a fixture for many years at Salters Steamers in Oxford, who run tours on the Thames. He was also very fond of the Great Western Railway, a.k.a 'God's Wonderful Railway', tragically nationalised by Germany's Clement Attlee after World War II.

These entirely proper enthusiasms communicated themselves through two generations to myself. I still fondly recall being taken as a boy to traction engine rallies. I still love steam engines, to the dismay many years ago of a lady friend who did not share my passion to the same extent. Sadly, she failed to appreciate to the requisite degree the delights of a run over the Settle to Carlisle Railway behind the London Midland and Scottish Railway's Stanier Pacific *Princess Elizabeth.*[1] My most exhilarating charge up the 1- in-100 'Long Drag' was behind Sir William Stanier's other masterpiece, the *Duchess of Hamilton*, of the celebrated *Princess Coronation* class.[2] Readers will be pleased to learn, however, that my love life does not feature greatly in this book. It's a history after all, not a tragedy.

The family regiment was the Oxon and Bucks Light Infantry. Great-uncle Harry John Shrimpton gave his life in 1916, having been decorated for his role in the Battle of the Somme. Less distinguished Shrimptons include General Sir John Shrimpton, Governor of Gibraltar, who sadly was found with his fingers in the till,[3] and Jack Shrimpton the highwayman. He was hanged, appropriately enough, on Deadman's Hill, on what is now the A40, near High Wycombe, Buckinghamshire. He thus started the family's association with the law.

The most glamorous member of the family, far more so than me, is the former supermodel Jean Shrimpton. She and her husband Michael ran the Abbey Hotel in Penzance, Cornwall. We are distantly related. If I may say so, her side of the family got the looks, whilst our side were lumbered with the brains.

From Elizabethan times my branch of the family, the Long Crendon branch, made industrial needles, including sail-making needles for naval and marine use. Long Crendon is a delightful village in Buckinghamshire, near Thame. We made the needles which sewed the sails that powered the ships of the line at the Battle of Trafalgar, although French distrust of this Shrimpton is probably not related to that particular historical titbit.

Lung disease brought on by the fine dust meant that the Shrimptons tended to live short but happy lives, whereas I am aiming for long and happy. They were reluctant to modernise and in the Industrial Revolution the needle-making industry moved to Redditch. The resultant hardships saw many Shrimptons emigrate, some to Nebraska and elsewhere in the States, others to Canada, Australia and New Zealand. At least one Shrimpton ended up in the Pentagon. His path and mine never crossed, doing his career no harm I am sure.

'Shrimpers' retired from the RAF as a Fight Lieutenant in 1963. He was a good pilot - fast jet pilots tend to be - and flew Meteors, Vampires and Canadair Sabres, as well as the storied Hunter. He served *inter alia* with the great Kiwi aviator Ray Hanna, of Red Arrows fame, in the Ferry Squadron at RAF Benson. For many years Benson was home to the King's/Queen's Flight, until it was abolished as part of the government's drive to upset the Royal Family, not to mention the RAF. As an air force brat I lived on or near a succession of RAF bases and grew up around aircraft.

Dad's most notable escapade, related in the standard work on the Sabre in the RAF,[4] came after some with respect ill-advised orders saw him doing a low-level strafing run straight after returning from leave. He asked for and should have been given a familiarisation flight. Pilot Officer Shrimpton's

Sabre was in contact with rising ground at the end of the gun- butts after a fast, low-level run firing the fighter's six fifty-cals.

Her jet-pipe was bent and the pitot tube went west, resulting in a recommendation to eject. This was very properly ignored as the aircraft was over a densely populated part of West Germany. With assistance from his CO in a chase plane 'Shrimpers' got the bus back. Her tailpipe was red-hot, but the CO's face may have been even redder. It ought really to have been Air Force Cross time, but Dad, sadly, got the raw end of the deal. He never complained and it took nearly 50 years for me to get bits of the story out of him!

'Shrimpers' was the first Shrimpton to exceed the sound barrier. I later did it, in rather greater comfort, on Concorde - the food and drink service on the F-86 was poor! I gather recommended - or, depending upon your point of view, not recommended - procedure for going supersonic in a Sabre involved climbing to the fighter's ceiling, rolling off the top and putting her into a 20,000 foot or so power dive. After that, levelling off was encouraged, at which point you did a wing count. If the total came to less than two, you ejected.

The 234-squadron boys seem to have had a lot of fun on the front line in the Cold War. This included some illicit gun-camera runs on Premier Khrushchev's Tu-104 when he was flying to the 1956 London summit. I rather suspect Air Intelligence was behind the request. Unhappily, a slightly dim view appears to have been taken of this at Air House. In a slight failure of liaison nobody told the boys that the British Air Attaché in Moscow was on the 104. The plane was based on the Tu-16 Badger bomber of course, and had similar performance.

The Welsh Connection

Whilst the Shrimptons went aerial the Barnetts, or to be more precise my grandfather Jack Barnett MM, went underground. He was a coal-miner in South Wales, going to work for the Forestry Commission and farming a small holding after the lengthy 1926 miners' strike.

Sergeant Barnett served with distinction in World War I as a stretcher-bearer and ambulance driver in the Royal Army Medical Corps, being awarded the Military Medal for rescuing the wounded in heroic circumstances during the Battle of the Somme. He was also Mentioned in Dispatches, the Mention being signed by Winston Churchill, then Secretary of State for War. It had an honoured place in the Barnett family home at Orchard Cottage, Coychurch, near Bridgend in Glamorgan.

He served in the Home Guard in the second war and is said to have been responsible for a story, which went the rounds of the army, indeed as far as the Eighth Army in the Western Desert. Sgt Barnett's hopelessly ill- equipped unit was being inspected by an elderly cavalry general. When asked what he would do, if 'the Hun' invaded Sgt Barnett replied that "he would be up the nearest tree". When the shocked general asked "but what about your horse, man, what about your horse?" 'Gramps' replied, no doubt respectfully, to the effect that if he knew anything about his horse, it would be up there before him. The Barnetts were a wonderful family and I have fond memories of my many stays at Orchard Cottage.

Aunt Agnes served in the Queen Alexandra's Imperial Nursing Yeomanry throughout almost the whole of World War II, nursing the wounded from *inter alia* the Battle of El Alamein. She was in the Western Desert when she first heard the story about Sgt Barnett and his horse. In 1941 she was evacuated in turn from Greece, where she came down with appendicitis, and Crete, being in the last group of nursing sisters to leave the island. Devotion to the care of the wounded clearly ran in the Barnett family.

A District Nurse in the Vale of Glamorgan after the war Agnes rose to the rank of Lieutenant-Colonel in the Queen Alexandra's Royal Army Nursing Corps (TA), as it became. She was decorated with the Associate Royal Red Cross (ARRC) medal and the Territorial Decoration (TD). The visit to Buckingham Palace for the ARRC investiture was a proud moment for my grandparents.

In the next family visit to the Palace I saw my other maternal aunt, Zita, awarded the OBE by Queen Elizabeth II for services to midwifery. Zita taught in Yorkshire during the war, and did not lack a spirit of adventure. She ran a midwifery ward in Sumve mission hospital in what was then Tanganyika, followed by a stint as a midwife in Ghana, eventually becoming Chairman of the Board of the Royal College of Midwives. These two remarkable ladies were a great and positive influence on me. I loved them both dearly.

Agnes's unit was close-knit. Her wartime colleagues Mary Lynch and Blanche Atkinson, whose stepson David rose to the rank of Brigadier and became a distinguished head of military intelligence in Northern Ireland, became part of the family. Mary moved to Coychurch and Bill and Blanche's house in St Mark's Road Mitcham, in Surrey, became almost a second home for me. Bill too had done his bit in the war and was a man with sound conservative opinions, to which I eventually paid heed.

My uncle George went ashore with the Royal Marines on D-Day and was a fine man. A steelworker after the war in the great Port Talbot Steelworks in South Wales, he was Labour through and through. To the end of his days he recalled giving Geoffrey Howe a hard time when he came canvassing for votes, somewhat optimistically, in Aberavon, in his first, failed Parliamentary campaign.[5] It should come as no great surprise that as the grandson of a coalminer, I first joined the Labour Party, not least at a time of high unemployment in South Wales. What is more, in those days Labour, unlike the Conservatives, had a sensible European policy, i.e. withdrawal from the EEC. Long and enjoyable sessions with George at the Taibach Rugby Club no doubt helped.

The Move to Australia

After retiring from the RAF 'Shrimpers' emigrated to Australia with his young family. I was the eldest of six, sadly now only five, two of whom, Judy, now married and living in Brisbane, and Tony, presently serving as a Flight Sergeant in the Royal Australian Air Force (RAAF), were born Down Under. After training at Essendon Airport in Melbourne, Dad started a second career as an Air Traffic Controller, with the Australian Department of Civil Aviation.

The long (36 hours) flight out in a QANTAS Boeing 707-338 was my first, and a source of great excitement. The DC-6B (I think) down to Melbourne from Sydney was less exciting. Quite how Mum coped with four kids under the age of seven on this long journey is not entirely clear. The Australians are a hospitable lot and the warm welcome at Essendon from a nice lady with the Department, complete with large bars of Cadburys chocolate for us kids, is still remembered with affection.

'Shrimpers' served in Queensland, firstly at Eagle Farm, the main airport for the delightful sub-tropical city of Brisbane, then at Garbutt, the airport for tropical Townsville. Garbutt is also an important RAAF station. Dad later returned to Brisbane, sadly after he and Mum had separated.

I grew up in the lovely seaside suburb of Scarborough, on the Redcliffe Peninsula, 20 miles north of Brisbane. There were memorable visits to the Port of Brisbane, to meet and greet, and then wave farewell to, Gran and Grandpa Barnett on from memory Sitmar Line's MS *Fairsea* and MS *Fairsky* [6]. I also went on board the destroyers USS *Blue* (DD-744) and USS *Collett* (DD-730), on an R & R visit after bombarding enemy positions in Vietnam and doing other good work. At a tender age this was my first acquaintance with Americans and the US Navy. I came away greatly impressed. The US Navy are great ambassadors for America.

Mum's religion meant going to Catholic schools, including the excellent De La Salle College Scarborough. This was followed by two years (1973- 74) at De La Salle College Cronulla. Inspired by those who had taught me, I was contemplating a vocation as a teaching brother.

Whether the abandonment of this plan was a source of greater relief for the Catholic Church or myself is a matter for debate, but at least it afforded me an opportunity to meet Saint Mother Teresa, one of the two most remarkable women I have met. The late Margaret Thatcher was just as steely, but not perhaps quite as saintly, although she also was a good woman, with respect. Mother Teresa had the most penetrating eyes. She was small and slight but conveyed an impression of great inner strength and piercing intellect. You took her on at your peril.

School lore has it that one of my fellow pupils for a month or so in 1967 was the future Australian Prime Minister Kevin Rudd, although I have no recollection of meeting him. As a future politician and believer in global warming he would have been in the non-academic stream of course, no offence intended.

Shane Gould, the brilliant Australian Olympic swimmer, was a more glamorous classmate, albeit only for exams. De La Salle had a rather nice 50-metre swimming pool, built on the initiative of a wonderful man, Monsignor Bartholomew Frawley. 'Mons' Frawley served in New Guinea in World War II as a Catholic chaplain in the RAAF and never passed up an opportunity to cadge a helicopter ride to film his parish. I was one of his less proficient altar boys, indeed to my shame I once dropped the chalice. 'Mons' passed away in 2002, at the age of 98. It was impossible to spend money on him. He ran around Scarborough for years in a three- wheeled Messerschmitt bubble car. When the ladies of the parish bought him a Volkswagen he promptly raffled it! They should have made him a bishop.

Scarborough was a great place to grow up, and family holidays in Caloundra on the Sunshine Coast were always something to which to look forward. The home environment was never entirely settled, although my much-loved parents did their best. Strong support was provided by school-friends and neighbours, not least the wonderful Peut family at No 26 Seaville Avenue. We were at 22. Fred Peut had done his bit in World War II and drove for K.R. Darling Downs, the famous dairy concern, famous in Queensland anyway.

The summer heat and humidity of Townsville needed a period of adjustment and provided something of a contrast to Sydney. Swimming in the Coral Sea is not generally a good idea, unless there are nets, as poisonous Portuguese Men-of-War jellyfish are prevalent. Cronulla surf beach was much more enjoyable.

Living in Townsville and going to school in Sydney provided a splendid opportunity for lengthy railway journeys. Three day, 1,500mile journeys to be precise, on the comfortable and stately *Sunlander* of Queensland Government Railways and the crack *Brisbane Limited* express from Brisbane to Sydney.

Homebound trips afforded an opportunity to savour New South Wales Government Railway's famous meat pies. These were baked beneath Sydney

Central Station and in my humble opinion (and I am *very* humble!) are the tastiest pies ever served in a buffet car. Both the train and the pies, sadly, have gone. Their replacements are inferior. My most recent rail journey between Sydney and Brisbane, in 2002, on the XPT, a slowed- down version of Britain's Inter-City 125, was not nearly as much fun as my schooldays trips, nor did it offer such gastronomic delights.

The Draft

The 1972 election of the Australian Labor Party's Gough Whitlam sadly saw Australia pull out of Vietnam, prematurely. The Aussies distinguished themselves in 'Nam, ditto the Kiwis. Growing up in Australia, the war was far more prominent than in the UK. Harold Holt, whose assassination, is covered in Chapter 24, correctly decided in 1965 to take Australia in, the reason why he was assassinated.

Debates raged over Australian participation, the domino principle, US strategy or lack thereof and conscription. I assumed that my name would be included in the ballot when my time came and had no plans to scuttle back to Britain to dodge the draft. In the events that happened I missed Vietnam by about three years, although I could and probably would have volunteered after turning 18. You were only called up after your 20th birthday and only if your date of birth was drawn in a ballot. Only a tiny minority, about 2%, of those eligible to be called up ended up actually serving in 'Nam'.

The trip round Europe

In 1975 I took a gap year before they were called that, after working for six months at the Yabulu nickel refinery in North Queensland to pay for it. There I learnt useful life skills such as how to handle a fire hose and stir a tank of ammonium sulphate. Later in life I would put out the odd fire and do the odd bit of stirring. I headed home to Britain, then to Rome, courtesy of the Papal Nuncio, armed with the invitation to a general audience with His Holiness Saint Pope Paul VI referred to in the Preface.

Pope Paul made a great impression and is still the only Pope I have seen up close. The Garelli moped referred to in the Preface had to be pushed up the Alps. Loaded with gear for the six-week trip she would happily go up a steep grade under her own steam at full throttle, provided I was walking beside her. The trick was to yank back the throttle, or jump back on, before the road levelled out. Going down was easier, indeed she touched 50mph. For a 49cc moped that is fast.

Alone in Italy aged 18 I still recall the friendliness of a nice couple going down to Malta in their new, P-registered[7] Aston Martin V8, who spotted my P plate and pulled in for a chat and a rather more elaborate picnic than my coffee out of a Thermos. The trip was great fun, even at 35 mph, which at least gave me more time to savour the scenery. Arriving in Rome late at night with an inadequate map, after a long run, for a moped, from Civitavecchia, I was only too happy to be guided to the youth hostel by a delightful Italian couple in their Fiat Bambino. They showed me how to negotiate the Rome traffic.

I was given a most courteous reception at the Vatican. Return to Coychurch was via Florence (impressive), Milan, Switzerland, Germany, the Netherlands and Belgium, before hopping on a hovercraft. After a minor traffic violation (parking a moped where one shouldn't) produced a near hysterical response from a German police officer who, waved a sub-machine gun in my direction (it might only have been a pistol, but my recollection is that it was a sub-machine gun!), I was rescued by a charming English university student, studying German. Her charm calmed the policeman but excited me. I shall move on before I get wistful.

Autumn 1975 in Europe was a trifle chilly, at least if you were on a moped. I did not know it then, but the world was coming to the end of a cooling phase. I well remember being chilled to the bone on a visit to see the famous windmills at Kinderdijk, a scenic delight to add to the Louvre, the Eiffel Tower, Monte Carlo, the Leaning Tower of Pisa, the Colosseum, the Alps, the Black Forest and the Rhine.

Zita Barnett was close friends with a wonderful Dutch lady, Mieke, with whom she had served in Ghana. Mieke too was part of the family and regularly joined the wonderful family Christmases at Coychurch, although delicate negotiations were required in order to watch the Bond film on Christmas afternoons. The first Christmas back at Coychurch was in 1975 (I had lived there on and off as a young child of course, indeed it was at Coychurch that I heard the devastating news in 1963 of the assassination of President Kennedy). The Christmases, including the puddings, have never been bettered.

Aunt Agnes was something of a local legend. She had many friends, including a number of the local doctors, one of whom, Dr Farrell, an authority on the GWR, naturally enjoyed my esteem. The local police were forgiving of the occasional motoring lapse, a policy extended to my father, returning with Uncle George from a fairly serious party. Agnes, a wonderful character, never quite mastered the art of driving, but there were no casualties, not serious ones at any rate. My first encounter with a policeman was being entertained at age 5 after a slight brush between Agnes and a motorcyclist. This was near the delightful town of New Alresford in Hampshire, where we lived when Dad was stationed at RAF Odiham, flying Hunters.

The Law was a logical alternative calling to the Church. After returning to Australia in early 1976 I enrolled at the University of Queensland in St Lucia, near Brisbane, on the LLB course, combined with history. Australian undergraduate courses are four years, and Queensland University had a sensible policy of requiring law students to study another discipline in their first year.

There was a minor panic when the Queensland Permanent Building Society, in which I had invested the funds I had earned by 'hard yacker' at Yabulu, collapsed, inducing a lifelong reservation about financial institutions, more widely shared after the GFC. During this year I decided to complete my studies in Britain and read for the Bar. As student grants were not available to British students who had been living overseas for three years this meant working and saving to pay the fees.

There was a spluttering start with Gordon Lee & Co Pty Ltd, Townsville's GM-Holden dealer. The less said about this the better. I didn't make a very good car salesman and Holden at that time had a weaker product range than usual. It included an awful thing called the Sunbird, lumbered with the Opel 1900cc cam-in-head engine, Germany's revenge for the Rats of Tobruk.

I then landed a job with the fine old Brisbane firm of toy and sporting goods distributors, Alan Scott & Co Pty Ltd. So far as I know they are still going strong after more than five decades, no doubt due to their outstanding service, fair prices and friendly staff. Alan Scott was too shrewd a businessman to believe my profession of a lifelong dedication to the toy industry, but I did my best to add value to the firm in my short stint.

My sales territory was Queensland north of Mackay, i.e. North and Far North Queensland, and the Northern Territory. This was an area about the size of Western Europe. Transport initially was a battered old Valiant station wagon, complete with cross-plies and the lovely old 245 cubic inch Hemi Six engine. She returned around 9mpg when loaded to the gunwales with samples and luggage.

I picked her up in Brisbane and drove her to Townsville, opening some new accounts on the way. She took me to all sorts of places including Mount Isa, Julia Creek, Cairns and the scenic Atherton Tablelands. There I over-estimated (1) my driving skills at the age of 20 (2) the grip in the wet of the slightly worn cross-plies and (3) the handling qualities of a heavily laden Valiant wagon with a live rear axle, leaf springs and no 'slippery diff'.

Sadly, these lapses in judgment resulted in the rear end trying to overtake the front and the Valiant leaving the road, with me on board. Admittedly this was at night, after a long day, in a tropical downpour. Valiants were not so-called for nothing and I emerged, shaken but not stirred, without a scratch. The dear old Valiant suffered instead, sadly as she went through a barbed wire fence, down a slope and into a field, happily soft after all the rain.

The Valiant was replaced by a Ford XB Falcon with the powerful 250 cubic inch straight six. She could thunder from Mount Isa to Townsville in the North Queensland summer heat in a day, without the needle of the temperature gauge going much above middle. Standard schedule was to leave 'the Isa' about 0330 to make the first appointment in Hughenden for 0900, stopping for breakfast in Cloncurry, dodging bullocks along the way. They used to sleep on the road (warmer than the bush) and could be a bit tricky to spot, although spotting them and stopping was the recommended procedure.

In those far-off days the Flinders Highway was not sealed throughout. Judgment as to which track was the real road was occasionally called for in the wet season, the road trains making their own road as they went along. Road trains might be 150 feet long, and they could kick up a fair bit of dust, especially on the narrower outback roads. Recommended procedure for overtaking road trains on a dusty road into a setting or rising sun was to drop back out of the dust, move out, take a long, hard look for oncoming traffic, kangaroos and emus, signal your intentions clearly, wait for the signal to pass, drop the 'tranny' into intermediate, wind the old girl up and overtake blind, making sure that you had an exit off to the side should something solid materialise out of the sun and the dust. You then honked the horn to thank the road train driver as you passed. Great fun.

The best stretch of road for roo-spotting in those days, in my again humble opinion, was the run between Emerald and Dingo. The best time was the wee small hours - 'roos' all over the place. You quickly learnt that your average kangaroo doesn't have much road sense and can turn around and hop right back in front of you. Locals said that it was better for the 'roo' to go under the car rather than over the bonnet. If they came through the windscreen t'were better they were dead, as they could get a bit annoyed. Big reds can be fairly hefty animals and are definitely not for cuddling. If you want to cuddle a marsupial go to the Lone Pine Koala Sanctuary in Brisbane.

There were occasional misunderstandings in those pre-mobile days between myself, and dear old Jim Hinchcliffe, my sales manager. One involved Winton, in western Queensland. "I thought you said go to Winton, Jim." "No, Michael, I said *Ingham.*" They are over 500 miles apart.

Outback Queensland red-dirt roads in the wet are essentially elongated skid-pans. I well recall my hilarious manoeuvres on the old red top stretch between Winton and Mt. Isa. The locals said I'd never make it and they were right, although at least there were no barbed wire fences to go through this time. After the old XB turned 180^0 for the third time I decided that as she kept pointing back towards Winton she was trying to tell me something, as were the locals in the Emerald Hotel the night before.

Both the CIA and Hertz (nice black lady at the Hertz counter 'at' [strictly near] LAX: "OK, this is a one-way rental, drop off Boston? Sir, you do realise that Boston is on the *East* Coast?" "Ma'am all Englishmen know where Boston is") were a bit puzzled by my fondness for road trips. I have now driven four times across America and twice across Australia. Averaging 1,000 miles a week in outback Queensland in '77-8 is where it all began. Dawn or just before, window down, coffee in the cup-holder, favourite CDs in the stacker, open road and 600 miles to go – great!

Back home again

Australia is a wonderful place, and the Aussies are wonderful people, but it was nice to be back at Coychurch by September '78, ready for three further years of law study. Zita by then was in a senior midwifery position at the Morriston Hospital near Swansea. It is pure coincidence that the beautiful actress Catherine Zeta-Jones has a similar name, although apparently she was born on Zita's watch. Zita dropped me off at Bridgend railway station most mornings. A student railcard did the rest.

Cardiff is a good law school, and then had an excellent head of faculty with respect in Professor Sheridan. Intellectual rigour was the order of the day and there were some outstanding teachers, including Dr George Kanyeihamba. George had been Attorney-General of Uganda in her only honest administration between British rule and Peter Museveni, under Professor Lule. Professor John Wylie was a noted land law scholar and Professor Harry Calvert a fine teacher of constitutional law, a duty he shared with George.

I was elected Secretary and then President of the Law Society, whose annual dinner was of course black tie, with a band to play the first three bars of the National Anthem before the Loyal Toast. I tried to give something back, and our second-hand law bookshop did a roaring trade. Partly due to Lord Elwyn-Jones, former Lord Chancellor and President of University College Cardiff, the Law Faculty had a good relationship with Gray's Inn. I was active in the Cardiff Gray's Inn Students Society.

I recall one memorable trip driving a party of a dozen or so law students up to Gray's to dine. In those days you had to eat 36 dinners before you could call yourself a proper barrister. Sadly, standards have declined since. The Students Union had a small fleet of Ford Transit minibuses, some more clapped out than others. The law students were, of course, assigned the most clapped out, LBO, whose last journey this was to be.

Before setting out for London I checked the oil and pumped up the tyres, habits acquired when driving 1,000 miles a week in the bush. No one told me however that the engine was on its last legs and had consumed more than a quart of oil on its last trip, which was not as far as London. Sadly it seized in heavy traffic in rush hour just before the Hammersmith Flyover, about a minute after the low oil pressure warning light came on, followed by disturbing noises from under the bonnet.

The rest of the party went on via the Underground and home by train, whilst I looked after the bus and waited for the AA man. He was disapproving. Having missed my dinner and a visit to the Inn I was not of the most cheerful disposition and then I discovered what the AA meant by 'Relay'. Not a breakdown truck to carry one all the way home, but a series of trucks, which deposited the annoyed author plus broken-down minibus, at Leigh Delamere Services on the M4 Motorway at about 2 am. Here I waited several hours for the next truck.

Amongst the more successful efforts of the Student Law Society, apart from the 'Snoopy' Law Soc sweat-shirts, which may have involved a slight breach of copyright, was organising a debate on censorship between Mrs Mary Whitehouse and the chairman of some daft official committee on press freedom. The debate was lively and well attended. Mary Whitehouse gave a far better account of herself than most expected. She was a much warmer person than her media profile suggested, with a keen mind.

The law studies very nearly came to an abrupt end, thanks to Geoffrey Howe, then the Chancellor of the Exchequer. He introduced swingeing new overseas student fees, and applied them retrospectively to students who had already started on their courses. The local Tory MP did his best on my behalf, but nothing doing. Combined with family background, mass unemployment, the Thatcher Government's commitment to continuing EEC membership and the energising of the Labour Party by the Deputy Leadership battle between Denis Healey and the late Tony Benn (who came to Bridgend and gave a good speech) this swung me to the left.

My mistake was to suppose that Geoffrey Howe was a conservative, just because he was a member of a Conservative Cabinet. I had joined the Federation of Conservative Students in my first year and was elected chairman of its small UC Cardiff branch. I made my maiden political speech to a Conservative students gathering in Aberystwyth on the need to retain HMS *Ark Royal*,[8] *inter alia* to deal with the Argentinian threat to the Falklands. It still amuses me when the Falklands War is described as "unpredictable" or "unexpected", when 'blind Freddy'[9] could have foreseen an armed Argentinian attack on the Falklands.

The University of Wales Air Squadron

My favourite daytime activity at university was flying. I learnt to fly solo with the RAF in the University of Wales Air Squadron (UWAS) at RAF St Athan, which was the main Phantom (F-4) maintenance base - great! Of course you had to be a bit careful taking off in your little Bulldog[10] behind a Spey Phantom with the afterburners lit, but St Athan Air Traffic Control were very good at traffic separation. Sadly, I did not get much beyond the first solo stage as (1) my eyesight, good enough to pass an aircrew medical in 1978, started to go, to the point where I needed glasses and (2) as my QFIs (Qualified Flying Instructors) will confirm I am not a very good pilot. 'Shrimpers' senior is the hot-shot pilot in the family.

My CO was that nice man and good pilot, the eponymous Group Captain Adam Wise, later an ADC to the Queen. There were some great characters on the squadron, including Squadron Leader Johnny Mills, the Adjutant, and Flight Lieutenant Malcolm Hunt, a fine QFI who missed flying his beloved C-130 Hercules. Highlights included a summer detachment at RAF Abingdon, a visit to the F-111 base at RAF Upper Heyford, which included getting to sit in an F-111, but sadly not to fly in one, time in the VC-10 simulator at RAF Brize Norton and a trip down to Malta on a VC- 10 C Mk 1. Sadly, this was just as Britain was pulling out of Malta, at the insistence of the German spy Dom Mintoff, now an ex-spy of course.

The Malta trip was fun. Proof that my peripheral vision still worked came when I spotted out of the corner of my eye, whilst seated on the jump seat in the cockpit, an Air France 747. Her pilots had been jabbering away in French with Lyons Centre, climbing happily into the VC-10's airspace on what looked suspiciously like a converging course. This was the only occasion on which I have triggered a sudden change in rate of climb by a 747.

Cardiff-Wales Airport, at Rhoose, were near neighbours. Their ATC were positively thrilled to bits at having student pilots learning to fly and navigate right next to their airspace. You could sometimes sense the excitement in their voices over the radio.

Aberthaw Power Station was another near neighbour, with conveniently sited tall chimneys, on which I used to line up when flying the downwind leg. This was all very well, but the chimneys were to starboard of the correct line when flying downwind for landing on Runway 08. The heated air was also not good for light aircraft, as I discovered when attempting to turn onto base leg over said chimneys, prompting stern words of censure from the QFI seated beside me. He also made a sensible observation to the effect that as the aeroplane was only at 1,000 ft going downhill at 500 ft per minute was not perhaps the best policy. He was right.

First solo was fun, the second time. It was an anxious time for pupil, instructor and the RAF, who were reasonably entitled to wonder whether they were going to get their aeroplane back. Sensibly most flight instructors do not allow their pupils much thinking time before sending them solo. Usual policy is to get out and give a few last words of instruction about making sure to land the right way up, avoiding power station chimneys and so on. The trouble was that it was a breezy day, breezy enough to match my personality.

After completing my take-off checks and asking the tower for permission to take off I had to wait at the runway hold for about 20 minutes, keeping a careful eye on the cylinder head temperatures. Crosswind limit on the Bulldog, from memory, was 25 knots,[11] and the anemometer stayed stubbornly just above it. Eventually it was decided to abandon light aircraft flying for the day, by which time I was feeling a bit like Michael Caine's character in the film *Battle of Britain*, i.e. both pilot and engine were overheating.

Not the least drawback of part-time flying was that you could go several weeks between flights, whereas ideally you want to be in the air every few days. Things like law lectures got in the way however. Several weeks went by before I was sent first solo for the second time. This time I managed to get airborne, complete a circuit and land in one piece, with words of congratulation coming over the radio from a QFI who thought I could do it, an opinion not shared universally by his colleagues.

A fellow squadron member was on hand to photograph the landing, which wasn't a bad one at that, even if I do say so - not a three-pointer, but then again you're not supposed to do those in aircraft with nose- wheels. At the time I thought this was a nice gesture. It was only later that I realised that said fellow squadron member was probably expecting a crack-up and a much more interesting photo.

University Air Squadrons are a wonderful idea, which is why some in the MOD want to abolish them. In the 1930s they trained many of the pilots for the Battle of Britain. Aviation and the RAF in particular are in my blood and I loved my time on the squadron. I particularly recall an emotional moment, at sunset, on a deserted airfield, admiring a dear old Percival Provost[12] and thinking that all the effort to get back to Britain had been worth it.

Most cadet pilots do not go on to a career in the RAF, indeed these days there aren't that many careers on offer. Most, however, will retain an affection for the Service and a desire to give something back. Many years later I took particular pleasure in cracking who had set up the Stalag-Luft III executions,[13] many of the 50 victims being RAF officers, and uncovering the German spy who had betrayed the 1944 Nuremberg Raid.[14] I did not hesitate to offer help to Bomber Command veterans when the opportunity arose and I am proud to be an Honorary Life Member of Bomber Command Association.

This was also a sad time, as my beloved grandmother Frances fell ill with pneumonia and passed away. I was with her when she died, at the grand old age of 94. She had led a hard life, with two world wars, one depression and much tragedy, including the loss of all four of her brothers in World War I and its aftermath, including the Spanish Flu WMD Pandemic, but a good one. From Frances Barnett I learnt that a life devoted to the service of others is ultimately far more rewarding than a life devoted to service of self. My Catholicism had long since waned, but giving up religion and becoming an Anglican was delayed until after she passed away, lest it break her heart.

A wide variety of extracurricular activities, not all of which are suitable for detailing in this mini-memoir, meant that there was not quite as much devotion to my law studies as my long-suffering tutors might have wished. In due course, however, I graduated with honours, albeit only second class, and a generous second at that.

The swingeing increase in fees halfway through the course meant extra work in the vacations, but my experience at the Yabulu nickel refinery did me in good stead. I found work in the Avon tyre factory in Bridgend and elsewhere, including a spell in the National Health Service as a hospital porter. That was an opportunity to get used to dead bodies, as I was assigned firstly to the mortuary.

A trip to Aberdeen to find work on a North Sea oil rig as a roustabout was not a financial success. However it afforded an opportunity for a couple of fast runs on the East Coast Main Line behind a Deltic[15] and to meet Margit & Eve, two beautiful, charming and delightful Austrian twins, in the Aberdeen Youth Hostel. The days of 5-star hotels lay some years ahead.

---

1. A big, red, taper-boilered engine, Class 7, i.e. more powerful than most first generation diesels, the English Electric/Napier Deltics excepted. The Pacific wheel arrangement is of course 4-6-2.
2. Arguably the most powerful class of British steam locomotive ever built, with 250psi boilers (low by American standards but high by British), said to be capable of generating over 3,000HP at the drawbar. Steam engine power, is normally denoted by drawbar horsepower, i.e. discounting the power required to haul the engine. Diesels are rated by gross HP, making them seem more powerful than they are. Stand next to a *Princess Coronation* class doing a standing start on a grade whilst hauling 15 'bogies' and you'll understand that steam engines are not necessarily wimpish.
3. For the avoidance of doubt the sadness lay in the fact that he put his hand in the till, not the fact that he was caught!
4. Curtis, Duncan, *Sabre: The Canadair Sabre in RAF Service.*
5. Sadly, later campaigns succeeded, no offence intended. He became Lord Howe of Aberavon and sadly died in 2015. We actually got on quite well.
6. Lovely ships, each had been converted from a WWII CVE (escort carrier)!
7. British number plates were still logical in 1975, and still looked British - these days they tend to look European. 'P' was the suffix letter for 1975. When they ran out of letters they simply reversed the sequence and put the year letter first. After 50 years (you don't use 'I' or 'O') most of the 'A' suffix cars would no longer be on the road, so there was no need to change the system.
8. *Audacious* class, originally *Irresistible*, laid down 3rd May 1943, launched 3rd May 1950 and eventually commissioned in 1955. After a major refit she was able to operate a modified version of the McDonnell Douglas F-4 Phantom (with a longer nosewheel leg), an outstanding and versatile shipboard strike fighter. Crucially she also operated Fairey Gannet AEW aircraft (the name Gannet was originally proposed by the Royal Navy for the Grumman F6F Hellcat in WWII). The absence of the Gannets led to unnecessary ship losses in the Falklands War. It was partly the ability of *Ark Royal* to operate AEW aircraft and the lack of a Conventional Take-Off and Landing replacement ship that led me, at the age of 21, to propose retaining her, *inter alia* to deal with the Falklands.
9. This was a favoured expression of the distinguished late Channel 9 (Australia) cricket commentator and former England Test Cricket Captain Tony Greig. I have no idea who the original Freddy was.
10. BAe (ex-Scottish Aviation, ex-Beagle) Bulldog T Mk 1, a two seat side by side trainer, with a fuel injected Lycoming IO-360 opposed piston engine, generally very reliable but with a nasty habit of cutting out at low altitude, leading to the tragic loss of Flt Lt Jack Piercy and Midshipman Mark Simon in September 1978 on a Fleet Air Arm training flight out of RAF Leeming. Lovely little aeroplane, good for 'aerobatting', with generally very good handling qualities, although they stalled left wing low (from memory) and an unwary pilot could soon find himself, or herself in a spin. Unlike a Cessna 150 you got lots of warning of the approaching stall, however.

11. My understanding of crosswind limits stood me in good stead in 1995 when I spotted a porky told by the MOD to Buckingham Palace. I was organising the Battle of Britain Memorial Flight fly-past over Watermead, Buckinghamshire, where I then lived, on VE-Day afternoon in 1995 and was nervous about not getting the Spit, which has only a 15-knot crosswind limit, due to the narrow undercarriage track. That in turn, was a consequence of the aerodynamically advanced thin wing as the undercarriage legs had to be mounted inboard, near the fuselage. MOD, were too cheap to open up another runway, i.e. one on a different alignment to RAF Northolt, on a Sunday. The Spit was grounded at Northolt until the wind both lessened and veered around a bit, which didn't happen until the afternoon, thus no Spitfire over the Palace. The scuttlebutt was that MOD tried to fob off Buck House with a load of nonsense about engine failure. When I was sounded out, from memory by the very nice Vice Lieutenant for Buckinghamshire, John Pattison, the appearance of a Spitfire over my village on VE-Day afternoon and its absence from the sky over Buckingham Palace that morning having been noticed, I was happy to fill in the gaps in the official account.
12. A piston-engined trainer powered by an Alvis Leonides radial engine and made by the fine old firm of Percival Aircraft at Luton, in a hangar probably now full of orange Easyjets. Percival went on to make the famous Jet Provost of course.
13. Anthony Barber - he was the Abwehr's representative on the Escape Committee. They left that bit out of *The Great Escape*.
14. Duncan Sandys.
15. Wonderful devices, knocking out 3,300HP from 2 Napier 18-cyl diesels, originally geared for 110mph. They made a lovely noise. The prototype, made by English Electric, entered service in December 1955, hauling the *Merseyside Express*. She had a most attractive electric blue livery, which British Railways abandoned for the production engines, presumably on the ground that it was too attractive.

2

Student Politician

My involvement in student politics led eventually to an unopposed run for President of the Union in 1981/82. It was an interesting year, dominated by a student rent strike and student unrest throughout the UK, with lots of occupations, some including myself. Sadly, the Principal of University College Cardiff was slightly bent. He had been found by an official inquiry[1] to have, taken payments, i.e. bungs, for tenured appointments before they were advertised in the *Times Higher Education Supplement*. Rather than just say the students couldn't afford to pay higher rents I had a look at the costs base, found £50,000 in the housing account that didn't belong there and brought in the Students Union auditors to advise. There was a settlement.

Relations with Principal Bevan were a little bit strained after that, but that is not to say there was no respect for him at all. He was a good educator, the welfare of his students mattered to him and his dealings with me were always courteous. I hope that courtesy was returned.

'Bomber' Jenkins

I shared the great excitement over the Royal Wedding but a slight snag arose when HRH the Princess of Wales, whose outrageous assassination is dealt with in Part Three, made her first visit to Cardiff. The student body at University College happened to include the late John Barnard Jenkins, a retired Welsh terrorist. He was studying for a postgraduate qualification in social work, having obtained an Open University degree whilst in prison. Prime Minister Harold Wilson is reputed to have said that the Open University, which as its name implies does not require physical attendance, making it ideal for *inter alia* Category A prisoners, was the achievement of his government of which he was most proud. This was a fair enough observation, since apart from some nice stamps, which that nice man Tony Benn organised, it was its only achievement.

Fondly known to the student body as "Bomber", John Jenkins led the Welsh terrorist group *Mudiad Amddyffin Cymru* (Movement for the Defence of Wales, MAC) from about 1966 until 1969. MAC carried out a number of bombings, including a particularly controversial one at Abergele in North Wales. Urban myth has it that this was intended to blow up the Royal Train carrying HRH Prince Charles (who, by the way, learnt Welsh before John Jenkins did) on the way to his investiture as Prince of Wales on 1st July 1969. In fact the Royal Train, which passed safely through Abergele several hours before the IED was set off, was not the target.

John Jenkins assured me then, and stated many years later in an interview for the BBC,[2] that MAC had intended only to destroy property, not take lives. Since the only lives lost were two MAC members (one of the hazards, sadly, of setting improvised explosive devices, which is a very naughty thing to do), and the bombs were timed to go off when buildings were unoccupied, his assurance equated with the known facts. At any rate I accepted it then and still believe it to be true.

Special Branch took a slightly different view however and John was arrested in the early hours on the specious pretext of having taken part in a burglary. My assistance was sought and I gave it. After the keenly anticipated Royal visit to Cardiff was over John was released, without his shoes, for reasons which remain unclear. Wiser counsel might have been to let the incident pass, but umbrage was taken, not helped by the tapping of the Students Union telephone. These were pre-digital days and I was amused to pick up the phone and find myself talking directly to Cardiff nick!

I thereupon supported the election of John Jenkins as a member of the Student Union Executive. This prompted an outbreak of mild hysteria on the part of the Welsh Conservative Party and the local media. These unusual goings-on, for an Englishman at any rate, attracted the attention of Plaid Cymru, the Welsh nationalist party. I was invited to mid-Wales to meet my first German spy, although that's not quite how the invitation was framed, Gwynfor Evans. He was a charming and well-informed man, President of Plaid Cymru, the Welsh Nationalist Party, from 1945 to 1981.

German Intelligence has always taken a close interest in nationalist movements. As we shall see in Chapter 19 the successful splitting off of Eire nearly caused the Allies to lose World War II. Irish, Scottish and Welsh nationalist movements have long been associated with German intelligence, a strategy followed by Britain's European enemies for centuries. Welsh folk hero Owen Glendower was in cahoots with mad King Charles VI of France (who was even madder than Mitterand), Mary, Queen of Scots with King Phillip II of Spain (who was bad)(she was also close to the French of course and was the Dowager Queen of France) and her son James 1 with Kings

Henry IV and Louis XIII of France. As we have seen, the French bankrolled the 1715 and 1745 invasions of England and the 1798 rebellion in Ireland, during the Revolutionary War with France. This European support is usually downplayed by nationalists, of course. I should explain that Britain is not in Europe.

I do not believe in the politically correct new county names in Wales, let alone devolution, let alone Welsh 'independence', i.e. the creation of what would be in practice a German client state on England's west flank. Both at the time, and since, I have been challenged as to why I supported John Jenkins. In American politics I would be classified as a neo- conservative, i.e. a liberal who adopts conservative positions later in life, i.e. a liberal who rejects social and economic theories which are not supported by the evidence, i.e. a rational liberal, like Dick Cheney.

In 1981-2, sadly, I was on the left, thinking, as observed above, that Sir Geoffrey Howe QC MP, Margaret Thatcher's Chancellor of the Exchequer, was a conservative. We all make mistakes. I was also a law student and believed, as I still do, in the Rule of Law. The fact that some judges struggle with the concept does not mean that it is not valid jurisprudence (liberal senior judges, if that is not a tautology, tend to believe in the Rule of Judges, which is not quite the same thing).

John Jenkins had very properly been sentenced to ten years imprisonment for his crimes whilst leader of MAC. He served his time at HM Prison Albany, on the Isle of Wight, where by all accounts he was a model prisoner, singing in the prison choir. Whilst the rest of the Isle of Wight is a holiday destination, Albany Prison is not. The sentence no doubt stunned the defence and many in Wales, but was scarcely out of line with the sentencing guidelines of the Court of Appeal (Criminal Division), which then controlled sentencing policy. It has since been transferred to a quango, i.e. to the bureaucracy. You cannot go around blowing things up and not expect a medium to high tariff sentence.

He had however served his time and was entitled to the presumption of innocence thereafter. In many ways he was a reformed character, something that the prison authorities appeared to have accepted. He could not have studied for a degree, even in social work, without the permission of the Governor. He had been accepted by the university authorities and was admitted as a postgraduate student. John was also an intelligent, witty and personable man, whose company I enjoyed. If you are so insecure in your opinions that you cannot enjoy a discussion with someone holding different opinions perhaps you should revisit your own views.

On any view John's arrest was unlawful, as was the tapping of the Students Union telephone, although it would not have been unreasonable to apply for a warrant to tap the phone of the former leader of MAC. A new generation of militant activists had appeared, a disgraceful arson campaign against second (i.e. holiday) homes was just starting and former members of MAC were reasonably suspected of involvement. It would be truer to say that the new generation of 'direct action' activists were inspired by MAC's campaign but had nothing to do with MAC. By setting fire to people's homes, even out of season, when they were unlikely to be there, they were risking lives.

John Jenkins admired the Princess of Wales for her beauty and grace. The idea that he might have been party to an attempt on her life was just plain silly. When she was assassinated, logistics support was actually provided from within MI6, albeit by GO2, i.e. by German penetration assets. Cardiff Special Branch behaved like DC Plod, no offence intended. It looked like and probably was a case of Plod giving vent to ancient frustrations about the merry dance Jenkins had led them in the 60s. Admittedly he was in the Army and living in married quarters in Wrexham, not the first place you would look for a terrorist. In World War II the Special Operations Executive (SOE) would probably have had a couple of jobs over in Europe in mind for Mr Jenkins. I am sure that he would have done them, if asked nicely.

I am also part Welsh and am very proud of my Welsh heritage. I would have to concede that the Welsh nationalists, Gywnfor Evans excluded, had a point over the mass murder of Welsh schoolchildren at Aberfan by German assets in the National Coal Board (NCB) and the flooding of the ancient village of Capel Ceryn in the beautiful Tryweryn Valley to provide water for Liverpool.

There was real anger in Wales in the 1960s, indeed MAC's campaign was arguably the first 'water war'. I am a unionist, i.e. a strong supporter of national unity, but good unionists should have no truck at all with England throwing her weight around within the union. All good Englishmen should have sympathy for the underdog.

Capel Ceryn did not need to be flooded at all, as Liverpool and every other city could and should have been connected to a national water grid. That would have avoided the 1976 water shortages in Britain, for no more money than was wasted on EEC membership. The answer to dam controversies is not to flood beautiful Welsh valleys (and Tryweryn was hauntingly beautiful), but to build the dams underground, *inside* the mountains, not between them. You then combine the dams with pump storage power schemes as at Ffestiniog and Dinorwic. Pump storage is a great idea, effectively creating a giant water battery.

Underground dams are of course much more expensive to build, but they are inherently safe, as the water is contained by solid rock. As observed, they can be used for pump storage using reversible pump/generators as at Dinorwic and they reduce the need for quarrying, as the removed spoil can be reused. They generate far less opposition, minimise the loss of valuable agricultural land and have very little impact on the environment once constructed. If they are built near railway lines the local impact during the construction phase is much reduced and the community has the benefit of an upgraded rail link. Over the long term the economic and environmental benefits will far outweigh the extra costs upfront, without the political penalties of cack-handed surface schemes.

The Aberfan Disaster

Feelings in Wales about the Aberfan Disaster and its aftermath, including the unlawful removal of £150,000 from the Disaster Relief Fund by the National Coal Board to discharge its legal responsibility under the Rule in *Rylands v. Fletcher* [3] were still running high in 1981. The effective sanctioning of this illegality by the Liverpool-based Charity Commission, a notorious quango, the abolition of which is long overdue, which also did its best to obstruct relief payments to the parents of the murdered children, and the failure to prosecute the DVD's Lord Robens, did not help matters.

Robens was the Chairman of the Coal Board. He wasn't even stripped of his peerage, which was ridiculous. Of course had any official below Robens been prosecuted for the murders he might have turned Queen's Evidence, exposing his boss, one of Germany's most important political assets in post-war Britain. Thus there were no prosecutions at all, for the worst single incident of mass murder in British history until Piper Alpha. In 1981 the post-disaster machinations of Robens, who ought to have been hanged,[4] and the Charity Commission, were still concealed under a cloak of official secrecy, unsurprisingly. It is likely that Gywnfor Evans and senior figures within MAC knew more than the public, including the poor parents of the murdered children, had been told. This is one of those topics that would justify a book in its own right, but readers might find a brief explanation of the background to the murders and how they were committed helpful.

Aberfan is a Welsh village, formerly a mining community, near Merthyr Tydfil in South Wales. The main colliery was Merthyr Vale, which closed in 1989. The Federal West German government were well aware of the dangers posed by coal waste tips and the possibility of causing a tip to slide appears to have been appreciated by the Sabotage Section of the DVD sometime in the 1940s. At any rate the DVD file on Aberfan is believed to pre-date the disaster by some years.

After a careful study, the village of Aberfan was determined by the DVD to be particularly vulnerable. The waste tips were close by, there was a natural water source from several springs adjacent to the existing, more safely sited, tips and the terrain favoured terrorist use of coal slurry as a weapon. The tip and land contours meant that Pantglas Junior and Senior Schools were especially vulnerable and there was only one telephone line between the tips and the village below.

Local meteorological conditions meant that the valley was often shrouded in mist, which would prevent the villagers from seeing the tip slide towards their community, although they could of course hear it. Sound in fog can be directionally confusing however. A roaring flood of liquefied waste could easily be mistaken for an aircraft about to crash.

The Coal Board, which was effectively under German control, i.e. the control of a German penetration asset, deliberately placed a waste tip, No 7, on top of a known spring. The idea was to make it vulnerable to movement with a small explosive charge after heavy rain. The rain would both increase the amount of waste released and reduce ground friction, and hence time to target. The primary German targets were the Pantglas Junior and Secondary Schools, with the terraced housing along Moy Road the secondary.

The DVD's preferred time for setting the charges was a misty morning with reduced visibility from the valley floor, after morning assembly. This would maximize the number of child deaths, as the kiddies' classrooms, particularly in the junior school, would face the approaching slurry mass. A local (i.e. South Wales based) asset or assets mounted a campaign of sabotage against the vital telephone link, so that the severing of telephone communications would not stand out as unusual. GO2, the German operation in London, had a number of police assets in South Wales and one or more of these may have been used, as a policeman in uniform would arouse less suspicion. German political assets in Whitehall made sure that the sensible West German example of legislating to make coal tips safe was not followed. Lord Robens ensured that warnings from *inter alia* the conscientious local authority,[5] which could scarcely have conceived that Aberfan was about to move centre-stage in a brutal and ruthless geo-strategic powerplay, were ignored.

An area of low pressure was observed moving into the target area on or around 18th October 1966, bringing with it heavy rain. Conditions were 'ideal'. It is probable that Federal West German Chancellor Ludwig Erhard, who reported to the DVD, authorised the attack, on 19th October. It was probably linked to Prime Minister Harold Wilson's reluctance, for political reasons, to bend to covert German demands that the UK apply again to enter the EEC.

It was also intended to help drive a wedge between Wales and England and encourage moves towards devolution, i.e. a political break-up of the United Kingdom. The attack was finally sanctioned by Robens on or about the 20th. There was some urgency as Friday 21st October was the last day before the half-term vacation. The children would only be murdered in large numbers if they were concentrated, i.e. at school.

So far as I can ascertain the operational planner for the Aberfan attack was SS-Standartanführer Otto Skorzeny. His position in the DVD chain of command at that time was senior officer in charge of sabotage and terrorist attacks against the UK. Certainly, the outrage bears the grisly hallmarks of his work. He was then based in the Republic of Ireland, with the full knowledge and consent of the Eire government, although it is highly doubtful that anyone in Dublin was in the loop on Aberfan.

The vital telephone link that could have carried a warning to the village and permitted a precious couple of minutes of evacuation time, was severed on the night of October 20th/21st, probably by one of the DVD/GO2 team which carried out the attack. It would not have been entrusted to local assets. At or around 0815GMT 0915LT on Friday October 21st 1966 a series of shaped high explosive charges was set off on Waste Tip No 7, triggering a slurry slide which engulfed Pantglas Junior School and part of Moy Street.

Tragically, the children had reached their desks. 116 of them were murdered, along with five of their teachers and 23 other adults. The final death toll was 144. It is unclear whether the school was under active reconnaissance by the DVD/GO2 team before the attack. It is however highly unlikely that the charges would have been set off without the terrorist team leader obtaining visual confirmation that the school assembly, where the children had sung their last hymn together, *All Things Bright and Beautiful*, had ended. Apparently a higher than usual number of the children had not wanted to go to school that fateful day, almost as though they sensed the presence of evil.

Hopelessly inadequate counterintelligence work by the admittedly badly penetrated MI5, who should have had Robens arrested and hanged in World War II, meant that the attack was treated as though it were a natural disaster. It was in fact an Act of War by the Federal Republic of Germany upon Her Majesty and amounted to a repudiation by West Germany of both the unconditional surrender of German forces in the West in 1945 and the Treaty of Washington, usually referred to as the NATO treaty. It justified a resumption of hostilities by Britain against West Germany.

An ultimatum should have been issued forthwith to West Germany (there is no indication whatsoever that the communist East German authorities were aware of the attack). The RAF's V-Force should have been put on alert within hours of the attack, neutrals given 24 hours to leave West Germany and the British Army of the Rhine ordered to effect an emergency withdrawal to defensible tactical perimeters. Strategic conventional bombing of the Ruhr, Munich, Stuttgart and other key targets should have been commenced by no later than the night of Saturday 22nd/Sunday 23rd, when conditions over Germany were reasonably good for radar bombing.

Robens, by all accounts, was not unduly taken by surprise by the attack. Cold-bloodedly, he carried on with his investiture as Chancellor of the University of Surrey. He should have been arrested within hours and prosecuted at the very least on 144 counts of murder as an accessory before the fact. You could make an argument that as it was an Act of War by a foreign power it amounted to high treason, which then carried the death penalty, and rightly so.

As it is, the University of Surrey enjoys the unusual, and possibly unwanted, distinction of being the only British university to have had a mass-murderer as its chancellor. The appointment was about as appropriate, with respect, as making Dr Harold Shipman President of the Royal Society of General Practitioners. MI5 should also have had Harold Wilson arrested and interrogated to determine the extent of his foreknowledge of the disaster, although 'Box' would first have had to arrest its own Director-General, Sir Roger Hollis. He worked for the same agency as Wilson, i.e. the DVD. Sadly, the late, great Peter Wright, a friend of several friends of mine, had worked out that his boss was a spy, but had not got as far as finding out the agency he was really working for.

The attack on Aberfan sent a shockwave through the Federal West German Government. It collapsed within days, triggered by the resignation of the FDP leader, and future West German President, Walter Scheel. He was an intelligent man, who must have appreciated that the attack had been staged by the DVD and may even have obtained confirmation. Rather a nice man by all accounts, he flew with the Luftwaffe in World War II as a radar operator on Bf110 [6] night-fighters with III/NJG1, reaching the rank of Oberleutnant.

Entirely by coincidence, or possibly not, a very nice retired Luftwaffe Bf110 radar operator, who may or may not have flown with Oberleutnant Scheel, popped along to Watermead and was introduced to me after I had announced my decision to write this book. The subject of Aberfan did not come up however. If Walter Scheel did indeed obtain confirmation of German involvement he would have been horrified, not just by the loss of life (he was a humane man, who served his country honourably in the last war) but also by the consequences for his beloved Germany were the DVD's involvement to be discovered. It now has been, admittedly more than 45 years late.

The Labour Government, which was heavily penetrated by the DVD, as was the Cabinet Office, apparently banned HRH Prince Charles, now the King, from representing his mother Queen Elixabeth II at the mass funeral on 27th October. Officials piled further mental cruelty on the parents in the callous arrangements for identifying their dead loved ones. The Wilson government backed the Coal Board's illegal raid on the Disaster Fund,[7] and so far as I know failed to take legal advice before so doing. Indeed, they could not possibly have taken advice, as the Attorney-General was that nice man and fine lawyer with respect, my old friend Sir Elwyn Jones QC MP, as he then was.

Later, as Lord Elwyn-Jones, he was a distinguished Lord Chancellor. In 1945 he had been junior prosecuting counsel at the Nuremberg War Crimes Trials, which he told me were a mistake. Later he was lead prosecution counsel at the war crimes trial of Generalfeldmarschall Erich von Manstein.[8] Had Elwyn been consulted over the raid on the relief fund he would have advised very strongly against it, as it was clearly illegal. Generally speaking, the parents and other survivors were treated shabbily by official bodies, including of course the Charity Commission. (Many years later it covertly sanctioned the release to the Iranian regime of the names of dissidents being helped by one of the charities it was supervising, who were promptly bumped off.[9])

There was an inquiry, chaired by another nice man with respect, Lord Edmund-Davies, then Sir Edmund. His Lordship and I shared the same Inn of Court.[10] Sadly, however, it was the usual whitewash, again with respect. When we met many years afterwards Lord Edmund-Davies struck me as a fundamentally decent man who had been asked to bear too many burdens in a long and distinguished life.

His tribunal rejected with respect entirely proper observations by the great Desmond Ackner QC (another nice man, later a Law Lord himself and if I may say so a very good one) to the effect that senior Coal Board officials had shown "callous indifference" to the risks of placing waste tips on top of known streams. That was the very lowest at which it could have been put, given that the NCB Chairman was a German spy, the tip had been dangerously sited deliberately and 116 young children had been murdered.

The discovery of all this lay in the future when I weighed in on behalf of John Jenkins. All I and anyone in Wales, save for DVD assets, knew was that the Aberfan Disaster could and should have been avoided and that the grief-stricken parents had been given a raw deal. It should not have come as any great surprise that it was followed by a terrorist campaign directed against England. It was an entirely unnecessary campaign, as England was not to blame, save that those responsible for the safety of the kingdom and the welfare of her inhabitants, not least the littlest ones, were asleep on their watch.

In 2007, at the instigation of the then Chief Minister Rhodri Morgan, by all accounts a decent man, the Welsh Assembly finally restored the £150,000 unlawfully siphoned off from the Aberfan Disaster Relief Fund in an amount which fairly reflected the 43-year delay and lost interest, £2,000,000 (about $2,750,000). This followed an earlier, risibly inadequate, payment of £150,000, which took no account of inflation and interest.

It is a great pity that legal action was not taken at the time, as the Coal Board's raid on the Disaster Fund was a fraud on the public, carried out in gross bad faith, given that the NCB Chairman was concealing the truth about the disaster. Although the NCB had acted as the agent of the West German government, which had approved the attack and from whose territory it had been mounted, the DVD's Dachau headquarters being located in West Germany, the NCB was liable in its own right.

After the Crown Proceedings Act 1947 a government body the officials of which organise murder, as well as trespass to property, is liable to be sued in tort. Where officials act outrageously and commit grievous wrongs, as at Aberfan, punitive or exemplary damages may be awarded. Had the full facts been placed before a jury the NCB would no doubt have been wasted for the largest amount of exemplary damages ever awarded in Britain. Sadly however, our legal system proved as useless as the police, the intelligence services, the government and the media, who between them contrived to bury the truth as deeply as the Germans had buried the children.

Joining the Labour Party

It would be wrong to say that I was fat, dumb and happy in those years. I was actually quite thin, difficult though that is to believe now. Like the rest of the country I thought that World War II had ended in 1945, indeed that was the official position. I was unaware that nobody had told the Germans. Little did I know that the DVD had already opened up a file on me and would not be passing up any opportunity to jump all over me in the years ahead.

Joining the Labour Party seemed a natural move at the time. Unemployment had soared and the Thatcher Government managed to give out the impression that it did not care, unfair though that was. In one of her biggest mistakes with respect Margaret Thatcher stuck with membership of the EEC to which Labour were rightly opposed. The Labour Party were also more welcoming. Such Labour politicians as I met, including Tony Benn, seemed more genuine than the Tory politicians I ran into, including, very briefly, Michael Heseltine, when he came down to speak to students at Cardiff.

Lord Elwyn Jones was a strong influence, as was Gerry, later Dr Gerry Gadsden, the best student in my year. His doctoral thesis was expanded into the leading text on the Law of Commons, which it still is. Gerry was a mature student, retired farmer and BBC Wales personality, who ought to have been given a safe Labour seat but wasn't. This was probably because he failed the intelligence test, i.e. his intellect went through the informal ceiling applied by the major British political parties, i.e. he was considered too bright for the House of Commons. By the late 1970s the House had been dumbed down considerably. He and his charming wife Joan made me feel welcome in their lovely home on the Gower Peninsular near Swansea, still one of my favourite parts of the world. They later emigrated to Malta, where Gerry sadly died of a heart attack, far too young.

The National Union of Students (NUS) conferences were great fun and an opportunity to get used to speaking to large audiences in venues such as the attractive Winter Gardens at Blackpool. A number of the leading figures in NUS in those days went on to become MPs, ministers or public figures, including Trevor Phillips, the first black NUS President, later a major player in the race relations industry. Phil Woolas, later a Labour minister, was another.

Officially, Phil was disgraced in 2010 by an Election Court, although the court's findings with respect were thinly reasoned, difficult to sustain and ought to have been overturned on appeal.[11] Another distinguished, and very charming, NUS President was the future London *Times* columnist David Aaranovitch. In those days David was a fan of the fluffier form of communism practised in France and Italy. It's no wonder that he ended up working for Rupert Murdoch.

The Anti-Apartheid Movement

It was whilst I was President of the Union that I first became actively involved in the Anti-Apartheid Movement (AAM), whose cause I came to embrace wholeheartedly. I served on the Executive of the Wales AAM, helped to found Lawyers Against Apartheid, joined the Campaign Against the Namibian Uranium Contract (CANUC) and met many of the key players in AAM, the African National Congress and the South West Africa People's Organization, including a terribly nice lady SWAPO activist. Both the ANC and SWAPO Representatives in London impressed me, if I may say so. I met a great cast of characters, including dear old Ambassador Yusuf Maithama-Sule and the then Vice-President of Nigeria, Alex Ekwueme. He was later accused of corruption, unfairly. Nigerian politics *are* corrupt, but Dr Ekwueme left office poorer than when he started.

The whole concept of apartheid was just offensive and silly. The story of the ANC was in many ways a moving one, not least the loss of 607 young black South African troops on the SS *Mendi* on 21st February 1917, very likely a set-up involving German Naval Intelligence. In those far-off days I uncritically accepted the Official Version of Events (OVE), which was that it was a tragic collision, which just happened to befall the first troopship carrying loyal black South African subjects of King George V to France. This was just 15 years after a war in South Africa in which the Germans backed the losing Boers. In those days I also accepted the popular theory that Jan Christian Smuts worked for the Allies in World Wars I & II, i.e. I was quite naïve and ill-informed.

It was my affiliation with AAM that led to my first acquaintance with the United Nations. Not the least silliest policy of the Boer, i.e. apartheid, government was the setting up of client statelets called Bantustans. The idea was that all the 'blick' people could go and live there. It was what Afrikaaner strategists referred to as 'grand apartheid', as opposed to the petty apartheid of having separate beaches, toilets, park benches and so on. 'Petty' was the right name for that sort of apartheid, but 'grand apartheid' was a misnomer, to put it mildly. I was of course opposed to the racial policies of the Republic of South Africa government. The South Africans were the subject of a variety of UN sanctions, indeed sanctions busting was something of a hot-button topic at that time.

Notwithstanding this, dear old Principal Bevan cut a deal with the Transkei Bantustan to take a number of students on the Bachelor of Education course, hoping that no one would notice. I spotted it however, buried pretty deeply in some university paperwork. I checked it out and asked my long-suffering secretary Audrey to put a call through to the UN in New York, which she did. From recollection I spoke to that nice man Enuga Srinivasulu Reddy, for many years Principal Secretary of the UN Committee Against Apartheid.

At any rate I spoke to the right man and a telegram was soon on its way to the university from the UN. This apparently led to a minor outbreak of apoplexy in the Principal's office. When the College Council next met, including amongst its members a couple of MPs, including that nice man the late Caerwyn Roderick, and Vincent Kane, a senior chap at BBC Wales in Llandaff, also a nice man, the correspondence from the UN was overlooked. At least it was until a gentle reminder from myself to Registrar Moritz, asking, as one does, if anything had come in from the UN, which indeed it had.

Not all of these activities went un-noticed. The Special Branch file had probably started to bulge already. Possibly because someone at the Welsh Office thought that I would get on well with armed rebels fighting the Soviet invasion of Afghanistan I made my first acquaintance with the *mujahedeen*. These were nice *mujahedeen*, more like the character Art Malik played in *Tomorrow Never Dies* than the humourless, murderous Taliban. They were the kind of chaps who went on to found the Northern Alliance and with help from the Allies boot the Taliban out of Kabul after 9/11. I liked them, the lunch at the Welsh Office seemed to go well, and they didn't shoot anyone.

Running a students union meant opportunities to meet a great range of people, including Lord Fenner Brockway. He was very left wing, with some odd views on the British Empire with respect, but he was a gent nonetheless. There was also Professor E. P. Thomson, scion of the Campaign for Nuclear Disarmament and the Aldermaston Marches. E.P. was a nice chap, who had killed Germans. He was not a pacifist. Lord Brockway was polite about the Student Union accommodation, which was all the budget ran to, although I made sure the privation was mitigated with a decent bottle of Scotch.

Someone seems to have said some nice things about me to the late Michael Foot, who had succeeded that other nice man, Jim Callaghan, as Leader of the Labour Party. In any event when we eventually met I got on well with Michael, as indeed I did with Jim, although that came much later. They were both serious politicians, who stood for something other than themselves, in a way which Tony Blair, e.g. did not. I happen to know that both Michael Foot and Jim Callaghan enjoyed Margaret Thatcher's respect.

I had moved marginally to the right of centre, where I am now, and had long since left Labour for the Tories, when I met Michael Foot for the last time. This was at the memorial service in Westminster Abbey for our mutual friend, the great Labour statesman and opponent of EEC membership, Lord Shore of Stepney. Kind words were exchanged and I was greatly saddened to learn a few years later of Michael's own death.

Being a Students Union President was not all about student politicking. There were the bands of course, including the statutory Lindisfarne, plus greats of the 70s such as Alvin Stardust and Gary Glitter. I am aware that it was the 80s by then, but contemporary greats were a bit beyond a Students Union budget. There were also happy times in the Dyfed and Morgannwg bars. It was a time for serious drinking as well as serious thinking. A car, which by happenstance was clapped out, came with the job, justifying a new one, from memory a Ford Cortina estate car. She soon racked up the miles, including collegiate trips to the University Unions at Bangor and Aberystwyth.

Such was the bad blood between the English and Welsh-speaking students that Aberystwyth Union had split into two. This was another reason for swinging in so strongly behind John Jenkins after his wrongful arrest and false imprisonment, i.e. keeping the student body together. All talk of a separate Welsh Union at Cardiff ceased after an English-speaking President spoke up publicly on behalf of a convicted MAC terrorist and then supported his election to the Student Union Executive, nor was this done purely from political calculation.

I would not support the way John Jenkins was treated in 1981 today any more than I did then. Ham-fisted and unjustified police action does more harm than good, not least if it is unlawful. Although not Welsh- speaking, I love the cadences of the Welsh language, am half-Welsh, loved Wales then and still do.

Atalay's Case

One of the perks of being a Student Union President was that we had our own travel agency. If you sold the most tickets you got a free rail trip to anywhere in Europe and back, although the poor old Principal might have preferred a one-way ticket. The destination chose itself - Istanbul. Since the generals had recently seized power, Turkey was in the grip of a military dictatorship (again) and the long rail journey meant going behind the Iron Curtain, the choice was not immediately obvious to the aunts, Audrey, or the student travel office.

However, I was in good odour with the Turkish Military Government and had been invited to Izmir (Smyrna) by the family of a Turkish postgraduate electronics student, Atalay Pisil. How, I hear you ask, did an obscure 24-year-old student union president in Cardiff, who had never been to Turkey, let alone a shy and retiring one such as myself, manage to get in good odour with the military government in Ankara? It was all quite straightforward really.

When the military seized power, there was an interruption to the flow of funds from Turkey to Britain. It so happened that the PTT, the Turkish Post and Telegraph Office, were sponsoring Atalay and a number of other Turkish students at Cardiff. Atalay's leave to remain (visa) expired earlier than the others, from recollection because he had done a preliminary English language course. He could not renew his leave as a student without confirmation from the university that his fees had been paid, which they could not give, as things were fouled up in Ankara. The upshot was that Atalay over-stayed his leave and was prosecuted.

Now I have not acquired the reputation over the years of being overly fond of illegal immigrants or foreign citizens who overstay their leave to remain and thereby commit an immigration offence. I am not a dove when it comes to illegal immigration. Each case however turns on its own facts, and every illegal is entitled to be judged according to his or her merits.

Atalay had done nothing wrong, aside from committing a criminal offence of course. He had run out of funds due to circumstances which were wholly beyond his control and the military government were addressing the problem, indeed the funds eventually came through. He was a good student and his professors were supporting him. With strong faculty support I publicly condemned the decision to prosecute, which I saw as heavy-handed and unnecessary.

Unfortunately, Atalay's case came on before that august tribunal, Sir Lincoln Hallinan Bt, whose family lent its name to the establishment Cardiff law firm of Blackburn, Hallinan and Gittings. A great and much-loved character, he was the Cardiff Stipendiary Magistrate. With great respect, Sir Lincoln was eminently fair to everyone in his court, with the possible exception of Turks.

Atalay got a swingeing sentence (six months from memory) and was duly carted off to Cardiff Gaol, where I went to see him. With the help of the Turkish Students Society, who briefed me in on what newspapers to talk to and how, I soon had Atalay's plight mentioned in the Turkish press, but only on the inside pages.

Cardiff nick had been a bit slow in notifying the Turkish Embassy of Atalay's arrest. I decided that it would be a good idea to send telexes to the new President of Turkey, General Evren, and the general manager of the PTT. Telegrams were getting a bit passé by then and the Students Union did not have a fax machine, but British Telecom had a great scheme whereby you dictated your telex over the telephone to the international operator, who then sent your telex, complete with a reply address. BT then rang you when they had a reply.

The international operator was a bit surprised when I started to spell out the telex in Turkish, but as I explained I could hardly send a telex to the President of Turkey, whose telex number I had managed to acquire (and not from the Yellow Pages either), in English. Things started to happen. Memos started to fly.

Then some idiot racist in the prison decided it would be a good idea to have a go at Atalay. The next time I saw him his face was covered in bruises, which were coming out nicely. Now in those days only the front and back pages of the major Turkish papers were in colour. I decided that this was front-page news and arranged for a Turkish press photographer to come down from London, with colour film. The idea was to get the story into the Sundays. The Home Office beat me to it, Atalay was released, the funds came through and he got his masters degree. His grateful family invited me to stay with them in Izmir.

The rail journey was spectacular - at least the scenery was, if not the restaurant car. There wasn't one after Belgrade. The train was the old *Orient*

Express, not the posh modern one, nor the stylish one featured in the Agatha Christie movie, with proper engines, but the surviving service train, in its last iteration. Officially it had disappeared from the timetable, but in 1982 you could still get a through coach from Paris to Istanbul. It ran via Dijon to the Simplon Tunnel, through the Alps, Como, Milan, Venice, Zagreb, Belgrade, Nis, Sofia, and on to Istanbul.

This was my one and only trip behind the Iron Curtain, which I found a bit grim. Sofia Station was magnificent but lacked eateries and moreover a place to acquire some usable currency. Regular travellers knew to bring some US dollars with which to pay the food and drink vendors, who took advantage of the restaurant car coming off at Belgrade and congregated on the platforms. These were pre-*Lonely Planet* days however and the student travel office didn't do a lot of Iron Curtain business.

Most of the passengers after Zagreb were Turkish guest workers returning home from Germany for a holiday. They were kind, sharing their food. I was a bit peckish after Sofia. The 'express' was held up for eight hours at Edirne, on the Turkish frontier, for customs and immigration checks. This was my first encounter with Turkish troops, who boarded the train and stayed on till Istanbul, but their behaviour was correct and the standard of discipline impressive, not least by the standards of Cardiff Special Branch. The first glimpse of the Bosphorus between the minarets (and blocks of flats) was exhilarating. On arrival at Sirkeci Station you really felt as though that you had completed a journey, which after three days you had.

Atalay's family made me feel at home. Izmir, with the Sixth Fleet, or bits of it, in town, was fun, the beaches south of there rather good and the ruins at Ephesus haunting. I was sorry when it was time to go home. Johnny Turk is a good chap on the whole, and I encountered nothing but friendliness from the Turkish people. The guest workers that joined the train at Zagreb had come directly from Munich and that gave Shrimpton an idea. Could I change my ticket and return to Britain via Austria, Switzerland, Germany, the Netherlands and Ostend, and visit the twins in Salzburg? I could indeed. Turkish Railways were most accommodating when I returned to Sirkeci Station.

International calls from public phone boxes in Turkey in 1982 were not quite as digital as they are today and the conversations not quite as private. At any rate I got big grins and thumbs-up signs when I emerged from the phone box. The *Munich Express* to Graz, change trains for Vienna, which I wanted to see anyway, and on to Salzburg, where I was warmly received.

Having missed a restaurant car on the way down to Turkey and relied on snacks on the way to Vienna, I made up for it on a wonderful run from Salzburg to Zurich via Innsbruck. Austrian Railways are very good and the

Vienna-Zurich express had a superb restaurant car, which did a rather better lunch than British Railways. With the possible exception of the *Manchester Pullman*, which treated its passengers to fare you would not find on a British train in the 21st century, I have never dined so well on a service train.

The year was such fun and had been so rewarding I decided to run for a second term, having finished my first, unlike one predecessor who shall remain nameless, but was Neil Kinnock. The National Organisation of Labour Students (NOLS) were having none of it however and put up Bill Rammell, a future MP and Foreign Office Minister, to oppose me. A fully paid-up Labour Party member by now I withdrew, hopefully with grace.

It was now time to join the real world, although having travelled widely in the Australian Outback, done a few double shifts in a nickel refinery, seen the inside of a jail (as a visitor, of course), lugged lopped off arms and legs to a hospital incinerator, attended at a post-mortem, flown aircraft, been behind the Iron Curtain and visited Turkey during a military dictatorship I could reasonably claim to have seen a bit of the real world. I felt ready for the world anyway, although whether the world was ready for me was an open question.

To those who say that when I was a student politician I behaved like a student politician I would respond that there was a reason for that. I was a student politician. My complaint is not at student politicians who behave as such but at grown-up politicians who do. Sure, I made mistakes, like joining the Labour Party, but I would aver that the best time to make them is when you're young, partly because you've got time to correct them. Perhaps there is something to the old adage that if you're not a socialist when you're 18 you have no heart and if you're still a socialist when your 30 up you've got no brain. That's my excuse for my left-wing youth anyway, and I'm sticking to it.

1. By H. R. Francis QC, who also did the report, which led to one of the Rent Acts.
2. 4th July 2009.
3. (1868) LR 3 HL 330. The House of Lords held that a landowner is strictly liable for losses occasioned by unusual hazards on his land.
4. He could not have been hanged for arranging the murders, as capital punishment, idiotically, had been abolished for murder, but might have been hanged for treason, as the murders were an Act of War and could have been brought within the 'waging war' limb of the Treason Act 1351. Difficult to do with a single murder, but easier with mass-murder, especially of children.
5. Correspondence from responsible and caring local government officers is set out in Professor Maclean's page on the helpful and informative website, *www.historyandpolicy.org.*
6. Twin-engined and quite an effective night-fighter, although it failed miserably in its intended role as a long-range escort fighter in the Battle of Britain, indeed it needed escorting itself. There has been much controversy amongst aviation historians as to whether the correct RLM manufacturer designation for the 110 should be 'Bf' or 'Me'. For what it is worth my view is that it depends on when (i.e. to whom) the RLM awarded the contract. As the contract for the first 110s was issued to the Bayerische Flugzugwerke AG it should be referred to as the 'Bf 110'. Others are free to differ.
7. This is well covered by Iain Maclean & Martin Johnes, *The Aberfan Disaster.*
8. Elwyn and I did not specifically discuss the Manstein trial, but he probably thought it was a mistake as well. He was with respect undoubtedly correct about Nuremberg. The trial of Generalfeldmarschall von Manstein was particularly unfortunate, however much one might deplore the German scorched earth strategy in the invasion of the Soviet Union. Thankfully, the Field Marshal, who was an honourable man, was not sentenced to death, indeed Sir Winston Churchill very properly sanctioned his early release. Barristers are often asked to conduct daft or misconceived prosecutions, not least by the Crown Prosecution Service, and often have to suppress their true feelings in the matter.
9. An outrage brilliantly exposed by my friend Christopher Booker in a series of articles in the London *Sunday Telegraph*. The number of dissidents murdered is uncertain but was more than a few. No one was prosecuted, although the murder of the dissidents at the hands of one of the world's most brutal regimes was clearly foreseeable, raising the issue of whether officials at the Commission were guilty as accessories before the fact. The Charity Commission with respect is a pointless quango whose functions could easily be restored to the Home Office, which discharged them with distinction and would never have dreamt of treating the parents of the murdered children of Aberfan in the heartless way the non-eponymous Commission did.
10. Gray's Inn. There are three 'lesser' Inns, the Inner Temple, whose lovely church features in the *Da Vinci Code* by Dan Brown, Middle Temple and Lincoln's Inn, which is full of Chancery types.
11. Phil should have been offered a peerage, having first abolished the quango that vets life peerages, i.e. blocks appointments on political grounds. Democratic

parties should observe democratic principles and it is a basic principle that unelected and in most cases unelectable judges should be slow to overturn the judgment of an electorate and remove their choice as Member of Parliament. It really doesn't matter whether you are Labour, Conservative or Reform, or agree with Phil Woolas or not. The principle is bigger than the party or the man and the Tory Party is a party of principle or it is nothing.

3

The Bar

In England there are two types of lawyers. Of course there are short lawyers and tall lawyers, thin (mostly unsuccessful) ones and fat ones, good lawyers and lawyers who believe that the *Factortame* [1] cases were rightly decided, but your basic division is between barristers and solicitors. That is because the legal profession, happily, is divided, to the great advantage of the administration of justice and the public.

Perhaps the best way of expressing it in American terms is that barristers are trial lawyers and solicitors office ones, although that only holds true for a majority. Some barristers, e.g. the Chancery Bar, scarcely go near a courtroom, whilst some solicitors spend most of their day in the magistrates' courts, or driving between them, or ringing on their mobile phones for their cases to be put back as they have been held up in traffic. Barristers prefer death before dishonour, whilst solicitors prefer payment of their fee. Barristers may not practise in partnership, although the profession faced constant attacks on its independence since the notorious Green Paper of 1990,[2] which triggered the Bar Wars, a battle between the Bar and successive governments. To my dismay the new Labour Government appointed pro-Green Paper Law Officers in 1997, just about the last straw in terms of my membership of the Labour Party.

New Labour continued the policy of the Thatcher and Major Governments of attacking the Bar. This policy is firmly supported by GO2 and the Cabinet Office as it reduces the risk of fearless and effective representation at inquests, making political assassinations easier, as proved to be the case with the murder of Dr David Kelly CMG in 2003. Sadly, the English Bar struggled to find effective representation after the great days of Desmond Fennell QC and Peter Creswell QC in the early 90s. The ludicrous Legal Services Act 2007 remains an excrescence on the statute book, awaiting a government committed to the Rule of Law and the independence of the Bar, the first being dependent upon the latter, to repeal it.

Although there are solicitors in sole practice, most are in partnership, which in practice severely compromises their independence. The larger the firm and the greater the financial consequences of standing up to the executive, the more independence is compromised. This is one reason why you will not see small firms instructed as solicitors to inquiries in the outcome of which the executive has a stake, e.g. where a government minister or senior civil servant has sanctioned an assassination. If the solicitors are advising on covert, offshore Medium Term Note (MTN) transactions, where typically high fees are paid, they may be even less willing to upset the applecart.

As I once heard that fine judge with respect Lord Justice (Sir Patrick) Russell say, the continued independence of the Bar was of vital and fundamental importance. Its restoration is even more so. It used to be said that the first thing that any government committed to sustained illegality and criminality would do, would be to attack the Bar. They were right. Arguably one of the toughest and most competitive liberal professions in the world, barristers have to survive by using their wits and forensic skill, i.e. they have to think, in a way that politicians and journalists, who can resort to group-think, do not.

Wiser heads in Whitehall no doubt counselled government against turning on a profession with such forensic skill, especially if government wished to hide things, as most governments do, but they were ignored. There it is. No doubt there were also experienced men and women in Whitehall who cautioned the government against acting in bad faith, no surer way for any government to lose credibility with the Bar.

Barristers in independent practice work like actors, i.e. for a fee negotiated for each case, typically a trial brief fee topped up by daily 'refreshers'. As actors are said to be only as good as their last film, so barristers are said to be only as good as their last case. Just as Mel Gibson's career survived *Braveheart* (no offence), you can survive the occasional fiasco, just so long as you don't make a habit of it. There are differences between being an actor and a barrister of course. The principal ones are that actors have to stick to the script but get to wear different costumes whereas barristers can vary the script but have to stick to the same costume.

The notion that barristers are long-winded and pompous has long been put about by solicitors, but it is only partially true. Some barristers can be quite brief. Not all take brevity to the same length, as it were, as the late Barry Hudson QC, of immortal memory. Allegedly one of John Mortimer's inspirations for his fictional barrister [3] Horace Rumpole, a model for any young aspirant to the profession to follow, Barry, said to have been a favourite of the Queen Mother, holds the record for the shortest half- time submission ever made in an Old Bailey trial. "My Lord, this rabbit won't run."[4]

In 1982 the Bar's independence was unquestioned. It was a magnificent profession, with a generation of outstanding advocates, including Dickie (Richard) du Cann QC, Gillie (Gilbert) Gray QC, James Hunt QC and Lord Alexander of Weedon QC, each of whom I was privileged to know. Bob Alexander, who was then the President, was gracious enough to put me up for MCC. Sadly, each has now gone to the great robing room in the sky. If they are looking down now it could not be without misgivings. The law in England, home of the Rule of Law, has been hollowed out, lawyers and judges included, although there is nothing wrong that could not be put right by returning to the standards which prevailed as recently as the 1970s and repealing idiotic legislation like the Legal Services Act.

The Bar Wars however lay ahead. There was never any real doubt in my mind that my choice ought to be the Bar. As related, I was already dining at Gray's Inn before I went up to London in September 1982 to read for the Bar at the Inns of Court School of Law, an august seat of learning. The course lasted a year and I passed the Bar Finals, with honours but no great distinction, in 1983.

There were some very good teachers, both full-time and adjunct, the latter including that fine forensic scientist Professor James Cameron. The full-time teaching staff included David Barnard and Lindsay Megarry, daughter of the storied Sir Robert, then the Vice-Chancellor, i.e. professional head of the Chancery Division of the High Court, where intellectual rigour is the order of the day. Standards have declined a bit since but in those days only very good lawyers, like Sir Jeremiah Harman, with respect,[5] and the great Megarry himself, tended to be appointed.

Sir Robert Megarry V-C

As a junior barrister Robert Megarry, who had a piercing intellect, was so bright a prospect that he attracted the adverse attention of the DVD's British Section, GO2. Outrageously, DVD/GO2 assets in the Treasury prevailed upon the Inland Revenue to prosecute him at the Old Bailey in 1954 for alleged tax fraud. This followed an entirely understandable mix-up between his wife and his clerk as a result of which some tax, inadvertently, had not been paid. The amount was not large.

Fraud requires dishonesty, as any competent prosecutor would have grasped. Unfortunately, with respect, prosecuting counsel was Sir Hylton Foster QC, the Solicitor-General, and the trial went ahead. At any rate it started. Defence counsel was the great Sir Frederick Lawton QC, as he became, later a very fine judge. He was a man of sound opinions.

The prosecution, which would make most lawyer's lists of the top ten silliest prosecutions of all time, up there with the Salem Witchcraft trials and the Dreyfus case, was very properly chucked out at half time. There was no evidence at all of dishonesty. The mystery is how it ever got that far. It should have been dismissed at committal and the prosecution wasted in indemnity costs. The Megarry case was probably a turning point in the loss of confidence by Parliament in the ability of magistrates' courts to exercise their functions properly and fairly. At any rate they were largely stripped of their pre-trial powers in 1967[6] and Parliament has been reluctant to trust them with anything important since.

Sir Robert was elevated to silk a few years later and rightly so. Sir Hylton clearly had little future in the law after prosecuting such an eminent and honourable barrister with such a hopeless case, inflicting not insignificant damage on the reputation of the Law Officers in the process. Sadly, the idea that the Law Officers are fearless and independent legal advisers to the government is now seen as a joke. The current Attorney-General, Lord Hermer KC, has attracted huge controversy and damaged the Starmer Labour government in the process.

Only two years after the failed Megarry prosecution when the Prime Minister, Sir Anthony Eden, needed serious legal advice as to whether Britain could wage war against Egypt after the illegal regime in Cairo, which had seized power at the point of a gun, had unlawfully sequestrated the Suez Canal, he wisely bypassed the Law Officers altogether. He went instead to the Lord Chancellor. Disgraced, Sir Hylton Foster had to be found a non-job in the House of Commons.[7]

There is a saying that apples never fall far from the tree, and like many sayings it is derived from centuries of human experience. Lindsay Megarry greatly impressed me if I may say so and I began to have doubts about both the wisdom and ethics of her father's prosecution. These doubts grew after I had the pleasure of watching the Vice-Chancellor control his courtroom. This was an opportunity to witness a great judge in action and in retrospect pick up a few pointers for the day when I would have a courtroom of my own to control, albeit not as grand as the Vice- Chancellor's Court at the Royal Courts of Justice.

The case involved the National Union of Mineworkers (NUM) Pension Fund. Arthur Scargill, the firebrand mineworkers' leader, was conducting it himself, having wisely sacked the NUM's lawyers, on the grounds that they were professional, competent and had given him good legal advice. That's not quite how he put it to the learned judge, however. The NUM, not unreasonably, since mining communities are close-knit and sons often followed fathers into the pit, wanted the trustees to be free to invest what was by then a substantial fund in a way that benefitted the industry as a whole, rather than in a way that ensured the best return.

Thus a company making nuclear power stations might be a good bet financially but a poor choice from the point of view of a retired mineworker who wanted his grandson to have a job which did not mean leaving home. There were also moral and political objections, with which I sympathised, to the trustees backing companies investing in apartheid South Africa in the reasonable belief that the collective bargaining strength of their black workforce was weakened by having a white, racist government which was prepared to imprison trade union leaders and have them beaten to death in police cells.

Possibly because they wanted to have a go at Arthur Scargill, the National Coal Board over-egged the pudding. They were asking Vice-Chancellor Megarry for an injunction, when all they really needed was a declaration as to the obligations of the pension fund trustees. The NCB failed to get their injunction and the learned judge wisely declined to usurp the role of Parliament and change the law in the way that the NUM were demanding. The change they sought was not a bad idea at all and industrial pension fund trustees probably ought to be allowed to invest at least a proportion of their funds in ways which would benefit the industry as a whole, i.e. look to the long-term as well as the short. Sir Robert handled the case superbly, was perfectly courteous to Arthur Scargill, gave him his day in court, rapped the NCB on the knuckles for overstepping the mark and handed down a judgment which with respect was manifestly correct in every particular.

Two possible motives for the vexatious and malicious prosecution of Robert Megarry suggest themselves. Firstly, he was clearly a future Master of the Rolls.[8] The German masterplan for the post-war political and economic domination of Britain and Occupied Europe had been formulated in 1939/41 by a planning staff under Reichsminister Funk. It involved setting up a *Europäische Wirtschaft Gemeinschaft*, or European Economic Community.

Whilst the European Roman-Dutch, or Civil Law, legal systems were easy to subvert, Parliament's inability to bind its successors meant that EEC control over Great Britain would not be possible, unless tame judges could be found who would not uphold English law. Sir Robert Megarry with respect was about as far from being tame as a judge could get, without being over-bearing. He was brilliant as well as courageous. Put shortly, he posed a threat to the concept of supremacy of EEC treaty-based instruments over Acts of Parliament passed after a British EEC entry.

Secondly, Sir Robert had done excellent work in the critical Ministry of Supply in World War II, rising to the rank of Assistant Secretary. He was probably the most intelligent civil servant working on the British side of the

Civil Service. He played a role in blocking a number of attempts to suppress new technology, e.g. jet engines, the Meteor and Vampire jet fighters and H2S airborne radar.

The Germans and their assets in the Civil Service, including of course the wartime Cabinet Secretary and Permanent Secretary to the Treasury, and their protégés,[9] may simply have wanted revenge. Not being able to let things go is one of the great weaknesses of German intelligence and regularly delivers gifts to British counterintelligence.

President of AGIS

I was elected President of the Association of Gray's Inn Students (AGIS) for 1982/83. This seemed unlikely to land me in the soup. At any rate there was no precedent for an AGIS President causing even a mild political storm. That was about to change.

It will be recalled from the last chapter that I was strongly opposed to apartheid and was active in AAM. Now it so happened that Gray's Inn also had a Debating Society and a good one. If you can't debate you shouldn't be a barrister. My predecessor at AGIS and the President of Debates had carved it up between them that the Annual Dinner for 1983 would be a joint affair, with three speakers. This was a perfectly sensible arrangement, which we inherited.

So far, so good, but Debates had invited as their guest speaker one Rudy Narayan. Rudy, sadly no longer with us, was a radical black barrister from Guyana and a firebrand. His encounters with the Bar Council were already the stuff of legend. Some years later he sent along a nice young lady barrister to cover for him on a double-booked trial (whoops) in Birmingham.

This deeply upset both the learned Recorder of Birmingham, a lovely chap named Patrick Cox DSO, who had depth-charged a number of Germans in World War II, and the nice lady junior (she later married Keith Vaz MP, a future minister). Pat Cox got a solid return on his Asdic (i.e. sonar) and laid down a pattern, sending Rudy around to the Bar Council, again, where he was suspended, poor chap. Rudy was fond of a drink and was not a noted feminist, but he was a witty and entertaining after-dinner speaker, especially if the port came around early. Much of his wit was at the expense of the legal establishment.

These pertinent facts were well known to the Masters of the Bench of Gray's Inn and pressure was brought to bear on me to withdraw the invitation to speak. Now Rudy Narayan would not have been my first choice as a guest speaker, even in those days, but he was a barrister. I took the view, rightly or wrongly, that withdrawing an invitation already issued, even over a pint in the Gray's Inn bar, would be discourteous, so I declined.

A learned judge and Master of the Bench then came up with another argument for withdrawing the invitation to Rudy. AGIS had invited that nice man Paul Boateng, then a left-wing councillor on the Greater London Council, later an MP and government minister, and later still Britain's High Commissioner to South Africa. Since Paul too was black, so ran the argument, the speaker's panel was 'unbalanced'. Thus the invitation to Rudy should be withdrawn, on the basis that a panel of two black speakers and one white would be unbalanced, whereas one black speaker and two whites would, presumably, be balanced.

The young man whose task it was to present this 'argument' to me did not seem to relish his task and seemed to tremble as he spoke. What I should have done of course was go round to see the Treasurer,[10] a perfectly charming man, and come up with a compromise that would stop what had started out as a squall in a tea-cup from turning into a storm in a tea-cup. What I actually did was to enquire how many black speakers there had been at the previous year's dinner. On being told "none" I announced to the AGIS committee that I now accepted the principle of racial balance.

There having been no black speakers out of three the previous year, this year all three speakers would all be black. What was more, I had invited the distinguished black barrister Fennis Augustine, High Commissioner for Grenada and a friend of Maurice Bishop, the Prime Minister, who at that moment was busy upsetting the Reagan Administration by having a bunch of Cubans extend the island's runway.

It would have been a great dinner. Rudy Narayan had been upsetting the Bar Council, the GLC had been upsetting the Thatcher government and the Grenadian government had been upsetting the Reagan Administration. Nobody would have nodded off during the speeches, however good the port. AGIS could have sold tickets as far away as Reading, never mind London.[11]

A special general meeting of the student body was called however. Rather than use my casting vote to save my embattled presidency, a motion of no confidence being split down the middle, I resigned as President of AGIS. The invitation to Rudy Narayan was withdrawn, Paul Boateng very properly withdrew in protest at the treatment of Rudy and the dinner went ahead with a Circuit Judge as speaker. I gather that there were plenty of spare places in Hall.

To make up for my lost dinner Paul very kindly invited me to lunch in the Members' Dining Room at the GLC, which very democratically seemed to have been merged with everybody else's dining room. There I was introduced to Ken Livingstone, scion of the Labour left and future Mayor of London (not the Lord Mayor, the other one). Ken, known affectionately to the *Daily Mail* as 'Red Ken', is a great character (although Margaret Thatcher didn't seem to think so) and very personable. He once even stood me a pint in the GLC bar.

As it happened about this time the GLC were having trouble with the judges, some of whom disagreed with the policy of subsidising fares on the London Underground ("Fares Fair" it was called). Along with the idea of travelcards (i.e. fare zones - nowadays only a lunatic would design a mass transit system with individual fares between stations) it was actually quite a sensible policy. The judges were not obliged to like it or vote for it, but they were obliged in a democracy to accept it. What they actually did was to quash it, a classic case with respect of 'hard cases making bad law'. With respect their reasoning was hollow and the decision is unlikely to stand the test of time.

I heard a number of tales from judges over the years about how dodgy a barrister Rudy Narayan was, but I kept my own counsel. Years afterwards, during one of Rudy's suspensions, he needed leave to appear before the Immigration Appeal Tribunal (IAT). It so happened that his case came on before a tribunal chaired by myself. Rudy asked me for leave, as he needed to, clearly expecting a battle.

I just smiled and said words to the effect of "of course you may have leave Mr Narayan", turning to the Home Office Presenting Officer at the same time and saying "you don't oppose Mr Narayan's application, *do you*"? To the apparent surprise of everyone but myself, Rudy responded to the courtesy he had received from the bench with courtesy of his own. He conducted a difficult case both competently and professionally. Sadly, Rudy's liver eventually gave out and he died in 1998.

The Bar

Having eaten my dinners, lost my heart to a nice lady Bar student, at a time when I was still trying to persuade myself that I was heterosexual, stuffed things up with her completely,[12] and managed to pass the Bar Finals, I was finally called to the Bar, by Gray's Inn, at Michaelmas 1983. Dining in Hall was then, and still is, a requirement for being called as a barrister, and rightly so. It is a sensible custom going back to the Middle Ages, when students learnt the law from experienced barristers over dinner, rather than wasting time in lectures. It is a wonderful tradition and immerses students in *domus*, their professional home, and the ethos of the Bar. For some it is also their other home, as the Inns of Court still provide accommodation.

For several years I shared a room in Lord Campbell of Alloway QC's chambers in the Temple. A great character, he had been imprisoned by 'Jerry' in Colditz Castle in World War II, where he cut his teeth representing prisoners hauled up before the Commandant and German military courts. This was good training, some might think, for Tower Bridge Magistrates' Court. That nice man with respect Lord Taylor, then Lord Chief Justice of England, and Lady Taylor, lived upstairs. Peter was a pianist of not inconsiderable skill and when I was working late (in the days before everyone took their work and computers home with them) it was a joy to hear him tinkling away on the ivories upstairs.

Many years later I became a Senior, a great honour, and presided over Hall in the absence of the Masters of the Bench. Most Inns have Royal Benchers, HM King Charles being a Bencher of Gray's. There are four dining terms - Hilary, Easter, Trinity and Michaelmas. The most splendid occasion is Grand Night, when the Loving Cup is passed from hand to hand, and the health of Good Queen Bess is drunk. Queen Elizabeth I was a regular guest but on one occasion may have imbibed with respect just a little too much of the Inn's excellent porter. At any rate Her Majesty was unable to stand for the Loyal Toast, so ever since it has been drunk sitting down.

Albeit rebuilt, Gray's Inn Hall dates back to the Middle Ages, and is majestic. Legend has it that the wooden screen at the back of Hall comes from the timbers of a Spanish galleon wrecked on the west coast of Ireland during the Spanish Armada. It probably does. The decline in the required number of dinners, from 24 pre-call and 12 post-call, to just 12, is as regrettable as the Navy's abolition of the rum ration. Hopefully both decisions will be reversed before too long. Dining helps build the camaraderie of the Bar, which whilst fiercely competitive is a corps of advocates with deep traditions, sensible restrictive practices and the institutional loyalty of the Household Division. It is an institution which corrupt governments and dodgy civil servants attack at their peril.

Pupillage

You can't just get a law degree, read for the Bar and expect to be let loose on the public without some on the job training. All barristers have to study under a Pupil Master for 12 months, normally two periods of six months back-to-back, although 'third sixes' are not uncommon when a 'seat', or a tenancy in chambers, is hard to find. My 'first six' was in the chambers of the late Ian Macdonald QC and Owen Davies QC, at 2 Garden Court, Middle Temple. Neither Ian nor Owen had taken silk in 1983 and they shared the burden of having me as a pupil.

My 'second six', from March until September 1984, was with Tom Culver in the chambers of that fine barrister and lovely man John Platts- Mills QC. In his day, as a left-wing Labour MP, John had upset Clement Attlee, a man who as a German spy ought to have been upset. John Platts- Mills gave me some of the best advice I ever received when he counselled his young charges at

Cloisters that the best car for a barrister to buy was a Bentley (not a Rolls-Royce - they are for solicitors) and the right mileage, about 100,000. This is just after they have been run in, have depreciated sufficiently to make them affordable for a young barrister and are not so new some might consider them a bit flashy. Another way of putting it is that a barrister ought to be buying his or her Bentley from a footballer, not selling it to them.

John, who had been called to the Bar in 1932 and had vast experience, including the Great Train Robbery Trial and defending the Kray Twins, taught me another valuable lesson. You may be a radical barrister if you like, but you are still a barrister. Whatever the politics of the case you are not justified in departing from the ethics of your profession just to achieve what you think is the right result. Not all radical barristers agreed.

One of the cardinal rules of the Bar is the 'Cab Rank Rule' under which you *must* act for a lay client. The barrister's client is always the solicitor and he or she cannot sue for their fee, as it is an honorarium, not a contract, although the rule, sadly, has been watered down as of late, part of Whitehall's assault upon the profession. In the early 1980s some radical sets started adopting byzantine rules as to whom they would act for and whom they would not.

Thus they would not act for the defence (and since they would not prosecute, not for the prosecution either) in rape cases where the defence was consent, i.e. that the lady had agreed to share her favours. They would however act where the defence was one of alibi, i.e. that there had been no sharing of favours at all. Aside from the breach of the Code of Conduct this was open to serious practical objections. What would happen, e.g., were the defendant to change his instructions, a by no means infrequent occurrence? No doubt the radical sets would answer "that's easy, we would simply withdraw from the case", but you try triggering a mistrial by withdrawing in the middle of a case, on legal aid, on professionally dodgy grounds.

I received excellent instruction from each of my Pupil Masters and owe all three a debt of gratitude. When I became a Pupil Master myself I tried to teach my young charges as well as I had been taught. Each of my Pupil Masters had interesting cases, a couple involving security. Owen Davies acted for a very nice German lady terrorist/alleged terrorist, said by the very professional BfV[13] to be a member of the Baader-Meinhof Group, a front for the DVD. They had been going around Germany assassinating people who had been standing up to the DVD, although only the top leadership of the group knew that.

Owen also had an interesting case involving a slight legal problem with the firing range at RAF Gatow in West Berlin. MI5 popped along to chambers with a safe to secure confidential documents in one of these cases, and probably emphasised that I shouldn't be allowed anywhere near them. There was still a bit of annoyance over the John Jenkins affair at Thames House apparently,[14] based on reports from an even more annoyed Special Branch in Cardiff.

Relations with MI5 were a bit strained for years. There was a hilarious moment in 1992, shortly after my appointment to the Immigration Appeal Tribunal was announced. Someone, somewhere in Whitehall, had blown a gasket, leading to an urgent summons to see the Tribunal President, that delightful man, with respect, George Farmer. He was formerly Director of Public Prosecutions in Uganda, and a very good one too. The situation had calmed down however by the time I reached Thanet House, home of the IAT.

By late 1983 Ian Macdonald had just finished writing his seminal work on immigration law, *Macdonald's Immigration Law and Practice*, still the leading text. Ian was the country's foremost immigration lawyer and I got a good grounding in this fascinating area of the law, indeed I was doing immigration cases whilst still a pupil, for the Bar's Free Representation Unit (FRU). My first ever case was for FRU, on behalf of a widow, before the dear old Westminster National Insurance Local Tribunal in Parliament Street, Westminster. They allowed the appeal.

I did a fair number of cases for FRU between 1982 and 1984, gaining an understanding of welfare and employment law. My first appearance before a High Court judge was in front of Waite J., as he then was, a sound tribunal with respect and then President of the Employment Appeal Tribunal (EAT). I was acting on behalf of a Jamaican nurse sacked by the National Health Service for stealing a bottle of milk. Even if the allegation were true, the penalty was harsh. The EAT sat in the grand surroundings of Lady Astor's old town house, right next door to the Libyan Embassy.

Quite by chance I happened to be representing one of the Libyan Embassy's chauffeurs, who from recollection had been sacked by the Libyan press agency, during the Libyan Embassy siege. The case, for unfair dismissal, came on at Woburn Place, where the Industrial Tribunals (ITs) for London North sat. London South, used to sit in or very adjacent to the old Post Office letter-opening centre in Ebury Bridge Road. The EAT, which heard appeals from ITs, had of course been evacuated.

Now most lawyers will tell that you that gunning down an unarmed woman police officer in the street would make their Top Ten list of things they do NOT want their clients doing the day before the case starts. Most judges will tell you that "I am sorry, Your Honour, but my client is under siege by armed police and refuses to come out" would make the Bottom Ten in their list of 'good reasons for granting an adjournment'. The Libyans were represented by the least radical firm of solicitors they could find, in

Lincoln's Inn Fields. The settlement negotiations were the quickest I have ever conducted and consisted essentially of working out the maximum amount the IT could award.

My First Appearance on the BBC

I was still doing my first six when President Reagan decided that it would be a good idea to invade Grenada, which is in the British Commonwealth. Poor old Maurice Bishop, a Gray's Inn man, had been assassinated, indeed he was the first member of the Inn to have suffered that fate for many years, leading to my proposing a toast in Hall to his memory. The assassination triggered the invasion, which went slightly wrong when a mental hospital was accidentally bombed.

I took the view that the invasion was not only wrong but that there were some slight difficulties with it under international law. These I proceeded to expound on the BBC, to Ian Macdonald's surprise, since Nick Ross, who was presiding, was kind enough to refer to me as an "expert in international law". Ian might have put it slightly differently, but there it was.

The Tory on the panel, Julian Amery MP, was a great character. His brother Leo had been very properly hanged as a traitor in 1946 after broadcasting for the Germans, something viewed with even greater severity than broadcasting for the BBC. He expounded the traditional Tory view of international law, which was that "you can't obey it if the other fellow doesn't", which with respect he didn't get from the writings of Sir Hersch Lauterpacht. I was then a great admirer of Lauterpacht (this was before I discovered that he was a German spy) and begged to differ. There was also a nice lady Grenadian minister called Carol on the programme, who had been caught in London when the Americans went in. She was understandably upset.

I had been on TV before, indeed my TV debut was at the age of 15 on the school quiz show *It's Academic*, the Australian version of *Top of the Form*, but this was my first national appearance on 'the Beeb'. It was fun and I went on to do a fair amount of radio and TV work over the years, including appearances on CNN, Fox News, Al Jazeera, Russia Today and Sky News, where for a couple of years I was on the panel which reviewed the morning papers.

It was whilst doing my first six that I met my first alleged murderer, in Brixton nick, although in the end he was only found guilty of manslaughter, thanks to a skilful defence by Ian. It was an interesting experience, less stressful for Ian's lay client than it might otherwise have been of course, as by then the penalty for murder had been watered down to life. In those far-off days, when ITV's hilarious TV series *Minder*[15] was still being made and you were seeing the episodes for the first time, I was a firm abolitionist and paid-up member of Amnesty International. I still bought into the myth that the death penalty had no deterrent value, although any clerk in the Temple could have told me that the murder business had been getting steadily brisker since abolition in 1965.

Nuclear-tipped cruise missiles were all the rage back then. A lot of rage was directed at them, leading to an interesting case at Newbury Magistrates' Court. Being on the left for my sins, I had of course been along to RAF Greenham Common, offering encouragement to the charming ladies and a bottle of something to keep out the cold. I marched with Michael Foot and others from Greenham to Aldermaston and generally entered into the spirit of the occasion, believing, naïvely, that nuclear weapons were bad things and that one shouldn't go around dropping them on people.

A number of the ladies were charged with criminal damage, in connection with a spot of trespass onto the base.[16] They were not intending to steal anything. They only wished to score a point and annoy the MOD, who, generally speaking, ought to be annoyed, if not abolished. A stipendiary magistrate was parachuted in from London, with respect, to hear the cases, give everybody a fair trial and find them all guilty. The proceedings were a hoot, although the 'stipe' clearly didn't think so, not with a hundred or so Greenham Women chanting in his courtroom.

Tom Culver at Cloisters was another great pupil master. A Captain in the US Air Force JAG Corps he was opposed, for some reason, to the Vietnam War and emigrated to England, where he was very welcome and an adornment to his profession. A good jury advocate, he taught me a thing or two about jury trials. His pupils were usually entertained to steak lunches from time to time, if well behaved. The tenants at Cloisters then included the glamorous Anesta Weekes, later one of the first black women silks, who most assuredly was promoted on merit, and Michael Mansfield, who also made silk and with respect was almost as good an advocate as Anesta.

Pupils can do 'small' work in their second six. The *pro bono* work for FRU in fact meant that I had acquired quite a bit of advocacy experience, in over 50 cases, before getting on my feet for the first time for an actual fee.

The First Case

This advocacy experience did not prevent me dropping rather a large clanger in my first appearance in a criminal case, at the old Tower Bridge Magistrates' Court. This ought to have been a straightforward 'either-way' hearing to determine whether a drugs allegation against, as it happened, a young black man from Brixton, should go to the Crown Court or stay at magistrates' level. The usual rule is that fights go to the Crown Court and pleas stay in the Mags, where sentencing powers are less, although more serious 'triable either way' cases can be committed to Crown for sentence. Unfortunately, the 'stipe' at Tower Bridge in those days was Captain Jobling, formerly of the Pay Corps, from memory. He was not a racist - he just didn't happen to like black people. At any rate he managed with respect to convey that impression, fairly or unfairly, at least he did to my client. Not unreasonably, he decided to exercise his right to a jury trial. Captain Jobling was not amused and demanded to know why this particular defendant wished to go to the Crown Court.

Now the next case was being defended by that charming man Yusuf Seroogolugu, originally from Uganda. In the best traditions of the Bar he had given me every possible help in the advocates room beforehand, suggesting appropriate answers to likely questions from the bench. Since jury trial was a right, the bench was not entitled to have this particular question answered and so it was not covered.

I could have explained that jury trial was the right of every free-born Englishman and Jamaican, that the court was not entitled to an answer to its question, or that the Crown Court was just around the corner (which it was) and that the case wasn't going very far. What I in fact said was that the defendant might get a fairer trial there, or words to like effect.

Now this may well have been true, but it was not the answer that Captain Jobling wished to hear. The magisterial visage darkened with a thunderous expression. By this time I had started to appreciate that I might not have given the most politic answer. Glancing to my learned friend Mr. Seroogolugu for confirmation, I saw him with his head in his hands, which was all the confirmation I needed.

Some at the Bar might have referred to Captain Jobling as a 'medium to high tariff tribunal'. Reportedly he once told a woman defendant on a drink-drive charge, who had crashed her car after getting drunk, after her oncologist told her that she had just six months to live, words to the effect that "we all have to die some time, dearie". My recollection is that he proceeded to disqualify her from driving for 18 months (ouch), although amidst the uproar that followed the dying woman's appeal was allowed by the Crown Court.

Like an infantry commander, a barrister needs an exit from an exposed position. I managed to beat a graceful retreat. More importantly, my lay client got bail and an extension of legal aid, i.e. Captain Jobling dealt with the case perfectly fairly. The next time I appeared at Tower Bridge I made a point of being as nice as possible to him. Of course he may have been chastened a bit by the furore over his drink-driving sentence. With respect his bark was probably worse than his bite. Even his sentence of disqualification in the drink-drive case wasn't outrageously high if you put to one side the fact that defendant was not expected to live long enough to serve it, although as the appeal court seem to have accepted you couldn't.

The Miners' Strike

The National Union of Mineworkers set up a temporary law centre during the 1984 Miners' Strike, in the pit village of Ollerton, in the Nottinghamshire coalfield. As the grandson of a coal miner I was only too glad to help miners and their families *pro bono*. The work was varied and interesting, and included the longest session I have yet done in court – just under fourteen hours, including breaks for lunch and dinner. It is unusual for a court to sit until five minutes to midnight. They were bailing flying pickets back to Yorkshire and everybody was keen to get them back home. A lot of the radical Bar made their way up there.

The most entertaining aspect was conducting negotiations between striking miners and the police at power station secondary picket lines. There had been a little bit of police violence and the NUM wanted legally qualified observers. This role soon expanded into negotiations, the idea being to get out of the way if they failed and a pitched battle ensued. I was assigned mostly to the Trent Valley power stations, which were generally quiet. Relations between the largely law-abiding miners and the police were good, especially if the Metropolitan Police were nowhere in sight.

I nearly got to make my first *Habeas Corpus* application, on behalf of a miner illegally detained at a police station. The nearest High Court judge, from memory, was Mr Justice Anthony Lincoln, who was sitting at Nottingham. It was getting late on a Friday afternoon and His Lordship's clerk intimated that the learned judge was understandably anxious to return to London. I was on my way, *tout de suite*, when the police, lacking any sort of legal justification for the detention and not overly anxious to be on the receiving end of a *Habeas Corpus* writ, released the miner. His anxious family were grateful.

Since the learned judge had been good enough to make himself available I made sure that the release of the miner was communicated promptly to the court. If you ask a judge to make himself available for a Habeas Corpus application you don't leave him waiting around if the detainee is released.

Law Centres

I practised in law centres for the first five years after pupillage. They were and are still a good idea, similar to a Citizens Advice Bureau, but able to conduct litigation, with solicitors and barristers. Funding came from either the old Lord Chancellor's Department, now the Orwellian- sounding Ministry of Justice, or local authorities, with costs recovered in the usual way when cases were won. People did not have to pay and casework concentrated on areas of most interest to ethnic minorities or lower income groups, mainly social security, housing, employment and immigration law.

The Bar Council fully supported the concept and gave barristers employed in law centres a general waiver[17] provided the centre had an instructing solicitor. The Law Society, which then regulated solicitors, also supported the work of the law centres, but sensibly insisted on a supervising solicitor with at least three years' experience. As I tactfully pointed out, supervising did not mean supervising barristers! Since, the professions remained divided even inside a law centre, and rightly so, I insisted on a proper brief when instructed in litigation. Pink ribbon even made its appearance on the law centre's stationery list. John Platts-Mills QC would have approved.

There was then a vogue for advertising for black lawyers, to increase the diversification of law centre staff, the Commission for Racial Equality having granted a waiver. In case anyone has not noticed, I am white. Since there was a shortage of black lawyers willing to work in law centres I was offered a series of locum appointments, in the North Lewisham Law Centre in Deptford, South Manchester Law Centre, in Longsight, Manchester, Leicester Rights Centre, in the centre of Leicester and Brixton Community Law Centre. I finally secured a permanent position at the excellent Hillingdon Legal Resource Centre (HLRC) in Hayes, West London, in early 1986. All were sited in inner-city communities, or areas with a high percentage of ethnic minorities.

The caseload was enjoyable and the pay, on local authority pay scales, not unreasonably low, but law centre politics could be convoluted. This was especially so in Brixton, where supporters of the anti-Semitic American preacher the Rev'd Louis Farrakhan had a hold. I was elected to the Executive of the Law Centres Federation (LCF) and threw myself into the work. Taking over existing cases with no handover period meant getting up to speed quickly. On one occasion the first person in the door at the Leicester Rights Centre remarked that I was "in early", only to be told I hadn't been home yet, i.e. I had worked through the night.

1. The *Factortame* cases, were brought by a shell company set up by Spanish Intelligence with a view to undermining Parliamentary sovereignty. The House of Lords, nonsensically with respect, persuaded themselves that Parliament could bind its successors and that community law took precedence over British law. The Parliamentary Supremacy point was not argued however and in the later *Metric Martyrs* Case I was able to persuade the courts that the question of priority had to be decided according to English, not European Community, law. That must be right.
2. Published by Lord Mackay of Clashfern, a charming man with respect, who appointed me to judicial office (as His Lordship might say, his only mistake), this with respect shameful document drove a deep wedge between the Tory Government and the Bar. The then Chairman of the Bar, Peter Fennell QC, a very able and courageous advocate, was worn down by the battle against an obdurate government and bureaucracy. His health, sadly, was broken.
3. The rumour that I am included in that illustrious company sadly is unfounded. John Mortimer and I only met once, briefly, after the *Rumpole* books and TV series had achieved their richly deserved critical acclaim.
4. It didn't. You only make a submission of no case to answer at the end of the prosecution case (hence 'half-time') if there is insufficient evidence upon which a jury, properly instructed, could convict. They are normally a waste of time, as the judge is not the jury, the jury are. Judges are not entrusted with finding facts in important criminal cases for a reason. Old Bailey Judges are always as addressed as 'My Lord' by the way, whatever their rank.
5. Have a look at his argument in *Selangor United Rubber Estates v. Cradock* [1968] 2 All ER 1073. One test of a good lawyer is whether he or she falls for the nostrum that you need more than one term to define the genus in the ancient *Ejusdem Generis* Rule (general words take their meaning from a preceding particular word or words), which goes back to the late 13th century and with which every law student will be familiar. In contrast Lord Diplock with respect failed to avoid making this basic mistake in *Quazi* v. *Quazi* [1980] AC 744.
6. They still had the power to hold committal hearings (universally known as 'old-styles') but even that has now gone in relation to indictable offences and they were largely a ritual farce anyway, with respect. They have been replaced with interlocutory dismissal hearings, which frankly are a bit of a joke.
7. Speaker.
8. President of the Civil Division of the Court of Appeal in England.
9. The key Abwehr assets in the Civil Service in World War II were the Cabinet Secretary Sir Edward Bridges, later Lord Bridges, a protégé of the notorious Lord Hankey, and Sir Horace Wilson, who was close to Chamberlain and became Permanent Secretary to the Treasury after Churchill chucked him out of Downing Street. Tragically for the Allies, neither was hanged.
10. The senior Bencher, or 'big cheese' of the Inn, chosen annually and invariably a judge or silk of distinction.

11. That's Reading in the Royal County of Berkshire, not Reading Pennsylvania, i.e. not very far at all. It was a student dinner at the end of the day, not a state banquet.
12. As observed elsewhere this is an intelligence history, not a tragedy, so I am not dwelling too much on my romantic episodes, which sadly tended to be just that, i.e. episodes, at least until I met Henry.
13. *Bundesamt für Verfassungsschutz*, or Federal Office for the Protection of the Constitution.
14. HQ of MI5.
15. A great TV series from Euston Films, starring those fine actors George Cole and Dennis Waterman. The fictional hero, Arthur Daley, entered the language, along with his catchphrase "'er indoors", referring of course to the wife, who like Captain Mainwaring's wife Elizabeth in *Dad's Army* was talked about but never seen.
16. The MOD with respect stuffed up their case over trespass on the common itself by misusing their powers under the Military Lands Act 1892, leading to a successful challenge on appeal to the Crown Court at Reading, which the DPP, unwisely with respect, appealed all the way to the House of Lords. He lost in fine style, the case being reported as *R v Reading Crown Court ex p Hutchinson*. The case confirmed the principle that you may take a public law point - in this case the legality of the bye-law under which the defendant was charged - as part of your defence, i.e. there is no need to go to the trouble and expense of applying for judicial review. I later applied the decision in immigration cases, holding judicially that immigrants could raise public law challenges to ministerial decisions they were challenging on appeal.
17. In the mid-1980s this was contained in paragraph 33 of the then Code of Conduct. I always kept a copy handy in case my rights of audience were contested.

4

Into Politics

The Fight To Save the Settle To Carlisle Railway

Deptford (North Lewisham Law Centre) was fun, but a lengthy commute as I was sharing a flat on Putney Hill. No car then of course, and not a lot of parking in Deptford High Street anyway. Manchester was great and afforded the opportunity for trips back to London on the *Manchester Pullman*, the swishest train on British Railways. I had been nominated by the Inner London Education Authority (ILEA) to be a governor of Garnett College, the lecturers' training college in Roehampton, and ILEA paid governors first class. This meant full English breakfast on the up train and dinner on the down - great! There were also steam-hauled trips over the Settle to Carlisle Railway and some good runs, usually behind a Sulzer- engined *Peak* class diesel, through the Pennines to Leeds, York or Edinburgh, for political meetings.

The Settle to Carlisle is the most scenically magnificent railway in England. It is a wonderful tribute to her builders and still a vital alternative route from London to Scotland. It permits Euston-Glasgow expresses to be diverted via Hellifield should there be engineering works on the West Coast Main Line or an *al Qaeda* cell in say Oldham decide to pull a critical bolt from a set of points and derail an express. Steam-hauled runs up the 1-100 'Long Drag' on the S & C were a delight. Then some idiot decided to close it. This led to closure hearings before the Transport Users Consultative Committee (TUCC), initially in Appleby-in- Westmoreland, which is no longer in Westmoreland.

I agreed to represent the objectors *pro bono*, working with a very good London commercial solicitor, Ed Album. Our exploits are recorded in a couple of the books on the S & C closure battle,[1] the greatest in British railway history. It achieved victory after several years and halted, even if it did not reverse, the trend in rail closures. These had accelerated dramatically in the 60s under the notorious Dr Richard Beeching, who turned out to be a German spy. Excluding Jack the Ripper, who as we shall see didn't exist,

Beeching was arguably the most hated figure in British history since Richard III. Not even Tony Blair comes close.

The closure of the S & C made no sense. I, and others ripped into British Railway's economic case, showing, e.g., that their accounts were loading the entire annual maintenance costs for a locomotive onto the line even if it made only one journey over it in a year. Receipts for travel to or over the line were credited to the issuing office, so if you bought a ticket in Plymouth to go to Appleby, Western Region snapped up the lot. The estimated costs for repairing the great Ribblehead Viaduct, which had been allowed by BR to fall into disrepair through the simple expedient of not renewing the waterproof membrane protecting the hollow pillars, were ludicrously over the top.

The bridge consultant brought in by the objectors, who numbered some 23,000 people and a dog, Ruswarp, was Christopher Wallis, the younger son of the great Barnes Wallis. Barnes had annoyed the Germans in World War II by helping to design the Vickers Wellington bomber, [2] followed by the famous Bouncing Bomb for the Dambusters Raid, the Tallboy, which sank, or more correctly, capsized, the *Tirpitz* (I have met several of the crew who were on that raid) and the mighty ten-ton Grand Slam. That was a serious bit of kit. There is no better way of annoying a German than dropping a ten-ton bomb on him.

There was a neat symmetry in having a bridge-builder whose father was a bridge-buster. The most famous Grand Slam raid was on the Bielefeld Viaduct, south of Cologne. The footage is worth watching next time it comes around on the History Channel. It was a lovely bit of bombing, by 617 Squadron.

My opponent at the Appleby hearings was that nice man Michael Harrison QC, later Mr Justice Harrison. I raised a titter, in which the nice lady Chairman, a wonderful, old-fashioned country Justice of the Peace called Olive, joined, when I deferred to the other Michael on a point of procedure. I emphasised that he was probably right, as he was a silk, whereas I was just "a humble polyester".

The issue of whether Ruswarp, on whose behalf a ticket had been purchased, could lawfully be an objector was never resolved. He was a good dog. When his owner met an untimely, and slightly mysterious, death on a remote Welsh mountainside, Ruswarp stayed by the body for weeks. Happily, Ruswarp went to a good home. After he died a statue was erected in his memory, which you can see at Garsdale Station.

Richard Beeching

It is a fundamental rule of counterintelligence that you should not allow your personal feelings to affect your professional judgment, indeed it is a good rule in all professions. You might have met the person whom you have concluded is a German spy and liked him or her, and think it a dreadful personal tragedy that they should have got into such a mess, but you cannot on those grounds decline to give your true opinion. This happened to me when I was asked, entirely informally, on behalf of a certain regiment, to advise on whether or not an army officer, whom I had met and liked, betrayed several thousand men, many of whom died, to an SS Panzer Division in World War II. The answer, sadly, was yes, even though I would much have preferred to say "no, actually it was Edward Heath".

By the same token disliking what someone has done is no excuse for being less than objective. This is a different thing from saying that you cannot be pleased if you find out that a ratbag also turns out to have been a German spy. You *are* allowed to enjoy your work. The ratbag in question was of course none other than Richard Beeching, or as he is known by some in INTELCOM, 'von Beeching'. He spied for the Abwehr in World War II and the DVD thereafter. He assisted in technology transfer to Nazi Germany in four crucial areas:

(1) High octane aviation fuels (whilst at the Fuel Research Station, Greenwich), an area of great interest to the Luftwaffe.
(2) Advanced nickel alloys, of particular interest to JUMO[3] and BMW[4] in relation to the Messerschmitt Me-262 jet fighter[5] and Arado Ar-234 jet bomber programmes.
(3) Other advanced metallurgical research, in particular in relation to bomb casings and internal components for the German atomic weapons programme[6] (whilst with Mond Nickel), and
(4) High performance explosives, in particular plastic explosives for use by the Abwehr's Sabotage Section, headed by Skorzeny (whilst attached to the Armament Design and Research Establishment at Fort Halstead).

'Von' Beeching was the principal asset tasked with dismantling Britain's rail infrastructure, a mission he undertook with gusto, with his two notorious reports. Thankfully the Labour government sacked him in 1965 before he did any more damage. Beeching was paid absurdly high sums. No great intellect was required to produce his reports after all - they were essentially gibberish. He was used to trial a new method of paying spies, i.e. getting the target country to pay for them.

The S & C would have been closed under the Second Beeching Report and the 1985-89 closure battle, was essentially the Beeching Battle Phase Three. It was a terrible tragedy for Britain that 'von' Beeching was not spotted by MI5 in World War II and hanged, nicely of course. Interestingly, one of the

DVD Civil Service penetration assets assigned to Beeching was David, later Sir David, Serpell. He had previously worked on dismantling the British aircraft industry. Sadly, the Bad Guys got about two-thirds of our aircraft industry and half the railways.

If you expose a nice German spy, by the way, the correct procedure for dealing with him is set out by the great actor Sir John Mills in the famous old war film *Ice Cold in Alex*. He bought Anthony Quayle's character, 'Captain van der Poel', a cold beer in a bar in Alexandria, removed all his South African insignia ('der Poel' was masquerading as a Boer) and turned him over to the Military Police with a fake story about him being a captured German officer who had given his parole. This ensured that he wasn't shot. PBS should show the film in the States.

After Manchester

Manchester was followed by Leicester, where there was friendly rivalry with the Highfields and Belgrave Law Centre, where the solicitor was Keith Vaz. This was Keith's radical period. Later he became an enthusiast for the European Union, no offence intended. The short spell in Brixton (the law centre, not the nick) was notable for Operation *Cromwell*, a rather silly Met anti-drugs operation, which saw 300 police descend from a train parked on the embankment behind Railton Road.

From memory it netted a couple of wraps of a herbal substance that may not have been tobacco and an imitation firearm. GO2 had probably passed word along that the police were on their way and there may have been some activity on Railton Road beforehand. Half of Brixton seemed to have been arrested and it was several days before I got a square meal and a good night's sleep.

Transport was now an elderly (1968) but delightful Rover 2000TC, which I bought for a song. She drove like a dream, thanks partly to that wonderful De Dion rear suspension, and was great fun on runs from Leicester to Wales to see to the aunts. Sadly however, the sills fell out, a hazard with P6s. She was replaced by a stately and wonderfully comfy Rover 3.5 Litre (P5B) Saloon, complete with Connolly hide seats, picnic table under the dash, a gloriously old-fashioned instrument binnacle, white on black British Jaeger instruments and proper Bakelite toggle switches. The ex-Buick[7] V8 meant that she could pick up her skirts when required, as demonstrated to a doubtful Chairman of Horsham Constituency Labour Party in 1987.

As stated in the last chapter I was a bit left wing in those days, but I was not a loony. I never believed in man-made global warming, e.g. I made a point of trying to look like a barrister, as well as trying to behave like one. One of my slightly more radical colleagues in the South Manchester Law Centre took a dim view when my new, blue robe bag arrived from Ede & Ravenscroft, outfitters to the legal profession on Chancery Lane.

The robe bag, the Bar's version of the burglar's swag, is a jolly useful device - it swallows robe, wig tin, band box, papers and, occasionally, lunch. You just sling it over your shoulder. Silks have red bags and by tradition present one to a junior who has been of particular assistance. However, I have only been led by a silk three times, was of no assistance at all to my leaders and carried my wig and gown in a blue bag until wrongfully disbarred. Law centre barristers just weren't expected to turn up at court with a blue bag. They weren't expected to turn up wearing a black jacket and striped trousers either, but I did, although I may have overdone the conservative dress thing a bit when I allowed my then tailor, the late Stanley Ley, to sell me a bowler hat. This caused an adjournment of a Law Centres Federation Executive Committee meeting whilst everybody went outside for a photo.

Stuffy opponents expecting a bearded lefty to turn up in a rusty Renault clutching a file were sometimes taken aback when I rolled up in a Rover 3.5 Litre, complete with Fox-frame brolly, John Cleese 'Ministry of Silly Walks' suit with bowler hat, blue robe bag, papers neatly bound by pink ribbon and a proper counsel's notebook. Not all my law centre colleagues approved but I found that clients wanted a proper barrister, so I did my best to imitate one.

A poor persons' lawyer does not have to be a poor lawyer. In Manchester I joined the Northern Circuit, attended the Bar Mess and tried to behave in court as a lawyer should. Judges seemed to notice. At any rate I received an honourable mention at a judge's dinner in Manchester.[8]

Anti-Apartheid

AAM activities took up a lot of time in the 1980s. A few occasions stand out in the memory, the first being an Anti-Apartheid rally in Trafalgar Square. I was a steward and was up on the plinth, beneath the statute of Lord Nelson, looking after that nice man Alfred Nzo, then Secretary-General of the African National Congress (ANC). Later he was the first post-apartheid Foreign Minister of South Africa. He wrote me a lovely letter on his appointment.

Alfred was caught short and he and I, who had strict instructions not to lose the Secretary-General, went in search of a gents. The police, expecting trouble, had sealed off all the nearby conveniences however. By the time one was located, under Charing Cross Station, I needed to perform my ablutions as well, remarking to the Secretary-General as we went about our business that it was just as well we weren't in South Africa, otherwise we'd have needed to find two loos! It was not the wittiest of remarks, but Alfred thought it was funny. There were quizzical looks from fellow ablutionists as he burst out laughing. They probably thought he was laughing at something else.

The 75th Anniversary of the ANC in 1987 was the occasion of a great celebration at Alexandra Palace, graced by the rather stunning Zenani Mandela, if I may say so. I was again a steward, having managed not to lose the Secretary-General of the ANC, and was backstage, just like old times at the Students Union. Hugh Masekela gave the best live trumpet performance I have ever heard, seeming to derive extra energy from the audience. The apartheid regime had more money and guns, but AAM had the best bands.

I helped found Lawyers Against Apartheid, partly inspired by the late Kader Asmal, later a government minister. He was then a distinguished international lawyer in the peaceful surroundings of Trinity College, Dublin, although my motives for popping over to Ireland had more to do with a nice lady solicitor at a law centre in Dublin. Politics came into play however and there were strong moves to force me out of Lawyers Against Apartheid. HE the Nicaraguan Ambassador was a bit more appreciative, after I penned an article for the *Guardian* on the *Nicaragua v. United States* sea mines case. I was very amused to learn years later that a friend, as he became, in CIA, Duane Clarridge, had organised the mines!

In 1985 I flew to Bonn to attend my one and only conference at the West German Bundestag, hosted by the West German Green Party. One of my fellow delegates was Anton Lubowski,[9] a lawyer in Windhoek, who acted for SWAPO, the South West Africa People's Organisation. He was assassinated four years later by the CCB,[10] the first time someone I met (and admired) was assassinated, but sadly not the last.

The jovial SWAPO President (1960-2007) and future President of Namibia (1990-2005), Sam Nujoma, gave the keynote. He thought I was a bit premature in addressing him as "Your Excellency" but didn't seem to mind too much. By the way I think the Norwegians over-egged the pudding when they had a go at poor old Sam for ordering a presidential jet just after he'd appealed for some drought aid. What was he supposed to do? Fly South African Airways? Use up his air miles? Aid donors can be very picky sometimes.

If Sam Nujoma was the most impressive African political leader I met during this period the most impressive African military commander was General Roberto Ngongo, of the Angolan armed forces (FAPLA). Sadly, he later had a slight disagreement with Angolan President Eduardo dos Santos.

Hillingdon Legal Resource Centre

Hillingdon was my final law centre before setting up in private practice in early 1989. There were some interesting cases, two of which went to the Court of Appeal and one to the European Court of Justice in Luxembourg. The presiding judge at the local county court, Uxbridge, was that sound and efficient tribunal with respect, His Honour Judge Barr.

In one of my early appearances at Uxbridge I fell victim to an old trick, which might have been inspired by an episode of *Rumpole of the Bailey*. I was assured that His Honour liked nothing more than a nice point of law and always wished to be taken to the authorities. "Ah", said I, "I like a nice point of law myself, so this should be fun". I cannot now remember the point - it may have been something to do with equitable set-off by a tenant of arrears of rent. At any rate I rolled up to court with the Rover's boot full of law reports and legal texts, having given my opponent due notice. As the Rover had a large boot my learned friend might have started to regret the dodgy advice he gave me in the robing room after the earlier directions hearing.

The earliest case I cited was a decision by Judge Jefferies, of Bloody Assizes fame, who had very properly sentenced the Duke of Monmouth's surviving rebels to hang. A few polite words about Judge Jefferies, who like Captain Jobling was a medium to high tariff tribunal, and rather a better lawyer than most legal historians allow, raised a wan smile from the Bench. By now however I had grasped that the learned judge liked nothing more than agreement between the parties and a quick settlement. This was promptly achieved after a short adjournment, my learned friend viewing the lengthy row of law reports, all neatly tagged, with lots of paper tags sticking out, with as much suspicion as the judge.

My first appearance in the Court of Appeal, in 1987, caused some scratching of heads in the Civil Appeals Office. They had never heard of a law centre barrister exercising rights of audience in the country's second- highest court. Quite rightly with respect dear old Registrar Adams, Registrar of Civil Appeals, wanted chapter and verse from the Code of Conduct, so Paragraph 33 was read down the telephone the afternoon before the hearing. In fact a nice lady barrister, later a government minister, Barbara Roche MP, had got there first, although possibly in the Criminal Division.

The case was *Karim v. Sunblest Bakeries Ltd*. Mr Karim was a baker of Pakistani origins who had been unfairly sacked by Sunblest, makers it has to be said, rather than bakers, of bread. John Frost, a wonderful bloke, who had been a drummer for Manfred Mann's Earth Band but left them before their first hit (his timing was more effective on the legal stage), had won Mr

Karim's case before the Industrial Tribunal. That should have been an end to it, but Sunblest appealed.

It was one of those cases that might have gone either way at first instance, as under the Employment Protection (Consolidation) Act 1978 the employer had a fair deal of discretion. The Employment Appeal Tribunal however, presided over by Mr Justice Kilner Brown, allowed Sunblest's appeal, which with respect they had no business doing. No doubt they were led into their error by effective advocacy from Sunblest's counsel, Alan Wilkie, later Mr Justice Wilkie. He presided over a sensational murder trial, *R v Bellfield*, in 2011. Through no fault of his own, he was forced to hand down the usual soft sentence, to the dismay of the murdered girl's grieving parents.

John Frost sought my advice, which was to run the EAT ruling up to the Court of Appeal. The presiding judge was Lord Donaldson of Lymington, Master of the Rolls and nobody's fool, with respect. It looked like an easy win for the bread-makers, at any rate Alan Wilkie seemed to think that he hadn't got too much to do to earn his crust that day.

I respectfully piled into the EAT however, making the point that they were an appellate tribunal and had not the opportunity which the lower tribunal had of seeing and hearing the witnesses. Put shortly, whilst both the EAT and the Court of Appeal were entitled to think they might have decided the case differently, the IT's approach could not be faulted and there were no proper grounds for interfering. Things started going wrong for the other side when that splendid old tribunal with respect, Sir Roualeyn Cumming-Bruce, interrupted me (I didn't mind!) and remarked to his learned brethren "he's right you know, he's right!" Lord Donaldson had no need to trouble me in reply to my learned friend. As a High Court judge Sir Roualeyn had presided over the Tony Hancock divorce case. He was an artilleryman, with a distinguished war record in North Africa. His twin brother had been Governor of the Bahamas.

The *Page & Davis* Case

Page & Davis v Chief Adjudication Officer had a much longer history and a less happy outcome. HLRC's excellent welfare rights adviser, Steve James, came to me with a very troublesome case, later linked with the *Davis* case. The Department of Health and Social Security wished to recover overpaid benefit from Mrs Page, a widow, but she had done nothing wrong. Indeed, the DHSS accepted that her misrepresentation had been innocent. This is more common than might be supposed, as Britain's welfare system is Byzantine in its complexity.

Section 20 of the Supplementary Benefits Act 1976 provided that overpaid monies could be recovered if there had been a misrepresentation "whether fraudulently or otherwise". Praying in aid the *Ejusdem Generis* Rule (*mea culpa* if there is too much Latin) I advised that in the absence of words enlarging the ordinary legal meaning these words could not possibly mean "fraudulently or honestly".

The trouble was that this was precisely the meaning a Social Security Commissioner, who shall remain nameless, had given them, without argument, in a with respect dodgy decision back in 1981. By the late 1980s hundreds of millions of pounds of benefits had been clawed back unlawfully. We in the HLRC team had an uphill struggle on our hands.

The DHSS, ambitiously with respect, started out by saying that Lord Diplock had stated the law correctly in *Quazi v. Quazi* (1980). His Lordship had opined without argument that the *Ejusdem Generis* Rule, whereby general words must be read in context and their meaning cut down if specific cases are mentioned, could only apply where there were two or more words describing the genus.

This with respect was obviously wrong, not only as a matter of law but of logic, since the general words bring in cases which are alike but by definition are not identical to the specific examples. Thus the phrase "Tony Blair and other politicians" would apply not just to Tony Blair but to other ambitious, scheming politicians as well, no offence intended Tony.

I researched at least 25 cases where the rule had been applied to a 'one-word' phrase, including four in the House of Lords. The oldest example I found, covered in dust in the basement of the Middle Temple Library (the book, not me) dated from the turn of the 14th century. The rule itself is even older. There was an amusing episode before the Social Security Commissioner, when I cited an even earlier case, from 1292, and the Commissioner was convinced that I must have had said '1922'. The eventual loss of the case before the Court of Appeal was a blow. I intend no offence when I say that its ruling that "fraudulently or otherwise" means "fraudulently or honestly" is unlikely to stand the test of time.

Webb v EMO Air Cargo (UK) Ltd

The third of my cases from Hillingdon, which went to the Court of Appeal, *Webb v Emo Air Cargo (UK) Ltd*, went even further, reaching the House of Lords (twice!) and the European Court of Justice. The issue was whether or not it was sex discrimination to sack a woman because she was pregnant. You might think that was a 'no-brainer', but the EAT and the Court of Appeal, with respect, had managed to come up with the concept of the 'hypothetical pregnant man'. The idea was that it wouldn't be sex discrimination if a man with a 'disease similar to pregnancy' was treated in the same way.

One respected liberal lawyer even went so far as to suggest that a man with a venereal disease would be an appropriate comparator, presumably on the basis that pregnancy and VD, at least at the outset, both involve the 'wobbly bits'. With great respect to those taking the contrary view there were two tiny flaws in the 'hypothetical pregnant man' argument. The first was that pregnancy is not a disease. The second was that it was bollocks.

Carole Webb came into the law centre one morning late in 1987 seeking advice about her tenancy. The building society were about to foreclose. Her landlord had lied to the building society and stated that he was living in the house, whereas in fact it was a buy-to-let, a prevalent form of mortgage fraud on which the police, very properly, were cracking down. I happened to be working on reception, so it fell to me to fill in the Legal Aid form, for which I needed Carole's income details.

She told me that she had been sacked the previous week. That got my attention. When I asked why, without any prompting at all, she said it was because she was pregnant. I advised that sadly there was no defence against the building society and all I could do was negotiate extra time, as she was an innocent third party, but that she had a viable claim for sex discrimination.[11] I told my colleagues that the case could go all the way to Luxembourg, but they didn't believe me.

Carole, a very nice person by the way, made more money out of media fees than she did out of the case itself, and rightly so. On instructions, I tried to settle the case, but the employer, a decent man but not with respect a feminist, said it was a question of principle. Indeed it was. Whilst on the cusp of being a Eurosceptic I have never let any political opinion I might hold affect my legal opinion. The case could only be won on the European Sex Discrimination Directive, even though it was adopted after the Sex Discrimination Act. *Webb* established that an Act of Parliament may be interpreted in the light of the *travaux preparatoires*[12] of an instrument which Parliament intends to incorporate into law but whose formal promulgation post-dates the Act.

European Court of Justice rules on conflicting decisions by national courts are clear. There was a slightly tense moment at the Industrial Tribunal when the, with respect, somewhat incredulous Chairman asked me if I was seriously inviting the Tribunal to disregard, i.e. treat as wrongly decided, a recent decision of the House of Lords. Indeed I was, as it was in clear conflict with an ECJ decision.

The case lasted long after I left HLRC and was handed over, in turn, to Stephen Sedley QC (later Lord Justice Sedley) and Laura Cox QC (later Mrs Justice Cox). Carole Webb never forgot who had spotted the point in the first place however. Eleven years after drafting the 'IT1' originating application

I was counsel at the IT when compensation was finally agreed, in what was by now a famous employment law case being taught in every law school in the country.

Ironically the final amount was in line with what I had offered to settle for back in 1987. I never overstated the amount at stake, indeed I accepted throughout that compensation would have to be at the lower end of the scale. What I tried to keep at the forefront of my mind was the age-old distinction between liability and quantum. If a man assaults and batters you, but only causes bruising, his actions are no less unlawful than if he breaks your leg. You are not entitled however to the same level of damages, if you only suffer bruising, that you might receive with a broken leg.

The *Webb* Case was my first encounter with the Equal Opportunities Commission. They did not impress. They kept making the point that the case was "not strong on the facts", when what they meant was that it would not be a high compensation case. Well, no one was suggesting that it was. It was rather ironic really. Not even my best friend would describe me as a rampant feminist, yet here I was fighting for an important principle of sex discrimination law on which even the EOC had wimped out.

In one sense *Webb* was actually a strong case on the facts, because Carole's employer gave truthful evidence. A less honest man might have tried to lie his way out of liability. The Commission for Racial Equality, with whom I dealt more frequently, over race discrimination cases, were better than the EOC, but neither was particularly good. They were eventually rolled up into a pointless quango, the Equality and Human Rights Commission, which sounds like a UN body and does about as much good.

Spycatcher

Another interesting case, for me anyway, involved *Spycatcher*, which of course inspired the title of this book. (I could hardly call it *Spymaster*!). It too was written partly in Tasmania, by former MI5 Assistant Director Peter Wright, to whom I pay frank tribute. Peter personally dealt with J. Edgar Hoover in the FBI, although they didn't get along terribly well. The air in Tasmania is clear and seems to encourage clear thinking. The scenery is beautiful, the people hospitable, there are very few German spies about and unlike Thames Valley, it is efficiently policed.

Entirely by chance the first copies into the UK just happen to have been imported by one of my lay clients. Showing commendable enterprise, he had flown to New York with an empty suitcase and returned the same day, stopping only to buy lunch and a hundred copies of *Spycatcher*, which he proceeded to sell from a roadside stall in Westminster. He was moved on by the police (no surprise there) and ended up by the A40, the main road out of London for Oxford and Cheltenham, whereupon he was arrested for obstructing the highway, whereupon he was referred to HLRC.

Ambitiously perhaps, I advised that there was a public interest defence, i.e. the public interest in knowing what had been going on was greater than the public interest in getting home. The obstruction was not that great, since the lay client, not being a complete fool, had set up his stall beside the highway, not in it. The case went up to the Divisional Court, where that conspicuously fair tribunal, with respect, Mr Justice McPherson, departed slightly from his usual courtroom demeanour of great patience and humility, and offered me some valuable guidance. Sir William, a delightful man, who sadly passed in 2021, was ex SAS and 27th Chief of the Clan McPherson.

The *Spycatcher* team were forced into a tactical retreat, but the fine was low, the books were sold and some members of the public at least were better informed. Poor old Chapman Pincher, a gent if ever there was one, to whom Peter was introduced by the German spy Victor Rothschild, who was pretending at the time to be a British spy, never got the credit he deserved for the forerunner to *Spycatcher, Their Trade is Treachery.* Both books need to be read together, Chapman's being the more elegantly written tome if I may say so.

Peter never got his pension, not the full whack at any rate, and died not long afterwards, never knowing how close he got to revealing the DVD and blowing Roger Hollis's cover. Hollis was his boss at MI5 and was of course a German, not a Soviet, agent. Years later Chapman Pincher and I met for a most agreeable lunch but we had a slight disagreement over whether or not Victor Rothschild was a British or German spy. Strictly speaking, I suppose, he was both, i.e. a double agent. He was, however, quite a nice German spy. If you caught him, you would have had him straight round for lunch, not hanged.

Not long afterwards there was more family tragedy, sadly, when Uncle George, for whom I had enormous affection and respect, died of lung cancer, brought on partly no doubt by smoking, but not helped by decades of hard work in the Port Talbot Steelworks. Agnes and Zita nursed him devotedly in Orchard Cottage, but the diagnosis had come too late and nothing could be done. The poor man, strong as an ox in life and an ex- Royal Marine, was ravaged by what is a cruel illness, weighing less than eight stone by the end.

The 1987 General Election

My one and only general election campaign came in 1987, when I was adopted as Labour candidate for Horsham, the safest Tory seat in England. I increased the Labour vote by about 50% on the redrawn boundaries (the only two

Labour-voting wards had been lost to the neighbouring seat of Crawley, eventually won for Labour in 1997 by Laura Moffat). The Tory candidate was that nice man the late Sir Peter Hordern. The campaign nearly got off to a faltering start. Clare Short, the nice, left-wing Labour MP and later Cabinet Minister, who had principles (wrong ones with respect, but at least she had them), had to pull out of the campaign kick-off meeting. The meeting was in Billingshurst, West Sussex. Clare had to go to her own adoption meeting in Birmingham. These are arranged at short notice after an election is called and the prospective candidate always has to attend. At least it meant I 'drew' a large crowd, who of course had turned up to hear Clare, i.e. I had been booked as the warm-up act but was now the main event.

The meeting was due to start at seven pm. Expecting to drive well over a thousand miles in the course of a four week campaign in a large constituency by Home Counties standards, which stretched from Gatwick Airport to the South Downs, the first thing I did on hearing that the election had been called was to book the dear old Rover in for service. There was a firm injunction that she had to be ready by no later than 4 pm on the day of the meeting. "No worries Michael, we'll make sure she's ready in time."

Well they didn't and she wasn't, leading to increasingly frantic calls from Horsham and a plan to grab a taxi and be met half-way by the Chairman. He was on the phone at 6 pm when the long-delayed car finally arrived, the driver being met with a roared order through the window to leave the engine running and the bill in the driver's map pocket. I settled the "you'll never make it, you'll need a helicopter" "I haven't got a helicopter" argument by stating that I was on my way and breaking off the call, politely of course. I dashed out of the door, not forgetting my small kit and the back of the envelope on which I had sketched my speech notes.

I was then living near Hillingdon, i.e. in West London. The venue was 60 miles away, it was rush hour and traffic was leaving London, i.e. going the same way I was. I will never forget the look of astonishment on the face of the driver of a Lotus Esprit doing a ton in the fast lane of the M3, who had moved smartly out of the way as the elderly but powerful Rover roared up behind him, indeed had been forced to slow down.

The needle was hovering on 110 as the old girl swept majestically past, still accelerating, with a gloved hand acknowledging the courtesy of the Lotus driver in giving way (the poor man probably traded her in for a Turbo the next day). A well-tuned Rover 3.5 Litre will reach about 115 mph before the drag of that large frontal area kicks in and you start to encounter the law of diminishing returns, i.e. a brick wall.

With the big Lucas headlamps piercing what was by now night the old V8 just thundered away, never missing a beat. All done in complete safety of course, with no inconvenience to other motorists - the Chief Constable might be reading this after all. Dropped into intermediate a big Rover will overtake quite nicely and the two-lane A29 seemed to be a succession of overtaking manoeuvres, although for safety's sake I kept her to about 90. Aware that the press were there, anxious not to run over a voter with two tons of Rover, and wishing to convey the impression that running down to Billingshurst from Hounslow in just under an hour was a doddle, I remembered that ploy from *The Gumball Rally.* I slowed right down just before the 30 mph signs and swept majestically into the car park at a stately 20 mph or so, on the dot of seven. Anxious constituency officers were standing outside, trying not to look at their watches.

The campaign was a lot of fun, with a small but enthusiastic bunch of constituency workers. Lady Hordern complained to the effect that her husband had never been made to work so hard. Sir Peter said nice things about the Rover, which looked just right with campaign posters in the rear windows and loudspeakers on the roof. Nobody minded too much when I got the name of a village wrong, even though I was on the loudspeakers at the time (oops).

The cricket season had started and Sussex were playing one of their few fixtures at Horsham. I rang up Conservative HQ and suggested a truce for the duration of the match to the startled Tory at the other end of the line. My poor agent was equally doubtful, until I explained that every sensible person in Horsham and surrounds, including the late Christopher Martin- Jenkins,[13] would be at the match. I also explained that a truce did not mean that I could not wear my Labour rosette.

The 1989 European Parliament Election

Not long after the General Election I was adopted for the even larger West Sussex European Parliament constituency, the Tory candidate being the sitting MEP, Madron Seligman. He was a German agent, although that's not what he said in his campaign literature and I was unaware of the fact at the time. Selection well in advance of the election meant time for meetings with distinguished co-speakers such as Dennis Skinner, the firebrand MP for Bolsover, Jack Straw, future Home and Foreign Secretary and Tam Dalyell MP.

Tam was rightly exercised by what he saw as Defence Secretary John Nott's lies to the House of Commons about the position of the enemy cruiser ARA *General Belgrano* in the Falklands War.[14] The Royal Navy could have attacked her if they had found her off the Canaries, but it was wrong to mislead the House. It is now accepted that the House was misled, the Official Version of Events being that the misleading was unintentional on the part of the Secretary of State for Defence.

It was fortunate that I had turned down Dennis Skinner's offer of a pint, as I was hauled over for speeding (no admissions are made) and breathalysed, Dennis being anxious to make the last train from St. Pancras.[15] The police seemed not to believe the proffered explanation that the MP for Bolsover was running late for his train, until they looked into the passenger side of the Rover and found a highly amused MP for Bolsover scarcely able to contain himself. Dennis is a good bloke, with generally sound views on the European Union. He was a good constituency MP and his heart is in the right place, an observation I would also make of the long since departed and popular left-wing MP for Liverpool Walton, Eric Heffer.

Eric, a carpenter, and I seemed to get along just fine. Eric would never have dreamt of telling me how to conduct a case in court and I would never have dreamt of telling Eric how to make a fine piece of furniture. If you are ever near a set of shelves I have put up you would be well advised not to stand under them. Eric seemed to respect my profession and education and I in turn respected him for his obvious decency, patriotism, integrity and loyalty to his constituents.

Neither of us had much time for the trendy New Labour crowd, which was then trying to take over the party. Incidentally, my favourable view of Eric Heffer was shared by Lady Thatcher, who went to his funeral, which is more than I managed. Margaret always respected principled opponents who stood by their views. As a man Eric Heffer was worth more than half her Cabinet combined.

Since I was still living in London I offered to collect Tam Dalyell from the House of Commons for our meeting. The Rover felt right at home outside the Members' Entrance. It is often forgotten that in addition to the Great Storm of October 1987 (what a night that was) there was a Lesser Storm, which happened to be on the night of this particular meeting in Crawley.

Perhaps the memory is playing tricks, but the A23 and M23 seemed to be full of high-sided trucks and small European and Japanese cars weaving about all over the road, along with the odd tree branch, rubbish bin etc. It was an opportunity to demonstrate the P5's great stability in a crosswind anyway. With respect, I can well understand why the late Queen kept Her P5 for years.

On one occasion - this may have been just after the European Election - the late John Prescott, future Deputy Prime Minister, was unable to make a meeting on transport policy in Arundel. He asked me to stand in for him. This was a disappointment for the audience, but they seemed to bear it well. No voters were punched. John taught me a useful trick of the trade when I drove him to a meeting with the Civil Aviation Authority at the Beehive, a strange, round building near Gatwick Airport.

News at Ten were covering the story but the camera crew did not associate the stately Rover P5B with John Prescott, although he was a fairly stately sort of chap if I may say so. At any rate they weren't ready, so John shouted out the front passenger window that he was going to do the entrance a second time and suggested they might like to get the cameras ready. Naturally, as John's chauffeur for the day, I obliged. The footage made the national news that night from memory and is probably buried somewhere in the ITN archives.

Jim and Audrey Callaghan, both good people with respect - Jim was a naval intelligence officer in World War II - lived just outside the constituency. They were kind enough to come over for a few hours in support of my campaign. This seemed to surprise some of the constituency activists, not all of whom believed that Jim Callaghan would show up. He did. There is probably a photo in the *West Sussex County Times* to prove it.

Jim was in many ways an underrated Prime Minister. His victory over the Cabinet Office in getting a proper Silver Jubilee for the late Queen was a sweet one, a real triumph of Good over Evil. The Cabinet Office probably just wanted to send a card and buy Her a set of decanters. He looked after the Navy - the idiotic plan to scrap HMS *Ark Royal*[16] had to wait for the incoming Thatcher government, which walked into the Falklands War in a way Jim would never have allowed. Whatever your political views, at least the country knew that in Jim Callaghan they had a grown-up Prime Minister, which with respect hardly anyone would say today. The 1979 General Election was a repudiation of Labour and the trade unions, not Jim Callaghan.

Arrangements were made for candidates to visit European institutions, probably because someone at Walworth Road (Labour's then HQ), clearly unfamiliar with the EEC, thought it might make wannabe MEPs more pro-European. The visit to the European Parliament, apart from turning me off the idea of becoming an MEP, at least afforded me my only meeting, albeit a chance encounter, with a Holy Roman Emperor.

This was of course His Imperial and Royal Highness Archduke Otto von Hapsburg, arch-opponent of the Nazi *Anchluss*,[17] former Emperor of Austria and King of Hungary.[18] Very sadly His Highness died on 4th July 2011. Otto would have approved of the decision to sing the first verse of Haydn's beautiful anthem *Der KaiserHymne* at his impressive Requiem Mass in Vienna on 16th July 2011, even if the Austrian Government did not. He would also have approved of the laying on his casket of the 'Middle Flag', ensign of the countries represented on the Imperial Council. HIRH had of course been rescued as a child from the Hapsburg family hunting lodge at Eckertsau by Lieutenant-Colonel Edward Strutt, of British Intelligence, at the request of HM King George V. He was pro- British. It was nice, with respect, to see Otto properly addressed, i.e. as "His Imperial Highness", by the then Pope, His Holiness Pope Benedict, in the moving letter read out to mourners.

As the European Union collapses, restoration of the Austro-Hungarian Empire, in a loose federation with a constitutional monarchy, is clearly a viable option for post-EU European political and security architecture. The Empire's break-up led to a vacuum, which was filled firstly by Nazi Germany, then in part by the Warsaw Pact, then the EU.

The regular trips to West Sussex as a prospective European candidate afforded me an opportunity to see the 1988 West Indians play the Duke of Norfolk's XI at cricket, at His Grace's beautiful ground at Arundel, in the constituency. This led to a meeting with one of my cricketing heroes, Colin, later Lord, Cowdrey, former England Test Captain and future President of MCC. He approved of the Rover. Colin had been mentor to R. A. (Bob) Woolmer, another Man of Kent and like Colin a graceful batsman, who scored 79 and 120 against Australia in the Lords Test of 1977, whom I also met. I later took pleasure in identifying the Pakistani Inter-Services Intelligence Agency (ISI) agents who assassinated Bob in Jamaica in 2007. The Pakistanis still have no idea of how much upset that caused.

Cricket is one of my great loves and I played whenever I could. By sheer co-incidence one of my team-mates, in the Ealing College of Higher Education (later Thames Valley University) team was Ausbert Scoon. He was a good all-rounder and brother of Sir Paul, the late Governor-General of Grenada, who had 'invited in' US forces back in '84.

I taught as a part-time Senior Lecturer in Law at Ealing in the late 1980s and early 1990s. It was an enjoyable task, with good students and fine colleagues including the late Mike Molyneux, who presented the BBC's *Law in Action* program for many years. Mike was a sad loss to the law but it would wrong to say that I was a sad loss to cricket.

As indicated, the 1989 West Sussex campaign afforded an opportunity to study a German spy close-up, although I was not then involved in counterintelligence work and didn't know that Madron Seligman was a member of the Oxford Spy Ring. Indeed, I wasn't even aware that there *was* an Oxford Spy Ring. Madron lied to me about his visits to Germany and Poland with Sir Edward Heath in August 1939, just prior to the German invasion of Poland, placing them before Munich, i.e. at a much less sensitive time.

Jim Callaghan's visit to the euro-constituency probably created, if not waves, at least, a few ripples. Madron may have been trying to find out whether Jim had briefed me in. Jim must have suspected the truth, which may have been why he was happy to fire off a salvo in Madron's direction. The detail of the conversation about the 'camping' trip to Nazi Germany, not an obvious holiday destination for a young gay Jewish student, was filed away in my mind. It took me a while to get there, but I got there in the end.

The second German spy I encountered in 1989, although again it was some years before I found out he was working for the Germans, was the egotistical Sir Hartley Shawcross QC. He was then with the Social Democratic Party, which the DVD had sponsored to split the Labour vote after the Labour Party Conference voted to withdraw from the EEC. In those days the Labour Party was a democratic organization and conference resolutions actually meant something. Sir Hartley, who really ought to have been known as 'Sir Hartley Doublecross', was working as a consultant for a bank rumoured to have long-standing connections with German intelligence.

Notoriously, he had boasted to the House of Commons in 1946 that "we are the masters at the moment", although that nice man the late Lord Bruce of Donington, who was seated right behind him at the time, has stated that he actually said "we are the masters now"[19]. Many took this to be a reference to Labour but he was referring of course to the DVD, which took a firm grip on Whitehall after the July 1945 General Election, running the Prime Minister, the Cabinet Secretary and the Permanent Secretary to the Treasury. After a while they were able to set up and then replace Hugh Dalton, the patriotic Chancellor of the Exchequer, a nice man by all accounts, with Sir Stafford Cripps, who wasn't.

I had teamed up with Radio Mercury, the excellent local radio station in Crawley, to do a half-hour programme on the Acid Bath Murderer, John Haigh, and asked to see Sir Hartley. Haigh was a GO2 asset who had been dissolving old ladies in acid in Crawley and was very properly hanged for murder in 1949, forty years before. Sir Hartley was then Attorney-General, the second German spy to have held the post, after the notorious Sir Thomas Inskip, and had led for the prosecution. The very able David Neve, later President of the Immigration Appeal Tribunal and before whom I once appeared, was one of Shawcross's juniors, on a kite brief.[20] David was kind enough to grant me an interview as well, the idea being to speak to each of the surviving barristers who had appeared in the case.

Local radio in Britain is expected to confine its current affairs content to ads for lost cats and jam recipes, not make shattering revelations about high-level international espionage which would have been front-page news in Prince Rupert in British Columbia,[21] never mind in the *West Sussex County Times*. Radio Mercury however was an innovative local broadcaster and had decided to employ serious journalists. It was a worthwhile experiment, although it never caught on. It was probably viewed by the Independent Broadcasting Authority as a dangerous precedent.

The problem was that unbeknown to me, Haigh was on the German 'rent-a-psychopath' list. GO2 were paying him to bump off the nice old ladies and dissolve them in acid in the bath in Crawley. The insane German policy of renting nutters and psychopaths to disturb civil society continues to the present day. The most recent psychopath on the GO2 payroll to have committed mass-murder in the UK was Derrick Bird, who went on a shooting spree in what is now Cumbria (it should be called Cumberland of course) in June 2010. He murdered 12 innocent people before he was shot dead by police in order to silence him.[22]

There have since been others of course, most notably in Norway, Colorado and Connecticut. This is one of those areas of intelligence work where counterintelligence officers can have trouble in deciding, who is the more insane, the nutters on the payroll or the nutters who came up with the idea of employing them in the first place.

Radio Mercury tracked down, and over a bottle of good Scotch extracted some highly damaging admissions from, a senior *News of the World* journalist covering the case, later a distinguished editor of that now-defunct paper, Major Stafford Somerfield. These admissions included the interesting tit-bit that the *News of the World* had not only paid for but, controlled the defence.

The paper insisted on the choice of Sir David Maxwell-Fyfe, later Attorney General and, as Lord Kilmuir, Lord Chancellor, as counsel. Major Somerfield's colourful description of Sir David's abilities as a criminal defence advocate included the suggestion that he wouldn't have briefed him "on a charge of riding a bicycle without a light". Haigh was charged with multiple counts of capital murder. When Radio Mercury spoke to him, Stafford must have been one of only a handful of people still alive in England who had spoken to Haigh.

Haigh had a run at insanity, backed by none other than Sir Henry Yellowlees, later Chief Medical Officer, but this was put pretty feebly with respect in a slightly rushed but nonetheless fair trial at Lewes Assizes. The trial judge was that outstandingly fair tribunal with respect, Mr Justice Travers Humphreys. It looks as though GO2 were worried about Haigh's increasing instability and were afraid that he might blow the gaff if let off and sent to one of the rest homes for psychopaths run by the Home Office. It is standard practice for psychopaths to be told that they will not be hanged, or will be let out of prison early. Haigh probably thought he wasn't going to be hanged right up until the moment on the morning of 10th August 1949 when Albert Pierrepoint, the public hangman and a good one, walked smartly through the door of his condemned cell. Mr Pierrepoint didn't let the condemned suffer any more than was necessary and was an efficient despatcher.

The News of the World of course is no longer with us and frankly is not much missed. Its connections to GO2 seem to have run pretty deep. At any rate the fouling up of Haigh's insanity defence, such as it was, seems to have been coordinated with GO2.

Radio Mercury's lawyers apparently had a conniption fit when they heard the tape. It disappeared into a vault and has never been broadcast, although at least two copies may have made been spirited out of the building. Once again, I got close to unmasking a German spy, but not close enough. Stafford was a gent and may have worked for Military Intelligence - it's no wonder that Hartley Shawcross agreed to see me.

I simply didn't know about the DVD, or GO2, in 1989 and still thought that Admiral Canaris had died in 1945. We live and learn. To adopt a truism which appeared in a fortune cookie in a Chinese restaurant in LA whilst I was writing this chapter, "if you do not change your mind what is the point of having one?"

---

1. E.g. *The Settle to Carlisle*, by the late James Towler, a TUCC Chairman. James was a good chap.
2. The famous twin-engined medium bomber powered by Bristol Pegasus XVIII engines in the Mark 1C version. They were a bit slow with the 'Peggies' and the Hercules-powered Mark III offered improved performance. First flight 15th June 1936.
3. Junkers Motoren, maker of the Jumo 004 turbojets for the Me 262.
4. *Bayerische Motoren Werke*, makers of the BMW 003 turbojet, used in the Heinkel He-162.
5. The world's second jet fighter, after the RAF's Gloster Meteor – see Ch. 19.
6. Also covered in Ch. 19.
7. Hence the 'B'. All-alloy, the engine was one of the best General Motors ever designed, stretched to 4.4 litres by Leyland Australia for the under-rated P76 it remained in production for the Rover SD1, Range Rover, Morgan and TVR. It was discovered by Rover as a marine engine. They improved the breathing and never looked back.
8. That very good judge with respect Harold Singer was being honoured with a dinner upon his well-deserved appointment.
9. Anton Theodor Lubowski, 3rd February 1952 – 12th September 1989, trained at Stellensbosch and Cape Town Universities, an advocate and a good one.
10. Civil Co-operation Bureau.
11. There was no case in unfair dismissal, as the time limits had not long been extended, i.e. you had to be employed a certain time before your job was protected by statute.
12. Preliminary documents, which can be important in divining the intentions of state parties to an international agreement. The question of whether or not the UN Charter was intended to outlaw war (it clearly didn't), e.g., could probably be resolved by looking at the *travaux* alone, which almost certainly set out in terms the positions of all five proposed permanent members of the Security Council, which was that only an unjust war was unlawful.
13. BBC Cricket Correspondent and later President of MCC. I didn't agree with all of his opinions, or selections for the England team (he always seemed to do down Graeme Hick, e.g., who was a stylish and fine batsman), but he was a great cricketing journalist and respected broadcaster. Sadly, he died in January 2013.
14. Formerly the USS *Phoenix* and the last operational survivor of the sneak Japanese attack on Pearl Harbor, the *General Belgrano* was a *Brooklyn* class cruiser armed with 15 6 inch guns, displacing 10,000 tons. As the hostilities were general, i.e. not confined to the Falkland Islands and adjacent waters, HMS *Conqueror* could lawfully engage the Argentine enemy wherever he was found. The unwise limitations on her Rules of Engagement were imposed for political not legal reasons and reflected US practice in the Vietnam War, i.e. the endangering of friendly forces through excessive political interference in tactical decisions by the commander on the spot, who is usually in a far better position than an armchair admiral or politician thousands of miles away.

15. St. Pancras, a wonderful old station, was the old terminus for the Midland Railway and the trains for Derby, Chesterfield and Sheffield went from there. It is now the terminus for international passenger trains to Europe through the Channel Tunnel.
16. Of course she was old (she had been laid down in 1943 after all) and her hull was a bit battered by the end - the point is that she was scrapped without a replacement, indeed her replacement didn't enter service until 2020. Had Germany's Harold Wilson not cancelled CVA01 and 02, which were the intended replacements for *Ark* and her sister *Eagle*, then she could have been Laid Up in Ordinary, ready to answer her country's call, albeit after a refit. Jim would probably have ordered a replacement carrier if he thought he could get away with it, but he was lumbered with EEC membership and the economy had tanked. On the whole he and his Defence Secretary got along well with the Service Chiefs.
17. There was a later *Anchsluss* of course when Austria, at the urging of German assets in Vienna, joined the European Community. Otto von Hapsburg was the only person I ever met whom Adolf Hitler wanted to meet but didn't.
18. Whilst Otto had renounced the Throne of Austria and Austria, sadly, became a republic in 1918, largely to ease the problems of incorporating her into Germany (i.e. the *Anschluss* was being planned by German intelligence as far back as 1918), the position as regards Hungary is slightly more complicated. That is why the Hungarian fascist leader, Admiral Horthy, who feared and hated Otto, made himself 'Regent' not 'Führer' (Horthy would probably have quite liked to be Führer of Hungary). Officially Hungary is a republic but the Preamble to her latest constitution honours the Holy Crown of St Stephen!
19. *New Statesman*, 28th July 2003.
20. Kite briefs were a restrictive practice and a good one, sadly now discontinued as part of the government's drive to lower standards. The idea was that if there was a London leader there had to be at least one junior from the local circuit.
21. A nice place, where I had a very enjoyable stay in 1996 on my way to Alaska on the Marine Highway. The local supermarket stocked Froot Loops and for several years shipped them to me in England - I was one of their few export customers. Kelloggs may have noticed the spike in Froot Loop sales in Prince Rupert.
22. The Official Version of Events is that he shot himself but the problem with that is he appears not to have taken a gun with him when he abandoned his car, near the pleasant little hamlet of Boot (it is a lovely part of the world). There is also the little matter of the absence of sprayed blood and tissue, which we normally find when someone has shot themselves, which usually happens at close range. It's a bit difficult to shoot yourself at long range, unless you've got very long arms. Bird was being protected by GO2 assets in the Cumbria force, hence the ease with which he was able to 'lawfully' acquire guns and ammunition. Such shooting sprees are invariably accompanied by ritual hand-wringing about violent films - his GO2 handler instructed Bird to rent *On Deadly Ground*, starring that good man Steven Seagal (what if anything Mr Seagal had done to upset the Germans remains unclear) - and firearms controls. On this occasion the clamour to impose new and entirely unnecessary gun control

was resisted. The problem lies with having a German intelligence operation in London with assets in local police forces, not with firearms laws. America has the same problem, but with different intelligence sponsorship - the North Koreans e.g. sponsored an equally disgraceful shooting spree at the Virginia Polytechnic Institute on 16th April 2007, when a North Korean agent, Seung-Hui Cho, murdered 32 young people. The Denver cinema shooting involved a team of at least four - one to let the shooter in, a driver, the shooter himself and an explosives expert to rig the IED in his accommodation. There may have been a spotter as well. There were three shooters at Sandy Hook.

5

Onto The Bench

As explained, I returned to private practice in early 1989, initially with a slightly troubled set in Gray's Inn, which split, then with that nice man Harjit Singh in Temple Chambers. Harjit's set was viewed by the legal establishment, when they viewed it at all, as an 'ethnic' set, presumably because it had a lot of 'ethnics' in it - and very nice 'ethnics' they were too. Since I specialised in immigration law and many of my instructing solicitors were in law centres, ex law centre staff or ethnic minority solicitors, my practice thrived. I did not mind that it was not very fashionable. I do not follow fashion anyway.

Other barristers in the set included the courtly former Indian diplomat Jaswant Singh, a lovely man. He had been involved, from recollection on behalf of the UN, in the 1954 Geneva peace talks, which brought French involvement in Indo China to an end. Jaswant was the first man I knew who had personally dealt with the German spy Ho Chi Minh, although back then, for some reason, I thought that Ho Chi Minh was a communist. You can get these really weird notions when you're young.

The clerk at 41-44 Temple Chambers was another matter. Just before the new decade started - of course pedants assert that each new decade does not start until 1991, 2001, 2011, etc., but I am not a pedant - President George H. W. Bush, who was a German spy, decided that it would be a good idea to invade Panama.

I was still stuck in the BBC system as an expert on international law. Their flagship current affairs programme *Panorama* rang chambers asking if I could come into the Television Centre. The clerk reassured me when I got in from the Uxbridge Mags, or some other *palais de justice*, my rather bulky Technophone[1] mobile phone (for the benefit of younger readers mobile phones were not quite as common then as they are today) having run out of battery power, that he had treated the call as a hoax. Idiot! *Panorama* duly sent a car around (a Volvo from memory) and interviewed me. They did not include the clip in the programme but used the material I provided for some questions, which put a poor old US Senator on the spot.

The invasion was not entirely legal. Amusingly, when I later started having dealings with those nice people the CIA, and was having a Jack Daniels, or two, with the boys (I may have responded to some of the 'James Bond' ribbing you can get from the cousins when you do intelligence work by ordering a medium dry vodka martini, shaken, not stirred) one of them starting sharing a reminiscence about Panama, and his choice of music. I tend not to go in for intellectual dishonesty – one reason some may think why I never made it to the Court of Appeal and didn't get very far in politics. My view of the legality of the invasion of Panama hasn't altered very much from the briefing I gave to Panorama. It was a bit dodgy.

I can be diplomatic, although in my dealings with the Foreign Office and former Foreign Secretaries, of whom I have bumped into at least half a dozen, I have never been told that I am a loss to diplomacy, a surprising omission. I did not raise the subject of the invasion's legality at said drinkies. Something was said about a warrant, although warrants are not usually enforced with airborne troops, tactical aircraft and an amphibious assault force. Generally speaking, however, it is best to be diplomatic rather than get into an argument with someone, however nice, who is packing a .357 Magnum, especially when you're armed with nothing more powerful than a pen, and not one of MI6's funny pens either. By the way, if we want funny pens we tend to go to the Spy Shop.

The *Muboyayi* Case

Immigration applications were then the largest single category of judicial review cases in the Crown Office, which was later re-named the Administrative Court Office, so that (1) it sounded vaguely European and (2) nobody would know what it did any more. Almost all *habeas corpus* applications in the last 50 years, aside from imprisoned striking miners, have been immigration related in one way or another. The last time an actual writ had been issued was the *Soblen* case in the 1960s, when dear old Elywn Jones was counsel. Famously, the writ was issued late at night in Mr Justice Mocatta's drawing room.

The most powerful remedy in any legal system in the world, a writ of *habeas corpus*, commanding the gaoler to 'bring the body' before the court, can be issued *in extremis* (again *mea culpa* if there is too much Latin) by any High Court judge. Even a judge of the Family Division can issue it, at any time of the day or night, *ex parte*, i.e. with the other side not present. For many years, even after the decision in 1965 to encourage more murders by abolishing the death penalty, removal of a prisoner from the jurisdiction after a writ had been served was punishable by death, and rightly so.

Unlike judicial review *habeas corpus* is not discretionary, i.e. the judge cannot refuse relief on spurious grounds, i.e. it is a serious remedy. *Habeas corpus* applications also take precedence over all other business in court, as the law has no higher priority than safeguarding the liberty of the subject. Whitehall hates *habeas corpus* almost as much as Charles I did, and has been trying to abolish it for years. Thankfully all they have managed is to make a mess of the procedural rules,[2] most of which can be thrown out of the window in an urgent case anyway.

A harassed solicitor rang me on the Technophone one morning in 1991, whilst I was waiting for a train at South Kensington Underground Station. The lay client was a Zairean teacher, who had been refused asylum in the UK on grounds that seemed questionable, even though most Zairean (Congolese) applications are fraudulent. It is not unknown for asylum seekers to use *pro forma* case histories sold by human traffickers, who do a brisk trade out of Kinshasha. Mr Muboyayi was about to be put on a plane at Gatwick Airport. Could I nip down to the High Court and apply for judicial review? The instructions were that the client had fallen foul of Mobutu Sese Seko, the brutal Zairean dictator, who was all in favour of having his opponents dumped, in pieces, in the Congo, or fed to crocodiles.

Well it *might* have been true. It is not the place of a barrister to question his or her instructions. You can test them, ask searching questions, wrinkle your nose, make funny faces or noises, scratch your wig and generally indicate to the lay client and instructing solicitor that the instructions present conceptual difficulties ("I swear I didn't stab the bloke, guv, he just ran at me with the knife"), but at the end of the day you are bound by them.

Your lay client is entitled to his or her day in court, and you are there to present their case, not make up one of your own which might be easier to argue. I am well aware that barristers in commercial cases have been letting the side down in recent years by drafting witness statements (for which in the good old days they would have been run out of the profession) but even in commercial cases the witness statements are supposed to bear some resemblance to the actual instructions.

The instructions, in terms, in this case were that the lay client's life was at stake. Barristers should not run in the Temple, even to save their lay client's life, let alone their own, but the situation called for striding with best foot forward. Judicial review is a slow, bureaucratic and cumbersome remedy at the best of times, never mind where a life is said to be at stake. The situation called for an emergency application for a writ of *habeas corpus*, not just a summons to argue the case, but the mighty writ itself. I was aware that the great Habeas Corpus Act 1679 was still in force and that it was the duty of all who knew of a writ to do all in their power to prevent the prisoner's removal from the jurisdiction, on pain of death.

This included the senior duty air traffic controller at Gatwick and if need be the Military Controller at RAF West Drayton.

The application came on before the late Mr Justice Brooke, as he then was, whose father had been Home Secretary. He very properly gave the case priority over all the other business in his court. Equally properly with respect he issued a writ, for the first time in England in 35 years. This was despite counsel for the Home Office, who rushed into court half-way through the hearing, objecting that it was too late, the prisoner was already on board the aeroplane and the door had been shut. This message was repeated outside court, whereupon I advised that the writ be served by telex on the control tower at Gatwick. The solicitor, who was fast grasping what it meant to live in a country of laws, had obtained said telex number for use if need be. When told that the control tower would now be asked to rescind the aircraft's taxi and/or take-off clearance and if need be recall it, the Home Office discovered a need to make further inquiries. As a result of these it was established that *pace* what the learned judge had been told the prisoner was still in the airport terminal.

They appealed. The Court of Appeal allowed the appeal on the merits, but agreed with the learned judge's decision to issue the writ so as to allow the merits to be examined. The prisoner appealed forthwith to the House of Lords. Basing myself on the leading, indeed only modern, text[3] I advised that leave to appeal to the House was not necessary, as there was an ancient rule that mere general words do not impinge upon *habeas corpus*. If the executive want to mess with or suspend *habeas corpus* they have to go Parliament and tell it in terms what they are proposing. Parliament has never interfered with the right of appeal to the House of Lords in *habeas* cases.

I was told that the House was "interested" in the argument on leave, that the appeal very properly had taken precedence over all pending appeals and would I kindly present myself in Committee Room 1 at 10:30 (from recollection) tomorrow morning? I thought I could manage that (quick call to the clerk: "I've got a case in the Lords tomorrow, return the thing in Slough Mags would you?"). Counsel must give precedence to appeals before the House of Lords over cases in the Slough Magistrates' Court. The hearing in the Lords would have been only two days after the Court of Appeal had announced its decision. Indeed, it would only have been one day after the written judgments had been handed down, as the Master of the Rolls, still Lord Donaldson of Lymington, had stood it over until the following morning.

Whilst I was on my feet in the Court of Appeal sorting out costs, word came that the prisoner had escaped, from the Immigration Detention Centre at Harmondsworth. He went straight over the fence, we were told, and into a waiting black Vauxhall Astra, which was last seen disappearing down the Colnbrook Bypass. The escape had been very obviously set up by someone, indeed it is almost certain that the poor man was murdered by GO2.

Thirty years ago or not, I can still recall Lord Donaldson glaring at me as though *I* had set it up! Not only had I no notion that someone was organising my lay client's escape, thereby frustrating the appeal, I would still like to know who did and who exactly murdered my client. The case is reported as *R v Secretary of State for the Home Department ex parte Muboyayi*.

It so happened that one of the judges in the Court of Appeal was Lord Justice Glidewell, who thought I was holding out on the court on an authority. Counsel are under a duty to draw the court's attention to any case that might undermine their own argument. The rule only applies to *relevant* cases however. Some years before, another barrister, ambitiously with respect, had sought to use *habeas corpus* where not only was there no one in detention but his client was in Pakistan. Whoops.

The court ruled, quite correctly with respect, that that was a wholly inappropriate case for *habeas corpus*, which very clearly it was. What counsel really wanted was an Order of Mandamus compelling the issue of a visa, although it was at the very least doubtful that it was even a case for a visa. Since his lay client was not in jug it is not at all clear with respect where an order releasing him, which is what *habeas corpus* does, would have got him.

Lord Justice Glidewell accused me in open court of sitting on this earlier case, *Phansokpar*. I have a distinct recollection of Lord Justice Taylor, as he then was, intervening and trying to pour oil on troubled waters. Whilst this may sound an arcane dispute, Lord Justice Glidewell was levelling a serious accusation against me. Now the only two points of similarity between the two cases were that (1) there was an application for *habeas corpus* in each case (in the earlier it had been linked with a judicial review, making the reasons for applying for *habeas corpus* even more of a mystery with respect) and (2) each was an immigration case.

What Lord Justice Glidewell appeared to be saying with respect was that counsel applying for *habeas corpus* in an immigration case was under a duty to take the court to every failed application by an immigrant of which he or she was aware, which with respect can hardly have been the learned Lord Justice's real opinion.

I was ably assisted by a very nice junior, for whom I would have bought a red robe bag if I were a silk myself, Miss Judith Maxwell. When arguing a case in the Court of Appeal you have to give your list of authorities in advance, both to the court and your opponent, and summarise your argument in a written document (in America it would be called an appellate brief) known as a 'Skeleton Argument'.[4]

It was Lord Donaldson MR himself who had introduced the practice of filing Skeletons (if I were into weak puns, which I am not, this would no doubt be an ideal opportunity to refer to them previously having been left in the cupboard) in the Court of Appeal. Even Lord Donaldson however surely cannot have imagined that they would ever be used in the Uxbridge County Court. If counsel had told dear old Judge Barr that, "the skeletons were available" the learned judge would probably have assumed that it was a medical negligence case.

Judith and I together reviewed a large number of authorities. She was for putting *Phansokpar* in and I was against, on the ground that the *ratio decidendi* or basis for decision for that case could not possibly have a bearing on this one. She was right of course, which only goes to show you should listen to your junior. Even if a case is *not* material it is better to disclose it and have the court say "well that it is very proper of you Mr Shrimpton but it is hardly necessary" rather than have it ask "why have you not cited x, you must have been aware of it".

There it is. An argument about relevance was turned into an argument about my honesty. Relations with Lord Justice Glidewell were poisoned for years with respect (23 to be precise, until his death). Justifiably or not I resented the public attack on my integrity. When I applied for silk the following year I was refused, although several senior judges supported my application, including apparently Peter Taylor. The civil servant in charge of silk applications was, frankly, less than civil. Word reached my ear that Lord Justice Glidewell had blocked my application.

The Bar, applicants for silk especially, has always been told that a single judge could not block elevation to silk, but that seems to have been a sustained exercise in deception by Whitehall. Now the information may have been wrong, Lord Justice Glidewell may not even have known that I had applied for silk and if he did he may not have opposed my application, but that is what I believed.

Even though it was unusual to for silk to be granted on first application the process left a sour taste in my mouth. Not infrequently I was referred to erroneously by the media as a QC, without any encouragement on my part. I was not. I applied, was told where to go, and took the advice. There it is.

General Spears's old Rover

The dear old Rover had had her day by '92. Rover's first monocoque[5] design, they had a few rust-traps, especially the D-posts. So I traded her in. I still recall my sense of sadness as the old girl was trailered away. We had had some fun times together. Sensibly, the new car was a slightly *older* P5B, in the same colour, Arden Green. She was in very good condition, with much lower mileage. For over 12 years, I only owned Rover P5Bs, and why not? They are lovely cars, as British as they come. They have an interior like a gentlemen's club and an excellent V8 engine.

By another of those strange twists of fate the latest old Rover was first owned by Major-General Sir Edward Spears MC, Bt., Prime Minister Winston Churchill's key military intelligence adviser in World War II. Sir Edward was the intelligence officer chosen to accompany Churchill to the Western Front, twice, in 1915. He was also the intelligence hero of the Battle of the Marne 1914. It was he who got the warning through to Field Marshal Sir John French, Commander-in-Chief of the British Expeditionary Force, that the French commander, General Lanrezac, who was working for 'the Boche', was about to expose his flank.

General Spears was a man of very sound views, not to mention a good taste in motors. He was involved in the brilliant and highly confidential exposure of Lloyd George and Marshal Philippe Pétain, with both of whom he had worked in World War I, as German assets. Sir Edward was present at the crucial high-level meeting in Paris in May 1917 between Lloyd George, then Germany's highest-ranking political asset in London, Marshal Pétain, their highest-ranking military asset in Paris and later dictator of Vichy France, General Sir William Robertson, Chief of the Imperial General Staff (CIGS), Admiral of the Fleet Sir John Jellicoe, First Sea Lord, and French War Minister Paul Painlevé, briefly French Prime Minister later that year.

This crisis summit was triggered by CIGS's entirely proper concerns about the loyalty of Pétain and Lloyd George, both of them were traitors and each of whom should have been dismissed, tried and executed. As a general, Pétain was entitled to the military courtesy of being shot, but Lloyd George, as a civilian, should have been hanged, nicely of course. It was not Sir Edward's fault that Lloyd George was left in place to do even more damage, although as a damage control exercise Churchill was brought back into the government as Minister of Munitions and crucial intelligence was withheld from the Prime Minister.

In World War II Sir Edward Spears was *inter alia* British Minister in the Levant, where he worked with the great Lord Casey, later External Affairs Minister in Australia and a high-value target for the German enemy throughout his life. The DVD's Canberra Station probably sabotaged Lord Casey's Bentley in 1974 - he was not only a highly competent driver but an experienced pilot - although the investigation was so sloppy that those waters have long since been muddied.

Sir Edward and Lord Casey, who had been an intelligence officer during the Battle of the Somme, worked on the Macmillan case together. Harold Macmillan, who, like Lloyd George was eventually forced out of office, although again like Lloyd George not before he had done a lot of damage, came under suspicion after Intelligence became aware of a major leak out of Cairo into the German Embassy in Ankara, via Beirut. Macmillan was Minister Resident in the Middle East from 1942 to 1945. Prior to myself the Rover's only owners were the great Sir Edward himself, his second wife, Lady Nancy, who translated General de Gaulle's stirring speech on the BBC to the French people on 18th June 1940, and the landlord of their local. He had been promised the car after Lady Nancy's death by the general. Sir Edward sadly died in 1974 and Lady Nancy, heartbroken, the following year.

The 'new' Rover gave faithful service and always got me where I needed to be, being well looked after by Ivor Badrick and his team at Dutton Forshaw in Aylesbury. Ivor cracked the problem of fuel vaporisation, long alleged to be a design fault on the P5B, as the fuel line ran close to the exhaust manifold. It wasn't a design fault at all. It turned out that some idiot in Whitehall had decided that modern petrol should be made more volatile, presumably to stall classic cars on warm summer days. Insisting on lead-free petrol was a similar nonsense, given that the amount of lead in petrol had been reduced substantially. There was no evidence that modern levels of lead in petrol posed a health risk.

Since she was a working car, driving to courts like Taunton, an 0430 start from Aylesbury, modifications to cope with the decline in fuel standards since 1968 were acceptable. Ivor modified her with an SU electric fuel pump. There was some hilarity when SU, having been told the pump was required for a Rover 3.5 Litre, supplied a bl..dy great thing with a capacity of 25 gallons an hour, which must have been designed for an aeroplane. At any rate it was soon swapped for a more sensible bit of kit, as fitted to the Jaguar XJ6.

When the old girl was finally traded in, for the Bentley, I took a fond farewell photo with old and new side-by-side. She didn't look out of place and went to a good home, her new owner being kind enough to bring her up to Aylesbury a few years later. Sir Edward, apparently, loved the car. She was probably his finest steed since the horse on which he rode behind General d'Esperey, commander of the French Fifth Army, following the liberation of Reims in 1914.

The Immigration Appeal Tribunal

Although dealt with by the same government department, judicial appointments with respect were dealt with far more professionally than applications for silk. At the earliest age, in practice, for judicial preferment, 35 (I had to wait until my birthday before I could start sitting), I was appointed a part-time Chairman of the Immigration Appeal Tribunal. I had actually applied for a more junior appointment, as an Immigration Adjudicator (despite the name these were first instance immigration judges). The Lord Chancellor, Lord Mackay of Clashfern, was gracious enough to appoint me to the second-tier or appellate level, *ab initio*. The suggestion that I should apply for judicial office came from one of the Adjudicators in front of whom I had appeared, which came as a much-needed boost to my fragile ego.

Immigration is not an easy jurisdiction, as the number of deaths in office, Mark Patey OBE coming to mind, and the early retirement rate, of immigration judges will confirm. The Home Office at times could be very sloppy, administrative support was patchy and resources inadequate. The UK was rapidly losing control of her borders, indeed border control was largely lost in 1993 when asylum-seekers were given appeal privileges denied ordinary immigrants. Coupled with the inability of the Home Office to administer the system and their reluctance to deport failed asylum-seekers, chaos ensued. Eventually even the Home Secretary was forced to concede that his department was not 'fit for purpose'. The loss of control of our borders has played a major part in the rise of the Reform Party.

The chaos was organised, as most government chaos is, in the sense that it was the desired and predictable consequence of decisions advised by senior civil servants. One of my most valued judicial colleagues on the Tribunal was the late Ray Maddison, who warned the Home Office about the consequences of the dramatic undermining of immigration control in 1993. He was proved right.

Some might be surprised about the warmth of my tribute to Ray, as I was seen as a liberal immigration judge (this is not a misprint) and Ray a conservative, but there was mutual respect. The main rule seeking to prevent abuse of marriage, the primary purpose rule, was badly drafted, requiring appellants to disprove a negative. It would have been much simpler to exclude parties to arranged marriages, and marriages falling within the prohibited degrees of consanguinity under canon law, e.g. between first cousins, a fair percentage. Decisions on the primary purpose rule went back and forth. No one pretended that it was an easy rule to apply.

The Immigration Appeal Tribunal had an even wider territorial jurisdiction than the House of Lords, as it included the Crown dependencies of the Isle of Man and the Channel Islands, as well as Scotland and Northern Ireland. This had the unusual consequence, until the IAT sat in Glasgow (I wanted to accept a generous offer from that nice man Lord Hope of Craighead of a courtroom in Edinburgh, but there it is), of Scottish advocates travelling to London to argue cases before tribunals chaired by an English barrister.

I well recall readily deferring to members of the Faculty of Advocates in Edinburgh, in a case before me, on the Scottish Civil Evidence Act! I did not endear myself to the English Court of Appeal by preferring a decision on the primary purpose rule of a Scottish Court of Session presided over by that fine judge, with respect, Lord Prosser. There was nothing personal in it. The Scottish decision, with respect, had the merit of greater rationality than the confused and convoluted reasoning of the decision of the Court of Appeal, which the Home Office were trying to sell me. I wasn't buying.

There is no immigration control at Gretna Green and won't be unless Scotland withdraws from the United Kingdom. If that were to happen then of course there would have to be passport controls at the Anglo-Scottish frontier. As it was a UK tribunal, the IAT was free to follow which of two conflicting English and Scottish decisions it preferred, leaving it to the House of Lords to give the ultimate ruling.

The status of the IAT was increased when appeals from us went directly to the Court of Session or Court of Appeal as the case may be. Chairmen were empowered to grant leave, which I promptly did, in the *De Noronha* case, concerning a very nice Anglo-Indian gentleman, who had got caught up in a piece of bureaucratic nonsense. That fine author and MI6 officer Eric Ambler, who sadly deed not long afterwards, was a character witness in that case, although he wasn't called to give evidence. We did our best to make sense of a badly drafted rule. The point was arguable either way and I granted leave to appeal against our decision to the Home Office. They won their appeal, albeit with valuable guidance from the court to exercise discretion in Mr De Noronha's favour.

My first President was that nice man George Farmer, formerly Director of Public Prosecutions in Uganda. Had his advice on prosecuting Corporal Idi Amin for murder been followed (murder was and still is a capital offence in Uganda, and rightly so) several hundred thousand lives would have been saved. Amin of course was a DVD asset. Sadly, he had heavy duty protection in London. Nobody told the poor old DPP, i.e. George, who was only trying to preserve peace, order and good government in the colony and save Ugandan lives, that the Colonial Office had been penetrated by German intelligence. They were trying to reverse the result of World War I in Central Africa.

'Jerry' got his way in the end of course. His man took over in Kampala, with predictable consequences, i.e. dead bodies everywhere and a bunch of

Ugandans turning up at Heathrow. George was a brilliant administrator and could spot a backlog of appeals a mile off. His predecessor, David Neve, he whom I had interviewed for the Radio Mercury programme on GO2's 'von' Haigh, had also been a good administrator. The lay members were a great bunch, with vast experience of life and the colonies. The IAT in those days was a happy place to be.

Ray Maddison used to deal with most of the leave applications (i.e. leave to appeal *to* the Tribunal). He was very efficient and could knock over 30 in a day, getting most of them right. Bright-eyed and bushy tailed, I wanted to get them *all* right, which was a bit ambitious for immigration appeals. I therefore liked to limit myself to 12 a day, and introduced innovations like reading the papers and dictating (those were the days) individual determinations for each case.

Ray, being an older, wiser hand, 'looked' at the papers and used a *pro forma*. This created upset 'over the road'. A High Court judge, albeit a nice one, later a Master of the Rolls and a Supreme Court justice, was duly sent over to us at Thanet House to do a 'training session'. This was code for crushing judicial individuality and independence and imposing the High Court's way of doing things, no offence intended. It wasn't put quite like that of course.

His Lordship had a very polite go at the assembled chairmen for using a *pro forma* when refusing leave. Challenges to these refusals went by way of judicial review, i.e. to the High Court, rather than the Court of Appeal. Sad to relate, I agreed with the learned judge and then said something to the effect that some of us chairmen had been telling Ray that it was time that he changed his *pro forma*.

There was a left-wing conspiracy theory that immigration judges were all racists, which was complete nonsense of course. I gather they appointed a racist once, who was found climbing up the walls after a couple of weeks and quickly appointed to something less stressful, Crown Court Recorder probably. I bought into this conspiracy theory a little bit, in my early days at any rate, before my appointment. I recall gently preparing a nice Jamaican lady, who had a difficult appeal on behalf of her granddaughter (always heartrending cases), before John Housden, a retired colonial District Officer and Adjudicator of the old school, for the possibility that the judge might be, well, just a little bit racist.

John of course was as nice as pie. He ripped into the immigration rule in question as a nonsense, which badly needed revising, which it did, and allowed the appeal, leaving the Home Office Presenting Officer speechless. After the hearing the nice Jamaican lady gently chided me for making unfounded assumptions. She was quite right.

It was John, from memory, who caught out a bent Swahili interpreter one day at Thanet House. The interpreter was not only not translating the answers and making up his own, he was telling the witness, in his own language, what to say. Not for one moment did it occur to him that the Adjudicator was fluent in Swahili, until John instructed him, *in Swahili*, to be true to his interpreter's oath. As a District Officer, John had spoken Swahili all day long. He was completely fair and I only ever upset his decisions with the greatest of reluctance.

As a believer in the Rule of Law I hold strongly against judges making up the law as they go along. Some might say that this was another bar to my judicial preferment. I also hold strongly against judges allowing their political opinions to influence their judicial decisions, a major failing with respect of courts on both sides of the Atlantic in the Global War on Terror. I recall annoying the poor old President, who was a robust tribunal with respect, but did not interfere with his colleagues' judicial independence, by allowing the appeal of an Italian drug-peddler, who had very properly been sent to prison.

I held that if "anyone should be deported it is this appellant", i.e. my lay colleagues and I agreed that the appellant *should* be deported. The problem was that both Britain was then party to the Treaty of Rome, and there was an EEC Regulation in the way, which said in effect that he could not be deported. I advised my colleagues that we were duty bound to apply it, which we did. This was the only occasion when George Farmer queried a judicial decision of mine, as opposed to my lack of productivity in turning round leave applications when compared with Ray Maddison! The Home Office doubtless consulted the Treasury Solicitor, who doubtless sought counsel's opinion, who doubtless advised that they were lumbered with it, and would just have to look as happy as they could, or words to like effect. At any rate that was the last I heard of it. You don't have to like the decisions you hand down as a judge, so long as they are right. When it came to dealing with European Community law happiness was usually a bit too much to hope for anyway.

I also sat at first instance, to make up the numbers. A bright German barrister came before me one day, in the old Crown Court at Wood Green, and asked me to send a case to the European Court of Justice (ECJ) at Luxembourg. Not only had this never been done before, from my humble level of the system, but he was asking me to refer *inter alia* on the *German* text of the EEC/Morocco Co-Operation Agreement, sensibly. His case was stronger on the German text than the English, possibly because the latter had been badly translated.

Now it is a basic rule when you are construing an international treaty that the different language texts are equally authentic. If one text looks a bit dodgy you can undoubtedly look at the others. The Home Office, knowing me to be on the cusp of being a Eurosceptic, had only sent along a Home Office Presenting Officer, i.e. a civil servant, not counsel. I duly referred the case to Luxembourg.[6] The poor old H.O.P.O. nearly fell out of his chair.

Not only did I refer it but I, popped along to Luxembourg to observe the hearing, the ECJ having sat in plenary session to consider the point. Eleanor Sharpston QC, a specialist in EU law and later my honourable opponent in the famous *Metric Martyrs* case, was representing the UK. She informed the assembled judges that I was present in court. They did not smile very broadly however.

All good things come to an end and eventually it was decided that the IAT should have a High Court judge as President. With great respect to the new President, administrative efficiency and judicial independence went out the window and morale plummeted. There were no more leave applications to deal with, as I was applying the test in the rules, an arguable point of fact or law. The incoming President, again with great respect (he is a very nice chap), wanted to apply the High Court's own, tougher, test when refusing what was now called 'permission' for judicial review.

The backlog grew so great a bunch of live files were apparently locked away in a filing cabinet. At any rate there was a panic on at Field House, the IAT's new home (somebody forgot to renew the lease on Thanet House) one day. I was told that a new manager, who did not realise that he was not supposed to open *that* filing cabinet, opened it up for a look- see. The story went that he was nearly knocked over by the cascading files. For weeks afterwards the poor old full-timers had looks of despair on their faces as their desks groaned under the weight of files.

George Farmer would (1) have kept track of what was happening in his own tribunal and (2) if a backlog of leave applications had started to build would simply have pulled in the part-timers and given 30 files to Ray and 15 to me. (I met George half-way in the end and got my daily rate up to 15.) My case of course was that my bespoke leave decisions rarely went over the road and were quashed on even fewer occasions, i.e. in terms of resources things tended to even out in the long run.

The Immigration Appeal Tribunal was abolished in 2005. Everybody with any sense told the government that they were making a mistake, which indeed they were. They back-tracked eventually, after the High Court was flooded with judicial review challenges, which were dealt with by non-immigration specialists. However, the system was a mess by then. Anyone with a brain in Africa or Asia knew that (1) the UK was a soft touch for human traffickers and (2) the Home Office, with respect, couldn't run a whelk stall. There is now an upper tier again, under a new name, but with respect it lacks the ethos and expertise of the old IAT. Public confidence in the immigration appellate system, understandably, has collapsed, although that could probably be said of Britain's legal systems as a whole, sadly.

The greater independence of part-timers and full-time specialists was amply demonstrated, it is submitted, by the meek way with respect in which the judges caved into pressure from Downing Street during the Blair years. I was told, and have no reason to doubt, that monthly disposal figures were actually sent to Number 10. At first instance they actually circulated the adjournment rates of each individual adjudicator by name, i.e. pressure was brought to bear to keep disposal rates high.

I often used a first hearing to knock a case into shape, if it needed it, and send it away with directions, much as I had seen dear old Judge Barr do years before at Uxbridge. For this I was roundly criticised. Never mind that if the case was in a mess the decision could easily be wrong. Hammering appellants who might not be able to speak English for mistakes made by their representatives, not all of whom had legal training, was not only unfair it was an invitation to further appeals, clogging the system even more. Unsurprisingly sitting became more stressful and there were cases of extended sick leave.

Part-time judges are allowed to be politically active (a number of Recorders are MPs, e.g.). Had anyone in my then party tried to influence a judicial decision however I would have referred the papers to the Attorney-General.

There had always been some pressure at first instance. I recall being told by one Regional Adjudicator, who shall remain nameless, that "we don't grant bail at Hatton Cross", only to be met with the rejoinder, "well, I just have". By the end however it was getting ridiculous. Bail was always a thorny topic. You should always deal with custody cases first and it was my practice to have everybody in, find out what was happening and take any bail applications.

I was sitting, on high, in the lovely old magistrates' court at Gravesend one day (you peered down at the lawyers), when I was told that a surety had missed his connection at Birmingham. It was a renewal, the appellant had complied with his conditions and it was manifestly a case for further bail. The H.O.P.O. made the mistake of telling me that I "could not grant bail" unless two sureties were present. This was "the rule at Gravesend". Bail was granted and I announced a new rule. Applications for bail at Gravesend would henceforth be dealt with on their merits, in accordance with the applicable law, each case falling to be treated on its own facts.

The Bruges Group

I joined the Bruges Group, named after Margaret Thatcher's famous Bruges speech on Europe, whilst still in the Labour Party, which under Neil Kinnock's leadership was rapidly going in the wrong direction on the EEC. This allowed the mostly Tory Bruges Group to present itself as 'all- party', which it now was. The intellectual rigour of Bruges Group meetings was refreshing. Under the influence of great economic thinkers like the late Ralph Harris (Lord Harris), of the Institute of Economic Affairs, and Professors Patrick Minford and Tim Congdon, my economic views gradually became more sensible.

The Bruges Group was very active in opposition to the disastrous Maastricht Treaty. In conjunction with Conservative Eurosceptic barristers the late Leolin Price QC and Martin Howe, (who later took silk – he is an intellectual property specialist and has a lot of it himself), I provided much of the legal analysis of the treaty, and its constitutional implications, to the rebels. These included Sir Bill Cash MP, later Shadow Attorney-General, and Iain Duncan Smith MP, an officer and a gentleman. Iain was later an unfairly maligned Leader of the Tory Party. If he had become Prime Minister he would have avoided most of the blunders made by David Cameron.

It was through the Bruges Group that I met the distinguished former Prime Minister and Foreign Secretary, Lord Home of the Hirsel KT. As Lord Dunglass, Alec had been a member of the German spy Neville Chamberlain's government. He accompanied Chamberlain to Munich, although that was not an episode of which Lord Home, a patriot, was particularly proud.

A lovely man, he did not of course know in 1938 that Chamberlain was working for 'Harry Hun', indeed I don't think he found out until years later. As the Earl of Home, he was the most recent member of the House of Lords to have been appointed Prime Minister.[7] He was also the only Prime Minister to have played first-class cricket, being a useful batsman and fast-medium bowler. He toured Argentina with the MCC in 1926-7 and was President of MCC in 1966.

It has been asserted endlessly by left-wing academics that the last peer to serve as Prime Minister was the 3rd Marquess of Salisbury, in 1902, but that is simply untrue. As we have seen with global warming, endless repetition of a falsehood does not transform it into a truth. Lord Home confirmed to me that his decision to re-enter the Commons[8] was taken on political, not constitutional grounds.

Put shortly, some of the Tory grandees, including Lord Hailsham, had convinced themselves and in turn Alec, against his better judgment, that the Tories would get more votes if he were presented as a commoner, which he clearly wasn't. My view, from which Alec did not demur, was that he might have won the 1964 General Election had he stayed as the Earl of Home.

Some left-wing commentators have summoned the sheer gall and impertinence to suggest that Queen Elizabeth II only appointed Alec on the basis that he would surrender his peerage. Lord Home also confirmed to me that the only pressure to reduce his status to that of an MP, i.e. re-enter the Lower House, came from his Cabinet. The suggestions of pressure from the Palace were wrong.

The constitutional position is clear beyond a peradventure. Whilst the Prime Minister must be able to command the support of a majority in the Commons he or she may serve from either House. In fact, there have only been four great Prime Ministers from the House of Commons: Pitt the Younger, Benjamin Disraeli, Winston Churchill and Margaret Thatcher. Spenser Perceval might have been a great Prime Minister but he was assassinated on 11th May 1812, on the orders of the Emperor Napoleon, although the assassination was disguised through the usual 'lone nutter' route.[9]

As the political class becomes ever more discredited and politics ever more sordid, with lies, assassinations, cover-ups and what have you, it is quite likely that the country will turn once again to the House of Lords for a leader. The Earl of Home, with respect, embodied the qualities of decency, loyalty and honour so sadly lacking in the machine politicians who made up most of the Blair government and dominated the despised Coalition Government. In fairness Gordon Brown had a solidity that Blair, Cameron and Starmer lack, no offence intended.

Another great political figure I got to meet, indeed know, through the Bruges Group was that nice man Mr Enoch Powell. Unlike Heath, who ought to have been shot in World War II, Enoch was a patriot, who would have made a splendid Prime Minister. He was no more a racist than Oprah Winfrey. He was of course set up by Heath, who instructed Conservative Central Office to get the chairman of the infamous meeting at the Midland Hotel in Birmingham's New Street on 20th April 1968, to alter what was never more than a classical allusion from the original Latin. It ended up in English as "foaming with much blood", which the media exaggerated to "rivers of blood". As a literal translation of the original it was inaccurate. As a reflection of dear old Enoch's true meaning it was a grotesque parody.

The media were tipped off and the Sunday papers jumped all over Enoch, notwithstanding the wide public support for what he had said, not that public opinion has ever counted for much in the immigration debate. Politicians and senior civil servants who supported uncontrolled mass immigration were aware that their views lacked democratic legitimacy and simply resorted to lying and massaging statistics, to the point where official statements on immigration are now generally regarded as worthless.

Enoch and I stayed in touch until his sad passing on 8th February 1998. For the avoidance of doubt Enoch never sought to influence the discharge of my judicial functions as a Chairman of the Immigration Appeal Tribunal, nor would it have occurred to him, nor would Enoch have stood for any individual immigrant being treated less than decently or fairly.

I regularly used to chair Bruges Group events at the Conservative Party annual conference, even whilst still in the Labour Party. They were great fun, as well as intellectually stimulating. I had my eye on Crawley, a marginal seat, for the 1992 General Election, and had some local support. There was panic at Walworth Road however, and I was blocked, the popular local mayoress, Laura Moffat, being prevailed upon to enter the race, having initially ruled herself out. It was made clear to me that my opposition to Britain's membership of the European Community was an effective bar to my being a Labour candidate again, i.e. I had no future in the Labour Party.

---

1. Last hope of the British mobile phone industry, Technophone were based in Camberley in Surrey, and made stylish mobile phones with cutting-edge performance for the day. Sadly, they were taken over and you would be hard put to find a British-made mobile these days.
2. The courts are now lumbered with a daft document, with respect, called the Civil Procedure Rules, designed to Europeanise the law, i.e. make it less effective and more expensive, which was sneaked through by the Rules Committee when Parliament wasn't looking. The old *habeas corpus* rules were in Order 54 of the superbly drafted Rules of the Supreme Court (which need to be brought back and fast).
3. *The Law of Habeas Corpus*, by that nice man Judge Robert Sharpe, later a Justice of Appeal in Ontario.
4. This too should be filed in advance. I have some recollection of being against David Pannick QC, in another *habeas corpus* case, and being handed his Skeleton as he walked into court. The proper thing to do in those circumstances is to ignore it, give it to your solicitor to file, and if asked whether you have read it tell the judge 'no', explaining that you were only served at 1025, or whenever. If there is any point in it worth arguing your opponent will usually mention it to the judge, without commenting on the cogency or otherwise of Mr Pannick's arguments in that particular case. Sadly, with respect, there was a miscarriage of justice (i.e. he won!).
5. I.e. without a separate chassis, where the body itself is load bearing. Strictly the P5's were semi-monocoque, as they had a massive sub-frame at the front on which the engine was mounted – anything you hit, stayed hit.
6. The case was *El-Yassini v Secretary of State for the Home Department.*
7. Appointed by HM Queen Elizabeth II on 18th October 1963, the Earl of Home did not give up his peerage until the 23rd, nearly a week later.
8. As Lord Dunglass. Alec had of course been an MP from 1931 until 1945 and again from 1950 until 1951, when he succeeded to the peerage. Dunglass was an honorary title, as Alec was the son and heir of an Earl. It is not unknown for MPs to have an honorary title in this way, the most recent being Lord Cranbourne.
9. He was a nutter alright, a French nutter.

6

Into The Tory Party

Neil Kinnock very properly resigned as leader of the Labour Party after managing to lose the 1992 General Election, helped by that very silly rally at Sheffield. Neil - you're supposed to have the victory rally, if you must have one, *after* you win the election, not before! His main contribution as leader had been to give some good ideas to then Senator Joe Biden's speechwriter.

I backed that nice man Bryan Gould MP in the leadership election that followed. Bryan was intelligent - a former Rhodes Scholar - and had sensible views on the European Community. John Smith won however, and after an awkward meeting with him at the 1992 Labour Conference in Blackpool the informal message conveyed after I had been blocked at Crawley was confirmed. There was no place for me in the Labour Party.

Bryan Gould came to much the same conclusion and returned to New Zealand, where Waikato University were lucky enough to have him as Vice-Chancellor. Ironically, John Smith was murdered by his own side, i.e. the 'Jerries', two years later. He had stated at a Bilderberg Group meeting that in his judgment it was no longer politically possible after 'Black Wednesday', when the pound broke free of the European Monetary System, ensuring 15 years of prosperity, for a Labour government to destroy sterling. He was right.

There was no point my joining the Tory Party at that point, since (1) the pointless (with respect) John Major was its leader (2) its European policy was just as ludicrous and unpatriotic as Labour's and (3) I held myself out as a serious professional. By 1992 the Tories had spent several years waging war on the professions and the Bar in particular. The farmers, officers and gentlemen had largely left and it was mainly a party, then, for spivs and real estate agents. No serious professional would want to be seen going anywhere near it.

It was about this time that a nice member of the Trilateral Commission, a former Labour MP, sounded me out about joining the Commission, although he could not have been aware that it was a front for the DVD and certainly did not put it in those terms. After an amicable chat over a couple of pints in the *The Two Chairmen*[1] it was mutually agreed that I was not for the Trilateral Commission and the Trilateral Commission was not for me. These mutual conclusions were undoubtedly correct. If my name had got back to Dachau it would have provoked an outbreak of mild hysteria.

The Maastricht Treaty

The Maastricht Treaty was very sensibly rejected by the Danish people in a referendum, on 28th June 1993. 'No' votes don't mean very much where the EU is concerned however, and a second vote was called. In the EU you can only vote 'yes' and if you get it wrong you have to keep voting until you cave in to the Germans. Brexit was the exception which proved the rule.

In an effort to hoodwink the Danish electorate into believing that they were voting on a different treaty to that which they had already rejected, the heads of government of the European Community, meeting in Edinburgh at the European Council, concocted an elaborate fraud called the 'Edinburgh opt-outs'. The idea was to pretend that the Maastricht Treaty had been amended by the addition of an additional protocol designed to meet Danish objections.

The problem was that this scam had been tried before, by the DVD's Harold Wilson, in an effort to win the 1975 referendum in Britain on whether or not Britain should withdraw[2] from what was then the EEC (it keeps changing its name). There had of course been no referendum before Britain went in - it would have smacked of democracy. Informed by the 1975 experience, Bill Cash MP asked Leo Price QC, Martin Howe and myself to have a look at the conclusions of the Edinburgh European Summit.[3] This was published under the title *Edinburgh European Council – a Legal Assessment*, which was made available to the Danes as a courtesy, translated into Danish and published in a Danish national newspaper.

It seems as though the Foreign Office had bought into their own propaganda, i.e. hadn't read their Goebbels. They believed that we Eurosceptics didn't like Europe, didn't know where it was and would never work with any Europeans. They had obviously never met Sir Bill, who is from the millionaire 'Cash Tapes' family and is as cosmopolitan a politician as you could wish to meet. They may also have believed that English barristers could not survive on a diet of pickled herrings.

As the '*tre Engelske jurister*' were told, when we rolled up in Copenhagen the Danish Government thought they had the local media firmly under wraps. That's what they told the Germans anyway. Our conclusions were presented at a televised press conference in the *Folketing* (Parliament) in Copenhagen. I was properly dressed (the *Observer* described me as a "Dickensian character wearing a clanking gold watch chain" - high praise indeed) and explained in my speech that the Maastricht Treaty sought to create the first political union between England and Denmark since the reign of King Canute. I didn't know how to say "King Canute" in Danish but that problem was solved the following morning, as the quote was on the front pages.[4] The press conference made the evening news and we were invited to meetings all over Denmark.

Under public international law it is possible to have an additional protocol to a multilateral treaty. It was done in 1977 with the 1948 Geneva Conventions I-IV, e.g., indeed that was the Second Additional Protocol. That was an example of an optional protocol. The Treaty on European Union (i.e. the Maastricht Treaty) was self-executing however, and an optional protocol was a non-starter. Here the politicians gathered at Edinburgh encountered a real problem, which could not be washed away even with copious quantities of Scotch. A protocol, to be binding, would have to be agreed by each state party to the treaty. That meant reopening the controversial ratification process in each Member State. Oops.

What is more the agreement the leaders cobbled together did not even purport to amend the treaty, which a protocol would have done. It wasn't even called a "protocol", for the very good reason that it wasn't. Moreover, the European Council as a body had no jurisdiction under community law to propose amendments. It was not then a community institution, it was purely intergovernmental.

In public international law, as plenipotentiaries of the Member States, they could have got around that problem by amending the treaty, but the amendment would have been fairly complex, more than a one-liner anyway. However, as Martin Howe, with respect eloquently, pointed out in his speech in Copenhagen, the Edinburgh Agreement was so devoid of content - it was basically waffle - that it didn't actually say very much at all. Most certainly it did not give the Danes any opt-outs, which is how it had been spun.

The sensible thing for the EEC/EC/EU to do would have been to respect the democratically expressed will of the Danish people and scrap the ratification process. This would have meant abandoning the idea of creating the euro. Since the euro was a silly idea anyway and is bound to collapse in the end, no harm would have been done. Moreover, the EC would have been able to preserve the pretence that Western Europe was democratic and had learnt the lessons of 1945. By disregarding the result of the Danish referendum the EC revealed itself as essentially fascist. Strictly it is neo-fascist, since there are no uniforms or concentration camps, although as we saw with John Smith, the assassination of political opponents is part and parcel of the project.

This lesson was not lost on Moscow, which came to realise that the EC was about as democratic as the USSR. At Maastricht the nation states of Western Europe took a giant step backwards to the Bismarckian era of blood and iron. After Maastricht, if you could think straight you joined the intelligence community, if you could shoot straight you joined the army, if you liked messing about in boats you joined the navy and if you liked dropping things on people you joined the air force. Of course it takes time for things to work their way through. Apart from anything else the Germans in the mid-90s had the best tank[5] and these days it takes at least 10 years to bring a new weapons system into production.

As it turned out there was more on Danish menus than pickled herring. Myself and my colleagues were shown great hospitality, doing our best when pickled herring *was* served to look pleased and say "ahhh, pickled herring", or words to like effect. Lasting friendships were made. The first trip started to take on some of the attributes of a resistance convention - the highly principled Danish 'No to EU' group was essentially the old, Danish Resistance, minus Sten Guns. They were very nice people. One of the nicest was Professor Kai Lemberg, who had been betrayed to the Gestapo (no doubt by a future 'Yes' voter) and had done time in a Nazi concentration camp.

The conclusions of *A Legal Assessment* were rubbished by the Brussels establishment of course. Then someone in the European Commission very helpfully wrote to someone in NATO expressing agreement with the assessment and saying nice things about its authors. This was then very helpfully leaked to the press a week before the second referendum, triggering a mini panic in Copenhagen and Brussels. The 'Yes' camp dropped nearly 10 points in the polls. They were able to pull back however, and won.

Leo Price was a Chancery man, and a good one, and Martin, as we have seen, was an intellectual property chap. I was a public lawyer, although well versed in the interpretation of treaties. For much of the 1990s I was applying international conventions, either the European Convention on Human Rights, the UN Refugee Convention, or the Treaty on European Union, each almost as silly as the other, on a weekly if not daily basis, as an immigration judge. I spotted that the Danish Government were trying to pull a flanker, with respect.

The Maastricht Treaty was all about politics and governance and very little to do with economics or free trade. Freedom of movement of goods, labour and capital, disastrously, had been established in the original Treaty of Rome in 1957 and the so-called 'single market' (in everything except lamb of course) had been set up by the Single European Act in 1986. To incorporate the latest treaty into Danish law the Danish government clearly needed to amend the Constitution of the Kingdom of Denmark Act 1953.

Apart from anything else the two Maastricht referenda had been held only in Denmark. The loyal people of the Færoe Islands and Greenland, which were part of the Kingdom of Denmark, although they had home rule, had been excluded. It did not matter that Greenland had been the first territory to withdraw from the EEC's clammy embrace, in 1980, forty years before the UK. Greenland was part of Denmark even though she was not part of the EC. What is more there was a gate, in Article 88 of the Constitution, which was the amending provision. You couldn't just have any old referendum, you needed a proper referendum. The Danish government's view, which was wrong with respect, was that since the dodgy referenda had each been endorsed by the *Folketing* that was it, i.e. the *Folketing* could pass any law it wanted, like the British Parliament. "Ah", said I, "that ignores the principle in the great United States Supreme Court case of *Marbury v Maddison,*[6] which holds that where an elected legislature draws its authority from a written constitution it is as much bound by that constitution as anybody else, and under the doctrine of Separation of Powers the independent judiciary established by the same constitution may quash any acts of the legislature which are unconstitutional". The act providing for a second referendum was contrary to the Constitution of the Kingdom of Denmark Act and could therefore be quashed by the Danish Supreme Court. So went the reasoning.

My view was expounded over coffee and some tasty Danish pastries (what else?) in a café in the famous Tivoli Gardens in Copenhagen. Present were the June Movement's conspicuously able lawyer Christian Harlang, who now has his own firm in Copenhagen - very much a 'go to' firm these days - and a very nice and very senior Danish lawyer. He held the equivalent of the old English rank of Serjeant-at-Law, an ancient rank, abolished in a senseless change in the 1870s. It had been abolished in Denmark too, but this was their revenge. In addition to being a very good lawyer he was also the proud owner of, from recollection, a Derby Bentley. Put shortly, this was one of the biggest carve-ups in Copenhagen since VE-Day.

A constitutional challenge to the dodgy referendum act was mounted forthwith, seizing the imagination of the Danish public and causing a seizure in the Danish Ministry of Justice. They must have choked on their pastries when the writ came flying in. Not only did Denmark have a serious constitution she also had a serious chief judge with respect - Chief Justice Pontoppidan. Aside from being un-biddable and unbribable he was a good lawyer - rare qualities in a senior Danish judge, let alone amongst senior English judges.

The case, *Fischer and ors v. Prime Minister Rasmussen*, went first to the Eastern High Court in Copenhagen, who essentially said with respect they weren't being paid enough to decide it (a decision in favour of the plaintiffs would have tanked the euro), so off it went to the Supreme Court. The case had been split, the first issue being jurisdiction, i.e. could the courts strike down an unconstitutional act of parliament? In a landmark decision, the court, presided over by the great Chief Justice Pontoppidan, ruled against the government and upheld the right of the courts to enforce the constitution against the *Folketing*. So much government furniture needed replacing after that there was probably a boost to Denmark's furniture industry.

Sadly, however, Pontoppidan was not on the Supreme Court panel that decided the substantive issue. Having been present when the case was first discussed, I was invited over to Copenhagen and was present in court when the final ruling was handed down. The government won, a serious blow to the Rule of Law in Denmark.

The Danish Constitution may not be a complete dead letter however, as the Supreme Court laid down a marker. The 2011 fiscal compact, stitched together in a last-ditch effort to save the euro by transferring powers over budgets to Brussels, probably fell foul of the Danish constitution, although disappointingly there was no legal challenge. The problem may be that after *Fischer*, confidence in the Danish courts, sadly, has collapsed, just as confidence in the British courts, with respect, collapsed after the *Factortame* cases.

The first requirement for a judge is courage. If a judge doesn't have that quality it doesn't matter how good a lawyer he or she is. When the stakes are high, without the courage to apply your real opinion it's worthless. The written constitutions of the EU member states are just paper constitutions and will remain so until judges can be found who are willing to uphold them in the face of external demands from the EU. In practice this means demands from its controlling state, Germany. The same applies to European frontiers, which at the moment are just lines on a map, with the result that parts of Europe are now in the Third World, not the First. The *Legal Assessment* and constitutional challenge were also covered by the Swedish media. The British legal team were invited to Stockholm, indeed as we were heading to Copenhagen's efficient Kastrup airport for the flight home we heard a reference to the "*tre Engelske jurister*" on the radio. Our taxi driver informed us that we were going to Stockholm! We weren't, not then, anyway. It was the only time in my life I found myself on my way to the airport in a taxi and heard a change in my flight announced over the radio.

We got to Sweden soon enough however, and addressed the issue of the constitutional implications of EU membership for Sweden. The Swedish government had been playing these down, i.e. they had not explained to Swedes that joining the EU meant trashing the Swedish Constitution. Symbolically, one meeting was in Olaf Palme's old cabinet room in the delightful Swedish Parliament building. As major players in Swedish intelligence well know poor old Olaf was assassinated on German orders. Firm and lasting friendships were made on these Scandinavian trips.

The British team received friendly greetings wherever we went. One of the more notable personalities I met was Jan Myrdal. Both of Jan's parents won the Nobel Prize, a rare distinction. Of greater interest to me, he had a splendid train set.

The distinguished Stockholm lawyer Erik Göthe and his delightful partner Ragnhild were also most gracious. In 1997 I enjoyed a wonderful sailing voyage amongst the delightful islands of the Stockholm Archipelago (thanks Erik). This was followed by a driving holiday in Norway, combined of course with business in Stockholm and Oslo. Sadly, Sweden joined the EU, although the Swedes must wish by now that they hadn't. The decision ended up costing the life of the rather lovely Swedish Foreign Minister, Anna Lindh, who as we shall see was cynically assassinated by the DVD.

Watermead

The practice was going well and I bought my first house, on Watermead, near Aylesbury, in Buckinghamshire, in 1992. Watermead was the brainchild of Rob Clarke, of Royco plc, and was a lovely place to live. The water meadows after which it was named drained into two artificial lakes. Unfortunately, the Major government decided to have a recession. Royco, having shelled out six million pounds on the lakes and open spaces, went under.

I had no role in the Labour Party with John Smith as its leader. John Major was strangling the life out of the Tory Party with his idiotic European policy, no offence intended. This included hitching sterling to the deutschmark in order to help German exporters. Slightly against my better judgment I agreed to become Chairman of the Watermead Village Residents Association (WVRA).

Any hopes that chairing the residents' committee might be confined to mowing the open spaces and organizing the summer fête were dashed when a nightclub operator moved in. He was hoping to open a nightclub on the shore of the north lake, which sent residents into apoplexy. Putting the matter as delicately as one can, residents' concerns were not allayed by the contents of a report by a private investigator on the nightclub operator. He had however missed a trick. He applied for planning permission (zoning) without buying up the land on which he was hoping to build.

At my instigation WVRA promoted the formation of a company, Lakeside Land Ltd. We raised £30,000 to buy the land, exchanging contracts with an hour to spare. I had negotiated an exclusive 30-day option with the receivers to Royco plc. The nightclub operator did not take defeat gracefully. There was friction for a decade afterwards, with encroachment on boundaries, eggs being thrown at my house, and so on. At one point I was thrown bodily, into one of the lakes by a group of about a dozen trespassers. They were operating loud jet-skis on a lake the community had bought with its own money, right in front of our local old-folks home. The police and Crown Prosecution Service (CPS) did nothing, despite the attack taking place in broad daylight in front of eyewitnesses. This confirmed my low opinion of Thames Valley Police and the CPS.

I should explain that Aylesbury is the county town of Buckinghamshire. We used to have an efficient police force, the Buckinghamshire Constabulary, but in a disastrous decision in 1968 it was merged with four other forces to create Thames Valley Police. The idea was to make policing more remote, more corrupt and less responsive to the needs of the community. It worked. In practice the new force reported to the Cabinet Office, although that is not the official position.

The CPS was another silly idea. It was set up in 1986, the idea being to have the Civil Service take over the conduct of criminal prosecutions. That was all very well, but the Home Civil Service has low ethical standards, with respect, and lacks managerial competence. The 'service' has been a disaster.

It wasn't all about being beaten up, however. Lakeside Land bought a John Deere ride-on mower. This gave splendid opportunities to mow some of the 25 acres of parkland we had bought. There were also carol concerts every Christmas and trapped ducklings to rescue. Watermead is a wildfowl centre. We even had that nice man the late Rolf Harris visit one day. This gave me an opportunity to tell him what pleasure his show had given us as children, and to complement him on his great skill as an artist. (His conviction was a joke, as the jury, at Southwark Crown Court, was probably tampered with, as in my case.)

VE-Day 50th Anniversary

8th May 1995 was the 50th anniversary of VE-Day. I decided that Watermead should (1) celebrate it in style and (2) honour World War II veterans, who had fought so long and so hard to defeat our community partners. The lakes were just right for a Lancaster fly-past, although when I announced to my committee that I thought I knew where I could get my hands on a Lancaster for VE-Day afternoon they thought I was making it up.

The Lancaster duly arrived, along with a Vickers-Supermarine Spitfire and a Hawker Hurricane, on VE-Day afternoon, as promised. This was courtesy of the Royal Air Force's excellent Battle of Britain Memorial Flight. They even did a second fly-past, doing a 'U-ie' (i.e. a 180^0 turn) over the nearby village of Bierton, roaring back over the lakes. The ground rises behind Watermead, so the Lanc's pilot gave her mighty Merlins a boost. They made a tremendous sound. Well-tuned Rolls-Royce Merlin engines make sound, not noise.

Quite what the good people of Bierton thought when a WWII Avro Lancaster roared over their village at 500 ft on VE-Day afternoon is anyone's guess. There were no complaints, however. We put up red, white and blue bunting in the village square, a crowd of over 3,000 roared their approval and a brass band struck up the *Dambusters March* as the aircraft made their approach. Watermead has an attractive bandstand, built over the north lake. Great. The veterans, from Bomber Command Association, were nearly in tears, as was I.

There was a collection for Bomber Command funds. People gave generously, especially the young. Many of them were seeing a Lancaster, a Spitfire and a Hurricane for the first time. The local radio station Mix 96, were forewarned. They did not quite believe that it was actually going to happen, but they sent along a reporter and sound man just in case. When they saw that the spine road into Watermead had a temporary closure order on it, the Fire Brigade and an ambulance were on standby, stewards in yellow jackets were everywhere and people were running around with air-band transceivers, they started to get a clue. There were urgent calls into the studio. As the flypast commenced a mike was thrust into my hand and I was told to get going with my first live commentary.

The following year (1996) we had a joint Fireworks Night/Remembrance Day event, which saw the first collaboration between myself, and the Rolls-Royce Enthusiasts Club (RREC). This led in turn to my purchase of a Bentley, the battle to keep Rolls-Royce British, the intervention of the DVD to capture the marque for the fatherland and their exposure.

It all started with an act of kindness and generosity on the part of RREC towards the Queen's deputy representative for Buckinghamshire, the Vice-Lieutenant. He was John Pattison, an extremely nice man. It would not have been necessary but for a mean-spirited official decision to deprive the Lieutenancy of Buckinghamshire of an official car.

Although Britain is a constitutional monarchy and a democracy, senior officials at both Whitehall and county level try to govern her as though she is a quasi-dictatorship, with the Cabinet Secretary as quasi-dictator. They tend to pay lip service both to government ministers and elected local councillors, who are treated as rubber stamps. No opportunity is passed up to snub the King, or His representatives. This was demonstrated too me by Thames Valley Police, when their officers insolently refused to salute the Vice-Lieutenant, even though he was on official duties.

This particular piece of effrontery may not sound significant, and wasn't in the great scheme of things, but it was symbolic. It called the patriotism of senior Thames Valley Police officers, and their commitment to the Rule of Law, into question. Peace officers in Britain hold office from the Sovereign. They are sworn to uphold His laws. Thames Valley Police, one of the least efficient and most corrupt forces in Britain, should be broken up into more accountable county forces. Sadly, the problem with the police in Britain is not confined to Buckinghamshire, Oxfordshire and the Royal County of Berkshire.

Naturally, the Queen's Representative could not be seen to arrive in any lesser conveyance than a Rolls-Royce. John Pattison thought that the 'Royce' was a lovely gesture. He was properly dressed, i.e. in full dress uniform, complete with sword. There was a brass band, of course - the Band of the RAF Regiment, no less. The national anthem was played upon John's arrival, all three verses.

A public-spirited resident was kind enough to lend his balcony for the occasion. We brought the bunting out again with more funds being raised for Bomber Command Association, who by now were beginning to sit up and take notice, as I suspect was the local MP, David Lidington. Once again, the crowd was huge, and enthusiastic.

A previous fireworks night, not, I hasten to add, involving me, made the national press, sadly for the wrong reason. The fireworks, for some reason, had been placed on a barge. They caught fire and exploded, and the barge sank. The operators had to jump into the lake. This time the fireworks were fired safely, by a team of professional operators, over the main lake, from the opposite bank. They were quite spectacular.

Bomber Command

In a most gracious gesture, Bomber Command Association awarded me an honorary life membership. The presentation was made at the RAF Museum in Hendon by that very nice man the late Marshal of the Royal Air Force Sir Michael Beetham GCB, CBE, DFC, AFC, who bombed Germany. Sadly, the Blair government continued Whitehall's German-influenced policy of insulting Bomber Command veterans by depriving them of a campaign medal. A medal was richly deserved, given that they suffered the highest ratio of losses of any Allied combat command in World War II. Bomber Command made a huge contribution to the Allied victory. Very frankly the clasp was too little, too late.

They ought to be have been awarded a series of medals, one for the Strategic Bomber Offensive, with a clasp for each tour[7] and additional medals for special operations such as the great 1,000 Bomber Raid on Cologne in May 1942, or the famous Dams Raid. Bomber Command Association were wonderful people, sadly almost all gone now, and I count myself privileged to have been associated with them.

The post-war attempts to belittle their great achievements, and those of their valiant comrades-in-arms, the USAAF Eighth Army Air Force Bomber Command, by German assets such as J. K. 'von' Galbraith, were simply outrageous. The post-war assessments of the effectiveness of Allied strategic bombing are not even remotely serious historical documents.

The time has come for an unbiased assessment, which could start by ditching the myth, still propagated by the *History Channel*, that British and American heavy bombers were unable to hit their targets. If there were any truth to the German-influenced official claims, when allied troops entered Germany they would have found intact or nearly intact targets, surrounded by fields full of holes. Most of the targets were of course flattened and rightly so. Of course, if the Germans did not wish to be bombed, they should not have invaded Poland.

More Interesting Cases

I think these cases are interesting but you can always skip this bit! In one case, a section 18 wounding with intent, tried before that splendid tribunal, with respect, His Honour Judge John Slack TD, at Aylesbury Crown Court,[8] my instructing solicitor included the following immortal phrase in my instructions: "it was at this point that our client's knife unfortunately accidentally entered the victim's chest for the third time". Many trial lawyers will tell you that this was not the most promising of starts.

Luckily, the lay client, a nice black man from Milton Keynes,[9] who had had been cutting chicken with a machete at the time, as one does, was not represented by a silk. Silks have a terrible tendency to impose their view of the case on the client. Sometimes they also forget which side they are acting for. When defending, they can start acting as though they are leading for the prosecution.

I fought the case according to my instructions. I did not chicken out by asking the learned judge to leave the lesser charge of wounding, under s. 20 of the Offences Against the Person Act 1861, to the jury. Our case was that there had been no stabbing at all, i.e. that although the alleged victim's chest had been penetrated three times by a knife held in the defendant's hand each of these penetrations was accidental.

The great forensic pathologist Professor Austen Gresham, fresh from the Julie Ward murder trial in Kenya,[10] did a rather more thorough analysis of the wounds than the prosecution (CPS again) with respect. He demonstrated to the jury that the defendant's account of the 'victim' running onto the knife, and the second and third cuts happening as he backed away, was consistent with the evidence of the wound sites. The jury acquitted, and rightly so.

The defendant burst into tears when the verdict was read out. This is always a better sign than having your client give a high five to friends in the gallery and leaping out of the dock grinning from ear to ear. Juries have an amazing facility for getting it right, partly because, unlike judges, they tend to apply the correct standard of proof.

This is one reason why I do not associate myself with the widespread criticism of the jury in the *Florida v. Casey Anthony* murder trial in 2011. Indeed, some might think that was one of those cases where the prosecution ought perhaps to have been arresting one of their own witnesses. There it is. In fairness to the prosecution, they seemed to lose confidence in their case as they went along. I have always maintained, albeit controversially, that when prosecuting you should think about your case before you open it.

The *New York Times* were kind enough to print a letter from me defending the jury in the O. J. Simpson murder trial. Their verdict, by the way, was consistent with the subsequent verdict the other way in the civil trial, since the standards of proof were different. If the jury in the criminal trial had been asked the same question, whether they thought the defendant had probably killed the victim, they might have said 'yes'. The issues in the civil trial were also broader. In the criminal trial the prosecution nailed themselves to murder one, which I always thought was a stretch. Had I been prosecuting I would have gone for involvement as an accessory. That was as far as the admissible evidence seemed to go.

In my letter to the *Times* I was seeking to make the point that an English jury would probably have reached the same verdict, on that evidence. As presented, there was clearly a problem with the prosecution case, as the able defence advocate Johnnie Cochran, sadly no longer with us, fairly pointed out. My only respectful criticism of his conduct of the defence was to do with his choice of ties, which were perhaps a trifle frantic. Defence advocates on both sides of the Atlantic probably make too much of supposed racial bias on the part of the jurors, a problem more perceived than real in my experience.

Public Interest Immunity

Another memorable win was in Birmingham. That's BIRMingham, in the English Midlands, not BirmingHAM in the great state of Alabama. This touched upon the thorny issue of Public Interest Immunity certificates. These scandalous documents, which permit the trial process to be subverted by the suppression of evidence, were brought into disrepute in the notorious *Matrix Churchill* trial. In that case, in the 1990s, decent and patriotic company directors, who had agreed to help the intelligence services, were left swinging in the wind after political pressure was brought to bear on MI5 and MI6. They are still angry about it, not least because the impression was given out that if you help British Intelligence you will be left to rot if anything goes wrong. That only holds good if GO2 have been allowed to get in the way.

Whitehall was anxious to cover up its role in the shipment of the three ex-South African nuclear weapons to Iraq and some other stuff (which I have no chance of getting into print). The other stuff may have included protecting the brilliant Canadian ballistics expert Dr Gerald Bull from being exposed as a German (DVD) agent. At any rate, the poor old Matrix Churchill directors were hung out to dry.

The courts have always accepted that you can suppress the identity of sources. The jurisprudential justification for this was the notion that the identity of sources, as opposed to what they say, is not relevant to the issue before the jury. If the jury are told the truth it does not matter where the truth comes from and there is no real injustice.

The idea that you could distort the outcome of a trial by suppressing *material* evidence goes back to the *Thetis* Disaster of 1939. The Cabinet Office and the Germans wanted to turn the British public off the idea of war. Ninety-nine men were drowned within sight of shore after the brand new submarine *Thetis* was sabotaged by the Abwehr. The Official Version of Events was that a valve, which happened to be of German manufacture, had "malfunctioned". The facts are starting to be obscured by the mists of time, but it looks as though political interference was run on the rescue operation. If not, it was remarkably ham-fisted, given that the *Thetis*, which was on her trials, had gone down in shallow water, less than the length of the submarine.

The Chamberlain government, secretly, had been helping Germany to re-arm. In addition to wanting casualties, the Cabinet Secretary, whom it will be recalled was a German spy, was understandably anxious to hide the extent of technology transfer to Germany. He also wanted to cover up arms purchases by pro-German British company directors, mostly linked to the notorious Federation of British Industry, from Nazi Germany.

The House of Lords was prevailed upon to sanction the cover-up, under a bogus national security pretext. The case was *Duncan v. Cammell-Laird* [1942] AC 624. All that was in fact needed was for Whitehall to agree to pay fair compensation to the *Thetis* widows and children. They were treated abominably, as my late friend Eric Heffer well knew.

The uncompromising brutality of their treatment is of course one indice that the original sinking was not a malfunction of the German valve at all, but sabotage. Typically, you get German assets in Whitehall blocking compensation to victims of Abwehr or DVD sabotage. The viciousness and sheer nastiness of German intelligence is a gift to counterintelligence, i.e. they like to keep bashing their victims long after security considerations should have dictated a halt. Holding up recovery efforts whilst the survivors asphyxiated would also have helped with the cover- up, as the officers and petty officers, i.e. those with the most technical knowledge, would have been last off the boat. Sensibly, although he must have hoped he would soon be re-united with his comrades, *Thetis's* intelligence officer was off the boat early. He had an urgent despatch from her captain, Lieutenant-Commander Guy Bolus, for the Admiralty, and for the Naval Intelligence Department.

The *Thetis* was sunk twice, which is unusual for a warship. She was refloated and commissioned as HMS *Thunderbolt.* Sadly, she was eventually sunk by our community partners, 'the Eyeties' on 14th March 1943. Before she slipped beneath the waves for the last time however she had avenged the men who died in her in 1939 and given the enemy something to think about.

The *Thetis* widows and children would best be honoured by scrapping the PII system, making similar official cover-ups more difficult. The system was extended, without argument, to criminal trials and then incorporated in the Crown Court Rules. Every conviction obtained by this unconstitutional withholding of material evidence should be quashed by statute.

If any of the widows and children of the *Thetis* survive they should be paid just compensation, with interest, so that their last years may be made as comfortable as possible. Compensation should also be extended to surviving family members of the widows and children who are no longer with us. Our British tradition, as in America, is that wrongs should be righted. The sooner this grievous wrong is righted the better.

When the Department of Trade and Industry indicated to the learned Recorder of Birmingham in my case that they were applying for a PII certificate I respectfully indicated that I was reserving my position on the correctness of *Duncan v. Cammell-Laird*. That is to say I was indicating my willingness to attack one of the most shameful decisions in British legal history, with respect, in the House or Lords, if need be. Indeed I would have subjected it to savage attack. Although there were several Court of Appeal decisions on PII procedures the argument that PII did not apply in a criminal trial had been allowed to go by default, as it had in *Matrix Churchill.*

Aside from being wrong, *Duncan v. Cammell-Laird* was a civil decision, i.e. on the face of it had no application in a criminal trial at all. That view was apparently shared by Lord Kilmuir, formerly our old friend Sir David

Maxwell-Fyfe. When Lord Chancellors of his ilk make a statement they usually mean it. David Kilmuir may not have impressed Major Somerfield as a criminal defence advocate but he was too well informed, with respect, not to have known or least suspected the dark secret behind *Duncan v. Cammell-Laird*. He must have appreciated that the spotlight might be shone onto the *Thetis* sabotage if an innocent man were sent to prison after the prosecution had deliberately and consciously withheld material evidence from his counsel and the jury.

The CPS, which has willingly gone along with this nonsense, will have to go, as well as PII certificates. Each county council should be asked to set up prosecuting solicitors departments, or retain reputable local firms of solicitors to do the work, as the Benson Royal Commission once wisely recommended. Aside from any other consideration the CPS apparently did nothing to ensure that the attention of the courts which first extended PII certificates to criminal cases was drawn to the views of Lord Kilmuir.

Whitehall also took care to suppress the true facts of the *Thetis* disaster from every court which subsequently considered *Duncan v. Cammell- Laird*. Had they been told the truth those courts would probably have 'confined the decision to its special facts', judicial code for 'don't go near'. In my Birmingham case the DTI backed down and showed the documents to me on a counsel-to-counsel basis. I was satisfied that they were not material to any issue in the case and so advised my lay client. The ability of barristers to trust each other in this way means that quite a few PII cases could be settled without argument. Very often the documents that a government department is trying to suppress aren't germane in any event, in which case they are not admissible into evidence anyway, or they do not in fact assist the defence.

Sometimes the only reason the defence think there might be something in secret documents is because of the effort being put into suppressing them. As in this case, they can actually turn out to be quite boring when you finally get to see them. Of course, lay clients have to trust their barrister, but that's why we have free choice of counsel.

The facts of the case were not entirely dull. The defendant had sold the assets of his company, which was failing, for £50,000, about $80,000, on the basis that he would pay off the creditors. He walked out of a bank with the £50,000 in cash, in a briefcase, having given a false address. He and his charming wife then spent the money on themselves, not the creditors. Sadly, the DTI summoned the impertinence to accuse him of dishonesty. The learned judge agreed that there was a *prima facie* case to go to the jury - I cannot remember why.

The defendant explained that it had all been a misunderstanding. He went on to blame the purchaser's solicitors for drafting a contract that was unclear and did not fully reflect the underlying business discussions. The jury, having heard him and his wife give evidence, very properly acquitted him. In fact, when we looked at the contract it was not at all clear. A lawyer could understand it, but the defendant had no legal training.

He was a hands-on businessman who left the business of drafting documents to others, in this case the other side. The defendant did not leap gleefully from the dock when the verdict of Not Guilty came in and I rather thought that justice had been done. It was the sort of case a judge might get wrong nine times out of ten and a jury not at all. The DTI still went away muttering however.

My Defection to the Tories

In the 1997 election the Tory candidate for Aylesbury, David Lidington, later Minister for Europe, expressed the view that it was about time I went over to them. He was right. There was no role for Shrimpton in the new Labour government, led by my 'learned friend' Tony Blair. Tony has never been a fully paid-up member of my fan club anyway, not that it's the size of Madonna's. Moreover, as I explained in the last chapter, Tony appointed pro-Green Paper law officers. One of them later keeled over with the strain, poor chap.[11] The way was now clear for a barrister to join the Tory Party without feeling that he or she was letting the side down.

It was clear that the new government was going to be a disaster and was not going to govern in the British interest. There had been a moment in the campaign when I thought I could get John Prescott, Labour's Deputy Leader, to persuade Tony Blair to see sense over Europe. I even sent a fax to John's battle-bus proposing a serious European policy instead of the silliness which had found its way into the manifesto. The fax was no doubt screwed up and is still littering the side of some motorway somewhere.

Sadly, the stress of a close campaign proved too much for the poor old Member for Uxbridge, who died. I had my supporters in the Uxbridge Constituency Labour Party and was actually nominated by one of the branches. The party machine imposed a Blairite however, who duly went on to lose the by-election to John Randall and rightly so. John now Lord Randall, is a first- class chap and was an excellent constituency MP, although he didn't always remember who his friends were. Democracy in the Labour Party had clearly had its day. I had finally had enough and went over to the Tories, notwithstanding a poignant plea from the great Peter Shore, Lord Shore of Stepney and a former Secretary of State for Economic Affairs, to stay.

John Major, thankfully, had gone. There could be no question of joining a party led by one of the architects of the Maastricht Treaty. Conservative Central Office backed my defection, sending a Shadow Cabinet member, Andrew Lansley MP, later Lord Privy Seal and Leader of the House of Commons, to make the arrangements. The BBC *Today* programme were a bit baffled. Andrew and I were amused to hear John Humphries (from memory) on the radio, on the way down to the press conference, querying who the "mystery defector" might be. In a tongue-in-cheek response to a question at the press conference from a slightly gob-smacked *Guardian* journalist (this was not a career move after all) I explained that I thought it was time for "a move to the left".

Tony Blair, unusually for a serving Prime Minister, had chosen that day to campaign in the by-election. He may have made a mistake when asked by Independent Television News about my defection, by attributing it to "sour grapes". I had been keeping my usual low profile and Tony could probably have got away with pretending that he had no idea who I was. I was now a fully paid-up Tory, having brought my chequebook with me. To prove it, I was presented by Andrew Lansley, a nice man, with a complimentary party tie, although I stopped wearing it some years ago. Shortly thereafter I was put up for membership of the Carlton Club and became a proper Tory.

I go on a fishing expedition

For many years I was Honorary Constitutional Adviser to Save Britain's Fish, a campaigning organisation defending the rights of Britain's fishermen. These had been trampled upon, at German insistence, when we joined the EEC. Spanish entry after the death of the fascist dictator Franco was being contemplated even then. Their access to Britain's rich fishing waters was a key demand, although boats from other European states were interested in raiding them as well.

Fishing became a key constitutional battleground, with the geo-strategically important *Factortame* cases. Spanish Intelligence, acting through a front company and backed by Germany, mounted an assault on the vital Merchant Shipping Act 1988. This was done in an attempt both to destroy the Supremacy of Parliament and force Spanish boats into British waters. The Spanish argument, which was absurd, was that Parliament was no longer supreme and that the courts had a duty to 'set aside' any Act of Parliament, even one *post-dating* EEC entry, which contradicted an EEC directive.

The loss of the FV *Gaul*

No fewer than 15,000 British fishermen gave their lives in the world wars started by Germany in the 20th century. Germany's man Beeching made a special point of cutting off the fishing ports such as Peterhead, home to the late, great Bill Reid VC, of Bomber Command, from the national rail network. Bill always pronounced it 'Peeterheed' by the way.

GO2 probably planted an IED on the deep-sea stern trawler FV *Gaul* (ex-*Range Castor*). She may have been involved in intelligence-gathering work on behalf of GCHQ, as part of Operation *Hornbeam*. The *Gaul* was sunk in the Barents Sea, in the Soviet Red Banner Northern Fleet's operational area, on the night of 8th and 9th February 1974, with the loss of 36 lives.

The families of the lost fishermen have been treated with a casual disregard by Whitehall. The original Wreck Commissioner anticipated the film *Perfect Storm* and concluded, somewhat vacuously with respect, since no Mayday message was broadcast, that the *Gaul* had been swamped by a series of 'giant waves'. Whilst the long-range tanks fitted for her important intelligence-gathering task marginally affected her stability, and there were heavy seas that night, no other vessel was lost. Fans of *Perfect Storm*, a great film, will recall that it wasn't just the brave Gloucestermen in their sword boat who ran into trouble.

The official finding does not explain the absence of a Mayday signal, nor indeed did the equally vacuous, with respect, findings of the second wreck inquiry. That was prompted by the discovery of the wreck itself. Since a visual examination of the wreck did not suggest that her radio aerials had been carried away, we can exclude any cause other than a sudden, catastrophic event. The Cabinet Office are totally opposed to any attempt to raise her, presumably for fear of what might be found. It cannot be anything to do with not wanting *Hornbeam* exposed, since the *Hornbeam* files are now available for public inspection in the National Archive, the silly new name for the Public Record Office. With great respect, the findings of both Wreck Commissioners may safely be confined to the deep.

The *Gaul* went down not far from where the German battlecruiser KMS *Scharnhorst*[12] was sunk by Vice-Admiral Sir Bruce Fraser (later Admiral of the Fleet Lord Fraser of North Cape) on 26th December 1943. That was the famous Battle of the North Cape. It is entirely possible that 'Jerry', who likes his little hissy fits, was making a point, in his usual unsubtle way. Very few British surface vessels went that close to Soviet waters in the Cold War. Russian Naval Intelligence, are believed to have concluded that it was an IED. No Soviet vessels were involved in the disaster. The *Gaul* could not have snagged SOSUS[13] cables, as some have suggested, since she was not on a fishing expedition, not for fish at any rate.

No explanation fits the known facts as well an IED planted on board by GO2, with a radio or time-delay fuse. The DVD at that time could fuse for about 30 days, using solid-state electronics. Their main fuse supplier was based in Switzerland and was exposed some years later, leading, apparently, to a discreet, nocturnal visit from the CIA. Their alarm system may not have been as good as their fuses.

My own little fishing expedition was in the North Sea and North Atlantic, in the slightly chilly winter of 1997/8. This was on board the stout Peterhead demersal trawler, the MV *Veracious II*, whose master and crew made me feel very welcome. It was a splendid opportunity to watch the risible Common Fisheries Policy in action, although it cost me a perfectly good dinner. There turned out to be no quota fish to the west of the Shetlands. The skipper, quite rightly decided to head about and plough back through the Pentland Firth, between Caithness in Scotland and the Orkney Islands, against the weather, in a Force 7-8. This is a manoeuvre best done before dinner. Unfortunately, I had already had dinner.

Yes, I did help out on the fish-deck, or, to be more precise, I tried not to be too much of a hindrance to operations. I chopped the heads off a few fish (just think of them as politicians and the time flies by) and stood watch. Whilst the Navy admittedly have come under heavy pressure from Whitehall to behave badly towards our fishermen, one lesson of this trip was that they have been too effective in disguising their distaste for enforcing the CFP. Careful study of the behaviour of the Norwegian and Danish police during the German occupation will reveal the correct procedures for flouting reprehensible and idiotic laws whilst pretending to enforce them.

There was also time in the second half of the 1990s to appear on a couple of *Newsnights*, in particular a special programme on withdrawal from the EU, chaired by that splendid chap Jeremy Paxman. *Newsnight* is BBC2's flagship current affairs programme. It's a bit like *60 Minutes*, without the objectivity (yes, it's that bad!). That wretched woman Edwina Currie MP, no offence intended, was one of the pro-European team. That nice man, and former BOAC Douglas DC-7C Seven Seas pilot, the late Norman Tebbit, was part of the pro-British team. Edwina - John Major's former mistress - would no doubt say that we British are Europeans, but what would she know? She actually thinks that Britain is in Europe.

Trial By Conspiracy

The most interesting book launch I attended in this period was for *Trial By Conspiracy*, by the investigative journalist Jonathan Boyd-Hunt. In the run-up to the 1997 election, which brought Tony Blair to power, a nice Tory MP and former minister, Neil Hamilton, was falsely accused by the late Egyptian financier Mohammed Fayed of taking cash to table questions in Parliament. The allegation was widely believed and repeated *ad nauseam* (*mea culpa* again if I am using too much Latin) by the media. The problem was that none of them troubled to investigate it, partly no doubt as it suited the media agenda of painting the Tory Party as sleazy.

There was a libel trial, but the truth failed to come out - not for the first time in a libel trial. Jonathan smelt a rat. In a fine piece of investigative journalism he demolished the allegation, or rather the several different versions of it. Indeed a forensic comparison of the different versions was his starting point. One would have thought the media would sit up and take notice, but both the book and Jonathan were studiously ignored. So far as I know no newspaper which printed any of the versions of the 'cash for questions' allegations put forward by Mr Fayed at different times even tried to grapple with the points Jonathan made.

He tried to get Granada Television, for whom he had worked, interested. Granada, are based in Manchester. They are famous for the long-running soap *Coronation Street* and not much else. In desperation Jonathan resorted to using the creaking media complaints machinery and then a legal challenge by judicial review, at one point instructing myself. It would be fair to say that no one in the media or officialdom was remotely interested in whether the original allegation was true or false. Their attitude was that the smear had served its purpose and that was that.

The left-wing media in particular were carried away by the scale of Labour's victory in 1997. They had no conception of how bad the Blair government was going to be and seemed to think that there could never be another Tory government. As Neil and his charming wife Christine were Tories (then) they were seen as fair game. They defected to the United Kingdom Independence Party of course, the main difference being that the Tory Party drink gin and tonics, whereas UKIP drink beer. They are very nice people.

The media and those responsible for its oversight lost their moral compass. Not until the News International scandal broke in 2011 did we hear the flapping wings of the first chickens flying home to roost. At the same time as casually printing smears against Neil Hamilton without doing even basic checks, such as whether the latest version of the smear was consistent with the ones printed earlier, and if not why not, scandals involving New Labour were firmly suppressed. One editor of a Sunday newspaper privately admitted to me that he had four affidavits locked in his safe from rent-boys who had been servicing a Labour politician. He couldn't use them, as the proprietor wouldn't wear it.

Several Scottish newspapers knew which Scottish politicians - not all Labour by the way - had got caught up in the Dunblane scandal. An unstable paedophile called Thomas Hamilton had been supplying boys from his boys clubs to politicians, judges and senior policemen. He was paranoid and insisted on firearms controls being relaxed in his favour. When someone finally summoned the courage to rein him in he lost the plot and shot up the local primary school, Sandy Hook style.

The police had to execute him to reduce the risk of the truth getting out. Officially he shot himself, but then officially he was still supposed to be alive, several minutes after firing a round through the roof of his mouth. You are *not* encouraged to try this at home, but generally speaking it is difficult to miss your brain if you put a powerful handgun into your mouth and pull the trigger, even if your brain is small.

If we in INTELCOM had the same regard for the truth as the media, governments would be operating even more blindly than they are now. I was starting to lose my naïvety by 1997 but even I was shocked by the utter, casual disregard for the truth shown by the media and Whitehall. Of course I apply the same standards to myself as I do to others. I am not remotely interested in saying or printing anything unless (1) I believe it to be true and (2) it is in fact true. I am not so conceited as to believe that I am immune from error but like any intelligence professional I am aiming for the centre of the target.

---

1. An agreeable watering hole in Dartmouth Street, London, rebuilt in the 1750s. The title refers to sedan chairs.
2. The tactic appears to have failed and resort had to be had to rigging the count, which was placed in the hands of another DVD agent, Sir Phillip Allen, later rewarded with a life peerage as Lord Allen of Abbeydale. Although the actual counting was done regionally by returning officers, who are generally incorruptible (they are local government officers, not civil servants) they were barred from declaring the results, which were 'tallied' centrally. Since no one kept a video record of the regional counts (the votes are paper and are bundled - you can get a reasonable tally just by counting the bundles, i.e. there are no problems with hanging chads) no one knows what the actual result was. Doing the best one can, having spoken over the years to returning officers, local officials and people from both the 'Yes' and 'No' camps, it looks as though the 'No' campaign performed broadly in line with poll expectations, winning narrowly, by about 52.5% to 47.5% of the unspoilt votes. Phillip Allen was instructed to give the 'Yes' side a wide margin in a failed effort to try and close down debate on EEC membership.
3. Strictly, since the UK was included, it was an Anglo-European Summit.
4. For those interested (this cannot be a large class of persons) it's *Kong Knud.*
5. The Krauss-Maffei Leopard 2, a jolly nice little panzer, with the Rheinmetall-Borsig 120 mm gun, an exceedingly useful bit of kit, particularly in its latest, 55 cal. guise (see Jackson, p. 90).
6. The Maddison in question of course later became President. The case is reported at (1803) 5 US 137.
7. A tour with RAF Bomber Command was not quite the same thing as a bus tour. It was thirty ops. USAAF tours were 25, as commemorated in the excellent remake of *Memphis Belle*. There were remarkably few technical errors in that film - P-51Ds instead of P-51Bs e.g. (the 'D' model came later). Even those were probably driven by a lack of flying models of the correct aircraft.
8. A nice old court, especially Court 1, where a number of death penalties were handed down in the good old days. The Great Train Robbers were tried there, at least the ones who didn't get away. Fans of the TV series *Judge Deed* will recognize the front of the building. Some idiot in the Ministry of Justice (no offence intended) decided to close the court and it now sits in what used to be Aylesbury Magistrates' Court.
9. A planning error in Buckinghamshire.
10. The locals claimed that Julie Ward had been eaten by lions. In fact she was murdered. Dear old Professor Gresham was retained by her father, who showed great moral courage and perseverance in going after the truth.
11. Gareth Williams, Lord Williams of Mostyn. I well recall trying to persuade him to a more sensible view about the Green Paper when we shared a first-class train carriage on the way back from a Midland Circuit mess in Birmingham.
12. I know 'Jerry' and some pro-German historians class her as a fast battleship, but she was a battlecruiser.
13. Sound Surveillance System.

7

Rolls - Royce

The Bentley

The Bar practice, combined with the judicial income (I was being invited to sit, or deal with leave applications on the papers, up to five days a week) was sufficient to allow me in 1997 to purchase my first Bentley, just a small one, of course. I was only a poor, humble barrister after all. I was her third owner. The car, a 1987 Turbo R, was a glorious device, sorry though I was to see the Rover go. Bentley Turbos are great Q-cars.[1] Other drivers tend to underestimate the speed with which two and a half tons of Bentley can accelerate.

The turbo installation, designed by my friend Ken Lea, a brilliant engineer, had almost no throttle lag at all. This was in the days when turbocharged cars had more lag than an underground train. Many a Volkswagen Golf (Rabbit) GTi driver was surprised, as the Bentley roared majestically past. Gestures were responded to with a toot from the twin air horns. These had a 'country' (i.e. upsetting VW drivers) setting.

Her engine was the 412 cubic inch (6.75 litre) Jack Phillips all-alloy V8, with a great big Garrett truck turbocharger, and fuel injection. Top speed was a shade over 160 mph; horsepower something over 300 and torque around 500 pound ft. The only gear she could legally be driven in the UK at the red line was first.

She was a very green car of course. A pleasant shade of metallic Forest Green in fact, with Spruce leather top roll and seat piping, green wool carpets and dark green lambswool over-rugs. "Lovely, jubbly" as Del-Boy from the BBC comedy *Only Fools and Horses* might have said,[2] although of course he ended up buying a Rolls-Royce. Since about 75% of a car's lifetime energy consumption is spent in her construction, if you include the energy used to make the steel and light alloy, of which there is rather a lot in the average Bentley, large, long-lived luxury cars are environmentally sensible.

The Phillips V8 engines are good for about a million miles if looked after, with a top overhaul at half a million. The majority built since they first made their appearance, in 6,230cc carburettor form in 1959,[3] are still on the road. Their CO2 emissions are probably sufficient to increase crop yields, another social and environmental benefit.[4] The cars are an antidote to the 'use and throw away' mentality. Beautifully made by craftsmen and women who took pride in their work, they were designed to last a lifetime.

The massive, under-stressed engines do not do much more than tick over in the fast lane of a motorway, although that's partly because motorway speed limits in Britain are absurdly low, even sillier than New York's.

The Battle

As I explained in the Preface, the 1997 sale announcement of Rolls-Royce Motors by Vickers came as a shock. The Customer Buy-Out was conceived shortly afterwards, at a technical weekend for owners at the impressive Paulerspury HQ of the Rolls-Royce Enthusiasts Club in Northamptonshire. Nobody gave us a chance but the public announcement at Paulerspury, with the courtyard full of pre-war Rolls- Royces, received worldwide publicity. I could write a book just about the bid battle. Suffice to say the discovery of leveraged, high-yield Medium Term Note trading programmes, the method used to get past us, came as a shock.

The Swiss bankers who opened up a private channel to me (not for nothing was I renting Lear Jets and flying off to Switzerland on short notice) were also clearly concerned. They were right to be. The exposure by the Germans of their main intelligence agency, i.e. the DVD, and the trading programmes has had long-term strategic consequences.

Mike Penning, later a minister in the Department for Work & Pensions, was then a PR man and a good one. He was present one day in my home on Watermead. He had an equally distinguished colleague, sadly no longer with us, with him, when one visit to Switzerland was arranged, at about two hours' notice. He had to go home and fetch his passport! He may recall the number of times my phone rang whilst he was there. At times it was an intense battle. I well remember coming in from a series of meetings in the City of London and finding 33 messages on my answering machine.

There was tremendous help from Rolls-Royce insiders, Rolls-Royce and Bentley owners worldwide, and the dealer network. British Intelligence came on board pretty quickly. It became clear from *inter alia* telephone intercepts by GCHQ that German Intelligence was backing the attack on Rolls-Royce. The company supplied cars to our Head of State (then the Queen), and was a national icon.

The German bids were hostile in every sense of the word. A revanchist Germany, reunited, with her economy boosted at Anglo-American expense by the massive offshore trading programmes, was flexing her muscles again. She was engaging in nothing less than economic warfare against Great Britain. There was no post-war economic miracle by the way - it was largely bankrolled by us (i.e. Britain and America) offshore.

The Germans seem to have been a bit shocked by the strength of public opinion. They shouldn't have been. The Blair government seemed to get a bit rattled as well. Although New Labour was backing the Germans, and trade union leaders were told to distance themselves from the British team, the late Gwynneth Dunwoody, the redoubtable Labour MP for Crewe, was supportive. The 'Hun' backed down from his original plan to seize the tooling, close down the plant at Crewe and transfer production to Germany.

Coupled with the Maastricht Treaty, which created the euro, the take-over of Rolls-Royce signified that the hand of friendship that Great Britain and the British people had extended to Germany after World War II had been spurned. From now on it was war. Never mind that Vickers had put the company on the market. Vickers had been penetrated by German intelligence for years. Germany's Lord Robens, who sanctioned the mass-murder of the children at Aberfan, was Chairman of Vickers at one point.

The shockwave went right to the heart of the British Establishment. By that I do not mean the lightweights in Parliament, or the heavily penetrated Civil Service. They are a joke, although they have been able to inflict a lot of damage. I refer to those great and good people who have the true interests of Great Britain and her people at heart.

It gradually came to be appreciated that the Cold War, or at least its intensity and duration, was a mistake, that the Arabist bias of the facile Foreign Office was ridiculous and that our true interests lay with our war-time allies and with the State of Israel. From the heart of the Establishment the hand of friendship turned away by Germany was extended once again to America, Canada, Russia, Australia, South Africa, New Zealand and Israel. The Russo-Ukrainian War, which I predicted in November 2020 has seen sympathy for Russia decline of course, but a great deal of intelligence has yet to emerge, e.g. about the German (GO2) poisoning attack, using BDX nerve agent (*not* novichok), at Salisbury in 2018.

Within four years of the attack on Rolls-Royce the armed forces of Britain and America went into combat together against Germany's ally Mullah Omar in Afghanistan. Within five years we went to war against the key German asset in the Middle East, the Iraqi war criminal Saddam Hussein. He was soon swinging at the end of a rope, and rightly so.

Not much more than ten years later a contingent of British troops marched for the first time in Red Square, in celebration of Russia's great victory on the Eastern Front in World War II. They were cheered on by friendly Muscovites. Deep inside the Russian military establishment authorisation was apparently given for a discreet search for a restorable Hawker Hurricane,[5] a survivor of the sturdy fighters donated by Britain in World War II. In 2012 the intelligence on the planned German nuclear attack on London came from the late Colonel-General Igor Sergun, as he became, then head of those nice people the GRU.

Contingency planning began for war with Germany. Official support for British membership of the EU began to drain away, slowly but surely, eventually leading to Brexit. There were no official announcements, but there rarely are when countries change direction. When even a Prime Minister as weak as David Cameron, no offence intended, was able to veto the proposed EU fiscal treaty in 2011 many in Whitehall were taken by surprise. Strategic thinking has never been Whitehall's strongest suit.

As I indicated in the Preface it was during the battle to save Rolls-Royce that those very nice people the Mossad and the CIA first opened up to me.[6] There was an intelligence aspect to the battle anyway, but there were also practical issues, such as assistance with due diligence. Mossad and the CIA do not carry out assassinations of course, save in a proper case. For the avoidance of doubt at no time was it suggested that the battle go kinetic. Although at some briefings, e.g. when dealing with Medium Term Note (MTN) trading - firearms were carried by the Allied intelligence officers present, they were purely for defensive purposes.

It was no great wonder that Swiss bankers started to get cheesed off. They have made a lot of money on MTN trading over the years. The plan to use an MTN programme to capture Rolls-Royce for Germany caused understandable alarm in Zurich. The Swiss must also have been anxious about the intelligence war between Germany and Britain getting so far out into the open. Not so far that the media would notice (not that they notice that much), but far enough.

Although the Swiss understood that Germany had been waging a covert intelligence war against Britain since the German surrender in 1945, the whole idea of a covert war is to keep it quiet. The thought of British Intelligence fighting back caused a few anxious frowns in Switzerland, never mind the German Foreign Ministry. They understood that intelligence wars have a nasty habit of becoming hot wars.

Vickers did their best to be obstructive, at one point leaking the British team's bid figure to BMW. Had they known how good my sources were inside BMW they might have thought twice. I didn't mind too much, since I had

BMW's own bid figure. As indicated above, the frontal attack on Rolls-Royce caused high-level alarm in Germany. We got quite a bit of assistance from friendly Germans and Bavarians.

Bavaria suffered badly in both world wars. Major players in that country were well aware not only of the DVD (it is based near Munich after all), but its methods. Since these include carrying out political assassinations, sponsoring terrorism and the sabotage of civilian airliners and merchant ships, some of these players began to question whether or not it was worth risking a third round of suffering for Bavaria. The DVD's methods are undoubtedly such as to justify target countries, including the United States and Great Britain, in declaring and waging war on Germany. BMW is the most important manufacturer in Bavaria, although Siemens runs it close. The location of its factories is well known to the RAF. They would be legitimate targets, as would Munich's central business district. The RAF could barely flatten Slough at the moment, but that was equally true in 1938. Britain is capable of rapid ramp-up, as the Germans well know. The drawing up of discreet plans in Bavaria to break away from the Federal Republic of Germany goes back to the late 1990s. Bavarians are not Germans. It has been made abundantly clear to me since 1998 that they do not favour German methods. In the event that the existing intelligence or quasi war with Germany goes hot, there is a strong case for special treatment for Bavaria. This would be on the basis that she broke away from Germany at the start of the war and permitted access to Dachau, so that the DVD could be closed down. It would be nice to think that Bavarian casualties could be avoided if possible. Pope Benedict XVI, a lovely man, with respect, was aware of the issues.

The City of London in 1998 was generally useless, but they always are when it comes to manufacturing. It wasn't until the Global Financial Crisis a decade later that the British people as a whole came to appreciate how foolish it was to neglect manufacturing and rely on the City for overseas earnings, not least given the instability of most of our major banks. The same is true in America. To say that the City in 1998 thought only in the short-term would be an under-statement - most bankers thought long-term meant after lunch.

We had our supporters in the City however. There was an amusing moment when I learnt that plc (as Rolls-Royce aeroengines are known) had put together a £500 million line of credit that morning. This suggested to me that they were finally coming to the party, heavy government pressure notwithstanding. I rang that nice man Sir Ralph Robins, the Rolls Chairman, and not through the Buckingham Gate switchboard either.

I asked Sir Ralph if the capital raising signified that the Rolls Board had sanctioned a bid for Vickers. Ralph, a gent, was slightly taken aback.

He muttered something about only having secured the line of credit that morning and asked how I had found out about it so quickly. Sadly, this was followed by the disappointing news that 'plc' were simply rearranging their debt. Designing and building aeroengines is a capital-intensive business.

One quite serious British multimillionaire had a private landline in his shower (generally only multimillionaires have this). He nearly fell out of the shower when he found me at the other end of the line ("where did you get this number?"). Rolls-Royce plc told me an amusing anecdote about how they had saved their Spitfire from the receivers after the German- sponsored bankruptcy, by hiding it in a hangar, from memory at Hucknall. Someone on the receivers' team told me about how they had noticed a strange-looking shape under a tarpaulin at the back of said hangar. They pretended not to notice that it was, by 1971, quite a valuable aircraft. That is what we lawyers call 'exercising discretion'.

One of the interested parties was the late, great Joe Bamford, a noted taxpayer and a great character. He was the founder of JCB, Britain's answer to Caterpillar. He was hiding behind dear old David Wickes, of British Car Auctions fame. Wickesy was another buccaneering character, to whom I took straight away. He was flying between Majorca and England with messages from Joe, who didn't know I knew who the "Swiss Syndicate" was.

Sir Anthony Bamford, Joe's son, (Joe of course was the "J" in "JCB") had expressed an interest early on. Crewe were horrified and had visions of their lovely cars being painted yellow and fitted with mechanical diggers in front. To put it politely, Joe and Sir Anthony decided not to work together. This is another way of saying that Sir Anthony may not have known that his old man was also in the race to save Rolls-Royce from the 'wily Hun'.

Throughout this turmoil Crewe were working on a beautiful new drophead convertible, which was being kept strictly under wraps. Not so strictly however that I was not given a little briefing. It was just as well that the senior Rolls executive I praised the looks of the new car too was not driving it when he took my call, otherwise there might have been an expensive crash.

There was a call early one morning from a Rolls-Royce fleet customer (there aren't many of those) in Hong-Kong. He had just been given a preview of the new Rolls-Royce Silver Seraph, complete with the ghastly BMW V12 engine. He didn't seem overly impressed. He was however interested in my idea for a Phantom VII, on the 144-inch stretched Silver Spur wheelbase, with a proper, British engine.

As I put the phone down I was a bit annoyed. The media were portraying the British CBO team as a bunch of amateurs. Yet here was a *fleet* customer, whose opinion was being sought *after* the car had been designed, who seemed to find the idea of a management willing to listen to customers *before* they designed a new product refreshing. Not for nothing had Vickers been trawling British Leyland for their senior management at Crewe.

Professional and judicial sitting obligations still had to be filled of course, although with a slight difference. I had a courtesy Rolls-Royce Phantom VI, complete with chauffeur, waiting outside court. It is amazing what parking liberties your chauffeur can get away with in a Phantom. Barrington, my highly competent chauffeur, who had an equally competent sidekick, who used to drive King Khalid's Rolls-Royce, told me one morning that none other than Sir Richard Branson had knocked politely on his window, asking to know whose Phantom this was. Of course, Barrington may simply have mistaken a passing pop star for Sir Richard. Even in the City however a Phantom VI got noticed.

The pressure was so intense at the height of the battle that I went without a meal for a couple of days, apart from snatched bowls of Sugar Frosties at breakfast (this was before I was diagnosed with Type 2 diabetes of course). No Froot Loops in Britain, of course, at any rate not then (Tescos gave them a try a few years later). It was getting a bit ridiculous, and I was famished. Happily, it was half-term-holidays. The nice couple opposite had a young daughter, who had asked, very politely, for a ride in what must have seemed to her to be a very big Rolls-Royce. Since the Phantom was over 20 feet long, she *was* a very big Rolls- Royce. They have never gone for sub-compacts. I dashed across the road between phone calls, with a 'tenner' in hand. I asked the nice couple if their delightful daughter would (1) like a McDonalds (2) be kind enough to get me a cheeseburger and large fries at the same time and (3) like a ride in the Rolls. The answer to all three questions was yes.

Barrington promptly drove her to the McDonalds in Aylesbury High Street. He waited on the double yellow lines outside whilst the victuals were obtained and people took photographs. Who the small crowd, which may by then have included a traffic warden, were expecting to see emerge was unclear. Eventually a little girl emerged, according to Barrington with a huge smile on her face, to be seated in triumph in the back of the Phantom. I expect that Barrington carried out his instructions to doff his peaked cap and hold the door open for her.

There was a very funny episode early in the battle. Toyota crunched the numbers, presumably with a view to eliminating competition for their top of the range Lexus. They are nice enough cars, but at the end of day are just badge-engineered Toyotas. Some idiot in Toyota HQ came up with a preposterous figure, north of £600 million, for "urgently needed investment". When a baffled author caused inquiries to be made, through a Japanese financial journalist in Tokyo, word came back that this figure was largely made up of new industrial robots.

This suggested that someone on the Toyota Board had only a loose grip, if not on reality, then at least on Rolls-Royce brand values. Had some fool of a manager gone into the radiator shop at Crewe and told the chap in charge "Bert (not his real name), we're going to replace you with a robot", and been whacked on the head by Bert with his soldering iron, no jury in England would have convicted.

Poor Princess Diana had not long been assassinated. The battle presented an unexpected snippet of intelligence when two major players, who officially never met, each of whom was close to the murders of Diana and Dodi Fayed, did in fact meet. Neither was aware that I was talking to the other. I was able to work out that they had met by the fact that each was heading for the same RV[7] at the same time. Ho-hum. One of the major players, Mohammed Fayed, has since snuffed it, no offence intended.

The near 24-7 nature of the operation had its advantages. I seemed to impress one nice Canadian billionaire by ringing his office in Vancouver just as the working day *there* was finishing. It was 3 am in England. The 'Hun' won, but he knew he had been in a battle.

Misconceptions

There were a number of misconceptions in the media and elsewhere about the bid to save Rolls-Royce for Britain. It is high time a few of these were cleared up:

(1) The British CBO team were putting together a bid for Vickers plc, not trying to buy Rolls-Royce Motors from Vickers. Being a defence company the 'Jerries' could not go there. Provided Vickers still owned it the car company would come across with the rest of Vickers, i.e. there was a window of opportunity between the decision of the Vickers Board to accept BMW's bid (which it eventually turned down in favour of a higher offer from 'V-Dub' anyway) and completion to save the company.

(2) The offer documents were sent to the British team's advisers, who were required, not unreasonably, to demonstrate their seriousness of purpose by identifying, in strict confidence, some of the owners to whom they were talking. Since one of these had a net worth ten times Vickers' market capitalisation, their merchant bankers, Lazards, gulped and sent over the documents to the CBO team's merchant bank.

(3) The CBO team *did* have a plan for the tanks. After discreet talks with GKN about their taking the tank division off our hands failed

there was an equally discreet briefing from a nice tanker general. This was the one over a brandy from the cocktail cabinet in the back of the Phantom as she glided one night around St. James's. The general suggested there might not be enough orders to keep both the Leeds and Newcastle tank plants open, so I had a retired general, who knew the Middle East well, sounded out about joining the Board. My plan was that he would lead an export drive to friendly Middle East states within range of Iraq who could see an invasion coming and could do with a few decent tanks. The idea was to repeat the success of the Shir[8] and offer the British Army a seriously upgraded and already paid for Challenger III, with a new engine, a fire control system which worked first time round and possibly some guided AA kit to assist in control of the air-land battlefield. The armour needed a bit of work as well. The intent was to keep both tank factories in production.

(4) Plc (i.e. Derby) were sounded out, informally, about a nice little package intended to build on the synergies between the car and engine companies, with cross-equity not ruled out. Areas for discussion included a joint pension scheme, marketing, a joint apprentice training scheme, Cars latching on to the superb engine parts distribution network ("but our parts are needed urgently by airlines Michael" "Yes, but *our* parts will be needed by the CEOs of the companies buying *your* parts"), shared facilities for overseas offices and borrowing Trent-800 engine blade technology for a new turbocharger ("but you don't need cooled titanium fan-blades in a car turbocharger Michael" "No, but you don't buy a Rolls-Royce because you *need* one, but because you *want* one, and we want a turbocharger with an R-R badge on it, which won't just be ahead of the opposition, it will blow them into the weeds").

(5) The need of the workforce for stability was fully understood. RRMC had been through a period of underinvestment, bankruptcy, associated instability, flotation and takeover since the 1960s, being largely starved of investment after the launch of the superb Silver Shadow in 1965. The decision to go with BMW engines and the sale process itself had introduced further instability, since it was unclear whether Rolls- Royce cars would ever again be powered by Rolls-Royce engines, indeed Vickers management intended that there should never again be a Rolls- Royce car engine. They had bought into the nonsensical argument that the company was "too small" to develop its own engines, although it had been making world-beating engines

to its own design since 1904 and the Phillips V8 had been the Gold Standard for car engine design for nearly 40 years. The CBO team opened up channels of communication to senior trade union officials from the get-go, as well as maintaining links with Gywnneth Dunwoody, who had sound views on Europe. (She had teamed up with my old friend Peter Shore in the 1983 Labour leadership contest - she would have made an excellent Speaker of the House of Commons and it was a tragedy for the House that MPs preferred the, with respect, disastrous Michael Martin.) Not only would all jobs have been preserved, the intent was to give workers who had been made redundant their jobs back.

(6) The car company would eventually have been floated, with a 51% minimum requirement that the shareholders be British, similar to plc,[9] but in order to get there a small and manageable group of major players amongst the owners first needed to get control of Vickers. They would not have had to wait until the flotation for their exit as a book would have been opened by Butterfields (our nice merchant bank) and the equity sold down.

(7) Very careful attention was paid to the management structure. Although the intention, after some reflection, was to retain Graham Morris as CEO for reasons of business continuity the CBO team had a very credible alternative CEO already on board in the shape of Ken Lea, who had Rolls Main Board experience. Plan A was to put his considerable engineering skills to good use in leading the design team for the Medium Sized Bentley (MSB) and then the new large engine, and bring back a very capable manager who had been forced out during the bitter internal dispute over abandoning engine production and going down-market, i.e. to BMW, for the engines for the Silver Seraph and the new Bentley Arnage. There would have been overseas Boards and a powerful Main Board, with some familiar names on it, and

(8) There was not only a well-thought out business plan, parts of it were subsequently lifted by BMW (e.g. rear-opening doors for the Phantom - the safety and engineering case for these had already been looked at by the British team, plus bringing back the Phantom name itself) and VW (replacing the BMW engines in the Silver Seraph and Arnage with the wonderful old Phillips V8). The engine would have had an advanced new engine management system, using Formula 1 technology. The CBO team's views that this engine *could* be made Euro Phase III emissions compliant and would easily fit into the Seraph/Arnage bodyshell were subsequently confirmed

to be correct, in fact I had already obtained quotations for the minor tooling changes involved.

The planned new cars

There would have been a Phantom VII on the existing 144-inch stretched wheelbase, with the great John Blatchley, stylist of the immortal Silver Cloud and Phantoms V and VI as consultant. The offer was to take clay models, sketches, etc. to him at his home in Hastings. BMW later accepted his recommendations for their Phantom but consulted him at a later stage than our team would have done. The first car off the line would have been offered as a gift to HM the Queen. A new convertible was on the way anyway and it would have been continued with. Subject to a detailed feasibility study Rolls-Royce would have moved to an advanced 24-volt main electrical bus, leading the world and making full use of the light aircraft industry's experience with 24-volt.

The Medium Sized Bentley project would have been resurrected on a new platform, utilising the excellent 5-litre engine Ken Lea's team had designed in the 80s, when the Main Board were concerned about possible fuel economy restrictions in the States.[10] It would have had Turbo and convertible versions and no loss of Bentley brand values. Sadly, the brand was damaged with the glorified VW Phaeton, i.e. the Continental, which I christened the "Bentwagen".

This would have been followed by a new large engine, probably a V8, for torque, although V10 and V12 configurations would have been looked at, along with a modular, turbocharged or supercharged V8/V12 mix for Bentley/Rolls. There would have been a new platform for the full- size cars, which would probably have been code-named Malaya, modular with the new platform for the MSB.

Full use would have been made of the latest computer-controlled soft-tooling technology. This would have avoided the problems encountered with the graceful Azure, where the number of body shells was artificially limited by the tooling. At least it was limited by the original tooling. It could have been replaced, as the company making it quietly confirmed to me in a little tête-a-tête in Geneva.

There it is. As I remarked to someone on the design team for the "Bentwagen" at least Volkswagen hadn't put the engine in the boot! Whilst the 'Hun', a.k.a. Volkswagen, was unfriendly, the Bavarians (i.e. the Beamer boys) behaved like gentlemen, as one would expect of Bavarians. I was glad to lend some weight behind the scenes to moves to replace Ferdinand Piech, CEO of VW, with that nice man Bernd Pischetsrieder, the capable BMW

CEO. A member of the BMW Management Board (there were also discreet contacts with the Supervisory Board, via Switzerland) told me that they were gathered around a television set in 'BMW Towers' in Munich as the battle to stop VW reached its hectic climax. It was a bitter defeat, but the war is not yet over, indeed VW are in financial trouble as I write. Wolfsburg may yet be flattened again.[11]

As I explained in the Preface the tactical victory for 'Harry Hun' may turn out to have been a strategic defeat, rather like Operation *Barbarossa*. Admiral Canaris, who was already running the Communist Party of the Soviet Union, sensibly tried to stop that, partly because he was a sensible chap. The opening up of the DVD, their failed assassination attempt on me, which just irritated me,[12] and the exposure of MTN trading programmes and their control from Frankfurt have all had long-term adverse consequences for Germany.

These included exposure of the role of the DVD in devising and controlling 9/11, the subsequent loss of their main Middle East asset, the brutal Iraqi dictator Saddam Hussein, and the exposure of German control of the Provisional IRA. Although I could see that the post-war Anglo-German friendship, already strained by Maastricht, was over, not all of the strategic consequences were clear in 1998. There was much work still to be done.

It should not be thought that I am anti-German. As I explained in the Preface, I am no more anti-German than Bomber Harris was. It's just the way the Germans behave. I have always enjoyed my visits to Germany. The individual 'Jerries' I dealt with in the battle to save Rolls-Royce were generally charming (I never met Piech). When the then German Ambassador to the Court of St James's, that nice man Dr Jürgen Oesterhelt, invited me to the German Embassy for drinks I was only too happy to accept. Indeed, it would have been discourteous (*nekulturny* as the Russian SVR might say) to refuse. Britain and America may be in a quasi-war with Germany, but war is no excuse for discourtesy.

Concorde

An Englishman is not expected to complain just because someone had tried to murder him. However, the DVD's assassination attempt on me and the Gastro-Oesophageal Reflux Disease that foiled it, knocked me about a bit. I was glad of a Thanksgiving holiday in 1999 with a dear friend, a lady, in the beautiful mountain village of Bailey, Colorado. As suggested in the Preface the name should be familiar to fans of *South Park*, as its creators hail from nearby Conifer. They often manage to work in local place names, the pleasant and friendly town of Fairplay being another. Colorado is my favourite state, even if Texas runs it close, and I have now visited most parts. Her high mountain passes in winter are great fun.

Flying home after Thanksgiving threatened not to be such fun however, when the captain of the British Airways 747 reported sick (come back BOAC,[13] all is forgiven). BA cancelled the flight, on the Sunday of the Thanskgiving holiday - shades of *Planes, Trains and Automobiles*![14] Declan O'Brien, the harassed but efficient BA manager at Denver, had been solemnly assured that there were no seats out of Denver that night on *any* airline. This only made the First and Business class passengers (being just a poor, humble barrister I was slumming it in business) more determined. Two went in search of flights to New York whilst Declan and I had a chat, the outcome of which was the block-booking of all 17 stranded First and Business class passengers on Flight BA002, the morning Concorde from New York.

Frontier Airlines, bless them, had a policy of not stockpiling spare parts at Denver, indeed it was not clear with respect if they had a policy of stockpiling spare parts anywhere. As a result, one of their 737s, for La Guardia, was running *ten hours* late. Some 40 of their passengers had managed to find another plane headed east, grab a Greyhound bus, or go home in disgust. Thus there *were* some seats headed east.

It was then just a simple matter of block booking the Concorde party (and any Economy passengers who wanted to come along) onto Frontier and booking an airport hotel at JFK. "Why do we need a hotel Michael, why don't we just hang around the BA terminal waiting for the Concorde lounge to open at 7 am?" "Trust me, by the time we get to La Guardia it will be 3 am and you'll be grateful for a shower, two hours blanket drill (sleep) and breakfast." They were. Declan did well, so well in fact that I dropped a kind word about him round to the British Airways CEO.

Concorde was my favourite airliner. That first trip took just 3 hours 20 minutes, New York to London. The take-off was spectacular, with great views of New York, poignantly including of course the Twin Towers, which the DVD even then were planning to bring down.

The 'arguments' used against Concorde were rubbish. Of course they were noisy. They used turbojets after all, which are noisier than turbofans,[15] but there were so few of them the noise scarcely mattered. Their rate of climb was such that the noise footprint was quite low anyway. They did not hang around, in other words. The seats were smaller than first class seats on a 747, but they were scarcely cramped. The plane was so fast you would have been very unlucky to get deep vein thrombosis! Leg room wasn't that bad in fact, and the seats were quite comfy.

Yes they used a lot of fuel - supersonic cruise does that - but the world oil price is a phony anyway. The answer, then as now, was to bring fuel prices back down to a more sensible level, not scrap Concorde. Engine-out performance was superb. The criticism of the rudders (there were two) was overdone, like all criticism of Concorde (there would hardly have been any at all if she had been a European aircraft).

The effect of rudder deflection into the supersonic slipstream seems to have reduced the fatigue life of the component, but that was a simple matter of replacing them well inside their revised fatigue life. The problem with the tyres and the vulnerability of the fuel tanks to tyre debris on take-off had been fixed, at least on the British Concordes. Air France dragged their heels, contributing to the Paris Air Disaster.

That was very much a French disaster, whitewash notwithstanding. The plane took off some 6,000 lbs overweight,[16] downwind, i.e. on the wrong runway, with a spacer missing from an axle on the port undercarriage bogie, so that the aircraft tracked to the left, hitting the runway lights. It only narrowly missed President Chirac in a 747, waiting at the runway hold position on a taxiway, not that he would have been irreplaceable loss, with the greatest of respect.[17] The flight engineer, sadly, shut down a perfectly good engine (No 1), in response to a false engine fire warning, probably generated by the increased temperatures in the port engine bay. Engine No 2 was only giving intermittent power because its fuel supply was being interrupted. The engine itself did not fail.

This might not have been disastrous but Nos 1 and 2 were on the same side, i.e. the shutdown exacerbated the asymmetric flight condition caused by the power loss from No 2. The Control Tower were no help to the captain, as they appear to have concluded that the aircraft was on fire. She did catch fire eventually, but only after she crashed onto the unfortunate restaurant.

The flames you see on the famous amateur video are streaming *behind* the aircraft and show fuel vapour from the leaking tanks being ignited by the exhaust from the afterburners. Even downwind and overloaded as she was F-BTSC could probably still have made her emergency alternate at Le Bourget on three engines. On two they were toast, sadly. French toast.

If you try and operate *any* airliner, let alone a high-performance machine, overweight and downwind, with bits missing from the undercarriage, you are inviting a crack-up. Primary cause of the Paris Concorde crash was the French failure to maintain the aircraft properly, leading directly to impact with the left-hand runway lights. This was exacerbated by the failure to follow the manufacturers' recommendation on the tyre-debris guard, operation of the aircraft outside of its design envelope, the use of the wrong runway and the decision of the Flight Engineer to shut down an engine developing full power at a critical phase of the flight.

One would have more sympathy for the French if they hadn't tried to lie their way out of it by blaming the Americans, i.e. the Good Guys. There was a load of nonsense about a piece of wear strip, allegedly from the starboard (No 3) engine cowling from Continental Airlines DC-10 N13067, the first photographs of which only appeared with the BEA (French accident bureau) report in 2002. The DC-10 didn't actually *have* a corresponding piece of engine cowling missing when she arrived at Houston.

Sometime after the crash the BEA, NTSB, FAA and the airline went through the ritual of examining an engine with a conveniently missing strip. I passed a warning to Continental to double-check the maintenance records on their bird and did not get a denial that on inspection she was not found to be missing any bits. When the engine cowl was opened on 25th August 2000, *after* the crash, no reference to a missing wear strip was entered into the maintenance records.[18] The infamous wear strip was probably lifted from an old UTA DC-10, which had identical cowlings to Continental's DC-10-30s.[19]

1. Q-Ships did good work in World War I. Relying on the preference of the 'Hun' to attack unarmed merchant ships the idea was that a ship would pretend to be unarmed. Then, when the 'Hun' duly surfaced, licking his chops in anticipation of an easy kill, our jolly Jack-Tars would drop the screens, swing out the guns and give him what for.
2. The great comic actor David Jason's character in the BBC's *Only Fools and Horses* comedy series. If they're not showing it on PBS they should. David Jason also played the hero, Skullion, in *Porterhouse Blue*, the TV series based on the late Tom Sharpe's wonderfully funny book. Skullion got to kill the liberal.
3. In the Rolls-Royce Silver Cloud II and Bentley S2, designed by John Blatchley. Lovely cars, I seriously considered an S2 as an alternative to the Turbo, but they are not quite as useable as daily cars.
4. CO2 is a plant food, not a pollutant.
5. Russian pilots loved the Hurricane - obsolescent in many ways by 1942 they were well armed, could absorb tremendous battle damage and still get their brave pilots home. Their sturdy, wide-track undercarriage was ideally suited for operation from forward airfields.
6. In fairness to Mossad and the CIA, it should be pointed out that the officers in question were only helping out in their spare time.
7. Rendezvous that is, not recreational vehicle. They could each afford hotels.
8. The upgraded Chieftain main battle tank, sold to that nice man the Shah of Iran before the nutters took over in Teheran. It had the then-secret Chobham composite armour, a greatly improved fire control system and a decent engine in place of that horrible Leyland donk in the Chieftain. It later became the Khalid, for the Royal Jordanian Army – that nice man King Hussein knew a good tank when he saw one - and in turn the Challenger, with a few mods.
9. The company did a small amount of defence work – not all of the factory was given over to cars. Although this area was reserved in the offer documents, by buying Vickers the CBO team would have got around the reservation and the defence work could have been integrated. This made restrictions on foreign ownership easier to defend against a legal challenge based on community law.
10. Unaccountably, this engine was apparently not considered for the MSB, which was underwritten by a major player in Jakarta, i.e. having spent a lot of money designing a smaller engine, which was then abandoned, for the larger cars, the Board did not resurrect it when they decided to design a smaller car. With respect this is what is described in the better business schools as disjointed thinking.
11. It's a wonderful target, easy to distinguish, with good bombing runs at low-level from most points of the compass, a fairly gentle run-in from the North Sea coast, lying within unrefuelled range of our main bomber bases in Lincolnshire, permitting maximum bomb loads and minimal payload wastage on drop tanks.
12. The attempt, not that it failed!
13. A.k.a. 'Better Off on A Camel', successor to Imperial Airways. State- owned after 1945, thanks to that idiot Attlee, no offence intended, merged with British European Airways, in another act of stupidity, in 1974, by another idiot (Heath).

14. The wonderfully funny film starring Steve Martin and the late John Candy. The scene at the rental car counter is a hoot, along with the bit where John Candy offers his Casio to the motel owner, in my opinion anyway (and if you don't want my opinion you shouldn't have bought this book). John, a serious talent, is much missed in Britain and I am sure in America as well.
15. The first turbofan was the Rolls-Royce Conway, designed initially for the cancelled Vickers-Supermarine V-1000/VC-7 - fuel-efficient and powerful, they later replaced the Armstrong-Siddeley Sapphire in the Handley-Page Victor V-Bomber and powered the beautiful Vickers-Supermarine VC-10, together with the -40 version of the Douglas DC-8 and the Boeing 707-400 series. There is a school of thought that at supersonic speeds turbofans are not much more fuel-efficient than turbojets. They create more thrust pound for pound but you have to allow for the higher drag.
16. I have had heard different figures, but about 3 tons overlimit seems about right.
17. There was speculation in INTELCOM that Chirac may have been the target, i.e. the thing may have been a set-up (shades of the staged runway collision at Tenerife in '77). It was scarcely wild speculation, since the way the Concorde was being operated was a long way removed from normal airline operations, i.e. was anomalous, and there *was* that near miss with Chirac's plane. The first-class section in which Chirac was seated (the President of France does *not* fly economy) was most at risk, but the Concorde was never likely to veer that far over to port, so the intent cannot have been to take him out, only to make a point. Whilst the Tower delayed granting take-off clearance until the 747 was in position, or approaching the hold, a hit would have been a long way from being guaranteed, i.e. way too messy. It *is* just possible that the German black agency in Paris were sending Chirac a message and seeking to demonstrate their reach. It was probably a classic French snafu, but the DVD file on the disaster would be worth reading.
18. BEA accident report into the crash of BAC/Aerospatiale Concorde F- BTSC at La Patte d'Oie in Gonesse, English language version as released by BEA, p. 107.
19. The -30 was the long-range version of the -10, readily identifiable by the additional undercarriage bogie. Continental also used DC-10-10s for domestic flights, e.g. to Honolulu. I once flew into Honolulu on one. Continental's Business First was an excellent product, with a rather better selection of brandies and liqueurs from memory than BA First Class. They were a classy outfit, although their domestic First Class service wasn't quite as good. I recall sitting myself comfortably in a First Class seat on a Continental DC-9 out of Anchorage Alaska in 1996. Having replied "a glass of champers would be nice, thank you very much" on being asked by the nice lady flight attendant whether I wanted anything to drink, I was met with the pitying response "you haven't flown with us before, sir, have you"? Not only was there no champagne, but they lost my luggage.

8

General Pinochet

The intelligence connections built up during the Rolls-Royce battle gave me a tap into MI5, MI6, GCHQ, CIA and the Mossad. These came in very handy in October 1998, when Robin Cook, whom I had known slightly during my Labour days, decided to mount a bid for the leadership of the Labour Party. Robin was then Foreign Secretary. The darling of the Labour left, in Parliament at any rate, he was planning a Ken Livingstone style coup, i.e. winning an election behind a leader from the right, then dumping him soon afterwards.

Now it may be protested that there wasn't a vacancy for the Labour leadership in late 1998. Robin and I, however, were, shall we say, each aware that circumstances might change, another way of saying that MI6 had briefed him in on the same bio-leverage on a leading member of the government later used to persuade the Labour government to go to war with Iraq. Robin was quite a nice chap and I was saddened by his brutal assassination in 2005.

Had Tony Blair been forced out Robin's main challenger from the right would have been Jack Straw, the Home Secretary. Jack and I shared a platform back in my Horsham days. Indeed, I also shared a platform with Ken Livingstone, in Horsham Town Hall. Ken had been held up in London and was late. I was on my feet when noises backstage signified his arrival, affording a golden opportunity, which was not missed, to say, "ah, Mr. Livingstone I presume". Happily, Ken was not within earshot.

Robin was briefed in that that nice man General Pinochet, quite the nicest dictator with whom I have ever dealt, but who was heartily disliked by the left, was coming to London for medical treatment. The left wing of course had fallen for the conspiracy theory about General Pinochet torturing people in Chile. As Robin well knew (he had gone European by then and had built up a number of political contacts over in Europe) an overmighty left-wing Spanish judge, Baltazar Garzón, had persuaded himself that he had jurisdiction over General Pinochet. This was notwithstanding that the general was a former head of state and senator for life of the Republic of Chile.

Robin and the then Spanish Foreign Minister, Abel Matutes, not such a nice man, with respect, apparently got together over the telephone and formulated a cunning plan.[1] If the Spanish would be kind enough to issue a warrant, it could be served on General Pinochet in London. Jack Straw and the Home Office would be reluctant to extradite. Jack's standing on the left would plummet. Never mind the general's age, the possible effect on his health, the damage it might do to Anglo-Chilean relations and the discouragement extradition would give to any dictator wishing to hand over to civilian rule. It was straight out of Machiavelli's playbook. The general was cleared by the Foreign Office to come to London, in the full knowledge that he would be arrested.

The problem was that the circuits between London and Madrid were leaky. The calls between Cook and Matutes were intercepted by those very nice people the National Security Agency. For the avoidance of doubt the NSA has a strict privacy policy and it is not suggested that the intercepts were intentional. It just so happened that recordings of the calls simply found their way onto a hard drive at Fort Meade Maryland.

As related in the Preface, a very nice Chilean military intelligence general popped round to my chambers for tea. However, it was some time before it was appreciated in Santiago that my advice was correct. They had a faith in the British legal system that was touching but outdated, although they soon got up to date when the first House of Lords decision had to be set aside because of problems with bias. Lord Hoffman, a nice but liberal peer, with respect, failed to disclose his links to the notoriously left-wing Amnesty International organisation. Amnesty had been bitterly opposed to the military government led so ably by General Pinochet, which turned Chile from a Third World to a First World country. They also have dodgy views on the death penalty.

After my walk in the garden with the general in the house at Wentworth, Chilean military intelligence starting putting some calls through to the CIA. Word on the street was that they verified the intelligence briefings I had given re the problems inside New Labour. Arrangements were made to fly me to Washington.

An awfully nice former National Security Adviser to the President, the late Dr Henry Kissinger, gave me that direct dial number to ring at the White House. They were in a slightly delicate situation of course. Officially President Nixon had ordered Henry to order the CIA to haul their bottoms out of Chile in '73. Unbeknown to Henry (at the time, no doubt he found out eventually, being the very well-informed chap that he was) a couple of the boys had stayed behind, to lend a hand with the change of regime. ("Coup" is such a strong word.) One of these chaps was known to 'Bill', introduced in the Preface, who was in London, investigating the money transfers to the East Coast for what became 9/11.

I received the usual death threats, including word of a plan to blow me away with a .32 at Dulles Airport. Presumably they were referring to a .32 ACP, although they might have meant H & R Magnum.[2] This didn't impress the CIA boys much, since they were carrying .357 Magnums, but they advised me not to enter the United States unarmed. They were kind enough to explain the unusual Customs procedures involved. These apparently, and entirely by coincidence, also lent themselves to smuggling in extra duty-free bottles of Scotch, possibly something to do with the prices in the CIA canteen. (I am told that the food is better in the NSA canteen, but if you're on a diet for heaven's sake avoid that fried chicken steak).

Naturally, as is my wont, I observed the duty-free limits, and made sure any carriage of firearms was strictly compliant with applicable local laws. This again was in accordance with my policy. Happily, Savile Row tailors (you can't go driving around in a bespoke car without a bespoke suit) tend to be well informed. Without asking, my tailors had allowed extra room in my jacket, so that a holster would not spoil the line of my suits.

The flight out to Washington, for my first visit there, was comfy. The Chileans had been kind enough to put up a Club World ticket on British Airways, but Lady Thatcher knew someone in the Chairman's office.[3] I was upgraded to First. The new lie-flat bed was rather nice and there was a welcome spot of VIP treatment at the airport. This sometimes happens with airlines when the Chairman authorises your upgrade.

Happily, there was no shoot-out at Dulles.[4] Europeans probably think shoot-outs happen at Dulles Airport on a daily basis. In my experience however, it is rare to see people shot whilst waiting at luggage carousels at US airports. You are more likely to hear the sound of gunfire on a Saturday night in Oxford than you are in downtown Washington. This is partly, of course, because unlike Thames Valley, Washington has an efficient and well-armed police department, the Metro Police.

My driver seemed to be carrying an adequate amount of artillery (fully comprehensive insurance, as it were). I thought I saw at least one Chevy Suburban with smoked windows a discreet couple of car lengths behind, with another in front. It was all great fun, even if there was no shoot-out at the airport, and a pleasant change from Uxbridge Magistrates Court.

For the avoidance of doubt, the CIA were not officially involved. Any participation was on a deniable basis. The US had no dog in this fight, the boys at the airport just chanced to be there on their day off, plane- spotting, and the Suburbans (should that be Suburbia?) were delivering parts to a used car lot in Maclean, Virginia.

The meeting with General Walters - seriously good people by the way - went well, monitored by MI6, CIA, the Chileans and hell, just about everybody. I popped along to the Hill for a quiet chat with that nice man Senator Jesse Helms's people, and was entertained to lunch at the Mayflower by that very nice man Ambassador John Bolton. He turned out to have very sound views, although sadly we have since fallen out, at any rate officially. (I'm in good company, as John has also had a slight falling-out with President Trump.)

There were some other meetings as well. When I was invited into to the Chilean Embassy for the tea referred to in the Preface I was told that there had been "developments". Indeed there had been. It turned out that the general had suddenly become unwell. As related, the first medical report was just coming off the fax machine as I was shown into the office. Her Majesty's Government had suggested on the backchannel to Santiago that they might wish to apply to have the general repatriated on compassionate grounds, and why not.

The Spanish however kicked up a fuss. In my experience they are always kicking up a fuss about something. Later on, they got a bee in their bonnet about Gibraltar, of all places, belonging to them. (They'll be claiming the Isle of Wight next.) Robin and the Foreign Office dragged their heels in getting the general back home however, so a second visit to Washington was arranged.

Enter Lieutenant-General William Eldridge Odom, US Army (retired), graduate of West Point (class of '54), Vietnam veteran and former Military Assistant to President Carter's National Security Adviser Zbigniew ('Zig') Brzezinski. On my first visit I had popped my head around the door of Zig's office, in his diplomatic absence (this allows messages to be passed without actually meeting). Zig, funnily enough, knew Dick Walters.

Bill Odom had been Assistant Chief of Staff for Intelligence for the United States Army between 1981 and 1985, and a good one. He was deservedly promoted by President Reagan to be Director of the National Security Agency. By another one of those funny coincidences General Odom had worked with General Walters during the Reagan years, when Dick Walters was a regular visitor to the Oval Office.

By another strange coincidence (these can happen) General Walters had recommended General Odom's name to President Reagan when the President was wondering whom to appoint to be the next Director of the NSA. "Boomps-a-daisy", as the nice NCO said in the film *Battle of Britain*, at the point where somebody was trying to land his fighter with the under-cart up.

By means which need not be described, but which did not involve dialling 411, the unlisted number for General Odom's holiday home in Lincoln, Vermont, was passed to me. I rang it, at an arranged time, when the General and his good lady wife Anne were not at home and the answerphone was not left on. The reaction at GCHQ was apparently a little like the scene in the Bond film *The Living Daylights*, when the dodgy KGB general goes through the pipeline to the West. Lights starting flashing and noises were heard.

Telephones were rung, even though it was late on a Friday evening. It is entirely possible that the Director of GCHQ even rang the Director of the NSA, who at that time was that very nice man General Ken Minihan. Had such a call been put through (and here I am merely postulating a purely hypothetical situation) General Minihan might well have explained that:

(1) General Odom was now a private citizen and nothing whatsoever to do with the NSA - he just happened to be a former Director that was all.
(2) That the NSA, as GCHQ perfectly well knew, had a strict privacy policy and did not tap diplomatic communications, and that if they did the State Department might get upset.
(3) GCHQ knew how careful NSA were about not upsetting the State Department.
(4) That if there were any transcripts of conversations between the British Foreign Secretary and the Spanish Foreign Minister they could only have been obtained by accident, as the result of a computer glitch.
(5) That GCHQ knew the problems Meade had been having with those damn Data General computers.
(6) If General Odom, General Walters or Mr Shrimpton were to obtain any transcripts it could only be as the result of a leak, and
(7) That if, disgracefully, there were such a leak the Director of GCHQ could rest assured that there would be a thorough investigation.

If my first visit to Washington had been conducted with my usual tentativeness my second, in January 2000, was a little more sure-footed and slightly more high-powered. There was a snow-storm, the East Coast was socked in from Philly to Jacksonville and the Governor of Maryland, sensibly, had called out the National Guard. As my Virgin Atlantic 747 approached Washington the captain announced that Dulles had just been closed, the Air France plane ahead was going to be the last plane in and he was expecting to be diverted to Orlando. A groan went up throughout the Upper Class cabin.

A few minutes later, in a pleased but slightly puzzled tone, the captain announced that Air France had just been diverted to Orlando and we had been cleared to land. If the opposition had turned up with .32s (which are girls' guns anyway) they'd have been seriously outgunned – if not by the National Guard, as they had only been called out in Maryland, but by the good old Virginia Farm Boys. Happily, the Bad Guys were snowed off. After a few adventures in the snow, which made up for the lack of a winter holiday that year, I ended up in the pleasant little community of Chevy Chase, Maryland. Here I bumped into a retired senior Pentagon official.

There then took place one of those high-level, informal, strategic intelligence exchanges between the United Kingdom and the United States, which oil the wheels of the Special Relationship. Shortly thereafter the Fuerza Aérea de Chile (Chilean Air Force) received orders to dispatch a Boeing 707, with military doctors aboard, to RAF Northolt air base west of London, to take General Pinochet home, later switched to RAF Waddington. The Foreign Office were instructed to convene a committee to plan the departure arrangements and three years later the Labour Government and the Foreign Office were left with nowhere to go in Iraq except downtown Baghdad.

On returning to London I had the FCO on the blower, inquiring about the departure arrangements. As the Foreign Office have never said to me but might have done, had they thought about it, I am a loss to diplomacy. Normally I am only too willing to accommodate them[5] but by this time I was a bit hacked off. Thus the arrangements I proposed on behalf of General Pinochet were of the High Diplomatic sort, i.e. ones, which had the dear old boy chuckling over his afternoon tea (he quite liked his cuppa). A few facts should be explained by way of background.

The Falklands

It so happened that General Pinochet and the Chileans had been exceedingly helpful during the 1982 Falklands War. The full extent of that help still has not been made public. The arrest of the General nearly caused a second Falklands War as a small team of Chilean military intelligence officers was dispatched to Buenos Aires. They opened up a strategic dialogue, which led eventually to a settlement, of sorts, of the Beagle Channel dispute between Chile and Argentina.

One of the topics for a discussion was Chilean support for a second Argentine invasion of the islands. The plan was to seize RAF Mount Pleasant, the large airbase built after the war. As both Chilean and Argentinian military intelligence knew full well the Blair government, idiotically, had left this crucial base without an adequate defence. Dear old Jim Callaghan, who as I explained in Chapter 4 was one of Vice-Admiral Godfrey's[6] boys from World War II, must have been, indeed was, appalled.

In return the Argies proposed supporting a military coup in Santiago, on a back to barracks basis (i.e. civilian government would be restored after hostilities between Britain, Chile and Argentina had ceased), cutting Santiago in for 50% of the oil. The South Atlantic oil field is allegedly eight times the size of the North Sea's. General Pinochet, who was under effective house arrest near London, was unaware of this secret mission to Buenos Aires. When the plan was put to him at Wentworth, he promptly vetoed it.

Admittedly he didn't have much choice, since good friends of Britain in the Chilean Navy had tipped me off, in deniable fashion of course. This was via a roundabout route, indeed via a roundabout more complicated than the silly one in Swindon (a town in Wiltshire noted for its silly roundabouts). The naval officers concerned were good Catholics. The arrangements involved those nice people *Opus Dei*, a nice man at the Vatican (later elected Pope), a couple of Hapsburgs and the Defence Intelligence Staff (DIS).

I hinted to the Chilean Navy that a *Trafalgar* class nuclear hunter-killer submarine had been dispatched to the South Atlantic. This was a bit of a gambit, as the Navy hadn't nearly enough submarines, the b****y thing was in a dockyard somewhere and she'd have taken weeks to get down there. At the same time I got on the blower to counsel for the CPS, who were representing the Spanish government, and suggested, diplomatically, that the CPS might want to introduce a new policy and think about they were doing.

At one point, since it was unclear whether or not the joint invasion plan was actually in the process of implementation, there was a quiet weekend briefing to a startled duty officer at RAF Mount Pleasant. This was followed by an entertaining series of conversations with the Intelligence Staff, which started out with a Flight Lieutenant and ended up with an intelligence one-star. At some point that weekend someone seems to have lost track of bits of the Chilean Navy.

The Departure Arrangements

By 'High Diplomatic' I mean treating General Pinochet as he should have been treated all along, i.e. as a former Head of State, travelling on a diplomatic passport or equivalent. He was a serving member of the Chilean Senate and an honoured guest, who had helped save British lives. His arrest may have been in Robin Cook's political interest and may have pleased the Spaniard, but it was not in the British interest.

As I told the dismayed FO man who rang me on my mobile phone I had arranged with a very nice Chilean Air Force colonel, later a very nice Chilean Air Force general, to have General Pinochet's No 5 Full Dress Winter Uniform, complete with medals and regalia, pressed and put on the plane. Someone had also kindly given me a direct line number for the Central Band of the Royal Air Force. I chanced to discover that they had the hymn sheets for the Chilean National Anthem, which they may have been practicing.

It was apparently going to be possible to have live TV coverage in Chile of the General's departure, which of course was now going to be from Waddington, a former V-Bomber base. Since he would be in full uniform, with a band playing the rousing *Himno Nacional de Chile*, I thought that the Chileans would probably quite like a fly-past. I thought a 'battle four' formation of Hawker Hunters would be nice. The Hunter held a sentimental association for the General.

The FO man spluttered something about the Hunter no longer being in service. I explained that I knew a nice, retired Air Marshal, who knew a chap in Gloucestershire who had some Hunters, which he could probably lay on for the price of the petrol. Not too bad, all in all, for a former member of the Chile Solidarity Movement, probably the only one ever to have taken tea with General Pinochet. I had long since ceased to think like a student politician, i.e. I was starting to think like a grown-up. Very frankly this is more than could be said for the Foreign Office.

Sadly, Whitehall scotched these modest and sensible proposals. The General was bundled out of Britain in a low-key manner, with an inexcusable lack of diplomatic courtesy, to the lasting shame of the Foreign Office. They couldn't even manage a band. I helpfully explained to the Chileans that nobody in Britain knew on whose side the Foreign Office was - we just knew it wasn't ours.

The DVD and Chile

As I explained in the Preface, General Pinochet was such a nice man that I stopped buying into the facile nonsense about him authorising unnecessary human rights abuses that I had bought into as a student politician. It was clearly a pup, as was the conspiracy theory that he was a fascist. General Pinochet was no more a fascist than Tony Blair. If anything, in my humble opinion, no offence to Tony intended, he was less of a fascist, and a much nicer man to boot. He was never a fan of the EU, e.g. there had to be something deeper, more sinister at work.

An entirely informal, international counterintelligence investigation was commenced. During it I met former members of the Chilean intelligence agency DINA, Chilean military intelligence officers, retired CIA personnel with operational experience in Chile, and 'Mr T'. His name does not begin with a 'T', of course. He had one of the smartest brains in the US intelligence inventory, if I may say so, and counterintelligence experience going back to the Kennedy Assassination. 'Mr T' moreover had encountered the German DVD and knew who they were.

The intelligence was reviewed to see what had been missed, i.e. there was a wash-up. The undoubted excesses at the football stadium and elsewhere pointed to the DVD and strongly suggested that DINA had been penetrated. Suspicion was not proof, however.

It took a while, but deep background checks on ex-President Salvador Isabelino Allende Gossens, including his political views before he claimed to be a Marxist (his 1933 doctoral thesis makes interesting - and for his left-wing supporters not entirely comfortable - reading) revealed that he had been recruited as a young man by the Germans. This all happened at the University of Chile in the 1920s. Allende became an Abwehr agent, becoming part of Karl zur Helle's[7] extensive network.

Although Allende was paid via the German Embassy in Santiago, Chile, he ultimately reported to the German Head of Station Buenos Aires. This officer also ran Juan Perón of Argentine military intelligence, later the pro-Axis dictator of Argentina. Perón sheltered many DVD assets after 1945, including Dr Josef Mengele (so evil he could have run the NHS) and Adolf Eichmann. He probably sheltered Martin Bormann as well, at least for a short while until the DVD shipped him back to Germany, although some maintain, absurdly, that he died in '45'. (The man who died was a doppelganger.)

Chilean counterintelligence reports on the contacts between Perón and Allende are said to be worth studying. Allende, who recognized Communist China, then under the control of the DVD's Mao Tse-Tung, was also in contact with a high-ranking member of Fidel Castro's nominally communist government. A significant number of Cuban assets were brought into Chile between 1971 and 1973, along with arms and ammunition. Many of the dead in 1973 were actually killed in running street battles. They were not all unarmed.

The DVD were not backing General Pinochet in 1973, they were *backing Allende*. General Pinochet was first and foremost a Chilean patriot. DVD methods used to undermine the junta not only included standard economic sabotage tactics, but a well-worn German intelligence tactic, also used by the DVD's penetration assets inside the Iranian SAVAK to undermine the Shah. Go over the top, torture a few poor wretches at random, and you can discredit a government.

No professional military intelligence officer would have recommended the roundup of harmless students and left-wing activists that took place in

1973. Most were guilty of no more than naïvety. DINA officers loyally obeyed orders, but with a high level of professional discomfort.

What was done was not in dispute. What our team wanted to find out was why, and who was giving these over-the-top orders, which in turn were justified by outright lies. "Why did we shoot Pedro, his cousin's in the army?" "Oh, we found out he was working for the Cubans." Lower down the chain of command of course the lies would be different. "We have to shoot Pedro, the orders come right from the top."

The DVD's Head of Station in Chile, who played a key role in the torture and assassination of young left-wingers supporting his own side, in order to make the other (i.e. Chilean) side look bad, was eventually identified. He was the German war criminal and paedophile Paul Schafer. At least that was the identity he used in Chile. There is some doubt that this was his real name, although he used the same ID in the American Sector of Germany, and then West Germany, between 1945 and 1961. Schafer was part of the Gehlen Organisation, Gehlen of course being a senior DVD officer.

The Gehlen Organisation effectively went on to become the BND, the overt West German external intelligence agency, who are generally very pleasant people to talk to. They are however deeply penetrated. A number of senior BND officers are double-hatted, i.e. both BND and DVD. One way of telling how many hats they wear is to start talking to them about the DVD. If they look at you blankly they are either single-hatted, i.e. BND, or well trained.

Experienced counterintelligence officers will be more interested in how they react when the subject of the DVD first comes up and less interested in what they say after more than 30 seconds has elapsed. If you're chatting over coffee and the cup starts rattling (I've had this happen – I was talking to a senior intelligence adviser to Chancellor Merkel, someone at the same conference saw their face go white and came up afterwards wanting to know what on earth could have produced such a shocked reaction) you know you've made your point.

Schafer ran a German colony 320 klicks south of Santiago, where he abused both German immigrant and local children. 'Suspects' were taken there for torture and execution in 1973 and afterwards. Schafer was of course, protected by Allende, indeed it was more a case of Allende reporting to Schafer than protecting him. The child abuse, which was of the worst sort, went on for years until a young local lad escaped in 1997. He went to the Chilean civilian authorities, sadly not knowing that some of Allende's, and Schafer's protégés had got back into power after the junta restored civil government. Although charged (he was later convicted *in absentia* on multiple counts of child abuse, including rape) Schafer was tipped off via

Santiago. Arrangements were made for him to go to Argentina, where he enjoyed the protection of the government until the gaff was blown on 10th March 2005. This was no doubt down to good intelligence work by someone.

Interestingly, one of the key players in the Pinochet case, a nice French aristocrat, was nearly murdered in a staged car crash, involving a truck (they usually do), in Argentina shortly after the General returned home. Schafer was on the shortlist of DVD officers who sanctioned the hit. My aristocratic friend, who owned a lovely chateau, survived, thankfully, but only just.

Although the Argies initially kicked up a fuss, Schafer was extradited to Chile. He held joint German and Chilean nationality, i.e. was under a duty of loyalty to the Republic of Chile whilst continuing to work for German intelligence, i.e. was guilty of treason. This was an offence formerly carrying the death penalty in Chile and rightly so. Schafer died on 24th April 2010, officially of a "heart attack". Unofficially, it may have been staged, like the car crash.

Chinese Walls and wet-work

Executions, both official and unofficial, are part and parcel of counterintelligence work. Sadly, they are necessary in a civilised society *pour encourager les autres*, as Voltaire famously put it, when commenting, albeit elliptically,[8] on the perfectly proper decision to trigger a by-election in Rochester by executing Vice-Admiral John Byng by firing squad. He was shot, in the nicest possible way of course, since he was an admiral, on 14th March 1757. Byng had let an entire French fleet escape. He also managed to lose Minorca, and, what's more, we've never got it back, although it's on the list if there's another war with Spain.

Unhappily, he should probably have been known as Admiral Bung, although officially he was acquitted of the more serious charge of disaffection, i.e. working for the French. An advocate, by the way, is entitled to feel a sense of disappointment, if not as keenly as his or her client, if he is acquitted of the more serious charge, but sentenced to death on the lesser. Even today there are some who say that the decision to shoot Admiral Byng was harsh, although they tend to forget that as well being a Vice-Admiral, the man was an MP. The execution *was* nicely done however. It still serves as a valuable precedent on the correct procedure to be followed when shooting admirals, or for that matter MPs, by firing squad.

I am sometimes asked if I lose any sleep when a traitor is executed as a result of a counterintelligence operation to which I may have contributed some analysis. My answer is "not a wink". There are four basic reasons for this:

(1) Save in dictatorships like China the test applied before the death penalty is imposed is one of moral certainty (I am not certain what test they apply in China but given the number of executions it cannot be all that strict - probably down to the sort of standard magistrates' courts apply when convicting motorists).

(2) It is bad counterintelligence practice to execute someone on the basis of the opinion or analysis of a single intelligence officer or analyst - apart from anything else it is bound to put a strain on the man or woman concerned. More than that, a single opinion may be wrong. Invariably, decisions to execute are based on a careful analysis of evidence from multiple sources.

(3) I have to be separated from decisions on sentence and mode of execution, since the only advice I could properly give would be to try the individual concerned in a court of law. There has to be a Chinese wall between decisions as to who is working for whom and why, and the ultimate disposal of a case. Taking the high road and putting a traitor on trial is not always possible. To take Admiral Byng as an example, there would have been a lot less sympathy for him had he been charged with, and convicted of, taking a bribe to let the French fleet escape. There would also have been a lot less pressure on the government and less impudent criticism of His late Majesty King George II, a fair man, for not exercising His undoubted Prerogative of Mercy. That however would have meant exposing our highest-ranking asset in Paris, i.e. the man who shopped Byng, to torture and certain death, and

(4) Each state is sovereign and at the end of the day must make its own decisions. Although terminations with extreme prejudice may look extrajudicial a senior lawyer or retired judge is often called in to look at the papers, especially where the civil or military authorities are compromised by the suspect's own agency and a fair trial (i.e. fair to both prosecution and defence) is not possible. This is always done with care and concern, not just for the suspect, but the poor intelligence officers who have to carry out the execution. It's not nice work and, so I am led to believe, is usually messier than in the movies.

Personal Life

I struggled a bit with ill-health for about a decade, roughly between 1994 and 2004, with two major operations. The first, on the NHS, led to a romantic encounter with a nice divorcee, Sarah, courtesy of mixed-sex wards. Sadly, after my discovery of the DVD the pressures were such that living with someone outside INTELCOM was almost a non-starter. Even simple things, like checking under the Bentley for bombs, having a remote-engine start when such things were not usual (it's much better if the car blows up when you're not in it - being blown up can be jolly irritating), having the house electronically swept for bugs, receiving threatening calls from gents with Irish accents ringing from masked numbers in Northern Ireland, or at least from numbers they thought were masked, and having the CIA ring at three o'clock in the morning tended to cause visiting lady or gentleman friends to freak out.

There was also constant low-level harassment from a drugs distribution network in Aylesbury linked to GO2 and Iran - nuisance phone calls, eggs thrown at the house, having Mercedes-Benzes try and run you down in the local pub car park, that sort of thing. The Gastro-Esophageal Reflux Disease was finally fixed with a brilliant piece of surgery, at a nice private hospital near Reading. It had been causing severe bouts of bronchitis, particularly in the winter, thanks to stomach acid tipping over into the lungs, via the oesophagus, not helped of course by the damage to my oesophagus courtesy of the DVD. The damage was so bad that I was wrongly diagnosed with Barrett's Oesophagus (you can live with it but, trust me, you don't want it) before the biopsy results came back.

These were minor complaints however compared to the suffering my poor aunts went through. Dear Zita died of motor neurone disease in 1998 and Agnes from Parkinsons Disease, aggravated by her age (she was 88), and a bad fall, in 2001. No one could persuade her, after Zita's death, to wear the panic alarm around her neck the NHS had thoughtfully provided. Sadly, it was many hours before she was discovered by a kind neighbour. I was in Northern Ireland at the time, and of course had long since ceased to live at Orchard Cottage. By the time she was found, poor Agnes, who had nursed many wounded in her time, helped a great many people and lived up to the high standard set by her beloved father Jack on the Somme all those years ago, was just about all in.

Steam Engines

There was time however to fit in the odd run behind a steam engine, including a nostalgic trip back to the Settle and Carlisle. For many years I was a member of the Duke of Gloucester Steam Locomotive Trust. The *Duke of Gloucester* was one of the most famous rescues from Dai Woodham OBE's Barry scrapyard. Dai Woodham was a patriotic, kind- hearted Welsh soul, who refused to cut up hundreds of steam engines and allowed groups of enthusiasts a generous length of time in which to save them.

Technically interesting (she was British Railways' only Class 8 Pacific, and was fitted with energy-saving Caprotti valve gear), the *Duke's* rebuild revealed valuable economic intelligence. Britain has vast coal reserves, but prior to North Sea oil, only a miniscule oil output. She also had some of the world's greatest steam engine designers. In the space of a few decades great men like Sir William Stanier FRS of the LMS, Sir Nigel Gresley of the LNER, George Jackson Churchward of the GWR and R. A. Riddles of British Railways rebuilt the British locomotive fleet.

The world speed record for steam traction, 126 mph, set on Stoke Bank in 1936,[9] is still held by the beautiful LNER A4 Pacific *Mallard*, thankfully preserved by the National Railway Museum, which is well worth a visit. Many of the engines scrapped so brutally in the sixties had decades of life in them, *Duke of Gloucester*, which was barely run in when she was scrapped, being one. There were also thousands of skilled engine drivers and firemen. Having been invited onto a footplate and taken my turn with a shovel I can confirm that firing an engine is not quite like lighting a coal fire at home.

'Blind Freddy' could have worked out that the most economic strategy for motive power in Britain was to keep using steam, except for shunting, where diesels worked well. Once the main lines were electrified the more modern steam engines could be decanted onto secondary lines, bringing in tourism revenues at the same time.

The mostly lovely branch lines all had infrastructure for steam. Understressed little tank engines could have chuffed along quite happily for another 50 years or so, with happy punters in the carriages too. The *Duke*, the last great British express passenger steam locomotive for 50 years (until the remarkable achievements of the A1 Steam Locomotive Trust brought forth the magnificent *Tornado*[10]) threatened a Whitehall strategy which promised to do lots of damage to the balance of payments and cause distress to millions.

She had to perform badly and she did. It is surprising that someone in the economic warfare department of GO2, which took its strategy from the economic warfare section of the DVD in Frankfurt, did not think to have the *Duke of Gloucester* cut up or dropped off the end of a train ferry. All they could manage was to have her sent to the 'wrong' scrapyard, Cashmores, by mistake. Happily, she was spotted by a former fireman, Maurice Shepherd, God Bless him, and rescued,[11] although a Good Guy might well have asked Maurice to find the missing *Duke.*

Her rescue from Dai Woodham's scrapyard (once he had retrieved the engine he had paid for), and rebuild, were remarkable feats. It was then discovered that her performance had been *held back* by British Railways, e.g. by fitting wrong specification dampers and chimneys. Dai, a great hero, had his contacts and might well have been asked to save the Barry engines. He was eventually given an honour and rightly so. A knighthood would not have been out of place, or even a small peerage.

Returned to the main line, where she belongs, the *Duke* turned in some impressive high-speed running, even with heavy loads on. The *Duke's* true power output (i.e. when not artificially held back by a daft directive from some lunatic in the Ministry of Transport reporting to GO2) turned out to be greater than a High Speed Train power car. You could have hitched most of the early diesels behind her and the *Duke* would probably have towed them up a gradient with the diesel trying to go the other way on full power.

My favourite moment behind her came on a *Shakespeare Express* from Stratford-upon-Avon, courtesy of a generous decision on the part of the signal controller for Oxford. He gave her a fast approach and a clear run through the station on the line adjacent to the up (London) platform. It was the end of term and the platform was crowded with university students. Judging from their expressions they had been misinformed (they were Oxford students after all) and may have thought that the steam era on the main line in Britain had ended, if not with Celia Johnson and Trevor Howard in 1945, at least in 1968.

At any rate they did not appear to be expecting a steam-hauled express train to come thundering through the station, whistle screaming, at the line limit or perhaps a shade above. Well-handled, the dear old *Duke* gave her all. With 14 bogies on, i.e. a total train weight of something over 500 tons, clouds of steam billowing behind her for about half a mile, enough CO2 coming out of her Kylchap double chimney to save on the heating bill for the Balliol Common Room if the quacks' theories on global warming were right, she must have been quite a sight. Great fun. Grandpa Shrimpton would have loved it.

The Harrow Rail Disaster

The *Duke of Gloucester* was of intelligence interest for another reason besides the sabotage back in the fifties. Not easy to spot sabotage by throwing a spanner in her works, but the more subtle kind, like building in a headwind. She had been ordered as a one-off, which itself was absurd. She ought to have been the first of a class allocated to hauling crack Anglo-Scottish expresses on the West Coast Main Line.

Officially, she was a replacement for 46202 *Princess Anne*, the re-built *Turbomotive*. This engine herself had held out great possibilities for steam traction, since her design built on the huge pre-war technological progress with high-pressure marine steam propulsion, which made the fast battleship possible.[12]

Princess Anne was destroyed on 8th October 1952 in the Harrow Rail Disaster. Driver Robert S. Jones of British Railways, at the regulator of ex-LMS *Princess Coronation* Class Pacific 46242 *City of Glasgow*, was ordered to run the 2015 up sleeper express from Perth though the outer home signal for Harrow and Wealdstone Station in suburban London at danger, at speed, on the up fast main line. Either he had been told to obey the inner home signal, also set at danger, to make it look good, or the fireman, sensing danger or responding to the strange behaviour of the driver, slammed on the brakes. With over 150 tons of locomotive and tender, a Scottish sleeper express behind them, and the 0731 local from Tring stopped in the station ahead, as scheduled, it was too late to avert disaster.

The G02/German intent was that the wreckage would be strewn across the down main line in the path of the double-headed 0800 down express for Liverpool and Manchester, as happened. The lead engine of the down express was the *Jubilee* class 4-6-0, 45637 *Windward Islands*. Indeed, given the weight of a *Princess Coronation* class Pacific and the comparatively light construction of outer suburban stock, no other pattern of wreckage distribution was likely. It took three days to get the bodies out. Tragically, 112 people died, including Driver Jones and his fireman. 340 people were injured.

It was the worst rail crash in Britain since the Quintinshill troop train disaster, also arranged by German intelligence, in 1915, and the worst peacetime rail disaster on the British mainland since the 1879 Tay Bridge Disaster. By the way, the widely accepted view[13] as to the cause of that may have to revisited when the German Secret Service files from 1879 become available, or a more sophisticated stress analysis of the Tay Bridge design than the fairly rudimentary affairs conducted to date is done.

Automatic Train Control, as adopted on the GWR decades before, would have prevented the Harrow Rail Disaster. The brakes would have been tripped by the outer home signal at danger. German assets in the Treasury however blocked its adoption, including an updated version of it, on the nationalised railway, precisely because its absence made disasters much easier to arrange. This didn't apply to the Western Region of course, inheritors of the proud traditions of the GWR. The staging of major crashes there would have to await the computer age, as well as the abandonment of the safe methods of working of the Great Western Railway.

The official inquiry into the Harrow disaster was the usual farce, with respect, but eyebrows were raised at the time. It seems that, concerns were raised privately with military intelligence by the Chief Inspecting Officer of Railways, George Wilson, who later died unexpectedly whilst investigating the Lewisham Rail Disaster, and Colonel Arthur Henry Trevenix-Trench, who did good work in Mesopotamia in World War I. Colonel Trevenix-Trench was an experienced former Investigating Officer of Railways himself. Partly because of concerns about German sabotage,[14] Inspecting Officers of Railways were always military officers, usually drawn from the Royal Engineers.

The problem was that neither George Wilson nor Colonel Trevenix-Trench were made aware, as they should have been, of the existence in Britain of a covert German sabotage unit specialising *inter alia* in rail sabotage. Partly to make it easier to stage 'accidents' the investigation of railway disasters was later watered down, being handed over in turn to the pointless Health and Safety Executive and the equally pointless Office of Rail Regulation, with respect more 'Off-the-Rails' than 'Ofrail'. His Majesty's Inspectorate of Railways should of course be restored and made completely independent of Whitehall, with Inspectors being appointed by the general officer commanding Royal Engineers.

There is little point concentrating the blame on Driver Jones for the Harrow Rail Disaster until it is known precisely what pressure was brought to bear on him and his family. GO2's methods are German, unsurprisingly, since it is a German agency. They include not just blackmail, bribery and threats of violence to the individual, but threats, including of sexual violence, to family members, including children. Because they are false flagged via the UK and GO2 have Whitehall and the police thoroughly penetrated, an individual train driver, signalman or anyone else targeted in the rail industry, is bound to feel vulnerable.

Digressing if I may, there is an urgent need not only to restore proper, i.e. military, railway accident inspectors, who are not only unbribable but have had firearms training, can carry sidearms if need be and would be comfortable with Royal Military Police escort at disaster scenes, but to implement a confidential reporting system. This has been used successfully in civil aviation.

The restored HMRI should have formal liaison with military intelligence and GCHQ, permitting a review of relevant COMINT[15] and SATINT, including before and after overheads of disaster scenes. In future these should be secured by armed military police. Too many lives have been lost, there have been too many cackhanded inquiries into rail disasters and the railway companies themselves have proved too vulnerable to pressure from Whitehall.

The Case of the Metric Martyrs

In the mid-nineties I advised the board of a nice carpet retailer, which was concerned about the EC's plan to force a reluctant Britain to go fully metric. As the Directors explained to me everybody's houses in Britain are measured in feet and metric carpets wouldn't fit, not least as the EC wanted them measured by the whole square metre. Few people would know what they were buying anyway, since many did not know what a square metre was, and why should they? People would go out to buy a new carpet for the bathroom and end up with enough for the living room, or buy for the living room and end up with a rug.

In order to avoid Parliamentary debate and not tell anybody that the mad dash to metrication was being foisted upon Britain by Brussels, Whitehall came up with a cunning plan. Why not do what His late Majesty King Henry VIII had done and simply bypass Parliament, save for the formality of 'scrutiny' of delegated legislation?[16] The trouble was that by design the Henry VIII Powers[17] in the Weights and Measures Act 1985 (WMA85), which was enacted to preserve the Imperial system side by side with the metric, giving business and consumers a choice, were insufficient. In order to carry out Brussels' orders to destroy the Imperial system, Whitehall had to resort to the master Henry VIII Power in the bitterly controversial s. 2(2) of the European Communities Act 1972 (ECA72), since repealed. It is axiomatic however that a Henry VIII Power can only affect statutes *already enacted*, not future statutes. That is because Parliament is supreme and cannot bind its successors, who remain equally supreme. The power of Parliament cannot be fettered by anything a previous Parliament has done. The new metrication regulations were clearly illegal and unconstitutional and I so advised the retailer.

Sadly, a deal was done with Trading Standards, who agreed to turn a blind eye to the marketing of carpet by the square yard, with a fractional metric equivalent. Basically, all the big carpet retailers had to do was to give the price per part of a square metre as well, which was the reverse of what the EU wanted and what the regulations, on their face, required.

Battle was postponed until 1st January 2000 when the metrication regulations were extended to loose goods sold in bulk, i.e. fruit and veg. Trading Standards, even when backed by Whitehall and Brussels, were unwilling to take on the big boys, but licked their chops at the thought of crushing corner shops and market traders. The big retailers for their part wanted no part of a constitutional battle with Brussels and the government - no High Street Hampdens there.

The Six knew full well when we joined the EEC that Parliament could not embed its statutes and would therefore be free to override community law. Even if their foreign ministry lawyers were so grossly incompetent that they did not know that, the rule that Parliament cannot bind its successors is a fundamental principle of the UK's internal law, of normative force. Under international treaty law, state parties to treaties are taken to know the fundamental constitutional principles of other state parties. Otherwise, they could simply be undermined by treaties, which are intergovernmental.

Parliament only enacted the ECA72 after assurances that its supremacy would not be affected were given by Sir Geoffrey Howe, as he then was, the Solicitor-General, in the House of Commons. Lord Hailsham of St. Marylebone, the Lord Chancellor, gave similar assurances to the House of Lords. With a view to encouraging parliamentary support for the European Communities Bill Lord Diplock, a senior, albeit not widely respected, judge stepped into the political arena. In those days that was much rarer than it is now, thanks to the constitutionally undesirable politicisation of the judiciary. In a speech to the Association of Public Teachers of Law, which was widely reported and relied upon by the government in pushing the bill, Lord Diplock assured Parliament that if it backed EEC entry the judges would continue to uphold its statutes.

Sadly, as we saw in Chapter 6, the judges went on to make a liar of Lord Diplock by purporting to set aside the Merchant Shipping Act 1988 in the notorious *Factortame* cases. Thankfully their ruling lacked binding status as the then Solicitor-General, Sir Nicholas Lyell QC, a nice chap, but with unsound views on Europe with respect, declined to argue the point.[18] The *Factortame* ruling was of course wrong with respect, the law having been correctly stated by Sir Geoffrey Howe QC S-G and Lords Hailsham LC and Diplock back in 1971. It was the duty of the House of Lords in its judicial capacity to uphold the statute and the duty of the Royal Navy to enforce it against the Spaniard, by lethal force if necessary. It was of course an unreasonable fear of war with Spain, should the Spanish fleet sortie to protect the *Factortame* false-flag boats, which led Nick Lyell to decline to argue the point, i.e. the Implied Repeal point was not pressed for political reasons. Although Spanish owned, the *Factortame* boats flew the Red Ensign, in defiance of the express wishes of the Queen in Parliament.

This was arguably the most insolent show of defiance on the part of the Spaniard since Spanish coastguards brutally hacked off Captain Jenkins' ear,[19] leading to global war with Spain[20] and rightly so. The *Factortame* boats should have been boarded, with cutlasses drawn,[21] any offending Spaniard run through and the rest arrested. Had the Spanish fleet sortied it should have been brought to battle and sunk. Instead the controversy was allowed to roll on.

Official anxiety to avoid debate about the unconstitutional use of the 1972 Henry VIII Power, which raised serious questions about the governance of Britain, clashed with the desire to rub British noses in it.

There was a crackdown. On 4th July 2000 (what a date to choose!) Trading Standards officers, backed by police, seized the Imperial weighing scales of a courageous Sunderland market trader named Steve Thoburn. He had been observed by an undercover officer using them to weigh out bananas (what a fruit to choose as well - *and* after the EU had legislated against excessively bent bananas). Steve, a wonderful bloke, who tragically keeled over from a massive heart attack after the final appeal, on commercial free speech grounds, was thrown out by the European Court of Human Rights in Strasbourg, was quickly dubbed the 'Metric Martyr'.

I was lead counsel for the defence, ably assisted by Miss Helen Jefferson, who added brains as well as beauty. Steve's solicitors were the reputable old Sunderland firm of McKenzie Bell, who were unbiddable, as a good firm of solicitors should be (well done Frank!).

The *Thoburn* case was covered all over the world. Even the *Washington Post's* London Bureau Chief made it up to Sunderland. Barristers, like badgers, are shy, gentle and retiring creatures, who tend to come out only at night. All the publicity naturally came as a terrible burden to me, but I bore it as best I could. To their credit some of the commentators grasped that the case was not just about bananas, but the way in which Britain was governed.

In asserting the undoubted right of Parliament to enact what it wished, the Metric Martyrs (Steve was soon joined by others - there were five in all) were seeking to stabilise the British Constitution, which had been rocked by the *Factortame* decisions, and restore battered public confidence in the judiciary. The idea was to present the judges as honourable men and women who would uphold the law, come what may. Thousands of people wrote in support, many sending cheques. The prosecution throughout used the threat of costs as a weapon. The defendants, none of whom were wealthy, needed the protection the well- run Metric Martyrs Defence Fund afforded. The lay bench of magistrates who dealt with the initial hearing did not seem too impressed, with respect, with the idea of prosecuting a man, in effect, for selling a pound of bananas. The charge against Steve was using Imperial scales but it came to the same thing - three of the other martyrs were charged directly with selling a pound of fish etc. The defence toyed with the idea of inviting the bench to reserve, i.e. hang onto, the case, but there was little prospect of their being allowed to.

A District Judge (the fancy new name for a Stipendiary Magistrate) was always going to be parachuted in. The task fell to D.J. (M.C.) Bruce Morgan, a nice man, who with great respect was wrong but courteous. At the end of the trial in the Sunderland Magistrates' Court, with the agreement of the prosecution, we presented the District Judge with a small gift, the original of a very funny Matt cartoon (if that is not a tautology) about the case in the London *Daily Telegraph*. For the avoidance of doubt the gift was presented after the decision was announced! Bruce Morgan handled the hearing well, with respect. The atmosphere in court was as it should be when great issues are being discussed, with mutual respect amongst the Bar, and between Bar and Bench.[22]

Steve's conviction was immediately appealed to the Divisional Court, where it first came on in front of Lord Justice Scott-Baker, who later handled (some would say mishandled) the inquest on the assassination of the Princess of Wales. Lord Justice Scott-Baker was a *Factortame* man, i.e. he had managed to persuade himself with respect that the House of Lords had stated the law correctly. Again with respect, where he got that notion from is unclear. It certainly wasn't from Blackstone.

The substantive hearing was in front of the late Lord Justice Laws, an abrasive personality with respect. As readers will have gathered I, in contrast, have an emollient personality(!). The second judge was that nice man with respect, Mr Justice Crane. It really ought to have been listed in front of a five-judge panel, with the Lord Chief Justice presiding. Lord Justice Laws had a go at me, accusing me of being "passionate" about the case. With respect His Lordship misunderstood what I was being passionate about, which was the British Constitution and in particular the bedrock principle of Parliamentary Supremacy. I was also accused, if it was an accusation, of citing a "library's worth of authority".

We relied upon statements of constitutional principle by *inter alia* Sir Edward Coke, Sir William Blackstone, Professor Dicey QC, Sir William Anson KC and Sir William Wade QC. The chances of those five great scholars agreeing and getting it wrong were not high. Behind the scenes Sir William, who sadly has since passed, was working with me. Indeed I sent the case papers up to the great man in Cambridge. Bill's former students included the late Lord Bridge of Harwich, who with great respect had fallen into egregious error in *Factortame*. Bill did not describe Nigel Bridge as his brightest pupil.

The case was controversial enough, with Brussels and the government backing the prosecution, and the opposition the defence (the Shadow Cabinet sent Andrew Lansley up to Sunderland), without the Divisional Court departing from normal procedure. With respect they deprived the defence of a fair opportunity to put their case.

It is a fundamental rule that all of Parliament's statutes are of equal status, if not importance. The Dangerous Dogs Act 1991 is just as much law - and just as daft - as the Human Rights Act 1998. Having stopped me from developing this point, as the court agreed with it, they then changed their mind, *after* argument had concluded and without calling counsel back, relying on authorities which had never been shown to counsel.

This was an unprecedented breach of protocol with respect. I had never seen it done and am unaware of any other reported instance of it happening. The late Lord Bingham, who presided when the case on for argument in the House of Lords, on an oral application for leave to appeal, did not seek to defend the way in which the Divisional Court handled the case. Had the Divisional Court reconvened, both myself and Eleanor Sharpston QC, for Sunderland, who correctly with respect had not taken the point, would have been able to point out, respectfully of course, that the cases relied upon by the court were 'not in point'. That is legal code for 'nothing to do with this case, M'Lud'.

Ironically, in a case which is now a leading modern authority for the proposition that a decision is not binding if a point is not argued (although you would not guess it by reading the headnotes in the law reports, which with respect are incomplete to the point of being misleading), *Thoburn v. Sunderland City Council* itself is not binding. That is because the point on which it was eventually decided was never put to counsel.

With great respect to the Divisional Court and the House of Lords, the Law of the Constitution is quite clear: Parliament may enact any law it pleases and cannot bind its successors. Whether it *should* enact any particular legislative proposal is another question of course.[23] As the great Professor Dicey explained in his magisterial *The Law of the Constitution*, merely because a law is legally valid it does not mean that it is constitutional, in the sense of complying with the spirit of the Constitution. The 1972 Henry VIII Power on which ministers sought to rely was clearly unconstitutional, the ministers who promoted it unfit for public office and the civil servants who advised it unsuitable for the public service, but the power was nonetheless valid. That is, provided it was only ever used in respect of existing statutes.

Shortly after the Divisional Court, with respect, fell into error the Public Records Office at Kew (not the hothouse - that's down the road) released the advice[24] to the government in 1971 of all four Law Officers of the Crown[25] as to what would happen in a *Metric Martyr* situation. Their unanimous advice was to the effect that in accordance with the settled Law of the Constitution the courts would be obliged to give effect to a *later* act, even if it was inconsistent with community law. Thus in a situation where community law mandated the use of the kilogram and Parliament after 1972 made it lawful to sell by the pound, the later law enacted by the Queen-in-Parliament Assembled would prevail.[26] The decision of the Divisional Court was not only wrong with respect it was unconstitutional.

Sadly, a supine House of Commons, whose members seemed more interested in fiddling their expenses than defending the Constitution, rolled over without a murmur whilst the judges with respect once again trashed an Act of Parliament. There are three dangers in this, the first being the macro-economic impact of constitutional instability. After three centuries of comparative constitutional stability, the UK, sadly, is now unstable. That in turn impacts on business confidence, although these things are comparative. In an unstable world the UK, apart from Scotland, does not stand out.

Secondly, once you start trashing Acts of Parliament, where do you stop? If the Weights and Measures Act 1985 is, as the Divisional Court in effect held, a worthless piece of vellum which the judges will not recognise, what about other acts? Why should the intelligence services, e.g., not follow the judges' example and start to pick and choose which laws to obey?

Some of them, e.g. the restrictions on the use of torture in the UK, are frankly a bit onerous, and in the Global War on Terror started to look a bit dated. Why not just ignore them? After all, now that *judges* have started to ignore the law who are they to lecture to anybody else? There is no point the judges pointing to the ridiculous wording of s.2(2) of the ECA72. As the Solicitor-General in effect told the House of Commons, and the Lord Chancellor told the House of Lords, that section, in so far as it looked to the future, was so much gibberish.[27]

Thirdly, the judicial attack on the privileges of Parliament was hardly going to stop at refusing to apply the WMA85. As we have seen they went on to attack the privileges of the House of Lords in the *So-Called 'Hunting Act' Case*, where the judges held that the House of Commons can expand its powers at the expense of the House of Lords almost at will. The new Supreme Court went on to assert the right of the ordinary courts to try not only former members of Parliament, but a serving member, of the Upper House,[28] in relation to their Parliamentary business. In so doing they drove a coach and horses through the Bill of Rights.

Rather like the impertinent prosecution, with respect, in Chicago of Lord Black of Crossharbour, led by the over-ambitious Patrick Fitzgerald, the first time that an American judge locked up a serving member of the British Parliament, this was rank interference in our democracy. The House of Lords forms an essential part of that democracy. The powers of Parliament are so great they could never be entrusted to a single chamber. As any sea captain, with the possible exception of Italian cruise ship captains, knows, if you dump the ballast you risk capsizing the ship.

What if there were to be a crucial division and Lord Taylor's, or for that matter Lord Black's, vote might have carried the day? The intellectual gymnastics with respect by which the so-called 'Supreme' Court (the High Court of Parliament remains Britain's highest court) managed to persuade itself that the ordinary courts have power to try both former and existing members of Parliament in respect of their Parliamentary dealings not only lacked intellectual rigour, they ended up depriving the defendants of a fair trial. That was because their defence could only have been a political defence, which could only be understood by men and women of affairs.

The Parliamentary expenses scheme wasn't an expenses scheme at all, but a backdoor means of paying MPs and peers after the government of the day decided, for party political reasons, that it couldn't force through a decent pay increase. As it was a stitch-up it was never reduced to writing, but rightly or wrongly that's what was done.[29] Try telling that to a jury though and you'd be laughed out of court. The judges who dealt with the cases with respect naïvely assumed that Parliamentary expenses worked like their own not ungenerous scheme, i.e. had to be related to expenditure actually incurred. That was never the intention, but it was politically convenient to hang a few bunnies out to dry, so they were.

The new expenses scheme by the way is hopelessly bureaucratic and cumbersome. What's more it's run by an unaccountable quango, unaccountable to Parliament at any rate. It is no longer uncommon to see MPs sleeping in their offices. If an MP or a peer offers to buy you lunch these days make sure you have a good breakfast first.

The former MPs and Lord Taylor should never have been sent to prison. The Supreme Court - not only a misnomer, for the reason given above, but an idiotic idea, as I submitted in evidence to the House of Lords committee that examined it - should be abolished. The defendants ought to have their costs paid by the CPS and should be compensated from public funds for the time they spent in prison, wrongly. The easiest way to quash their spurious convictions would be by Royal Pardon. Although technically a pardon leaves the original conviction intact, it becomes a technicality, like a speeding ticket.

Incidentally, it was a thoroughly bad idea - put forward by a German spy[30] of course - to deprive peers of their ancient right to be tried by their peers, i.e. by the House of Lords. I well recall discussing the last trial before the House of Lords with that lovely man, the Canadian peer Lord Shaughnessy. He was the last survivor of the peers who had been present. Lord Shaughnessy ascended to the peerage whilst very young, in the middle of an Atlantic crossing (on a Canadian Pacific liner of course), to attend HM King George VI's Coronation.[31] This was a rare case of someone's name having to be amended on their ticket mid-voyage. His Lordship assured me that he had considered the evidence against his Upper House colleague with great care and deliberation, before voting for an acquittal.

Very frankly, if the Crown Court is going to make a habit of sending lords to prison then the privilege of being tried, literally, by their peers should be restored, and the sooner the better. Someone also needs to tell the Justice Department that they should not be prosecuting members of the British Upper House, for the same reason that the Metropolitan Police turn a blind eye every time a gay Senator ends up in a spot of trouble with a rent boy in London. It is never a good idea to go around prosecuting members of the legislature of a fellow democracy, partly because you invite retaliation.

The Justice Department need a rap over the knuckles for banging up Lord Black. No offence, but they are going to be made to look a bit foolish as the truth about PanAm 103 gets out. Hopefully, that will send the right message and encourage them to be a bit more respectful of Britain's sovereignty in future. No doubt someone in London is biding their time for revenge against the Senate.

The best time to arrest a senator, preferably a northern Democrat (not a nice southern one) would be when there is a crucial vote coming up on the Senate floor. If they haven't actually got into trouble with a rent boy no doubt MI5 could always be asked to lend one of their tame ones for the occasion. Since Lord Black was fitted up,[32] the senator could hardly be heard to complain.

The judges with respect are making the same mistake as King Charles I, who of course became an ex-King. Just because the House of Commons is full of MPs of straw and you can push them around easily it doesn't mean that you should. That is because there are such things as elections and every once in a while serious MPs, such as that nice man Nigel Farage, get elected. Parliament is not only the highest court in the land, it is at the moment the only one able to impose sentence of death.[33] The judges with respect need to back off, with as much grace as they can muster.

The split with the Bruges Group

Speaking of stitch-ups, sadly, I was forced out of the Bruges Group by a former Chancellor of the Exchequer, who shall remain nameless but was not that nice man Lord Lawson of Blaby. He was working with a former Prime Minister, not that nice lady with respect the late Baroness Thatcher, who should have been made Countess of Grantham (by convention distinguished former prime ministers are offered an earldom[34]). These 'grandees' acted through my friend Ralph Harris, Lord Harris of High Cross, who being a gent was terribly apologetic about it all. Happily, before he died he spilled the beans.

It was sad, since I enjoyed my time in the Bruges Group, which had played a major role in informing opinion in the Tory Party on Europe, although it had less success with Labour. The Group then rubbed my nose in it by leaving my name off the list of former chairmen, i.e. they tried to airbrush me out of the Group's history. That was a tactic often used in Moscow, when the German spy 'von' Stalin was in charge.

1. Apologies to Tony Robinson, a.k.a. Baldrick in the *Blackadder* TV series.
2. Harrington & Richardson - see Hartink, p. 39. It's an old calibre, but the new, slightly longer cartridges introduced in 1984 are much more effective.
3. The Chairman.
4. Named after the German spies Allen Welsh and James Foster Dulles, known in England as the 'von Dulles brothers'.
5. Strictly the FCO, since the Foreign Office captured the Commonwealth Office in a Whitehall coup some years ago, essentially in order to stuff up the Commonwealth, in much the same way they've stuffed up our foreign policy, no offence intended. It's now known as the FCDO, as they wanted to stuff up overseas aid as well.
6. Head of Naval Intelligence, known to generations of moviegoers as 'M'. His PA happened to be one Commander Ian Fleming.
7. See Bisher, Jamie, "German and Chilean Agents in Peru: Entwined by a Yen for Espionage", *International Journal of Intelligence and CounterIntelligence*, Vol. 6, Issue 2, 1993, p. 205, for an interesting account of 'zur Helle's' extensive Latin American network, which became part of the Abwehr network in 1933 and the DVD in 1945.
8. In *Candide*, which was a novel. Since Byng was on the French payroll it's no wonder that they were upset.
9. Full use of course was made of the slight (about 1 in 200) downhill gradient of Stoke Bank (that's why it's called Stoke Bank), but that was within the rules. Nothing should be taken away from Driver Doddington and Fireman Bray of the LNER, who had been checked going through Peterborough and did not get a clear run at the bank. *Mallard* was probably good for a few mph more, indeed Driver Doddington thought he could have cranked her up to 130. *Mallard* performed well out of Waterloo Station in the famous 1948 locomotive trials, thundering through Clapham Junction in not much over six minutes and putting in a timing that would be considered respectable even today.
10. An LNER Class A1 Pacific, built from the original blueprints. Immensely graceful and powerful locomotives, their scrapping was a particularly egregious piece of economic sabotage.
11. *Steam Railway*, No. 396, Dec. 2011, p.65.
12. The American *Iowa* class, e.g., had 600 p.s.i. boilers, which not only meant more power but less weight and space for an equivalent amount of horsepower - they were as fast as some destroyers. The impressive *Essex*-class fast carriers had marine propulsion nearly as advanced and the next generation of big carriers went even further. Even the mighty *Mallard* was limited to 250 p.s.i. Main-line steam locos after the war really ought to have gone to 400 or even 500 p.s.i., at which pressures safe, regular and economic 125 m.p.h. running on the East Coast Main Line and 110 m.p.h. on the West would have been possible. There is no recorded instance of a British (we eventually caught up with the US Navy, with the 650 p.s.i. powerplant for the *Daring* class destroyers) or American high-pressure naval boiler exploding.

13. Although it is noteworthy that neither the Inspecting Officer of Railways nor the other member of the inquiry, supported the Chairman's damning conclusions as regards the highly respected civil engineer Sir Thomas Bouch. I'm no civil engineer but his design was probably sound.
14. Which in 1861 led Parliament to provide for the new and serious criminal offence of endangering the safety of the railway, although the section is rarely used. Metal thieves who steal copper from signal cables, e.g., are invariably charged with the lesser offence of theft, presumably in order to encourage the illicit trade (the copper usually ends up in the PRC). Clearly criminals who disable railway signals are willing to endanger the lives of passengers.
15. COMINT was apparently useful in the parallel intelligence investigation into the causes of the *California Zephyr* Rail Disaster near Fallon, Nevada on 2nd June 2011, when AMTRAK's magnificent *California Zephyr* long- distance express from Chicago to San Francisco (Emeryville Terminal) was rammed by an 18-wheeler. Despite private urgings by myself the analysis of communications to and from the truck prior to the ramming was not made available to the Nevada Highway Patrol, nor the efficient AMTRAK Police Department, which then took railroad safety very seriously indeed under the able leadership, with respect, of Chief Johnson. So much for the 9/11 Commission's call for greater co-operation with law enforcement on the part of INTELCOM. The call, sadly, has largely gone unheeded.
16. Scrutiny of delegated legislation is a farce – it mostly goes through without debate, and hardly any MPs or peers bother to read it, with a few honourable exceptions. The purported metrication regulations went through on the nod.
17. A Henry VIII Power is an unconstitutional device whereby ministers are given power to alter statutes, i.e. they set the Executive above Parliament. Not dissimilar to the Nazis' Enabling Act they are hugely controversial and were rightly condemned by a great Lord Chief Justice of England, Lord Hewart of Bury, in his important book *A New Despotism*, well worth a read although sadly most copies by now have been destroyed. My copy was saved from disposal and from memory came out of the old Supreme Court Library. It is the most powerful book ever written by a British judge, hence the efforts to suppress it.
18. Under the ancient Rule in *Rex v. Warner* (1661) it is part of the Doctrine of *Stare Decisis*, or Precedent, that the *ratio decidendi*, or deciding principle, of a legal authority is not binding if the point is not argued.
19. There is a left-wing conspiracy theory that poor Captain Jenkins' ear was not cut off at all, although it was produced in a jar to the House of Commons. MPs then, unlike now, were generally men of sober judgment and good character, all except for the Whigs of course. There is no reason to doubt their conclusion. Captain Jenkins moreover was an officer of the Mercantile Marine, courageous, a fine sailor and a man of honour, and he was minus an ear. There are no grounds whatsoever on which to impugn his integrity.
20. The War of Jenkins' Ear of course, which in turn led to the War of the Austrian Succession. The Good Guys (that's us) won.
21. I respectfully and entirely agree with the 2011 ruling from the Pentagon, no doubt prompted by the resurgence of marine piracy, requiring US Navy Petty

Officers to take their cutlasses on board ship and I am pleased to hear that they are keeping up their cutlass drill. They can be jolly useful weapons in close combat as they are more flexible than a firearm, i.e. you can run through your Somali or Houthi pirate without killing him, or chop a couple of bits off. Although he might hop about a bit and complain he won't be dead - it makes life easier for the US Ambassador to the UN.

22. I was pleased to see the good relations between the prosecution and defence teams in the fraught *Florida v. Casey Anthony* murder trial. Personal attacks on your opponent usually rebound and are never dignified, unless they've come after you and you are firing the odd brickbat back. The prosecution team were fair, indeed their very proper doubts about their own case came across.
23. There have been some fairly crazy statutes in recent years, not just the ECA72 and the HRA98, but also the Climate Change Act.
24. PRO reference FCO/30/1049. The advice is dated 14th June 1971.
25. The Attorney-General, the Solicitor-General, the Lord Advocate and the Solicitor-General for Scotland.
26. Under the Rule in *Princes* Case (1602) Parliament consists of the Sovereign, the House of Lords and the House of Commons. Having advised at an earlier stage in the proceedings, and having the considered the matter in an Opinion for several Peers, including that nice man the late 11th Duke of Devonshire, which was lodged by another nice lord, with respect, Lord Clifford of Chudleigh in the House of Lords Library, I am well aware that the Rule in *Princes* Case was attacked by the House of Lords in the *So-Called 'Hunting Act'* Case, reported as *Jackson v. Attorney-General*, but the confused and contradictory reasoning, if reasoning is not too strong a word with respect, of the House is unlikely to survive. The much sounder analysis with respect of the Judges in *Princes* Case is to be preferred and is far more likely to stand the test of time.
27. Of course the answer is not to enact gibberish in the first place. Section 2(2) should never have been passed in those terms, but then the ECA should not have been enacted, period.
28. That charming man Lord Taylor of Warwick, a former judicial colleague of mine in immigration appeals. Slightly bent sadly, on the basis of his own plea of guilty to an offence of dishonesty in relation to his Parliamentary expenses, but no more bent than the average life peer.
29. The sensible thing of course would be to do what was suggested in a *Yes Minister* episode and link MPs' and ministers' pay to a senior civil servant - say the Cabinet Secretary, with MPs paid a proportion below, Cabinet Ministers the same and the Prime Minister and Lord Chancellor a proportion above. No civil servant should be paid more than the Prime Minister.
30. Clement Attlee, although it probably originated with his Abwehr and DVD colleague Hartley Shawcross, who as we have seen ought perhaps to have been called Hartley 'Doublecross' (it's always a bad idea to recruit agents with 'cross' in their names).
31. The peer in question, Lord Cliffard, had been accused, quite unnecessarily as it turned out, of motor manslaughter - he was very properly acquitted. You try running the same defence before the Crown Court today and see how far you

get ('Your Honour, my client is a lord, the bloke he ran over wasn't, the widow's been taken care of, he didn't mean to run the poor fella over, he's a decent chap and clearly ought to be let orff').

32. It is a basic rule of company law that shareholder decisions are made by a majority of the voting shares, not a bare majority of shareholders (otherwise Vickers could never have sold Rolls-Royce). It is also a basic rule that a company's Articles of Association are a public document and that shareholders, who are not obliged to buy the shares after all, accept the rules for corporate governance set out there. There were also serious problems of jurisdiction in the Lord Black case - if there were to be a prosecution at all it should have been brought in Canada. There are by the way sensible reasons why there was no prosecution in Canada. The offence was compounded by the lack of courtesy shown towards Lord Black, with respect, by both the prosecutor and the learned trial judge, e.g. in their mode of address, the learned trial judge conspicuously failing to address His Lordship as 'Your Lordship'. Mr Fitzgerald was even ruder. The judge might well reply that the American colonies had done away with lords in 1776, but the point is that Britain hasn't. I am quite sure that George Washington took care to address Lord Cornwallis correctly at Yorktown.
33. By Act of Attainder, i.e. State Trial. The usual mode of execution is decapitation by axe, usual venue the Tower of London. Traditionally the prisoner's escort keep their axes turned outwards before sentence and inwards if, as usually happens, the accused is convicted, after a fair trial of course, and sentenced to death. The sentence is normally carried out with a single stroke (in practice these days the executioner would be a retired NCO from the SAS Regiment, i.e. someone with valuable experience of killing people), but if someone has made a particular nuisance of themselves - Mary Queen of Scots e.g., or the Duke of Monmouth - the executioner is instructed to chuck in an extra stroke or two, for an additional fee.
34. That is why Harold Wilson was only offered an ordinary peerage and Edward Heath and Tony Blair none at all - Harold Macmillan got one but Lady Thatcher was not told that he was a German spy. It was a great shame that poor old Jim Callaghan was not offered an earldom - he should have been, but they felt a bit constrained, unnecessarily so, after Wilson was only given a life peerage. Winston Churchill was offered a dukedom (Duke of London) but as his late grandson Winston confirmed to me the offer was only made after the great man had indicated that he would turn it down. This was a pity. Had the younger Churchill been in the Lords, as the 3rd Duke, as he should have been, subject to a minor amendment to the Tory Party's constitution, he could have run for leader after Iain Duncan Smith's untimely resignation, when the Right were looking for a heavyweight about whom they could unite to block Michael Howard (David Davis is a nice chap but with respect lacks bottom – he has dodgy views on capital punishment e.g.).

9

9/11 And Its Aftermath

My first encounter with *al Qaeda al Subbah* ("The Base"), as related in the Preface, was over their attempt to get some U-235 out of Mindanao in the Philippines, although officially it never happened. The air strike on the Islamic 'Jolo Liberation Front', which was in cahoots with *al Qaeda*, was real enough however. It was preceded by a little bureaucratic win, at one remove, over the Department of Energy. It was a tricky case. Anything involving missing nukes usually is, especially when you're not dealing with intelligence professionals.

Law enforcement officers, e.g., not least in Thames Valley, tend to have no idea what is missing and what is not, lack the security clearance to access the intelligence and can get very aggressive when their uninformed opinion is challenged. Generally speaking, the less intelligent a policeman is - and, sadly, intelligence is seen as a bar to promotion in Thames Valley - the more belligerent he will be when his opinion is challenged. It's usually a 'he' - in my experience women police officers tend to think with their brains rather than other parts of their anatomy. Intelligence analysis is a collegiate business. Once it degenerates into a competition between competing views the quality of the product suffers. That is because the better view may be a synthesis of competing views. Thames Valley Police got it spectacularly wrong in my case, of course, charging me with a 'bomb hoax' when the bomb was actually present.

Sadly, President Truman and the Democrats with respect made the same mistake after World War II as the Allies did after World War I, and NATO after winning the Cold War. They ignored Vegetius's time- honoured and correct maxim *si vis pacem para bellum*[1], rushed to disarm and sent out a message of weakness.

When Germany's Mao Tse-Tung and Chou En-Lai threatened victory over the pro-Western Chiang Kai-Shek, not a bad man by all accounts,[2] Chiang made a desperate plea to Washington for help. He was too smart to waste his time asking Britain of course, as the German spy Attlee was running the show. Chiang had already seen all he needed to see with the Attlee government's pathetic climbdown over the unprovoked attack on HMS *Amethyst,*[3] which still has not been avenged to this day.

The US Navy in particular was run down idiotically. No fewer than three of the outstanding *Midway* class armoured attack carriers[4] were cancelled following the great victories in the Battles of the Philippines Sea and Leyte Gulf, along with a number of still to be completed *Essex* class,[5] the final two *Iowa* class fast battleships[6] and the entire *Montana* class of super-battleships.

Truman was left with insufficient battle-ready conventional forces to go to the aid of the Chinese government, even though Chiang had been a valuable ally against Japan and was facing defeat by a German-backed communist insurgency. It is doubtful that Truman appreciated that Mao and Chou were DVD, indeed their DVD colleague General Marshall, as Secretary of State, would have taken great care to keep the President as ill- informed about foreign affairs as possible. MI6 played a similar game with the Foreign Secretary, Ernest Bevin.

Truman's advisers came up with the bright idea of repeating the success of the atomic bomb attacks against Japan, which would not have been necessary of course had Britain and America smelt the coffee and rearmed in time. Sadly, politicians tend to see nukes as a cheap alternative to adequate conventional forces. This is not to say that Truman was not strategically correct in his decision to nuke Hiroshima and Nagasaki, a decision forced on him by prewar mistakes in both London and Washington and massive American casualties at Iwo Jima and Okinawa. The casualties would have been much less of course had the Japanese not been warned by 'von' King that the Good Guys were on their way.

It is still not clear exactly what target list they came up with, although it is reasonable to assume that the communist capital Peking was at the top. In great secrecy, two Boeing B-50 Superfortress bombers, America's latest,[7] were dispatched to the Far East, under the command of a general, complete with second-generation nukes and instructions to bomb the hell out of the commies. Sadly, the mission was known to General Marshall, who was of course still working for Admiral Canaris and wanted the German-backed communists to take over.

Marshall's backing of Mao was probably the great betrayal at the heart of Washington which so exercised Senator Joe McCarthy. The good Senator, who was a patriot, knew more than he let on in his committee, although exactly how much more must remain a subject for speculation. He suspected Marshall but did not have proof, unsurprising since at that stage only the Russians knew for sure that Marshall was a German spy. McCarthy sure as hell wasn't talking to 'those damn Russkies'.

Tragically, the B-50s were intercepted and shot down over the Philippines by ex-Luftwaffe pilots working for the Chinese. These were probably some of the *Zerstorergeschwader* 26 boys, probably flying Me- 410C long-range bomber destroyers with the Junkers Jumo 213 two-stage supercharged engines and four-blade paddle props. Officially these were never built,[8] but they seem to have turned up over Mindanao nonetheless. These crash sites became known to a young, and ambitious Filipino lawyer and intelligence operative named Ferdinand Marcos. He hung onto the nukes, partly why he was so powerful, as even in their damaged and non-operational state they gave him a hold on Washington.[9] 'Bill', Frank Powers[10] and the boys spent hours in U-2s trying to find the crash sites, but the wrecks were of that difficult to find type, in ravines, with jungle canopy on top. You would be surprised how rugged some bits of the Philippines can be.

The idea of *al Qaeda* getting hold of fissile material from a couple of missing American nuclear weapons, which were originally going to be dropped on *inter alia* Peking, had official Washington in a bit of a flap. I've never seen a Defense Secretary move so quickly. At one point I was woken up early by Henry Kissinger's office. (Henry was providing the White House with some deniability.) I was asked to stand by my fax machine and ring back to confirm safe receipt.

My protest that I was alone in the house, that the office with the fax machine in it was secure, had only one door and was protected by a separate alarm, and could I make a cup of tea whilst waiting for the fax to come through, was brushed aside. It was sad that I was alone, but you can see why friends staying the night sometimes ended up having hysterics, despite warnings that there might be early morning calls if another nuclear weapon had gone missing. Washington can get its priorities wrong sometimes - even with a couple of missing nuclear weapons there was time for a nice cup of tea. Happily, on that occasion the fax came through pretty smartly. You would be amazed how difficult it can be just to organise a simple air strike.

Islamo-fascist terror was very much on my radar before 9/11. I was not one of those who had never heard of *al Qaeda* before 2001, indeed 'Bill', 'Mr T' and others had been tracking large inflows of funds into the Eastern Seaboard since late '98/early '99. Almost certainly this cash was bankrolling the reconnaissance cells in New York and Washington - at least two, probably three, with one assigned to the Twin Towers, one to the Pentagon and one to the White House. There is an argument that the White House may not have been added to the target list until after the November 2000 presidential election. At the time, however, no one knew what the targets were. We just had a sense that something was happening and that a big attack was due.

The Iraqi-backed *al Qaeda* attacks on the US Embassies in Nairobi, Kenya and Dar-es-Salaam, Tanzania and the destroyer USS *Cole*[11] gave fair warning. Sadly, tackling terrorism was a long way down most political to-do lists. Both the Clinton Administration and the Blair government in Britain were obsessed with the notion that terrorism was a law enforcement, not national security issue. It is ironic that a section of the radical left rejected the notion that terrorism is state sponsored, then convinced itself that the 9/11 attacks had to be backed by a state, which could only be the US. This was a bit like blaming Pearl Harbor on poor old Admiral Kimmel.

The idea that terrorism is a spontaneous phenomenon and therefore, just a policing issue, like double-parking, reached the height of absurdity when the FBI were given the lead on the investigation into the attack on the USS *Cole*. That was a state-sponsored attack on a warship where she had every right to be, and an Act of War by Iraq on the United States. Quite how the FBI were going to arrest Saddam Hussein in Baghdad was never explained, although such was the interference run on their investigation by the DVD's Correa Group the issue never arose. The Clinton Administration's feeble response to the attack on the *Cole* gave the DVD, Saddam and bin Laden the green light they needed for 9/11.

9/11

No doubt 9/11 could have been prevented had serious people been put in charge of the West's counterterrorist effort, but that was never likely to happen. 9/11 itself wasn't enough to trigger more than a couple of with respect pointless official inquiries and a rearranging of the deck chairs on the *Titanic*. Thankfully there was a brief period of lucidity, down to those nice people President George W. Bush and Vice-President Dick Cheney, who launched the Global War on Terror and rightly so, with respect.

When American Airlines Flight 11 went in I was upstairs in my office at home, working at my day job. My director at the Bruges Group rang to tell me to switch on the telly, as a plane had crashed into the World Trade Center.[12] My first thoughts were that it had to be a light plane, or perhaps something the size of a B-25.[13] I rushed downstairs to turn on Fox News (which I preferred to the BBC, for its fair and balanced coverage) in time to see the United Airlines Flight 175 going in. Not navigational errors, then.

By then I was sufficiently tapped into INTELCOM to be able to get hold of the CIA that afternoon, which is how I learned that the CIA were distributing internally, and presumably to State, an initial assessment of 50,000 dead. That was an interesting figure, which seems to have originated with the

Correa Group in Frankfurt. Thankfully, it turned out to be no more than a fantasy figure on the DVD's wish list.

I was able to express sympathy to, and offer help to, another CIA officer, whom I got a hold of on his cell-phone as he was boarding a Gulfstream at Langley Air Force base, at a time when not a lot of planes were getting airborne. He was in the process of shepherding some innocent members of the bin Laden family back to Saudi, a wise precaution at a time when Sikhs were being mistaken for Muslims and beaten up. Their chances of getting on a commercial flight, when they resumed, with that moniker, were not high. "Hi, my name is bin Laden and I'd like to book a first-class seat on the first plane out of JFK for Saudi Arabia." "Shirley, send for security."

The White House and Pentagon were thinking Iraq and rightly so, but they wanted a smoking gun, or at least a second smoking six-shooter. The Pentagon quickly confirmed from ELINT and SATINT analysis that the Iraqi armed forces had been placed on heightened alert before the planes went in (hello). Nobody else was on alert, apart from a well-timed exercise in the States, which of course got the conspiracy theorists going. In fairness that might have been triggered by chatter or other intel hinting at something happening. There usually is. The trick is identifying the target in time.

There were of course official investigations, but they quickly ran into the sand, getting hung up on the Huffman Aviation thing (Cessnas in uncrowded skies in sunny Florida). To his everlasting credit President Bush, a former pilot and a good one with respect (he flew Convair F- 102s[14] - you were either good, out, or dead) never bought into that nonsense. The 9/11 pilots were clearly experienced on, or had been specifically trained on, the Boeing 757 or 767.

Neither the Joint Congressional Inquiry the 9/11 Commission nor the absurd Chilcot Inquiry in the UK, each of which rejected the idea of Iraqi involvement out of hand, had an actual pilot as a member, so far as I know. I had brief dealings with all three. They may even have been labouring under the misapprehension that you can programme the Honeywell autopilot on a 757 or 767 to exceed the aircraft's flight envelope, or the 250-knot speed limit below 10,000 ft. Perhaps they watched too many of those films where one of the passengers boldly steps up to the plate and flies the plane.

I accepted an invitation to join a panel of national security experts in Washington in November 2001, put together by those very nice people the Jewish Institute for National Security Affairs (JINSA). Apart from myself of course (this is my natural, unassuming modesty taking over again) this was not a low-powered panel. It included a retired air force general, with command experience of special operations, and up and coming Congressman Eric Cantor, later the very able House Majority Leader. (I used to be thought of as 'up and coming' politically myself, but sadly I am now 'been and gone'.) Eric had to break off to go to the White House for the signing ceremony on the very sensible Patriot Act.

I didn't know it then, but a summary of my conclusions as to where the pilots had been trained was later put before the President. The panel was one of those meetings with armed police on the door and intelligence types in the audience. Somebody thought my speech worth putting on the Internet, which kind of ended any idea of pretending that I only did my day job.

'Bill'

As will be recalled from the Preface, one of the nice spies I represented was 'Bill', one of the finest pilots America has ever produced, let alone the CIA or the NSA. The U-2 programme by the way seems to have been more of an NSA programme than CIA, but it was flagged through Langley. You won't find 'Bill' or the other NSA U-2 pilots in published books on the U-2. Most of his missions, which included flying over Communist China, North Vietnam, Cuba and the USSR, are still classified.[15] 'Bill' seems to have started his flying career in the Strategic Air Command. At any rate he was a personal friend of the formidable General Curtis LeMay, another nice man, who bombed Berlin and Tokyo. As Commander 20th Army Air Force in the Marianas, Curtis was in charge of the atomic bomb raids on Hiroshima and Nagasaki.

So far as I can tell the first plane 'Bill' flew operationally was the wonderful old Convair B-36 Peacemaker,[16] the world's first and so far only ten-engined bomber (hence "six turning and four burning"). You had to be a pretty good pilot to handle those. At nearly 200 tons, with a wingspan of 230 feet, they were a lot of aeroplane. With first-generation power controls, it probably wasn't too difficult to over-rotate on take-off, and they were a bit tricky to land when asymmetric, especially if you had two engines out on the same side. 'Bill' went on to the U-2, indeed he was on the shakedown programme. He helped teach Frank 'Gary' Powers to fly, indeed, as related he was offered the Powers flight before Powers.

The early U-2s, i.e. the A model with the J-57 engine, were a trifle underpowered. Later models with the J-75 were a lot better. They could be a real handful at altitude. There were good U-2 pilots and very good U-2 pilots, but no bad U-2 pilots. The missions were long. Peshawar, Pakistan to Bodo, Norway is a pretty long haul in a subsonic aircraft on any definition.

After the U-2 'Bill' was chosen for the SR-71[17] shakedown programme. The 'U' in U-2 stood for "Utility" by the way, as in UC-64A, the Noorduyn Norseman,[18] i.e. it was a cover designation. The SR-71A was no joke to fly either, especially before the boys at the Skunk Works (great people) got the fuel leaks sorted. They were fine once they were warmed up, it was just that bit before they got warm.

Put shortly, 'Bill' knew a fair bit about flying. So did 'Mr T', who'd done some time with Air America in the good old days, with no frequent flyer miles to show for it, sadly. (How could the CIA not offer frequent flyer miles?) 'Mr T', famously, had been in a 'Gooney Bird'[19] which ditched in the South China Sea, on a mission which officially never happened. With the cargo, about which the less said the better, off-loaded, she stayed afloat for three days. They couldn't tell the Navy, as she wasn't supposed to be there. *Air America* was not so much a film as a documentary.

In the aftermath of 9/11, and with my Washington speech coming up (which the boys had kindly arranged would be taped, i.e. bugged - I hope someone told the general[20]), 'Bill', 'Mr T' and myself sat down in London over a bottle of Jack Daniels. We chewed the fat on pilot training and whole Iraq-9/11 thing.

The 9/11 pilot training

Nobody with any sense in the aviation intelligence community was buying Cessnas in Florida. Equally, nobody had been able to find an airline that had lent *al Qaeda* or the *Mukhabarat*[21] a Boeing 757 or 767 to practice on. The 75' and 76' were designed with cockpit and systems commonality, so that pilots could easily transition between the two. The fact that *al Qaeda* had confined their choice to those two airliners, when a Boeing 747 or 777 would have supplied much more accelerant (i.e. fuel) and kinetic energy[22] seemed significant.

By way of explanation there are several differences between flying light and heavy aircraft. For one thing there are a whole lot more 'knobs and switches and stuff'. CIA officially seized on the unintentional broadcast of a PA announcement to the passengers, which suggested a lack of cockpit familiarity on the part of the hijackers. However, Boeing apparently confirmed privately to them that there were minor radio switchgear differences between the 757 and 767 and between international and domestic models, which could account for the confusion. Obviously, I talked to Boeing as well, but they clammed up tight on the subject of variations in radio switchgear.

More importantly, heavy transport aircraft do not respond to the controls in the same way that a light aircraft does, as any pilot who has transitioned between fighters and bombers, or light and heavy civil aircraft, will tell you. With an airliner or bomber you have to wait for the ship to respond to your control input. If you do not, you can quickly get into trouble through over-controlling.

When I first took the controls of a Vickers-Supermarine VC-10 C Mk 1 in the simulator at RAF Brize Norton I made the right rudder, throttle and control yoke inputs for a Rate 1 turn[23] to starboard. Nothing happened. So I did what every rookie pilot does and gave her some more right rudder and aileron, boosting the power as I did so. A turning aircraft needs more power if she is to maintain altitude - dropping height in turns is another standard rookie boo-boo.

Then things started happening, all too quickly, as the 'plane' caught up with the controls. What started out, as a gentle Rate 1 turn became a steep starboard bank, from recollection requiring TOGA[24] power just to maintain altitude, at which point I absorbed another lesson. The mighty Conways[25] did not spool up to full power just because you'd yanked the throttles forward. When the power did kick in I discovered I had too much of it, and I'd recovered too far, i.e. I now had the 'plane' banking, quickly, to port. What was more I was nowhere near the heading the instructor had commanded. At this point said instructor showed me how to do it without upsetting the crockery in the galley and having the passengers behaving as in *Airplane.*

The next point of difference is that all heavy transport aircraft since the great Lockheed Constellation[26] have had power, i.e. hydraulically assisted, controls. A Cessna 172 has simple cable-operated controls, which are far more responsive and analogue, i.e. they give a proportionate feedback. In a modern airliner the feedback is built-in, i.e. artificial, with no direct connection between the pilot and the control surfaces. Earlier power-assistance, as on the Constellation, was just boosting, but the De Havilland Comet introduced fully powered controls. We then moved to fly-by-wire, with Concorde.

Fourthly, an airliner's instruments are much more complex. The Flight Director, e.g., will give you a lot more information than the simple version in the 172. Compared to a Cessna you are bombarded with information in a 757/767 cockpit, much of which you don't need, but get anyway.

Fifthly, the aircraft will not let you crash it without letting you know. You can crash a Cessna and never hear a peep until the terrain starts coming through the prop, you say "oops" and the passengers start saying "ouch". There are several aviation disasters in recent years where the pilots' minds have clearly been scrambled by a multiplicity of aural and visual warnings. Indeed, I would suggest that simplification of warning systems is a live aviation safety issue.

On the final approaches to the Twin Towers and the Pentagon there would probably have been master alarms, ground proximity warnings, overspeed warnings, TCAS alerts and all sorts of flashing lights. You can cancel alarms, but you need to know how. The good folk at Huffman Aviation aren't going to tell you how to cancel an overspeed warning for a Boeing 767 whilst teaching you how to fly one of their Cessnas.

Sixthly, the autopilot on a Cessna, assuming your Cessna actually has one, is usually a simple three-axis affair, allowing you to select altitude and heading, and maintain level flight. It is not a programmable, smart autopilot like the Honeywell Flight Management System on the 757. The FMS will review your inputs and reject them if they exceed the flight envelope. No modern airliner autopilot is going to let you programme the aircraft for an overspeed condition at low altitude. The flying on 9/11 had to be manual, and not out of the manual either.

Seventhly, it is very difficult to overspeed a piston-engine aircraft in level flight, i.e. crank on so much power that you are exceeding the structural limits of the airframe. One of the first things I did when starting to analyse 9/11 was to get a credible estimate of the aircraft speed prior to impact. In each case the aircraft were in overspeed condition, mostly way above, as well as exceeding the 250-knot limit below 10,000 ft, not that a terrorist would be overly concerned about observing the speed limit. Exceeding the airframe limit involves a bit more than just an FAA violation, however.

Eighthly, the power of the engines (typically Rolls-Royce RB-211s) on the 757 and 767 is a whole order of magnitude greater than that put out by Lycoming engines on Cessnas. Straight comparisons between piston- engine output, usually expressed in horsepower, and turbofan output, usually expressed in pounds thrust, can be misleading. Power on both types of engine varies with altitude, but you are looking at a difference of orders of magnitude – say a total of 80,000 HP on a 767 to 160 HP on a Cessna 172. Moreover, piston and turbofan engines work on such different principles that you are not going to learn anything about power management of a pair of RB-211s from the boys at Huffman, and what you do learn will work against you. A big turbofan is not nearly as linear in its power delivery as a small piston engine. Most of your power comes in the last 10% for one thing.

About the only thing that is the same is the throttle direction - i.e. forward is up and back is down.[27] If you were to ask your instructor at Huffman Aviation about compressor stall on a Cessna 172 he or she's going to (1) give you a funny look and (2) tell you that you do not need to worry about compressor stall on a Cessna, unless you're lucky enough to be flying a Citation.

Power management of a Lycoming aeroengine is admittedly bit more complex than power management of the Northstar V8 in a Cadillac. You've got mixture to worry about for one thing, and prop pitch. You also need to keep an eye on your cylinder head temperatures, especially on a long descent with power off, when it can be a good idea to 'blip' the throttle to keep your engine warm. However, it's not a lot more complicated. Light aircraft aeroengines are not much larger, or more powerful, than a large car's V8. My Bentley had a bigger engine (412 cubic inches) than the Lycoming in the Bulldog I flew in the University of Wales Air Squadron (360 cubic inches).

Managing a high-bypass ratio turbofan is a lot more difficult. If you forget the engine's need for air as well as fuel it will soon let you know. It needs a lot more air than it does fuel. When it stalls it will do so with a thump.

Lastly, putting entirely to one side the fact that airliners like the 757 are pressurised and have complex fuel systems, which need managing, factors that would probably not have come into play on 9/11, they are swept- wing, not straight-wing like a Cessna. The stall characteristics are quite different, so much so you have a new category of stall - high-speed stalls. You do not have to worry about high-speed stall on a Cessna 172.

Many years ago, RAF Flying Training Command, fully appreciative of the different characteristics of piston-engine and jet-powered aircraft, found that they were having to spend time detraining pilots converting to jets after they learnt to fly on piston-engine types. In those days they trained on kites like the lovely old Percival Provost, or the De Havilland Canada Chipmunk, on which my dad learnt to fly. Sensibly, the RAF moved to a jet as a basic trainer, the excellent Hunting-Percival Jet Provost.[28]

The on the record flying training for the 9/11 pilots, i.e. the training which left a trail even loveable old Sergeant Shultz from *Hogan's Heroes*[29] could follow, was enough to allow those two men to stooge around in relative safety in Florida's uncrowded and sunny airspace. As my late learned-friend John Mortimer QC remarked in one of his great Rumpole books, the Florida climate is just right for oranges. Over New York they have white, fluffy things called clouds.

The training was insufficient to permit smooth, manual, precision flying of turbofan-powered heavy jetliners on a terrorist attack mission in excess of the aircraft's VNE[30] for that altitude. Even less did it ready them for flying at low altitude, or a descent through crowded airspace, with no go-around, i.e. an accurate line-up on the target on first approach.

The phrase "those two men" is deliberate. The 9/11 Commission and the media, having fallen with respect for one of the oldest dodges in the book, naturally assumed that the pilots who had gone through the training in Florida etc., leaving a trail a mile-wide behind them, were in the command seats on 9/11. That assumption may not be warranted. There is no evidence, such as finding their remains in that position, nor from cockpit voice recordings, that those pilots actually took the left-hand seat. They may have done, but equally they may have been acting as copilots, i.e. in the right-hand seat, handling radio communications and PA announcements.

Some of the CVR and FDR[31] recorders probably did survive the impacts, although USINTELCOM is understandably cagey about that. That nice man Governor Jesse Ventura probably got close to the truth about the CVRs and FDRs in his interesting programme in the *Conspiracy Files* series.[32] Just because a 'black box' is recovered however (as the Governor rightly observes they usually come in a lurid hue of orange and are rarely in your basic black) it does not follow that the data, or all of it, is recoverable.

Black boxes are designed to survive high-speed impacts. They are not designed to survive a third of a million tons of masonry[33] falling on top of them. Generally speaking, if you are a pilot and have a crash, and then a third of a million tons of masonry falls on top of you, you are entitled to feel that you are having a bad day at the office. It is reasonable to assume that the terrorists identified by the 9/11 Commission were in the cockpits. It is not safe to assume they were in the left-hand seats.

I talked with a range of aviation and air intelligence experts before concluding that the training in Florida and elsewhere was an intelligence blind, but it helped to start with two of the best in the business, i.e. 'Bill' and 'Mr T'. Of course there are commercial pilots who are comfortable with the 9/11 Commission's conclusions, but I suggest they would be in a minority. There aren't too many takers in INTELCOM these days for the 9/11 Commission's findings, indeed judging from a private conversation with one of the Commissioners not everybody on the Commission itself was comfortable with the official line.[34]

It is entirely possible that the Commission were allowed to believe that you can programme the autopilot and autothrottle systems on the Boeing 757 and 767 to exceed the structural limits of the airframe, or that the Commission were simply unaware that VNE decreases with altitude, as the air gets denser. In the alternative, as is often the case with official inquiries (this is certainly true of the UK), it may simply be that the conclusions got denser as the inquiry went along and it became clear that the truth was politically unpalatable or unprintable.

Flight Into Danger

Another possibility is that those, like the Chilcot Inquiry members with respect, who concluded that you can learn how to fly a Boeing 767 into a skyscraper on your first attempt by flying a Cessna in Florida, have watched too many of those films where the courageous and pretty flight attendant takes over the controls and lands the aircraft. This can be done with or without the assistance of the late, great Charlton Heston.

This enjoyable genre of films, spoofed so hilariously in *Airplane*, had its genesis in Arthur Hailey & John Castle's very readable novel *Flight Into*

Danger. The book was turned into a Canadian TV film, remade in the States as *Zero Hour* (1957). The latter was the inspiration for the makers of *Airplane*. Unlike them however (I have never been entirely clear whether the piston-engine soundtrack for the Boeing 707 in the film was a genuine mistake or part of the spoof!) Arthur Hailey[35] knew something about flying, having served in World War II in the RAF.

Also unlike the *Airplane* films, which so far as I know have never been credited with a major contribution to aviation safety, save possibly discouraging shaving in aircraft toilets, *Flight Into Danger* actually made commercial aviation safer. It highlighted the dangerous practice of feeding the same food to the flight crew - not just any old food either, but *airline* food. This simply invited the incapacitation of the entire flight crew through botulism, even in the days before low-cost carriers. The sensible practice of having the pilots eat different meals came in not long afterwards.

It is not entirely clear, by the way, which aircraft the fictional C-5[36] in the book was supposed to be, but we know it was a piston-engine airliner,[37] we know it was the size of a DC-4,[38] we know it was pressurised, we know it was *not* a DC-4,[39] and the book was based in Canada. From all this we conclude ("come on class" I can hear myself saying, if I were lecturing intelligence students) that the airliner Arthur and John had in mind was probably the Canadair C-4 Argonaut, as it was known in BOAC service. Arthur Hailey must have flown in one. In Trans- Canada Airlines it was known as the North Star, a lovely old bus, if a trifle noisy,[40] with Rolls-Royce Merlin power.[41]

To give the plot some credibility our hero is a former military pilot. In fairness the plot has more than a little credibility, as the grizzled old airline veteran talking the flight down suggests what any experienced airline pilot would. Ditch the kite in the sea, in the hope of not losing most of a suburb of Vancouver and fishing a few bedraggled survivors out of the water before she goes under. Without any experience on type, long out of a cockpit and unfamiliar with the delayed control responses of a heavy aircraft[42] our hero credibly weaves her all over the sky like a drunken sailor, plonks her down on the runway any old how, slides off and cracks up the under-cart.

It was only a good landing in the sense that everybody walked away from it. That is one definition of a good landing admittedly, but not one adopted by most airline managements, with the possible exception of Ryanair.[43] Modern aircraft are much more sophisticated than the dear old Argonaut, but one thing has not changed since *Flight Into Danger* was written in the fifties. Flying airliners remains a job for the pilots, not the passengers.

Finding the Simulator

As far as I know I was the first to suggest folk started looking for a 757 or 767 simulator. It didn't take long to find. As I well knew, Kuwait Airways operated the Boeing 767, the dash 269ER version to be precise.[44] Three aircraft, 9K-A1A, 9K-A1B and 9K-A1C, at least two of which were seized by Iraq in August 1990, were delivered new by Boeing in 1986, along with a simulator. Kuwait City was so far from the nearest 767 training facility and so much pilot training is done on simulators these days there was bound to be one, but the Kuwaitis confirmed it. More than that, they confirmed that their 767 simulator - a big-ticket item - went walkies along with their 767s. Indeed, Kuwait Airways successfully sued in London for its recovery.[45]

I was of course aware of the lengthy collaboration between Iraq and *al Qaeda*, which made sense, since both Saddam and bin Laden were DVD assets. Not only was I aware that Saddam and bin Laden had held proximity talks at Baghdad International Airport when *al Qaeda* was being formed, the ground covered including the degree of intelligence assistance to be provided by Iraq, but it was me who dobbed in MI6 to CIA over this. (Six had very naughtily held out on the Americans.) Since Six monitored the meeting they were in a position to know what was going down.

For the benefit of the 'where is your evidence/you must identify your sources brigade' I am not risking my source's life by going any further, even though he was got out of Baghdad. Once again this is an area where you will have to make your own enquiries. Since bin Laden flew into Baghdad on a Boeing 707 owned by someone close to the Saudi royal family and many in the media and elsewhere have gone way out on a limb 'pooh-pooing' any suggestion of an Iraq/*al Qaeda* link it is a highly politicised and sensitive area.

Legwork still has to be done after you come up with a bit of analysis. It's a bit like an old episode of *Softly Softly*[46] where Detective Chief Superintendent Barlow briefs in the team and tells them to get cracking, before driving off in his Jaguar, usually a lovely old Mk. 2. I opined that the simulator had ended up in Salman Pak, the Iraqi terrorist training centre, but it took careful analysis of overheads to prove it. Unsurprisingly, Iraq's main terrorist training facility came in for a good bit of satellite attention, not least after the Gulf War.

My speech in November 2001 went down well, indeed as indicated I was told that a synopsis ended up in front of the President, although officially it didn't. The Bush Administration was so badly penetrated by the DVD however that I did not receive so much as an invitation to a White House Christmas party. Word went out that if you helped the Administration you got kicked in the teeth. It didn't stop me passing stuff over to them, as they were the Good Guys, but it was a thankless task. It might have deterred others, however.

---

1. If you want peace prepare for war.
2. I never met him of course, but that nice lady Madam Chiang and I had several mutual friends, including General Walters, who bumped into her a couple of times - nicely of course.
3. Improved *Black Swan* class sloop, 1,350 tons. She was first attacked on 20th April 1949.
4. 45,000 tons, before modernisation, great ships. They were very elegant, well protected and had a powerful AA battery.
5. 27,000 tons, smaller and lacking the protection of the *Midway* class, which incorporated the lessons of World War II, in particular the impressive survival of Stuka attacks by the armoured carriers HMS *Indomitable* and HMS *Illustrious*, both of which were repaired in the States, with the Royal Navy returning the favour by showing their US colleagues all over the ships. The *Midway* class were the first to be designed after those attacks (the *Essex*-class were enlarged *Yorktowns*) and along with the British *Maltas* (45,000 tons standard displacement) the first class to get carrier design right, combining battle-worthiness, large enough hangar and flight decks to operate a full-size carrier air group, high speed and a strong defensive armament. The *Maltas* of course were cancelled as part of the Attlee government's policy of weakness at sea and encouraging communist aggression, in which it was sadly all too successful.
6. USS *Indiana* and *Kentucky*, although *Kentucky's* bow got to go to sea after the Captain of *Missouri*, the only US battleship known to have been commanded by a German spy (Roscoe Hillenkoetter) decided to lose her bow in a ramming incident.
7. This is not a typo - there were two principal versions of the Superfortress, the original B-29 and the later B-50, which had sufficient improvements to justify a new type number, although it could and perhaps should have been called the B-29D. It was a less advanced aircraft than the Convair B-36 Peacemaker and Boeing B-47 Stratojet. The B-50 had the big (really big) Pratt & Whitney R-4360 'Corn Cob' three-row radials (same powerplant as the piston engines on the B-36), a taller fin and some other improvements. It was the model of Stratofortress you wanted to have.
8. They weren't, in Germany at any rate. The tools and blueprints went to the USSR from the Dornier factory in Munich, which licence-built the 410, in '45. The C version was produced in small numbers, apparently by MiG, which had a good working relationship with Willi Messerschmitt, although the design team was led by Waldermar Voigt.
9. I never met Mr Marcos, who was nothing to do with the Marcos car company by the way, but Mrs Marcos and I had a couple of mutual friends, indeed one sounded me out about taking on a 'lady in the Philippines' as a client. I quoted a fee structure which was fair but did not suit the 'lady in the Philippines', whoever she was, thus permitting a graceful exit - it's a tactic I'd used before, e.g. when an allegedly slightly dodgy banker, not unreasonably, since he'd allegedly had two other bankers shot in a cheap motel (never agree to RVs in cheap motels), thought he was about to be arrested. Fortunately for the banker he

had DVD connections and was able to evade justice. The CIA, who bugged the conference with a laser mike, later congratulated me on the advice I'd given, once they'd stopped laughing over my risible security precautions (it was a "we'll need to check the room for bugs for this one I think" "Michael, you're being paranoid" "No I'm not, have a look under that table whilst I unscrew this table lamp" type situation).

10. The world knows him as Gary Powers but in the CIA he was always known as Frank.
11. DDG-67, 6,800 tons.
12. That is how it's spelt - it was in New York, so it was a 'Center,' not a 'centre,' just as Pearl Harbor is not spelt 'Pearl Habour.'
13. Thinking back to the B-25, which hit the Empire State Building on 28th July 1945, sadly not an inspired piece of navigation (Mayor La Guardia certainly seems to have thought that it was a strange place to land).
14. An early Century-series fighter, supersonic, but hairy, with limited visibility and a narrow flight envelope, especially above Mach 1, when things could go wrong pretty quickly. J-57 engine. President Bush has always been derided for serving in the Texas Air National Guard, unfairly since (1) it was probably Daddy's idea anyway (2) National Guard units are not exempt from overseas service in time of war, i.e. there was no particular reason why the his fighter squadron could not have been sent to defend say Da Nang Airbase (nobody in that unit knew, then, that the Mig-21s were mostly being flown by Luftwaffe pilots and were under orders not to venture into South Vietnamese airspace) and (3) there are safer occupations than flying Century series supersonic fighters.
15. 'Bill's' name came up at the Pentagon a couple of times, including in a conversation in the SecDef's corridor. He is known personally to at least one living former US President, was probably known to President Eisenhower, as he was the CIA's first choice for the Powers mission on 1st May 1960, and was probably known by name to President Kennedy, as he flew missions over Cuba classified beyond Top Secret before, during and after the Cuban Missile Crisis. He also flew critical recon missions over Haiphong harbour and Hanoi, North Vietnam, from Kadena Air Force Base Okinawa, where Lee Harvey Oswald had been stationed. He was also known to the late President Johnson, indeed so far as I know 'Bill' was the intelligence officer detailed to brief in the President at Camp David, Maryland as to the CIA's and NSA's awareness of the President's prior knowledge of the decision to assassinate President Kennedy, following which briefing the President very sensibly took the decision not to seek the Democratic nomination for the 1968 election. Had he not done so a small team reporting to 'Bill' would probably have provided *Newsweek* and *Time* magazines with the phone logs of the critical calls out of the then Vice-President's office in Washington, which confirmed prior knowledge on the part of the Vice-President.
16. 6 P & W R-4360s and 4 General Electric J-47 jets.
17. Lockheed SR-71, capable of Mach 3.2 cruise, over 2,000 mph. It seems that it was Curtis LeMay who pressed for the SR-71 designation, 'SR' standing for Strategic Reconnaissance. The number was lifted, illogically, from the B series, following the North America XB-70 Valkyrie. The story that President Johnson misread

'RS' for 'SR' on TV seems to have its foundation in the failure to amend all the press copies of his speech.

18. Nice little bus, Air America apparently had a couple and used them in Laos, although there is an ongoing debate about that between myself and one of the Air America boys, who sent me a photo of him by the door and challenged my slightly creaky aircraft recognition skills (I once got my Devastators and Helldivers mixed up when being shown over the nice Pacific War display in one of the more public parts of Fort Meade). I said it 'looked like a Norseman' and I'm still waiting for the denial! The most famous Norseman casualty of course was poor old Major Glenn Miller, whose pilot wandered off course, sadly, into a bomb drop zone, and seems to have been hit beneath cloud by a rather large bomb, which even unfused would have been enough to crumple the wings.
19. Douglas C-53 Skytrain or, in RAF service, the Dakota. The 'Dak' had a number of USAAF designations and was also used by the Navy as the R4D (R for transport, D for Douglas and 4 for 4th Douglas transport). At least three different piston engines were fitted to 'Daks' (some were converted post-war to turboprops of course), the P & W, the Wright and, a very small number pre- war, the Bristol Pegasus. Douglas old-timers may tell you that the 'Peggies' were actually the smoothest of the three, a great tribute to Roy Fedden and his team at Filton. The R3D was the US Navy equivalent of the DC-5, something I got wrong in earlier editions of this book!
20. For the avoidance of doubt both CIA and the NSA had my consent to record my speech. Indeed, as I reassured a former General Counsel to the NSA they have my general consent to intercept and record my communications (it saves silly questions). All my speeches in the USA are on the record so far as NSA, DIA, CIA, ONI, MCIA, DNI, DEA, DHS, ATF and FBI are concerned, i.e. if there is anything in them any one in USINTELCOM thinks is of value they are free to use and distribute it with or without attribution - it's called professional courtesy. It can also be an informal discharge by the UK of our obligations under the UKUSA Intelligence Treaty, i.e. a means of telling an ally something which some clown on the JIC or in Whitehall has blocked for political reasons. Works a treat, even better than STP's radiator cleaner.
21. The Iraqi external intelligence service. I first encountered them in 1981 when I agreed to accompany some Iraqi students to their Embassy to lodge a human rights protest - they were slightly worried they might not be allowed out if they did not have an independent witness and they were probably right.
22. A Boeing 747-400 has a maximum take-off weight of 875,000 lbs, compared to only 255,000 lbs for a 757-200.
23. 180^0 a minute, i.e. a gentle turn. In practice commercial aircraft turn even slower, at 90^0 a minute, 'Rate One' is an expression more used by light aircraft pilots.
24. Take-Off and Go-Around Power, i.e. firewalling all four throttles - in modern aircraft there is usually a 'TOGA' switch to reduce pilot workload in the go-around, i.e. you have aborted a landing, or you are doing 'circuits and bumps,' in which case you will normally set go-around power after as soon as you have all three on the ground, especially on a short runway.

25. Rolls-Royce RB-80 Conway, 20,250 lb. thrust on the VC-10, as related above the world's first turbofan engine, selected for the long-range Boeing 707-400 and Douglas DC-8-40 as well, also the powerplant for the graceful Handley Page Victor B Mk2 V-Bomber: powerful, thirsty, noisy and wonderful.
26. Lockheed Model 49. The ultimate Connie was the Lockheed L-1649 Starliner - Lockheed model designation for the Constellation was '49', different models were the designated 049, 749, 1649 etc. Wright R-3350 Turbo-Compound engines in the later versions, supremely elegant, and fast for their time.
27. Unless you are flying a Bf109 of course, when if you want more power you yank the throttle back.
28. Powered by a little gem of a turbojet, the Armstrong-Siddeley Viper.
29. Played very skilfully by John Banner - smarter than he looked - who had done time in a German concentration camp, before going on to serve in the USAAF in World War II.
30. Velocity Never Exceed, i.e. the speed for which the airframe is rated. It varies with altitude, as air is denser at lower altitudes.
31. Cockpit Voice Recorders and Flight Data Recorder, i.e. the 'black boxes'.
32. 2006, BUT I wish the producers would do deeper background checks on those bringing stories to the Governor's attention: the interesting programmes tend to get undermined by the not so interesting ones, where someone is clearly trying to take the Governor, who clearly has a heart of gold, for a ride. Hopefully some of the bad faith contributors will get a metaphorical punch on the nose from the Governor at a convenient moment.
33. The weight of the Twin Towers has been the subject of some dispute - a dead load of about 1/6 million tons per tower sounds about right and the live load can't have been heavier than the dead load. A third of a million tons seems to be in the ballpark - the oft-quoted figure of half a million tons per tower seems a bit high. It may be that was a figure for both towers and the media got into a muddle somewhere along the way. As one or two journos have admitted candidly to me the media try not to let the facts get in the way of a good story.
34. Unsurprisingly neither the Joint Congressional Inquiry, the 9/11 Commission nor the Chilcot Inquiry had sufficient courage of their convictions to order tests. Unlike an autopilot/autothrottle you can actually programme a simulator to do all sorts of silly things. There is no obvious reason why you couldn't take a good student with an agreed number of hours on a Cessna 172 or similar aircraft, programme a 767 simulator to allow it to exceed VNE and see how they got on.
35. Apparently a very nice man, he lived in the Bahamas, near Nassau, where he and I had a mutual friend. Arthur died, sadly, in 2004.
36. There was a Canadair C-5, but it never went into service.
37. If you are a freshly minted, bright-eyed and bushy-tailed first officer on a 777 you will not impress your captain by asking where the mixture controls are - the only mixing devices on a 777 are the cocktail stirrers in first class.
38. Also easy to work out, since the flight was full and Arthur Hailey and John Castle helpfully tell us how many passengers were aboard.

39. The pre-landing checklist in the text refers to radiator shutters, which you won't find on a DC-4 (radial engines - no radiators). The DC-4 pre-landing checklist referred to cowling flaps.
40. Despite the crossover exhausts. These kept the exhaust away from the passenger cabin.
41. Merlin 622s of 1,760HP, about the same power as a Lancaster bomber, i.e. the C-4s were not underpowered and cruised at about 325 mph.
42. An Argonaut only weighed in at 73,000 lbs loaded, and from memory did not have power controls, the flight controls being derived from the Douglas DC-4, of which it was a version.
43. Apologies Michael!
44. Boeing allocate airline codes for their aircraft, so that a 767-200 ordered new by Kuwait Airways would be a 767-269, their 74's were designated 747- 269B and their 707s 707-369C and so on. However, their 707-321C was an ex-Pan Am aircraft, 21 being the code for Pan Am.
45. *Kuwait Airways Ltd v. Iraq Airways Ltd.* The simulator was listed in the schedule of property stolen by Iraq and not recovered.
46. A wonderful old BBC police drama, a spin-off from the more famous *Z- Cars*, starring the great Stratford Johns as DCS Barlow, backed up by a strong supporting cast including Frank Windsor as DCI Watts. It was well-written, well-acted, hugely popular and an export success, so the BBC cancelled it.

10

Analysing The War On Terror

HMS *Ark Royal*

In 2002 *al Qaeda* were tasked with sinking the aircraft carrier HMS *Ark Royal*,[1] then skippered by that nice man Captain Alan Massey. He was later deservedly promoted to admiral and made Second Sea Lord. This cunning plan, which clearly had not originated in a cave in Waziristan, involved a USS *Cole* style attack, presumably with Iraq supplying the explosives again, from the Spanish enclave of Ceuta in Morocco. The Spaniard of course insists that it's part of Spain. The idea was to sink the *Ark* as she passed through the Straits of Gibraltar, using fast motorboats. The cunning plan had one tiny, technical flaw however - it was 'bollocks'.[2] USS *Cole* was in harbour, i.e. *not moving* when she was attacked. Her captain and intelligence officer had also been left in the dark about the links between Iraq and *al Qaeda* and the extent not only of the latter's presence in Aden, but the degree of coverage the terrorists had from Yemeni officials. This was at the height of the "terrorism is a law enforcement problem" hysteria. The fact that terrorism is state sponsored was not widely appreciated.

Not only was *Ark Royal* a *moving* target but 9/11 had increased military awareness of the threat posed by Islamic terrorists. Warship captains no longer looked benignly upon approaching motorboats manned by chaps with beards, shouting *Allahu Akbar*. They now appreciated that the phrase did not mean that they were offering women, or had souvenirs for sale.

The difficulties of sinking an aircraft carrier on the open sea with a motorboat should not be underestimated. Whichever clown it was in the DVD or Spanish Intelligence who came up with that plan should have been invited to try it and reminded not to forget their water wings. The attack was aborted, but not before it attracted my interest. Upon being told that *Ark Royal* had been invited, on a NATO pretext, to visit Barcelona I concluded that she might be sailing into a trap. I was aware *inter alia* that:

(1) The German DVD controlled *al Qaeda*.
(2) 'Jerry' had not pulled out of Madrid after the falangist victory in 1939.
(3) The then Spanish Government, essentially, with honourable exceptions, were a bunch of warmed-over falangists.
(4) As demonstrated in the *Factortame* cases, where as we saw in Chapter 8 a front company controlled by Spanish Intelligence[3] mounted a frontal attack on a cornerstone of the British Constitution, the Supremacy of Parliament, Spain was a hostile state.
(5) There was a covert German intelligence organisation in Madrid.
(6) Elements of Spanish intelligence were in cahoots with *al Qaeda,* and
(7) Spain was secretly planning a military attack on Gibraltar if the surrender negotiations with the Foreign Office failed.

During the battle to save Rolls-Royce I turned my spare bedroom into a micro-operations centre. Having spotted a potential problem, it was a simple matter of preparing an informal intelligence assessment for distribution to a defence minister, the Defence Intelligence Staff and the Pentagon. They were a bit concerned about the NATO base at Rota, not to mention the possible implications for NATO of one member sponsoring a terrorist attack on a major warship of another member. I also alerted the Royal Navy, a simple matter of ringing an admiral.

Just in case the message was blocked it was a fairly straightforward task to arrange for a backup message for *Ark Royal* via an American aircraft carrier in the Indian Ocean, via a cutout in Washington, although you are not advised to try this at home. When I bumped into *Ark's* very nice captain a few years later there was a discussion about unusual use of the SATCOM network, but I will say no more than that. Alan Massey gave nothing away.

As usual the captain had been kept pretty much out of the loop. Officially, Spain is a valued NATO ally and was then a fellow member state of the EU. Officially Spain never planned to attack *Ark Royal*, or Gibraltar, and officially Spanish Intelligence are not in bed with *al Qaeda*. The shrapnel and shards of glass were real enough when *al Qaeda* were permitted to blow up a railway station in Madrid a few years later, however.

Facts interlock. If facts A, B & C are true and the subject matter is related, the pieces of the puzzle will fit together. Similarly, if theory A fits known facts B & C then that is support, even if weak, for the theory. Of course, if theory A fits facts B, C, D, E, F & G, then the support is stronger. Sometimes the supplier of a piece of intelligence will not know the big picture, nor how that particular piece of the puzzle fits. That's how the cookie crumbles.

Sometimes, as with a comment from a former Boeing B-52 Stratofortress captain on the similarities between the organisation of the air defences for Hanoi in the Vietnam War and Berlin during World War II, the big picture does not become clear for years.

The nice person who briefed me in on *Ark Royal's* intended movements may have thought that Spain was an ally, and may not have known that the Spanish were providing an *al Qaeda* cell in Barcelona with a safe house and Iraq a shaped charge powerful enough to blow a big hole in her. S/he also did not know that a naval staff officer attached to the Gibraltar invasion planning group in Cordoba had studied the Falklands War, entertained a justifiable professional concern about the capabilities of the Hawker Siddeley Harrier and Sea Harrier[4] and had asked Madrid if at least one of our carriers could be taken out of service during the invasion window. *I* knew however (never mind how), and put 2 and 2 together.[5] In intelligence work of course it's usually a case of adding 2, 4, 8 and the square root of 16, taking away 15 and adding 1.[6]

The *Ark* moved to, the Outer Harbour (the Spanish plan assumed that she would be in the Inner Harbour) and word was quietly passed to Madrid that they had been spotted. The *al Qaeda* cell was told to stick to desecrating Jewish cemeteries, visiting halal fried chicken shops, or whatever else it is that *al Qaeda* terrorists do when they're off-duty.

After a suitable interval to give Madrid some badly needed deniability, the cell members were arrested, the first *al Qaeda* cell I helped nab. I was already unpopular with *al Qaeda* after the Mindanao business and my Washington speech. This did nothing to increase my approval ratings in Pakistan (where the *al Qaeda* leadership, including Osama bin Laden, moved after their ejection from Afghanistan) or Dachau (where *al Qaeda's* operational planning is done), but I didn't mind.

Gibraltar

A puzzling development followed. Neither the Gibraltar Government (unlike Britain, Gibraltar is well-governed and usually has a serious chief minister), nor the Governor of Gibraltar, seem to have been briefed in that Spain was drawing up plans to invade Gibraltar, Falklands-style. Of course, there would only have been an invasion if the New Labour/Foreign Office plan to surrender sovereignty over the Rock come unstuck. Nothing was being done to restore Gib's run-down defences. Britain's defence posture in the Western Mediterranean remained unaltered.

Entirely by coincidence, I was invited down to Gib to give a speech at the impressive Casino there. The Governor, David Ducie, a nice man, some members of the Gibraltar Government, Joe Bossano, another nice man and Leader of the Loyal Opposition, and some UN types also happened to be attending. The event was to be covered by Gibraltar television. They were doubtless expecting another dull boring speech from me, but this seemed to me to be an opportune moment to alert Gibraltar and dob in the Spaniard.

The Governor and Joe Bossano were seated at the same table. It would be fair to say that the Governor's face wore a slightly greyish hue as I sat down. Joe Bossano, a lovely bloke, wore a more thoughtful expression, although in fairness Foreign Office types with respect rarely wear thoughtful expressions. It's probably something to do with group thinking.[7] There seemed to be a commotion over at the UN table and a couple of media types didn't stay for the coffee and mints.

Spanish Intelligence had my speech covered. There's a surprise. There was movement across the Gibraltar/Spanish frontier in both directions overnight. It turned out that there are some intelligent people in Spanish Intelligence, which was another surprise. An intelligent intelligence officer, which is not necessarily a tautology, popped across the frontier for an amicable chat, delivering assurances that the Spanish Defence Ministry had crunched the numbers and they were coming up a bit short for an all-out war with Britain. In my speech I chanced to slip in a reference to the outcome of the last battle between the British and Spanish fleets.[8]

This was the only speech I have ever given which upset Air Traffic Control. Apparently, some idiot in Madrid had concluded that I was in cahoots with MI6, which was ridiculous. I was actually in cahoots with the Defence Intelligence Staff. Madrid feared that we had moved some additional surface to air missile batteries to the Rock. I was told. by someone with a pained expression, that a McDonnell Douglas F-18 Hornet of the Spanish Air Force (Ejercito del Aire Espanol) had done a high-speed run over La Linea parallel to Runway 27/09 at Gibraltar Airport, in a transparent effort to get the boys to light up their fire control radars, *without* alerting ATC.

Naturally, as the son of an air traffic controller, I was distressed to hear that ATC were upset. In fairness they were not as distressed as the UN delegation had been the previous night. The UN lot were bothering the hard-working and long-suffering organisers[9] with silly threats of a walk out.

On reviewing the Ejercito's order of battle I noticed a Boeing 707 - a 300 series Intercontinental to be precise - that looked like it didn't belong. At least it provoked the question "I wonder what Samuel Spaniard wants with a 707, which is not fitted as a tanker"? The number of military uses for a 707 is limited. As any F-18 pilot will tell you, however, a 70' has five things that an F-18 does not:

(1) Space - lots of it.
(2) Electrical power - ditto.
(3) Big fuel tanks.
(4) A galley, for in-flight snacks.
(5) Toilets - very useful on an extended mission (the toilets on the F-18 are apparently a bit cramped)(memo to St Louis: fix the toilets).

Making a wild surmise I rather thought the 70' would have been stooging around just out of radar range on an ELINT mission. I was right. Again, as with DCS Barlow of *Softly, Softly*, it was a question of someone - in this case a Spanish-based US air intelligence officer - doing a bit of legwork. I am told that he popped along at short notice for a dekko. The Spanish had pulled most of the stuff from the racks but hadn't quite got around to going the whole hog with the "this is just a transport, Senor" bit. Bingo. They should probably have installed some inflight entertainment, to boost their cover story.

One of the tasks of an intelligence officer (of course I am not one of those) is to determine a potential enemy's capabilities and intentions. Sometimes you get a clue as to his intentions from the capabilities that your potential enemy has equipped himself with. This was just such a case. The Spanish Army had ordered 235 Leopard 2A5 Main Battle Tanks from Krauss-Maffei, allegedly to deal with Morocco's Steyr Sk-105 light tanks.

Now your Leopard 2 is a serious panzer, with a big gun - the Rheinmetall 120 mil. Without being unkind to the fine old company of Steyr-Puch, and whilst not as tiny as Lieutenant Gruber's[10] little tank in the BBC's hilarious WWII comedy *'Allo 'Allo*, the Sk-105 was fairly described in my informal intelligence assessment as "the Fiat Uno of tanks".

You do not need a Leopard 2 to deal with an Sk-105. In a duel between the two the Leopard commander's worry would not be so much how to pierce the armour of the Sk as how to stop the round going out the other side without exploding. The Spanish were clearly contemplating a war against somebody with a much bigger tank than a Steyr 105, something like a Vickers Challenger in fact. Not after my speech they weren't.

For the avoidance of doubt, as explained in the Preface, strict compliance with the Official Secrets Act (OSA) has always been my policy. OSA is often misunderstood - it only applies to *official* secrets. Officially, the Foreign Office weren't planning to surrender Gibraltar, they were merely negotiating with a hostile state over her future. Officially, Spain was not planning an invasion and officially Spanish Intelligence are not in bed with *al Qaeda*. So, there was no question of any official secret being leaked to me. Unofficial secrets officially do not exist, i.e. they are officially unofficial.

The Bentley goes to Windsor Castle

The highlight of 2002 was driving past Queen Elizabeth II and that lovely man, with respect, HRH the Duke of Edinburgh, on my first visit to Windsor Castle. The castle was wonderfully restored after the 'Jerries', a.k.a. GO2, set fire to it.

My Turbo was part of a parade of 500 Rolls-Royce and Bentley motor cars to mark the Queen's Golden Jubilee, organised by the Rolls-Royce Enthusiasts Club. That other nice man HRH the Duke of Gloucester drove a rather splendid looking Phantom, which was parked adjacent to my Bentley in the staging area. All in all, it was an impressive line-up. Naturally the Bentley was spruced up for the occasion and looking her best. I tried to spruce myself up as well.

My first visit to the State Department

I was a fairly regular visitor to Washington and the Pentagon in the years after 9/11, indeed from the time I represented General Pinochet. In 2001 the very sound Ambassador Bolton invited me to his swearing-in, on that occasion as Under-Secretary of State for International Security Affairs and Arms Control. It was a great occasion, in the splendid surroundings of the Benjamin Franklin Room at the State Department. Oddly, I seemed to be the only Brit present. Naturally, this being a diplomatic occasion and me being a diplomatic sort of chap, I turned out in my best black jacket and stripes. Fortunately, no one asked me for a gin and tonic. This actually happened to me once, at the book-launch for *AIDS And The Law*, which I co-wrote (I obliged with the g & t!).

Possibly the light was playing a trick, but I thought I saw Colin Powell, who had known John for many years, look more than once, with a degree of suspicion, in my direction. The general gave a witty speech, remarking that the President seemed to have sent John to the State Department to open up an American Interests section. The experiment was not repeated and State remained neutral in the Global War on Terror. As my friends at State might put it however, "even if we're not pro-American, at least we're not *anti*-American in the way that your Foreign Office is anti-British".

You can usually get a decent cup of tea at Foggy Bottom. The Pentagon (no offence boys) does lousy tea, but decent coffee, except at the McDonalds for some reason and the Office of Net Assessment (creamer only – no milk). I always tried to do the Pentagon in the morning and State in the afternoon. If you're ever invited to brief in staffers on the Senate Select Committee on Intelligence (nice people) take a tip from me and bring a Thermos flask. I've had better coffee in London. When we Brits understand coffee and the Americans understand tea then the Anglo-American alliance will truly be cemented. The Tea Party, sadly, takes its name from the sort of party where you throw the tea into the harbour, not put it into the pot, where it belongs.

Coffee at the White House was never a problem. It's heavily penetrated by DVD assets, or useful idiots - useful for the Bad Guys that is. It's even worse than the Cabinet Office in fact, so much so that the best course was to adjourn to the Starbucks on 17th Street - fewer eavesdroppers, and much better coffee. The big problem in Washington is not the Chinese holding too much American debt, but not enough fridges and too much creamer. Curiously, with all the money that was hosed around by the stimulus package, no one thought to get some orders down to the good folk at Kelvinator and install some fridges.

My Visit to Israel

Highlight of 2003 was undoubtedly my first visit to Israel, on the inaugural Lawyers Mission. This took in the West Bank, the Lebanese frontier, the Golan Heights and all the other tourist hotspots. Being shown over the battleground where his lads stopped the Syrians in their tracks (strictly they blew their tracks off) by that great tanker general, Major- General Avigdor Kahalani, was a moving moment. The Golan Heights are quite pretty by the way, and peaceful, when the Syrians are not invading that is.

INTELCON

Highlight of 2005 (sadly, there were no highlights in 2004) was the Intelligence Conference (INTELCON) in Crystal City, convenient for the Pentagon and handy for CIA, allowing you to dodge both the traffic and Air Florida. My speech was well received - this was the trip where I drove over 7,500 miles in just over a fortnight, as related in the Preface. It was preceded by that scare over the 15KT nukes that had gone walkies from South Africa at the end of the *apartheid* era. That was the one where some clown in Teheran wanted to blow up bits of Houston by sneaking one of those all too portable bombs into Galveston TX on a container ship. Hence the side-trip to see some nice nuclear weapons specialists at the Monterey Institute near San Francisco, with a spectacular drive back to LA via Carmel and the Pacific Highway, and the need to pop into the FBI Field Office in Houston. There were some other folk to see as well, including 'Bill' of course, by then officially retired. In the first editions of this book I suggested that he was living in North Carolina. That was to protect his identity. (He had after all survived an assassination attempt by the DVD, in Switzerland.) Sadly I understand that 'Bill' has now gone to the great intelligence fusion centre in the sky. I'm still not giving out his real name, as it might expose some former colleagues, but I can say that he lived in West Palm Beach.

INTELCON grew out of the concern expressed within INTELCOM itself, by Congress, the President and the 9/11 Commission, at the lack of coordination between intelligence agencies, law enforcement and independent intelligence specialists, which is where I came in. Just about everybody was there, including the Bad Guys, mostly at a discreet distance, although the DVD sent someone along to cover my speech, which happened to be about them, *inter alia*. As always at conferences, the serious work was done in the bars, the late-night pizza sessions and over working breakfasts.

Some of the boys, including myself, popped around to the Pentagon, as one does. The conference was a great success, although MI6 needed a period of adjustment to the comparative transparency – guys from CIA, e.g., walking round with badges saying "CIA", not that they really needed them with those suits. Had the conference been held in 2000 the DVD and Saddam would have had to cancel 9/11. We in the UK are way behind. Our arrangements for coordination between law enforcement and intelligence are primitive. The police in particular are next to useless at working with outside intelligence specialists. They see us a threat and are far more interested in protecting their turf than they are in combatting terrorism.

The networking and intelligence work done before, during and after INTELCON led directly to the location of Osama bin Laden's first safe house in Pakistan, which in turn led us to the Abbotabad safe house, as the move between the two was tracked by satellite. If I say that that was not the least successful outcome readers may get an idea why there was heavy interference on INTELCON '06.

Partly due to DVD assets inside CIA (Correa Group at Frankfurt again) there was an inter-agency bust-up. INTELCON split into two for 2006. This was a great shame, as neither conference was able to command the same attendance by spooks and spook shops. Still, some good work was done at the Intelligence Summit, at the same venue, in February 2006. Not everybody believed me when I responded to queries about where I was headed next by saying "oh, just down to Charleston WV for the weekend, then across to Norfolk to fly out to *Enterprise*".

My visit to the USS *Enterprise*

My hosts in Charleston were my good friends Allan Tweddle and Barbara Braun. Allan had been on the board of the Rolls-Royce Owners Club of North America and was a key member of the Rolls-Royce Customer Buy- Out team. Barbara was formerly an actress, although she is as modest as I am (!) and would simply say she had tried to build a career as an actress. She certainly has the beauty and the brains[11] for it.

Allan owned Marcel Dassault's lovely old Rolls-Royce Silver Cloud 11 lwb limousine. She still had the bullet holes in her from when the 'Jerries' had tried to assassinate him (Marcel that is, not Allan), and the West of England cloth insisted upon by Marcel's chauffeur. He was Hindu, worked for British Intelligence and knew how to drive his boss out of an ambush.

The Silver Cloud made a great sight berthed (you don't park a Silver Cloud, not a long wheelbase anyway) right next to RMS *Queen Mary* at Long Beach during the Rolls-Royce battle. (Normally visitors are directed to the car park.) She also seemed to create a good impression on the Los Angeles freeway system, with the Union Flag and Old Glory fluttering from the flag-posts on her front wings, symbols of the close Anglo-American co-operation during the battle to save the old firm from falling into the grasping hands of the 'Hun'. Allan and I also discovered during a visit to the excellent US Naval Academy at Annapolis Maryland that turning up in a gleaming, white Rolls-Royce limousine with the Stars and Stripes fluttering was one way of getting a good berth. Allan also owned a superb Bentley Continental.

Whilst they are by no means unusual, flying visits to nuclear-powered American aircraft carriers by British civilians don't happen every day. This is especially true if the carrier is working up for operational deployment, this case. Although he knew me well enough by now not to dismiss the possibility out of hand, and had heard me ringing those nice people at Hertz to arrange a Chrysler Sebring (Hertz don't do Rolls-Royces) with a pick-up at Yeager[12] and drop-off at Norfolk VA, I am not sure with respect that Allan quite believed it. That was until Naval Air Force Atlantic rang to confirm my reporting time at Norfolk Naval Air Station. The flight out, in a lovely old Grumman C-2A Greyhound COD[13] aircraft, was in the capable hands of a very nice lady pilot from VRC-40, the "Rawhides". Landing on an aircraft carrier is great fun. Not only is the aircraft moving, but the airfield as well. In a long North Atlantic swell in winter, staying lined up to the centreline and on the glidepath required constant adjustment. Close attention was no doubt paid to the FIDO, whose job it is to monitor the approach and give the wave-off, to which a pilot's response must be immediate, as in now.

Turbine engines must be spooled up to full power before impact (touchdown is too soft a word), as the runway on a carrier, even the world's longest,[14] is too short to permit spool-up to Take-Off and Go- Around power if the arrester hook does not engage one of the wires. Our landing was good - third wire, but there was a swell. With the powerful Allison T-56s at full power and a big thud (you don't kiss the deck on a carrier, at least not until after you've landed) it was *not* quiet.

Captain, later Rear-Admiral, 'Lips' Rice is a great carrier commander, CAG was great and *Enterprise* was a fine ship, of which her crew were justifiably proud. I still drink my coffee out of an *Enterprise* mug. In my humble opinion the Obama Administration's decommissioning of her made about as much sense. as transferring the last *Enterprise* (CV-6) to the Imperial Japanese Navy would have done in 1942.

I was made to feel like a VIP throughout, even though I am only an FIP (Fairly Important Person). I thoroughly enjoyed the visit, which wasn't even spoilt by the German U-Boat lurking off our port quarter, although officially she wasn't there. If she was officially there, then she was on her way to a 'show the flag' visit in Wilmington. There was a working breakfast with a very nice admiral, courtesy calls on the ship's impressive Intelligence and Combat Information Centers and some other stuff. She was a wonderful ship.

If landing on a carrier is great fun, taking off is even more so. I am used to getting up out of my seat after take-off, even on Concorde, but not *during* takeoff. The dear old Space Shuttle apparently pulled about 3G on lift-off. In a carrier launch pre-briefing you are told to expect about 3.5. In the Grumman Greyhound the seats, à la RAF Transport Command, of fond memory, face backwards, which is ideal for landing.

On take-off it means that you leave your seat, restrained only by the safety harness, which is why the crew check it before the bird is hooked up to the catapult. It's not an experience for nervous fliers. There's a great commotion of engines being tested, chains rattling (as the catapult is brought back) and the odd bump before take-off, which in our case was behind an F-18.

The McCann Case

The following year saw the tragic kidnap of poor little Madeleine McCann, and 2008 saw her disgraceful murder, as detailed in Chapter 29 and Appendix 8. For understandable reasons the case took over my life for a while. Madeleine was kidnapped on local election night 2007, when I won a seat on Watermead Parish Council. We had a breakthrough on the night I was due to sign my acceptance of office papers, her case took priority and I never got to sign them. This led to a casual vacancy, as in J.K. Rowling's novel, *The Casual Vacancy.* As with the fictional Pagford we on Watermead were trying to establish our identity and break free from the nearby town of Aylesbury. Unlike Pagford however, the church was on the hill in Aylesbury, not Watermead.

I was in touch with J. K.'s office (she was a patron of the excellent British Weights and Measures Association and apparently supported the Metric

Martyrs, which was kind of her). She had been gracious enough to contribute to the reward offer. We never met, however. I am quite sure the fictional church of St Michael in Pagford is not named after me. I've met a couple of saints in my time, but I am *not* saintly.

Her office were pretty unhelpful however, almost to the point of rudeness. They just recycled any enquiry back to Leicestershire Police, the out of their depth rural police force, which never got anywhere near finding poor Madeleine. What was worse they wasted time rubbishing the team, led by me, which did. They went to absurd lengths, denying e.g. that I had been involved in the Pinochet case, even though my visit to the general in the house at Wentworth was logged. They even invented a conversation with a nice Major-General, claiming that he had rubbished me to them. The general stated - and I believed him - that there was never even a conversation. They denied that Leicestershire Police Special Branch had sat in on the briefing I gave them, even though it was recorded and I noted the name of the Special Branch officer. They also put it about that I only had intelligence which was in the public domain, when they were getting calls expressing concern about my level of access and a rather silly e-mail from the Cabinet Office, asking to them to find out where I was getting my satellite imagery from!

The failure to rescue Madeleine demonstrated all too grimly the extent of DVD penetration in London, Washington, Brussels, Canberra, Rabat and elsewhere. It partly inspired the decision to write this book. INTELCOM speaks truth to power but cannot take the decisions.

The years from 2002-2015 were marked by repeated attempts by Germany and Iran to mess with my life, to the point where things became difficult. This private war might justify a book in itself, but I am holding fire, partly for legal reasons and partly because there might be collateral damage to institutions which I respect, like the Bar Council. It's a sensitive area, in part because some of the black hats involved were working with *al Qaeda* and were linked to 7/7 and 21/7. One, using the alias 'Hamid Reza Pardis' (taken out by MI5 in 2024), even met with Abu Musab al-Zarqawi in Turkey. It is by the way a complete coincidence that I chanced to be in the Pentagon in June 2006 when that nice man Gordon England, Deputy Secretary of Defense, went over to the White House to ask for presidential sanction to take al-Zarqawi out.

I warned a Metropolitan Police Special Branch officer, who came to my home on Watermead about midnight on 19/7, that London was one of two cities thought to be about to take a hit on their mass transit system on 21/7.[15] The uncertainty was due to only having a fragment of a three- letter *al Qaeda* city code.[16] My warning was ignored however, partly due to GO2 penetration assets in Thames Valley Police Special Branch and the Met, who ran interference on me. To this day the Met have not apologised to me for ignoring my warning, nor were the public told that the Metropolitan Police were given 36 hours warning of a possible terrorist attack on the London Underground on 21/7.

One of these clowns in GO2 successfully undermined me to Special Branch and SO13 (Counter Terrorism at Scotland Yard) at a crucial moment, achieving GO2's aim of giving *al Qaeda* a clear run. In the events which happened, the terrorists realised that they had been set up, or were suspicious, and only exploded the detonators, not the IEDs. Hence the small explosions on 21/7. If you're on a subway train and *al Qaeda* are riding with you, you only want them to explode the detonators. (You can ignore the Netflix documentary on 7/7 and 21/7 by the way – it's junk.)

Readers in INTELCOM will understand the sensitivities if they access the IMINT backtracking the Nissan Micra the terrorists used to go to Luton railway station to the location in Aylesbury from where they set out, the Riviera Restaurant, as was, run by none other than 'Pardis'. One of the terrorists, Germaine Lindsay, was Aylesbury-based. You can forget fairy stories about them going all the way down the M1 and somehow missing all the cameras on the section between the M1/M6 junction and Luton. You should also be suspicious of purported contemporaneous CCTV footage released several years afterwards. CCTV is easily tampered with, especially digital images.

If you're a British spook you will get an idea of the potential difficulties for officialdom if you access the old NCS (National Crime Squad) corruption files on Thames Valley Police, which went across to the old Serious and Organised Crimes Agency. Some of the files on 7/7 and 21/7 are code-word classified in the States, or classified above Top or Most Secret (in Britain we used to use Most Secret), or at GCHQ at the equivalent of the old *Spoke* classification. The satellite imagery of the Micra should only be at the old GCHQ *Penumbra* equivalent, however. Officially *al Qaeda* have never had inside help, so officially some of the files do not exist, which helps when it comes to fending off Freedom of Information Act requests. There it is.

Of course, I maintain an open house for Special Branch and always offer them a cup of tea. The officer on the 19/7 visit was a bit tense for some reason and seemed to be keeping an eye out for something. It was only a couple of years later that I heard about a silly conspiracy theory, which might have been the explanation, although it may be that someone at the Met had rubbished me to the officer. Possibly he may simply not have liked that nice man Bomber Harris (a couple of bomber prints signed by the great man hung in my living room).

Firearms policy and preferences

The silly conspiracy theory was that I was keeping an assault rifle at home without the necessary permit. Upon enquiry this turned out to be based on more than my known admiration for the products of the excellent Bushmaster Firearms International Company of Windham Maine,[17] in particular their .223 M4 assault rifle, one of which was used by the snipers in the Beltway shootings in 2002. I worked informally on that case, by the way, at the pre-arrest stage, there being a connection via weapon acquisition to an *al Qaeda* cell in the Caribbean.[18]

There was also a visit to a Bushmaster dealer, a subsequent visit to that dealer by a member of the aircrew of a stretched McDonnell Douglas DC-8 freighter, a flight by that freighter to Gatwick Airport and my Bentley being spotted on a back road near Gatwick a couple of days later. (I was on my way to give a speech.) People can get really paranoid sometimes, and leap to the wildest conclusions.

For the avoidance of doubt my policy is one of strict compliance with firearms controls in each jurisdiction in which I happen to be. In my experience firearms are as much a matter of personal preference as objective performance standards. What works well for one shooter may not work well for another, even if their requirements are identical. As I know diddly-squat about firearms my views don't count for all that much, but since I'm asked about them from time to time here they are anyway.

For a sidearm I think highly of the Sig-Sauer P229 semi-automatic, chambered for the Smith & Wesson .40 calibre cartridge, especially the newer model with the laser sight. Some of the boys still hang onto their Colt Python and Ruger .357 Magnum revolvers, preferences acquired in some cases in the field, in Vietnam, where their simplicity, ruggedness and reliability, combined with good stopping power, made them a pro choice. If firepower is the main consideration, even after 56 years the Ruger Blackhawk .44 Magnum is still competitive, especially if you don't mind hitting a low-flying aircraft after the first round. You really need big hands however, as they have a kick like a mule. You can get bigger sidearm cartridges of course, such as the .50 cal., but you're showing off if you pack one of those. In my view, expressed with my usual diffidence, a 'Big Sig' is hard to beat. The FBI like them, the DEA boys don't mind them either and they are less plasticky than Glocks, which also have that fiddly trigger safety. Some people like Glocks of course, especially down at Hereford.

I fully comprehend the arguments in the law enforcement community in favour of 10 mil. semi-autos. For regular shooters 10 mil. is probably a better bet, but for dilettante, occasional shooters like me the lower recoil of the .40 S & W cartridge is preferable. For a back-up weapon you could do a lot worse than Kel-Tec's excellent little P11, chambered for the Parabellum 9 mil. Only 20 ounces loaded - you shouldn't need the optional 12-round magazine - and nice and compact. The boys down in Cocoa, Florida really know how to make a gun.

For the frankly very rare occasion when an assault rifle or sub-machine gun is too bulky and there is a requirement for a short burst of automatic fire, the 9 mil. Beretta Model 93R will look after you if you look after it. You can get a 20-round mag. and the extendable front grip comes in handy.

The Bushmaster M4 is the best assault rifle on the market in my humble opinion - beautifully made and well balanced, you won't go far wrong with a Bushmaster. Optional extras include a grenade launcher, so I gather, although of course there is official hysteria in Britain over grenade launchers coming into private hands. Firearms officers can be a bit sticky about them.

For considerate shooters who do not wish to disturb the neighbours and require a silenced sub-machine gun, the Italian Spectre PCC, normally in 9 mil, is an under-rated weapon in my opinion. The compact, optional 50-round box magazine is a particularly clever feature. It has a good cyclic raid - not as good as the Ingram of course, but likely to get more rounds on target in the same time. At least it has an effective range which is longer than the barrel. There are, not however that many silenced sub- machine guns around which can outperform the dear old British Sterling L34A1. You would be unlikely to wake the neighbours with one of those. Part One has been a short (ish) summary of my life, with a few digressions, intended to give you a rough idea of how I came to know what I do. Parts Two and Three tell you what I know, in so far as I am allowed to say. Readers of a nervous disposition however, or who are one of the stupids, are advised not to plough on, as it will only upset them.

---

1. The fifth Royal Navy warship and the third aircraft carrier (if you discount the second *Ark Royal's* service as a seaplane carrier in World War I) to bear the name, 22,000 tons. Outrageously ordered to be scrapped by the Coalition Government.
2. With apologies to Captain Blackadder.
3. But not CNI, the Spanish internal intelligence agency, who are nice.
4. The manufacturer has gone through the usual succession of silly names but the Kestrel, the forerunner of the Harrier, was designed by the immortal Sir Sydney Camm, designer of the Battle of Britain winning Hurricane. The Harrier is a Hawker aircraft. The Spanish Navy uses the McDonnell-Douglas built version under the name Matador.
5. They add up to 4, just in case a member of the Chilcot Inquiry reads this book (no offence intended).
6. It still comes to 4.
7. The problem with group thinking is that everybody tends to leave it to everybody else to do the thinking - it's a bit like having group organisation of a picnic. Somebody always forgets the sausage rolls.
8. The Battle of Trafalgar, 21st October 1805. The Good Guys (us) won.
9. They were nice people and naturally I warned them that my speech, which was delivered off the cuff, might be a bit controversial. What I should probably have said was that it would be a bit controversial by my standards.
10. Wonderfully played by that fine actor Guy Siner, into whom I chanced to bump, as it happens, in the Garrick Club, and later on, accompanied by dear Henry, on the Severn Valley Railway. For those who are not fans, *'Allo 'Allo* is a very witty series, with sensible observations on the Germans.
11. Acting requires more intelligence than some would have you believe, indeed some of the greatest actors also worked in intelligence - Cary Grant, e.g. The media's patronising view of actors may partly explain their under- estimation of President Reagan.
12. The airport for Charleston, named for the great American pilot Chuck Yeager, first through the sound barrier, in level flight at any rate (there are stories, probably apocryphal, of late model Spits going past Mach 1 in power dives from over 30,000 feet during the war - the Spit had a very aerodynamically efficient wing, and Rolls had a hot version of the Merlin which knocked out 2,700 HP on 150 octane fuel. There were also higher-rated versions of the Griffon than those which made it into service, with advanced contra-props, but you are not advised to try this at home). The Bell X-1 owed more than Yeager or Bell cared to admit to the Miles M-52, cancelled by Germany's Clement Attlee, for fear of the great prestige breaking the sound barrier would bring to Britain. We were only first on film, and a slightly silly film at that, which would have done better to acknowledge Yeager as the first and tell the true story of the pioneering work done by the great Miles Company.
13. Carrier On-Board Delivery.
14. As *Enterprise* people will tell you with pride their ship was the world's longest warship, just shading the shorter *Nimitz* class.

15. The other was Chicago, where it turned out there was an *al Qaeda* presence. Chicago PD are good and someone's nose at the Met was really put out of joint when they put a call through to me, prompted by a very nice retired Special Forces general.
16. *Al Qaeda* have now changed their codes, and have been degraded significantly, so there are fewer constraints on my talking about them. In 2005 *al Qaeda* were still using three-character target codes for cities. They were using the dark web, which a team reporting to me were monitoring.
17. Sadly, as was, as the operation there was closed in 2011.
18. Law enforcement officers working the case would not have known of my involvement, or even of INTELCOM's involvement, since cutouts were used, nor was the *al Qaeda* connection explored in court (the older of the two shooters was very properly executed of course by the Commonwealth of Virginia). The intelligence interest arose because the shooters were working their way around towards a naval facility in the Catoctin Mountains in Maryland. Before anyone in INTELCOM sends a postcard, I got the ultimate target right but the location of the planned shoot wrong. One out of two wasn't too bad however in fact it was probably two out of three, as I had a line on the licence tag. It was one of those cases where a lawyer needed to be in the loop at the intel-gathering stage so as not to foul up the legality of any vehicle search. Sometimes it's much easier to do these things off-campus. It saves on the paperwork and adding to the burdens of busy agency general counsel.

Part Two

GERMAN INTELLIGENCE PRIOR TO 1945

11

The Nineteenth Century

Historical Introduction

Much of the world of secret intelligence remains hidden, at least to historians and the long-suffering public. This may seem an obvious statement. Saying that secret intelligence is secret should be like saying that King Alfred was not a good cook, or that Sir Keir Starmer is not a good Prime Minister, no offence intended, but it isn't. Most historians, politicians and commentators simply cannot grasp that someone living a hundred, let alone a thousand, years ago might have been intelligent, let alone smarter than they are.

As I suggested in the Preface, historians still treat the disgraceful kidnap in 1192 of King Richard the Lionheart, England's greatest king, by Leopold V, Duke of Austria, working on behalf of Phillip II of France, as one of those things. It's as though Leopold's boys woke up one morning, asked themselves "what shall we do today" and one said "I know, why don't we kidnap the King of England"?

The intrigues behind that kidnap, which was sanctioned by Richard's evil younger brother John,[1] an even worse leader than David Cameron, no offence intended, were at least as complex as any modern-day plot. John had secretly agreed to be King Phillip II of France's vassal, with Vatican backing. King Richard's eventual assassination, arranged by the French, may have given them temporary ascendancy over England but it led to the great revolt of the Barons, Magna Carta and centuries of bitterness between England and France. This culminated in the Hundred Years War, during which we gave them a good thrashing at Agincourt.

King Richard's principal intelligence officer was later immortalised by Sir Walter Scott as Sir Wilfred of Ivanhoe, in his famous Waverley novel *Ivanhoe*. He wasn't called Ivanhoe, but that there was such a knight, or more likely several knights of which the fictional Sir Ivanhoe was a composite, is not in doubt. Like Field Marshal Erwin Rommel in World War II, the

Lionheart's justified reputation as a military genius owes much to the good intelligence he received. Unsuccessful military commanders often have good intelligence officers as well. The difference is that they don't listen to them.

When the Bad Guys started the rumour going that good King Richard had died in captivity in Europe (it is remarkable how quickly silly rumours can spread - just look at man-made global warming) it was a courageous intelligence officer, a knight of course, who got back to England and brought the people the joyous news that King Richard lived. The intelligence background to the Crusades - such as Richard's discovery of the origins of Islam[2] - resonates today in the Global War on Terror. Indeed, the Saudis still keep that particular snippet under close wraps.

Saladin, the 11th century's answer to Osama bin Laden, had his intelligence advisers as well, probably including some from the Vatican. Vatican theologians had written the Koran[3] and set up Islam, for geopolitical reasons. The multiple authorship of the book, by the way, explains why the earlier chapters cannot readily be reconciled with the later. Forensic linguistic analysis is an important intelligence tool.

Following the money trail ("always follow the money", as 'Mr T' once cautioned me) for Islam's invasion of the Holy Land throws up some interesting eastern connections as well, as did the Persian invasions in the time of Darius and Xerxes. Invasions have to be bankrolled, even if you're saving money on troops by using religious zealots as cannon fodder. The trails from China to Persia are ancient and are not all about trade. Genghis Khan was just one invader who did his banking east of the Great Wall of China, and not with HSBC either.

The Holy Crusades have a political resonance a millennium later, to judge from the Islamic and left-wing overreaction to President George W. Bush's well-judged description of the Global War on Terror as a "crusade", which it was. Good Guys against Bad Guys, just as in the good old days. It would have been more stylish to have-called it, "The Tenth Crusade", but that might have led to more letters to the newspapers. It was never a war on a concept by the way, more an intelligent recognition, based on sound advice, that terrorism is a state sponsored phenomenon. The only way to defeat it is to defeat the states that sponsor it.

Richard the Lionheart was not the first King of England to have had access to good intelligence advice. One of England's most successful intelligence officers, and the only one to date to have been elected Pope, was Joan. She penetrated the Vatican all the way to the top. They were so stung by that one that the French transvestite, who finally swung the Hundred Years War France's way, before being burnt at the stake by our gallant allies the Burgundians, took her name.

That episode by the way demonstrated the perils of disguising yourself as a woman. A chap could not be convicted of witchcraft. To this day, as portrayed, rather well I thought, in the excellent television mini-series *The Borgias*, the Vatican still check that the chap they've elected Pope is actually a chap, i.e. has the necessary wobbly bits.

If accused of turning history upside down I would simply respond by saying that I'm putting it back the right way up. I'm not rewriting history, just correcting a few errors that have crept in along the way. The intelligence structures of most powerful states are never as advertised - it stands to reason that the most effective intelligence agency is one whose very existence is a secret. That has been the key to the DVD's success, although thankfully it was so successful that it eventually overreached itself and went three steps too far by backing Germany's grab for Rolls- Royce and attacking in turn New York and London.

There is no shortage of historical precedents for going too far. Attila the Hun overreached himself by crossing the Rhine and invading first Gaul and then Rome. Islam overreached itself by invading the Holy Land, backing the Holocaust and allowing itself to be used as the cover for the attacks on New York and London. Attila's successor as leader of the 'Huns', Adolf Hitler, overreached himself by trying to conquer Russia, which only served to annoy the Russians. One of Hitler's successors as leader of the 'Huns', Helmut Kohl, who reported to the DVD, overreached himself by pushing the Treaty of Maastricht and triggering the Balkan Wars of the 1990s. At least by arranging to kill a few hundred thousand Europeans he helped the EU to win the Nobel Peace Prize.

The German Empire

With the German Empire it was not so much a question of the state being created and then establishing internal and external intelligence services, as the intelligence services creating the state. Germany is and always has been an intelligence state. The Second, Third and Fourth Reichs, counting the Federal Republic of Germany as the Fourth, have always been controlled by intelligence agencies, usually covert, like the DVD. Ironically, they came more out into the open during the Third Reich. In many ways the Third was the most transparent of all the Reichs. Adolf Hitler, on one view, was one of the more honest German Chancellors, albeit not necessarily the nicest. (At least he was nicer than Helmut Kohl.)

The DVD's origins go back to at least the 1830s and probably 50 years beyond, when one considers the secret societies associated with it such as the Illuminati, founded by Adam Weishaupt in Bavaria in 1776. There have been reorganisations and splits but there has also been continuity.

The Illuminati are nothing to do with lizards, unless the odd member happens to collect them. It is a dangerous secret society, but it has always acted as a front for more powerful interests behind it, these days the DVD. Bad Guy spook shops love secret societies. They provide great cover. What journalist, having penetrated a secret society, would think of moving down to the next layer? The rituals are a marvellous excuse to persuade men (it's usually men, although there are a lot of women in Common Purpose in Britain, which doesn't do rituals) to get their kit off, providing plenty of opportunities to acquire blackmail material.

This does not apply of course to nice secret societies like the Freemasons, who are (usually) the Good Guys, although you can get German Masons. Erwin Rommel was one, and quite a senior one too, 33^0. The secret societies at British and American universities tend to be fronts for German Intelligence, who are usually good at spotting young men and women with leadership potential, identifying weaknesses of character, and dividing them into those who can be blackmailed and those who cannot.

They then try to block the careers of the latter. Margaret Thatcher, e.g., encountered constant interference, both when she was searching for a seat and after she joined the government. The rituals have usually given the Bad Guys a good guide as to who is gay and who isn't, who likes having their bottom smacked, and so on.

The First, Prussian, Reich was a rather more liberal state than many might suppose and was on the right, i.e. British, side in the Napoleonic Wars. The formidable Marshal Blücher, not a military commander who ignored intelligence advice, made a vital contribution to the defeat of Napoleon. Bonaparte was of course a Bad Guy indeed these days he would have been a supporter of the EU. The German Empire, which collapsed in 1918, was the Second Reich. Everybody knows about the Third. The decision not to name the Federal Republic of Germany the Fourth Reich, for presentational reasons, was probably the right one.

Bismarck's Spymasters

The key Prussian spymasters were Karl von Hinckeldey and Wilhelm Stieber, who made Bismarck look better than he was. Their methods, including assassination, penetration of potential enemies and sabotage, are still used by the DVD. The assassination of President Kennedy, dealt with in Chapter 23, was straight out of the Prussian Secret Service's playbook. They set up the most serious of the assassination attempts on Queen Victoria, the first coming after HRH Prince Albert went over to Britain. They also knocked off Prime Minister Peel's Private Secretary,[4] set up the Liberal Party to control British policy and hold back the development of the British Empire (an operation which was largely successful) and ran at least six brothels, in Oxford, Cambridge and London.

The Whigs had always been largely anti-British. Lord Palmerston was that rare bird, a sensible and patriotic Whig, with sound views on gunboats. The formation of the Liberal Party marked a changeover in Whiggery from French (and, earlier, Spanish, that nasty piece of work Sir Horace Walpole having been on the Spanish payroll) to German sponsorship. After Palmerston it was a rare leader of the Liberal Party who did not report to the 'Hun', Sir David Campbell-Bannerman being the only non-German asset in charge of the Liberal Party between Palmerston and Grimond. Even the latter had decidedly dodgy views on the EEC, of which Lord Palmerston, a great statesman, would not have approved.

The reason there were six brothels rather than three is because Stieber ran male brothels as well. "Brothel" is perhaps the wrong word, since the aspiring young men Germany was seeking to recruit were not paying customers. Since students are usually young it follows that the Germans were recruiting quite young men and women to provide the sexual services.

Key German academic assets such as Professor Arnold Toynbee, later a notorious supporter of the League of Nations, helped with the recruitment, no doubt identifying the type of establishment to which the young men should be steered. Having friends on faculty no doubt helped come exam time. There was no shortage of cash to make undergraduate life easier for the chosen few, most of whom repaid Germany handsomely, sometimes with British lives, once safely ensconced in office.

Brothels and honeytraps were also used in Germany and Washington. The strategy is used by the Bad Guys to this day. The Good Guys use honeytraps as well, for visiting bankers and so on, but it is a dangerous tactic, which can blow up in your face if you are not careful. It necessarily involves corruption of the young, indeed the KGB, who learnt the tactic from the Cheka, who learnt it from the Germans, who set up the Cheka, famously had schools for women, and men, engaged in this line of intelligence work. The Czech StB were also very good at it, recruiting at least one future British Prime Minister.

In the 20th century blackmail techniques came to involve covert recording. Germany wasn't the world leader in developing audio and video tape technology for nothing. In the 19th century they used photography, both overt and covert, the more compromising positions being reserved for the latter, and letters.

The Prussian/German operations, not being commercial brothels, although they may have taken in paying punters to meet running costs, were not quick 'in and out' affairs with someone knocking on the bedroom door and saying, "your half hour is up". The young men and women were encouraged to build relationships with the people they were entrapping. If German (in those days there were no immigration controls - they did not come in until 1905 and even then were extremely lax, not applying to first class passengers) they would be fluent in English. They were instructed to write to their targets, as love letters make excellent blackmail material, if you're foolish enough to go in for blackmail in the first place. The perils for intelligence agencies of blackmailing politicians are nowhere better demonstrated by the case of 'Jack the Ripper.'

The Ripper Affair

You have to protect your assets from exposure, all the more difficult if like William Ewart Gladstone your asset is out on the town on his own account, i.e. not just using your prostitutes. Gladstone was a sexual predator of the worst sort, whose proclivities were, shall we say, a trifle exotic for Mrs Gladstone. The Liberals and their German backers put it about that Gladstone was a 'humanitarian', whose interest in 'fallen' women was not remotely sexual.

Not only was his interest sexual, it was violent. The Home Secretary of the day, a Tory but a dodgy one (the German Secret Service had their claws into the Tory Party as well, which is why naval and military expenditure was so low, sensible measures to defeat cholera faced constant frustration, etc.) had to cover up repeated incidents of bleeding women being found on the streets or taken to hospital. At least two of these unfortunates appear to have died.

Just how odious a business blackmail can be was dramatically revealed in Durward Street, East London on the stormy night of 30th and 31st August 1888. Whilst one team of German agents started distraction fires in the London Docks, another team, effectively a death squad, accompanied by a German military surgeon, murdered and savagely mutilated a common prostitute, Mary Ann (Polly) Nichols. She had serviced Gladstone, then Leader of the Opposition.

An alcoholic, chronically short of cash, poor Polly apparently made the mistake of going to Fleet Street, in the hope of selling her story. It is also possible that she was friends with one of the working girls penetrated so violently by Gladstone that she bled to death. Sadly, he was not the sort of man to send for a doctor, indeed he just left the helpless women to die in alleyways or yards. The idea that he was interested in the welfare of prostitutes is as silly as the idea that he was interested in the welfare of ordinary working men and women. So far to the contrary, he was a keen proponent of driving up unemployment by lowering tariff barriers against predatory German imports.

Tragically, Polly was fatally unaware that Gladstone was at that time the highest-ranking political penetration asset of the Imperial German Secret Service in the British Empire. He had secretly backed the German-sponsored Mahdist Revolt in the Sudan, sold Major-General 'Chinese' Gordon down the Nile River as far as the delta and exported hundreds of thousands of British jobs to Germany, a policy he first supported as a member of Peel's government. That government had repealed the so-called 'Corn Laws', favouring European agrarian interests over British, under the guise of cheaper food. Sadly, Polly was also unaware that German influence on Fleet Street was even greater then than it is now.

It did not take long for the German Head of Station in London to become aware that their man Gladstone was threatened by a story that would not only destroy his career but most likely take the pro-German Liberal Party down with it. Not content with murdering poor Polly Nichols the Germans went on to murder at least four other working women, Annie Chapman, Elizabeth Stride, Catherine Eddowes and Mary Jane Kelly.

They were not the only sex workers murdered in 1888/9, i.e. there may have been more murders by the German death squads. Each was mutilated, with some skill, by a military surgeon. The murders were intended as a warning to the many women who had serviced Gladstone, whose sexual appetite was enormous, not to go to either the police or the press.

They have come to be known as the Ripper Murders. The police and the press, not to mention a veritable industry of 'Jack the Ripper' books and TV films in the century and a third since, have fallen into what Professor Stephen Law[5] calls an 'Intellectual Black Hole'. This is an opinion not supported by the facts, from which their limited powers of reasoning permitted no escape, rather like a spaceship in a Disney science- fiction movie.

They treated the atrocities as an ordinary, as opposed to state- sponsored, crime, committed by a single deranged criminal without a motive. Rape has never seriously been suggested as the motive. This criminal is supposed to have suddenly decided to go about mutilating and murdering prostitutes in the East End, having never done such a thing before. The Intellectual Black Hole guaranteed that the crimes would not be solved. They were in fact committed by a rogue state, i.e. Germany, for a political motive.

Had Whitehall wanted the murders solved the investigation would never have been left in the hands of the police of course, rather like the kidnap and murder of poor Madeleine McCann 120 years later. The episode is illustrative of the extent to which the Gladstone and Salisbury Governments wanted to help Germany. The idea that they were governing Britain in the

British interest and the British Empire in the interests of its inhabitants is simply silly. The only serious British politician in this period was the great Randolph Churchill, who was assassinated by the German Secret Service.[6]

At a time of an emerging threat to Imperial security from Germany, Britain, the world's greatest power, had no official internal or external intelligence service. German assets in Whitehall also made sure that military and naval intelligence were starved of funds. For much of this period the Empire was effectively blind, stumbling from one military disaster to another. Then, as now, the best intelligence work was done out of Whitehall.

Clearly any well-governed state, confronted with a series of grisly murders alarming the public and damaging its national prestige, would assign the investigation to its principal internal intelligence service. The Metropolitan Police Special Branch had been set up in 1883 to deal with the German-sponsored Fenians, but it was essentially a 'two man and a dog' operation.

They never even worked out who was sponsoring the Fenians (perhaps they thought it was the Belgians), let alone a method of dealing with them. The investigation into 'Jack', as the press dubbed him (Fleet Street was no brighter then than it is today and pulling the wool over its eyes was child's play for the 'wily Hun'), wasn't even handed over to this primitive intelligence service. It was so weak that it couldn't protect itself, let alone the Met, from German penetration.

The farcical police investigation into the 'Ripper' murders was brilliantly parodied by the late Ronnie Corbett and Ronnie Barker (*The Two Ronnies* - their show was so good that it was cancelled by the BBC, much to their disgust) in a six-part mock serial in Series 1, *The Phantom Raspberry Blower of Old London Town*. It's a pity that the Metropolitan Police in 1888 didn't have anyone as bright as Ronnie Barker on the strength.

Perhaps I should explain that whilst the Met has always had a minimum height requirement it has never had a minimum intelligence requirement, although the problem was cured to some extent when policewomen started to be recruited in numbers. In fairness, the Met did experiment with having a highly intelligent senior officer, with the appointment of Sir David Veness QPM. The integration of intelligent leadership into a non-intelligence led force was always going to problematic, however. The experiment has never been repeated.

In the years since, numerous candidates for 'Jack' (who did not of course exist) have been suggested by the Ripper industry, even a member of the Royal Family. Perhaps we should be grateful that they left out dear old Queen Victoria, as likely a candidate as some who have been mentioned. The intellectual gymnastics indulged in to try and fit the facts to the lone killer theory have been quite impressive. Proponents of the lone killer theory not only have to explain how the same man can have been in two places at once but also how a single man could have carried out the murders.

You are not advised to try this at home, but should you try to disembowel somebody alive, whilst they are fully conscious, without anaesthetic, you will find that they tend to kick up a fuss. None of the victims were found tied up, nor was there any evidence of ligatures having been applied. It would have taken at least two strong men to hold the poor women down and gag them. People tend to scream whilst they are being disembowelled, which can attract the attention of bystanders.

Anyone who thinks that Germans would not be capable of such brutality is advised to revisit the hideous medical experiments conducted at *inter alia* Dachau Concentration Camp. Sadly, German medicine is not always about making people well, rather about finding new ways of making them die horribly. Poor Hugh Gaitskell found this out in 1963 when he was assassinated with a bioweapon developed at Dachau.

It is not my intention, by the way, to undermine all fairy tales. We are still left with *Alice in Wonderland*, the Dracula stories, Hans Christian Andersen's wonderful tales, *Winnie the Pooh*, Harry Potter and the Liberal Democrats' last election manifesto. My point is that it should not be the function of the police, nor the media, to fall for fairy tales when investigating, or reporting on, a series of murders. Fairy tales are essentially for children. Grown-ups, at least periodically, ought to act and think like grown-ups. The lone killer theory for the 'Ripper' murders is and always has been Alice in Wonderland nonsense.

Other German Assets

Gladstone was not the only high-ranking German political asset of course. Sir William Harcourt, the Chancellor of the Exchequer who notoriously introduced death duties, was another. Death duties were aimed at the aristocracy. They were a classic German decapitation tactic (carried to extremes at Katyn), which caused much social and familial disruption and distress, without raising much if any net revenue. They are expensive to collect and if anything had a negative impact on GDP. Onerous taxation is about bringing people and economies down, not raising revenue, as the great American economist Arthur Laffer demonstrated.

The Germans did not limit themselves to recruiting current or future politicians. Lord Hankey[7], known in the trade, for obvious reasons, since he was a paedophile, as 'Hankey Panky', was their most successful ever Whitehall asset. He eventually became Cabinet Secretary. Indeed, the

Cabinet Office was created for him, by another German asset, David Lloyd George. Britain was still suffering from Hankey's protégés as late as the 1960s.

Other Myths

Supermen able to hold women down single-handed and remove their internal organs at the same time were not the only enduring myths to emerge from the Victoria era. It is right that I should emphasise that I am not encouraging Jamie and his able *Mythbusters* colleagues, should they bring it back, to find a couple of volunteers willing to allow themselves to be disembowelled single-handedly to test the myth.

The Zulus single-handedly defeating the British Army at Isandlwana is another. They were of course advised by German military and intelligence advisers, as indeed was General Robert E. Lee, which helps explain why he suddenly became a great military commander, showing a brilliance which with respect had not always been apparent in his earlier military career. The South's key strategic adviser was none other than Field Marshal Helmuth von Moltke, of course, although he left that bit off his resume.

Well over a century later the identities of King Cetswayo's German intelligence advisers were such a sensitive secret that the DVD asked the South African National Intelligence Agency to assassinate a British historian, fluent in Zulu. MI6 are of course a bit short of Zulu speakers ("anyone here speak Zulu?" "No, but I've seen the film"). He was David Rattray and he was researching Germany's involvement in the Zulu Wars.

As indicated in the Preface the 'robbers' thankfully missed the backup memory sticks (jolly useful devices, memory sticks). In case you were wondering how much intelligence you can download onto the memory sticks you can't buy in the shops it was over 1TB by 2010. It's now over 4TB. That's a big memory stick.

Covert German activity was not confined to Africa. The Muslim troublemakers who incited the Indian Mutiny, e.g., had deep links to the Prussian Secret Service. Red Indians were another popular German ally and an enduring source of myths. The 'Hun' picked up on the tactic of using native allies, which was first tried on a large scale in Canada in the Seven Years War.

General Custer contributed to his own defeat at Little Big Horn but he wasn't just up against Chief Crazy Horse, whose previous combat experience had largely been with buffalo. The guns were largely infiltrated via Mexico (*plus ça change*), an important German station from the 1870s. Bismarck, correctly, saw America as a strategic competitor, although he never grasped that the Americans, being the Good Guys (they were formerly British after all), and a democracy, would never use aggressive war to further their ends, nor have they. The Spanish-American War is included in that observation. That war was started, insanely, by Spain, by blowing up the USS *Maine*.

The American Civil War

The strategy of using Indians to try and stop America's march west (it is remarkable how many Indian attacks were directed against lines of communication, such as stagecoaches and railways) replaced the failed strategy of trying to divide America into two, a.k.a. the Civil War. The South followed the classic Prussian pattern of short, carefully planned and prepared wars against ill-prepared opposition, the 1864 invasion of Denmark, where the 'Hun' seized Schleswig-Holstein,[8] being the classic example.

This time it blew up in their faces, as the invasion of Denmark would have done had the Prussians not had so many assets in London. Clearly Britain should have gone to the aid of Denmark, in pursuit of her traditional foreign policy objectives of upholding the rights of small nations and the Rule of Law, and preventing the domination of the Continent by a single aggressor.

Historians tend to treat Jefferson Davis, President of the Confederacy, as a complete idiot, indeed they tend to treat most people as idiots, including their readers. Clearly, he wasn't and equally clearly he did not start a war (historians will have you believe he started it accidentally, as though he were a drunk driver) against a much stronger opponent without first securing the covert backing of a great power. In this case it was one with the world's most powerful intelligence service, and moreover one with assets in place in Washington. The South would have preferred overt backing from Britain, which given the strength of the Royal Navy would probably have meant no war at all, but we very properly declined to intervene in America's internal affairs.

The British objection to slavery was as real as the Union's. Not content with being the first country to abolish it (only in the colonies of course – slavery was never legal in Britain itself[9]) the Royal Navy spent much of the 19th century suppressing the odious and inhuman trade. President Lincoln was both aware of and appreciative of the British rejection of the approaches from the South, both prior to the war and towards its end. In 1865 Southern blockade-runners carried messages to London and Paris, seeking intermediaries, in a despairing effort to reach a deal. The blockade-runners were of course primarily intelligence ships, mobile phones in those days being non-existent.

The Lincoln Assassination

The Prussians hated losing, and also wanted to drive a wedge through the newly re-united country. One of their agents, John Wilkes Booth, assassinated President Abraham Lincoln in the Ford Theater in Washington. Prussian assets in Washington first made sure that the President's security was compromised, not for the last time. In a neat historical allegory, just under 100 years later, the Prussian Secret Service's successor agency, the DVD, assassinated President Lincoln's successor, President Kennedy, in a Lincoln, in the South. His Secret Service protection too was pulled, although happily the DVD were less successful when they tried to assassinate President Ford.[10]

Marx

Ideas are a more powerful weapon than bullets. Unfortunately, this holds true for bad ideas as well as good ones. The Germans have always understood this. Their most successful agent of influence, Karl Marx (who had meetings with Stieber in London - as Stieber was leaning on Sir Robert Peel, he had the Home Office covered and could come and go from Britain at will) caused over a century of chaos. A whole bogus ideology was named after him.

No other spy in history has ever inflicted so much damage on his nation's enemies, nor, when one thinks of the havoc wreaked in Germany after World War I by the communists and the disaster which was East Germany, so much collateral damage on his own. Engels, the bagman, also worked for Stieber of course. It is a charming thought that the Home Office permitted houseroom to Marx and Engels because they believed in free speech. The reality is that someone senior was taking his orders from Berlin. The Home Office are not wholly committed to freedom of speech even now.

The Germans did not confine their interference in internal affairs to Britain and the United States. They are wholly opposed to self-government and cannot abide the thought of any country actually being allowed to govern itself, one of the drivers of the EU. They did terrible damage to Russia also, using the same strategies - assassination, trying to get their people into the Royal Family by marriage and adapting Marx's bogus ideology to a largely agrarian society.

Marxist historians have tied themselves in knots trying to explain the adaptation of Marxism to a largely non-industrial society. The answer of course is that the books were a nonsense anyway and simply a means to an end for the state which paid for them. When Germany turned her attention eastwards it was a simple matter to adapt the ideology to Russia. There were no anarchists as such, not real ones anyway. As with all terrorist groups they were simply a cover for the sponsoring state. The great Tsar Alexander III was assassinated on German orders. His successor, the weak Tsar Nicholas II, was inveigled into marrying a German asset, nearly lost his throne to a German-sponsored revolt in 1905 and succeeded in losing it in 1917. He and his family, the Tsarina included, were brutally mass-murdered the following year, again on German orders, Lenin being one of theirs. German Intelligence has always been willing to sacrifice its own people in order to cover its tracks, as Osama bin Laden found out to his cost in 2009. The 'Hun' does not hand out tickets on 'sealed' trains just because you've rolled up to the booking office and asked nicely. (The train wasn't that sealed – Lenin could get on and off.)

Russia was also weakened by war with a German proxy, as were Britain (the Zulu and Boer Wars) and the USA (the American Civil War). The proxy in Russia's case was Japan. Japanese battleships were built in Britain in a strategy supported by German assets in the Tory and Liberal Parties, including of course Asquith and Lloyd George.

The pro-Japanese strategy reached its apogee in 1942 with the surrender of Singapore. That military disaster, Britain's greatest ever, was decades in the planning, including not just technology transfer to Japan but a deliberate weakening of the Royal Navy and the defences of Singapore. The Japanese alliance in World War I with Britain, France and Russia was a phoney.

Economic disruption

Stirring up discontent in the working class, propagating fake ideologies and forcing down tariff barriers against predatory German imports were not the only means used to undermine the British economy, and with it her ability to defend herself and her Empire, in the 19th century. The Bank of England was a prime target for penetration, easily achieved given German control of the Treasury through assets such as Gladstone and Harcourt. These people liked to portray Britain's relative economic decline in relation to Germany as an inevitable process at the same time as they were promoting it.

A similar process is at work in Washington today, as pro-Peking politicians seek to build the Chinese economy by lowering tariff walls, a process now being reversed by President Trump. Control of the Bank of England allowed control of interest rates, helping Germany to force Britain into recession in the 1890s, following a deep agricultural recession. The recession strategy was assisted by the lowering of tariff barriers, once again in the name of cheap food. Low-cost food is not much good to you if you've been forced off the land and into the workhouse, another German innovation by the way. It was firmly backed by the Liberal Party and promoted by a sadistic crank who should not have been allowed anywhere near policy formulation.

Sometime in the last quarter of the 19th century the German central bank diverged the German economy into onshore and 'offshore', using Switzerland. The Swiss Federation increasingly became a German client state. The Germans set up a rigged market in financial instruments, usually Medium Term Notes, rigged in the sense that the first or primary purchase, always off the bank's books, is not made until an exit had been secured. You do not commit to a buy ticket until your sell ticket is in place.

The purchasers were usually British or American banks or financial institutions, which were able to buy for less than face value and thought they were getting a good deal. What they did not know and were not told was that both the bank and the seller were leveraging their initial commitment, secure in the knowledge that no trade would be entered into without an exit. In some cases the banks, whilst nominally British or American, were under the control of German assets such as J. P. Morgan. As we shall see in Chapter 13, he got into the mass-murder business in 1912, not that it did him much good. He died horribly a few years later, a physical and mental wreck, sadly not soon enough.

Moving the money offshore was simplicity itself. You just blocked the funds in one account and a Swiss bank, for a fee of course, extended a line of credit against it. There is no such thing as a free lunch however. Both Britain and America suffered from an uncontrolled increase in the money supply, with resultant inflation, a situation that continues to the present day. Unfortunately, as some of the principal German bankers, such as their branch of the Rothschild family (there are also nice Rothschilds of course, i.e. British ones), were nominally Jewish, the antics of German banks helped generate anti-Semitism in the West.

The Germans have always made good use of their Jewish assets, ditto the Prussians before them. One of the best Prussian agents in Warsaw in the 19th century was an interesting chap, Abraham Miliband. His direct descendant eventually led the Labour Party. Unusually, some might say, for a Labour leader, he was not a German spy, unlike Keir Hardie, Ramsay MacDonald, George ('let's disarm and give Hitler a clear run') Lansbury, Clement Attlee and Harold Wilson before him. Ed Miliband's grandfather Samuel[11] and father Ralph both worked for Germany however, the latter being infiltrated as a 'refugee' in 1940.

Being Jewish was wonderful cover for the Abwehr whilst Germany was conducting a pogrom against the Jews - none better in fact, as you could always claim to be fleeing Nazi persecution. No one ever checked with the Nazis to see if they were persecuting such and such an asylum-seeker. In retrospect it is odd that Ralph Miliband was not spotted by MI5 before his death in 1994. He was far too intelligent to be a Marxist, which had to be a legend, intel-speak for cover story. You can either be intelligent, or you can be a Marxist – you can't be both. Ralph Miliband was no more a Marxist than Karl Marx, or Fidel Castro if it comes to that.

---

1. These days He would be a single currency supporter. He is rightly reviled as England's worst ever king, despite the best efforts of revisionist historians to portray Richard as some sort of Frenchman and gay, although why that should make Him a bad king they do not say (He was probably bisexual anyway), and John as some sort of hero.
2. It was created by the Vatican and tailored to cater for the Arab tribes in what is now Saudi Arabia.
3. It's just as well that I haven't appeared on *Who Wants To Be A Millionaire*, a classic illustration by the way of how suspects can collapse under interrogation. The question in one show was 'in what language was the Koran first written?' and Latin was included with Arabic as one of the answers. Latin was the correct answer. Arabic is only officially correct. Islamic theology holds that the Koran was first written in Arabic and dictated by God, which it cannot have been of course, as it wasn't dictated in English.
4. Drummond. The Prussian agent involved was a Scot, Daniel M'Naghten. The case led to the famous M'Naghten Rules on insanity that have stood the test of time. Unsurprisingly, M'Naghten had heavy-duty Liberal Establishment representation at his trial. Drummond's assassination was linked to Prussian pressure on Peel, whom Queen Victoria disliked, for good reason.
5. *Believing Bullshit*. The examples of pseudo-profundity are classic - the pseudo-intellectuals quoted should be drafting global warming reports for the IPCC. Rather than quote them I would prefer to increase the Professor's sales by encouraging readers to buy his excellent book.
6. The old mistress with asymptomatic syphilis trick, first used by the Vatican to commit regicide against King Henry VIII. An old favourite, it allows you to both humiliate your victim and make sure he dies a lingering death. If he is having sexual relations with his wife (Lord Randolph wasn't, fortunately for her) you get the wife as well. Discussing the matter with Randolph's great- grandson, the late Winston Spencer Churchill, it seems that Randolph's son, Sir Winston, a titan, was unaware that Germany had brutally murdered his beloved father. Thankfully for Christendom and the Empire Sir Winston survived all three German-sponsored assassination attempts on his life and went on to avenge the murder of his father, even if unknowingly. The younger Winston Churchill, Sir Winston's favourite grandson, sadly died of cancer in 2010, after a long and brave fight.
7. A. J. P. Taylor, the greatest British historian of the 20th century, grasped the importance of Hankey (see e.g. his seminal *English History 1914-45*) and probably knew he was a German asset, not that he could ever have got that it into print. At least, not if he wanted to remain an Oxford don.
8. They still haven't given it back. Control of Schleswig-Holstein was critical for the Prussian and in turn German Navies, because it allowed a canal to be built (the Kiel Canal) linking the Baltic and the North Sea, thus avoiding the Skaggerak and the Kattegat, which are easily mined and can be dominated by shore batteries.
9. Hence the famous *Somersett Case* in 1789, where Lord Mansfield, a serious judge (he was Scottish) issued a Writ of *Habeas Corpus* in favour of an escaped slave.

Slavery is contrary to common law and in theory any slave held in England was entitled to a Writ of Habeas Corpus. Trading in slaves through British ports was outlawed in 1833. Since slavery was never legal in England it is a nonsense to talk of it having been abolished.

10. On 5th and 22nd September 1975. It is noticeable in the first attempt that Lynette 'Squeaky' Fromme appears to have ejected a .45 cal. round from the chamber of her weapon, i.e. there is a serious argument as to her actual intent. Nervous after the official explanation (i.e. the Warren Commission's lone gunman theory) of the Kennedy Assassination had been treated with justifiable derision by the American public (although you still find it trotted out with a straight face by CBS, ABC, NBC and CNN) the DVD, thankfully, made the mistake of staying too deep in the background. Fromme cannot have known for whom she was working and seems to have had no clear idea of why she was trying to assassinate poor old President Ford, who was harmless enough. Indeed, she does not seem to have had any actual intent to shoot the President. She was however linked to a known DVD asset named Charles Manson, another one of their tame psychopaths. In fairness to them, the DVD officers planning the Ford assassination had to contend with political infighting in their own agency as Canaris's powers waned. Vice-President Nelson Rockefeller, whom the controlling faction in the DVD were trying to install, was opposed by another powerful faction. Ironically, they later took control and had Rockefeller assassinated (the old 'fix him up with a woman and make it look like he had a heart attack on the job' trick, although again the nice lady involved may not have known for whom she was working). Fromme is by no means a sympathetic character but the time she served was probably disproportionate to the actual degree of criminality she showed. From the counterintelligence perspective it might have been better to try and get her to cooperate by offering a greatly reduced sentence, as she was in a position to supply valuable intelligence on Manson, although she would not have wished to harm him. She was a seriously confused young woman with respect, but not intrinsically evil. I am inclined to believe her statement that she wrestled with her conscience before setting out from her home on 5th September, decided that she would not carry out the instruction to shoot the President and ejected the round deliberately. On the Colt M1911A1 this requires a positive action on the part of the weapon handler. I am glad that she has been released and hope that she can now find some peace. It is a cardinal principle of counterintelligence in a democracy that you must act fairly and defensibly, and a basic rule of counterintelligence anywhere that you work upwards from those who are left to carry the can to those controlling them, taking a merciful view if need be.
11. A rare photograph of Samuel (and his brother David, who also worked for the Abwehr), taken somewhere in Europe, appeared in the London *Sunday Telegraph* on 11th October 2009, page 34. By then Ralph's cover had been blown and there was increasing intelligence interest in the Miliband family. The name 'Miliband' appears to have been a fake ID, originally used by Abraham Miliband - which is you why won't see a lot of names in the Miliband section of the phone book. When he was Foreign Secretary (a disastrous one with respect, favouring

the EU at every turn) David Miliband, amusingly, was known in the State Department as the 'Man With No Name'. By then the Bureau of Intelligence and Research paper file was starting to get a bit thick, and the electronic files were multilayered, with high-level clearances needed to get to the really interesting bits. In the leadership election following Labour's defeat in 2010, the Labour Party essentially had a choice between "smart Miliband" and "nice Miliband", no offence intended to either. NOT being a nasty party, then, they chose the nice one, which was the smart move. Nice party leaders can always bring in smart advisers. You can always add smart, but you cannot add nice.

12

1900 - 1912

The McKinley Assassination

German influence in Washington was increased after they arranged for the assassination of President McKinley, the 25th President and a highly intelligent one, on 5th September 1901. The poor man was deprived of adequate medical treatment and lingered for nine days. At the time Britain was tied up in a full-scale war against the German-backed Boers in South Africa.

Both Britain and America made the same mistake. We failed to recognise that we were up against a common enemy, which was prepared to violate international law at will and showed precious little regard for international norms. The 'Hun' also had an utter disregard for the democratic will of the electorates in the Western democracies, indeed still does. The German Empire of course was no more democratic than the Federal Republic of Germany or the EU.

Sponsoring emigration has been a standard German tactic since the middle of the 19th century, initially of Germans, then of German allies, such as the Italians or Japanese, or more latterly, Muslims. By 1900 there were enough Germans in America for the German Secret Service to make its move and stage what was effectively a coup in Washington, the ultimate intent being to catch the Royal Navy in a pincer movement. As late as the 1920s the United States had a war plan for war with the British Empire. The Great White Fleet of 1907-9 was *inter alia* an intelligence- gathering exercise, including on British ports. Napoleon had a similar strategy. His secret service, working closely with the Vatican, persuaded Congress to invade Canada and open up a new front in the Napoleonic Wars in 1812.[1]

It is still unclear what deal if any was cut with Vice-President Theodore Roosevelt, the immediate political beneficiary of McKinley's disgraceful assassination. There is usually a deal with the Vice-President before the

Germans shoot the President. If there was, it may have been along the lines of the deal Benjamin Franklin cut with the French in exchange for bankrolling the American Revolution.

You will have to ask the French whether they told Ben Franklin that they were paying British politicians to stir up anti-British sentiment in America, including passing the ridiculous and constitutionally improper Stamp Act.[2] Like George Washington with the French, Teddy Roosevelt probably strung the Germans along, citing political difficulties with an anti-British alliance. Roosevelt later accepted German cash, laundered via George Perkins and Frank Munsey, to fund a new party (the Progressive Party) when he agreed to block the re-election of Taft in 1912 and get in Germany's preferred candidate, the woeful Woodrow Wilson. Taft of course had upset Germany's J. P. Morgan.

The media's response to the McKinley Assassination was as naïve and ill-informed as the earlier response to the Lincoln Assassination and the later to the Kennedy Assassination. The 'lone gunman' theory seems to have a fatal fascination for the media, even more fatal of course for the American statesmen cruelly sacrificed to appease Germany's desire to control events in Washington.

In fairness, the British media's response to all three assassinations was just as witless and ill-informed. From the Drummond assassination in 1843 onwards no assassination sponsored by German Intelligence has ever been seriously investigated, either officially or by the media. Thankfully, as we have seen, not all succeeded, the sponsored, i.e. serious, attempts on Queen Victoria and all three attempts on Churchill failing.

German Intelligence/Vatican Co-operation

This period was also marked by increasingly close cooperation between Germany and the Vatican, helped by the fact that the covert Prussian and Bavarian intelligence services were merged in or around 1871, Bavaria of course being Catholic. The Illuminati secret society, founded in Bavaria, was effectively a front for the covert Bavarian service, which always reported to the King's spymaster.

The merger allowed Prussian, now German, intelligence, and the Jesuits, to form a powerful and dangerous axis. Their most successful joint operation was the outrageous assassination of His Highness Archduke Franz Ferdinand and his lovely wife, the Archduchess Sophie, in 1914. Her marriage to Ferdinand had been bitterly opposed by the ageing Emperor Franz Joseph, not nearly as nice a man as Franz Ferdinand with respect, although the latter was perhaps a trifle too keen with the hunting rifle.

Moving forward briefly to 1914, Gavrilo Princip was a Jesuit asset, recruited by a Jesuit agent, Father Anton Puntigam, who coincidentally (or not) happened to be on hand to 'deliver the last rites', Jesuit speak for making sure that the targets were mortally wounded. No doubt there was a back-up plan had Princip missed. It is unclear who recruited the driver, who was later paid off, but it was probably Puntigam himself. He was close to the Royal Family, who trusted the Society of Jesus, at least they did then (if you talk to a Hapsburg now, don't mention the Jesuits).

No one in INTELCOM fell off their chairs, unless they were very junior or very stupid, when Princip's 9mm Browning Model 1910 semi- automatic, serial number 19074, turned up 90 years later in a Jesuit monastery in Styria, Austria. No doubt it had been a prized possession.

The Archduke's driver, Leopold Lojka, was instructed to reverse into the alley where Princip was waiting, of course.

Historians, who must take their readers for fools, will have you believe that serendipitously Lojka just happened to reverse into the very alley where Princip, complete with late-model, short-range semi-automatic (it had a barrel less than four inches long and a muzzle velocity of less than 1,000 ft per second) just happened to be waiting, in a café. No doubt he was hoping that the heir to the throne of Austria-Hungary might pop in for a cup of tea with his wife.

At a time when German troops were already moving up to their holding areas near the Belgian frontier, in preparation for their flank attack on the French Army, and Germany was looking for a *casus belli*, since the Belgians, who were not insane, were not planning to invade Germany, Lojka just happens to stop outside the café and then chances to stall a car with which he was very familiar, whilst a Jesuit agent shoots his employers. Getting the principals shot is not normally a career move for chauffeurs, but instead of being arrested and shot himself Lojka ends up trousering enough Austrian Crowns to buy himself a pub in Brno, courtesy of German ally Emperor Charles 1. I have already made the point about fairy tales.

I am not implying by the way that all Jesuits are nasty or involve themselves in starting world wars. I have met several nice Jesuits, mostly connected to the excellent Georgetown University in Washington, and I am sure there are more. My point is that from 1871 onwards there was close co-operation between German Intelligence and the Vatican, which came out into the semi-open with the carefully staged assassination of the Archduke and Archduchess. The Jesuits are still playing silly games today, as the successful attempt in February 2013 to force out that awfully nice man, with respect, Pope Benedict XVI, demonstrated.

German Naval Expansion

The development of Medium Term Note trading programmes by German banks including the central bank was linked into German naval expansion, Krupps and Thyssen being key participants. The German taxpayer did not directly fund all of Germany's naval expansion. Achieving superiority at sea over the Royal Navy, ultimately in conjunction with the Imperial Japanese Navy, was a major German ambition. As indicated in the last chapter, Japan's alliance with Great Britain was a phoney.[3] Amongst other things it would permit Japan to take over Germany's Pacific bases in the event that Germany lost the war she was planning. Japanese territorial ambitions *vis à vis* Russia were actually quite limited and the Russo-Japanese War was designed to serve Germany's strategic interest rather than Japan's.

There were six major obstacles to Germany obtaining supremacy over Great Britain at sea. None of these were ever fully overcome by the 'Hun', resulting in the humiliation of the Imperial German Navy at the Battle of Jutland, when they had to run for home, the internment of every major surface combatant in the German Fleet at Scapa Flow in 1919 and the ultimate loss of every German capital ship in World War Two. These were:

(1) Britain's technological supremacy, particularly as regards fire control, protection, i.e. armour plate, and propulsion, reflected in the revolutionary, turbine-powered, fast (for her day) battleship HMS *Dreadnought*. She rendered existing German (and American[4]) battleships obsolete.

(2) British doctrinal supremacy. Unlike the Americans, with their brilliant Admiral Mahan, the Germans never fully grasped Sea Power. They were and remain a continental power, landlocked in their thinking.

(3) The Royal Navy's superior training (the Germans understood this, hence the closure of Manadon[5] by German assets in Whitehall and the current pressure to close down Dartmouth).

(4) Germany's inferior strategic position (not much that the 'Hun' can do about that - he can invade other people's countries and annex them to the Fatherland, but he cannot move Germany).

(5) Britain's wonderful shipbuilding industry and huge shipbuilding capacity (latent but recoverable), allowing her to out-build Germany once her assets in Whitehall were outmanoeuvred, and

(6) The 'Hun' does not like getting his feet wet.

There was not much German intelligence could do about (2), (3), (4) and (6) but they had enough assets in Whitehall, including Lloyd George and Geddes, to be able to:

(1) Transfer British technology to Germany.
(2) Prevent the Royal Navy exploiting the latest British technical developments.
(3) Insist on building-in design weaknesses, particularly as regards protection and fire control, on British warships, and
(4) Slash British naval expenditure. After World War I they also used penetration assets in Washington to help force Britain into the disastrous Washington Naval Treaty, the silliest arms control treaty in history, which only Britain fully observed[6] and which ended up costing tens of thousands of lives. It must also have cost at least one hundred million pounds in lost revenue and material damage for every million 'saved'.

Thus, the brilliant Parsons turbine and Pollen Fire Control Clock were transferred to Germany, the former overtly, under a ludicrous licence insisted upon by German assets in the Treasury. The latter was transferred so covertly that the fire control equipment had to be removed from every major German surface combatant before they sailed to Scapa Flow to surrender, in order to protect German agents in London, principal amongst them Lloyd George.

He of course reported to Max Warburg, head of the Imperial German Secret Service, both the overt and covert agencies, making him an extremely powerful spymaster. It was Warburg who paid for the champagne and provided the mistresses. In return, as Chancellor, Lloyd George was able to make sure the Royal Navy never got the Pollen Clock. For readers unfamiliar with battleship fire control[7] the Pollen Clock was not a timepiece but the world's first fully synthetic, gyro-stabilised, electro-mechanical fire control computer, the forerunner of today's advanced digital computers, capable of integrating the data streams from both the firing ship and the target, such as range to target, speed, direction and rate of turn, length and height of target etc. This enabled battleships to both fire and manoeuvre.

Lack of fully synthetic fire control computers tragically allowed a large number of 'Huns' to escape the fire of the Grand Fleet Battle Line at Jutland. Admiral of the Fleet Sir John Jellicoe's[8] squadrons were forced to cease fire whilst they executed a very necessary battle turn, to the utter frustration of their Gunnery Officers. The lack of fully synthetic fire control continued to hamper Royal Navy main battery gunnery until the last great big-gun battle with the 'Hun', the Battle of North Cape, on Boxing Day 1943.[9] It materially contributed to HMS *Hood's* inability to hit *Bismarck* with her 15 inch battery whilst executing her final battle turn to port in the Battle of the Denmark Strait.

Asquith, Lloyd George and the Liberals did their best to hold back the naval building programme in order to help the Germans. It should be remembered that the Liberal Party was created as a front for the Prussian Secret Service. When that was discovered by Joseph Chamberlain they split, the patriotic Liberals, a minority, aligning themselves with the God- fearing Tories.

That they did not do more damage is a tribute to the fine work of the Navy League, public pressure and the constitutional crisis of 1910, triggered by the Liberals themselves, which cost them their majority in the House of Commons. They also had to tread carefully, lest their links with German Intelligence be exposed.

MI5

Asquith was gay and very much in the closet. Moreover, he liked his men young. His demands, combined with Lloyd George's philandering, meant that the Liberal Government lived in constant fear of exposure of either or both of its major players, with possible adverse consequences at the polls. They also had to keep promoting Liberals in the know, such as Sir Rufus Isaacs. He was eventually made Marquess of Reading, no less, and what's more didn't have to pay Lloyd George's bagman, Maundy Gregory (later sent to prison and rightly so) for the privilege. They also had to make Isaacs Viceroy of India.

After the war the well-informed Sir Gordon Hewart, who drafted most of the Treaty of Versailles, largely in accordance with German instructions run through Lloyd George, had to be made Lord Chief Justice of England. In fairness Hewart turned out to be a great Lord Chief, the second best of the 20th century after Lord Goddard, although neither was exactly up against stiff competition. Both were conspicuously fair men, Lord Hewart being responsible for the famous *dictum* that 'justice must not only be done, it must be seen to be done'.[10] The *dictum* must have frightened the pants off that old goat Lloyd George, not that it took much to get his trousers off. He could have been hanged many times over.

Understandably, the Liberals starved the intelligence services of funds. This is usual procedure when the Chancellor of the Exchequer is a German spy. When eventually forced to set up the Secret Service Bureau, forerunner of MI5 (a title which only came into use during the Great War, when the military, who sensibly did not trust the SSB, took over) the Liberals turned to Max Warburg for advice. He recommended one of his best agents, Vernon Kell. He would hardly recommend a British spy, could he?

The military takeover of SSB during the war, which meant they got the files, was to the serious discomfiture of Asquith, as someone seems to have discovered both his liking for young men and links with Germany. At any rate the decision was taken by Military Intelligence to have his eldest son Raymond shot, in the usual way.[11] It was decided that shooting Asquith himself, whilst a much better idea, might have led to a fuss (letters to the *Times* and so on). Raymond Asquith was duly shot on 15th September 1916, during the Battle of Flers-Courcelette.

The Strange Case of Dr Crippen

Kell was a cold fish, who kept a tight lid on Asquith and Lloyd George's sexual shenanigans, but he nearly lost control in 1910. Some of the young men Asquith buggered were brought over from Germany (the exemption of first-class passengers from immigration control was largely for intelligence reasons, so nobody would know who was in the country and who wasn't). This solved one problem - finding young gay men willing to be rogered by the Prime Minister - but created another. They had to be found safe houses, preferably not with gay men, so as to avoid potential complications.

There was an almighty panic in Number 10 and the newly created SSB when a delicate, young, German rent boy, who had been servicing Asquith, and of whom Asquith was rather fond, seems to have refused sexual demands from a married, gay, homeopathic doctor with whom he was being housed. The quack's name was Dr Hawley Harvey Crippen. Obviously, the Wilhelmstrasse had read too much into the fact that the doctor was married, to a German/Polish woman, christened Kunigunde Mackamotski. Ostensibly he had a mistress, named Ethel Neve, but she was his handler. At any rate there was a blazing row, during the course of which the rent boy seems to have been thrown down the stairs and died. The rent boy's pyjama bottoms were found in Dr Crippen's bedroom, there being no chain of evidence to support the proffered explanation for this discovery. The prosecution at the subsequent trial wisely chose not to dwell on the size of the said pyjamas, which seem to have been a trifle small for the good doctor.

The famous pathologist Sir Bernard Spilsbury, who very properly told the jury that he could not determine whether the remains he examined were those of a male or a female, found traces of the drug scopolamine, said to be the cause of death, although the dosage does not seem to have been fatal. Aside from being used, recklessly, by some intelligence agencies as an aid to interrogation (please do not try this at home), scopolamine was the world's first 'date rape' drug. It is not only a muscle relaxant, it can induce temporary memory loss, as the German Secret Service's medical section discovered whilst researching its usefulness, on unwilling subjects, as an aid to interrogation. It is not only an aid to female rape, but male rape as well, something of which Sir Bernard was probably unaware, since scopolamine was not widely used in Britain in 1910.

Being an agent of German intelligence, the young rent boy might well have been familiar with the uses for scopolamine, indeed he might have used it himself, to make his encounters with the Prime Minister more bearable than otherwise they might have been. Just because a particular Prime Minister happens to be fond of a particular rent boy it does not follow that the rent boy is fond of the Prime Minister. Dr Crippen undoubtedly purchased a quantity of scopolamine before the incident, for which as a homeopathic doctor he could furnish some sort of explanation to the chemist. Again, it does not follow that that was his only purchase, nor that only he had a use for it.

Rather than inform the Imperial German Secret Service that he had just knocked off one of their rent boys, and upset the Prime Minister into the bargain, Dr Crippen panicked. He tried to bury parts of the body under the basement, as one does. However, there was a problem. Kunigunde, a.k.a. his second wife Cora, understandably alarmed at these developments, fled to the United States, in January.

This put Dr Crippen in a slightly delicate position, i.e. no wife and a dead body in the basement. When Scotland Yard showed up, under very firm instructions from high up the payroll to conduct a cursory search only, Crippen panicked and fled with his alleged mistress Ethel to Brussels. Here Ethel was able to arrange a quiet chat with a somewhat perturbed German Head of Station, who given the compartmentalisation for which the Wilhelmstrasse was famous, was almost certainly unaware that the Home Office were in the loop.

The detective who had missed the body in (strictly under) the basement and had decided not to arrest Dr Crippen was none other than Detective Chief Inspector Walter Dew. He was one of the Met's most corrupt officers, and was able to retire on the proceeds of the Crippen trial. These included handsome payments from Fleet Street laundered as libel settlements, augmented by libel damages from a newspaper whose faith in British justice proved not to be justified. Readers will not be surprised to learn that earlier in his career he had been one of the detectives who had failed to find 'Jack the Ripper', for which failure he was promoted.

Brussels Station swiftly arranged transatlantic passage on the first available liner, the elderly SS *Montrose*, and a disguise for Ethel Le Neve. As a trained agent she may not have been wearing disguise for the first time of course. Sadly for Dr Crippen, there were five problems with this cunning plan:

(1) The *Montrose* was a Canadian Pacific liner and she was going to Canada, not the United States.
(2) She was single screw and made only 12 knots.
(3) Her complement included an intelligence officer.
(4) Her master, Captain Kendall, 'recognised' both Crippen and Le Neve, i.e. was alerted to their presence by Naval Intelligence and
(5) She carried radio, surprisingly for such a small liner (less than 7,000 tons) in 1910, or possibly not, given the amount of intelligence activity associated with Antwerp. Captain Kendall of course had her radio officer alert the authorities.

The 'wily Hun' moved swiftly to plan B. Chief Inspector Dew was sent ahead on the White Star liner *Laurentic* and the decision was taken to sacrifice Crippen. Dew duly 'verballed' him, i.e. made up a bogus confession, a task he may not have been carrying out for the first time. Sadly, the 'Met' then was no more honest or professional than it is today. The Director of Public Prosecutions was a bent Liberal, if that is not a tautology, Sir Charles Matthews KC. Indeed, he was a former Liberal parliamentary candidate. He owed his ethics to the profession of politics rather than the Bar. Of course he owed his appointment to the Liberal Government, the same one that might have found itself in difficulties had the truth come out.

There were several problems with the prosecution of Dr Crippen, one being the complete absence of any female bits on the prosecution's prize exhibit. Another was the fact that the alleged victim was still alive. Generally speaking, the victim still being alive is a good defence to a charge of murder. Take it from me, if you're prosecuting a murder you don't want defence counsel calling the 'victim' as a witness. The judge is bound to be confused and the jury will look at you strangely.

It seems as though someone got hold of Pinkertons and had them trace 'Cora' Crippen in the States. There was also the inconvenient matter of the passenger manifests for January, when she suddenly disappeared from London. The checking of such records is a basic step in a missing person investigation.

Naval Intelligence, who had access to said records, started to take an interest, not least since Le Neve was a known German agent. Sadly, they were penetrated, indeed the German spy (strictly an Austrian spy working for the Germans, since he was Austrian born) Prince Ludwig (Louis) von Battenberg, had been made Director of Naval Intelligence in 1902. (Battenberg and his father, also a German spy, chanced to have a dinner engagement at the Winter Palace with Tsar Alexander II on the evening in 1880 when the German agent Stephen Khalturin blew up the dining room, although the Battenbergs wisely missed being blown up by being late for dinner, no doubt pleading a previous engagement.[12])

At this point Whitehall went into overdrive cover-up mode. They must have been terrified lest prosecuting counsel, Sir Travers Humphries, found out. Sir Travers was the straightest prosecutor in England, but a man of limited imagination. They later made him a High Court judge, lack of imagination not being a bar to judicial preferment. Dr Crippen was duly hanged on 23rd November 1910, for a crime he hadn't committed, indeed for a crime that no one had committed.

Poor old Travers Humphreys found out some years later and was shocked to the core. He seems to have told his son, Christmas, who became England's leading Buddhist. Buddhists are opposed to the death penalty on religious grounds. They had to make him a judge as well, in 1968. He never tried a capital case, because as related in Chapter 24 capital punishment was abolished for murder in 1965.

The three most controversial cases that undermined public support for capital punishment in England were those of Timothy Evans, Derek Bentley and Ruth Ellis. Prosecuting counsel in all three was Christmas Humphreys, his Buddhist beliefs notwithstanding. He also prosecuted in the Tokyo War Crimes Trials, which were capital cases.

Nearly a century passed before someone organised a DNA test and confirmed that the remains of the person found in Dr Crippen's house were male, not female. He should have been charged with manslaughter of the hapless young German, not murder, let alone of his still-living wife. Crippen was doubtless keen to save himself, but must have been aware that he wouldn't last very long if he told the truth. His choice really lay between a quick, near-painless death at the hands of a British hangman and a slow, painful one at the hands of the Germans.

There was also the possibility that German assets in the Civil Service, of which there were many, would arrange for a bent hangman, i.e. one willing to take an extra fee on the side to get the length of the drop wrong. Depending on whether it was too short or too long that would result in death by decapitation or strangulation. Dr Crippen, who had after all been housing one of the Prime Minister's rent boys, would have known how deeply corrupt the Asquith Government was. It is also possible that he was given bogus assurances that he wouldn't actually be hanged. Stringing people along before stringing them up is a well-known German tactic.

Tying-up Shipyard Capacity

The one serious figure in the Liberal Government was Winston Churchill, who strongly backed the Navy. To its relief he was made First Lord of the Admiralty on the outbreak of war. The Fleet he inherited however was ridiculously small. This was partly because the Liberals had British shipyards spending part of the decade between the laying down of HMS *Dreadnought* and Germany's decision to start World War I building battleships for Latin American countries (such as Chile[13]) and German allies such as Turkey and Japan.

Thankfully the 'Hun' started the war before the Turkish super-dreadnought *Sultan Osman I* was delivered. She was taken over for the Royal Navy (preposterously, this was used by Turkey as a pretext for entering the war, as though that had not been carved up with the 'Hun' years before) and rendered sterling service as HMS *Agincourt.* Her main battery of no fewer than 14 12 inch guns (mounted in seven turrets) made a tremendous racket, as well as a splendid sight, especially at night. She was much loved in the Fleet.

Germany would not have dared to start the war had the Royal Navy not been starved of funds by the Liberals. In the so-called 'naval race' between Germany and Britain the Germans were running whilst Britain, thanks to the Liberals, was only taking a walk in the park. Since British banks were buying Medium Term Notes at silly prices, Britain was also indirectly bankrolling German naval construction.

Ireland

Asquith and Lloyd-George were desperate to give Germany a free hand to invade France and came up with a cunning plan, which they sold to Max Warburg in Berlin. If they could force Irish Home Rule, a key German strategic demand, as the German Navy could outflank the Royal Navy and would have Atlantic bases, which their U-Boats eventually put to devastating use in World War II, they could trigger a civil war. This would tie up the British Army in Ireland, giving Germany a free hand against the French.

Since the Liberals were in power, they could also make sure the British Army ran into trouble by getting some of the loonier unionists to commit atrocities against the Catholics. This was the strategy Lloyd George used to terrible effect after the war. He armed the Black and Tans and gave them outrageous, covert instructions to rape and kill every Catholic they could lay their hands on, to the utter despair of the Chief of the Imperial General Staff.

There was one major problem for the Liberals however. The House of Lords, as symbolic of decency and patriotism as the House of Commons was symbolic of corruption and treachery, stood in their way. Lloyd George, as Chancellor, manufactured a clash between the two houses by pushing an inequitable and iniquitous land tax, which the Lords rightly threw out. That gave the wily Welshman the pretext he needed to push through the ridiculous Parliament Act 1911, which in turn allowed the Commons (under German control) to ram through the Government of Ireland Act 1914.

The great Marquess of Lansdowne, formerly Governor-General of Canada, Viceroy of India and Foreign Secretary, led a principled opposition in the Lords to this wholly unconstitutional legislation, which threatened to turn Britain unicameral. Lansdowne had good access to intelligence and must have suspected that Asquith and Lloyd George were traitors. He knew that Asquith was being serviced by rent boys, may have known they were being supplied by Germany and that Lloyd George was living well beyond his means, financing a number of mistresses.

Unfortunately, the Liberals had foisted another traitor, Lord Stamfordham, on King George V, as His Private Secretary, a standard German tactic. Stamfordham, impudently, took it upon himself to represent to Lansdowne that the King was willing to flood the Upper House with *ersatz* peers, even more than Tony Blair created. This would have been both unconstitutional, barring wholly exceptional circumstances, and pointless, since the House of Lords control the rate of admission. They could easily have slowed down the rate at which the phoney peers became eligible to vote.

Sadly, the Tories in the Lords, roundly abused by Liberals and left-wing historians as 'ditchers', backed down. Great man though he was, Lansdowne proved too cautious. He was not the first and certainly not the last to make inadequate use of powerful intelligence he had in his possession whilst waiting for further confirmation of it. The Liberals however lost ground in the country, throwing away their majority. Although the ditchers lost the battle, their courageous and principled stand helped win the war. By the time the so-called 'Government of Ireland Act' was forced through, without the approval of the House of Lords, the 'Hun', unwilling to wait until the spring, had already started World War I.

Civil war preparations in Ulster, which were advanced, were abandoned, as was the offensive 'Government of Ireland Act' itself. Not having been approved by the House of Lords it was not a proper act of course. Ulster is still part of the UK, as the majority of her people wanted, then and now. The Germans got their civil war in Ireland, but they had to settle for war in the south instead of the north. Not until 1969 did they get to turn Ulster into a killing ground.

An appreciation of the German machinations over Ulster is essential to a coherent grasp of their strategy. This was not to have a world war, but a series of short wars, as between 1864 and 1871. Kaiser Wilhelm II, Bismarck, Tirpitz and Warburg each wanted to roll over France, Russia, Britain and America in turn, probably in that order. Keeping Britain out was essential to this strategy and would allow German forces to redeploy from the Western Front. This would take advantage of Germany's internal lines of communication. The German rail network is geared to rapid troop movements from east to west. To this day travel on that axis is easier than north-south.

Instead, hoping for a quick victory against the French, by outflanking them through Belgium, they ended up fighting a two-front war against three of the strongest powers in Christendom. Of course, they ran slap bang into Field Marshal Sir John French's immortals of the British Expeditionary Force. Bismarck would have avoided a strategic blunder of that magnitude. To turn what was already looking like a disaster, especially after their advance on Paris was halted, with great bravery, into a complete fiasco, the Germans followed a naval strategy of using U-Boats against civilian targets. This cheap substitute for fighting the Grand Fleet eventually brought in the United States.

Just because the Germans lost World War I does not mean that they planned on losing. They actually started the war hoping to win. They also had ambitions of winning World War II, in which they replicated the failed strategy of their first war. Once again, they got caught in a drawn- out conflict, of their own making, on two fronts. Since they started both world wars, and blamed everybody else, from the Royal Navy to the Poles and the Jews, we needn't be overwhelmed with sympathy.

The Agadir Crisis

German long-range planning for what became World War I started at least 20 years before. It included base acquisition, including covert naval bases, a huge naval building programme, backed by increases in ship-building capacity, improvements to railways to transfer troops and ammunition between the western and eastern fronts, doctrinal development and the notorious Schlieffen Plan. Not everything went to plan, however.

The Agadir Crisis saw the plan for a permanent naval base in Morocco abandoned. Grand Admiral von Tirpitz's ambition was to have naval bases straddling the western approaches to the Mediterranean. Germany took control of Portugal after Warburg had King Carlos I and his heir, the 23rd Duke of Braganza, brutally assassinated on 1st February 1908. The pro-British monarchy was eventually overthrown by a German-backed coup (if that is not a tautology) in 1910, since when Portugal has been a German client state.

British Intelligence, particularly Naval Intelligence, had not been idle. This was despite the interference being run by the chief German spy in the Admiralty, Prince Louis von Battenberg, and his protégés. The Empire was alerted to the growing German menace by a brilliant naval intelligence officer, Erskine Childers. His superb book *Riddle of the Sands* was published in 1903, directly influencing public perception of the menacing German moves against Morocco. There is still strong German influence in Rabat by the way, which in 2007 helped frustrate the attempt to rescue little Madeleine McCann. The DVD's Generalleutnant Otto Ernst Remmer organized a brutal coup attempt there in 1971.

The Financing of World War I

The most critical component of German war planning was financial. You do not start a world war, or even a series of small wars, without cash. Central to getting the cash were:

(1) Expanding the Medium Term Note trading programmes, which were directly linked into the German military-industrial complex, and
(2) Obtaining gold from the huge covert stockpiles in East Asia, in particular from China and Japan.

The gold was mostly transferred by warships, including Japanese, once the war had started. Intelligence missed a trick here. They bought into the official line from the Liberals and the Foreign Office, which has always had trouble distinguishing Britain's enemies from her friends, that Japan was an ally.[14] Almost all the official gold reserve figures from the Far East were phoney. They still are.

That's what Wilhelm Canaris was doing with the German East Asiatic Squadron in China in 1914. It also explains why SMS *Dresden*, on which ship he happened to be, along with a large quantity of gold, broke away from the squadron when Admiral Sir Frederick Doveton Sturdee's mighty battlecruisers[15] caught up with them in the Falklands.

Having American financial institutions participate more fully in offshore Medium Term Note trading, buying up the notes at inflated prices (they still do), was critical to the expansion of the system. That expansion was in turn essential for the funding of the war. There was a problem, however.

Blocking funds in US banks could not be done, especially at this level (Medium Term Notes typically have a face value of $100 million) without alerting the US Treasury. The same applied to moving large quantities of dollars offshore, or repatriating trading profits onshore. The answer was to set up a central bank under German control, i.e. have Germany take over the monitoring of US dollar movements.

To this end, Nelson Aldrich and Frank Valderclip of Rockefellers, Henry Davidson, Charles Norton and Benjamin Strong of J. P. Morgan and Paul Warburg of Rothschilds met on beautiful Jekyll Island, off the coast of Georgia, in 1910. Paul Warburg's brother was Max, head of the German Secret Service. Each of these banks was German-owned, German- controlled or had close connections to German intelligence.

There were however powerful opponents of setting up the proposed Federal Reserve System, which to this day is so closely involved in monitoring Medium Term Note trading that many bankers, brokers and others believe it actually controls it. In fact, all MTN trades have to be OK'd via Frankfurt, which is able to pull the rug from under a bank fairly easily if it can sucker it in to moving too much cash offshore. Some famous names have gone south in this way.

Prominent amongst these opponents were John Jacob Astor, Benjamin Guggenheim and Isidor Straus. They had to be eliminated, but in such a way as to make it look like an accident. The problem of course with staging a series of accidents is that the more you stage the less accidental they look. What the German Secret Service really needed was to get them all in the same place at the same time.

1. The official American explanation for the War of 1812, a very silly war in that it saw Good Guys fighting Good Guys, appears to be that the Canadian colonists invaded the United States, a point of view not accepted in London or Ottawa. There was manufactured concern in Congress over the Royal Navy's hardworking press gangs offering career opportunities to dual nationals, i.e. sailors with a close connection to both Britain and America, to serve in the Royal Navy. No doubt in the confusion the odd American sailor (only sailors could be impressed) ended up serving in the British Navy. Since the food and the company were good, the discipline fair, the ships state of the art, with the very latest in sailing technology, and there were plenty of opportunities to kill Frenchies, it is unsurprising that the Admiralty recorded very few complaints.
2. Whilst Parliament had the legal power to legislate for the colonies and Virginia (which was a self-governing dominion - historians refer to the "thirteen colonies" when they should be referring to "the twelve colonies plus Virginia") each colony had representative government and the Act should not have been promoted without meaningful consultation with them. In relation to Virginia the Stamp Act went way beyond improper and was unconstitutional to the point where King George III would have been entitled to refuse Royal Assent. Unfortunately, His Majesty was broke. Some years later He needed Lord North's support for the Civil List, an idiotic arrangement foisted upon the King by dodgy politicians and equally dodgy civil servants in the Treasury, a government department almost as dodgy as the Cabinet Office, no offence intended. It is very doubtful that the King knew that Lord North, who kept the Stamp Act in place when he should have promoted its repeal, was a French spy, as otherwise He would dismissed him. North of course should have been given a fair trial by Parliament and beheaded. (Kings of England, by the way, get capital letters.)
3. A clue to this is to be found in *World Peace or World War: which way is Germany to turn?,* written in 1907 by Count Graf Ernst von Reventlow, close to German Naval Intelligence and a mouthpiece for von Tirpitz. This was quoted in the *Los Angeles Times* for 19th March 1907 under the heading *German says Hawaii is Weak Naval Base*, which sadly it was. Von Reventlow was scathing about America's naval strength *vis-à-vis* Japan and predicted that the Imperial Japanese Navy would defeat the US Navy. He sure got that one wrong. It was not of course a coincidence that the German spy Admiral Ernest King pushed for the US Pacific Fleet to be transferred to Pearl Harbor. I am indebted to Drs Michael McMaster and Kenneth Hagan of the US Naval War College satellite at Monterey, CA for their article in praise of the great Admiral Sims, "His Remarks Reverberated from Berlin to Washington", *Proceedings*, Vol. 136/12/1,204, December 2010, p.66. The charming town of Monterey is of course a great jumping-off point for the glorious drive to LA along the Pacific Highway, but fill up with gas before you set off!
4. The US Navy will tell you that they had ordered dreadnoughts of their own and they weren't far behind. They would be right.
5. The Royal Naval Engineering College. Many in the Navy could not understand the decision, quite reasonably, since it had no rational basis, unless of course you were German.

6. Emphasis on "fully". The Americans, being white hats, made an effort, and had to build in serious weaknesses into their cruisers to keep them within the silly 10,000 ton limit, which was designed to make them easier to sink by Japanese cruisers which went way over (as did 'Jerry' and 'Eyetie' cruisers). American hull stress levels were still too low even after Washington, hence the weak bows of the otherwise impressive *Cleveland* and *Baltimore* classes, as revealed in the famous typhoon. Another typhoon by the way afforded a British admiral, Rawlings from memory, the opportunity to respond to a 'how did you guys do in the storm?' type signal with a 'storm, what storm?' type signal. When it came to battleships the Navy Department, sensibly, threw the absurd 35,000 ton limit overboard. The *Washingtons* and the *South Dakotas* officially had a standard displacement of 35,000 tons. 41-42,000 would be nearer the mark. To maintain the deception the mighty *Iowas* were officially listed at 45,000 tons, which since their full load displacement was 57,000 puzzled many observers. The Director of Naval Construction at the Admiralty was not puzzled, however. He jotted down a few figures on his blotter and came up with 51,000 tons standard displacement, which was about right. He was a brilliant naval architect.
7. Norman Friedman, a nice man, into whom I have bumped, is the most informed and erudite author on this subject and readers are respectfully referred to his seminal work, *Naval Firepower: Battleship Guns and Gunnery in the Dreadnought Era*, London: Seaforth, 2008.
8. Admiral of the Fleet Sir John Jellicoe, a 33^0 Freemason and a nice one, but too political, and too inclined to cut Admiral Sir David Beatty, who was not a Mason, out of the loop. The Admiralty's Names Committee quite properly proposed to name the fourth unit of the mighty *King George V* class fast battleships after him, but there was opposition on the spurious ground that capital ships cannot be named for living persons, which came as news to King George V, who was very much alive when the first *KGV* was laid down. His son King George VI wanted the lead ship of the next class named in His father's honour. Sadly, there has yet to be a HMS *King George VI*. The fourth ship was eventually named *Anson*. Tarrant (*King George V Class Battleships*, London: Arms and Armour Press, p.15) suggests that the name change was due to the ongoing controversy over Jellicoe's disappointing failure to sink more 'Huns' at Jutland.
9. Bruce Fraser's boys in HMS *Duke of York* were able to blow the KMS *Scharnhorst* out of the water, but by jove they used up some ammunition.
10. The case is *R v. Sussex Justices ex p. McCarthy* [1924] 1 KB 256 [1923] All ER 233.
11. By a trusted NCO or sniper reporting to Military Intelligence. Usually, it's not too difficult to find volunteers to shoot officers. Traitors, or sons of traitors, are usually shot in the back, in the field, at long range, with a German rifle, just in case anybody digs the bullet out. Raymond Asquith however was shot in the chest, possibly because he was running away from the enemy at the time. He had a comfy staff billet and had to be ordered to the Front. Since he was an officer and a gentleman, of sorts, the usual procedure, of allowing him to 'apply to rejoin his regiment', was adopted. Sons of Cabinet Ministers can throw their weight about and their units are normally pretty relieved to be shot of them, no pun intended. Asquith got a nice headstone. GHQ probably sent flowers.

12. Tsar Alexander's head of intelligence was no fool. Once he heard that the von Battenbergs were going to be late he had the dining room evacuated and the Tsar moved to safety. The subsequent meeting between the Battenbergs and the Tsar must have been interesting. The usual practice on these occasions is to have an intelligence officer present when the late-arriving guests are told that the Tsar is looking forward to receiving them and they are asked to step around the dead bodies as there hadn't been time to clear them away yet.
13. This had hilarious consequences when the dreadnought *Almirante Cochrane*, building for the Chilean Navy, was taken over on the outbreak of war. She was converted, eventually, into an aircraft carrier, HMS *Eagle*, whose engine room instruments were in Spanish! So far as is known however she never went backwards when she was supposed to go forwards. She was a good ship, part of the aircraft carrier squadron whose aircraft sank the Italian battlefleet at Taranto. Sadly, she was sunk on the *Pedestal* convoy to Malta, in August 1942. A young relative of my grandmother is said to have gone down with her, aged 18.
14. If you want to check how much Japan contributed to the Allied victory take a grand tour of Japanese Great War memorials. It won't take long.
15. HMS *Inflexible* and HMS *Invincible.* The 'Hun' was shocked. He knew they were coming but hadn't banked on Sturdee making such good time. As we shall see in Ch. 14 Naval Intelligence fed false progress reports through von Battenberg, who by then had been spotted as dodgy.

13

The Titanic

Jekyll Island

It seems to have been agreed at the Jekyll Island meeting that Astor, Guggenheim and Straus would need to be eliminated before the end of 1912. The attack on France had been pencilled in for May 1914, i.e. as soon as the ground conditions were firm enough for large-scale military movements. As we saw in the last chapter, in the events that happened Asquith's delay in getting a civil war under way in Ireland held things up. The German General Staff were of course worried about the onset of winter. They wanted to be in Paris by the end of autumn, hence the August start. Ideally however they wanted to start their world war in the late spring.

The problem was that all three targets had fairly good security. Whilst the Germans could have assassinated them semi-overtly, i.e. murdered them one by one whilst staying in the background, hiding motive but not the fact of murder, even the press might have smelt a rat. How to get them all in the same place, assassinate them and make it look like an accident? We shall have to wait for the German file to be opened up to confirm who came up with the cunning plan to build a grand ocean liner with a weakness in her hull, make sure she didn't have enough lifeboats and sink her in mid-ocean when no other ship was near. Whoever it was - it might even have been Tirpitz himself - should have been told to keep taking the tablets.

The plan clearly involved mass-murder. No one would buy just the financiers being left on the ship to drown and a liner grand enough to attract all three would need room for at least 1,000 passengers. However it was done some one would be bound to work it out sooner or later, even if took 100 years. Germany's name would be mud.

It would be the disaster of the century and would be bound to be the subject of both books and the new-fangled films. If Germany lost the war which she was planning so carefully it might be difficult to prevent the victorious allies uncovering the truth in the intelligence yield. As Sir David Omand, former Director of GCHQ, explains to anyone who will listen, the golden rule in intelligence is only to do that which you can defend if it gets out. It probably will.

To the planners in German Naval Intelligence however, it must have seemed a cakewalk. J. P. Morgan, one of theirs, happened to own a shipping line, International Mercantile Marine. They happened to own White Star Line, whose ships sailed under the British flag, who happened to want to build a new fleet of grand ocean liners to match Cunard's superb *Lusitania* class. Germany's Asquith and Lloyd George ultimately controlled the Board of Trade, which regulated British shipping. They could make sure it kept the antiquated rule on lifeboats, which 'Blind Freddy' could see needed updating, and which the Board itself wanted to update.

They could always find a tame British judge to make sure that the inevitable inquiry was a whitewash. They had just got a man hanged for murdering a woman who was still alive for heaven's sake and must have thought they could get away with anything. British Naval Intelligence was heavily penetrated, thanks to their man Louis von Battenberg, who in fairness never pretended very hard to be British anyway, unlike his son. Lord Mountbatten (it sounded less German) of course carried on the family tradition of working for Germany. Indeed, as we shall see, he went even further than his old man and had a shot at becoming military dictator in the abortive 1968 coup.

German assets in Naval Intelligence could be relied upon to lean on any surviving officers and crew, as in the events that happened they did. Everything could be co-ordinated by radio. All they needed to do was buy up or blackmail a Marconi operator or two, child's play for an agency that was blackmailing the Prime Minister and had already bought the Chancellor of the Exchequer. You can get an awful lot of Marconi operators for the price of a Chancellor.

The steel grilles

Germany's sinking of the RMS *Titanic* is worthy of a book on its own, followed by a serious film, to make up for the last one. It cast a slur on the British Mercantile Marine and the White Star Line in particular, by repeating the lie[1] that the *Titanic's* Third Class passengers were imprisoned behind steel grilles. The theory is that they were prevented from reaching the Boat Deck by gates, insisted upon for immigration ships by the US authorities, until the First and Second Class passengers had had their pick of the lifeboats. The sources of funding for any film, which repeats this canard (in fairness to 20th Century Fox and Paramount *Titanic* was not the first film to recycle this particular piece of anti-British propaganda) should always be looked at carefully.

German influence over Hollywood is indirect but strong. Most film finance is arranged in New York, not Los Angeles. East Coast banks are generally beholden to the Bundesbank, and the DVD's operations in Frankfurt, for continued access to Medium Term Note trading. This is one reason why we British, who are white hats, so often get portrayed as black hats by Hollywood, to the point where British cinema goers these days would be disappointed if the villain did not have a British accent. At least the American *Titanic* did not incorporate footage from the Nazi-era propaganda film of the same name, unlike *A Night to Remember*.

In fairness to Hollywood they are also anti-American, in particular anti the American military. Hollywood rarely misses a chance to bash the good folk at the Pentagon or the nice National Security Agency. Hollywood is also usually kind to RAF Fighter Command, as in *Pearl Harbor*. Since the film had the Japanese bombing the Pacific Fleet rather than the Fleet Air Arm it could not fairly be said Hollywood is prepared to ditch historical accuracy completely.

The *Titanic/Olympic* switch theory

The plan to sink the *Titanic* was amongst the most insane and immoral any intelligence agency has ever put forward. It was so baroque, requiring at least three ships, that it was bound to go wrong somewhere, as indeed it did. We now know the broad outline of what actually happened that cold and dark night. At last we can put an end to fairy tales about lookouts not having access to binoculars, the *Titanic* ramming the iceberg accidentally, J. P. Morgan having missed her sailing because he came down with a provident 'illness' and the latest piece of nonsense, courtesy of Lady Louise Patten no less,[2] about the helmsman not knowing which way to turn the wheel in order to turn the ship. Generally speaking, the helmsmen of great ocean liners will have discovered which way to turn the wheel by the time they have left harbour. Car drivers will often have made the same discovery by the time they have backed the car out of their drive.

We can also put paid to the theory about the *Titanic* really being the *Olympic* and being sunk as part of a gigantic insurance scam,[3] although there is still a degree of mystery about the ramming of the *Olympic*. In fairness to those who have pushed the *Olympic* switch theory there are very few photographs of *Titanic*. Apart from her trials, she only sailed on two voyages, sadly, from Belfast to Southampton and from Southampton to the iceberg.

With a typically casual disregard for the facts, newspapers printed photos of the *Olympic* as the *Titanic.* No doubt some newspapers had the *Lusitania* standing in for *Titanic.*

Journalistic standards in 1912 were no higher than they are today. So far as newspaper editors were concerned they just wanted a photo of a big ship. It didn't matter which ship. Perhaps we should be grateful for small mercies and thankful that no newspaper printed a photo of a paddle steamer and captioned her as the "*Titanic*". The result is that printed newspaper photographs of "*Titanic*" departing Southampton are of no forensic value at all.

In each case you need to have a look at the original photograph. I have refrained expressly from using the term "conspiracy theorist" to describe those pushing the switch theory, however. It was not an unreasonable theory, in the sense that there have been such scams, albeit not on that scale, and the two ships *were* half-sisters. They looked very much alike, there are contemporaneous printed photographs of "*Titanic*" which are clearly of the *Olympic*, the latter *had* been badly damaged in a collision and the ultimate owner of both hulls was one of the dodgiest financiers there has ever been, no offence intended. The theory just happens to be wrong, that's all.

It's not actually that difficult to tell the two ships apart. The most obvious point of difference externally was that the forward part of the Promenade Deck was enclosed on *Titanic* but open on *Olympic.*[4] In fairness to the newspapers of the day standards of modern TV documentaries are not much higher. I have lost count of the number of times I have heard a voiceover referring to another ship and seen the dramatic footage of HMS *Barham's* sinking. I have given up trying to persuade documentary-makers of the importance of historical accuracy.

RMS *Titanic*

At 882 feet long and 52,310 tons standard displacement the *Titanic* was a beautiful and well-made ship. She was not only, with her sister the *Olympic,* the largest ship in the world when launched on 31st May 1911, but the largest manmade moving object ever built. She was bigger than the *Bismarck* and not much smaller than *Queen Elizabeth 2*. If, as has been alleged, there were weaknesses in some of her rivets they were latent defects unknown to the legendary Belfast firm of Harland & Wolff, then the world's greatest shipbuilders, who built her.

The persistent myth that a shipyard worker wrote, "I defy God to sink this Ship" then plated over it seems to have been pushed by the German station in London. The 'Hun' of course knew full well who had sunk her, but could not resist rubbing it in. This is a German failing for which we British are grateful, as it helps us work out what the Germans have been up to.

It is also a myth that either Harland & Wolff or White Star Line proclaimed the ship to be 'unsinkable'. It would have been an odd claim to make just after the *Olympic* had sustained serious damage after being rammed by HMS *Hawke*. It was the press, who knew nothing about it, which pronounced her 'unsinkable', although the very papers that said she couldn't sink did not tarry with the news when she did.

Even with the design weaknesses insisted upon by German intelligence, whose asset J. P. Morgan, it will be recalled, controlled the company which owned the ships, *Titanic* and her sister (strictly half-sister) *Olympic* were the safest and strongest ships afloat. The great strength of their hull design was demonstrated when the *Olympic* took a midships hit at speed from an armoured cruiser equipped with a ram, a very old-fashioned piece of kit even in 1912, and stayed afloat. Most liners of the day would have gone down. A modern cruise liner would not have stood a chance.

Titanic's impressive stability was demonstrated when she sank. Even after sustaining tremendous asymmetric damage from the initial ramming of the iceberg, with further strain being imposed on her hull by Captain Smith's entirely correct decision to steer towards the big, darkened ship he could see nearby, which opened her hull further, she stayed upright till the end.

Electric power was available almost until the generators flooded. There was enough light at any rate for the band to read their music sheets on a very dark night. Sadly, I cannot resolve the controversy over whether they played ragtime or the moving hymn *Nearer, My God, To Thee* at the end. The better view seems to be that they started out with ragtime. As the scale of the impending tragedy became clear, and the great ship sank inexorably beneath the waves, Wallace Hartley and the brave boys in the band, in their last moments, seem to have played the great hymn. This might have been chosen for the soundtrack of *Titanic* for the ship's death- throes, had the filmmakers with respect had more soul.

In fairness to Fox and Paramount, and the makers of the rather better-acted TV film (with George C. Scott playing Captain Smith it could hardly fail to have been better-acted - Lord Olivier would have trouble out-acting the great George C.), not to mention *A Night To Remember*, their scripts are no less far-fetched than the fatuous Mersey and US Senate inquiries. We have probably now reached the stage where the words "fatuous official inquiry" are a tautology.

The collision with the iceberg

It should come as no surprise that the officers of the British Mercantile Marine, as a body, never bought into the findings of the inquiry chaired by the carefully chosen (by the same government which knowingly made sure there were as few survivors as possible by manipulating the lifeboat regulations) Lord Mersey. No doubt some did, particularly those ships' officers who made a habit of colliding with icebergs or anything else in their ship's path. When safely out of sight of land however, whenever the subject of *Titanic* came up there were mutterings, or so say the old sea- salts who have spoken with me. The findings of the official inquiries are strictly for politicians, journalists, moviemakers and anybody else who doesn't know one end of a ship from another.

It was that wise old 'ancient mariner' (I have not corresponded with any wiser!), Captain Graeme Boxall MNI, formerly of the Mercantile Marine, who came close to the truth with his letter in the London *Daily Telegraph* on 28th September 2010. He was responding to Lady Patten's with respect risible suggestion that Quartermaster Robert Hitchins, at the helm of *Titanic*, didn't know his Rudder Orders from his Tiller Orders, i.e. didn't know how which way to turn the wheel. As I observed above, if he didn't know how to steer the ship before he boarded *Titanic* he would have found out by the time he'd steered her out of Southampton harbour, in 1912 one of the world's busiest.

The iceberg was sighted four minutes out, just under 1.5 nautical miles at 22 knots. As Captain Boxall explained, "at these distances Murdoch would have had ample time to avoid the iceberg". At the point of impact *Titanic* had swung 20 degrees to port, which would have taken just 37 seconds at 22 knots at full left rudder, using the data obtained from rate of turn trials on *Olympic*. Captain Boxall was clearly puzzled, although I do not suggest that he has rejected the accident theory.

If First Officer Murdoch was trying to avoid the 'berg it suggests that the lookouts high up in the crow's nest on the foremast, with an excellent field of vision, on a starlit night, against which the 'berg would have shown up as a dark shape (never mind sea conditions being still, i.e. no waves lapping at the foot of the 'berg - they would have seen it in plenty of time and did) would only have spotted it from about two cables. That is just one and a half ship's lengths away. Even *Titanic* does not push such an outlandish notion. For those who prefer to work in the inferior metric system, a cable is about 185 metres.

The answer of course is that Murdoch was trying to *hit* the iceberg, not avoid it. He ordered the helm put over only so far as would ensure a glancing collision with the target, which had no doubt been carefully reconnoitred by the third ship out there that night. That only makes sense once it is appreciated:

(1) That this was an intelligence operation and that Murdoch was working for the German Secret Service, and
(2) That he was armed and must have had support from other German agents on the ship.[5]

British officers do not go around their ships shooting the passengers. One of the intriguing questions about the *Titanic* sinking is just who Murdoch and the other German agents were shooting at. It is tolerably clear that shots were fired and there is no evidence that any of the passengers were shot. They would not have shot the primary targets, i.e. the financiers, as their bodies might have surfaced, as the band master's did. Bullet holes would have tended to disprove the 'accidental collision with an iceberg' line the 'Hun' was pushing.

Even as musical comedy a proceeding as Lord Mersey's inquiry, with respect, would have had trouble explaining how an iceberg shot a banker.[6] We do however have a missing Captain, for the later stages of the disaster at any rate. Most experienced intelligence officers would ask themselves if these events (i.e. shots being fired and the most experienced ship's captain in the Mercantile Marine going walkies in the middle of the most sensational peacetime sinking in maritime history) were connected.

One thing that we can be sure that Captain Smith did *not* do, was carry on sleeping through the collision. Captains of ships at sea tend to be very light sleepers. Having felt the collision, he would not have yawned, said to himself "Murdoch is a good officer, no doubt he'll make a note of what he's hit in the log and I'll read about in the morning", and gone back to sleep. Captain Smith would probably have felt the sudden change of course - captains of ocean liners tend to notice such things - and tried to make his way to the bridge *before* the collision.

President Taft's closest intelligence adviser, Major Archibald Butt, was on board, not entirely by accident. He had been to Europe and indeed he had popped down to the Vatican to see the Pope, in an effort to stave off war. There was no obvious reason for him to return from Europe to the United States via England. There were ships, Italian ships admittedly, from Naples to New York, but at least there would have been pasta for dinner and a decent bottle of Chianti to wash it down. He was never seen again. Major Butt was on board for intelligence reasons, not because he didn't like spaghetti.

The Admiralty's Naval Intelligence Division assigned an intelligence officer to all White Star and Cunard liners, who would ordinarily have kept a sidearm in his cabin. There was, therefore, at least one British intelligence officer aboard *Titanic*, who was also never seen again. The intelligence officers, Major Butt included (the British officer would have introduced himself as a courtesy, knowing that Major Butt would be in the loop regarding intelligence protection for ships on the Atlantic run, the US having similar arrangements) would have made their way to either the bridge or the radio room as soon as the ship stopped, knowing that something was up.

Whilst Archibald Butt, being Army, might have thought that colliding with icebergs was an ordinary hazard of transatlantic operations, and might have supposed that passengers mingling at New York docks regularly asked each other how many icebergs their ships had hit, the naval intelligence officer would have known better. Since each would have been armed this raises the intriguing question as to whether any shots were exchanged with the German agents.

All we know for certain is that there was at least one British and one American intelligence officer on board *Titanic*. They would have had handguns. There were at least three German agents on board (Murdoch and the two radio officers), probably more, not counting Bruce Ismay, who was unarmed (and so weak he would have been more a danger to himself with a gun than anybody else). Each intelligence officer would have been armed, shots were fired, and they weren't fired at the passengers.

Jack Phillips, the senior Marconi officer, is said to have died of hypothermia, but the evidence for that starts to falls apart as soon as it is scrutinised. Harold Bride, the junior Marconi officer, who survived, continued to perform radio intelligence duties (monitoring of German communications) for the 'Hun' in World War I.

Almost all the key witnesses to what transpired on the bridge and in the radio room, the key areas, at the most critical times, including the gallant Captain Smith, were murdered, either by shooting or being thrown overboard (who would have noticed another body over the side in all that confusion?). In the alternative they drowned with the rest of the unfortunate victims.

Phillips and Bride have been portrayed as heroes and it would be pleasant to record in their favour that they were. This portrayal however rests on the naïve assumption that the radio log is as found by the Mersey Inquiry. Since this omits all the communications with the third ship, including the incoming messages, that log is obviously incomplete. There is no published log of the traffic on the emergency frequency at all. One thing we do know - each was a competent radio officer and neither would have ignored an ice warning as suggested in the film *A Night to Remember*.

Father Browne SJ

Before turning to the second and third ships out there that night (readers dying to know more, especially Jesuits, could always skip the next few paragraphs, which are bound to be upsetting for Jesuits anyway) I should deal with a point raised in the anti-Jesuit tract *The Secret Terrorists,* published by the Truth Triumphant Ministries. I intend no offence when I say that their very title is a bit off-putting - not being religious,[7] I am a bit wary of the more fundamentalist churches. This lot sound worse than the Methodists.

They claim that Captain Smith, who was Catholic, was a Jesuit agent. He *was* Catholic, but that does *not* mean that he was a Jesuit. Their point, picked up by *Titanic* commentators such as Doug Yurchey,[8] that a known Jesuit agent, Father Francis Browne, went on board *Titanic* on the day she sailed, and disembarked at Queenstown, is however a good one. Intriguingly he was given access to the radio room.

If SSB or Naval Intelligence had been on their toes the very appearance of a Jesuit agent on board *Titanic,* given the passenger list, should have been enough to justify a priority signal to the Admiralty and a battlecruiser escort. Indeed, the Admiralty missed a trick in not laying on a battlecruiser anyway. She could have intercepted the radio signals passed to and from the third ship by Phillips and Bride, triangulated the enemy's position with the Marconi station at Cape Race and raced ahead to engage the 'Hun', not that the 'Hun' would have stayed on station by the ice field had he sighted the fighting top of a British battlecruiser bearing down upon him, battle ensigns flying, with her gun crews closed up.

It is a leap too far to say, however, as the Truth Triumphant Ministries and Yurchey do, that Father Browne met Captain Smith, although the good friar clearly had access to the operational areas of the ship. It is far more likely that he met with Ismay, Phillips, Bride, Murdoch or all four. There is photographic evidence that he was close to Bride at one point, as he photographed him in the radio room.[9] Father Browne may also have been conveying a message from Pope Pius to President Taft via Major Butt. In fairness to Captain Smith there is no evidence that he was ever a Jesuit. Even if he was, one should not be paranoid. Many Jesuits are not involved with German intelligence at all and as I have observed some are even quite nice.

As I have learnt in my own, admittedly very limited, dealings with the Vatican you have to be careful to draw a distinction between the Good Guys and the Bad Guys, who go around raiding private apartments and seizing chaps' private papers. It is also important to avoid anti-Catholic prejudice, not too difficult for me as I was raised as a Catholic and invited into the Vatican when I was aged just eighteen, for a General Audience with Saint Paul VI. Some very silly points, e.g., were taken against Pope Benedict XVI, the last but one Pope and an awfully nice chap with respect, if I may say so. His Holiness was most definitely a Good Guy, notwithstanding his enforced membership as a boy of the Hitler Youth. At that stage they were essentially the German equivalent of the Boy Scouts, with guns.

Religion is, undoubtedly, a core function of the Vatican. With the Jesuits it is merely a cover, albeit a very good one. Thus between 1912 and 1914 we have the Jesuits trying to start World War I, and succeeding (since their man Princip fired the starting pistol, as it were). The Pope was trying to stop it, as President Taft understood, hence the ostensible reason for the presence of his senior intelligence adviser and backchannel on board the *Titanic*. Archibald Butt would also of course have been liaising with, and helping to protect, Astor, Guggenheim and Straus each of whom went down with the ship like a gentleman, and properly dressed too.

Founded in 1540, as a response to the Reformation, with a view to stopping it, the Society of Jesus (great name - they probably wanted to call the Nazi Party, which they helped set up with their Bavarian connections, the Truth and Justice Party) was the prototype black intelligence organisation. Their first big murder was the regicide of King Henry VIII (the old mistress with asymptomatic syphilis trick), although they failed to knock off Martin Luther. Their involvement in the *Titanic* operation was a long way from being their first excursion into mass-murder.

Far more people died in the Great Plague of London in 1665 and the Great Fire the following year. The Jesuits had a sophisticated understanding of germ warfare long before the term came into general use. It was no accident that Dr Mengele's work in this area was conducted in Catholic Dachau, very much home turf for the Society.

The setting of the Great Fire by French Jesuit agents by the way, aside from leading to a new discipline (town planning) and leading, eventually, to the creation of the Fire Brigade, led to the Bill of Rights, the throwing over of the Catholic King James II, England's last Catholic king, and the Protestant Ascendancy. The Jesuits have been trying to undermine that ever since.[10] Jesuit agents do not wander on board ships which are about to sink, especially not if the German Secret Service is going to be doing the sinking, because they want to take the air. There is no credible motive or reason for Father Browne to have travelled from Southampton to Queenstown on the *Titanic*.

The Second Ship

The second ship out there that night was the SS *Californian*, of the Leyland Line. That line was also controlled by Germany's J. P. Morgan. Her Captain, Stanley Lord, was also on the German payroll, indeed he demanded more money as the price for his silence and retired early in 1927, having received an 'unexpected legacy', a.k.a. a pay-off from the Abwehr. No doubt the 'Jerries' considered murdering him to ensure his silence, but they could not be sure that the truth about the *Titanic* had not been set down into writing as insurance. It would have been a much better policy than he could have obtained from Scottish Widows.

It was the barrister Leslie Reade who exploded the frankly silly arguments advanced on behalf of Captain Lord down the years. He wrote an excellent book, *The Ship That Stood Still,*[11] in which he derides ideas such that the rockets fired by *Titanic,* might have been mistaken for an early celebration of Guy Fawkes Night, or whatever. Rockets at sea, whether white or red (the *Titanic* carried both, this being the changeover period from white to red for distress rockets) had then, have now and always will have only one meaning: a ship in distress and urgent need of assistance. They are *not* a sign that the captain has decided to throw a party.

Any Mercantile Marine or naval officer witnessing, as did Captain Lord's watch officers, the firing of rockets at sea, not being engaged in another rescue, e.g. of another ship foundering in the same storm, is under an immediate duty to go to the assistance of the ship firing the rockets, with the utmost despatch, rendering every assistance which they are able to give. Only the fact that the inquiry was a whitewash prevented Captain Lord from being stripped of his ticket and prosecuted for as grave an offence as a Master Mariner could commit. Indeed, the soft treatment of Captain Lord is evidence that the inquiry was not being conducted as a Wreck Inquiry should be, with respect.

Caution should be exercised, by the way, before assuming that the *Titanic's* last surface position was the same as, or even adjacent to, the position of the wreck on the ocean floor. There is no reason to doubt that her position as broadcast in the first CQD (Distress) call, at 0015 hours ship's time on 15th April 1912, 41.44 N 50.24 W, was worked out with reasonable accuracy, probably to within three ship's lengths. The revised position (41.64 N) may simply reflect the ship's movement after the collision, as Captain Smith tried to put her alongside the third ship. It would be both logical, and correct procedure, to work out a revised position, having moved the ship.

Of course, the circumstances were far from ordinary. Stanley Lord should have been given a fair trial at the Old Bailey and hanged as an accessory to murder both before and after the fact. Whether he was aware that as many as 1,517 passengers and crew would die is very doubtful, but to the eternal shame of her captain, her crew, the Leyland Line and IMM, the *Californian* stood still whilst over 1,500 men, women and children died. She was carrying very few passengers and her cargo included 3,000 warm, woollen blankets. That suggests that at least some if not all of the British officers persuaded to go along with this madness were told that the passengers would be taken off *Titanic* and well looked after. That is standard practice with German Intelligence, which has a lot of form for telling people what they want to hear.

Had Captain Smith known that there was a ship from a sister company sitting less than 10 nautical miles away (now we know that Lord was working for the Germans it is not necessary to resolve the controversy about how far away the *Californian* was - she was close enough to be able to observe *Titanic's* lights, the distress rockets and her sinking, that is to say her lights assuming an odd angle and then disappearing, which to a mariner at night amounts to pretty much the same thing) with plenty of room for his passengers and a cargo of blankets, he would have been both relieved and suspicious. He was probably suspicious anyway.

He must have asked the lookouts why they hadn't passed a warning to the bridge in sufficient time for the iceberg too have been avoided. Why on earth wouldn't he? He was the captain of the world's greatest ship, was about to preside over the world's greatest-ever maritime disaster and quite possibly lose his life into the bargain. Wouldn't you be just a little bit curious as to how this disaster had come about out on a bright, starry night in a calm sea?

On being assured by the lookouts that they had passed a warning down in good time (which indeed they had), there must have been some conversation with Murdoch, if only to pass the time. Perhaps a gentle enquiry as to what he thought he was doing setting a course (port 20) to hit the iceberg to starboard, instead of say port 30, which would have cleared it by a wide margin, or even port 45. As Captain Boxall pointed out to the readers of the *Daily Telegraph*, by implication at any rate, Murdoch had nearly enough time to have reversed course 180 degrees and start heading back to Southampton.

It is doubtful that First Officer Murdoch would have risked his captain's wrath (it would be fair to surmise that Captain Smith by this time was *not* a happy bunny) by suggesting, as was suggested to Lord Mersey's inquiry, that he thought he'd try and 'port round' the 'berg, i.e. manoeuvre around it. This might have produced a response along the lines of "have you suddenly taken up wildlife painting Mr Murdoch? Was there a polar bear on the ***** iceberg that you wanted to sketch"? There was no need to sail around the iceberg as though it were a tourist attraction and the *Titanic* on a polar cruise. It could simply have been avoided, had Murdoch wished to avoid it.

The Third Ship

The criticism of Captain Smith for restarting his engines and moving off, thereby straining the hull, is misconceived. There was another ship out there, slightly to the north, off *Titanic's* port bow, and Smith, or the lookouts, saw her. She was a German warship or U-Boat, operating under darkened ship, i.e. wartime, conditions, understandably, since she was involved in a military operation, if murdering over 1,500 unarmed civilians without warning on the high seas in peacetime can be described as a military operation. Her outline would have stood out against the stars, just as the iceberg would have done. In particular, she would have been visible to the lookouts from their vantage point high up on the foremast. If you are in any doubt about the advantages of height at sea, go up as high as you can on the next ship you are on and compare the view with that from the main deck. I well recall the difference in visibility between the flight deck and the navigation bridge of the *Enterprise*.

The German warship or U-Boat was oil-fired or diesel fuelled, and had been on station for longer than planned, requiring refuelling from the German tanker *Deutschland*.[12] Her role of course was to liaise with the Marconi Company officers in *Titanic's* radio room re the coordinates of the iceberg, monitor radio traffic and ensure no other ship, including *Californian*, interfered with the operation. She was also to report to Berlin, in code, once *Titanic* had rammed the iceberg and again when she sank, and if need be, shoot any survivors.

She is the probable source of the unidentified low-powered transmissions on the night of 14th and 15th April, which cannot be reconciled with the radio logs of commercial traffic, which of course was identified by call-sign. *Titanic's* call-sign was MGY, although Phillips and Bride would not have used her call-sign when sending the low-powered transmissions to the cruiser on the emergency set. A low power setting would have been selected to reduce the risk of interception. Incidentally, the fact that the radio officers were using *both* sets, and were under immense stress, particularly once they realised that the passengers were *not* being taken off by the *Californian*, helps explain the abruptness of some of their responses.

To those who would say "ah, but the Germans are nice people, they would never shoot survivors in the water", I would respond: "try telling that to the relatives of the hundreds of helpless men murdered by repeated Stuka attacks on the RMS *Lancastria* in 1940, after she had turned turtle". For that matter try telling it to the relatives of the thousands of other men and women machine-gunned in the water by the Germans in World Wars I and II, or who drowned after their ships were torpedoed whilst stopped to take on survivors. The disreputable tactic of interfering with rescue operations eventually rebounded on the 'Jerries' of course, when a U-Boat alert forced the heavy cruiser HMS *Dorsetshire* to break off rescuing the survivors of the *Bismarck* in 1941.

It is a matter of historical record that the oiler *Deutschland* was out in the North Atlantic that night. Having run out of coal (!) she had to be towed by the J. P. Morgan owned Leyland Line freighter SS *Asian*[13] to Halifax, at least according to the *Asian's* radio logs. These cannot readily be reconciled, as they put 500 miles between her position on the morning of Monday 15th April, and the *Titanic's* final position, where the *Asian* had been, on Saturday 13th April. Her reported speed, with the *Deutschland* in tow, was only 5 knots.

Five knots is about what we would expect, given her single screw and low-powered, 555HP triple-expansion engine, indeed it was probably close to her best speed. Not only can the *Asian's* reported positions not readily be reconciled but if they are to be believed her daytime radio range (her messages were supposedly being picked up at over 500 miles) was more than twice that of the 5 kilowatt sets on the *Titanic* and the *Olympic*, very nearly the most powerful then afloat.

What Captain Wood and the *Asian* were doing adjacent to the iceberg, whose position they reported to Bride and Phillips on *Titanic*, aside from confirming its position (so that Murdoch knew where to steer for) and rescuing the *Deutschland*, have never been made clear. The fact that the *Deutschland* should need rescuing mid-ocean at all is cause for comment. Running out of coal in the North Atlantic is not quite like running out of petrol on the motorway. There are chief engineers on board ships with engines, who do things like check the fuel consumption, nor is a coalbunker quite like the fuel tank in a car. You only have to look at it to know that the coal is getting low. The *Deutschland's* requests for assistance have a phoney look about them as well. The reality is that two days before the collision there were no fewer than three ships or submarines at or near the reported position of the *Titanic's* sinking, each of them German-flagged or German-owned.

The higher-powered (i.e. longer-range) exchanges between the cruiser, the *Deutschland*, the *Asian*, the *Californian* and Berlin were monitored by the US Navy, which had radio sets of its own. It was also able to triangulate, i.e. take different bearings on a transmission, allowing the position of a transmitter to be calculated. President Taft was monitoring the voyage anyway, hence the presence of his senior intelligence adviser on board.

The fake radio messages from the *Asian* would have raised eyebrows, ditto the presence of a German tanker. "Who's she tanking?" would be the first question any naval intelligence officer would ask, not least as most oil-fired ships in 1912 were warships and diesel-powered submarines were just coming in to service. Add to that mystery transmissions of non-commercial origin directly ahead of *Titanic* and the taking in tow of the *Deutschland* after she *ran out of coal,* duty naval intelligence officers would have been reaching for their telephones. Tankers running low on coal head for port, unless they are remaining on station for a refuelling at sea.

Unsurprisingly, in the circumstances, but almost ignored by historians, President Taft ordered a military response. The US Navy sortied two cruisers on the morning of the disaster, USS *Chester*[14] and USS *Salem*[15]. Between them they were more than a match for the German warship or U-Boat, which would not have been looking for a gunfight with an American cruiser squadron on their side of the Atlantic anyway. The US Navy, i.e. the Good Guys, were going to sea and they did not leave the ammunition behind. What's more they weren't hanging around, in fact they made such good time it raises a legitimate question as to when their captains first ordered their boilers lit.

Perhaps I should explain that sortieing a *Chester* class cruiser wasn't quite like sending out a modern gas turbine powered warship, or backing your car out of the garage. Steam-powered ships need steam (no s**t Sherlock). That means lighting the boilers well before you leave harbour. I would not be surprised if the classified White House and ONI files on the *Titanic* show that the American squadron sortied *before* the *Titanic* struck the iceberg, whatever the official logs might say.

If historians mention the deployment of this cruiser squadron at all they tend to assume that it was sent out to search for survivors, or enquire after Major Butt, which is nonsense. All the lifeboats were picked up by the *Carpathia*, whose radio officer was kept very busy. The American squadron did very little searching at all and there would have been no point anyway, since the water temperature was such that survival for more than a few minutes would not have been possible. Maximum survival time that night was probably not much more than half an hour. Enquiries about Major Butt could have been, indeed were, made by radio. There was not the slightest reason to suppose that he had been rescued by RMS *Carpathia.*

In the events which happened there was enough German influence in Washington to ensure that whatever orders the Commodore had when he charged out of Norfolk were reduced to basically saying hello to the 'Hun' should he catch up with him. As already indicated, later that year German political interference in the USA extended to discreet financial backing for Theodore Roosevelt, the third-party candidate in the presidential election. As planned, he attracted sufficient support[16] to get Germany's preferred candidate, a justifiably obscure Democrat named Woodrow Wilson, elected.

The Germans, who wanted war, naturally wanted a powerful potential enemy led by a man who wanted peace. Any potential aggressor would want someone as fluffy as WW in the White House. Saddam Hussein would have paid for his TV ads.[17] President Taft had nowhere near as much room to manoeuvre as First Officer Murdoch. Like him, he ended up trying not to inconvenience the Imperial Germany Navy by damaging one of its units.

As any experienced intelligence professional could and should have told the Kaiser (who cannot have been out of the loop on something as big as this), and Warburg, the whole scheme was madness. The timetable could not be guaranteed. As it was there was a coal-strike, which German assets in the trade union movement could not get settled in time to ensure an on-time departure by *Titanic*. That meant that the cruiser or U-Boat, which had to return to Germany directly, had to stay out there at least a further 24 hours.

The delay meant that the nice empty mid-Atlantic envisioned by the boys in the Wilhelmstrasse was starting to get a little crowded. In particular, it meant that a British liner, which on the original timetable would have been too far away, was able to race to the rescue. This in turn ruled out any question of waiting until first light to machine-gun the survivors in the lifeboats. That could only be done in the early hours of course for fear of missing a boat. Even the press might have smelt a rat if a boat got away under cover of darkness and reported a warship or U-Boat strafing people in the water, and bodies being weighed down to stop them resurfacing.

RMS *Carpathia*

Captain Arthur Rostrom was everything Captain Lord was not, i.e. a Britisher to his bootstraps, a fine seaman and a credit to the Mercantile Marine. He raced heroically to the rescue, ice and all, in the old *Carpathia*, cranking up her engines as they hadn't been cranked since she'd done her high-speed trials. Unsurprisingly, since the Liberal government appear to have wanted *Titanic* sunk and everybody dead - as it was the surviving crew had to be gathered together in Southampton and gagged very effectively by one of Battenberg's boys - this gallant master mariner was given only grudging acknowledgement by Whitehall. In particular, he was not decorated, as he should have been, with the Sea Gallantry Medal.

HMS *Hawke* and SS *New York*

It looks as though Naval Intelligence got wind of what was going on and tried to stop it, in the usual, ineffectual, oblique, "let's keep the whole thing under wraps and for heaven's sake let's make sure we don't upset anybody" intelligence way. With the government and the White Star Line under effective German control there wasn't much they could have done anyway, save for advising a battlecruiser escort for *Titanic* in the strongest possible terms.

The ramming of the *Olympic* in a way in which no one was likely to be hurt and the ship was not likely to sink, by almost the only ship in the Royal Navy still equipped with a battering ram, looks just a bit too coincidental to be a coincidence. Her Captain, Commander Blunt, does not seem to have suffered unduly.

Normally, for a professional naval officer to ram the world's biggest ocean liner broadside, in harbour, in good visibility, would not be a career move. Naval officers are not encouraged to test the point. Captain Blunt's career however does not appear to have suffered unduly. It is not a defence that your ship had a great big battering ram sticking out in front of her, since the larger the ram the more careful you are expected to be as to where you put it, as it were. In retrospect the whole episode looks like a shot across the bows of J. P. Morgan and the 'Hun', who was annoyed with HMS *Hawke*. At any rate she was ambushed by U-9 and sunk in 1915 with heavy loss of life, at a time when she was too old to have any military value.

Then there is the curious business of the SS *New York*, which tried to ram *Titanic* in Southampton. *Titanic* would not have sunk of course – she was too big and strong for that - but the damage would have prevented her from sailing. The musical comedy Mersey and Senate inquiries glossed over this and put it down to 'propeller suction', an explanation which would hold water, as it were, had the *New York* been a dinghy, or possibly even a tugboat.

The SS *New York* was a 17,270 ton liner. Moreover, she was tied up at the time, i.e. the theory is that *Titanic's* prop-suction was so great that she was able to exert enough force on *New York* to snap her mooring hawsers (we are not talking bits of string here) and move a mass of over 17,000 tons several hundred feet. No practical experiments, involving e.g. the *Olympic*, were ever carried out to test this remarkable proposition, reported by historians as though it were fact.

The *Titanic's* three engines were massive, but not exceptionally so. Her horsepower was 46,000 SHP, compared with say 70,000 SHP for the contemporary *Lion* class battlecruisers, which were at least five knots faster, and 144,000 SHP for the near-contemporary HMS *Hood*, laid down in 1916.

Hood, about the same size as *Titanic*,[18] was not known for sucking passing tugboats, freighters, ocean liners, or even the Isle of Wight ferry, into her propellers every time she left harbour.

Captain Smith would not have called for maximum revolutions on the engines as he was manoeuvring *Titanic* out of harbour anyway. He only comes across as a complete lunatic because intelligence-illiterate commentators have allowed themselves to be drawn into the theory that the *Titanic's* sinking was an accident, making wild allegations of recklessness against officers of the White Star Line, in a desperate effort to fit the facts to their preferred conclusion. Facts which cannot be made to fit - like untraced non-commercial radio traffic from a source on *Titanic's* line of advance - are usually ignored by the accident theorists, whom no one could accuse of intellectual honesty.

Again, it looks as though someone was trying to avert a disaster. There is little point asking why they did not go public - INTELCOM was as media illiterate then as it is now and the media were just as naïve anyway. They would never have printed the story, nor was there much point in telling the government, since the government already knew.

Conclusion

A century after they were murdered it is time for justice to be done for the lost souls of the *Titanic*, all of whose crew and passengers are now at peace. To those who say that the Germans should be allowed to get away with the murders and that telling the truth now may stir up anti-German feeling and cost Volkswagen a few sales, I would respond that if Germany felt genuine guilt over what was done by her naval and intelligence services in her name she could have disclosed her files on the *Titanic* long before now.

Instead, the Third Reich and the Federal Republic of Germany in turn were content to adopt the operation and continue to take advantage of German influence over the Fed. Furthermore German-influenced banks in New York have continued to fund anti-British propaganda, e.g. the lie about the third-class passengers being imprisoned below decks. The film *Titanic* has simply served to inflame British public opinion even more, at the same time as reminding the world what a magnificent ship she was and how dramatic her end.

The best memorial to Captain Smith, his passengers and crew, and the White Star Line, apart from resuming ocean liner construction in Great Britain, with Admiralty subsidies,[19] ending flags of convenience, bringing back the Mercantile Marine and in particular the White Star Line[20] in all their glory and naming the first, subsidised, new White Star Liner RMS

Titanic II, would be to clean up the Fed and the Bank of England. Offshore Medium Term Note trading should be stopped. Those banks and high net worth individuals who have not declared their offshore high-yield earnings should be made to pay the back taxes they owe. This would provide more than enough cash to reopen Britain's shipyards.

In the events which happened the primary German targets Astor, Guggenheim and Straus were assassinated, and their murders were covered up by two of the most facile official inquiries ever to be conducted, each of which made the Warren Commission and the Diana Inquest look like searches for the truth, no offence intended. Opposition to setting up the Federal Reserve System under covert German control melted away. Medium Term Note trading accelerated, backed by the gold transferred from the huge off-books stockpiles in the Far East, the idea with MTN trading being that you use the asset, make your cash and then get your gold back, i.e. you don't have to sell it. The Germans were able to start their war. Thankfully, they managed to lose it, but that's the next chapter.

1. The producers had access to the original plans of the ship, which do not seem to have been followed, and they also consulted with Harland & Wolff's historian. In February 2012 I asked Paramount Pictures and 20th Century Fox, who made the film, to justify their assertion that third-class passengers were imprisoned below decks in such a manner as to jeopardise their safety, in particular by identifying the location on the plans of the grilles which appear in the film. No British official, even under a Liberal government, would have approved such a dangerous feature in the design, although US immigration laws mandated strict separation of third-class passengers for 'health' reasons. Remember that the plans had to be submitted to the Board of Trade for their approval. Neither Paramount nor 20th Century Fox have been able to back up their slur on White Star and the British Mercantile Marine. I was in LA at the time and offered to meet James Cameron or an assistant and go over the plans of *Titanic.*
2. *Daily Telegraph*, 22nd September 2010, p 27. Lady Patten is married to the former politician Sir John Patten, a failed Secretary of State for Education, no offence intended (he had the opportunity to bring back grammar schools but preferred to condemn another generation of schoolchildren to mediocrity). She is the granddaughter of the *Titanic's* Second Officer, Charles Lightoller, who prepared a report for Naval Intelligence.
3. *Gigantic* was one of the names considered for *Titanic*. White Star liners always had names ending in 'ic'.
4. Matsen (*Titanic's Last Secrets*, New York: Grand Central Publishing, 2009) gives a good summary, although with respect there is nothing in the theory about the expansion joints being weak - they were above the hull girder anyway and in no way contributed to the sinking. The hull was in fact quite strong as the steep angle before her final dive demonstrates. Matsen queries the angle but there is no reason to doubt the evidence of eyewitnesses that her hull rose-high out of the water. It's not the sort of sight a witness would be likely to forget.
5. Intriguingly something similar is hinted at in *Britannic*, the film about the sinking of the third ship of the class, the hospital ship HMHS *Brittanic*, torpedoed by a German U-Boat on 21st November 1916. To cover up this war crime the Germans claimed that she had struck a mine, a claim which was blown out of the water as high as the *Britannic* herself by the celebrated French diver Jacques Cousteau (almost the only celebrated Frenchman of the postwar era), who found no traces of a mine when he dived on the wreck in 1975. They were added later, i.e. the Germans were still sensitive about the crime after 60 years. Always go for to the first description of a controversial wreck site.
6. It's a pity that Gilbert and Sullivan weren't still around - poor old W. S. Gilbert had died the year before. They could have given the inquiry to them (they had done *HMS Pinafore* after all) and had it set to music.
7. As I have observed elsewhere, I am an Anglican.
8. See e.g. *Who Sunk the Titanic, www.world-mysteries.com/doug_titanic1.htm,* accessed in October 2010.

9. What is described, probably accurately, as "the only known photograph of Titanic's Marconi room" appears on a website dedicated to the radio aspects of the disaster, *The RMS Titanic Radio Page*, accessed 28th February 2012.
10. Given the history of Jesuit involvement in regicide, especially the assassination of King Henry VIII, the recent proposals to end the Ascendancy are dangerous, since they may be linked to the acceleration of Catholic claimants to the Throne, or claimants married to Catholics, through the assassination of Protestants ahead of them in the Line of Succession, indeed one such cunning plan, involving an attack on the Opening Ceremony of the London Olympics, which was attended by the Queen, the Prince of Wales and Prince William, was spotted by a team lead by myself (Operation *Vulcan*) leading to the seizure, as it happens, of an earlier draft this book, not to mention my imprisonment on a trumpery bomb hoax charge. There is still a nexus between the DVD and the Bad Guys at the Vatican, who forced out Pope Benedict in February 2013.
11. Revised edition New York: Norton, 1993, edited by Edward De Groot.
12. 1893, 3,796 tons. She had a triple-expansion engine and carried sails. She was sold after World War I to the pro-German Standard Oil Company of New Jersey.
13. 1898, built by Caird & Co., Greenock, 5,515 gross registered tons (a Board of Trade measure, usually lower than standard displacement, which is why many think that the *Titanic* was smaller than she was, as the tonnage figure usually quoted is the lower GRT figure).
14. CL-1, 3,750 tons, 2 5-inch and 6 3-inch guns.
15. CL-3, a sister-ship to the *Chester*, placed in reserve at Boston five days after the sinking. Senator Smith accepted that she sortied and I respectfully agree. Most accounts of the sinking downplay the associated naval activity indeed Major Butt's presence on board is usually glossed over.
16. The Good Guys, a.k.a. the CIA, might have had a small hand in running this type of operation the other way round, in '92, when that nice man Ross Perot was able to block the re-election of President George H. Bush, who was a disastrous President. Other than his own supporters, nobody in CIA wanted him back in the White House, in particular nobody with any brains in CIA (and there are some pretty smart operators down there in Langley) wanted Bush 41's proposed choice as head of CIA. Clinton was never going to be an effective president (no offence) but at least he wasn't going to cause any actual damage, except in the Balkans, and apart from CIA and State nobody in Washington, then, knew where they were anyway (they're in South-East Europe, to the right of Italy and below Austria). With respect, O. J. Simpson would have made a better president than Bush 41. In the events that happened Clinton made that nice man Jim Woolsey Director of Central Intelligence. Jim is good people and was liked by the intelligence professionals at Langley, to whose opinions he always listened with respect.
17. I am of course aware that in 1912 we British had not yet invented television (there was a transatlantic division of labour - we did television and the Americans invented colour, game shows and Lucille Ball).
18. HMS *Hood*, the 'Mighty Hood', was the world's greatest warship from the time she was launched until the time she was blown up (see Ch. 17). 46,680 tons full

load displacement, 860 feet long, main battery 8 15-inch 42 cal. Mk 1 guns, at the time of her commissioning equal to the most powerful afloat.

19. These were needed to build RMS *Queen Mary* and RMS *Queen Elizabeth*, which both went on to serve as troopships in World War II, using their high speed to evade U-Boats. Operating outside enemy fighter range and too big to be sunk by the long-range but lightly armed Focke-Wulf Condors, with powerful surface combatants providing long-range cover against raiders (the sailing of a Queen did not go unnoticed by Naval Operations), in practice they could only be sunk if they stopped. A German attempt on 2nd October 1942 to get *Queen Mary,* carrying over 15,000 American troops of the 29th Infantry Division, to stop so that she could be torpedoed by a waiting U-Boat, by setting up a collision with the anti-aircraft cruiser *Curacoa* (in theory her escort, which was a joke as there was no air threat sufficient to justify an anti- aircraft cruiser and as rebuilt the 'C' class cruisers could only do 25 knots) failed when her Captain, Commodore Sir James Bissett CBE RNR, obeyed orders and maintained speed. He correctly sensed an ambush, and equally correctly put the lives of the GIs, who were too numerous to be safely evacuated, ahead of the poor survivors of *Curacoa*, who were left in the water. The kinetic energy of the *Queen Mary* at nearly full speed (28 knots) and under war overload conditions was such that most of the troops she was carrying barely felt the collision. HMS *Curacoa*, a 4,000 ton cruiser, was cut in half. 'Jerry' was desperate not only to stop Operation *Torch,* the invasion of North Africa, but to damage the Democrats in the mid-terms. The Germans got their revenge on *Queen Elizabeth* by having their communist Chinese allies set her on fire in Hong Kong Harbour in January 1972 (her hulk was used in a famous scene in the 007 film *The Man With the Golden Gun*). The value of using liners as troopships was again demonstrated in the Falklands War, when SS *Canberra* and the *QE2* did sterling work. They also have other emergency uses, although sadly Cunard did not respond to my suggestion that the new *Queen Mary* and *Queen Elizabeth*, who were in steaming distance, be despatched to Lyttelton Harbour for earthquake relief after the second DVD earthquake attack on Christchurch. Intriguingly, there was a plan to build a near sister of the original, *Titanic* in China, by that nice man Clive Palmer, but nothing came of it.
20. Germany's Stanley Baldwin could not stop the Queens being built but finished off White Star by forcing a silly Cunard takeover as part of the deal.

14

1914 - 1916

1914

There is an old military saying that no plan of action survives first contact with the enemy. Like a lot of old sayings, it has a kernel of truth. General von Schlieffen, who did the staff work for the German offensive in the West, which was designed to outflank the French army by hooking through Belgium, did not allow for Field Marshal Sir John French and his brave lads in the British Expeditionary Force (BEF). We British had done a bit of advance planning of our own. 'Blind Freddy' could see that war was coming, never mind Naval and Military Intelligence.

The Royal Navy shipped the BEF and its ammunition to France in impressive time, covered at long range by the battleships of the Grand Fleet. The German High Sea[1] Fleet was not going to risk a battle near the English Channel. The 'Hun's' flanking manoeuvre was in turn out-flanked and he was held up on the Marne. Paris was saved and von Schlieffen's carefully worked out cunning plan was in tatters. The outcome was four years of trench warfare, a pattern only finally broken in 1918.

The German Army had greater success in the East, winning the battle of Tannenberg against an Imperial Russian Army whose war preparations had been seriously hampered by German penetration assets in Moscow, including, critically, the Tsarina. She, sadly, was a vastly more successful German lady spy than Mata Hari. The so-called 'mad monk' Rasputin, who was bad not mad, also worked for Max's boys on the Wilhelmstrasse. Since Rasputin and the Tsarina both reported to Max it was not surprising they worked together as a team, slipping dodgy advice to the poor old Tsar.

Long-term planning in Berlin for the October Revolution seems to have started after the Battle of Tannenberg. This was not quite the comprehensive victory that Field Marshal Paul von Hindenberg had hoped for, but at least he got a big balloon named after him. This time the 'Hun' would have greater success than he had in 1905. It was not of course an historical accident that the 1905 revolt happened in the same year that Russia was engaged in the East with Germany's covert ally Japan. The 1917 revolution also served Germany's strategic aims, by taking Russia out of the war in advance of the planned spring offensive in the West. Only historians tend to believe in historical accidents.

British Naval Intelligence sadly lacked a sound grasp of the way that Germany was funding the war. This was not too surprising, since Lloyd George had moved the notorious German spy Montagu Norman into the Governorship of the Bank of England, virtually guaranteeing the two and a half decades of economic instability and underperformance which followed. Norman, who was fully in the loop regarding German Medium Term Note trading, was very careful to suppress this knowledge from Intelligence. He also made sure that loans from J. P. Morgan and others were on the most unfavourable terms possible. Like all too many Governors of the Bank of England he was keen to hold back British economic performance as much as possible. He succeeded.

It was also no accident that Germany's von Battenberg was made First Sea Lord. Churchill was never told that Battenberg was working for the Germans. 'Winnie' had been made First Lord, or political head, of the Admiralty, on the outbreak of war, in an effort to convince the public that the Liberals actually wanted Britain to win. As First Sea Lord von Battenberg had access to Britain's naval plans and was able to influence appointments to key positions. As we have seen, he was spotted. He was forced out, but not soon enough, nor was he shot, as he should have been, nicely of course.

The damage limitation exercise was inadequate. Key German assets, at least three of whom became admirals - Reginald Ernle Drax,[2] Hugh Sinclair[3] and Palliser[4] - also escaped being shot, which was ridiculous. Amongst the ships sacrificed through this poor counterintelligence work (not a single German spy in the Admiralty was shot during the whole of the war, although, absurdly, poor shell-shocked squaddies were - tragically, our firing squads were in the wrong place, shooting the wrong people) were the old armoured cruisers *Crecy*, *Aboukir* and *Hogue*. They were set up for a U-Boat ambush.

It was not a coincidence that the first major naval actions of both world wars took place in, or not un-adjacent to, the South Atlantic. Both Admiral Graf von Spee and the pocket battleship named after him were up to much the same thing - shipping gold from the Far East, either directly, or through trans-shipment points, back to Germany. The idea was to use it to back trading programmes run out of Switzerland. Gold shipment was the primary mission of the *Deutschland* class pocket battleships, partly why they were fitted with diesels, for endurance.[5]

Battenberg would have been fully aware of the importance of getting the gold the Asiatic Squadron was carrying back to Germany. He made sure that the squadron sent to intercept von Spee was wholly inadequate. They were wiped out, as intended, in the first major naval battle of the war, Coronel, on 1st November 1914. The British ships, under Rear- Admiral Sir Christopher Cradock, a first-rate chap if not a first-rate brain, put up a splendid fight, however. None fought more bravely than HMS *Monmouth*, last seen drifting into the mist, ablaze from stem to stern. None of her crew was ever seen again, but they died as Britishers should, with their boots on, battle ensigns flying, blazing away at the 'Hun' for all they were worth.

Battenberg had exposed his true loyalties. He was forced out on 27th October, sadly not in time to reinforce poor old Cradock's squadron. The great Jackie Fisher was recalled and organised a spectacular British response, although naturally Battenberg warned Berlin that a powerful British battlecruiser squadron was on its way south. The flagship, HMS *Invincible*,[6] flew the flag of the formidable Vice-Admiral Sir Frederick Doveton Sturdee, ironically not a supporter of Fisher's. He ought to have succeeded Sir David Beatty as Flag Officer of the Battlecruiser Squadron. Disgracefully, he was never made First Sea Lord, probably because he had sunk too many German ships.

Battenberg's warning was relayed to von Spee by Buenos Aires, then as now on the 'Hun's' side, although ever willing to take British cash for corned beef, at the expense of Australia. The great speed of the British battlecruisers was underestimated however, probably because Battenberg was being fed false position reports.

Von Spee tried to starve them of fuel by seizing all the coal (later battlecruisers, such as the *Lion* class,[7] were partly oil-fired, but von Spee knew which ships were after him) from the important coaling station at Port Stanley, in the strategically situated Falkland Islands. The islands' development had of course been held back by the Liberals in order to make German shipping movements around Cape Horn easier.

Whilst SMS *Dresden*, with the all-important gold (and that wiliest of 'Huns', Wilhelm Canaris) on board was sent in one direction, von Spee made off in the other. His alert lookouts had spotted the fighting tops of Sturdee's battlecruisers at anchor in Port Stanley. Von Spee must have been doubly shocked - not only was he up against a British battlecruiser squadron, but he must have appreciated that Germany's network in the Admiralty had been fed false intelligence, i.e. had been spotted.

The battlecruisers were fast, with centrally directed main batteries. Even without fully synthetic fire control, they were able to win a great victory, soured only by the failure to sink *Dresden* and capture both the gold and Canaris. With better intelligence, Sturdee would have sent say *Inflexible* after *Dresden*, whilst the rest of his powerful squadron, which included the armoured cruiser HMS *Kent*, went after von Spee. Still, a brace of enemy armoured cruisers wasn't a bad bag with which to see out the year.

The Battle of the Falkland Islands was a triumphant vindication for Jackie Fisher (Admiral of the Fleet Lord Fisher of Kilverstone), who had championed the battlecruiser concept. Sensibly, Fisher had wanted to go after the 'Hun' at least five years before, correctly appreciating that he was hell-bent on war. He may well have known that the 'Hun' had sponsored the Zulu and Boer Wars and had been waging a quasi-war on the British Empire for decades, not to mention all-out economic warfare, much of it disguised as 'free trade'.

His view, which was strategically correct, was that it would be better to tackle him from a position of relative strength. He also seems to have had his doubts about *Titanic*, the sinking of which was an Act of War by Germany against both Britain and the United States. The pressure applied by German assets in Naval Intelligence to the surviving crew was too strong not to have gone unnoticed and as we have seen Lightoller, the *Titanic's* senior surviving officer, had been debriefed by Naval Intelligence in any event. Charmingly, both of Lightoller's daughters went into intelligence work, Mavis in the First Aid Nursing Yeomanry (FANY) and Doreen in political intelligence. FANY *did* do first aid, just as Jesuits hold masses, but they did a lot more besides.

The battlecruiser concept - high-speed, long-range capital ships with battleship-calibre main batteries, too fast to be caught by any ship able to sink them and powerful enough to overwhelm any ship able to match their speed, was sound. The German Navy adopted it, eventually ordering the powerful *Mackensen* class. They also used it to justify the pocket battleships, although they were slower than HMS *Lion*, never mind the last generation of British battlecruisers ordered during World War I, including the 'Mighty Hood', which attained 32 knots on her full-speed trials.[8]

Had Fisher's proposed HMS *Incomparable*, a daring, 1,000 ft long design, which was to mount 6 20-inch guns, have four Brown-Curtis turbines pushing out 180,000 SHP, do 35 knots and have global range, been built there would have been far fewer problems with the German battlecruisers *Scharnhorst* and *Gneisenau*, in World War II. The pocket battleships would have been hopelessly outgunned. Critics of the battlecruiser concept, who rarely acknowledge that it was proven in the Battle of the Falkland Islands, keep emphasising the lack of protection. In so doing they fail to grasp the point. Like the later pocket battleships, they weren't intended to engage battleships.

Incomparable would have had better than heavy cruiser armour anyway. Nothing but a battleship would have had much chance of staying operational after a single hit from one of her main battery guns, which were intended to fire projectiles weighing more than 4,000 pounds, not so much the size of a Volkswagen as a Range Rover. In World War II she would have been a superb fast carrier escort. She would have required investment in dry-docks, but that was needed anyway, and as we have seen Britain was operating 1,000+ ft ships by the end of the 1930s (the *Queens*).

Of course, had the Royal Navy been allowed to develop the 20-inch gun, and not subsequently been forced to hand it over to the Japanese, like the 18-inch, another of Jackie Fisher's good ideas, then there might not have been a World War II at all. On the same basis Germany would never dared start World War I had Fisher, England's greatest admiral since Nelson, been listened to by the Liberal Government.

1915

It is impossible to understand the events of 1915 unless one appreciates that both Asquith and Lloyd George were working for the Germans. Indeed, until one understands that fact it is impossible to make sense of World War I, in particular how long it took to beat the Central Powers, who could and should have been rolled over by 1916. The British and Russians were not alone in having been penetrated by the German Secret Service of course - the 'Boche' had a major asset in the French Army, in Philippe Pétain, who had been blackmailed over his homosexuality since he was a young man.

The blackmailing was done with Jesuit assistance (the fact that Pétain was gay was picked up at school and passed on down to the Vatican). There were high-ranking German assets in the French government as well. As indicated in Chapter 5, Pétain was spotted by the great Sir Edward Spears, who was present at most of the important Anglo-French military conferences of the war. He was fluent in French, with a near-flawless accent.

Lloyd George was particularly nervous of Churchill, a man of high intelligence. The wily Welshman schemed to embarrass him, force him out of the Admiralty and end his career.

The Dardanelles Amphibious Operation

Churchill, a strategic genius, was appalled by the carnage in the trenches, in which he was later willing to serve, unlike his Liberal Cabinet colleagues, none of whom knew the first thing about war. The trench systems stretched all the way from the Belgian coastline to the Swiss frontier. Italy had chosen to stay neutral. The 'Hun' could only be outflanked by an amphibious assault on the Belgian coast, which would have been a marginal military operation at best, through the Balkans or via Turkey.

An attack on Turkey might take her out of the war, liberate Palestine, break up the Ottoman Empire and safeguard oil supplies from the Middle East, all desirable strategic outcomes in themselves. In Churchill's words it would also expose Germany's 'soft underbelly'. If successful, it would certainly have opened up the war, broken the deadlock and created opportunities for manoeuvre warfare.

The idea of an amphibious operation was daring. None had ever been tried on such a scale before. Long before 'jointery' was promoted as a concept, it emphasised Army/Navy co-operation on an unprecedented scale. By attacking the Dardanelles the Ottoman capital of Constantinople was exposed, with the potential, if only German assets in Military Intelligence could be kept out of the way, for an enormous intelligence yield.

This might have included interesting snippets on the origins of Islam (i.e. whether or not it was sponsored by the Vatican) and the identity of the Vatican and European assets in London who cooperated in permitting Barbary Pirates to enslave so many English men, women and children over the centuries. The intelligence he found in Constantinople was later the key to Ataturk's power of course. With Turkey knocked out of the war there was the potential for a major Allied offensive against Bulgaria, which in turn would expose the right flank of the Austro-Hungarian Empire.

The impact of a successful amphibious attack on neutral opinion, especially American and Italian (Italy had not yet joined the war when Churchill and the Admiralty were planning the Dardanelles attack) would have been impressive. Russian morale would been boosted. It would not have been necessary for Allied troops to fight all the way to Vienna. The Austro-Hungarian Empire's enthusiasm for the war was muted, not least amongst the major players in Vienna who knew that Warburg, the Wilhelmstrasse and the Jesuits had been behind the assassination of Archduke Ferdinand.

As they did in 1917 after the new Emperor, Charles I, into whose son I happened to bump many years later,[9] discovered that Germany had set up the Sarajevo assassinations, Vienna would most likely have opened up separate peace negotiations. Never forget that Max Warburg and the Jesuit Provost, or Superior, General Franz Wernz, had ordered that the Archduchess Sophie, a very sweet person, be put to death as well, i.e. there were two assassinations not one, each of shocking brutality.

Sadly, of course, Charles had no one to negotiate with in London in 1917 as Lloyd George was working for the Germans. The Emperor's intelligence service would have so advised him, along with the Cardinal Archbishop of Vienna, Cardinal Piffl, who was as well-informed with respect as his successor Cardinal Schornborg (and just as nice a man by all accounts[10]). Woodrow Wilson wanted to break up the Empire, i.e. hand it over to the Germans (Democrats don't do kings). After the capture of Constantinople however, with Asquith and Lloyd George out of the way, Churchill as Prime Minister would have cut a deal with Vienna, leaving the Empire intact and Germany isolated.

The Italians would have been able to reinforce the Western Front, via Ventimiglia, and the Germans would have needed to weaken it in order to shore up the Eastern Front. Numbers varied but the Austrian Army provided a large number of both infantry and cavalry divisions against the Russians. The war would have been over by 1916, probably in sufficient time to limit the disruption of the cricket season.

The fly in the ointment of course was Lloyd George, who was well aware of his deficiencies as a war leader. The Army wouldn't have put him in charge of a platoon, never mind the entire war, even if they hadn't suspected that he was working for the enemy. He was desperate both to force Churchill, the most serious war leader Britain had, out of the Cabinet and to block him from taking over from the ineffectual Asquith. The latter's contribution to the war effort was even less than his son's, putting the matter at its lowest.

Had the Dardanelles Offensive succeeded Churchill would probably have succeeded Asquith as Prime Minister, saving tens of millions of lives, indeed he would have probably have remained Prime Minister for two decades, avoiding World War II and saving another 50 million lives. When you have a statesman as brilliant as Churchill you put him in charge, not in a trench. Putting Churchill in a trench and Lloyd George in the comfort of Number 10 threw away lives by the million.

As I have confirmed privately with 'Johnny Turk', Lloyd George betrayed Churchill's brilliant plan to the 'Hun'. This gave him time to move reinforcements to Turkey, fortify and mine the straits and ambush the British and French Navies when they turned up to commence their powerful preliminary bombardment. The traditional explanation - that 'Harry Hun' and 'Johnny Turk' were warned of the impending land attack by the naval bombardment - is risible nonsense. Defensive preparations were well advanced by the time the Anglo-French fleet rolled up. The key thing is to focus on when the 'Hun' *started* to fortify and reinforce the Dardanelles, not when he finished.

Lloyd George was also keen to drive a wedge between Australia, New Zealand and Britain. He was particularly anxious that the combined Australian and New Zealand Army Corps (the immortal ANZACs) suffer heavy casualties, which tragically they did. The Turk was given ample warning of the landing at Anzac Cove on 25th April, still commemorated in moving dawn ceremonies in Australia and New Zealand nearly a century later.[11] Betraying the operation to Germany was not the only way Lloyd George was able to run interference.

Churchill could ensure that a competent naval commander was chosen but had no influence over the War Office. They were prevailed upon to select the most useless commander they possibly could. General Sir Ian Hamilton was a genial old duffer - no better man if you were in the Sudan and surrounded by 'fuzzie-wuzzies'[12] – but would have been no more out of his depth had he leapt overboard from the flagship, HMS *Queen Elizabeth*. She, incidentally, was the most powerful warship in the world. With every respect he had as much idea of how to run a major amphibious operation as Corporal Jones from the wonderful BBC comedy *Dad's Army*. The brilliant Australian general, Sir John Monash, would have been a far better choice. Again, one of the problems with having idiots in charge in London was that they tended to appoint other idiots to take charge elsewhere.

As indicated, the first British intelligence officer to pick up that there was a major problem in London was probably Sir Edward Spears. He also became aware the Germans had high-level penetration assets in Paris as well and that Pétain's loyalty was in doubt, to put it mildly. He sacrificed over a million French troops at Verdun pursuant to a deal struck with the Germans, who were willing to sacrifice a few hundred thousand of their own in order to bleed the French Army dry.

It was an utter tragedy for the British Empire and the Allies that Lloyd George was not publicly exposed and hanged. The French, similarly, could usefully have shot Pétain, but chose instead to sacrifice a large chunk of their army. The losses eventually doomed the Third Republic, as the French had had the stuffing knocked out of them by the end of 1917.

Fewer German outrages caused more upset than the raids on quiet English seaside towns such as Scarborough, which had no military significance and were not legitimate targets. The operations were all to do with exerting psychological pressure by killing civilians and causing damage to beautiful and much-loved seaside towns. They were nothing whatsoever to do with trying to bring the Grand Fleet to battle.

Von Battenberg had ensured that there were enough German assets in Naval Intelligence to be able to warn Berlin if the mighty Grand Fleet, or the fast Battlecruiser Squadron, set sail. Although von Battenberg had been forced out his protégés were still in place. Only once, at the Battle of the Dogger Bank, were Beatty and his battlecruisers able to get to grips with the 'Hun'. Pre-warned, most of the German squadron were able to make good their escape, the old cruiser *Blücher* being offered as a sacrifice.

The Germans also tried to cause panic and terror through bombing, mainly using Zeppelins, again not of military objectives, indeed half the time they were bombing through cloud. As long as they killed people they did not seem to mind, although the Germans were full of captious criticism when they suffered collateral casualties from RAF bombing of strategic targets in Germany in World War II. The difference of course was that the RAF were careful where they dropped their bombs.

Nurse Edith Cavell

At around 0500 hours local time on 12th October 1915, in an atrocity which aroused the Empire and appalled the rest of the civilised world, and which confirmed to informed opinion that whatever else he was the 'Hun' was not civilised, a German firing squad shot the brave English nurse and intelligence officer Edith Cavell. This outrage rightly led to a fine statue of Nurse Cavell just off Trafalgar Square in London, and to the naming of a beautiful, 11,033 feet mountain in the Canadian Rockies after her.[13] You just don't put nurses up against a wall in the cold light of dawn and shoot them.

There is a slight snag with the official narrative however. The Germans didn't shoot Edith Cavell. They shot a woman they thought was Edith Cavell, i.e. someone dropped a very large clanger. Warburg, who authorised the execution, was probably hoping to acquire intelligence in exchange for clemency. This is a standard and of itself not unobjectionable tactic (which many years later I myself suggested to a legal adviser acting for Saddam Hussein), provided you don't end up shooting nurses. You have to make sure that your execution is justified in the first place, both legally and morally, which the Brussels execution was not. Appeals to legal technicalities do not assist the 'Hun'.

There can be no suggestion that Edith Cavell was a coward. So far to the contrary, her intelligence operation had saved many lives, not just those of the Allied escapees her escape run helped over the lines, but through the intelligence some of them carried back. Battling an enemy as heartless and as given to hissy fits as the 'Hun', Edith Cavell cannot have been under any illusion as to how she would be treated if betrayed, as she was. This was probably thanks to someone in London. The cold and calculating Vernon Kell, who had access to military intelligence, is in the frame for the betrayal of Edith Cavell.

My understanding is that she was strongly opposed to the plan to substitute one of her nurses for her, particularly as this girl was very close to her, but she was overruled from London. Since she was officially dead it also meant that she was unable to resume her former life. The swap wasn't terribly difficult, courtesy of forged papers. The 'Hun' tends to attach great weight to his official documents. If your papers said that you were Nurse Edith Cavell that's who you were. Of course, the swap created problems postwar when a statue was proposed.

Edith Cavell, so far as I know, was still alive and living under an assumed name in Belgium (too many people in England might have recognised her). Of whom should the statue be? Edith Cavell, or the equally courageous young woman who went bravely and stoically to her death in her place? The latter by the way almost certainly did not utter the words attributed to her by the Revd Stirling Gahan, who was acting for Warburg and was trying to cut a deal. Sensibly, it was a statue of Edith Cavell, but not everybody who attended the opening ceremony was briefed in. A general with connections to military intelligence who had seen a file photo of the poor woman who was executed nearly gave the game away, until he was kicked in the shins. It is always important to have a few shin-kickers at these turnouts.

Betrayal of the tank

German assets in London, including the notorious Maurice Hankey, were also involved in betraying British weapons concepts to the 'Hun', such as the tank. Hankey was directly involved in that operation. Thus, when the British commenced the world's first large-scale tank operations they found the Germans waiting. One has to distinguish of course between initial German confusion at the tactical level and preparedness at the intelligence and staff level. The latter were not always willing to share intelligence lower down the food chain, indeed they dare not, lest they expose their assets in London.

Development of the ponderous (and very German-looking) A7V Sturmpanzerwagen started in 1915. The traditional explanation - that 'Harry Hun' responded to the initial British use of tanks in the Battle of the Somme by whistling up a brand new panzer just like that - is nonsense on stilts. Of course the 'Hun' took great care to add a year or so to the date of the blueprints, to fool historians in the future.

The Admiralty and technical innovation

The lead department on the development of the tank by the way, just as it had been on the aircraft (the world's first air strike was carried out by Sopwith Tabloids of the Royal Naval Air Service) was the Admiralty. More rubbish has been written about this department than any other. Churchill was technologically literate and had a progressive approach towards new technology. He found keen support in the Admiralty. The Tabloid was the world's first militarily capable aircraft, beating the Fokker Eindecker and the French Nieuport Scouts by months. The Army's Royal Flying Corps was promoting stable but slow reconnaissance aircraft such as the BE2c and RE8,[14] which were easily shot down by the new Fokkers, with their interrupter gear,[15] an idea stolen from the French.

The Admiralty were alive to the threat posed by submarines and had ordered their own, whilst being realistic about their limitations. No British capital ship or cruiser was sunk by U-Boat in either world war without first being betrayed. Most sinkings were ambushes. They also developed the world's first practical submarine detection device (Asdic[16]) and anti-submarine weapon (the depth-charge).

They also supported the invention of the computer (the Pollen Clock fire control computer, which as we have seen was essentially an electro-mechanical analogue computer) and ordered the conversion of the world's first aircraft carrier. When you consider that they had also taken the lead in developing the modern battleship (HMS *Dreadnought*, with her centralised fire control), the turbine, oil-firing and the destroyer, it wasn't a bad record. No modern British government department is remotely as progressive in its willingness to embrace new technology, unless it doesn't work, in which case it tends to be promoted with vigour.

The Admiralty had integrated the world's first aircraft carrier, HMS *Furious*, into the fleet by 1916, ordered the world's first specialist shipboard fighter, the Sopwith Camel F.2b, by 1917 and planned the world's first carrier strike, on Zeebrugge, by 1918. Along the way they invented the torpedo bomber (the Sopwith Cuckoo, built to Admiralty requirements).

The Sinking of RMS *Lusitania*, on 7th May 1915

I am *not* saying that the record of German Intelligence was one of unalloyed success. Had they been better they would have warned the Kaiser against starting World War I, indeed the smart move would have been not to try and take down the British Empire at all. For all its cleverness German Intelligence has never obeyed Sir David Omand's first rule of intelligence, i.e. never do anything you can't defend when it gets out. The second rule is that it *will* get out, sooner or later.

The sinking of the *Titanic* in 1912 was a short-term success, if murdering over 1,500 innocent men, women and children on the high seas can be called a success. It ensured sufficient participation in Medium Term Note trading by American-based banks to fund World War I, or at least get it started. However, I believe the long-term consequences for Germany of this crime will be grave.

I am not so egotistical by the way as to assume that the single chapter in this book on the *Titanic*, no more than a short summary, will be sufficient on its own. It builds on material that is in the public domain anyway, reflects doubts held in the Mercantile Marine over many years, and is no more than a step towards the full truth being known to all the world. These deaths will haunt the Germans for centuries long after Germany has ceased to exist. There will probably be a memorial service for the *Titanic* victims in 2512. The cover-up, which has dragged in Whitehall, Washington, the Third Reich and the Federal Republic of Germany, if not worse that the original crime, has seen a great many accessories after the fact.

The ludicrous plan to torpedo the *Lusitania* counts amongst the Wilhemstrasse's silliest errors. This time it had immediate strategic consequences, in that it helped bring America into the war. The infamous warnings in the American press were of course promulgated in full knowledge that a U-Boat would be lying in wait off the Irish coast to torpedo the great Cunarder, ordinarily far too fast for a U-Boat. She could steam at 25 knots. The U-20, which sank her, could only do 9.5 knots underwater.

The sinking, on 7th May 1915, was essentially a decapitation exercise, aimed at embarrassing Churchill and forcing him from the Admiralty. He posed a high order threat to the Central Powers - and an even greater one were he to replace the ineffectual Asquith. The Dardanelles Offensive still had the 'Hun' worried.

The devious and villainous Lloyd George, then Chancellor and shortly to be made Minister of Munitions, arranged for some munitions to be placed aboard the *Lusitania* in New York, a militarily pointless exercise. British weapons were generally a different calibre to American. The British Army in 1915 actually used very little American kit, indeed that position did not alter greatly after the United States entered the war two years later. Munitions could have been placed on board fast freighters via Halifax if need be. Strenuous efforts have been made to argue the military value (e.g. of the 13-pounder guns) of the munitions placed aboard the *Lusitania.* The reality is they were of no material significance to the war effort at all.

The munitions were not there for their military value of course, but their political value. As has been explained, the Admiralty was thoroughly penetrated. Not only had the previous First Sea Lord been a German spy, but many of the Admiralty's officials were civil servants, not naval officers. That is to say they had lower ethical standards and less moral fibre. This came to the fore in the subsequent, disgraceful treatment of Captain Turner, *Lusitania's* Master, which of course gave Lord Mersey (no surprise there) ammunition to embarrass the Admiralty at the subsequent inquiry, another musical comedy. Captain Turner was understandably bitter at Churchill, but never appears to have considered:

(1) That whilst he knew, obviously, that there were munitions on board his ship Churchill did not, and
(2) That there were German agents in the Admiralty, indeed Churchill himself was not fully briefed in, yet another case of someone who needed to know things being left in the dark.

Lloyd George's plan was to have Churchill make a statement to the House of Commons, in good faith, denying the presence of munitions, then have pro-German officials pull the rug out from under him. German assets in Whitehall have long pushed the idea, which has no basis in the British Constitution, that a minister can be forced to resign, i.e. take political responsibility for, misconduct by officials of which he has no knowledge. It sounds fine in theory until you realise that it's a perfect way for a hostile state which has penetrated the Civil Service to get rid of ministers who actually know what they are doing, not that there are many of those.

The intent was not to sink the *Lusitania*, partly because the 'Hun' was shocked by the worldwide reaction to the sinking of the *Titanic*. Captain Smith's humane, correct and thoroughly British instruction to give priority to the women and children, including those travelling in third-class, the stoic way in which the male first-class passengers went to their deaths, the heroism of the *Titanic's* crew, who stayed at their duty stations[17] until the end and most of whom drowned, and Captain Rostrom's gallant dash through the night to rescue the survivors, created powerful images. They are still able to stir the emotions a century later.

The German Head of Station in Washington would have been alarmed at any suggestion of killing American civilians, especially women and children, on the high seas, whilst going about their lawful occasions, on an essentially unarmed ocean liner. A sneak attack from a submerged vessel in breach of the Laws of War would especially be calculated to arouse emotions. In the next world war, the Japanese picked up a few hints about how Americans view sneak attacks.

As someone in German Naval Intelligence ought to have pointed out this cunning plan suffered from one tiny, technical flaw - it was bollocks.[18] All that was required was a change of course for a firing solution aimed at hitting the target in the bows to turn into a midships hit. Since the Germans themselves had arranged through their assets in Whitehall to load munitions on board *Lusitania* and since she was coal-fired, which meant coalbunkers, which meant coal dust, the risk of secondary explosions was obvious. This was not least because in order to further embarrass Churchill and the Admiralty, the munitions, such as they were, had not been properly packed.

That is what happened. Captain Turner, unaware that a U-Boat was lying in wait with orders to torpedo his great ship, albeit with a single shot, ordered a change of course, throwing out the firing solution. Recklessly, Kapitänleutnant Schwieger fired anyway. The *Lusitania* took a fatal hit and 1,198 people lost their lives. A stronger President than Wilson - an FDR or a George W. Bush - would have asked Congress to declare war on Germany immediately, indeed American troops had already engaged with a German client state on her southern border.

Wilson however seems to have had no idea whom he was fighting down south, even when a German freighter showed up with guns (in 1916 Pancho Villa went so far as to invade New Mexico - as his boys were eating burritos Wilson correctly concluded that they were Mexican, the bit he missed was who was bankrolling them). Aside from being distracted by German machinations in Mexico, Wilson was also worried about the 1916 election. For the time being the 'Hun' was allowed to get away with killing Americans, at least until the next electoral cycle.

Since the *Lusitania* had sunk there could be no 'surprise' discovery of a small shipment of munitions after she limped into harbour. The 'Hun' and his supporters have banged on about munitions ever since however, omitting the small but vital detail that it was a German asset who arranged for them in the first place. The endless bashing of the Admiralty continues to the present day.

Unsurprisingly, since it had been betrayed, the Dardanelles Offensive failed. Tragically, there was great loss of life, including many brave Australians. Churchill, unfairly, since the blame lay with the traitor Lloyd George, took what he thought was the honourable course and resigned. This was not long after the *Lusitania* was torpedoed and sunk, her loss clearly being a factor.

Lloyd George escaped the noose, sadly. This was one of the greatest counterintelligence bungles in recorded history, but he lived long enough to see his nemesis save Britain, the Empire and the rest of the West in 1940, and go on to take a major role in inflicting a second crushing defeat on Germany. The old goat finally snuffed it in March 1945, just before VE-Day. Understandably praised by his friend Adolf Hitler for his role in pulling Germany's irons out of the fire in 1919-1922, he had inflicted a lot of pain and heartache on the peoples of the Empire.

The U-Boat Campaign

The 'dastardly Hun' as ever was on the search for cheap solutions that did not include combat with the Grand Fleet. The idea of sneak attacks on unarmed merchant ships had powerful attraction for an enemy whose navy tended to run at the sight of a British Battle Ensign. The effectiveness of the 'unrestricted', i.e. criminal, U-Boat campaign is frequently over-estimated however. It depended on the willingness of neutral countries such as Germany's new client state Portugal to supply bases (German U-Boats in World War I had insufficient range to be able to operate into the Atlantic from Germany[19]). It also required a continued flow of intelligence from German assets in Britain, so that convoys could be ambushed.

That the U-Boats inflicted heavy damage from 1915 onwards is not to be denied, but with better counterintelligence they would not have been nearly so effective, indeed they were heavily dependent on Germany's assets in Whitehall betraying the convoys. Convoys maintained strict radio silence, there were no long-range aircraft then and the Zepps were misused for indiscriminate terror bombing of civilians instead of the one task of military value on which they could have been engaged. They bombed from such a height that they couldn't hit a military target even if they wanted to. Precision bombing had to await the development of gyro- stabilised bombsights and radar bombing in World War II.

The one thing they could do was long-range reconnaissance over the Atlantic. The very fact they were not so used emphasised that the Germans didn't need reconnaissance. They knew when the convoys sailed, what their cargos were, what escort they had if any, where they were headed and what course they would take. It would be 1943 before Naval Intelligence finally woke up to what was going on and convoys would suddenly change direction in mid-Atlantic for no apparent reason. Two of the German assets who helped to get our ships sunk in that war went on to do further damage as Prime Minister.[20]

Bureaucratic warfare

Two other ploys made their appearance early in the war, also used to great effect in World War II. The first was to have unnecessary rationing. The British Mercantile Marine was the largest in the world and had a capacity that would be impressive even today. The United Kingdom, including Ireland, was a rich agricultural nation, whilst the British Empire had immense capacity to produce food, from the vast prairies of Canada, to the huge cattle stations of Australia and the farms of New Zealand. At no stage did the Royal

Navy ever lose control of the sea, nor were merchant shipping losses ever heavy enough to stop enough food arriving at British ports.

Very little food actually needed to be brought across the Atlantic, the only sea-lane threatened by the U-Boats. Most food could be brought in from Australia (beef, mutton, sugar, fruit, jam, wine and grain), New Zealand (butter and lamb), East Africa (tea and coffee), India (tea), Ceylon (tea and spices) Mauritius (sugar) and if need be South Africa (fruit and wine) through the Suez Canal and the Med. After HMAS *Sydney* brilliantly blew SMS *Emden* apart there was very little the 'Hun' could do to stop food reaching Britain via the Indian Ocean.

The Austrian Navy, being run by gentlemen, of the sort portrayed in the classic, semi-fictional, heart-warming film *The Sound of Music*, didn't go in for sneak attacks on merchant ships. Unlike the 'dastardly Hun', your Austrian generally doesn't go in for waging war on unarmed civilians, although he may occasionally lock up his children in his basement.

With millions serving abroad in the Forces, and no reduction in food production in either Great Britain or Ireland, there was no need for rationing at all, except possibly in 1917. There was no difficulty in bringing foodstuffs across the Irish Sea, no reduction in coal output or closure of railway lines. The 'Hun's' air arm, which was essentially tactical anyway and part of the German Army, couldn't hit a railway line from height even if it aimed at one. The only way the Germans were ever able to interfere substantially with rail travel in Britain was to get their man Attlee to set up British Railways.

Put shortly, a system which was allegedly designed to make sure everybody had enough to eat, ended up making sure nobody did. It was all about punishing the British people for supporting the war effort and trying to make them war weary. In the end all it did was to make them thoroughly browned off. Since it was 'Harry Hun's' war they tended to be browned off at the 'Hun' rather than anyone else.

There were few private motor cars and motorcycles. Britain controlled much of the world's oil supply (in the Middle East) and the railways ran on coal. No diesel engines were built by any British railway company before 1918 – the first diesels didn't start running on the main line until after World War II, when they promptly broke down. The Empire had massive refining capacity. There was, therefore, no real need to ration petrol either. It was simply regulation for the sake of it.

Now if there is one thing the 'Hun' does understand it is how to gum up the works with pointless regulations. The European Union is the prime modern example, but he's been at it since World War I. This was the period when Whitehall really got going with pettifogging bureaucracy. The huge wartime increase in regulation had four aims:

(1) Creating non-jobs for civil servants, especially jobs which gave them an excuse not to do any fighting.
(2) Slowing down the economy.
(3) Draining the Exchequer, and
(4) Annoying people.

Led by Hankey, Germany's grey men in Whitehall achieved all four.

1916

In 1916 the 'Hun' came up with another cunning plan. Not content with controlling the main government departments (he had been in a position to push his people since Gladstone was Chancellor of the Exchequer), he decided to concentrate Civil Service power in a new, overarching central department. Hankey was just the man to lead it.

This new department was of course the Cabinet Office. The first Cabinet Secretary was indeed our old friend Maurice Hankey, a.k.a. 'Hankey Pankey', for the assorted naughtiness he got up to in the 'Hun's' male brothels. Hankey and his principal protégés Edward Bridges, Norman Brook and Burke Trend did enormous damage for over 50 years. Again, it was a tragedy that he was not spotted over the tank and shot, nicely of course. As an officer, of sorts, he was entitled to a firing squad. The 'wily Hun' is not called the 'wily Hun' for nothing. In both world wars he was more than happy to pick a few bunnies who couldn't shoot straight, and wouldn't have been much use on the front anyway, and send them to England to be captured. It was the height of complacency for MI5 to assume that they were rounding up every German spy sent to England. In both world wars they only caught the ones the 'Hun' wanted them to catch.

The betraying of their own people reached farcical proportions in World War II (tragically for the agent concerned, who was hanged) when a U-Boat commander, probably on instructions, famously gave a spy being landed by rubber boat a sausage. No doubt the U-Boat officer had stinted on breakfast. Turning up on a Scottish railway platform in heavily rationed 1941 eating *any* sort of sausage, let alone a *German* sausage, was guaranteed to arouse suspicion. They may as well have kitted out the poor agent with a spiked helmet, with orders to goose-step up to the booking office and ask the clerk for a ticket to London with a teensy-weensy bit of a German accent. "*Schnell, schnell dummkopf, ze zug* is coming!" "Angus, send for the Home Guard."

The funny "*Spy v. Spy*" cartoons in *Mad* magazine continue to exercise a fevered grip on the public imagination. The German spies who did the real damage to Britain and the Empire tended to be recruited at Oxford and

Cambridge, not in Germany. Similarly, those who did the most damage to America tended to be recruited at Harvard or Yale.

The damage is ongoing. Four things your really dangerous German spy will not be are:

(1) German.
(2) Dressed like a spy.
(3) Carrying a bomb, and
(4) Carrying a sketch map and camera.

The dress code for German spies in Britain - *ersatz* Edwardian gentleman - was set by Harold Macmillan. As for sketch maps and cameras what is the point when the Cabinet Secretary and Permanent Secretary to the Treasury are German spies and can not only get complete specifications of the things being photographed but get them altered, or for that matter not built at all?

Jutland

The precise role, played by German Secret Service assets inside Naval Intelligence, and the secret war waged against them, in the lead up to and during the Battle of Jutland is still not known, although the German file on Jutland will tell us a lot. What we do know is that significant interference was run on communications. Admiral Beatty was denied the aircraft sighting report of the German High Sea Fleet bearing down upon him, Admiral Scheer's idea of course being to ambush Beatty's battlecruisers.

As explained, battlecruisers were never intended to engage battleships. The tactical concept was that they would use their high speed to get out of enemy gun range. Once they were in a gun duel with battleships of equal or greater firepower their thin armour made them vulnerable, especially to plunging fire. They were big cruisers with battleship firepower, not battleships, and had no place in the battle line.

The Admiralty wanted better protection, in particular stronger armoured decks. That applied to each class of battlecruiser a member of which was sunk at Jutland. Lloyd George as Chancellor insisted that the Treasury have access to the detailed plans of all Royal Navy ships and submarines. These were promptly handed over to Germany. Never again must the Treasury be given sensitive military information - one may as well e-mail it to Berlin.

The German Navy were worried about the Royal Navy's battlecruisers. They posed a high order threat to German 'raiders' and in turn to Germany's ability to ship gold from the Far East to underpin their trading programmes, thus, the protection specifications for the battlecruisers were dictated to Lloyd George by German Naval Intelligence (I understand at a dinner at the Reform Club, attended by the German Naval Attaché). Put shortly, the Germans not only knew where the weaknesses were in British ships, their assets in the Liberal Government had put them there in the first place. Those in the know in the Navy were livid.

It is sometimes said that it was important that Jellicoe was a Mason whereas Beatty was not, although that didn't prevent the latter from being promoted to Admiral of the Fleet and replacing Jellicoe. It is more likely that Jellicoe had been forced to do a deal with Asquith whereby he did not chase the High Sea Fleet, which as history records (without explaining why) was able to make good its escape. The traditional explanation – fear of mines – holds no more water than the *Seydlitz* did after taking the Grand Fleet's shellfire.

Thanks largely to Churchill the British had the immense advantage of the 15-inch 42 calibre Mark 1 gun, with which the *Queen Elizabeth* class super-dreadnoughts were armed. There should have been a class of ten rather five, however. The 15 inch 42 was not only heavier than any gun in the High Sea Fleet, which had to buy from Krupps and was generally lumbered with their rather inadequate 28 cm (11 inch) and 12-inch guns, but had a longer range as well. It was a super bit of kit.

The Battle of Jutland was still a British victory, although it came at a grievous price. It is not true to say the High Sea Fleet never ventured out of harbour again except to surrender, but it only went out when it knew the Grand Fleet was at anchor *and* was confident German naval intelligence would warn the admiral should it set sail. Jutland ensured British control of the North Sea and North Atlantic. If it didn't win the war in an afternoon, it at least made sure that Germany couldn't win at all.

The next long voyage the High Sea Fleet made, minus the fire control clocks of course (which would have given the game away), was to surrender. That too was a farce, as there were sufficient German assets in the Admiralty to allow them to get away with scuttling their ships, ironically at the same time as Germany's Sir Eric Geddes was scuttling the Royal Navy's, many less than ten years old.

The Danes no doubt took note of what was happening off their coast. Admiral Fisher's highly original but possibly too bold plan to attack the 'Hun' on his Baltic flank, land troops and take Berlin really needed Denmark. It was an interesting concept, though. The North German Plain is ideal for manoeuvre warfare and if the Kiel Canal were blocked the High Sea Fleet would have been marooned on the North Sea coast.

The Danes however were still annoyed by the disastrous decision to leave them in the lurch in 1864, when Prussia invaded. Copenhagen was no doubt thoroughly penetrated as well. Since Fisher would not have proposed the plan without squaring it away with the Danes it rather looks as though he had some contact with Copenhagen, with a view to ensuring that Denmark did not stay neutral.

Admiral Fisher's Baltic plan left the Royal Navy with three shallow-draft light battlecruisers, HMS *Glorious, Courageous* and *Furious*, the latter being the first capital ship in the world to mount an 18-inch gun.[21] The twin 15-inch turrets (two each) on *Glorious* and *Courageous* were landed after the decision was taken to convert them into carriers. This was sensible - arguably the world's first littoral combat ships they were no use outside the littoral, being a handful in any sort of sea.

The guns were eventually fitted in HMS *Vanguard,* Britain's most recent battleship. She survived until Macmillan had her scrapped in 1961,[22] in order to weaken the Royal Navy and reduce British prestige, which was suffering pretty badly as it was with him as Prime Minister. When the last 15-inch Mark 1 was scrapped, fifty years after it was designed, there was only one better operational piece of heavy artillery in the world, the US Navy Bureau of Ordnance's great 16-inch 50 calibre.[23]

The Somme

The Somme was also a victory, but at even greater cost, and not as decisive. It would have been decisive had Lloyd George not tipped off 'Basil Boche', who thus had time to deepen and harden his trenches. The Royal Artillery were not stupid, nor for that matter was Field Marshal Sir Douglas Haig. The massive artillery bombardment, which preceded the great attack on 1st July 1916, was calibrated by a careful intelligence- gathering exercise on the depth and strength of German trench systems.

Knowing exactly when and where the attack would come gave the 'Boche' a decisive advantage. Smarter counterintelligence work would have seen Asquith, Lloyd George and Hankey spotted, left in place for the time being, whilst their telephones were tapped and their movements carefully monitored. A case for high treason could have been built, whilst the attack was switched to a weak section of the German lines.

The great Field Marshal Earl Kitchener of Khartoum, assassinated, with Lloyd George in the loop, on 5th June 1916, after his ship, HMS *Hampshire,* was blown up by the German agent Fritz Duquesne,[24] knew that there was a leak out of the Cabinet. Lord Kitchener wasn't sure who it was, but was closing in, the reason he was murdered of course. Had he survived he would most probably have switched the Somme attack.

Since German troops were being pulled out of other sectors in order to reinforce the Somme salient there were plenty of opportunities. Leaving Lloyd George and Hankey in place (Asquith was eventually forced out, to spend more time with his rent-boys, although that is not quite how it was put in the press release) virtually guaranteed that every major British offensive of the war was betrayed to the enemy. Whilst the Home Office and War Office were lecturing everybody about security, a German spy was not only attending every meeting of the War Cabinet, but taking the minutes. A complete set probably resides in the DVD's archives.

One of the reasons the Somme Offensive was persisted with was to get artillery and intelligence officers into the German trenches. We had to know how so many 'Huns' had survived the initial bombardment. Sir Edward Spears had been making himself unpopular warning Kitchener and others that there was a leak in London, and a major one at that. After the summer of 1916 he was listened to with greater care.

It took far too long however for the leaks to be traced to Lloyd George, who was not forced out until military intelligence finally, at long, long last briefed in the suits in the Tory Party. This was done over dinner in the Carlton Club. The Tories promptly pulled the rug from under the Welsh traitor (hence the title of the powerful backbench 1922 Committee).

Even then Hankey was left in place, which was absurd, as was the decision not to hang Lloyd George. In exchange for his miserable life he offered nothing in return, blaming the generals for casualties he himself caused. The popular image of British generals in France is reflected in the wickedly funny *Blackadder Goes Forth* television comedy series, starring *inter alia* the late, lugubrious Geoffrey Palmer as Field Marshal Haig and Stephen Fry as the 'Haig-like' General Melchett. (Geoffrey and I once bumped into each other, on a Metropolitan Line train to Baker St.) It is important to remember however that like the Official History of World War I, *Blackadder* is a work of fiction. Lord Haig was the standout military commander of the war. He would have won it in 1916 had his great offensive not been betrayed from London.

Einstein

1916 saw a mini-coup for the German Secret Service when they sponsored the publication, by one of their tame publishers (it would probably be fair to say that *all* publishers in the German Empire were tame - there were not a lot of radical books-shops in pre-war Berlin), Verlag von Friedrich Viewheg &

Sohn, of the greatest scientific hoax of the 20th century until global warming. This was *Uber die spezialle und allgemeine Relativitatstheorie*, written by their chief scientific adviser, a chap named Albert Einstein. Naturally the book was translated into English (in 1920), under the title *The Special and General Theory of Relativity*, to which great acclaim was accorded, partly because no one understood it.

Like his earlier Secret Service colleague Karl Marx's *Das Kapital, The Special and General Theory of Relativity* is a marvellous example of what Professor Law calls 'pseudo- profundity',[25] a posh name for bollocks. Like *Das Kapital*, which was junk economics, and the later junk science of global warming, the junk science of the theory of relativity, in which Einstein was essentially trying to persuade us that when a ship steams away and disappears over the horizon it is shrinking, had a kernel of truth, or profound insight.

Most businessmen today talk in terms of adding value and when Marx talked about workers adding value to a product he was right. The whole point of having a worker in the first place is to add value to a business, but the rest was nonsense on stilts. Einstein got the mass-energy equation right, so people made the mistake of assuming that he had to be right about everything else.

The big lie is in Chapter 12,[26] where Einstein asserts that the speed of light is "an unattainable limiting velocity", although the wily old scientific spy carefully avoids saying how, if the speed of light is unattainable, light can attain it. Sadly, his stock rose at an even faster velocity. For nearly a century this collection of old cobblers held science in its thrall.

It certainly lasted a lot longer than the similar theory that you couldn't go faster than the speed of sound, in which case there must have been something wrong with my watch the last time I flew Concorde. That took just 3 hours 15 minutes from JFK to Heathrow. Perhaps it was just a poorly calibrated Machmeter (they had one at the front of the cabin).

In fairness, NASA were not taken in by Einstein, at any rate not the very smart folk down at the Jet Propulsion Laboratory in Pasadena. Apparently, they were puzzled at his 'error' about the speed of light at least until I popped along[27] to explain that he was a German spy. His book was largely an exercise in scientific disinformation, which would have done credit to the UN's IPCC.

The only way to get scientists who didn't work for NASA to consider the matter rationally was to persuade a few helpful subatomic particles to trot around the Large Hadron Collider in the Swiss Federation at faster than the speed of light. This was duly done, publicly at any rate, in 2011. I am nothing if not fair to 'Harry Hun' however and I believe that the credit for being first to walk a few particles faster than the speed of light should go to two brilliant German physicists, Drs Gunter Nimitz and Alfons Stahlhofen at the University of Koblenz, that rather lovely city on the Rhine. There have been official denials of course, and mutterings about the Hadron Collider's time measurements, as though they used cuckoo clocks.

German Intelligence started showing an interest in acquiring uranium not long after Einstein's first book came out. These facts may not be unrelated. German atomic research, partly thanks to Einstein, was well ahead of Britain's and Denmark's. The structure of matter, i.e. the existence of sub-atomic particles, was well understood by 1916. Einstein was quick to grasp the military potential of atomic energy.

He was also careful[28] in his book to try and undermine Newton, which suggests that he was worried about the potential for combining the vast potential of atomic energy with Newton's Third Law of Motion. If a stream of subatomic particles is fired at above the speed of light in one direction, then an interstellar ship could advance at greater than the speed of light in the other, opening up at least the nearer stars to human exploration.

Sabotage of space programmes has been a priority for German Intelligence since they murdered Virgil 'Gus' Grissom, Edward White and Roger Chaffee, the Apollo 1 astronauts, on pad 34 at Cape Canaveral on 27th January 1967. Sadly, it was years before Einstein, whose priority was the military exploitation of atomic energy for Germany, not the Good Guys, was spotted. By then he had passed every atomic secret of importance to emerge from the Manhattan Project (so named because the first intended target was Lower Manhattan[29]) to Germany.

---

1. Most historians describe it as the 'High Seas Fleet', but 'Sea' is correct. The 'Hun' appreciates correctness.
2. Partly exposed by Ian Fleming, who gave the surname 'Drax' to the evil German villain in *Moonraker* - it's amazing what you can get away with in a novel.
3. Who put up the money for Bletchley Park. It was an amusing conceit of GCHQ for many years that its forerunner Bletchley Park was never penetrated, when it was in fact owned by German Intelligence. Sinclair didn't use his own money of course.
4. Whose late son Sir Michael, a nice chap, became an ambassador. Unusually for the FCDO, he was not a German spy.
5. Hitler insisted her name be changed and it was (he could be a very insistent chap), to KMS *Lutzow*. It would be interesting to know why - the official explanation, that the blow to morale should a ship named for the Fatherland be sunk would be too great, is unconvincing to say the least.
6. 17,250 tons standard displacement, 8 12-inch guns.
7. 26,270 tons standard displacement, 8 13.5-inch Mk V guns, 28 knots - wonderful ships. They were mainly coal-fired but used oil as well, in fact the oil could be sprayed onto the coal, i.e. their propulsion was a transition to the full oil-firing of the *Queen Elizabeth* class.
8. HMS *Hood* Association website, which is very good by the way. They give 32.07 knots at 42,000 tons on the Arran Mile in a Force 6 and 31 knots average top speed on 144,000 SHP at 197 revolutions, presumably clean hull in temperate waters. In her final engagement, badly in need of refit (indeed she needed rebuilding, as the Admiralty wanted, never mind a refit) she was barely able to make 28 knots and was even slower than *Bismarck*. She looked wonderful, however.
9. In Strasbourg in 1989, as related in Ch. 4. This was of course HIH Archduke Otto von Hapsburg, an awfully nice man, who gave rise to the only joke to come out of the European Parliament, that is if you discount the Parliament itself. Austria were playing Hungary at football in the European Championship, Otto was asked whether he was intending to watch the 'Austria Hungary match' and quick as a flash is reported to have responded 'who are we playing?' It was quite a nice old Empire and should be brought back. As indicated, its collapse left a void that led to Nazi, then Communist, control of much its former territory, and a series of wars in the Balkans. If the Liberals had done the right thing and gone to Denmark's aid in 1864, Austria- Hungary might well have attacked Prussia from the East - Britain and Austria- Hungary had of course been valiant allies together against Napoleon. Historians tend to confuse the Empire's decentralised and quite liberal structures with weakness. It worked, whereas its successors didn't. Most of his former subjects would have wept for joy had dear old Otto been restored to his rightful inheritance. Certainly, fewer of them would have ended up in gas chambers or basements.
10. His Eminence and I have not met, but we had mutual friends.
11. I attended one in Perth in 2011, by the sea. It was very moving.

12. The British Army's affectionate, non-racist, nickname for the Mad Mahdi's army, who if they weren't mad were certainly a trifle keen. Over a century later an Army officer sent out to the Lebanon as a peacekeeper, who had probably forgotten to pack his sun helmet, went ever so slightly off his rocker and started shooting wildly, thinking that he was 'surrounded by fuzzie-wuzzies', which of course was silly. He was over 1,000 miles from the Sudan.
13. It's near Jasper in the loyal province of Alberta, many of whose bravest sons and daughters went on to avenge her execution. It can be seen by passengers on VIA Rail's superb *Canadian*, at over 2,750 miles the longest rail journey in North America and by far the classiest way to travel from Toronto to Vancouver. The view from the dome cars as you go through the Rockies is magnificent. The *Canadian* of course was originally a Canadian Pacific express - it is a great shame they pulled out of long-distance passenger trains.
14. The dear old RE8 should be familiar to most readers of the Biggles books, written by that great air intelligence officer Captain W. E. Johns, who was murdered by GO2, the German operation in London, in 1968. They are full of sound advice about how to land spies at night, deal with restless natives and so on.
15. A mechanism whereby a machine-gun could fire through the propeller, it being a bad idea, generally, to shoot your own propeller off.
16. It is a myth by the way that this came out of the 'Anti-Submarine Detection Investigation Committee' - that was a little ploy by the Naval Intelligence Department.
17. This may not include the radio officers Phillips and Bride. Whilst they probably broadcast the first distress calls, on Captain Smith's instructions, they may have refused to broadcast later calls. No one has ever published the analysis of *Titanic's* radio traffic, some of which (particularly the low- powered emergency set transmissions) was never intercepted anyway. *Californian's* radio officer only ever monitored one frequency, but as we have seen the *Titanic* had two sets. The naval intelligence officer aboard would have been fluent in Morse, ditto Major Butt, and many of the Mayday transmissions may have been theirs. It is noticeable that there were changes in style, e.g. from the use of the older CDQ distress code to SOS, which was the correct code. It had been agreed as far back as the 1906 International Radiotelegraphic Convention and was first used at sea in 1909. The idea that it had only just been introduced seems to have been pushed to distract attention from the fact that there was a change in the style of the transmissions. Morse operators can be identified from their 'signature'. The change in the ship's position may not be accounted for entirely by the distance she covered as Captain Smith sought to bring her alongside the German cruiser or U-Boat, which was of course moving away at high speed. Since they were working for the enemy, the radio operators may have altered the position deliberately, as well as used an out of date distress code. They were no doubt expecting to be rescued by the *Californian*.
18. With apologies again to Captain Blackadder, played very wittily of course by Rowan Atkinson CBE.

19. U-20 had a cruising range of just over 5,000 nautical miles e.g., which sounds a lot until you look at the map and factor in operations, which tended to require full speed, and the need to stay on station for extended periods. Unlike World War II there were no German bases on France's Atlantic coast or in southern Ireland.
20. Harold Wilson and Edward Heath.
21. Two in fact, in single turrets, which without fully synthetic fire control and triaxially stabilised directors, which the Treasury wouldn't allow the Admiralty for fear that the armament might actually be made to work, were a case of 'great gun, shame about the fire control'. So far as is known the Navy never actually managed to hit anything with them, not at sea at any rate, but they made impressive splashes. The Germans asked Lloyd George to give the gun the to the Japanese, who improved and metricated it and installed it in the IJN *Yamato* and *Musashi,* which thanks to the Washington Treaty and other assorted idiocies ended up as the largest and most powerful battleships ever built, on paper at any rate. Fortunately, the Japanese didn't know how to use them and only managed to build two. They rather pointlessly, indeed completely pointlessly since they didn't have any aircraft to put on her, converted the third, the *Shinano,* into an aircraft carrier, rather making my point that they didn't really understand battleships. Their battle line in World War II had a daft mix of 14-inch, 16-inch and 18-inch - the US Navy wisely concentrated on the 16-inch and brilliantly managed to fit the stonking 2,700lb Mk 8 projectile into the short (45 calibre) barrel, giving them a very integrated and easy to control battle line. Unsurprisingly, since they had a couple of admirals who actually understood battleships (Lee and Oldfield they won their two big-gun battles with the Japanese. They also beat the French - the famous gunnery duel in 1942 between the USS *Massachusetts,* the only American battleship in history to fire on a French ship of the line, and the FS *Jean Bart.* The French score it as a draw but the 49ers said that about the 2013 Super Bowl. The Good Guys, i.e. the Americans, won.
22. Sadly, she wasn't used at Suez, partly because the German spy Mountbatten was involved in the planning and was reluctant to kill Egyptians, Colonel Nasser of course being a fellow German spy. Strictly, he should have been called Oberst Nasser. *Vanguard* would have been a wonderful asset in the Falklands, indeed what was left of the enemy forces on East Falkland would probably have surrendered after a single night-time bombardment.
23. It was one of dear old HMS *Warspite's* 15-inch (42 cal.) which scored the longest-range combat hit of World War II, 26,000 yards, on *Giulio Cesare* at the Battle of Calabria - brilliant gunnery. The 'Eyeties' still say that it was a fluke of course, but what else do they think that *Warspite's* gunnery officer was aiming at, the Leaning Tower of Pisa?
24. Fritz Joubert Duquesne had tried to assassinate Kitchener in the Boer War. The debate about Kitchener's sexuality has dragged on long enough. He was bisexual, and a very nice one too.
25. *Believing Bullshit.*

26. P. 45 of the Folio Edition, 2007, itself a reprint of Methuen's 15th ed., published in 1954.
27. Purely informally, for a cup of tea. It was an afternoon meeting, following one at the Skunk Works, which are just up State Highway 14 at Palmdale, where my response to the question "where are you headed next?" ("just down to Pasadena to see NASA") fractionally raised a couple of eyebrows. There was no question of a consultancy fee of course (that would have raised alarm bells in Washington), but I popped into the well-stocked little gift shop by the entrance and purchased a very nice NASA mouse-mat, used when writing the first editionmuch of this book.
28. See Ch. 30, where he attacks Sir Isaac Newton.
29. This is not the official explanation, according to the Department of Energy.

15

1917 - 1918

1917

No commander can control the weather of course, at least not until scalar high-energy weapons came along at the end of the 20th century. The great Flanders Offensive in 1917 suffered from wretched weather, although again it would have helped had the Germans not known we were coming. The BEF learnt from the Somme and a new tank doctrine started to emerge at the Battle of Cambrai in November.

It had Haig's complete support, i.e. the commander generally portrayed as unimaginative, stubborn and out of date presided over the invention of armoured warfare. It is likely that the British breakthrough would have been exploited had the Germans not being waiting with their own tanks, having been warned in sufficient time to reinforce the Cambrai sector in depth. Sadly, a cousin of Henry's, Willie Robinson, a gunner in a Vickers Mark IV tank in H battalion of the Tank Corps, lost a leg at Cambrai, which was a nuisance. (Apparently it didn't slow him down very much.)

The entry of the United States into the war in April largely sealed the 'Hun's' fate, although of course it should not have been necessary. The war would have been won by the end of 1916 but for the degree of penetration in London and Paris by the German Secret Service.

Any lingering resistance in the Wilhemstrasse to deploying Lenin and organising a further revolt in Russia melted away after America's entry. Both Ludendorff and Hindenberg appreciated that Germany had one last chance to break through in the West, in the spring of 1918. It is still unclear whether Hindenberg was aware of the Secret Service's plan to augment the offensive with a new biological weapon. It came to be known as Spanish Flu, but ought to have been called German Flu. I suspect that Ludendorff kept Hindenberg, who was a gent, largely out of the loop. Germ warfare wasn't really the Field Marshal's cup of tea.

With fresh American troops reinforcing the Western Front it was all the more vital that German troops be recalled from the East. The Wilhemstrasse made their move.

The October Revolution

It is impossible to understand any part of the history of the Soviet Union, including the close German-Soviet military and intelligence cooperation after 1919 and the Molotov–Ribbentrop Pact, without appreciating that the October Revolution was bankrolled and sponsored by the German Secret Service. Lenin of course was one of theirs. The whole idea was to help Germany win World War I.

It is not clear if Churchill understood this at the time, although correctly he appreciated the need to stand up to the USSR. Adolf Hitler died in ignorance of German sponsorship of the October Revolution, having spent decades railing against the Bolsheviks, Germany's own party in the east. That is not to say that Hitler was stupid, he was merely ill- informed. He was a politician after all.

So far from being stupid, he was a military intelligence officer. Stupid officers tend not to last very long in military intelligence, although they have fared better in other branches of the military. He reported directly to Ludendorff from very early on in the postwar period. There was a fascinating period in 1917 when Hitler's regiment, the 16th Bavarian Reserve Infantry Regiment, came in for special attention. It would be interesting to know why. I do not pretend to have *all* the answers, just some of them.

HMS *Vanguard*

German Naval Intelligence were always on the lookout for sabotage opportunities. On 9th July 1917 they were able to blow up HMS *Vanguard*. Thanks to German penetration of the Treasury the 'Hun' had a complete set of plans for the *St. Vincent* class battleships. It is doubtful if their man - probably Duquesne again - spent a lot of time searching for the best place to put the IEDs. This happened to be in the cordite rooms adjacent to P and Q magazines. There were multiple explosions, two of them probably primary, i.e. two IEDs are indicated.

It is a popular myth that battleships regularly blow up spontaneously. It was not as though Commanders-in-Chief, upon hearing a loud bang, were wont to say "whoops, there goes another battleship", or words to like effect. If a battleship suddenly blows up, like USS *Maine* in 1898, or HMS *Vanguard* in 1917, it is usually because somebody has blown it up. To every rule there is an exception. Neither British Naval Intelligence nor the Office of Naval Intelligence appear to have blown up the Japanese 16-inch gun battleship IJN *Mutsu* in the Inland Sea on 8th June 1943. That seems with respect to have been an entirely Japanese cock-up, which must have come as a great annoyance to Captain Miyoshi.[1] The Imperial Japanese Navy's conclusion that a suicidal crewman was responsible carries some weight, however, i.e. it does not appear to have been a spontaneous explosion.

There has been a tendency to discount the IJN's board of inquiry as an exercise in wartime propaganda and it may have been. Equally however they would have been anxious to find out if there *was* a flaw in their ammunition handling procedures or the design of the *Nagato* class, not least as the class leader, *Nagato*, remained in service. I tend to attach more weight than most historians to the IJN board of inquiry's conclusions. Staying with the subject of exploding battleships I also reject the accusations of bad faith casually levelled at the US Navy Board of Inquiry into the sinking of the *Maine*.[2]

Halifax explosion

On 6th December 1917 German Naval Intelligence had a big success in Canada, blowing up the ammunition ship SS *Mont-Blanc* in the great harbour of Halifax, an assembly point for convoys to Britain. The explosion was laundered through a staged collision with a Norwegian freighter. Warburg's people in Ottawa were able to cover-up the sabotage, and the murder of 2,000 people.

Since then, the idea that munitions ships blow up spontaneously in key harbours in the middle of wartime has entered the public consciousness, with assistance from intelligence illiterate historians and media. If the theory were valid people driving past harbours would regularly be hearing booms and saying to each other "uh-huh, another munitions ship gone up".

Just because an idea is widely accepted does not mean to say that it is right. It was a widely held belief in North Korea that Kim Jong-il could change the weather, as though he were an American driving an SUV. The belief was neither valid nor rational.

The Zimmerman Telegram

The big intelligence success of 1917 was of course the decoding of the Zimmerman Telegram. This was an exceedingly silly telegram from the German Foreign Minister to the German Ambassador in Mexico, at a time when the Germans wanted Mexico to join the war officially. Pancho Villa had been helping out already of course.

The strategy wasn't completely silly, if you discount the silliness of waging war on the United States in the first place. If you're the Bad Guys, you're in Europe (which is where the Bad Guys mostly come from) and you want to invade America, buying up Mexico, at Mexican prices, and invading from the south makes a lot more sense than landing on Long Island. What *was* completely silly was giving it away in a telegram, even an encrypted one. Even after 96 years it isn't clear what Zimmerman was thinking. Since he was a foreign minister, perhaps he wasn't thinking at all.

German intelligence has always tended to leave German politicians in the dark, with the hilarious consequence in 1941 that the German Government committed over three million troops to invading a country already controlled by German intelligence. This was the silliest invasion since the Chinese-bankrolled Persian Emperor Xerxes invaded Greece. It's not just British and US intelligence which sits on vital intel and watches an avoidable disaster unfold.

Neither British nor American intelligence at the time picked up that the 'Hun' had set up and was bankrolling the absurdly named Institutional Revolutionary Party (IRP), i.e. that Mexico was a German client state.

Zimmerman himself may not have been told, on the 'need to know' principle, which has blown up more intelligence operations than German Naval Intelligence has blown up battleships.

The intelligence failure over the IRP was to cost hundreds of thousands of young American lives in the years ahead,[3] due to German-sponsored narcotic trafficking across America's poorly defended southern frontier, came along, poorly defended at least until President Trump came along. Opposition to his border fence is not a bad litmus test by the way if you're looking for politicians closer to the Germans than they should be. On the basis that every able-bodied illegal immigrant exported north is a working-class job exported south, this intelligence failure also cost millions of American jobs, not to mention billions of dollars in unnecessary welfare payments.

Intelligence getting it right was only the first part of the equation of course. Intelligence is only of value if it is used. Intelligence is *not* about gaining knowledge for its own sake, however much knowledge may flatter the ego of an intelligence bureaucrat, intelcrats please note. Had MI6 sussed that Mexico was a German client state it wouldn't have made very much difference in 1917, as the Prime Minister and the Cabinet Secretary were German spies. Telling them would just have got a few of our agents south of the border shot, assuming that the local boys hadn't already spotted them. It's a rare MI6 officer who looks good in a sombrero.

Had American intelligence sussed it they probably couldn't have done much with it either. They would have needed to persuade either President Wilson or Secretary of State Lansing to invade Mexico (again). They were Democrats, i.e. in the fatal grip of the standard narrative of the American Revolution, the one which omits to mention that it was sponsored by the French. That was of course a partially successful effort to reverse the result of the Seven Years War. Sadly, politicians in Washington have only got to see a revolution to leap to the conclusion that it is an authentic popular uprising.

You can get them of course - as in Syria, subject to arguments about Turkish sponsorship - but they only tend to succeed if they are state-sponsored. That is unless you can split the military and turn the uprising into a civil war. Previously over 100,000 Syrian lives were thrown away uselessly whilst politicians in Washington and London continued to test the theory that you can have a successful, non-state-sponsored revolt to destruction, sadly other people's.

The obvious and correct response to the Zimmerman Telegram was for the United States to declare war on Mexico as well as Germany and invade Mexico, rather than wait for the Mexicans to invade them. Mexico City remains one of the largest German overseas stations. In World War II it helped to arrange for the covert supply of Mexican oil to Germany, which was done via fascist-controlled Portuguese or Spanish colonies in the Atlantic.

1918

Spanish Flu was particularly lethal for fit young men, i.e. troops. It first made its appearance (putting aside German tests on live subjects in 1917) amongst British troops on the Western Front, coinciding with Ludendorff's spring offensive. Somebody might have put these facts together and popped up to Cambridge or Oxford to ask the boffins, if they could find any who weren't working for Germany that is, whether the 'dastardly Hun' might not be up to something

Not finding out that Spanish Flu was a bio-weapon[4] was, in retrospect, a singular failure of the imagination. If that sounds a harsh judgment, remember that the German-sponsored pandemic cost between 50 and 100 million lives, more than the war itself. That is an awful lot of lives to throw away on an intelligence failure.

There are a number of reasons for the failure. I respectfully suggest, with my usual humility, that the five principal ones, each of which partly reflects German success in frustrating efforts to access her scientific secrets were:

(1) Poor intelligence co-ordination in London (the Joint Intelligence Committee came later), not unrelated to the fact that the Cabinet Secretary was a German spy (the last thing Hankey wanted was effective intelligence coordination - he might have been hanged).

(2) The failure to accord scientific intelligence the importance it deserves, a theme which was repeated throughout the following century (there is still no dedicated scientific intelligence agency in Britain and there is no Director of Scientific Intelligence - had there been the British Government would not have wasted so much time and money on global warming, as investigation of scientific hoaxes would be one of the duties of a DSI).

(3) The charming but naïve assumption that German science works in an open and transparent way, even though the rest of Germany doesn't, which in turn led to a woeful underestimation of the true state of German science. German medical scientists had discovered the secrets of the human body's auto-immune system in the latter half of the 1890s, finding a way to trigger it into an overreaction being the key to the success Spanish Flu.

(4) The lack of appreciation of the potential, for the Bad Guys, of biological warfare, in itself a reflection of earlier counterintelligence and scientific intelligence failures, such as the failure to pick up that *phytophthora infestans*, the so-called 'potato blight', which had shattered Ireland's agriculture in the 1840s, with appalling human and economic consequences, had been bred and spread deliberately. This in turn meant that disease spread patterns were not studied and no one picked up that the distribution pattern for Spanish Flu was more consistent with a deliberately spread bio-weapon[5] than a natural pandemic, and

(5) Their mad scientists were better than ours.

The Spanish Flu pandemic was the greatest crime in history, exceeding the later Holocaust, which goodness knows was bad enough, by a factor of between 8.25 and 16.5. Germany became the first state to murder more people than its entire population. With every respect to the Germans, it's not an achievement to be proud of.

The sad end of the Royal Naval Air Service

The intelligence failure to pick up German sponsorship of the so-called 'independent' Boer Republics, which in reality were German client states, had five serious consequences:

(1) The British Empire was perceived as the aggressor. The true aggressor was the 'Hun', who was seeking to drive the British out of South Africa, seize control of her raw materials, in particular gold and industrial diamonds (needed for machine tools for armaments production) and interdict the sea route around the Cape.
(2) An enduring and terrible fascination with the concept of 'independent' states in Africa, all of which have started out or ended up as client states of Germany, or German allies such as the People's Republic of China.
(3) A grotesque underestimation of the degree of German intelligence involvement in South Africa, which allowed the Abwehr to obtain large quantities of industrial diamonds[6] in World War II, keeping the German military-industrial complex going.
(4) Apartheid - the old National Party was effectively a German front organisation and its election in 1948 effectively a reversal of the result of the Second Boer War. The South African Bureau of State Security (BOSS) was a sister agency of the DVD and the collapse of the apartheid regime in practice reflected a switch in DVD support to the once pro-British African National Congress (ANC), and[7]
(5) Last but not least, the failure to shoot Field Marshal Jan Smuts, for many years Germany's highest-ranking spy in South Africa. Smuts did a lot of damage to the Good Guys in his intelligence career, but the greatest damage was in April 1918, when the RNAS was abolished.

The Imperial German Navy was badly rattled by the Royal Navy's world-leading use of air power in the Battle of Jutland. Correctly, since no aircraft in service was capable of carrying a weapon powerful enough to damage, let alone sink a battleship - a state of affairs only remedied by the Admiralty itself, by ordering the Sopwith Cuckoo - the Admiralty concentrated on reconnaissance and air defence.

So keen were they on naval aviation, and so quick to grasp the potential for using aircraft at sea, that at one point the Royal Navy even launched fighters from lighters towed at high speed behind destroyers. Not content, by the way, with ordering the brilliant little Sopwith Tabloid, the RNAS went on to deploy some of the finest combat aircraft of World War I, including the Sopwith 1 1/2 Strutter and Sopwith Pup, from which the Camel, the war's finest fighter,[8] was developed.

As better aircraft became available, such as the Camel, which was powerful enough to be able to carry an offensive load, the Royal Navy went one step further. As we have seen they organized the world's first carrier air-strike, nearly a quarter of a century before Pearl Harbor. All of this progress was called to a halt by Smuts, who recommended, in bad faith (he knew what he was doing and had fully grasped the significance of naval air power), that the dear old Royal Flying Corps (RFC) and the RNAS be merged. The Germans never grasped the importance of strategic air power and were not too worried about the creation of the world's first independent air arm. They must have started to have second thoughts when the RAF dropped its first bombs on Berlin in World War II.

As Smuts intended, the RAF, almost inevitably, concentrated on strategic air power and the air defence of the homeland, relegating naval air power almost to the status of a sideshow. Some of the damage done by Smuts was repaired when the Fleet Air Arm, initially part of the RAF, was created in 1923. The culpable neglect of Britain's naval aviation over two decades left the Fleet Air Arm in an appalling state by 1939, however.

This was bad enough in the North Atlantic, where it took four years to organise enough naval aviation assets to provide adequate air protection to convoys. Resort was had to desperate expedients like launching clapped-out Hawker Hurricanes from catapult-equipped merchant ships.[9] It also meant the innovative air strike on the Italian Fleet at Taranto lacked enough punch to deliver a knock-out blow. For the Far East Empire, which was handed over the Japanese, the decision to scrap the RNAS had catastrophic consequences.

This is not to say that setting up the RAF was a bad idea. So far to the contrary, it was a wonderful idea and helped win World War II. The mistake lay in depriving the Fleet of its organic air power, thereby sacrificing lives by the tens of thousands, warships by the dozen, merchant ships by the gross and cargo by the hundreds of thousands of tons, not to mention our entire empire in the Far East. It was recovered only briefly, before being handed over to German or Chinese clients.

The Admiralty - and the US Navy, which sensibly carried on using battleships until 1991[10] - were quite right by the way to insist that capital ships remain the backbone of the fleet. The farcical tests sponsored after World War I by Brigadier-General Billy Mitchell merely demonstrated that undefended, thinly armoured and out of date battleships could be sunk from the air, provided that they were at anchor, which the Admiralty and the US Navy could have told him anyway. This would have saved the cost of the bombs. The record of land-based bombers against battleships in World War II was poor, HMS *Prince of Wales* being the only fully worked up battleship sunk at sea by land-based airpower in the entire war.[11] Even she would probably not have been sunk had she not been betrayed.

The much-maligned Admiralty, by the way, also went on to fit high-angle anti-aircraft guns and aircraft catapults to every major warship, invent the world's first dual-purpose gun, the 8-inch Mk VIII[12] and the first effective close range anti-aircraft gun, the formidable eight-barrelled two-pounder 'pom-pom'. This mounting could fire 920 rounds a minute. It was still a pretty useful tool in 1945, nearly two decades after it first appeared.

The Dragonfly Ploy

The last year of the war saw the emergence of another cunning plan by the 'Hun'. Alarmed by the appearance of serious aeroengines such as the Rolls-Royce Falcon and Eagle, and the Wolseley Viper (which powered the second-best fighter of the war, the SE5a[13]) he came up with the bright idea of wasting public money and precious resources on an engine that didn't work. This gave his assets in the Treasury an excuse not to spend money on engines that did. All he needed was (1) an engine which didn't work and (2) some idiot directors to insist that it did. The latter were needed to provide cover.

Enter the ABC Company, complete with silly engine, which it called the Dragonfly, after the flying insect. Sadly, the insect flew a lot better than their engine. Whitehall naturally lavished funding on it. Even better, engineering delays meant that none actually reached the Front before the end of the war, although lots of cash reached ABC. Historians have tended to blame Whitehall stupidity, in particular on the part of Sir William Weir, a protégé of Lloyd George's. As is so often the case, the antics of stupid civil servants, of which there has never exactly been a shortage, provided excellent cover for civil servants who knew exactly what they were doing. All they had to do was try and keep a straight face and pretend that they were helping the war effort. They were - the German war effort. Sir William of course was promoted. It is almost impossible to throw money away in Whitehall and be demoted. The entire programme was a waste of money from beginning to end. It is even possible that the engine, with its daft copper cooling fins, was designed in Germany. The internal vibration was a quite a clever feature and looks like 'designer vibration'. If so, the only real hazard for the Germans was the risk of the blueprints getting wet and smudging as the designers shed tears of laughter.

The Special Air Service

Intelligence may have missed the odd trick during World War I, such as the facts that the Prime Minister, the Cabinet Secretary and the Director of MI5 were all German spies, but they had a few tricks of their own. One was a marvellous thing called the Special Air Service, which as its name doesn't imply, was part of the Air Force (after 1st April 1918), not the Army. A huge success, which is why it was disbanded, the SAS dropped agents behind enemy lines. They included the 'Ace of Spies', Sydney Reilly. He kept popping up in unexpected places, to which the SAS had flown him by amphibian from a secret island base in the Baltic. The 'Hun' kept looking for airfields, because the planes had to land to drop Sydney off.

Another grateful SAS client was T. E. Lawrence, a.k.a 'Lawrence of Arabia', a brilliant British intelligence officer, who kept 'Johnny Turk' on his toes. He too had a habit of popping up in unexpected places, to which he happened to have been flown by the SAS in a Bristol Fighter.[14] When Intelligence wanted him in Iraq a few years later, at a time when the wily 'Hun' was stirring things up in Baghdad, the chap in charge of the recruiting depot in London to which he was directed turned out to be none other than his old pilot, Captain W.E. (Bill) Johns.

There are no inverted commas around his rank for a reason. Johns had been temporarily promoted to Major in the RFC, then ended up as a Flight Lieutenant, equivalent to Captain, in the RAF. Because he was doing intelligence work and his promotions were never gazetted, he was later unfairly accused of claiming a rank to which he was not entitled. He was one of the most patronised and unfairly criticised intelligence officers in history.

Lawrence was an odd sort of chap - many of the best intelligence officers are - and his own sternest critic. Unfortunately, he took things a bit too far and went in for a spot of self-flagellation, although he was not above asking his young Arab boyfriend, with whom he had many adventures in the desert, to do a bit of flagellating for him. This left scars on his back. The Medical Officer would never have passed him without Bill's valuable guidance.

When the SAS who had been flying agents into what was now the USSR (Good Guy spies are called agents, they're only 'spies' if they work for the Bad Guys) was disbanded, Bill took to writing the 'Biggles' books. Before the disbandment he had been doing air intelligence related police work for the great Marshal of the Royal Air Force Lord Trenchard, the best Commissioner of the Metropolitan Police to date.

The air intelligence officer in the books, Major, later Air Commodore, Raymond, was modelled partly on Bill John's wartime and later Yard boss, Hugh Trenchard. Major, later Squadron Leader, James Bigglesworth, known to generations of air-minded young boys and girls as "Biggles", was partly modelled on himself, of course. The full-length books were basically expanded short stories, most of which were written in the 1920s and 30s.

Bill carried on working for Intelligence (Air Intelligence & MI18) until the 'Hun' (a.k.a GO2) finally got him, in 1968. He subsidised his work by having a Biggles book a year published, peppered with clues to covert German bases all over the world. Hilariously, Bill, whose publishers didn't know one end of an aeroplane from another, was able to get away with leaving clues as to when the books were really written, e.g. by having a Hawker Hunter with a wood and fabric fuselage.[15]

Even after a new series of books, featuring a lady pilot ("Worrals") was written at Air Ministry request during World War Two, to encourage women to take to the air, he was still accused of promoting himself to Captain. It never seems to have occurred to his left-wing critics that the Air Ministry might actually have had access to his personnel file (or some of it at any rate). Bill's greatest contribution to the West probably came in the 1930s, when at Trenchard's request he briefed in Churchill on the expansion of the Luftwaffe. Apparently, this was done over the odd convivial glass of brandy at the Royal Aero Club at the old clubhouse on Piccadilly. Perhaps the best tribute to Bill's memory would be to film the books in a properly funded television series.[16]

Two great unsolved mysteries remain from World War I. Firstly, why were the high-level German penetration assets in London, Moscow, Paris and Washington not picked up? Secondly, having failed to get rid of any of them, however did the Allies manage to win?

1. He was blown up.
2. The Spaniard doesn't really do mines and it's a fair bet that the 'Hun' came up with the idea of mining the poor old *Maine*, at a time when he was seeking to undermine the United States.
3. Everybody has their own numbers on this, but dangerous narcotics seem to cost roughly 300,000 American lives a year and has done so at that rate for at least a decade. 100-200,000 a year is probably a more realistic figure for the 1960s and 1970s. The Germans would think it a bad week if they didn't knock over at least 5,000 Americans. Until Donald Trump, the only US President smart enough, and well informed enough, to know what was happening was President Richard Nixon, hence his 'War on Drugs', but he wasn't democratically minded enough to take the American people into his confidence. LSD was invented by Mengele's mob in Dachau and tested there on live subjects. An American lefty later took credit for it, no doubt for a fee.
4. One of the best-, informed military scientists in the US on this subject, in my as ever humble opinion, is Dr Jeffrey Taubenberger, formerly of the Armed Forces Institute of Pathology in Washington. For the avoidance of doubt, he and I have never met and have had no dealings with each other, although we may have mutual friends. The discovery that Spanish Flu was a bioweapon was part of the intelligence yield from the victory over Iraq. The death from influenza of the German spy Allen Welsh Dulles might be worth a second look. If it was a coincidence it was more than ironic.
5. It was also handy for assassinations, especially in the middle of the pandemic, when one more death was scarcely noticed, the most prominent victim being the distinguished diplomat and intelligence officer Sir Hugh Sykes, who had done good work in the Middle East.
6. Famously shipped out on one occasion in a long-range FW200 Condor, which landed at night on the high veldt - there were probably others (there were hardly any night-fighters in South Africa and no one thought to set up a chain of radar stations across the continent - sensibly there ought to have been at least two chains, at the SA border and another from British West Africa, dog-legging down to Entebbe then across to Mombasa).
7. Naval Intelligence really needs to take a closer look at the tragedy in the Channel when over 1,000 black volunteers from South Africa, recruited partly by the ANC, drowned, after a suspiciously convenient collision, admittedly in fog, but no naval intelligence officer would think of trying to set up a collision in broad daylight. Scarcely any of the men could swim and they went bravely to their deaths singing the moving African hymn *Nkosi Sikelele Africa*, a favourite of King George VI's.
8. It could turn on a sixpence, especially in a torque-assisted turn to starboard to starboard using the power of its rotary engine, and shot down over 1,000 'Huns'. Later marks used the first Bentley engines (the Bentley Rotary BR1 and BR2).
9. On which they could not land of course - you try landing a Hawker Hurricane on a catapult and see what happens. The brave pilots had to either find a ship and ditch beside her, or if in range, fly to the nearest air base. Since the whole

idea was to try and provide some organic air cover outside of fighter range, i.e. far out to sea, the idea of having them land on land was a trifle optimistic. It would have been much better to have saved weight and reduced drag by removing the undercarriage altogether, using the space vacated in the wings for self-sealing long-range tanks, which when empty would have provided extra buoyancy on ditching. Using tired airframes was all very well but they should have been reengined and thoroughly over- hauled, with anti-corrosion paint. Low-powered VHF transmitters on the motherships and VHF radio compasses in the fighters might have been an idea worth exploring as well.

10. The most recent combat engagement involving battleships, albeit only on one side, was in the Gulf War - so much for all the talk about the Battle of Midway (in which, by the way, most of the carriers engaged were sunk but none of the battleships, albeit partly because the Japanese didn't know what they were for and didn't use them) marking the 'end of the battleship era'.
11. The RM *Roma,* which was not fully in commission, was hit and sunk by German stand-off weapons in 1943 and the KMS *Tirpitz* was sunk (strictly capsized) by RAF Lancasters in 1944, whilst at anchor (I knew at least one of the pilots on that raid, the late Squadron Leader Tony Iveson DFC). None of the boys would claim to have been able to hit her had she been able to manoeuvre, part of the problem being that the target would not only have moved after the great Tallboy bombs had been dropped but would have had time to alter course. The Luftwaffe never sank an operational battleship and the Japanese were only able to sink American battleships if they were at anchor and on peacetime routines.
12. Shame about the fire control. The Mark VIII also needed faster elevation and training, weaknesses probably insisted upon by the Treasury. Their maximum elevation was an impressive (for 1928) 70^0 - see Whitley, M.J., *Cruisers of World War Two,* London: Arms and Armour Press, 1995, p. 84.
13. The best was the Camel of course. The Fokker DVII comes in third, just ahead of the Spad and the Albatross.
14. The war's best two-seater, fast and manoeuvrable, a lovely bit of kit.
15. See *Biggles in the Terai.* The original manuscript would make even better reading. Bill probably had 'Algy' flying a Hawker Hart. The books have evocative descriptions of prewar airports and the prewar aviation scene. The publishers can't have flown abroad for their holidays - Bill was able to get in references to flying out of Croydon Airport years after London Airport was moved to Heathrow.
16. There was a rather disappointing film, starring Alec Baldwin as Biggles and that fine actor Peter Cushing as Raymond, and an earlier series, in 1960, starring Albert Whiting.

16

The Inter-War Period /1/

The Failure to take Berlin

The German Secret Service knew the war was lost when Ludendorff's spring offensive failed. They didn't wait for Haig and Foch's brilliant counter-offensive. Foch had been preferred to Pétain, as the French weren't completely stupid. They wanted a heterosexual in command, who wasn't being blackmailed by the Germans. The Wilhemstrasse made their dispositions accordingly. Unlike 1945 they didn't need to move out of Berlin, partly because they had enough political leverage in London, Paris and Washington to make sure that the Allies did not invade the fatherland. Haig was livid. Like the decision not to follow up the defeat of the Iraqi Army and Republican Guard in 1991 by going on to Baghdad, the decision not to march on Berlin virtually ensured there would be another war. It was a no-brainer. The potential intelligence yield alone was worth more than had been spent on the entire war to date by all the Allies combined. Knowledge of German trading programmes and how much cash had been shifted to Switzerland would have avoided all discussion of reparations.

Without the intelligence yield the Allies had no chance of being able to regain control of their own countries. This applied in particular to their commercial and central banks, state bureaucracies and intelligence agencies. Without control of interest rates they could not prevent further German-sponsored recessions. This time the 'Hun' was planning a real doozy. Without stopping the madness of trading programmes the Allies could not control the supply of money into their economies and therefore could not control inflation. The Allies thus bought into a whole bunch of industrial strife and insane economy drives, which were to make Jim Hacker's in *Yes Minister* look sensible.[1]

Like lambs going to the slaughter, or chickens being stalked by velociraptors,[2] the Allies condemned themselves to two decades of economic and social upheaval, military weakness and a further war, whilst the dead dropped around them by the million in the nastiest and sadly most successful campaign of biological warfare to date. Wholly ignorant commentators, if that is not a tautology, unaware that the Germans were knocking over people at the rate of about a million every fortnight anyway, exercised themselves over the thought of further casualties were the Allies to march on Berlin.

Since we had the 'Hun' on the run, he could barely feed his army let alone re-ammunition it, and it was falling apart anyway, it is not entirely clear how many further Allied casualties there would have been. They would probably not have been more than a few hours' worth of Spanish Flu. The pandemic could only be stopped from where it was being run – Berlin.

When you've got the enemy on the run, and your supply chain is able to keep up, you keep going. You don't stop and let him regroup. If he's German you'll have to fight him sooner or later anyway. You may as well do so on advantageous terms.

Of course, the British and French - particularly the French - populations were war-weary. They would soon have bucked up however as news came in of further massive allied advances and the casualty lists got shorter. One reason they were war-weary was that they didn't have enough to eat. That was easily fixed, by lifting rationing, indeed in a few months Whitehall would probably have started an anti-obesity campaign.

As the BEF advanced on Hamburg and the U-Boat bases on the North Sea, to which the U-Boats had to return eventually, U-Boat operations would simply have ceased. They could only be refuelled and re- provisioned in their lairs in Portuguese and possibly Mexican waters. They could not be refitted and those MAN diesel engines needed a lot of attention. They could scarcely operate out of Germany's Baltic bases. You can easily bottle up the Baltic.

There would have been very little public support for the absurd armistice had it been explained that:

(1) Letting the 'Hun' off the hook virtually guaranteed that their children would have to fight another war, at vastly greater cost in human life.
(2) There was something very strange about Spanish Flu and the boffins thought it might be a fiendish plot, i.e. being spread deliberately by the 'dastardly Hun'.
(3) The Royal Navy and United States Navy had licked the U-Boats and rationing, including petrol rationing, was being lifted with immediate effect.
(4) The Allies needed access to the intelligence yield, to discover who had financed the war and how, who had set up the assassination

of Archduke Ferdinand and his Archduchess and who in London, Paris, Washington and Moscow had been giving aid and comfort to 'Harry Hun'.

(5) The only way to ensure a peaceful, stable Europe and make sure this really was 'the war to end all wars' was to break up Germany, which could only be done if she were occupied, and

(6) Stopping before the job was finished risked throwing away the tremendous sacrifices that had already been made.

Instead, the decision was made to call a temporary halt to the fighting - that is what an armistice is - and have another world war later. This would allow the 'Hun' time to rebuild his strength, whilst his penetration assets ensured that the Allies had disarmed sufficiently to make it easier for him to win.

The League of Nations

The League was a particularly clever ploy by Warburg, later repeated in 1945 of course, when the new, improved Mk 2 League, a.k.a. the United Nations, was set up. Both had the same aim - to deprive the Allies of the fruits of victory and ensure that Germany and her allies dominated the postwar world. There have been new washing powders with more meaningful improvements than the UN represented over the League. Rather than being headquartered in London, the obvious location, where Britain could have kept an eye on it, the League was based in a German client state, Switzerland. Her banking system depended heavily on continued German-controlled Medium Term Note trading.

It was put in charge of a couple of German spies. The first was the notorious Sir Eric Drummond, a senior Foreign Official, later a key supporter of Mussolini and the Italian invasion of Abyssinia (as British Ambassador in Rome). Naturally enough for a supporter of fascism, he became deputy Liberal leader in the House of Lords.

The second was the even more notorious Jean Monnet, a deeply unpleasant man, who later supported the Holocaust and the EEC. In World War II Monnet worked hard for a German victory as an armaments broker, an odd occupation for a man who believed in world peace. At least it would have been had he actually believed in world peace. The whole idea of the League of course was to make sure there was another world war, which this time the Germans would win.

Another key German asset in the League secretariat was Arthur Salter, later Lord Salter. By coincidence he was from the family that owned

Salters Steamers in Oxford, where my paternal grandfather William Ewart Shrimpton worked. Salter and Monnet had collaborated closely together on the Allied Maritime Transport Council, a front organisation for German Naval Intelligence set up at the end of 1917. The AMTC was a vital adjunct to the U-Boat campaign. Its main task was to collate shipping intelligence on behalf of Germany so that convoys could be ambushed.

Unsurprisingly, Neville Chamberlain appointed Salter, by then MP for Oxford University, as a junior minister at the Ministry of Shipping in 1939. He was charged with getting as many British ships sunk as possible. In 1941 he was appointed to a shipping coordination role in Washington, with a view to strangling Britain's transatlantic lifeline. Unfortunately, he was never tried and hanged. He died peacefully in 1975 at the age of 93, much more peacefully at any rate than the many Mercantile Marine officers and seamen for whose deaths he was responsible.

President Wilson also believed in world peace, which was nice. Sadly however, it was not obtainable by any policy that he supported, with the exception of finally entering World War I on the side of the Allies, i.e. the Good Guys. At the end of the day the President's views on world peace were not much more sophisticated than those of Sandra Bullock's charming fellow contestants in *Miss Congeniality*[3] (not that Miss Bullock isn't charming of course). They were just expounded at greater length. It is not entirely clear who sold the idea of the League to Wilson, but it was supported by German assets in State Department and the very dodgy 'Colonel' Edward House, who never commanded so much as a platoon. He was a key adviser to Wilson and an enthusiastic proponent of the decisions not to invade Germany and not to shut down German intelligence. House was probably aware that German agents were spreading Spanish Flu in the United States, but sadly he did not catch it. You will not find many strong denunciations of Adolf Hitler or Benito Mussolini from this man of peace.

Being a Democrat, and not understanding that corrupt politicians were the villains of the Stamp Act nonsense, not nice old King George,[4] Wilson didn't do kings, let alone emperors. In the context of central Europe that meant he didn't do stability, which meant in turn that he didn't do peace. 'Blind Freddy' could see that breaking up the Austro-Hungarian Empire meant handing it over to Germany piece by piece. In the end it only took 22 years.

Democracy was not on offer, save as a cruel deception designed to keep the member countries of the Imperial Council quiet until the Germans could take over. For Emperor Charles 1's subjects the choice of future leader really lay between His Highness's heir Archduke Otto, who was an awfully nice chap, and Adolf Hitler, who wasn't.

For 150 years the choice in Europe has been between having Germany or 'peace, order and good government'. You can have one or the other, but you cannot have both. If you are a neighbour of Germany and you're not Switzerland, i.e. not doing their banking, you know that sooner or later you are either going to be invaded or invited to join the European Union. The Versailles Treaty is in vigorous competition with the Treaty of Rome, the Treaty of Maastricht and the Kyoto Protocol for the title of 'the silliest treaty in history'. Although it's up against some pretty stiff competition it probably takes the title, or the biscuit.

German/Soviet Cooperation

This was not something which suddenly started with the 1939 Molotov–Ribbentrop Pact, which only startled those who did not know who bankrolled the October Revolution. Having bankrolled it, German intelligence was scarcely likely to lose control of its new client state in the east. The Rapallo Treaty of 1922 was only the public face of the close military cooperation between the USSR and Germany. There was significant covert cooperation as well.

Both Stalin and Trotsky were German assets. Stalin and Canaris probably had Trotsky murdered for fear he was about to blow the gaffe on 'von' Stalin. Mexico was a German client state of course, a trick Trotsky may have missed. Unfortunately for him the chap with the icepick[5] didn't. In the late 1930s, as the Wehrmacht planned the invasion which eventually got underway in 1941, the staff work for which took years, Stalin was ordered to decimate the Red Army's officer corps. It was promptly culled in a murderous pogrom. As a Georgian, Stalin was not overly worried about the fate of Russian officers.

The 1922 Washington Naval Treaty

This was another piece of nonsense sponsored by German intelligence, the covert aims of which were to ensure that (1) there would be a second world war and (2) Germany and Japan would win it. The treaty's mostly pro-German backers noisily promoted the idea that there was a 'naval building race' between Britain, Japan and America.

They did not explain that the Japanese were going to build what they wanted anyway and were intending to sign the treaty in bad faith. The French and the Italians were broke and only signed the treaty so they would not be left behind. The Italian signature didn't make much difference since German intelligence had come up with a new 'ism' - fascism - and were about to lumber the Italians with Mussolini. He reported to German intelligence until the DVD and their man Menzies, then Head of MI6, had him shot.[6]

There was no race, although there may have been some friendly competition between Britain and America, who were now of course allies. The treaty's proponents never deigned to explain whether they thought Britain was going to attack America, or vice versa. Whilst each maintained war plans for an Anglo-American war, by 1922 they were no more than paper contingency plans. The Royal Navy's contingency plans were simply left to gather dust after 1917. Thanks in part to the great American admiral William Sims working relations between the two navies in 1917-1918 had been excellent.

If you visit the Naval Club in Mayfair you can still see the famous painting of British officers and crew lining the decks of the ships of the Grand Fleet to cheer the arrival of USS *Texas* and the other battleships of the American battle squadron. It was fully integrated into the Grand Fleet and counted it an honour to be so. It was an honour to have them. Naval Intelligence made sure that Assistant Secretary of the Navy Franklin Delano Roosevelt, the only member of the Wilson Administration with strategic grasp, dined with Winston Churchill, the only member of the British Cabinet with strategic grasp. The historic dinner took place, as it happens, in my old Inn of Court, Gray's, the intelligence Inn. No functioning democracy has ever waged war on another.

Capital ships needed to be bigger for several reasons. As we have seen, the great British admiral Jackie Fisher had decided that the next generation of battlecruisers needed to be 1,000 ft long, with a full load displacement of over 50,000 tons. He was right. There had been tremendous progress in naval and aircraft technology during World War I. Progressive sea services, such as the British and American navies, fully understood that they needed to adapt to the advent of aircraft.

Small-tube, high-pressure boilers, such as those planned for HMS *Incomparable*, meant that much higher speeds could be obtained. Longer engagement ranges (the idea that the Admiralty, which introduced the first long range gun, the 15-inch 42 cal. Mk 1, did not understand plunging fire ought only to be stated for its absurdity to be apparent) and the increased power of aircraft introduced a requirement for stronger deck armour. In turn that meant stronger hulls.

Heavier-calibre guns, such as the 16-inch fitted to the IJN *Nagato* and *Mutsu*, which were contemporaneous with the Washington Treaty, and the 18-inch fitted to HMS *Furious*, were now available. As we have seen, the DNC was planning to move to 20-inch. Prewar dreadnoughts were starting to look old-fashioned, indeed HMS *Dreadnought* herself played very little active role in the war. She was only 8 years old in 1914. She fell eventually to the Geddes Axe of course, wielded by that particularly nasty and supercilious German spy, who cost the Royal Navy more ships than the entire High Sea Fleet. Sir Eric also thanked brave men who had given their all in the war by throwing them on the dole queue, taking care to lie about the reasons, in the hope that they would be bitter at their own country, not the enemy.

The Germans understood all this. They were chafing at the 10,000-ton restriction on armoured warships in the Versailles Treaty, not that they ever had any intention of being bound by it. They came up with the idea of a 35,000-ton limit for battleships, chosen as it was impossible to build a modern fast battleship of 35,000 tons or under. They would either be under-gunned, underpowered or weak. The 10,000-ton limit for heavy cruisers was similarly unrealistic. It proved impossible to build a cruiser to that limit which could do everything which would be asked of it. That outstanding naval architect, Sir Tennyson d'Eyncourt, came close with the famous, three-funnelled 'County' class, one of which, HMS *Dorsetshire*, had the privilege of delivering the *coup de grâce* to *Bismarck*.[7] They were a good compromise, but still sacrificed speed (Sir Tennyson had wanted 100,000 SHP, e.g.) and protection to get a reasonable main battery and commodious hull.

Unsurprisingly, no Axis battleship was ever built to the Washington Treaty limits, the hope being that they would only ever encounter inferior opponents. The Italian *Littorios* weighed in at about 41,000 tons,[8] the *Bismarcks* at about 45,000,[9] and the only Japanese battleships built after the treaty entered into force,[10] the two *Yamatos*, at a whopping 64,000, although estimates for the latter vary.

In the events which happened the only battleships built to the 35,000-ton limit were the British *Nelsons.* Innovative ships, they were the first to have all their secondary armament (12 6-inch) mounted in turrets above the weather deck and to feature a combined armoured conning tower and bridge. The latter permitted superb command and control. The Director of Naval Construction ingeniously mitigated the lack of available tonnage for protection by mounting all three 16-inch main battery turrets forward of the tower. This allowed him to concentrate the armour and provide a reasonable degree of protection, although the 'C' turret firing arcs were a bit limited. There was no real loss of fighting ability, as British battleships chased the enemy, not the other way round.

The most powerful warships in the world for nearly two decades, they had a heavier broadside than the *Bismarcks*. The dear old *Rodney* absolutely smashed the *Bismarck* in 1941. At least one of them should have been preserved.[11] Their excellent main armament and good protection came at a cost, however. Their engines put out less than a third of the power of the previous British capital ship, the *Hood*, at only 45,000 SHP. They could only do 23.5 knots, clean hull, in temperate waters, preferably downhill, with a following wind.

The next British battleships, the *King George V* class, were faster and better-balanced ships, but their main battery was seriously compromised by the decision to go down to 14-inch. This retrograde step was forced on the Admiralty by the mad decision to stick with the Washington Treaty limit after the Axis powers had clearly signalled they were treating it as a joke, which it always was - a German joke. And they say that the 'Hun' has no sense of humour.

Just to make things worse, under heavy pressure from Germany's Stanley 'von' Baldwin in Downing Street, heavily backed by Chamberlain, then Chancellor, the Admiralty were forced to restrict the 'B' mounting to a twin. This not only cut the broadside by 1/6 when it was already a bit light thanks to going down to 14-inch, but necessitated a brand-new turret. Anti-flash precautions meant that by 1936 a battleship turret was a highly complex piece of machinery. The delay was unacceptable.

The 'B' mountings were still giving trouble in 1943. HMS *Duke of York's* gunnery officers, including Sub-Lt Henry (later Admiral Sir Henry) Leach in 'A' turret, a friend of several friends, were rarely able to call on all ten of her big guns at any one time during the Battle of North Cape. This must have been very frustrating when the enemy was in sight.

Thankfully the German asset Herbert Hoover[12] lost the 1932 election to the patriotic FDR.[13] The Department of the Navy were able to lose the Washington Treaty (why couldn't have it been signed in Newark or Hackensack?). The first true post-Treaty class of American battleships were the elegant and powerful *North Carolinas*.[14] USS *Washington* made a fine sight steaming alongside HMS *King George V* in the Home Fleet in 1942.

She attracted great professional admiration from the Royal Navy, not least from the C-in-C, that fine battleship admiral, Admiral Sir John Tovey, victor over the *Bismarck*. They were only 35,000 tons officially. The Pentagon is still a bit sensitive on the subject but 42,000 tons standard displacement, around 44,300 tons full load, would be nearer the mark. The *KGVs* as built were also over the 'limit', by some 3,000 tons, every one of which was vital, but none of the class was in service before World War II.

In fairness to FDR and the US Navy, it must be emphasised that by June 1938, when *Washington* was laid down, ONI intelligence assessments would have made it clear that the *Takao* class cruisers had been built way over the 10,000 ton 'limit,' by at least 20%. These assessments would also have made it clear that the Japanese government could not have believed in good faith that the ships would comply with the treaty. Even today it is not uncommon to see completely unreal displacement figures for the *Takao* class cruisers.[15]

Under public international law when countries sign a treaty in bad faith the other state parties are no longer bound, although the better course is to formally denounce the treaty rather than ignore it. It is impossible to argue that the Treaty of Washington limits had any binding status by 1938. The treaty was never worth the paper it was written on.

Baldwin and Chamberlain knew perfectly well that Japan and Italy had each signed the treaty in bad faith, but they wanted the Royal Navy to lose the next war in the Far East. Each wanted to surrender Britain's Far East Empire to the Japanese. They were comfortable with the loss of life that would entail.

In the events which happened neither the Germans nor Japanese were able to achieve their wet dream (as it were) of lining up battleships built in bad faith and way over the treaty 'limit' against a squadron of weaker opponents. The Axis lost every big-gun battle of World War II except the Battle of the Denmark Strait, in which they were up against an elderly battlecruiser (HMS *Hood*) badly in need of a rebuild and a battleship (HMS *Prince of Wales*) that still had not been completed.

One thing the whole sorry episode of the Washington Treaty demonstrated was this. Arms control treaties are a joke without proper verification. Washington was a complete farce from beginning to end. In Great Britain it marked a willingness of politicians to engage in deliberate deception of Parliament and the public over defence, a trend that sadly has continued down to the present day, the Starmer Labour government included. Some of the deception verged on the pathetic, such as the sustained attempt to say that the new 14-inch gun outranged its 15-inch and 16-inch predecessors, without pointing out that the figures were taken from different elevations, and that the maximum elevation of the mountings of the older 15-inch gunned ships was being increased as they were rebuilt.

German Inflation

Not the least absurd aspect of the Versailles Treaty was that Germany was to pay reparations in German marks, i.e. Germany got to control the amount of reparations she actually paid. If she wanted a discount all she needed to do was to devalue her currency. The Allies may as well have given the Germans vouchers. Reparations were a dubious idea anyway, although they were popular with the punters.

It would have been far more sensible to have located Germany's offshore assets, seize them and stop Medium Term Note trading. As it was, the ordinary German people suffered, the reparations were never collected in full anyway and of course their value fell with the German currency.

Historians tend to blame the runaway, Zimbabwe-style inflation in Germany in 1923 on the German reserve bank's decision to print more money. This assertion has never actually been tested, e.g. by computer modelling of the German economy, having first established how much cash was actually printed. Another crucial piece of economic modelling would be to match the inflation and currency distribution rates. You would probably find that the currency was being printed in response to the inflation, i.e. the central bank was playing catch-up.

As Professors Sir Patrick Minford and Tim Congdon, both very nice chaps, demonstrated in the 1980s (they were surprisingly knowledgeable about economics, despite being economists):

(1) Inflation is caused by loss of control over the money supply, and
(2) Money supply is more than just the amount of cash in circulation (hence M3 and other advanced definitions of money).

We shall need to see the German files, but it looks as though the inflation was caused by a reckless decision to run MTN programmes backed by cash instead of gold. This could no longer be brought in from China (the German Secret Service did not sponsor the Boxer Rebellion for nothing[16]) or Japan,[17] or at any rate not in the same amounts. One of the problems in running trading programmes off the back of borrowed gold from the families in the Far East (they know who they are) is that they usually want it back.

It's also best if you've assured holders of gold (probably 90% of the gold mined in the last 5,000 years or so is still around - you would be surprised how durable the stuff is and how careful people are not to lose it) before you start your war that you can't lose it, that you actually win. Investors in failed wars can get even more annoyed than investors in failed dotcoms.

The Civil War in Ireland

Another German wet dream, the civil war in Ireland, was brought about fairly easily, with Lloyd George making sure that anti-British sentiment was stirred by the paramilitary Black and Tans. Downing Street stayed well in the background of course. At the same time Lloyd George was able to prevent a serious military strategy to deal with the revolt.

Ireland was not a British colony, but part of the United Kingdom, sending MPs to Westminster, whilst the Irish representative peers sat in the House of Lords. These points are rarely grasped in Washington, where politicians tend to talk nonsensically about 'British rule' in Ireland, not very much more logical or constitutionally correct than talking about 'Irish rule' in Britain or 'American rule' in Florida.

The treaty which brought the war to an end was signed by the rebels, led by a German agent named Michael Collins, in bad faith. The new Irish Free State was intended by Germany, Collins and Lloyd George to be a German client state, just as the French Revolutionary Government wanted to open up a second front in Britain's rear in the Revolutionary War, by sponsoring the Wolfe Tone revolt in 1798. If you were invited by Tone to a working breakfast, you would probably have been offered croissants. This was after Washington, the chap, had booted the French out of Washington, the city.

Most importantly for Germany, Collins and Lloyd George (since both parties were reporting to German intelligence and understood that the other was as well the treaty negotiations were quite cordial, unsurprisingly) was that the Royal Navy be denied future access to Irish bases. These were the so-called treaty ports. There was never the slightest question of the Royal Navy being granted access to the treaty ports in wartime, although that didn't stop Whitehall foisting the idea on the Navy in a sustained campaign of deception.

Lloyd George, who was technologically illiterate (he only really understood three things - the black arts of politics, champagne and women) had not grasped the importance of the new sensors and anti- submarine weapons the Admiralty developed in World War I. He had been convinced that the Imperial German Navy would win the first Battle of the Atlantic and was astonished by the defeat of his beloved U-Boats, not least given that every convoy across the North Atlantic was betrayed. He was also surprised at the speed with which the Canadians got Halifax back into the war after the *Mont-Blanc* sabotage. Lloyd George, Monnet, Salter and German Naval Intelligence had set great store by that operation. They were determined that the Royal Navy would not defeat the U-Boats a second time.

Lloyd George's successor, Neville Chamberlain, also a German asset of course, equally understood that the civil war in Ireland had been driven by German strategic objectives and resisted Admiralty attempts to get Eire to adhere to her treaty obligations. What was worse, having misled the Admiralty into believing that the treaty ports would be available, he only made funding available for short-range escorts. Hence the little *Flower* class corvettes, whose shortcomings were portrayed memorably in the stirring film of Nicholas Monsarrat's novel *The Cruel Sea*, although the sea was not nearly as cruel as Monsarrat was to the Admiralty. Like many of the Admiralty's critics, he forgot that he who pays the piper calls the tune.

The detailed specifications and numbers of all Royal Navy warships were determined by the Treasury, who ought perhaps to have been made to go to sea in them, not the Navy. The Treasury has enough trouble understanding economics, never mind defence. It's not just a question of German penetration. The Treasury long ago fell into an Intellectual Black Hole, far too deeply to permit escape, its groupthink being that it is cheaper to have wars than to spend money on defence deterring them. Huge (and expensive) losses were incurred before the Admiralty got the long-range escorts it had always wanted and the Navy needed. The *Flower* class were glorified armed whalers,[18] really only suitable as escorts for coastal convoys. It must have taken immense courage and skill to sail them to Murmansk and back.

Ironically there was a second civil war, in which Collins died (served him right). He could never explain to the Irish people that he was working for Germany, that the Irish Republican Army (IRA) was effectively a force of German irregulars and that the Easter rebellion had been staged at German request to take pressure off the German Army on the Western Front. Even less could he explain that he supported the atrocities committed by the Black and Tans (who were yahoos who should never have been allowed anywhere near a gun) for their propaganda value and that the 'Irish Free State' was going to be neither Irish, free nor a state, as opposed to a German-controlled statelet.

German intelligence replaced Collins with De Valera, who openly supported Hitler. He was so upset when the Führer reportedly topped himself that he went to the German Embassy in Dublin to sign the book of condolence. Even in Dublin in 1945 he didn't have to queue for long. Not everything went to plan for the Germans, however. Lloyd George was desperate to have Churchill assassinated, but the IRA death squad assigned to the task made a complete hash of it, thankfully.

The Munich Putsch

There was another German intelligence lash-up at about the same time, in Munich. Ludendorff wanted to be President of Germany. He and intelligence backed a military coup by a strange little party obsessed with Jews, started by a strange little chap called Streisser, which Ludendorff persuaded his intelligence colleague Adolf Hitler to take over. It is still not entirely clear what they thought they were doing, since the capital of Germany was in Weimar not Munich. The putsch failed. German intelligence learned a lot from that - later coups were far better organised. Vatican and intelligence influence in the Bavarian police and judiciary was sufficiently strong however to allow the plotters to get away with light sentences.

Whilst in jail Hitler took the opportunity to read a book intelligence knocked up for him, called *Mein Kampf*, which he then pretended was his own. Nobody in the West thought that he took could take over Germany on his own and they were right. He couldn't. The problem was that he wasn't acting alone. The Nazi Party was just the latest in a long line of political parties set up or taken over by German intelligence, which has started more parties than Roy Jenkins.

It is rather ironic that the two main parties of the left in Britain between the wars, the Labour and Liberal Parties, each of which never missed an opportunity to shout down the Tory Party as 'fascist', were set up by essentially the same intelligence organisation that sponsored the Nazi Party. Commentators at the time who had not grasped this fact were puzzled - commentators often are - by the Lloyd George/Hitler meeting at Berchtesgaden in 1936. This was of course set up the man to whom each then reported, wily old Admiral Canaris.

Herr Admiral came out into the open as head of the Abwehr after Hitler took power, but it is unclear when he took over from Warburg, whom he later sent to the United States to head up his operation there. There may have been a director in between, probably Ludendorff. Warburg's stock had fallen of course after the defeat in 1918, even though he had successfully set up the League of Nations and secured a good deal for Germany at Versailles.

The Muslim Brotherhood

The Brotherhood was set up in Cairo in 1928 by the German agent Sanni al-Banna, the aim being to undermine not just Egypt but also the new, pro-British monarchies in Saudi Arabia and Iraq. The principal strategic aims were to reverse the defeat of Germany's ally the Ottoman Empire by creating German client states throughout the Middle East and seizing control of energy supplies to the West. This was particularly true of oil, but the covert Scientific Section of what became the Abwehr, led of course by Einstein, were also worried by natural gas and the British invention of the gas turbine. The gas turbine had huge potential for use in aircraft, power generation and locomotives. Powered by LNG, which was cheap and plentiful, they would have been very useful in power stations. That is still true even today, as reflected in the unnecessary linkage between oil and natural gas prices, intended to drive up the price of the latter.

The Muslim Brotherhood remains a German front. Trying to understand the Middle East without knowing that is like trying to understand the Cold War without knowing that the October Revolution was bankrolled by German intelligence and that the CPSU was a German front (at least until the GRU finally worked it out and knocked off Stalin). The terrorism strategy that worked so well for the Germans in Ireland with the IRA was applied to the Middle East, with even more murderous consequences.

All Palestinian and Islamic terrorist organisations, including *al Qaeda* and Hamas can be traced back to the Brotherhood. The co-called 'Arab Spring' in Egypt reflected a withdrawal by the DVD of its support for Hosni Mubarak, and a switch to the Brotherhood, not that that fact emerged in Mubarak's trial, which was something of a farce.

The Great Depression

Germany's plans for war were already being formulated by the end of the 1920s. The Rapallo Pact and German/Soviet military co-operation were all to do with military expansion. It didn't just suddenly happen when the Nazis were installed. At the same time Canaris and the cabal of bankers and industrialists with whom he was working wanted to weaken Britain, Canada, Australia and America.

Organising depressions had been a standard German tactic since before World War I. This time they wanted a really big one, with the hope of shutting down great swathes of Western industry. They succeeded, but not beyond their expectations, thanks largely to two men - the brilliant British economist Maynard Keynes,[19] who worked out that the counter to deflation is reflation, and FDR, who put America back to work. More importantly, FDR cut a deal with the Chinese to back the dollar, having access to some very good intelligence advice. The secret history of the New Deal is even more interesting than the open history.

If you're a mean German spymaster, and you want to throw lots of good people out of work and off their farms, you don't just come into work on a Monday and say you want a recession tomorrow and a depression by Wednesday. Depressions, especially great depressions, take a lot of careful planning. There are three main modalities for starting a depression:

(1) Organising a stock market crash.
(2) Having a credit squeeze, and
(3) Crashing a bank, preferably a big one, or a couple of medium sized banks.

To get a really good stock market crash going you need a bubble, i.e. you want to get the price of stocks inflated above the value of the companies into which the idiot investors are buying. You also need idiots of course but there is no shortage of those in the City or on Wall Street. This is an old ploy, which the Spanish and French, working together, tried in the 1740s, with the South Sea Bubble, encouraged of course by that nasty piece of work Horace Walpole. He was Britain's first Prime Minister, and a Spanish asset.

Walpole was unusual, being the only Prime Minister to have been bought up by the Spanish. The Tories eventually worked him out after he took no action in response to the brutal atrocity committed in 1731 by Spanish coastguards on gallant Captain Jenkins, the poor chap whose ear was cut off.

By October 1929 stocks were overpriced and conditions were ideal. It helped that the Fed and the Bank of England were under German control (Sir Montagu Norman was fully committed to the depression policy and later tried to deflate the Australian economy by giving insane advice to the Australian government, who must have thought that he'd been at the sauce), not to mention the White House. Herbert Hoover, a.k.a. Hoobert Heever, not a nice man (his treatment of the poor White House staff was inexcusable) was, as we have seen, a German asset. There is still some doubt surrounding the wife, but the better view is that she was probably in on it.

In Britain the Germans went one step further, provoking a mutiny (the Invergordon Mutiny, straight out of the French Revolutionary playbook) with a grossly unfair reduction in the sailors' wages. They were scarcely overpaid. Ramsay MacDonald was of course working for Germany, as was George Lansbury, who pushed disarmament in the face of the rising fascist menace, precisely in order to encourage fascist aggression. As we have seen, Stanley Baldwin was also working for 'Jerry'. Like Harold Macmillan, Baldwin went in for the patronising, avuncular style.

MacDonald and Lansbury both claimed to be pacifists, but their objection was not to killing *per se*, just killing Germans. Baldwin, who took over as Prime Minister on 7th June 1935, supported by MacDonald, encouraged Mussolini to invade Abyssinia,[20] making sure that the Royal Navy were not allowed to stop Italian supplies reaching the Horn of Africa.

Britain should of course have declared war on Italy and sent the RAF to defend the Abyssinian capital of Addis Ababa and bomb the 'Eyeties' in Eritrea to bits. The Navy should have been ordered to bring the Italian Fleet, then quite weak, to battle, launch air strikes on and bombard Naples, Taranto, Genoa and La Spezia and blockade Italy until Mussolini sued for peace. Mussolini of course wasn't stupid. He made sure that he had a green light from Baldwin, delivered via our old friend Sir Eric Drummond. Since the League of Nations had been designed to encourage aggression Sir Eric must have been pleased with its non-performance.

Staying briefly with Abyssinia, British forces were able to kick the Italians out in 1940. The best intelligence officer on that operation was Major, later Major-General, Orde Wingate, assassinated in 1944, with Mountbatten's support. (His plane was sabotaged by German agents in India.) Britain failed to give Emperor Haile Selassie the backing he deserved in 1973 - The DVD's Edward Heath was of course Prime Minister by then and he was understandably anxious to reverse the British success of 1940. Poor old Haile Selassie was betrayed twice by German assets in Downing Street. The coup, naturally, was organised by the Germans, Colonel Mengistu, who pretended to be a Marxist, being DVD. Britain should have sent in the SAS and airborne troops and sorted Mengistu out, i.e. had him shot, nicely, of course. Predictably, Abyssinia, now renamed Ethiopia in the hope that no one would know where it was, descended into civil war. Hundreds of thousands ended up starving and if that wasn't bad enough, they had to be rescued by Bob Geldof, no offence intended (his heart was in the right place). The Emperor's rightful heir still hasn't been restored and the republican government in Addis later 'decided' to have another famine.

The Lindbergh Kidnap

It is doubtful if Admiral Canaris ever grasped how upset the West gets when rogue states like Germany organise the murder of defenceless children. Colonel Lindbergh, a courageous man and great flier, if not a great intellect, who famously became the first man to fly solo across the Atlantic,[21] was sympathetic to Germany. He was the leading member of America First, an isolationist, i.e. pro-German, organisation.

Its policy was that America should abandon her democratic former allies across the Atlantic, Great Britain and France, allow the United States Navy to be caught in a pincer movement between the Kriegsmarine, reinforced by French ships after France's surrender, and the Italian Navy, in the Atlantic and the Imperial Japanese Navy in the Pacific. After that the Germans could invade via Mexico. That's not quite how they put it in the leaflets of course. American isolationism has always been about making sure that America would have fight to *in* isolation, having abandoned all her allies.

Colonel Lindbergh however was holding out on Canaris. It's not quite clear on what issue the Admiral was pressuring the Colonel, but it was big. Lindbergh had good intelligence connections (no surprise there) and may have been briefed in that Hoover was a German asset, at that time Germany's most valuable stooge in Washington.

He may also have been briefed in that Germany had orchestrated the Great Depression, which *inter alia* had done significant economic damage to the American aircraft and car industries. It also gave the lie to the isolationists' argument that if America did nothing to upset the Germans, they in turn would leave her alone. The Germans never leave you alone. For whatever reason, the Abwehr's Head of Station in Washington decided that it would be a good idea to kidnap Colonel and Mrs Lindbergh's baby.

This criminally insane plan, which might have led to war between America and Germany, in which the British Empire would have swung in behind the Americans, should have been stopped by a more balanced intelligence professional in Berlin before it landed on Admiral Canaris's desk. It should then have been dropped in the wastepaper basket, where it belonged.

Canaris sanctioned it, however. The kidnap, which was a doddle (babies tend not to put up a lot of resistance), went ahead, on 1st March 1932, and the Abwehr ended up looking after an 18-month-old baby, at least for a short while. There is some doubt about whether the remains found near the Lindergh home were in fact those of Charles Jnr and more doubt over the time of death. Pressure was applied to Lindbergh, on whom the Abwehr had quite an extensive file, i.e. there was no risk of his going public.

Quite what thought had been put into looking after Charles Lindbergh Jnr is unclear. It is doubtful if the Abwehr were overly supplied with baby food and nappies. Lindbergh backed down, but the operation was badly botched.

The poor baby ended up dead, his skull bashed in, probably after somebody panicked. If the remains near the house *were* those of the little chap they might have been moved there. It is wildly improbable that Canaris ordered the murder, indeed he probably turned even colder than usual when he heard that the Lindbergh baby had been killed by his agents.

The scale of public interest in the case shocked both Canaris and the German Foreign Ministry, which must have been doing its nut by this stage. Fortunately for them, the US media were as obsessed with the notion of a lone kidnapper as the British media were over 75 years later in the Madeleine McCann kidnap, also set up by German intelligence. It was easy to cover up German involvement. William Randolph Hearst probably knew, i.e. in his case it was more a case of censorship than ignorance. There was an element of rough justice therefore when his own granddaughter was kidnapped 42 years later.

The Abwehr needed a sacrificial bunny. Bruno Hauptmann, a low-life criminal and ex-soldier exported to the States nine years previously, suited the bill perfectly. Hauptmann was probably strung along until just before he was fried on 3rd April 1936. He would have been told that German assets in Washington would save his sorry behind. There has been a fatuous 'Bruno was innocent' campaign ever since, which has been grossly unfair to the State of New Jersey, His Honor Judge Trenchard and the jury, who got it right. He was clearly guilty.

Equally clearly, Hauptmann did not act alone, as New Jersey Governor Harold Hoffman concluded, apparently after visiting Hauptmann in prison on 16th October 1935. Governor Hoffman was one of the few to consider the case in the round, but he had no help from Washington, least of all from the BOI, predecessor of the FBI, which is still pushing the absurd lone kidnapper theory decades later. The FBI with respect has always got organised crime wrong, i.e. has never grasped that organised crime is organised by the intelligence agencies of rogue states. This is not just a failing by individual agents but an institutional failing, rendering the agency wholly unsuited to the task of investigating state-sponsored crime. German penetration of the Justice Department makes reform unlikely.

Thanks to Governor Hoffman, the New Jersey State Police investigation was more sophisticated, indeed the BOI seem if anything to have been a nuisance. They hampered the investigation with their rigidly fixed view that it was a single-person crime. There are question marks however over the role of Norman Schwarzkopf Senior, whose son became a much more famous general. Schwarzkopf Senior was a German as well as US citizen, who spoke German fluently and later worked for the CIA. As Superintendent of the New Jersey State Police, Schwarzkopf was in charge of the state police investigation. His basic strategy was to give the kidnappers a free hand until the discovery of the body, then go after Hauptmann. The storming Norman was definitely the son.

In fairness to Director J. Edgar Hoover, the BOI's failures may not have been due to a lack of professionalism or an inability to view the case objectively, as Governor Hoffman had done. There would have been intense political pressure on Hoover to avoid embarrassing Germany and German assets in Washington. The big mistakes were made in Washington, not Trenton.

1. For those who are not fans of this brilliant BBC series - so good it was scrapped - Jim Hacker was a bumbling John Major/David Cameron/Rishi Sunak style Conservative machine politician, no offence intended, played by the late, great Paul Eddington CBE, who died, after a deliberately delayed diagnosis of cancer, in 1995. In *The Economy Drive* (Series 1, air-date 3rd March 1980) he was persuaded by the wily Sir Humphrey Appleby, his Permanent Secretary, superbly played by the late Nigel Hawthorne, another very fine actor, to have an 'economy drive', with predictably disastrous consequences. At a Rotary lunch in New Hampshire many years ago I tried to persuade an official of the Public Broadcasting System to broadcast the series in the States, sadly to no avail. They are the funniest training videos ever filmed. Sky TV brought out a new series in 2013.
2. No need to e-mail the publishers - I do appreciate that this was not technically possible, as chickens came along some time after the velociraptors died out.
3. 2000, directed by Donald Petrie, also starring two other great actors, Sir Michael Caine and William Shatner, who should have been given an honorary knighthood long ago. Absolutely hilarious - the scene where Miss Bullock's character calls for tougher penalties for parole violators is a hoot.
4. He was actually rather jolly, until He came down with a touch of porphyria, poor chap, at which point everybody said he was mad, which he wasn't. He was a lot saner than his doctors.
5. The Abwehr's Ramon Mercader, although he was false flagged through the NKVD.
6. Officially MI6 only captured him and handed him over to the partisans, indeed some accounts even say the partisans captured him. MI6 did hand him over, but he was already dead. The partisans kindly agreed to fire a few rounds from a Sten gun (essentially a bit of piping with a slot for a magazine, accurate to about the length of the barrel) into the body to make it look good. The assassination was set up by Canaris's deputy in the DVD, von Lahousen, who having previously made sure that he was rescued - Standartanführer Otto Skorzeny worked for Herr Admiral - wanted Benito out of the way. Since Menzies, the wartime head of MI6, was Abwehr then DVD it was simple enough to arrange.
7. 'Jerry' of course claims that he scuttled her, but she sank just after *Dorsetshire's* last torpedo went in - funny that. The 'Counties' were swift, elegant, habitable, good steamers and mounted an excellent main battery gun, the famous 8-inch Mk VIII, which as explained in Chapter 15 could theoretically shoot down aircraft (they could be elevated to 70 degrees, astonishing for a medium-calibre gun designed in the 1920s). HMS *Cumberland* showed the class's strengths in her spirited dash from Port Stanley to the Plate to join Rear Admiral Sir Henry Harwood's squadron in 1939. They also had good workshop facilities, making them independent of bases for long periods, and hangars for their aircraft. This was an important consideration in the Far East, with its typhoons, and the North Atlantic, with its gales. All this came at a price however, and their belt and deck armour were inadequate.
8. All these are standard displacements.

9. Germany was not a party to the Washington Treaty (just the instigator of it) but became bound under the equally silly London Naval Treaty.
10. The rest of the Japanese battlefleet in World War II were older ships that had been rebuilt, such as the British-built *Kongos.*
11. They were both scrapped, on Attlee's orders, an act of sheer malice, probably in revenge for the *Bismarck.* Either would have made a wonderful memorial to the men who built and served on them.
12. Memorably described as 'Hoobert Heever' by that fine comic actor Harry von Zell, who pretended that it was a slip of the tongue. He had intelligence connections (a lot of actors do) and knew what he was doing.
13. I am marginally to the right of centre and a member of Reform, but this does not prevent me adopting a bipartisan approach. Hoover, a nasty piece of work, who was in the loop on Pearl Harbor, would have been a disastrous choice - his first term was bad enough. FDR was a great American and a great President, like JFK a statesman rather than a politician. The fact that they were both Democrats is beside the point.
14. USS *North Carolina* (BB-55) and USS *Washington* (BB-56).
15. Wikipedia, e.g., in March 2012 were giving a standard displacement of under 10,000 tons and a full load displacement of over 15,000. The full load figure is in the ballpark, but the standard displacement is a fantasy with every respect to the editor who put it there. Amusingly, Wiki were also loyally sticking with the 35,000 ton standard displacement figure for the *North Carolinas.*
16. About the first thing they did was shoot up the poor old German Ambassador, usually a sign that German intelligence is doing the revolt. MI6 missed a trick here in Libya - perhaps they should have got the rebels they were covertly backing to shoot the British Ambassador, then again perhaps not. It simply wouldn't have been British.
17. It would be interesting to know if anyone tracked the Japanese destroyers which were deployed to the Med in 1918 - it would not be surprising if one or more went walkies for a few days. They certainly weren't there to fight Germans.
18. They were in fact based on a whaleboat. It wasn't a bad hull design, if you wanted to go fishing. They displaced 925 tons, were 205 feet long (or short) and typically carried a single 4 inch and a 2-pounder pom-pom aft. They had no AA director, so could only be waved uselessly in the general direction of the enemy. At Treasury insistence, they had cheap reciprocating engines, pre- Dreadnought style, with a single screw, knocking out 2,750 installed HP. They were capable of 16 knots, with a following wind. It would have made more sense to intern Treasury officials at the start of the war rather than Germans.
19. Famously referred to as 'Milton Keynes' by Richard Vernon's character Sir Desmond Glazebrook, in *Yes Minister.*
20. My old friend (we were members of the same club), Sir William (Bill) Deedes, a gent and a decent old stick, sadly no longer with us, covered the invasion, which was absolutely disgraceful, for the *Daily Telegraph,* of which he was later a most distinguished editor. Bill's reports of the shocked response of Abyssinian officials, and the Emperor Haile Selassie, whom he met (Haile Selassie had excellent tailors by the way - mine) are very moving.

21. The first nonstop crossing of the Atlantic, i.e. not refuelling in the Azores, was of course by Alcock and Brown in 1919 in a converted Vickers Vimy bomber, powered by two dependable Rolls-Royce Eagles. The US Navy were first across, in Curtiss seaplanes, before the war.

17

The Inter-War Period /2/

The Bodyline Operation

Whilst the 'Hun' would not score many runs if he tried it himself, as he does not play with a straight bat, he does understand the importance of cricket to the English. So much so he made sure that he was able to interfere with the selection of the England cricket team. The principal German asset in the cricketing establishment for many years, recruited at Oxford (he was an Oriel man) was Trinidadian-born Sir Pelham Warner. Sir Pelham captained MCC in Australia on the 1903/1904 and 1912/13 tours. Marylebone Cricket Club is the custodian of the laws of the game, and as late as the 1970s overseas tours were conducted in our name. Our colours are an attractive shade of red and yellow.

The intelligence about Sir Pelham would have come as a great disappointment to his coach at Rugby School, Tom Emmett, but might not have surprised his superior in intelligence at the Foreign Office in the latter stages of the Great War, John Buchan. He of course wrote the spy novel *The Thirty-Nine Steps*, of which several rather good films have been made, the best (in my, as ever, humble opinion) in 1959, starring that fine actor Kenneth More. Any intelligence officer who has ever had to deal with dim-witted policemen will find himself or herself instinctively sympathising with Kenneth More's character.

Admiral of the Fleet Earl Jellicoe, who interrogated Warner, in a very gentlemanly way of course, in the flag quarters of HMS *New Zealand*, *en route* to Alexandria, after the war, would not have been surprised either. It is not usual for members of the MCC Committee to be invited to join former First Sea Lords on battlecruisers. Warner found himself batting on a sticky wicket, albeit not for the first time. In 1908 he scored 64 not out, out of 95, for MCC on a very sticky wicket against Yorkshire.

It was John Buchan who first suspected Warner, indeed he was forced to resign from the Foreign Office, under the pretext of poor health. A. C.

Maclaren, Sir Stanley Jackson, C. B. Fry and the great Prince Ranjitsinhji[1] all refused to tour Australia with him in 1912/13, which ought to have said something to Intelligence. Sadly, the liaison between Intelligence and the MCC Committee was not then all that it should have been. (It's improved since.)

So far as is known to British Intelligence, emphasising that I have only ever had lunch with British Intelligence, and the odd drinkies, and am not part of it, Sir Pelham is the only German spy ever to have scored a Test Match century. That was a fine 132 not out in the First Test Match against South Africa on Lord Hawke's tour. Had MI6 offered to play German Intelligence at cricket Sir Pelham would have been an automatic choice for the 'Hun' for many years.

He was the archetypal gentleman spy, indeed he played for the Gentleman, at Lords in 1901,[2] putting together a century opening stand with C. B. Fry, the only England cricketer ever to have been offered the throne of Albania.[3] It would have been quite wrong to hang him. He had sound views on maintaining the distinction between amateurs and professionals, which was not abolished until after his death. Quite properly, the dreadful news was held back until just after he died, to avoid upsetting him. It is very poor form to upset a chap on his deathbed.

The Japanese were very worried about the possibility of the Australians moving a couple of divisions to Malaya to hold up their long-planned advance on Singapore. Every capital in Asia had noted the fine performance of the Australian Imperial Force in the Great War and appreciated that an Australian division was likely to be a crack unit, worth at least two Japanese divisions. This proved to be the case in World War II, when the Aussies smacked the Japs back across the Kokoda Trail in New Guinea. The RAAF was also shaping up to be an effective fighting force, which would be able to contribute to the air defence of Malaya and Singapore.

Downing Street were desperate to come up with a way of surrendering Malaya and Singapore to Japan and get away with it. Starving the defence of funds, particularly to build airfields and radar stations, and refusing to supply high explosive shells to use against the invading Japanese, were two of the ploys used by Number 10 and the Treasury in the decade up till the surrender.[4] Understandably, Ramsay MacDonald backed a cunning plan thought up by Sir Pelham to force Australia out of the Empire.

In the Australian summer of 1928/9 a powerful new Australian batsman, Donald Bradman, had emerged. He went on to score 300 runs in a day on the Australian tour of England in 1930. England however had a possible counter, in two of the fastest bowlers ever to play Test cricket, Harold Larwood and Bill Voce, both of Nottinghamshire. When they needed a new fast bowler in Notts they 'whistled down the pits'.

In those days there was no restriction on how many fielders you could have on the leg, or body side, of the batsman. Sir Pelham was one of the few in the game who had seen leg theory, or bodyline as it came to be known, in action. It was called 'bodyline' as the bowling was on the line of the body, not the wicket. It was first used by W. B. Burns, for Worcestershire against Middlesex, at Lords, in 1910. Sir Pelham, quite properly, objected.

The facts are obscure, but it seems that the umpires asked Burns's captain, Harry Foster, of the famous Malvern cricketing family, to ask Burns to desist, which he did. Although within the laws, it was clearly not a tactic of which a gentleman could approve, and Harry Foster was a gentleman. Indeed, he captained the Gentlemen that year against the Players, a great honour, far greater than being invited to join the Cabinet, e.g. Sir Pelham realised that with Larwood and Voce England could fire in fast, short-pitched, rising balls at Bradman and the other Australian batsmen, i.e. bowl bodyline. It was of no use at all unless the bowler was fast, as otherwise runs would simply have been gifted on the leg-side. Shrewd observers of the game in the Long Room, if that is not a tautology, had observed during the Lords Test of 1930 that Bradman had a slight tendency to back away towards leg if the bowling was fast and short- pitched. The Long Room is a wonderful place from which to watch cricket, by the way. If a batsman has played well, you applaud him back in, whether he played well for England or the opposition.

If the bowlers could be instructed (Harold Larwood and Bill Voce were both sportsmen and would only bowl in this way if so ordered by their captain) to bowl fast at the body, not the stumps, they could not only restrict the scoring but might injure the batsman. You have to pitch the ball up if you want to hit the wickets, as they are only 28 inches high.

Of course this needed a captain who did not like Australians. Warner had just the man in mind, a dour Scot, if that is not a tautology with respect to the Scots, named Douglas Jardine. He was a gentleman, but Scottish. For Jardine, winning mattered more than playing the game. This is a compliment to a Scot but a dreadful accusation to level against an Englishman. It is possible that Warner and Ramsay MacDonald (but not Jardine) were hoping that Bradman would be injured.

As it was, poor Bert Oldfield, the brave Aussie wicketkeeper, was badly hit over the heart and never fully recovered. Justifiably, his widow Ruth still blames the terrible blow for shortening his life. Had he, or another Aussie batsman, died, Australia might have left the Empire. She nearly did anyway. This would have made it easier for Japan to seize Malaya and Singapore, in turn exposing Australia.

In the events which happened the US Navy was able to step up to the plate, but when the Bodyline tour was being planned Herbert 'von' Hoover was President and was expected to win in November '32. He would have greatly weakened the US Navy. Not a single major American warship was laid down when Hoover was in the White House.

German assets in Canberra desired the same outcome as Ramsay MacDonald. Japan was mainly interested in Queensland and Western Australia's mineral wealth. Key civil servants in Canberra, sympathetic to the Axis, were prepared to surrender all of Australia north of a line drawn from Brisbane to Perth. A version of this plan was later adopted as defence policy in the event of a Japanese invasion and was known as the Brisbane Line. Canberra is still penetrated, although Germany's key ally in the Far East is now China and DVD agents in Canberra are trying to turn Australia into a Chinese client state, à la Indonesia.

The MCC[5] tour of Australia, from 2nd December 1932 to 28th February 1933, has gone down in history as the Bodyline Tour. The tour manager, of course, was none other than Sir Pelham Warner. The new tactics, which simply weren't cricket, caused uproar and rightly so. Unfortunately, very few members of Nottingham County Cricket Club were involved in intelligence work and when bodyline was trialled at Trent Bridge[6] the problem wasn't picked up. Someone should have had a quiet word with MCC and had Warner replaced.

Intelligence did however have Members in MCC, indeed for many years both MI5 and MI6 had boxes at Lords and rightly so. At times Lords has seen more useful intelligence work done than the Joint Intelligence Committee. The whisper is that the Treasury objected to the boxes, which shows that they know no more about intelligence than they do about defence, nor for that matter about how to run an economy. Sir Pelham was spotted by the covert agency MI18, of which John Buchan, who had penetrated the Foreign Office for British Intelligence in the world war, was a member.

Someone also spoke to Admiral Jellicoe, now advanced to the 33^{0} of Freemasonry. Word was passed back to Canberra on the defence net, bypassing MI6, which was of course under German control. Instructions were given to Jardine to cool it and nobody died. Thankfully, a breach with Australia was avoided and the only Japanese invasion there was mounted after World War II by Toyota, Nissan and property developers buying up real estate on the beautiful Queensland coast.

Warner was furious. He took it out on poor old Larwood, who settled in Australia, where he lived to the ripe old age of 90, and Voce, each of whom was a decent man. They were treated badly after their return to England, particularly Larwood, with Sir Pelham pulling the strings.

This wasn't the only interference by the dastardly 'Hun' in the running of cricket. Warner was seriously worried by the great Gloucestershire batsman

Walter Hammond, whose qualification for Gloucestershire he held up, using the most spurious of pretexts. Germany's busy Kingston station, which later tried to murder MI18's Ian Fleming, tried and failed to murder Hammond on the 1930-1931 MCC tour to the West Indies.

Thankfully, Hammond, who was poisoned, survived, as he did the second attempt on his life, a car crash staged by the DVD-controlled South African intelligence agency BOSS, in 1960. At least Sir Pelham could console himself that he topped the Abwehr's batting averages.

The Maginot Line

The problem with having your government and bureaucracy penetrated by the enemy is that once inside the gate he can influence the design of your fortifications. This is why the Maginot Line ended at the Belgian frontier. The average junior officer in the French Army, never mind the general staff, could see that there was not much point in having a defensive line with a great big hole in it. It would be like having a border fence across the United States that left out New Mexico.

This suited 'Basil Boche' in two ways:

(1) It fitted in neatly with the Oberkommando der Wehrmacht's (OKW's) battle plan for the third invasion of France, which was to hook through Belgium, again, and outflank the French, again, and
(2) It drained the military budget, so that there was not enough left over for tanks and towed, i.e. mobile, artillery.

Your 'Boche' will always come up with ways of wasting your defence budget, so much so that any defence proposal, which any idiot can see is going to waste money ought to trigger a counterintelligence investigation. If it is proposed by a genuine idiot it can always be referred to human resources. In fairness to the French general staff (and I am nothing if not fair to the French) where the Maginot Line did not have a hole in it, it was well-designed. The 'Boche' understood this. He had the plans after all, courtesy of his many assets in Paris. When he attacked France, again, in 1940 he carefully avoided the Maginot Line.

The oft-repeated point that it was an anachronism in the age of the tank is a bad one. The fortifications were expressly designed to stop tanks, which would have been caught in crossfire from guns in armoured turrets that tank guns of the day could not hope to knock out. Not only that, but your average 1930s panzer was at a huge disadvantage when engaging fixed guns because its gun was not stabilised and lacked fully synthetic fire control. It could fire or manoeuvre, but realistically could not hope to do both. If you want to get an idea of how complex a device an electro- mechanical fire control computer really is have a look at the Admiralty Mk VI Fire Control Table in HMS *Belfast*. It fills an entire compartment and needed several crew and an officer to operate.

It was not really until the 1960s that Main Battle Tanks like the Chieftain came along with proper fire control. Even as late as the Challenger Mk 1 the fire control was not fully sorted - ask any tanker in the Gulf War. (The excellent, but thirsty, American Abrams[7] had better fire control, and it's been uprated since.) Put shortly, most 'Boche' panzers attacking the Maginot Line would have been sitting ducks, firing not very penetrating rounds, which would have bounced off the fortifications, whilst the defenders poured in lethal fire. The French knew what they were they doing, which is why the Germans stopped them.

Germany by the way only had one serious tank gun in World War II, the admittedly excellent 88 mil. modified flak gun, but that wasn't used in tanks until 1941. Thanks partly to Donald Sutherland in *Kelly's Heroes*[8] it has an inflated reputation. It was rather too good for the M3 Sherman (the later M3A1 had improved protection), but the 88-mil. armed Tiger and its successor, the rather more formidable King Tiger, of which only a few were made, were heavy tanks, whereas the Sherman was a medium tank.

The British 3.7 inch was a better gun (it also started life as an anti-aircraft gun) and the Russian 122 mil. D25 better still. The eighty-eights, don't forget, were only 3.5 inch, hardly what the Royal Navy would call a gun. It fired a shell about the weight of a baseball bat, when the average British and American battleship fired a shell the weight of a Volkswagen (and at supersonic speeds too, which made the daft theory that you couldn't exceed Mach 1 all the stranger[9]).

The Fairey Battle

Britain had the English Channel, so there wasn't much point in building a Maginot Line, but she had her equivalent - the Fairey Battle light bomber. This was a nice bit of kit, for 1936. It had a Rolls-Royce Merlin engine, similar to the Spitfire, pushing out about 1,000 HP, and could trot along at about 240 mph fully laden with a small but useful bomb load of about 1,000 lbs. It was pleasant to fly, had few vices and even fewer defences.

It was ideal for bombing tribesmen in Iraq and would have been just the ticket for strafing the wily Fakir of Ipi (who reported to the Abwehr – he was a very wily old Fakir indeed). The Fakir of course had no fighter defences. So far as Europe was concerned, it was obsolescent by 1938 and more of a danger to its crews than the enemy. Thus it was ordered in huge numbers.

Politically Number 10 needed to be seen to be doing something about the massive build-up of the Luftwaffe. Ordering lots of Battles, regardless of their military usefulness, allowed them to play the numbers game. It also allowed them to help the Germans by tying up factories, machine- tools, light alloys and precious Merlin engines, which could have gone into Spitfires, Hurricanes and Fairey Fulmar shipboard fighters instead. Each of them was armed with eight 0.303 machine guns. An added advantage for Chamberlain, who took over from his fellow German asset Stanley Baldwin on 28th May 1937, and his Civil Service side-kick Sir Horace Wilson (an odious little man, no offence intended) was that should it come to a war the Battle would be unlikely to kill many Germans.

The Navy's Fairey Fulmar, based on the Battle, was slow - it was a large, two-seater reconnaissance fighter rather than an out and out fighter – but it had pleasant deck-landing qualities, reasonable endurance, lots of guns and was only going to have to shoot down Italians. Unlike the RAF's airfields, except during the retreat from France, the Navy's floating airfields, i.e. its carriers, moved. This put a premium on finding them. In the days before radio navigation, which couldn't be used without betraying the carrier's position anyway, this meant a second seat. Given the likely sea areas in which they were going to operate, where the weather could be marginal (different considerations applied in the Pacific), the Admiralty's thinking was sound.

Multirole shipboard aircraft always make sense, as a carrier can only carry so many aircraft. Since the Royal Navy's carriers were expected to operate in the Med, within range of land-based bombers, and with the fleet rather than behind it, they needed to be armoured. Of necessity this meant fewer aircraft per carrier,[10] although the DNC cleverly addressed the problem by having double hangar decks in the *Indefatigable* class. The Americans preferred wooden decks, until kamikazes started coming through them, after which they moved to British-style armoured decks.[11] Spitfires, Hurricanes and Fulmars would have been a vastly better investment than Battles. The claim by Chamberlain's defenders, who tend to be ignorant of the fact that he was a German spy, German spies themselves, or persons with pronounced pro-German sympathies, that the Munich debacle allowed time for more fighters to be built is nonsense. Chamberlain was careful to appoint fellow German spies as Air Minister (one of them, the pointless Sir Kingsley Wood, fatuously objected to bombing private property in Germany, although in fairness that probably wasn't because he held shares in Krupps) and tried very hard to block the Spitfire. It actually started life as a private venture. He did everything he could to make sure that the RAF didn't get the kit it wanted and got kit it didn't need.

The Amelia Earhart/Fred Noonan Shoot-Down (July 1937)

This is only a mystery if you haven't read *Lost Star: the Search for Amelia Earhart* by Captain Randall Brink[12] and *The Search for Amelia Earhart* by Fred Goerner.[13] They and others have done the heavy-lifting on this, including researching the only known US photograph (there are further photos in the Japanese naval intelligence file) of the modified Model 10 Electra aircraft after it was shot down (a US aerial recon photo of Taroa Island taken in 1944[14]) and a rare post-capture photograph of Amelia Earhart, taken not long before her execution.

For the avoidance of doubt, I am not claiming to have 'solved' the mystery, which was cracked by Fred Goerner as far back as the sixties, and was known to ONI and British Naval Intelligence at the time anyway. I can however add a few intelligence snippets, which after all is the purpose of this book, i.e. to supply the odd snippet of intelligence here and there and fill in the occasional gap in the historical record.

Neither Fred Goerner nor Captain Brink had access to the Japanese intelligence files. The main one is their black naval intelligence file (i.e. the real one, not the fake one inserted into the records for the Americans to find). It has photos of both Amelia and Fred after their capture, photos of the Electra on the deck of the IJN *Kamoi* and IJN *Koshu* (the Japanese Navy produced false logs for these vessels), a summary prepared by the senior intelligence officer on the carrier, together with a brief combat report by the pilot who shot them down. He was apparently instructed not to use tracer rounds, making aiming more difficult. The file also contains interrogation records and the dates of their executions, together with details of the name and rank of the executioners. These were apparently an NCO in the case of Fred Noonan and an officer in the case of Major Earhart.[15] It is thought that the Japanese later posted the pilot to China, where they arranged for him to be shot down.

The truth might have emerged before 1960 but for the unfortunate habit Washington has of surrendering territory hard won with American blood. The people of the Marshall and Marianas islands, which absurdly did not become US territories like Puerto Rico (leaving Okinawa in the hands of the Japs was a similar mistake) knew perfectly well that the Japs would be let back in, and indeed they were, albeit by the back door. There has been quite a bit of intimidation of eyewitnesses on Saipan and in the Marshalls over the years, although one Saipan woman was brave enough to go on NBC television in 1990.[16]

Amelia Earhart was both a wonderful person and a superb flier. The theory that she couldn't fly a plane or navigate - she flew solo across the

Atlantic without radio aids for heaven's sake - is just offensive nonsense. The same goes for the theory that Fred Noonan, who had helped pioneer Pan-Am's trans-Pacific route, couldn't navigate. There is more substance to the theory that he was an alcoholic, but as Mary Lovell[17] reveals, he was only a bottle a day man (scarcely an alcoholic then).

Their aircraft was not an XC-35 as has been asserted,[18] but a specially modified Model 10 Electra with military-specification, highly supercharged Pratt & Whitney R-585 radials. These were designed to allow her to outrun Japanese fighters, although sadly that didn't work as their mission had been betrayed and the Japanese were waiting for them. The Electra was fitted by Skunk Works personnel, including Robert T. Elliott, with Fairchild electric high-resolution cameras in the lower fuselage bay. Their mission was to photograph the Japanese naval base at Truk and illegal Japanese fortifications in the Marshall Islands. These were supposedly League of Nations mandates, although that was a complete farce, as of course was the League of Nations itself. Amelia Earhart was sworn in as a Major in the Army Air Corps Reserve, a photograph of her swearing-in ceremony appearing in Captain Brink's book. Fred Noonan of course was already a reserve officer, in the US Naval Reserves, attached to ONI.

British Naval Intelligence was in the loop. The brand-new light cruiser HMS (NZ) *Achilles*[19] was sortied from Devonport near Auckland to support the mission, by providing radio bearings, up to date weather reports and medium-calibre naval gunfire support if needed. Unfortunately, the IJN sortied a carrier task group and even the *Achilles*, with 8 6- inch guns, was outgunned.

The Admiralty should have sent at least a battlecruiser, preferably the *Hood*, which could have sailed from the Med via the Suez Canal and Singapore, supported by a fast carrier, such as HMS *Glorious*. She was used to forming fast carrier task groups further to tactics developed in the Med by the outstanding C-in-C, Admiral Sir Reginald Henderson.[20] Dear old *Hood* would have seen off the Japs. She could have rescued Amelia and Fred, who broadcasted from Mili atoll, where they ditched, for at least three days. Their frantic Mayday calls provoked a panic on the part of the German network in the United States, which went into overdrive cover-up mode.

The US Navy sortied the fine 16-inch gun battleship USS *Colorado* (BB-45) and 'Lady Lex,' the magnificent USS *Lexington* (CV-2), with her sister USS *Saratoga* (CV-3)[21] the world's largest aircraft carrier. Unfortunately, they were not sailing together in the initial stages, depriving the *Lexington* of heavy gunfire support and the *Colorado* of air support. It looks as though *Achilles* was in the best position. She was racing, covertly, to the rescue when hauled off by Horace Wilson in Number 10 via German assets in the Admiralty.

The Captain of *Achilles* was instructed to falsify both his log and the radio room log, but fortunately Naval Intelligence, at MI18 request, had a backup intelligence officer on board. His identity had not been disclosed to the Captain, in accordance with the usual practice (the Captain was normally only told the identity of a ship's official intelligence officer). This agent, a petty officer, was apparently able to secrete a photograph of the original radio log in the forward boiler room.

It was a measure of Horace Wilson's lack of morality that he was quite happy to allow a woman to be captured, tortured and executed by the Japanese. If anyone was to be tortured and executed, it should have been Sir Horace. The broad outline of events is tolerably clear:

(1) The Japanese were secretly building military bases in the Mandated Territories.

(2) Major Earhart and Lt-Cdr Noonan agreed to overfly the targets *in daylight* and switch their proposed west-east round the world flight at the Equator to an east-west flight, dog-legging the Equator, so as to overfly other targets of intelligence interest, including French and Italian targets. This would allow the all-important film to be handed over to ONI at Camden Island.

(3) ONI put up the funds for the plane, channelled through white hats including Victor Bendix and the patriotic folk at Purdue University.

(4) Lockheed built a brand-new Model 10 Electra fitted with Fairchild electric cameras and the uprated military-specification R-585 motors specified for the XC-35. The original Electra, serial number N16020, was broken up for spares and her engines returned to Pratt & Whitney.

(5) The new aircraft had an economical cruising speed of 240 mph, a maximum cruising speed of around 275 mph and a maximum speed at combat power of around 300 mph.

(6) Her fuel capacity was 1,100 Imperial gallons,[22] giving a still-air endurance range of approximately 4,800 statute miles allowing for take- off and climb to 10,000 ft and say 15 minutes at combat power.

(7) Amelia was instructed to fly at 140 mph so as to create the impression that it was the original Electra, but delays at Fort Lamy in Africa on the way out due to a leaking oleo strut meant that she had no choice but to open her up, so as to avoid a dangerous night landing at El- Fasher, which was unlit. This run alone confirms that it could not have been the original aircraft, but a much more powerful one. In practice she cruised at about 160-175 mph, using

some of the extra power available to her, but not so much as to tip the wink to journalists covering the flight. The good flight times were put down to 'tailwinds' even though the revised route meant she was mostly flying *into* wind, given the prevailing winds at the Equator.

(8) The mission was betrayed to the Japanese via their Head of Station Berlin, having been betrayed to Berlin by the senior Abwehr agent in the US Navy, Captain, later Admiral King.

(9) At least two other Abwehr assets were involved: William T. Miller and James Forrestal. Miller was exposed at the time and was probably taken out in World War II. Forrestal apparently was not exposed until after World War II, when he was very properly sanctioned by President Truman. He holds the dual distinction of being both the first Secretary of Defense and the first to be thrown from a high floor at Bethesda Naval Hospital.

(10) The Japanese ambushed the flight near Mili Atoll in the Marshall Islands.

(11) The intercepting aircraft was a Mitsubishi A5M Claude, launched from a carrier. Some sources state that the carrier was the IJN *Akagi*, although officially she was still in refit (records were altered for all of the Japanese warships involved in this highly covert operation - her refit looks suspiciously lengthy when compared with that of her sister *Kaga*).

(12) The pilot had instructions to force the Electra down to permit interrogation of the crew, recovery of the film and the cameras, and an opportunity to inspect the state of the art engines. He shot out the port engine, which caught fire.

(13) Amelia was able to feather her No. 1 prop and pull away even on one engine, at combat power aided by the fact that most of her fuel had been consumed, whereas the Claudes had not long taken off. She was unable to put the fire out in No. 1 however and was forced to ditch, which she did, on a coral reef, part of Mili Atoll in the Marshall Islands. She was uninjured but Fred Noonan in the rear compartment suffered a blow to the head, cuts and bruising, which were later attended to by an IJN corpsman, Biliman Amaron. There was some storm cell activity, and she may have been able to use a squall to conceal her initial escape. She may also have hoped that rain would help put the fire in No. 1 out. The fire was serious and photo interpretation of the damaged Electra on Taroa in 1944 suggested that it had started to burn through the engine bearers, which from recollection were magnesium alloy. At any rate the

port engine detached itself from the airframe during the ditching, which was carried out with extreme skill.

(14) Fred Noonan was observed leaving the aircraft shortly after she ditched to bury a tin on the nearby beach, which was later recovered, its contents being suppressed. The Japanese never found out about the tin.

(15) Amelia with voice and Fred with Morse, as he was the more fluent Morse operator, broadcast repeated Mayday messages for at least 72 hours after being shot down.

(16) These messages were intercepted by *inter alia* operators on board the *Lexington*, *Colorado* and *Achilles*, the PanAm station at Midway Island, the US Navy at Pearl Harbor and by a number of ham operators in the States. There was a massive cover-up, with the assistance of Captain King at ONI and Chamberlain and Wilson in London, and a rescue was ruled out.

(17) Amelia and Fred were taken to Japanese-held Saipan, where they were held and interrogated in the military prison at Garapan in appalling conditions. In particular, no toilet facilities were provided in the cells.

(18) Fred Noonan was beheaded a short distance outside the prison in or about October 1937 after he flung some of his own faeces in the face of the Japanese Kempeitai NCO interrogating him. He was buried in a shallow, unmarked grave near Garapan.

(19) After Fred Noonan's brutal execution Amelia was released to the Koboyash Royokan Hotel, but was free to walk around the town, where she was photographed. Her execution was ordered by Tokyo in or around March 1938, probably at Admiral Canaris's request to protect Ernest King and James Forrestal, who were key assets, King later being made CNO and Forrestal Secretary of the Navy. They went on to play a major role in forcing up American casualties in the Marshalls, Marianas, Bonins, Peleliu, and Okinawa campaigns by betraying American invasion plans to Tokyo via Mexico City and Berlin.

(20) Amelia was executed by a single shot to the temple delivered by a Kempetai officer. She was blindfolded before being led to the execution site, which was by Fred Noonan's re-opened grave. The removal of her blindfold, which was seen by a Saipan eye-witness, was probably done for psychological effect as Fred Noonan's body would by then have been in an advanced state of decomposition. Her body collapsed into the grave, both her remains and those of Fred Noonan were recovered by a small party of US Marines

in 1944 under the supervision of an officer of Marine Corps Intelligence Activity (MCIA) and both Forrestal and King were implicated in the cover-up, which was supported by Treasury Secretary Morgenthau.[23]

(21) President Roosevelt was fully aware of and encouraged the overflight, his go-between with Amelia and Fred being Bernard Baruch. The overflight was also approved by Generals Westover and Arnold, as well as ONI. Because of Roosevelt's justified doubts about Morgenthau's loyalty[24] the Treasury Secretary, who controlled the Coast Guard, was not told, hence the confusion on board the USCGC *Ithaca*. She was waiting by the advertised destination, Howland Island, the real destination of course being Camden Island. The President was *not* told that ONI knew where the Electra was and had intercepted the Mayday messages, indeed the evidence is that the White House was frantically trying to find out what had happened to the brave American flyers, nor was he briefed in, as he should have been, after the discovery of the Electra on Taroa by the USAAF (as it had become by 1944), the discovery of the remains of a man and a woman consistent with their being the remains of Fred Noonan and Amelia Earhart, on Saipan in 1944 and their subsequent verification by dental records, parts of the jawbones having been recovered[25] (there was apparently less certainty about Fred's identity but since he was buried with Amelia and her ID was confirmed the ID of the other remains was not difficult), and

(22) The fatal plane crash on 8th July 1965, involving Amelia's close friend, the Hollywood stunt pilot Paul Mantz (who had helped plan the first (wast-east) flight and saw the second Electra at close quarters, despite it being under military guard) whilst filming *Flight of the Phoenix*,[26] should be reviewed for evidence of sabotage, in particular weakening of the structure at the point of failure, together with the dubious finding by the FAA, based on post-mortem blood alcohol production, that Mantz, a highly professional stunt pilot, was intoxicated. The death on a ferry flight to Phoenix Arizona of his colleague Frank Tallman, also an experienced stunt pilot, on 15th April 1978 should also be reviewed, with specific reference to a fake ADF beam whilst the aircraft was under IFR conditions over the Santa Ana Mountains.

As the Japanese bases at Truk and in the Marshalls were being built in violation of international law, were not on sovereign Japanese soil and the

Japanese had executed ONI agents on previous missions, and furthermore had refused to comply with entirely proper US requests for access, which were supported by Great Britain, the leading League of Nations power,[27] it is doubtful that the overflight by an unarmed civilian-registered aircraft was illegal. It would have been different (*aliter*, as we lawyers say) if sovereign Japanese airspace had been violated.

Most public international lawyers would say that it would have been the better course to refer the matter to the League in Geneva. However, since the League bureaucracy was under the control of an Axis intelligence agency and was not willing to act in good faith, that course was not reasonably open to President Roosevelt. In my considered opinion it was reasonably and lawfully open to the United States, as a state reasonably fearing that an illegal armed attack might be mounted from *inter alia* Mandated Territories, to conduct the overflight. The concern that the islands were being fortified was fully justified - the illegal air and naval bases at Truk were massive.

Since the USA was the state of registry, the flight was conducted with the approval of the proper American civil and military authorities for a legitimate national security purpose and the crew were officers of her reserve armed forces, whose mission had been approved by their chain of command, it would be scandalous to suggest that some breach of federal aviation law was committed by Major Earhart and Lt-Cdr Noonan. In fact, as we now know, the Bureau of Civil Aeronautics co-operated fully.

Its officer, William Miller, who also reported to ONI and the Abwehr, approved the substitution of the civil registration N16020 on the second Electra, and the falsification, for reasons of security, of the manufacturer's construction number, the engine serial numbers and power ratings on the certificate of registration.

There are no grounds for criticising Lockheed, a great company, Kelly Johnson or the Skunk Works team, as they became known. Burbank did an outstanding job of work. There are no grounds either for criticising the Administration or the Admiralty, who needed to find out what was going in the Mandates. Neither the White House nor the Admiralty was responsible for the disgraceful decision to abandon Amelia Earhart and Fred Noonan to their grisly fates at the hands of the Japanese.

There is no doubt about the criminality of both executions, nor has the Japanese government ever sought to assert that they had some legal right to execute Amelia Earhart and Fred Noonan for espionage, a crime with which they were not charged. Their executions were a brutal atrocity, pure and simple. If Tokyo is worried that increased knowledge of the truth may cost Toyota and Nissan some American sales the answer is not to be brutal, construct illegal fortifications or plan armed aggression in the first place.

The attacks on Amelia Earhart's flying ability had gone way beyond outrageous before the summer of 1937 was over. Let the record state that along with Britain's Amy Johnson and Germany's Hanna Reitsch,[28] Amelia Earhart was one of the three finest woman pilots who have ever lived. Her flying skills were at least equal to those of Colonel Charles Lindbergh (at one time they were the only two fliers to have flown solo across the Atlantic), as her last take-off demonstrated. That was from the short dirt runway at Lae, at combat power, under high temperature, still air and war overload conditions.

The Munich Agreement

Chamberlain and the *ersatz* aristocrat Arthur Woods, a.k.a. Lord Halifax (it was a slightly dodgy peerage, courtesy of the Liberals), who also reported to Admiral Canaris, were keen to surrender Czechoslovakia to Germany. They were also keen to see total German domination of Europe and were planning to surrender chunks of the British Empire, the idea being that they could run a puppet government in Britain.

The Czechs had rather better tanks than the Germans, indeed their Skoda tanks were often preferred by the Wehrmacht to German ones. They also had an excellent steel industry (which helped fill in the gaps in the British steel industry left by the Geddes cuts and the mad Washington Treaty by supplying specialist armour plate for the *KGVs*), a defensible frontier and a first-class army. They could have withstood a German offensive, with British and French support from the West. The German High Command (OKW) understood this.

Nothing could be gained by waiting a year. The obvious strategic choice and the correct moral choice - was to go to the aid of Czechoslovakia if she were attacked. With strong British and French support of course she wouldn't have been. So far from being a "far-away country of which we know nothing", in Chamberlain's notorious and unforgivable phrase, London and Prague had been in close communication. The key link man between British and Czech Intelligence was our old friend Sir Edward Spears, who was fluent in Czech. Firm friendships were later made with the Czech pilots who served, very bravely, in the RAF, some in the Battle of Britain, for which they were punished severely by the pro-German 'communist' government after 1948.

I have only ever met one participant in the Munich conference, the Earl of Home, then Lord Dunglass. It is not entirely clear whether Chamberlain agreed that Czechoslovakia could be taken over in two stages, although he probably did. He understood the importance to the Wehrmacht of the Skoda armaments works and would have been anxious to cut off the supply of Czech armour plate to the Royal Navy. We know that the key participants were Chamberlain, Daladier (also a German spy) and Joachim von Ribbentrop, the German Foreign Minister, each of whom, reported to Admiral Canaris, as did Hitler's interpreter, Paul Schmidt.

Hitler was essentially the meet and greet man at Munich, more like an American Vice-President, whose role, traditionally, has been to go to weddings and funerals, make the odd speech, teach children to spell, or try to, and join in with the Germans in planning the assassination of the President.[29] In 1938 Hitler was only a Führer in title, although with the seizure of the Austrian gold reserves following the first *Anschluss* the Nazis were starting to assert their independence from Canaris. The Germans signed the agreement in bad faith, of course. The whole shameful exercise was a total waste of time.

The Durban Test

There was an alarming development for Chamberlain and Wilson the following March, just as the 'Hun' was about to march into what was left of Czechoslovakia. South Africa had set England a seemingly impossible 654 to win the final Test, in Durban. No team had ever scored more than 332 in the fourth innings to win a Test Match. Pitches deteriorated and normally took spin by the fourth day. These days they are covered and tend to last longer.

The final Test however was a timeless Test, i.e. England could take as long as they wanted to score the runs. It was a ballgame without a time limit. The gritty Norfolk-man Bill Edrich DFC got the impossible run chase off to a cracking start, with an outstanding score of 219. It is still one of the highest scores in the final innings of a Test. As the score mounted and the Test went into an eighth, ninth and then tenth day the Empire held its breath. Reports from Durban were flashed all around the world. Downing Street went into a panic, fully aware that the boost for morale would be enough to start a world war when our community partner the 'Hun' occupied the rest of Czechoslovakia, which Chamberlain had agreed could go ahead on March 16th.

Immense pressure was applied on MCC to force the great Wally Hammond, Captain of England (almost as important a position as Prime Minister, who was a mere party politician, invariably an idiot[30] and apart from Alec Douglas-Home couldn't normally hold a bat anyway[31]) to abandon the run chase. The patriotic Union Castle Line, whose ships were amongst the fastest in the world, were holding the turbine-powered liner RMS *Windsor Castle* to Hammond's order at Cape Town, the MCC having booked passage home on her for the England team. Although not their fastest or newest vessel she had recently been refitted. The plan was for her to make up time and sod the fuel consumption. There was plenty of bunker fuel in Freetown anyway.

The first-class passengers would have had their ears glued to the radio. They would not have dreamt of asking her Captain to sail without Hammond and the team, who were heroes and very welcome in the first-class dining room. The very idea was unthinkable, and completely un-British. The second-class and foreign passengers would have been told to wait and like it. The foreigners could always have sailed on a foreign ship if they didn't understand cricket.

Sadly however, Union Castle caved in, under very heavy pressure from Downing Street and the Board of Trade. Their sanction was needed to lay down future vessels, as construction was normally subsidised and rightly so. Union Castle ships were designed to be taken over as troopships, indeed the gallant and elegant *Windsor Castle* herself was torpedoed whilst on war service, on 23rd March 1943, off North Africa. Pretoria, who could easily have smuggled German agents aboard to blow up the ship, also added pressure. Tragically, the Test was abandoned. England were just 42 runs away from their target, with five wickets still in hand. Such a thing had never happened before and has never happened since. It is still the record score for the last innings of a Test Match and will probably stand for centuries.[32]

The cover-up began almost immediately, with Union Castle and the team management being forced to lie to the press and claim they needed to catch a train (they could have been flown to Cape Town in a chartered South African Airways aircraft if need be) to catch the *Windsor Castle.* Downing Street of course stayed deep in the background, content that others were lying on their behalf. The whole sordid episode deeply upset poor Hammond, an honourable man, who later abandoned his beloved England for South Africa, where, as we have seen, the DVD-controlled intelligence service BOSS badly injured him in a botched assassination attempt in 1960.[33]

The *Thetis*

The Kriegsmarine were deeply worried by the British *T* class submarines, a huge improvement on the *S* class, which also posed a threat to the IJN. A number of British businesses, including Cammell-Laird, were close to the Germans. As we saw in Chapter 6 the new class used a torpedo tube valve of German design, although that fact seems to have been concealed from the Admiralty.

Cammell-Laird made sure that key shipyard personnel were on board the doomed *Thetis* on 1st June 1939, a highly irregular procedure. It should have triggered an immediate security alert and a destroyer escort. As indicated in Chapter 6 it was a dreadful tragedy, made worse by the appalling treatment of the widows and children. It is inconceivable that either Chamberlain or Wilson did not OK the Abwehr's sabotage of the *Thetis*. Aside from anything else someone high up the payroll in Whitehall had to be in the loop, to frustrate the rescue effort.

---

1. After whom the Ranji Trophy, the Indian first-class domestic cricket competition is known. He became the Maharajah Jam Sahib of Nawanagar in 1907 and represented India at the League of Nations.
2. There is rather a good profile of him on www.cricinfo.com, to which website all Englishman are indebted, as it allows us to keep up with Test Match scores when abroad. I well remember tearing around Vienna in 1982 trying to find an English newspaper with the cricket score and wasting, from memory, 30 shillings on a copy of the *Financial Times*, only to find in disgust that it did not have a sports page. I have rarely bought it since.
3. Some have questioned whether the offer was made, but C.B. was neither a German spy nor a politician and there is no reason to doubt his word. He would have made a very good King of Albania.
4. It is a myth that the firing arcs of the heavy 14-inch guns did not cover the land approaches. Whitehall simply refused to supply the right ammunition.
5. England's overseas cricket tours were organised by the MCC, hence 'MCC tour of Australia 1970/71 etc.' The MCC were later pushed out by the Test and County Cricket Board, a retrograde step. Originally the MCC Cricket Committee selected England's tourists, but Warner was able to force a change to a small panel of selectors, which allowed him to block the great Frank Woolley from the 1928/9 tour of Australia, an outrage which still has not been forgotten in Canterbury. It was the cricketing equivalent of banning the Archbishop from Evensong in the Cathedral. If things aren't broke, don't fix them - the MCC should again take charge of England's overseas tours and the Cricket Committee, composed entirely of eminently sensible members with respect, should take charge again of invitations to tour. The Cricket Committee, once the most important committee in England after the Cabinet and the Committee on Imperial Defence, would never have made the mistake of appointing professionals to captain England, which has led to a sad decline in standards.
6. Nottinghamshire's lovely home ground, by the River Trent. I once saw Allan Lamb score a fine hundred there against New Zealand.
7. Named for General Creighton Abrams, a fine tanker general, who did good work against the 'Hun' in World War II and the Hunnish North Vietnamese in the Vietnam War, where there was a lot more armoured warfare than Jane Fonda would have you believe.
8. *Kelly's Heroes*, 1970, director Brian Hutton. Great theme tune, great cast, with Carroll Connor and Clint Eastwood, and a very believable plot too, at least if you're in intelligence, where less crazy things have happened. It also has some handy tips on how to knock out a Tiger tank. One acquaintance of mine (British, SAS) was in a group instructed to liberate some gold from a bank in Elisabethville during the Congo civil war and set out from Lusaka in a Land Rover. The CIA were tipped off and got there first, as they had a plane. One of the CIA pilots happened to be 'Bill'. The SAS never knew what happened to the gold, until I told my friend. 'Bill' wasn't told the SAS boys were on their way to safeguard it. There was no question of the gold being stolen of course, there was just a concern that it might fall into the wrong hands. The CIA had the codes to

the large safe and locked it up afterwards. The SAS corporal who spent some time blowing it open, with great care, was understandably annoyed when the door fell off to reveal an empty safe.

9. Most rifle rounds are actually supersonic, so the speed of sound was probably being exceeded in World War I at least a million times a day. Still, some 'experts' proclaimed that the speed of sound was a 'limiting velocity', long after it had been exceeded. Once it had been exceeded in manned aircraft (the whole point of the theory being to hold back aeronautical advances) no doubt the same experts shifted their ground and claimed that the speed of light was the 'limiting velocity'. Now that has been exceeded, we wait with bated breath to hear what the next 'limiting velocity' will be. (A prize of a free trip to the next *Star Trek* convention to the first idiot who says "Warp 8".)
10. HMS *Illustrious* was originally fitted to operate an air group of only 36 aircraft. Through deck-parking and the use of outriggers (i.e. parking the tailwheel over the edge of the deck) this was increased by the end of the war to 57.
11. In fairness to the Bureau of Ships the US Navy picked this point up before they entered the war, after a careful study, facilitated by the Royal Navy, of HMS *Illustrious* whilst she was being repaired in the States after being bombed in the Med. The *Illustrious* class influenced the design of the next generation of American carriers, the magnificent *Midway* class. Sadly just too late to see action in World War II, they performed superbly off Korea and Vietnam. They were supremely elegant ships - *Midway* can still be seen, preserved, in San Diego.
12. London: Bloomsbury, 1994.
13. Originally published in 1966, re-issued by Doubleday in 2000. Fred Goerner's sources included General Vandergrift, who learnt that she had met her death on Saipan from General Tommy Watson, who commanded the 2nd Marine Division on Saipan. There is no reason to doubt the account of either of these outstanding US Marine commanders.
14. Brink, see pp. 144 and 155, indeed see Brink's book generally.
15. Yes there are British and American agents in Japan and no I do not have copies of the file. I can only give a summary of it. That's how it works. If you want to find out what happened, you can be told but you don't get the raw data, so there's no risk of blowing the agent who supplied it. If it's of any comfort to the Japanese, I gather that the files were photographed with a Japanese digital camera. If anyone in the Japanese Diet wants to go searching for the files the best advice I could give would be: 'don't, but if you do don't start your search in Tokyo'.
16. *Unsolved Mysteries*, presented by Robert Stack. I am not questioning her account, i.e. I consider it credible eyewitness testimony.
17. *The Sound of Wings*, London: Hutchinson, 1989.
18. The XC-35 was pressurised. Amelia's and Fred's Electra was photographed at Lae and was clearly not pressurised. Equally clearly it was not a standard Model 10 Electra and was not the same plane that was very skilfully crashed on take-off at Honolulu on the first, west-east flight. They needed a pretext to get the plane back to Lockheed and switch the direction of the flight from west-east to east-west.

19. HMS(NZ) *Achilles*, *Leander* class, 7,270 tons standard displacement. She was a great ship and did good work, not least in the Battle of the Plate.
20. A progressive, air-minded and intelligent admiral, he would have made an outstanding First Sea Lord and a far better choice than Sir Dudley Pound ('dodgy Dudley' as he is sometimes referred to intelligence circles), who came up with the dubious plans for Denmark Strait and Convoy PQ17.
21. 36,000 tons. *Saratoga* was much loved by the Royal Navy, with whom she sailed in '44.
22. As given by the refueller at Lae, Robert Ivedale. An Australian-run airfield, it used the larger Imperial gallon. The US uses the old Winchester gallon of 231 cu. inches, approximately 83.25% of an Imperial gallon. A number of writers have assumed that the top-up and fuel total figures at Lae were translated into US gallons, but they were in Imperial. Fuel load was 1,100 Imperial, 1321 US gallons. The tanks were full to the brim.
23. See the declassified White House and Treasury documents, including notes of telephone calls, reprinted in Brink.
24. About which he could do little, as Morgenthau had helped seal the deal with Chiang Kai-Shek, whereby several thousand metric tons of gold was transferred from China to New York, to back the dollar after 1933. There was nothing improper in this save for the falsification of US gold reserve figures, but all gold reserve figures are a fiction anyway, including the Bank of England's, which in the 1930s could have been put together by Agatha Christie. The Royal Navy only chased pirates when they hung on to more than their 10% + expenses. Pirate treasure was buried in the Bank of England, not on beaches in the West Indies.
25. Poor Fred Noonan's jawbone was of course separated from the rest of his skeleton, which had been substantially eaten away due to the acidic nature of the soil, partly no doubt why that burial location was chosen. The Japanese arrogantly failed to allow for the possibility of their surrendering the island to the United States Marines in less than seven years.
26. Great film, with a superb cast, featuring Dickie Attenborough (nobody better at playing dodgy characters, or directing films about them – *Gandhi* was superb) and James Stewart. The remake is fun and very watchable, but it's a remake.
27. *Quaere* whether Japan had any right to continue to administer Mandated Territories anyway after her withdrawal from the League. They should have been handed over, logically to Britain, as she was a Pacific power and a member of the League. The US was too sensible to join of course. The willingness to let Japan occupy and fortify the Mandates after her withdrawal from the League demonstrated what a screaming farce the mandate system, and the League itself, were. After World War I the Carolines should have been annexed by Britain and administered with the Gilbert and Ellice Islands, and the Marshalls and Marianas should have gone to the United States. This would have ruled out a surprise attack on Pearl Harbor. The Royal Navy from Truk could have helped protect Australia, with the RAN at Rabaul.
28. I like to be fair to the 'Hun'.

29. Dick Cheney was an honourable exception, being an executive Vice- President who gave strong and loyal support to the President, whom he did not try to assassinate.
30. *Plus ça change*.
31. The Earl of Home, Prime Minister 1963-64, and an awfully nice chap, was the distinguished exception to this rule.
32. No other team has come within 200 runs of it.
33. A staged car crash, a popular assassination method in South Africa, and with the DVD, who also arranged the assassination of the beautiful Princess Grace of Monaco, not to mention Princess Diana. The car crash in which the heavy-hitting Test opening batsman Colin Milburn was half-blinded (he was never the same batsman again) is worth a second look.

18

1939 - 1942

The Children of the *Athenia*

No intelligence chief ever cultivated his image more carefully than Admiral Canaris. He liked to portray himself rather as Anthony Quayle did, to Herr Admiral's approbation,[1] in the fine film *The Eagle Has Landed*. He was undoubtedly an officer who had ambitions to become a gentleman. Sadly, with respect, they were never realised.

He was helped by the confusion he was able to create about his true loyalties (which were always to Germany) by the clash of strategy with Hitler and our community partners the Nazis after 1938. Canaris favoured soft power to the point where he actually tried to forestall the invasions of Poland, Denmark, the Low Countries and the Soviet Union. That is not to say that he was soft - far from it. German intelligence wrecked millions of lives with its depression strategy, aided by control of Western central banks and at times governments. Germany's Stalin, a Georgian, murdered Russians by the hundreds of thousands.

The ruthlessness both of the Abwehr and the governments it controlled is nowhere better illustrated than with the sacrifice of the children of the *Athenia*. Unable to stop the war, although he had a last-minute try, ordering troops in early, in the hope of alerting the Poles, and hoping to deter Britain from taking active steps to aid Poland, Canaris arranged for dozens of British children to be murdered. Chamberlain, who was hoping that the loss of so many young lives would undermine public support for standing up to Germany, arranged for a party of children to be sent to Canada, ostensibly for their safety. They sailed on the elegant Anchor- Donaldson liner SS *Athenia*, Captain Cook in command.

Her course and precious cargo were of course betrayed to the Abwehr, probably via Dublin and Lisbon. There were all sorts of contacts between Number 10 and Berlin throughout August 1939 however, one of the intermediaries being the young German spy Edward Heath. He was then on a 'camping tour of Nazi Germany' with his lover, Madron Seligman, as related in Chapter 4.[2]

The *Athenia* carried no fewer than 1,103 passengers, including several hundred US citizens. Many of them were women and children. She was duly ambushed on 3rd September near Rockall, by the waiting U-30. The war criminal Oberleutnant Fritz-Julius Lemp was in command. Hoping for maximum casualties he fired two torpedoes, which with a target of just 13,465 gross register tons, probably would not have been survivable. With two hits she would probably have sunk rapidly, probably with secondary explosions and a breach of her fuel tanks, leading to bunker fuel on the water. Being heavy oil, bunker fuel does not disperse rapidly and it quickly clogs the lungs, i.e. survivors in the water would have struggled. Bunker fuel is really thick, almost tar-like. It should *not* be confused with petrol.

Thankfully, Lemp's second torpedo missed. The *Athenia* was able to stay afloat for over fourteen hours, a great tribute to her builders, the fine old Govan firm of Fairfield. The destroyer HMS *Electra*, Lt-Cdr Sam Buss in command, raced to the rescue, as did the American freighter SS *City of Flint*. There was also a Swedish yacht. The North Atlantic at the start of World War II, not un-adjacent to a war crime, was an odd place and time to be going on a cruise, but there it is. The Norwegian tanker MS *Knute Nelson* also went to the rescue.

Some 981 passengers and crew were rescued, including many of the women and children. The *Titanic* scale disaster Canaris and Chamberlain had been hoping for failed to materialise. As with the *Lusitania*, the crime blew up in the Germans' faces. The courage of the children, and the discipline with which they went to their boat stations, not only reduced the death toll but also inspired the nation and the Empire.

Canaris's chief spin doctor, a chap named Goebbels, frantically tried to fool people into believing that the Royal Navy had torpedoed the ship, or that she had been mined or, when some of the truth finally emerged, that Lemp had not known at what ship he was aiming. Goebbels of course reported to Canaris, as did Goering. The Nazi Party, as we have seen, was installed by German intelligence.

U-30's logbook was falsified, standard procedure for U-Boats. There was no doubt that U-30 had fired two torpedoes. It was quite clear that one of them crippled and sank the poor *Athenia.* What did not emerge at Grand Admiral Raeder's farcical postwar trial, unsurprisingly, since the prosecution team was penetrated, was that U-30 had specific orders to torpedo the *Athenia*. The fact that German assets in Whitehall arranged to put young children aboard in the hope of shocking public opinion into giving Germany a free hand in Europe was also suppressed.

How Chamberlain and Canaris between them managed to persuade themselves that waging war on defenceless children in this way was going to make public opinion less amenable to waging war on Nazi Germany is one of the great unsolved mysteries of World War II. Whilst Admiral Dönitz was fully in the loop and had issued the secret orders to Lemp, there is no reason to suppose Admiral Raeder was. Indeed, there is every reason to suppose that he wasn't. Our community partner Reich Chancellor Hitler clearly had not authorised the attack, indeed he was appalled. This was not just at the potential political consequences, although these were less than he supposed, as he was unaware that the murder of the American citizens had been cleared in advance with German assets in the State Department, but at the loss of young life.

This is not to say that Hitler was a humane man - he wasn't - but he was more humane than is usually portrayed, whilst Admiral Canaris was much less so. One of several problems with Hitler was that like so many politicians he was unstable. He could have sympathy for children drowned on the high seas one day and sanction a war crime the next, in a fit of anger. Hitler's culpability in the sinking of the *Athenia* was far less than Chamberlain's, indeed to his credit he promptly issued orders prohibiting U-Boat attacks on passenger liners whether sailing independently (as *Athenia* had been, in order to make her easier to sink) or in convoy.

To even mention the sinking in the shameful prosecution of Admiral Raeder, a veteran of Jutland (he was Admiral Hipper's Chief of Staff), at Nuremberg was completely ridiculous. The Nuremberg War Crimes trials were a musical comedy proceeding as it was. Unlike Canaris and Dönitz, Raeder was an honourable man. He was an enemy for whom we British retain considerable affection and respect.

Similar courage to that shown by the children on the *Athenia* was shown by the children on the *City of Benares*, another liner torpedoed by the Germans, in September 1940. They included the late Colin Ryder Richardson, son of the famous barrister, who was only 11 when he survived the sinking. His *Daily Telegraph* obituary records that one woman, a nurse, died in his arms and he had to help throw the bodies overboard from his lifeboat. He must have grown up rapidly that night.

HMS *Courageous*

A further cunning plan by the 'wily Hun', to deprive the Royal Navy of one of its pitifully small number of aircraft carriers (almost as small as today) and force Churchill out of the Admiralty in disgrace, achieved only its first objective. The carrier HMS *Courageous* was sunk off Ireland on 17th

September 1939 by U-29. Once again it was an ambush, i.e. Käpitanleutnant Schuhart in U-29 knew that the carrier was coming and a German asset in the Admiralty made sure that she was sent in his direction. Yet again there was heavy loss of life, yet more casualties in the Royal Navy's desperate battle with German assets in Whitehall. It continues to the present day, as the Navy fight off insane proposals to mothball one of our impressive new *Queen Elizabeth* class carriers.

Churchill had supported the concept, adopted by the US Navy in the 1950s, of having hunter-killer groups with aircraft carriers going after U-Boats. The problem was that the Royal Navy in 1939 did not have specialist anti-submarine carriers (the US Navy was able to use the WWII- vintage *Essex*-class carriers, which were getting a bit small for jet operations, by US standards at any rate). Thanks partly to Smuts and the RAF, the Fleet Air Arm also lacked specialist high-endurance anti- submarine aircraft.

The overarching problem with the concept however was the failure to plug the leaks out of the Admiralty and Whitehall. This meant that operations were being betrayed to Germany. The men of the *Courageous* were part of the terrible price paid for the dreadful, ongoing failure to hang the Whitehall Spy Ring - Edward Bridges, Neville Chamberlain, Arthur Halifax[3] and Horace Wilson, the key German assets in London.

There were lots of smaller fish as well. It is a basic rule of counterintelligence work however that if you can execute the big fish the tiddlers will usually swim swiftly into line, anxious to save their own scales. The lamentable failure to shoot the Directors of MI5 and MI6 was also continuing to hamper each agency's contribution to the war effort.

HMS *Courageous* was a valuable Fleet unit, as was her sister HMS *Glorious*, sacrificed to the battlecruisers *Scharnhorst* and *Gneisenau* in April 1940. The Navy was not really able to make up for their combined loss until 1944,[4] when the twin-decked *Indefatigable* class[5] finally entered service. They were old, but big and fast, and the Fleet was desperately short of fleet carriers throughout the war. Of course, more modern carriers should have been constructed. At least two units of the *Illustrious* and follow-on classes should have been laid down each year from 1936 and *Ark Royal* should have had at least one sister.

Not losing the *Ark* was a small mercy. Chamberlain had wanted her sunk as well but the 'Jerries' missed. They were desperately anxious to sink *Ark Royal.* Whilst she was of limited value as a fleet unit within range of land-based bombers, thanks to the successful blocking of the Admiralty by the Treasury of her armoured deck, she would have been very valuable in the Pacific.

The *Ark's* aircraft capacity has often been overstated by the way, which has tended to distort the armoured/non-armoured deck debate. Although often given as 72, in reality she rarely operated more than 60. The *Illustrious* class, which had fully armoured hangars (they were a strong armoured box above the waterline), usually managed to do better than the official figure of 36. Indeed, as we have seen they were operating an air group of 57 aircraft by the war's end, and big aircraft too, including the excellent American Chance-Vought Corsair fighter-bomber (F4U) and Grumman Avenger torpedo-bomber (TBF).

The Sinking of HMS *Royal Oak*

Not content with starving the Royal Navy of funds prewar, blocking modernisation of most of its capital ships and refusing funding for new aircraft carriers, which were desperately needed,[6] Chamberlain helped to get the venerable old battleship HMS *Royal Oak* sunk. She was torpedoed on 14th October 1939. He frustrated Admiralty plans to protect the vulnerable southern approach to the Home Fleet's great anchorage at Scapa Flow. German assets in Naval Intelligence had of course made sure that the Abwehr was kept fully in the loop, although the possibility of an attack by U-Boat through Kirk Sound had been spotted by naval intelligence officers on the Imperial German Navy's capital ships in 1919.

The death toll was 833, but great though that loss was it did not shatter morale in the way that Chamberlain had hoped. Churchill, who backed the Admiralty plan to send blockships north and was not responsible for the delay, was not unduly damaged. There were however several intelligence failures. As soon as the C-in-C, Sir Charles Forbes, learnt of the delay in sending the blockships he wanted to Scapa Flow, his fleet intelligence officer should have advised dispersal of the entire fleet. Instead, just the most valuable units were dispersed. Kirk Sound should also have been monitored, with a view to ambushing any U-Boat trying to get through.

Thirdly, naval intelligence should have arranged for the arrest of the taxi-driver whose lights famously illuminated U-47. That looks like and probably was a prearranged navigational beacon. The fact that the driver did not immediately raise the alarm gave probable cause for his arrest. A U-Boat entering the anchorage of the Home Fleet clearly was not there to pay a courtesy call on the C-in-C and was more likely to be carrying torpedoes than a case of schnapps.

Fourthly, there was a failure to appreciate the value of the *R* class battleships. Designed by Sir Tennyson d'Eyncourt, they had an excellent protection scheme and a powerful main battery, about the same as *Bismarck's*. The Mk 1 15-inch admittedly had a short barrel, but it didn't flex and was very accurate. The *R* class were ideal as convoy escorts, indeed they deterred several attacks by raiders. Moreover, they could have been rebuilt, along the lines of *Queen Elizabeth* and *Valiant*. I'd have gone for say eight 'between-decks' 4.5-inch dual-purpose twin mountings, increased main battery elevation, triaxial directors, fully-synthetic fire control and modern, high-pressure machinery, boosting their speed to say 25 knots whilst permitting more space below decks.

This would have allowed them to reinforce the Mediterranean Fleet's battleline, or the Far Eastern fleet. It would have given the Royal Navy five modernised capital ships in much less time than new construction could reach the Fleet. Since the largest class of carriers then building, the *Colossus* class, could only make 25 knots, they would have made an ideal fit. The value of capital ships was to be proven time and again in the six years of war ahead. The age of the battleship was to last for another 50 years, indeed only 33 of the 85 years of the Dreadnought Era had passed. Lastly, her captain and crew were even more valuable than the ship.

Fairey Battle K9271

The French not only rolled over in June 1940. German assets in Paris, some of whom later found themselves a home in the Vichyist Fifth Republic, actively sought to frustrate what limited operations the RAF were allowed to get away with in the aptly named Phoney War in 1939- 1940. On 27th September 1939 a formation of French Curtiss P-36 Hawk[7] fighters bounced and tried to shoot down a lone Fairey Battle, K9271, of 103 Squadron, which was on a reconnaissance patrol. The attack was coordinated with the Luftwaffe and poor old K9271 was finished off by a gaggle of Bf 109Es from JG152.[8] Her pilot was killed, or to be more precise, murdered. The Battle was a large, distinctive monoplane that could not readily be confused for any German type, nor is it easy to mistake the blue, white and red RAF roundel for a swastika. The usual explanation for 'blue-on-blue' shoot-downs - "tragic mistake, could happen to anyone, even the French" - was foisted on the public in a manner which would have done credit to a Pyongyang press release. Air Intelligence however was not so easily fooled. It was perfectly clear that the shoot-down was deliberate, and what's more had been ordered from Paris. Decisions to have a formation of aircraft bounce and shoot down an ostensible ally are not usually taken low down the payroll. A back-off warning seems to have been passed in the usual way to Paris and there were no further French attacks on British aircraft, but it took some time for the obvious conclusion - that the French weren't just unreliable allies but weren't actually allies at all - to sink in. The charming scene in the great film *Battle of Britain*[9] of a French pilot hopping a ride in a Hawker Hurricane to continue the fight was not complete fiction. There were some Free French pilots in the Battle of Britain. Sadly however, it was not typical. The shoot-down of K9271 seems to have influenced Sir Hugh Dowding in his opposition to sending further fighter squadrons to France. If the Germans were going to be told when RAF aircraft took off, what was the point? The French comeuppance came at the Battle of Oran of course.

Similar strategic illiteracy as regards Paris's 'good intentions' was shown during the Falklands War, where once again French units fired upon British forces, in the Balkans, where the Americans lost an F-117A Stealth Fighter[10] after Paris betrayed her mission to Belgrade, and by the Coalition Government in Britain. In 2011 they came up with an insane plan to share aircraft carriers with the French. Sharing kit with the French is difficult enough when you're on the same side. Even if the crew do not end up shooting at each other, what happens when the French surrender?

Dunkirk

This is only a puzzle to those historians who have failed to grasp that Goering reported to Canaris, not Hitler, and that Canaris wasn't trying to win the war with Great Britain. He was trying to make sure there wasn't a war at all, so he could crack on with winning the peace, as he did after 1945. In the postwar period he tied up Whitehall in more knots than there are on board HMS *Victory*. DVD assets were able to dismantle the Empire, wreck British industry, cut Britain's armed forces to ribbons and alter the face of British society. They did far more damage to London than the Luftwaffe ever did.

Throughout Operation *Dynamo* Canaris, Bridges, Wilson and Halifax were working to reverse the disaster (for them) of the installation of a serious British Prime Minister, one of only two in the 20th century, although Anthony Eden and Jim Callaghan were decent men and did their best. The last thing the Whitehall Spy Ring wanted was the British Expeditionary Force wiped out at Dunkirk. In practice this would have made replacing Churchill, who was not responsible, politically impossible. It was Neville Chamberlain who had sent the BEF to France and then insisted they remain on the defensive whilst the Germans defeated the Poles. Our community partner Hitler was sold on the idea that air power would do the trick. How the Luftwaffe's staffeln could take and hold ground was never explained.

Fortunately for the BEF, Hitler had about as much idea about air power as President Clinton. He swallowed Goering's nonsense, although in fairness the British perimeter would have put up a tremendous fight and General Guderian's panzers were in no condition for a sustained assault. The Royal Navy would also have been able to use its destroyers, which despite heavy losses were able to operate in and out of Dunkirk, rescuing far more troops than the justly famed 'Little Ships',[11] in the fire support role.

A 4.7-inch semi-armour piercing round would have gone through an early panzer's front armour like the proverbial hot knife through butter. Indeed, it might have even gone out the back and made a mess of the panzer behind. Targeting coordinates could have been supplied at the tactical level to naval liaison officers and radioed to the destroyers.[12] If a real firefight had developed (no doubt it felt real enough to the brave lads defending the perimeter) Churchill would probably have pressed for the remaining *R* class battleships to be brought up. They would have given a good account of themselves before being sunk by Stukas.

The Battle of Britain

This is an intelligence not a military history, the purpose of which, as explained, is to fill in the odd gap in official accounts, explain the occasional puzzle and expose a few German spies. There are plenty of published accounts of the RAF's great victory over the Luftwaffe. However, the vital role, played by Air Intelligence in winning the battle has never been explained. This is partly because it was largely done 'off- campus' by the Air Section of MI18, whose existence still has not been officially acknowledged. No doubt there was also a desire to avoid treading on Foreign Office toes.

The great mystery, up till now, has been why Goering switched the thrust of the Luftwaffe's air attacks from 11 Group's airfields to London. The traditional view, as put forward in the 1969 film *Battle of Britain*, although not always to a musical accompaniment of the same standard, is that a Heinkel 111 crew got lost. They then dropped their bombs by accident on London, which they couldn't see because it was dark. This then provoked the RAF into bombing Berlin, which in turn annoyed Hitler, so he switched the Luftwaffe's target priorities.

There are several problems with this theory, apart from the fact that it's bollocks. One is that there is a big river through London, called the Thames. It was too wide to disguise with blackout curtains, which would have got wet anyway. Another is that Hitler didn't control the Luftwaffe - Goering did. As we have seen the Reichsmarschall reported to Canaris, not Hitler. As late as 1943 Hitler couldn't stop Abwehr officers wandering up to his personal Fw 200 (not, as in the film *Valkyrie*, a Ju 52) with a bomb.

What actually happened was that MI18 fed false high estimates of Fighter Command losses to a high-ranking German agent in the Diplomatic Corps in London, i.e. they persuaded Goering that his boys had done the job and that the RAF were out of the fight. As with the best false intelligence this accorded with the enemy's own assessments, i.e. it confirmed a wrong opinion he had already formed. Neither Canaris nor Goering knew that their man, a former bootlegger named Joseph Kennedy, whom President Roosevelt had been prevailed upon by the State Department to make Ambassador to London, had been spotted. As we shall see no fewer than three of his sons were later murdered by the Germans, one to cover up the fact that he was a German asset.

A fourth son, Teddy, who knew about his father's working for Germany but was willing to cover it up in exchange for political favours, may have gone into the murder business on his own account in July 1969. He drove a car off a bridge at Chappaquiddick Massachusetts and a young girl named Mary Jo Kopechne, who may have overheard something that she was not supposed to, drowned. His explanation may have convinced the Edgartown Police Department, which with respect was no more competent than Thames Valley Police, and the media, but it has not convinced everyone in INTELCOM. The CIA used the leverage for 40 years. They usually felt able to call upon the distinguished senior Senator from Massachusetts for the odd favour on the Hill.

We British are still well disposed towards the late Senator's late father. Joe Kennedy was the best conduit for passing fake intelligence to the Germans Britain ever had. In the Battle of Britain he was worth a wing of Spitfires, a Chain Home radar station and a crate of gin. In fairness, he was a pretty reliable bootlegger and always filled his orders. Prohibition of course was pushed by German assets on the Hill, playing on the anxieties of social conservatives and Methodists. It gave German and Italian intelligence a leg-up in establishing their organised crime networks in the States.

Canaris and Goering would have been reluctant to act on Ambassador Kennedy's reporting alone. The switch in targeting strongly suggests that MI18 had spotted either Sir Archibald Sinclair, the incredibly dodgy Air Minister, or Lord Beaverbrook, or both. Beaverbrook, who owned the *Daily Express*, knew where too many Establishment skeletons were buried and was difficult to remove. Feeding him fake figures at the Ministry of Aircraft Production was a reasonable intelligence strategy. It was politically difficult for Churchill to get rid of Sinclair, who was the Leader of the Liberal Party and close to his fellow German spy, Churchill's old enemy Lloyd George.

Beaverbrook and Sinclair were heavily committed to Goering's strategy of making sure the RAF was equipped with obsolescent aircraft, one reason incidentally why the RLM (German Air Ministry) and the German military-industrial complex generally were reluctant to tool up for new aircraft.

They and the Luftwaffe suffered a heavy defeat at the hands of de Havilland and MI18 however when the RAF were able to get the fast, versatile, new DH98 Mosquito into production. They had more success in the bitter bureaucratic battle to delay it being reengined with the powerful new two-stage Rolls-Royce Merlin engine[13] and the bigger Rolls-Royce Griffon, with opposed props,[14] indeed the 'Mossie' never got the Griffon at all.

Ironically, Canaris's and Goering's complacency meant that it was the Luftwaffe which ended up flying obsolescent kites, like the Bf 109 and Bf 110, long after they should have been retired. They repeated the mistake with the P-51. They were so confident that their man Marshall (who exercised ultimate control over the Army Air Force, as officially it was part of the Army) could block it that when they eventually appeared over Berlin, escorting the mighty Eighth Army Air Force B-17 and B-24 formations, the Luftwaffe had no effective counter to it. That was until the jets came along, by which time it was too late.

Sinclair, a dreadful man, never forgave Dowding for winning the battle. He blocked his promotion to Marshal of the Royal Air Force. Dowding had of course made complete fools of those like Baldwin, who barely knew one end of an aeroplane from another and rarely flew in one, who had argued before the war that "the bomber would always get through". This was never based on any serious analysis of air defence. It was all about finding a further excuse to appease Germany.

The people in Whitehall who said the bomber would always get through were not slow to block the excellent Westland cannon-fighter, the Whirlwind, which had the potential to be a superb bomber destroyer. It could have been in service during the Battle of Britain. It used the promising Rolls-Royce Peregrine engine, smaller than the Merlin but with a very low frontal area. Rolls were ordered to stop its development. There was never a two-stage version.

The Halifax/Hess Coup

On 10th May 1941, the Deputy Führer, Rudolf Hess, flew to Britain in a Bf 110, from which he bailed out over Scotland. The intent was that he would be based in a Scottish safe-house, or rather safe-castle, whilst he negotiated a peace deal with a new government. Hess, a friend of a friend (who got to know him in Spandau Prison after the war), reported to Canaris, not Hitler, i.e. he was Abwehr, not Nazi. As Deputy Führer of the Third Reich, naturally he was a member of the Nazi Party, but that didn't mean that he was a Nazi. David Cameron is a member of the Conservative Party, but that does not mean that he is a conservative.

There were two extremely dangerous power moves associated with this astonishing development. Canaris wanted to seize power both in Berlin, by toppling Hitler, with the backing of the OKW and Generaloberst Jodl, who also reported to him, and in London, installing his man Halifax. Sir Edward Bridges, the Cabinet Secretary, Sir Horace Wilson, by now the Permanent Secretary to the Treasury and Sir Stewart Menzies, 'C' of MI6, all backed the proposed coup.

So too did Sir Dudley Pound, the First Sea Lord, Sir Charles Portal, the Chief of the Air Staff and General Sir Alan Brooke, Chief of the Imperial General Staff, none of whom were loyal to Churchill.[15] The Service chiefs backed the coup on the basis that Hitler would be replaced and there would be 'peace' with Germany. The terms would be dictated of course by Germany, which would be left in control of London, Paris and Moscow.

Canaris, Jodl and the OKW wanted to scrap the planned German invasion of the Soviet Union, which they correctly saw as pointless, since Stalin reported to Canaris. It also exposed Germany to the risk of a two- front war. The plan was to turn on the United States instead, which would be caught in a pincer movement between Germany, Italy, Vichy France and Japan. Japanese planning for the attack on Pearl Harbor was already advanced. Halifax agreed to hand over Britain's Far East Empire to Japan. Labor leader John Curtin was being lined up to play a similar role in Australia.

Much of the detail was agreed between Frank Foley, an Abwehr double-agent who was close to Menzies and was MI6's supposed 'expert' on Germany, and an Abwehr intelligence officer serving in the German Foreign Ministry, Albrecht Haushofer. The latter was well aware that Halifax and Bridges were on side. Foley flew out of RAF Whitchurch[16] on 17th January for two weeks of planning meetings in Lisbon and Madrid. He seems to have met with Lahousen and another senior Abwehr officer, possibly Canaris himself. Foley was highly regarded in the Abwehr.

Critical to this murderous and entirely treasonable plot, for which all involved should have been hanged or shot, was a planned savage blow against British prestige, the Royal Navy and Churchill, the blowing up of HMS *Hood*. The intent was that her entire complement would die.

On 19th May 1941 the new battleship KMS *Bismarck* and heavy cruiser KMS *Prinz Eugen* sortied from Gotenhafen, intending to rendezvous with the battlecruisers *Scharnhorst* and *Gneisenau* at Brest. It was never intended that *Bismarck* would act as a commerce raider on the North Atlantic, a role reserved for the accompanying *Prinz Eugen*. That is why *Bismarck* never topped up her fuel bunkers at Grimstadfjord in Norway when she had the opportunity to do so. With the Royal Navy out of the way (so they hoped) the intent was that as soon as the Japanese, with German assistance, were ready to attack Pearl Harbor, Admiral Gunther Lütjens would command a combined German, Italian and Vichy French fleet against the US Atlantic

Fleet. Lütjens' fleet would have included the new *Tirpitz*[17] and the French battleship FS *Richelieu.*[18]

Defeat of the Atlantic Fleet, assuming they managed it, would have been a prelude to landing German and Italian troops in Mexico, on a scale approaching Operation Barbarossa, and French troops in Quebec. The French were promised Canada and were eager to reverse the result of the Seven Years War, which they had never accepted. The idea was that President Hoover, a German asset, would rule the rump United States, the southern states having been restored to Mexico. He would effectively have been an Amerika-Führer, backed by Ernest King and George Marshall, the leading German assets in the US Navy and Army respectively.

It was not an accident that the German, French and Italian navies had all chosen the 15-inch gun, which made fire control in a battleline much easier. When this plan was prepared by Admiral Raeder's staff prewar, it embraced the three Italian *Littorios* and all four rebuilt Italian battleships of the *Cavour* class. Italian admirals, by the way, were instructed to avoid combat with the Royal Navy, i.e. it is slightly unfair to accuse the Italian Navy of cowardice. No doubt their hearts would have been in a fight with the US Navy. The French battleship *Jean Bart*, under construction, was also included in the plan.

There were also the two *Bismarcks* and the two *Scharnhorst* class battlecruisers, which Raeder wanted refitted with 15-inch guns in twin turrets, i.e. the same guns as *Bismarck's*. Their weakish deck armour would have been strengthened and speed would have come down to about the same as *Bismarck*, i.e. 29 knots. They would have been transformed into genuine fast battleships.

This would have given Lütjens, blue-eyed boy of the Kriegsmarine, a combined force of nine fast battleships, all armed with 15-inch guns, plus the French battlecruisers *Dunkerque* and *Strasbourg* and the four *Cavours*. They would have been backed by the proposed German carrier *Graf Zeppelin*, the proposed Italian carrier *Aquila* and a powerful cruiser-destroyer force centred on the remaining *Hippers*[19] and the Italian 8-inch cruisers. They were designed to fight with the *Hippers* and like them had been built in excess of the joke 10,000-ton Washington Treaty limit. Former President Hoover was a key part of this strategy. Power-mad and desperate to get back into a position of influence, he backed the Republican candidate in the 1940 election, Wendell Wilkie, disguising his backing by standing himself (he had 17 delegates). Wilkie would have held back the American fast battleship programme had he been elected, citing 'experts' who regarded battleships as 'old-fashioned'. Similar arguments were used in 1945 to cancel the seriously powerful *Montana*[20] class, which would have made the planned North Korean invasion of South Korea problematic.

Canaris and Raeder were well aware that Roosevelt's superb naval building programme meant that any combined Axis force would be outgunned by the US Atlantic Fleet, backed by the new *Essex* class carriers, by the end of the first half of 1943. This type of dangerous thinking – an utter rejection of democracy and the idea that a united Europe, with Britain neutered, could be more powerful than America – appeared again after the end of the Cold War.

HMS *Hood*

HMS *Hood* was duly sacrificed to Lutjens' squadron in the Battle of the Denmark Strait, on 24th May, Pound having made sure that the British response to *Bismarck's* sortie was divided. There was no need to use capital ships to patrol the Shetlands-Faeroes, Faeroes-Iceland or Iceland/Greenland Gaps, which could have been patrolled by aircraft or cruisers. They could have shadowed the enemy until capital ships could be brought up, using air strikes to slow him down.

Using HMS *Prince of Wales*,[21] which wasn't fully commissioned (she still had her builders on board, for heaven's sake, and her main battery was not fully operational, indeed it kept breaking down during the battle), was preposterous. Captain Leach correctly chose not to sacrifice her or her crew, executing a battle turn to break off the engagement, for which he was subjected to captious and ill-informed criticism.

The logical thing to have done would have been to keep the Home Fleet together, have Tovey, the C-in-C, wait at Scapa Flow until the enemy's intentions were clear, send the cruisers *Arethusa* and *Manchester* to patrol the Iceland-Greenland Gap, reinforcing Rear- Admiral Wake-Walker[22] and have every available aircraft patrol the Faeroes-Iceland Gap. Tovey could have been reinforced by the battlecruiser *Repulse* and the 16-inch battleship *Rodney*. *Repulse* and *Hood* could have formed a battlecruiser squadron under the capable and intelligent Vice-Admiral Lancelot Holland CB, to screen ahead of *King George V* and *Rodney*. If Pound still wanted to play silly battleships, *Prince of Wales* could have joined Tovey, but frankly she should have been in dry-dock.

Admiral Tovey would also of course have had the aircraft carrier HMS *Victorious*.[23] The battlecruisers could have engaged and sunk the *Prinz Eugen*, fulfilling the cruiser-smashing role for which they were designed. They could have brought their massive combined firepower of 14 15-inch 42 cal. guns to bear on *Bismarck* to help finish her off after she had been pounded to pieces by the battle squadron.

Even now that the wreck has been examined on the seabed, experts have been unable to determine the cause of *Hood* blowing up at 0601 hours on

24th May. It certainly wasn't plunging fire through her deck and it's highly improbable that a shell went under her main belt, underwater, as has been suggested. The experts broadly agree that the first explosion was near the 4-inch magazine but have been unable to link it to a shell from *Prinz Eugen* or *Bismarck*, not that the comparatively small 8-inch projectiles from *Prinz Eugen* are very good candidates for blowing up a battlecruiser so heavily armoured for her type that she caused the US Navy to invent the term 'fast battleship' for her. The *Wikipedia* entry for HMS *Hood* as of 2nd March 2012 fairly summarised the state of the OSINT, including the evidence from examination of the wreck:

"The discovery of the wreck in 2001 confirmed the conclusion of both boards, although the exact reason why the magazines detonated will forever be a mystery as that part of the ship was thoroughly destroyed in the explosion."

Like HMS *Hampshire* in 1916, the probable cause was a powerful IED, probably in the 4-inch magazine, planted by Abwehr assets in the Naval Intelligence Department. These were probably those sponsored by Admiral Sir Hugh Sinclair, whose early death on 4th November 1939 did not come as a disappointment to dear old Admiral Godfrey, head of Naval Intelligence and the inspiration for Ian Fleming's 'M', nor MI18.

A clue is to be found in Lütjens' extraordinary order to *Prinz Eugen* to shift her fire from *Hood before* she blew up. German influence over the media worldwide was as extensive then as it is today. HMS *Hood's* sinking, and the loss of 1,415 lives, was given worldwide publicity, more than the equally sensational sinking of *Bismarck* three days later - that was not reported by every neutral outlet with quite the same enthusiasm. The BBC disguised its disappointment well.

Churchill took a firm grip and made sure that *Bismarck* was sunk. MI18 appears to have spotted the problem with the *Hood* sinking and linked it to the Hess arrival in Scotland, which is what good intelligence officers do - they connect the dots. The coup was headed off, although MI6's role did not become clear until later. Himmler smelt a rat after the Hess flight and took a firm grip in Berlin as well, partly why MI6's Menzies, who feared exposure, made sure that Himmler's suicide pill was politely returned to him in 1945. Himmler of course had tried to surrender to British troops, negotiations with the OSS through his physiotherapist Felix Kerten having failed.[24]

The free world dodged a bullet, ironically in part because in Himmler Canaris had an opponent worthy of his mettle. He kept Hitler in power, thus ensuring Germany's defeat. Back in Britain, Foley took charge of Hess, to prevent Churchill acquiring priceless intelligence from him. It was nothing to do with MI6.

MI5 should have been in charge of the interrogation, but of course 'Six' didn't want 'Box' finding out that the head of 'Six' was working for the Abwehr. Foley pretended that Hess was mad, which he most certainly wasn't. Bad yes, but not mad. He was kept in isolation until his death in 1987. In case anything of value emerged from Spandau, sources close to the DVD put it about that he was an *ersatz* retired Deputy Führer.

The Royal Navy should name a major warship after Admiral Holland. All that Britain has managed so far is a pub in Banbury, near to where he was born. That was a splendid tribute, but we can do better than a pub, although I am told that it is quite a nice pub. When Britain resumes major surface combatant construction, which will of course require a government which understands sea power, i.e. a new one, the first guided missile battlecruiser should be called *Hood*.

HMAS *Sydney*

HMAS *Sydney* too was a fine ship, a light cruiser of the *Amphion* class. She had done wonderful work in the Med in 1940 and caused Mussolini and his boys much grief. Her loss on 19th November 1941 was a grievous blow to Australia. Even after her wreck was discovered in 2008 some issues remain unanswered, such as why Captain Burnett had not used his Walrus[25] for a recce of the dodgy-looking freighter pretending to be a Dutchman. The 'freighter' was of course the German raider *Kormoran*. Raiders could disguise themselves at sea-level but their guns and torpedo tubes were generally visible from the air.

German Naval Intelligence were keen to get the *Sydney* and they had assets in Canberra who could help. Her very able skipper was replaced with Captain Burnett, whose psychological profile suggested that he would make the mistakes which in fact he did. He was an able officer but not a team player and not air minded. He also belonged to the 'get up close' school of thought for dealing with 'Jerry' raiders, which was not so much a school of thought with respect as just a school.

Much better to do what Captain Oliver of HMS *Devonshire* did just two days later. Fly off your Walrus, stand-off 15,000 yards and use the inestimable advantage at long range of centralised gunnery control to smash your raider (in this case *Atlantis*) to bits before closing in the for kill with torpedoes if need be. *Atlantis* probably had so much gold on board 'Jerry' would have scuttled her anyway had the good old 8-inch Mark VIIIs not done their work.

HMAS *Sydney* suffered from a built-in defect insisted upon by 'Jerry's' men in the Treasury, a single electrical circuit for gunnery control. This was a bit like building a car with the brakes on one side only - it will still work, but not as well as with brakes on all four wheels. *Kormoran's* skipper, being a naval intelligence officer, would have known of this defect. He did the 'right' thing, tactically, for a 'Q' ship, but not under the Laws of War. He flew the Dutch ensign until *Sydney* was close then opened up, his German naval ensigns were so slow going up that he had already opened fire. Captain Burnett, in fairness, was also drawn in by the fact that the *Kormoran* was using the correct recognition signals, which had of course been betrayed to the Germans.

How do we know this when brave HMAS *Sydney* was last seen disappearing into the murk, crippled and ablaze, and none of her crew, tragically, was ever seen again? There were 'Jerry' survivors, including Fregattenkäpitan Detmers. He did the usual two reports for naval intelligence, the 'Janet and John' one for the Allies and the historians, and the real one.

It still sits in the DVD archives in Dachau, in the Kriegsmarine section, filed under the ship, not his name, although apparently there is a note in his personnel file, which is cross-referenced to the *Kormoran* file. This file is in turn cross-referenced to financial files on gold transfers from Japan, including gold seized from certain families in China. There is no point asking me how I know this, save to say that the Good Guys have benefitted from the faction fighting in the DVD and the odd DVD agent has agreed to do the occasional favour, for a small consideration.

I understand that Volkswagen have ambitions to increase their market share in Australia. Opel even had ambitions to have their brand replace Holden, although why any self-respecting Australian would want to be seen on the Eyre Highway in an Opel is not clear.[26] These ambitions would best be served by dropping the *Kormoran* file - the real one, with no weeding – around to Australian Naval Intelligence. They will give the BND Head of Station in Canberra a receipt.

HMS *Barham*

The Germans understand battleships, indeed they have a good grasp of artillery generally. Your 'Hun' has always made a good cannon. They were understandably anxious after the great Fleet Air Arm raid on Taranto[27] about the possibility of the British Mediterranean Fleet sortieing through the Suez Canal to reinforce Singapore. The answer was to sink Admiral Cunningham's great battleships, a priority in the last quarter of 1941 for German naval intelligence. The first to go was the poor old *Barham*, which was ambushed on November 25th by U-331 and blown up.

Somebody on the battleship ahead, HMS *Valiant*, made sure that the German triumph was recorded for posterity by Gaumont News cameraman

John Turner. This may come as a surprise, but generally speaking in World War II camera crews did not hang around on quarterdecks hoping to see the battleship behind blow up. Somebody missed a trick in not pulling in Mr Turner for a quiet chat. The death-toll on the *Barham* was 862. Once again, an IED is indicated.

Not only is the official explanation for the secondary detonation - 4-inch AA ammunition stored adjacent to the main magazines - weak but Oberleutnant von Tiesenhausen in U-331 was wholly unaware that he had sunk the *Barham*. He fired his fish close in so close that they may not all have had time to arm. Torpedoes can jam in the tube and if they do it is generally better for the submarine if they are not fused. It is quite possible that two of his three torpedoes did not detonate. At the range he fired he should have heard, but did not hear, three separate torpedo explosions, even if the sound of one ran into the other.

One of the German spies responsible was probably Harold Macmillan, who also betrayed HMS *Ark Royal* and was shortly thereafter made British Minister in the Middle East. Only one torpedo was used to sink *Ark Royal*. The Treasury insisted on weaknesses being built into her, i.e. German assets in Whitehall, having failed to block her building,[28] made sure that she would be vulnerable to a single torpedo hit. The single casualty probably came as a relief to Macmillan, who was afraid of exposure and didn't want a spy-hunt. This is a different thing from a witch-hunt by the way, where you are chasing phantoms. Spies are real. So is the damage they do and the lives they cost.

Macmillan, a bisexual, was internally conflicted over his treason. He felt the German blackmail pressure keenly. In World War I he tried a variant of 'suicide by cop' and led what was literally a suicidal charge against the enemy, who missed him. This was very irritating. This was the one time in World War I we actually wanted our community partner the 'Hun' to hit one of our chaps, and he goes and misses. We then had to give him a medal and pretend that we were pleased he got back alright.

HMS *Queen Elizabeth* and HMS *Valiant*

Macmillan also helped get the *Queen Elizabeth* and *Valiant* sunk. They settled on the shallow harbour floor at 'Alex' on 19th December 1941, after a skilful underwater chariot attack led by the courageous Count Luigi de la Penne. Famously, he was interrogated on one of the very ships he had mined. A plan of the harbour defences of Alexandria was passed to Italian naval intelligence[29] via the German Ambassador in Ankara, Franz von Papen. A failed politician, he was the one–time leader of the *Zentrum* or centre party. German intelligence loves centre parties. They're a natural home for unprincipled, middle-of-the-road machine politicians.[30] In a weak political system using proportional representation, controlling the centre party allows them to hedge their bets.

Von Papen was another one of Canaris's boys. The same went for the British Ambassador, the one with the dodgy cover story about the valet, which led to another intelligence film starring James Mason. Tragically, except for Macmillan of course, 'Supermac' was not spotted, given a fair trial and hanged, as he should have been. After *Barham*, *Ark Royal*, *Queen Elizabeth* and *Valiant*, Naval Intelligence, had they known at the time, might have asked MI18 to ring Heinrich Himmler on his private line (they had that number - it's always useful to be able to have a chat with the opposition) and ask to borrow some of his piano wire. They'd have given it back.

Pearl Harbor

This is another topic that could justify a book on its own. There is only space however to add a few intelligence snippets to what is already in the public domain:

(1) The raid was conceived by the Germans not the Japanese, although they did much of the staff work.

(2) The dive bomber pilots included German Stuka pilots, from the air group for the cancelled Kriegsmarine carrier *Graf Zeppelin*, who carried on training after she was cancelled (strange that). This by the way explains why there are very few close-up shots of Aichi Val[31] pilots on the raid, indeed much of the footage released (after careful sanitising by Japanese naval intelligence) was shot during training.

(3) The vulnerability of Pearl Harbor to torpedo and dive-bomber attack was appreciated by *inter alia* Admiral Ernest King, the highest- ranking Abwehr asset in the US Navy, who pushed for the US Pacific Fleet to be transferred there, i.e. the US battleships were funnelled into a trap (Admiral Husband Kimmel deserves credit for appreciating this).

(4) General Short was encouraged by General George Marshall, the ranking Abwehr asset in the US Army, to concentrate on sabotage, i.e. make sure the Army's planes were lined up ready for the Japanese.

(5) Reporting indicating a Japanese attack on Pearl Harbor was suppressed from the President.

(6) German assets in the Admiralty were aware but as in Washington vital reporting was suppressed in order to keep the national leadership in the dark. Churchill knew something was up and that Pearl Harbor was a possible target, but he lacked specifics. Such intelligence as the British had was passed over to the Americans but it mainly concerned the Japanese move on Malaya. In particular, the Admiralty did not know where the Japanese fleet was.

(7) The key Axis intelligence asset on the ground at Pearl Harbor was Commander Roscoe Hillenkoetter, later the first Director of the CIA. He was on the battleship USS *West Virginia*. In order to protect him special arrangements were made, including not fusing the bombs aimed at his ship. His intelligence was not passed to the Japanese consul (whose phones were being tapped) but went to Berlin via Washington and Mexico City. Whilst secure this routing meant that Japanese tactical intelligence was at least 72 hours out of date, probably more, on the morning of the attack. In particular, Admiral Nagumo, the Japanese strike force commander, was not up to speed on the sortieing of the Pacific Fleet's carriers. It is not impossible that someone in ONI came up with the plan to reinforce Midway to get the carriers out of Dodge, as a precaution.

(8) The original plan called for a third strike, to take out the oil installations and dry-docks. Wily old Nagumo knew that the US Navy was heavily penetrated (it seems that only Yamamoto of the Japanese naval high command was aware that King, whom he apparently met in the States in or about 1920, was working for the Germans). Fearing that one or more of these assets might have been turned, and an ambush involving both submarines and the missing carriers, he cancelled it.

(9) Hitler was briefed in by Himmler, who had the Abwehr penetrated, about Germany's participation. Both feared that it had been blown, as a number of Japanese aircraft were missing. It was these fears which largely drove his decision to declare war on the United States. Churchill was unaware of the German involvement, possibly until his death in 1965. Naturally he wanted the US to join the Allies against Germany, but he would have been aware that war against Japan did not necessarily mean that the US would declare war on Germany, indeed so far to the contrary there would have been military and political pressure on Roosevelt to concentrate on Japan.

The Betrayal of HMS *Prince of Wales* and HMS *Repulse*

The key Abwehr asset in Singapore was Rear-Admiral Palliser, who not only informed the Japanese in Saigon that Force Z, the battleship HMS *Prince of Wales*, flying the flag of Admiral Sir Tom Phillips, and the battlecruiser HMS *Repulse*, had sailed, but lured them into a trap with a fake report of enemy landings at Kuantan. Bridges in London was determined to get the ships sunk and the highly intelligent Tom Phillips drowned. The First Sea Lord, still Pound, a weak man with respect, did nothing to stop him. Churchill was lied to and retired late in the evening before Force Z was sunk, thinking that the ships were still in Singapore. They had in fact already sailed, on December 8th, and were sunk on the 10th.

Both were powerful units, despite the Washington Treaty and interference by German assets in Whitehall, led of course by Chamberlain. They made sure that the *KGV* class were under-gunned by two main battery guns and blocked the badly needed modernisation of *Repulse*. Although that meant that the latter lacked modern anti-aircraft guns (her sister HMS *Renown* had 20 'between-decks' 4.5-inch, an excellent dual- purpose weapon later used *inter alia* on the 'Battle' class destroyers, which remained in service for decades after the war ended) she had lost none of her speed.

Captain Tennant, a courageous and highly competent naval officer, who had done good work at Dunkirk, threw *Repulse* around the South China Sea like a destroyer. She stayed in the fight after the much more modern *Prince of Wales* went down. A total of 840 men were lost, including gallant Tom Phillips. Sadly, Palliser was permitted to live, a huge mistake.

The big unsolved issue re the destruction of Force Z is who ordered her Captain to ground HMS *Indomitable*, its carrier, in Kingston Harbour, Jamaica, by departing from the channel, on 3rd November 1941. What we do know is that she went aground. Since the Japanese knew about it in advance it was no accident. With accidental groundings we like the enemy to become aware of them *after* they happen, not before.

As she was a 'one and a half deck' armoured carrier, she had a larger air group than HMS *Illustrious*. Although still small by American standards, the ability to store most of the aircraft in hangars meant they were far less vulnerable to damage from enemy action and storms. Deck- parking meant that in practice a US carrier's air group could fall well below its nominal allocation by the end of a combat cruise. The air group included Hawker Sea Hurricane fighters,[32] whose 20 mil. British Hispano cannon would have made a terrible mess of the lightly built, inadequately- armed and unprotected Japanese bombers. They didn't even have self-sealing tanks, i.e. would swiftly have fire-balled.

The sinkings emphasised the importance of organic fleet air defence. The reliance in the end on the RAF was misconceived, even if their aircraft had not been held back and German assets in Whitehall had not made sure that Malaya and Singapore were no, defended by modern fighters. Britain and Canada had more than enough aircraft-building capacity between them in 1939-41 to ensure that modern Hurricanes, Spitfires and long-range Whirlwinds were available in adequate numbers to defend Malaya and Singapore.

Churchill's view that Force Z should be ordered to retire on Port Darwin or Sydney and await reinforcements, including *'Indom'*, was strategically correct. There was little they could do without adequate air defence. The troops sent out to Singapore were simply sacrificed to no purpose, by Bridges and Wilson, by December 1941 the key German assets in Whitehall. The base's mighty 14-inch guns were no use without the right ammunition.

The time to organise the defences of Malaya and Singapore was before the war, not during it. Of course, further work could and should have been done after 1939, in particular building radar stations and improving command and control. Tragically Air Chief Marshal Sir Robert Brooke- Popham's air defence skills - he had helped design the air defences of Great Britain – were wasted. There has never been a serious inquiry into the loss of Malaya, with its valuable rubber, tin and bauxite, and Singapore. The guilty men got away scot-free whilst tens of thousands died or went into cruel incarceration by the Japanese.

The Barber Betrayal

On 27th January 1942 Anthony Perrinot Lysberg Barber, date of birth 4th July 1920, later made an *ersatz* (life) peer as Lord Barber of Wentbridge, defected to Nazi Germany with his Spitfire PRIV, RAF serial number AA813.[33] Barber, who had a Danish mother, Mussie, (she died in a plane crash, cause imprecise, in 1945), had been recruited by the Germans whilst flying for 1 Photographic Reconnaissance Unit, which was under the control of the Abwehr's Sydney Cotton. Ironically Cotton, a Queenslander, was a much-loved, if colourful, figure in the RAF, until forced to resign his commission, after flying in German agents, disguised of course as French. He was overly fond of the ladies, and liked them young, hence the vulnerability.

The RAF were not of course told by counterintelligence that Cotton, inventor of the famous 'Sidcot' suit, was a double-agent. The ease with which he was able to do overflights of pre-war Nazi Germany with a 'concealed' camera (visible to anyone who carefully inspected the plane) very frankly ought to have raised suspicions. Having Field Marshal Albert Kesselring as co-pilot on one occasion might have raised an eyebrow as well. The camera controls might have been concealed under a seat, and the cameras under the cabin floor, but the cutouts for the camera ports would not have been too difficult for an air intelligence officer to spot.

It has long been rumoured that he carried another famous passenger, this time on a flight to England, during the Phoney War, none other than Reichsmarschall Herman Goering. Rolling up to an RAF station with Herman Goering on board would have raised an eyebrow, but I have not been able to confirm the story. It is even said in the RAF that the Reichsmarschall was invited to sign the visitors' book in the Officers' Mess, but I have not been given the station (I think it was Manston, but I am not sure). Sadly, I do not have a copy of the entry in the visitors' book.

Control of British photo reconnaissance was a priority for the Abwehr. They were not only able to starve Bomber Command, the Admiralty and the War Office of critical intelligence, but were able to rubbish Bomber Command's valiant efforts by pretending that they were not hitting their targets. Faking target intel was easily done. You just substituted a pre-raid for a post-raid photo, particularly if the real post-raid imagery showed that the boys were bang on target and had just pulled off a 'wizard prang', RAF-speak for "target completely flattened and dead Germans everywhere".

In 1941 a bogus 'study' was flogged around Whitehall by German assets in the Cabinet Office showing that the RAF was often not getting within five miles of the target. This 'study' puzzled Bomber Command, whose navigator bomb-aimers (bombardiers in the USAAF) and pilots were a lot better than that.

Tragically for Britain and the many young men condemned to die needlessly as a result of their treason, Cotton and Tony Barber, one of Cotton's blue-eyed boys, were not arrested, given a fair trial and shot. Defections – actually flying an RAF aircraft to a Luftwaffe air base - were rare in World War II. There was always a risk of the aeroplane being spotted from the air. In the events that happened however, it was not until long after the war that a post-defection photo of Barber's Spitfire emerged. The full extent of Barber's treason only became clear after his sadly long- delayed death on 16th December 2005, not long after that of his former lover and political mentor Sir Edward Heath.

The defection was prompted by an urgent Kriegsmarine requirement for intelligence on RAF Coastal Command's torpedo-bomber dispositions in advance of the so-called 'Channel Dash' by the battlecruisers *Scharnhorst* and *Gneisenau*[34] and the heavy cruiser *Prinz Eugen*. They were to be moved through the Channel from Brest in February 1942. Barber took with him the entire contingency plan for a breakout by the 'Jerry' squadron, handing it over to his friend Generalleutnant Adolf Galland personally, apparently at Le Touquet.

Barber's flight - a first from Gibraltar to UK, using drop tanks - should have been stopped of course. He had sufficient fuel, but there was no need to get the kite back to England. PR Spits were badly needed at Gib, where they could do overflights of the covert U-Boat bases on Spain's Atlantic and Mediterranean coasts and monitor the tankers bringing in Mexican oil. The whole thing was a rum show. At the very least somebody should have arranged for an air intelligence officer, with a sidearm, to check the Spit over before her flight and search Barber, on the usual pretext. "We just want to make sure that you haven't left anything in your pockets, sir." A lot of good men died trying to stop Operation *Cerberus*, including the Royal Navy's greatest aviator of the war, Commander Eugene Esmonde VC. He heroically led his pathetically small squadron of biplane Fairey Swordfish torpedo bombers[35] in a desperate attack on the battlecruisers as they emerged from the Channel. Sir Archibald Sinclair's office made sure that the fighter escort didn't turn up at the RV, indeed the whole RAF operation was snafued from beginning to end by enemy agents. Thankfully, Bomber Command had been doing a spot of 'gardening' (minelaying) and *Gneisenau* snagged a mine. That was pretty much the end of her war. *Prinz Eugen* didn't do much afterwards either.

This was not the last of Tony Barber's espionage activities on behalf of the 'Hun'. After a few weeks debrief and rest he was assigned to the notorious Stalag Luft III at Sagan in Poland. Here he represented the Abwehr on the Escape Committee, although that's not quite how he put it to Peter 'Hornblower' Fanshawe RN[36] and the rest of the boys. The famous 'Great Escape', immortalised in the film of the same name, starring *inter alia* those fine American actors Steve McQueen, James Garner and Charles Bronson (there was a powerful British cast as well, including Dickie Attenborough) was of course a German idea, having been introduced to the Escape Committee by none other than Tony Barber.

Mirish Films, an excellent company, which later made *633 Squadron*,[37] took a few liberties with the facts, as USAAF aircrew weren't assigned to Stalag Luft III until August 1944, after the escape. If we want to make films about purely British shows with a purely British cast however someone has to put up the money and take the financial risk. We should stop whingeing when Hollywood limits its financial exposure by introducing American characters in order to get bottoms on seats in Carson City NV and elsewhere. With that scene where Steve McQueen, sadly no longer with us (he was a really fine actor) borrows a Wehrmacht motorbike and leads 'Jerry' on a merry dance, very frankly complaining is simply churlish.

The trouble with working for German Intelligence is that apart from the BND and the BfV, who are nice, they're the Bad Guys. Sooner or later you usually get involved in the grisly business of murder, because that's the way the 'Hun' conducts his business. He shouldn't, but he does. Amongst Barber's dodgier colleagues on this operation, even dodgier than Edward Heath, was SS-Grüppenfuhrer Artur Nebe. Himmler eventually had him executed with piano wire (ouch) on 21st March 1945.

Nebe was ordered by Heinrich Müller, who reported to Canaris (he also had contacts with the Vatican) and whose death, like Canaris's, was faked in 1945,[38] to select 50 of the recaptured prisoners, mostly RAF. They were then summarily executed. The good Grüppenfuhrer later claimed that this caused him much distress, but he did well to hide it. At any rate he was probably more distressed when they strung him up on the meat-hook. The RAF did not send flowers to the funeral.

Sadly, none of those who were with Barber at Sagan are still with us. Sydney Dowse, Bertrand 'Jimmy' James, Wing Commander Tom Baker and Fl. Lt Mick Shand, sterling chaps all, have passed away in recent years. The arm of British Intelligence that assisted escapes and tried to spot 'stoolies' like Barber in POW camps was MI9. Their man on the Stalag Luft III Escape Committee was Lt Cdr. J. Casson RN. Sadly, Barber's interrogation on his return to Britain was not terribly incisive. In a rather serious breach of security it was conducted by his brother.

Sensibly 'Jerry' arranged for their man Barber to 'escape'. He turned up at his mother's home in Denmark, a rather obvious place to look for a chap on the run in Europe with a Danish mother. They were never troubled by the Gestapo. 'Jerry' had big plans for Barber after the war. He ended up as their number two asset in the British Government. It would not be surprising if von Lahousen decided that Barber's mother should be liquidated in order to protect Barber. I do not suggest that Barber was in the loop. So far as is known Barber bought into the accident theory. We will not know the answer until we get the intelligence yield.

Barber became Chancellor of the Exchequer in a slightly unusual way. Ted Heath was of course committed to taking Britain into the EEC, i.e. the German sphere of influence. That had after all been the German plan since 1939. His win in 1970 was courtesy of a deflationary budget by his DVD colleague Roy Jenkins, who was hoping to take over the leadership of the Labour Party from Harold Wilson. Jenkins too wanted Britain in the EEC and was prepared to chuck a general election in order to get his way. For political reasons Heath was forced to make the popular centrist Iain Macleod Chancellor.

Macleod however was briefed in by Treasury officials that membership on the terms proposed by Germany would be disastrous for Britain, as indeed proved to be the case. The common perception of Treasury officials as stupid is not entirely fair. As they predicted, there was stagflation. By 1976 Britain was forced to go cap in hand to the IMF, a serious blow to British prestige.

Sacking Macleod just after he'd been appointed wasn't on - the City wouldn't have worn it. Heath decided that it would be simpler to have him murdered. An agent from the German operation set up in London in 1945, GO2, which reports to Dachau, duly popped around to Number 11 with some poison, to add to the dinner. Unsurprisingly, Macleod took ill and snuffed it, poor chap. Thanks to GO2, British post-war politics have started to mimic an Agatha Christie book - dead bodies everywhere.

As in the best Agatha Christie the person who ordered the murder - Edward Heath - was first on the scene, in order to 'comfort the grieving widow'. That of course is intel speak for making sure that Macleod was really dead. The then Permanent Secretary at the Treasury, Lord Croham, was a German spy. Had he been interrogated by MI5 his cause would not have been helped by his close association over many years with the *Deutsche-Britische Stiftung.*

Tony Barber took over as Chancellor, backed EEC entry on the disastrous German terms and successfully derailed the British economy, with a carefully managed 'boom-bust' strategy. It worked a treat. Careful coordination with DVD assets, some of them pretending to be communists, in the trade union movement, helped cut British industrial production to three days a week. The German assets in the TUC by the way included Jack Jones. He had penetrated the International Brigade in the Spanish Civil War, being highly regarded by the Abwehr Station Chief in Madrid.

Convoy PQ-17

This infamous Arctic convoy from Iceland to Murmansk, was sacrificed by German assets in the Admiralty. They prevailed upon Pound to force Jack Tovey, Home Fleet C-in-C (and a superb sea commander) to order the convoy to scatter. Admiral Tovey, hoping to bag KMS *Tirpitz* (to add to her sister, the *Bismarck*) was sold a pup. *Tirpitz's* sailing was nothing more than an intelligence ruse. The idea was to disrupt the sea line of communication to Russia by destroying an entire convoy, ship by isolated ship, with aircraft and U-Boats. Thankfully the losses, whilst heavy, fell short of German expectations. After a brief hiatus the vital convoys were resumed.

Dieppe

This was another set-up, masterminded by the Abwehr's Louis Mountbatten, working with German assets in Ottawa. They wanted to pull Canada out of the war, or at least get her troops out of the invasion of Europe. The German idea was to sacrifice large numbers of Canadians and wedge the Empire, à la Gallipoli. Superb work by the RAF in the skies over Dieppe however meant that the Luftwaffe got a bloody nose and the losses were not all one way. The Germans also underestimated the Canadians' fighting skills and courage. Their losses were not nearly as severe as Mountbatten and Canaris had hoped.

The right response, having spotted what was going on, would have been to sucker in Mountbatten, secretly reinforce the Canadians with a British division and more commandos, sailing from a different port, and ramp up the air support. We could also have moved a squadron of *KGVs* up the Channel from the West to absolutely plaster the 'Jerries'. Ambushing ambushers is always a good idea.

There is no law, which says that just because the enemy has come up with a cunning plan you cannot respond with an even more cunning plan of your own. Had He been briefed in it is unlikely that King George VI (to whom Mountbatten was related, along of course with Kaiser Wilhelm II) would have raised any violent objection to saving the hangman the cost of a silk rope. Peers are more expensive to hang of course. The RAF could have 'offered' Mountbatten a tour of the battlefield, during the course of which he could have been afforded the opportunity of a closer inspection, i.e. of stepping out of the aircraft, *Where Eagles Dare* style. It's been done before.[39]

1. It was a bit tricky sending a bottle of Scotch and a thank you note around to Anthony Quayle of course, since Admiral Canaris was officially dead. So far as I know Quayle didn't know the viewers would include the man he was playing. Quite a few of the DVD boys enjoyed the film apparently. Although Otto Skorzeny did not live to see it he approved of the script. It was of course his wartime exploits that inspired it he was played with his usual brilliance by Sir Michael Caine.
2. It is surprising it took as long as it did to spot Heath and Seligman. It would be fair to say that the Nazis did not go out of their way to attract the pink pound and generally speaking gay foreign visitors sharing tents were not encouraged. No doubt it helped working for the same man as the head of the Gestapo, whose equal opportunities policy omitted sexual orientation.
3. With a silk rope. As a peer, Lord Halifax was entitled to the courtesy of being hanged with a silk rope. The earldom was brokered through Maundy Gregory, Lloyd George's peerage broker. The viscountcy was created for his grandfather, who was almost as dodgy, having been a Liberal Chancellor of the Exchequer. He opposed helping Ireland in the famine and probably knew that it was deliberate.
4. She would have been particularly valuable operating alongside her sister in the Med, using the tactical doctrines developed by Admiral Sir Reginald Henderson.
5. HMS *Indefatigable* and HMS *Implacable*.
6. Of the 13 capital ships laid down or commissioned during World War I only *Renown* of the three battlecruisers was modernised, and even that was done too cheaply, depriving her of the latest high-pressure steam turbines. Of the 10 battleships of the *Queen Elizabeth* and *R* classes only HMS *Queen Elizabeth* and HMS *Valiant* were fully modernised. HMS *Warspite* was rebuilt but the rebuild did not go far enough. In particular, she was left without a modern AA battery.
7. 285 mph. They lacked military equipment such as self-sealing tanks and were not very good. Fitted with the Allison V-1710 in-line V-12 engine, which was good at low altitude, the P-36 became the P-40B Tomohawk, which wasn't very good either, although it performed well in the tactical strike role, i.e. as a fighter- bomber. In fairness to the boys at Indianapolis the problem with the 1710 wasn't with the engine, it was with the supercharger, the specification for which was drafted by RLM in Berlin. It was handed via General Marshall to his predecessor General Malin Craig, the same General Craig who succeeded in persuading himself that the Douglas B-18 Bolo was a better bomber than the B-17. Many readers will never have heard of the B-18. There is a reason for that. They were the USAAC's answer to the Fairey Battle and so far as is known went through the entire war without killing any Germans. Although they managed to kill a handful of Japanese the Americans would have got more killed by handing their B-18s over to the Imperial Japanese Army Air Force.
8. Wainwright & Marshall, "Into Battle", *Air Classics*, Vol. 47, No. 9, 2011, p. 18 at p. 22 gives a good basic account, without going into the intelligence aspects. Wainwright treats it as a case of mistaken identity by the French, which is the OFVE (Official French Version of Events).

9. 1969, a hugely impressive cast including Sir Ralph Richardson, Sir Michael Caine, Kenneth More and Susannah York. They borrowed the Spanish Air Force (just about all of it) for the air battle scenes, the Ejercito being equipped, largely for sentimental reasons, with Hispano-Suiza built Bf 109s (called the Bouchon) and He 111s.
10. A superlative piece of kit, out of the famed Skunk Works (I have seen the prototype).
11. My late friend (this was towards the end of his life) Raymond Baxter OBE owned one of the 'Little Ships' and would far rather talk about Dunkirk than his own not inconsiderable exploits chasing V-1s, supporting the British aircraft industry and encouraging technological literacy in the young by presenting *Tomorrow's World*.
12. This is not as straightforward as it sounds, as Army radio sets were not intended for, nor really suited, to naval coordination, but if need be coordinates could have been signalled to the ships by landed naval yeomen using Aldis lamps. Command of the littoral brings with it a significant ability to influence the land battle within range of your guns. A typical British destroyer of the period would have had a main battery of 4 4.7-inch guns, greater firepower than a squadron of Tiger tanks, with more rounds per gun, better fire control and faster rates of training and elevation.
13. The Merlin 61, knocking out about 75% more power at altitude than the engines used in the Battle of Britain. Dropped into the Spitfire V it transformed the fighter, especially above 20,000 feet, turning it into a real Fw- 190 killer, especially when fitted with metal ailerons.
14. Just under 37 litres (2,240 cubic inches) versus 27 for the Merlin. Opposed rotation props made high-performance piston engine twins much easier to handle. There were logistical issues, as having the engine turn the other way meant a largely separate set of spare parts, but they were manageable.
15. It was this disloyalty that lay at the heart of their difficult relationship with the Prime Minister, rather than any alleged tendency to 'interfere' with the running of the war, which as Prime Minister was his ultimate responsibility anyway. In Britain the Armed Forces are under civilian control. Churchill was the only Prime Minister to have served as First Lord of the Admiralty, Secretary of State for War and Secretary of State for Air. He knew more about defence than any Prime Minister since the Duke of Wellington and unlike most had combat experience.
16. Near Bristol, in the West of England.
17. Sister to *Bismarck,* she was already in commission and then working up in the Baltic, another powerful piece of evidence against the theory that *Bismarck* was going on a near-suicidal lone hunt for convoys, which would have had battleship protection once she was out. This might only have been from an *R* class, but they had a main battery of 8 15-inch Mark 1 guns, i.e. the same calibre as *Bismarck's.* They would have been well able to stand up to *Bismarck* if not chase her. *Bismarck's* deck armour has been overrated (3.9 – 4.7 inches - by comparison HMS *Hood* had up to 3 inches, i.e. weaker, but not *that* much weaker) and would have been at real risk from plunging fire as she approached the

convoy. The *R* class also had catapult-launched aircraft for spotting, i.e. indirect fire control.

18. 38,500 tons, 8 15-inch guns - as fast and almost as powerful as *Bismarck* herself. With the Brest Squadron, *Tirpitz* and the Italian *Littorios* it would have been a powerful fleet.
19. *Admiral Hipper, Prinz Eugen, Blücher* (heroically sunk by a Norwegian shore battery in 1940) and *Seydlitz*.
20. True battleships, they were to be armed with 12 16-inch 50 cal. guns. They would still have been relevant in the Iraq War in the fire support and bombardment role. They would have been near-invulnerable to modern anti- shipping missiles, which have small warheads and are much slower than battleship shells, i.e. would have little chance of penetrating battleship armour, designed to resist supersonic shells, in the case of the *Montanas* about 7 times the size of an Exocet warhead. Modern bombs are generally too small for use against battleships, the Massive Ordnance Penetrator excepted. That really is a bomb - Bomber Harris would have approved. They were used in combat for the first time against Iran in June 2025.
21. *King George V* class, 38,000 tons standard displacement, 10 14-inch guns and 16 5.25-inch, 28.5 knots: a handsome, fine and powerful ship, despite the political interference. Given another 5,000 tons the DNC could have turned them into really useful ships, with 12 main battery guns, stronger deck armour, slightly longer hulls and more powerful machinery, for say 30 knots. The weight and space given over to aircraft could have been put to better use with more 8-barrelled 2-pounder AA mountings but they were designed before the carrier building program got under way and the DNC was thinking of spotting and indirect fire control, especially as part of the proposed Main Fleet at Singapore, which would have been short of carriers until the mid-40s.
22. Who inexplicably failed to engage *Prinz Eugen* with *Suffolk* and *Norfolk*, each of whose firepower matched the enemy cruiser, albeit that they suffered from the lack of protection problem identified earlier, inexplicable of course unless he had orders from Pound. Had Wake-Walker illuminated *Prinz Eugen* with star-shell as he should have done, and gone inside his zone of immunity to engage her, approaching bows-on to the enemy to present a smaller target, Admiral Holland would not have been confused by the switch in position of the German squadron. However, this would have upset the narrative Foley had agreed with the Abwehr back in January.
23. 23,000 tons standard displacement, sister-ship of *Illustrious*, laid down in 1937, she had just been commissioned, the lengthy delay being due to interference from civil servant assets in the Admiralty reporting to Wilson in the Treasury. Germany's war against *Victorious* lasted throughout her life and she was prematurely scrapped in 1969 after an arson attack. Officially this was down to a short circuit in a tea-urn, but short circuits are an old intelligence favourite.
24. There was an interesting but wrong article about this episode in the *Daily Telegraph*, 2nd July 2005, p.8.
25. Not his pet walrus, but the lovely old Supermarine amphibian, designed by R.J. Mitchell of Spitfire fame, very slow (it was said they could go backwards in a

strong wind, but it would have to be a Force 8) but lots of lift and very suitable to the task in hand. They also handled well on the water, which not all marine aircraft do.

26. Holdens were fine Australian cars, designed in Victoria and made in South Australia. The first one was the iconic 48-215. Some invincibly stupid clown in GM wanted to design them in America and build them in China, which would be a bit like selling Chiko rolls (a local delicacy) made in Sri Lanka.
27. When three 'Eyetie' battlewagons were crippled for very little loss by an extraordinarily small number of Fairey Swordfish torpedo bombers, which once again proved that it was a good weapons platform. High speed can be a disadvantage when launching torpedoes from aircraft - the angle has to be within narrow limits otherwise they will porpoise or dive.
28. There was a similar battle over the *Queen Elizabeth* class aircraft carriers. Once you win the battle to order them you face exhausting years of sniping and bureaucratic guerrilla warfare and then a fresh battle over the carrier air groups.
29. One of my sources on this is an Italian admiral - *grazie*, although he didn't actually want to be a source. This is one aspect of World War II about which the 'Eyeties' have been highly circumspect. The chariots were a clever concept, later adopted by the Admiralty. They were also used against Allied shipping at Gib, the counter-offensive being led by a brilliant naval intelligence officer, 'Buster' Crabb, of MI18, murdered by the DVD in 1956.
30. Like Roy Jenkins in Britain, who set up his very own centre party, the SDP, after Labour once again took a principled position on EEC membership.
31. Aichi D3A1.
32. A robust design, well-suited to shipboard work and superior to the Zero in a number of respects, e.g. protection, firepower and gunsight, but which lacked folding wings. With the Merlin 61 motor, folding wings and better drop tank provision the Sea Hurricane could have remained a serious shipboard fighter into 1943.
33. Some of the Air Ministry records for Barber's aircraft have been tampered with. This wasn't difficult given that no fewer than five successive Secretaries of State for Air were German assets: Sir Kingsley Wood (1938-1940), Sir Samuel Hoare (1940) - as Foreign Secretary he had given considerable comfort to Mussolini, he was sacked by Churchill but assigned by the Foreign Office as Ambassador to Spain, where he liaised directly with Canaris, Sir Archibald Sinclair (1940-45) a Liberal, Harold Macmillan (1945), and William Wedgwood Benn (1945-46). Benn was the father of Michael and Anthony - Michael was murdered by the Abwehr in 1944, his plane being sabotaged, to protect his father, apparently after Michael had returned home unexpectedly to the isolated family home on the Essex coast, on the Blackwater Estuary, which was used as a U-Boat rendezvous. Tony Benn, a nice chap, into whom I bumped into on more than one occasion, was never briefed in.
34. 32,000 tons, 9 11-inch guns. The Kriegsmarine claimed they were battleships, but the Admiralty designation of them as battlecruisers is to be preferred, as they emphasised speed and range at the extent of protection. Elegant

ships, especially with the 'Atlantic' bow, they were primarily designed for the intelligence role, e.g. shipments of gold, with a secondary role as commerce raiders. Wisely they avoided combat with the Royal Navy wherever possible and *Scharnhorst* was rapidly sunk in her first engagement with a British battleship, the dear old *Duke of York*. They should both have been caught and sunk off Norway in 1940, but sadly the Treasury had blocked Admiralty requests for higher-pressure steam turbines for *Renown*. As rebuilt, she had lost too much speed (she struggled to make 28 knots) and was unable to catch the Germans, much to Admiral Whitworth's frustration.

35. The Admiralty have been mocked for staying with the 'Stringbag', which despite its appearance was a contemporary of the sleek Spitfire, but they were tough machines with a solid under-cart, which could be landed on in all sorts of weathers. The biplane configuration conferred great load-carrying capability and a low take-off speed, which meant they could be operated from astonishingly short decks, e.g. on escort carriers, or the even smaller Merchant Aircraft Carriers of the *Empire Mac* class. Show a modern US Navy aviator a picture of an *Empire Mac,* tell them it was an aircraft carrier and they wouldn't believe you. There have been larger cross-channel ferries. The dear old 'Stringbag' didn't need much more room to get off than a VTOL Harrier, especially into a stiff wind. There were plenty of those in the North Atlantic in winter.
36. Played in the film by David McCallum, a rather underrated actor - *www.fleetairarmarchive.net*, accessed 9th September 2006 (this book wasn't researched overnight).
37. 1964, cracking plot, some good flying sequences with real Mossies and a wonderful theme tune, still played by the RAF Central Band. I met one of the production staff many years later at the Simon Wiesenthal Center in LA. A very nice man, unduly modest, he was pleasantly surprised to learn that the film was still remembered in Britain with fondness. They ought to show it more often on TV. It would be a valuable boost for morale.
38. When Müller's alleged coffin was opened up there were bits of three bodies inside - not a good sign, as any intelligence officer will tell you. They like one body per coffin thank you very much. If there are three, it's usually a fair bet that none of them will correspond to what it says on the box.
39. Trials are better of course, not least for the Bar, but they are expensive and there's the publicity to consider, plus you need to find a judge who hasn't been nobbled by the Germans.

19

1943 - 1945

The Sikorski Crash

On the evening of 4th July 1943, RAF Liberator Mk II AL523, of 511 Squadron, Fl. Lt Prchal, a Czech serving in the RAF, in command, crashed on take-off from Gibraltar. Sadly all on board, save Fl. Lt Prchal were killed, including the great Polish leader General Sikorski and two intelligence officers, Walter Lock and H. Pinter. Abwehr agents on 'the Rock' started circulating conspiracy theories about the crash, which was observed by the Abwehr monitoring station in Algeciras, within 24 hours, blaming Churchill.

An Abwehr double agent inside the American Office of Strategic Services, Colonel Charles Whiting, claimed in his book *Canaris* in 1973 that his colleague Kim Philby, then manning MI6's Iberian desk in London, had arranged the assassination of General Sikorski, whilst working for the Russians. Colonel Whiting of course took care not to mention that he and Kim worked for the same outfit.

Philby, like his notorious father Harold, was a *German* not a Russian spy - he was just false flagged through Moscow. As anyone who knew Kim will tell you the idea that he was a communist was just plain silly. In fact, he hated Moscow and popped over to East Germany, to see his old friend (also known to me) Generaloberst Markus Wolf,[1] as often as he could.

Churchill was hopeful that General Sikorski would become postwar President of Poland and keep Stalin out of Warsaw. He would much have preferred his son-in-law Duncan Sandys too have been in the Liberator, indeed it's a pity he wasn't. When the tragic news (not that Sandys was still alive but that Sikorski was dead) was broken to him by dear old Sir Frank Roberts of the Foreign Office, whom I had the privilege of knowing many years later, Churchill wept. Sir Frank was a delightful chap, by the way. He afterwards headed up the British Mission in Moscow and got to know Stalin quite well.

A 'Jerry' playwright, Rolf Hochhut (no Shakespeare, no offence intended) called Churchill a 'murderer' in his play *The Soldiers*, which also suggested that Fl. Lt Prchal was in on the conspiracy. The great actor Sir Laurence Olivier rightly canned it, leading to a silly dispute in the press and a television programme hosted by the late David Frost, on dear old London Weekend Television, which used to have the weekend ITV franchise in London and made some excellent programmes before losing the franchise for political reasons (Thames TV, another excellent company, held the weekday franchise). The programme on the Sikorski crash featured my late friend Winston Churchill, Sir Winston's favourite grandson.

Hochhut tried to palm Frost off with the old 'all ze evidence is in a safe deposit box in a Swiss bank und cannot be revealed until 50 years after ze accident' line, which Frosty didn't buy.[2] Nothing happened of course in July 1993, i.e. 50 years after the accident. Interestingly, LWT brought Prchal, then living in the States, over for the program. David Irving, the historian, (*not* a friend of mine, although we have met) also participated. Colonel Whiting's book famously contains the only known published postwar photograph of his boss Admiral Canaris, at p. 110. Allegedly taken in "1944" it shows a man rather older than 57, with his "two favourite dogs", oddly enough not dachshunds. Herr Admiral's dogs in '44 happened to be dachshunds. They used to accompany him from his home in the Schlactensee to the office (partly because his wife Erika, a friend of a friend, wasn't so fond of them), where they would play under his desk. Apparently, they were very sweet.

Age can be faked and a couple of friendly pooches can always be borrowed from the nearest pound, but one thing that cannot easily be altered is the size of the ears. They don't stop growing. The different isn't huge, but always look at the ears.

The most sophisticated analysis of the Gibraltar tragedy was undertaken by the late Captain Jan Bartelski in his leading text, *Disasters In The Air.*[3] It is always best when reviewing an air crash and trying to answer the question "accident or sabotage?" to listen to the views of an experienced pilot. Very few pilots could match Captain Bartelski's experience. Having joined the Polish Air Force in August 1939, after Poland's surrender he went on to fly with RAF Coastal and Transport Commands. In 1948 he joined KLM, flying with them until 1978, by which time he was a senior DC-10 captain. He also found time to serve, with distinction, as President of the International Federation of Air Line Pilots Associations (IFALPA).

I do not always agree with Captain Bartelski's conclusions, but only where I am in possession of air intelligence that was not available to the Captain. One example is the Abwehr's involvement in the assassination of

HRH the Duke of Kent KG KT on August 25th 1942.[4] Another is the presence of a Luftwaffe ground radar unit at Tenerife on 27th March 1977.

With the possible exception of intelligence emerging that the Abwehr's Sabotage Section chanced their arm and had someone put the loose mailbag in the Liberator - as observed above the 'wily Hun' can be very wily, which as is why we call him the 'wily Hun' - *Disasters in the Air* is likely to be the last word on the subject. The Liberator was brought down by a combination of:

(1) Bad luck (the mailbag jamming the port elevator).
(2) An understandable design defect (no bulkhead between the nose wheel housing and the rear fuselage, allowing air to rush through the aircraft when the gear was down, especially if the rear hatch was open) in an aircraft designed in a tearing hurry to meet an urgent military specification.
(3) Sloppy closing of the hatch.
(4) A warm previous night necessitating the RAF guard, Corporal Frank Hopgood, opening the hatch for ventilation.
(5) The need for a guard to have to spend the night in the aircraft in the first place.
(6) Prewar cheeseparing at Gib, with the result that the runway was ridiculously short for four-engine operations.
(7) Scheduled runway work.
(8) A short take-off run, that necessitated a higher than usual alpha angle on take-of, and
(9) The shortage of transport aircraft, resulting in the carriage of mail on a VIP flight when a second mail Liberator, or a Wellington, should have been assigned.

Fl. Lt Pyrchal's survival is easily explained. He was the only crew member wearing a full harness and being a good airman he tightened his straps. The passengers had inadequate lap belts, no more use in a high-g impact with water than the dinky little things they give you on airliners these days. There are no grounds whatsoever for criticising Ft. Lt Pyrchal's handling of his aircraft - with a jammed elevator the flight was doomed. The Sikorski crash is an illustration that accidents can happen. The trick is sorting them out from sabotage.

The Strategic Bomber Offensive

The measure of how hard this hurt the 'Jerrres' can be seen in the intensity of his propaganda attacks upon it postwar. Assets like the economist J.K.

Galbraith piled into the splendid efforts of Eighth Army Air Force Bomber Command. No lie was too outrageous in a smear operation that continues to the present day. Of course, Galbraith and his colleagues in the DVD's Propaganda Section (naturally German propagandists tended to enjoy inflated reputations courtesy of fellow German-sympathisers in the media) built upon the wartime efforts of Abwehr assets in the British and American bureaucracies. As we have seen there was significant manipulation of targeting intelligence.

Let the record show that both Bomber Command and the 'Mighty Eighth' attacked strategic targets only, took immense care to hit those targets, hard, and minimise collateral damage to purely civilian targets. That definition did not include war workers, who were active and generally willing participants in the German war machine. People who made panzers, U-Boats and Stukas could not be heard to say that they were not legitimate targets, however keen they may have been to earn good money enabling suffering to be inflicted on others whilst avoiding it themselves.

Moreover, the Allies generally hit their targets, hence the panic over stopping post-raid photo-imagery reaching air force commanders. It is unlikely that the great American air commanders Carl Spaatz and Ira Eaker were given any more reliable post-raid intel than dear old Bomber Harris was. As observed, if they believed Galbraith or the similar nonsense dished up by Whitehall, anyone visiting post-war Germany would have been expecting to see undamaged industrial centres (pro- German writers prefer to say "cities", as though the factories in the target areas were making *Märklin* train sets, china dolls and paper doylies) surrounded by fields with large holes in them.

The accuracy of Allied bombing should not come as a surprise. Every bomber had a fully trained navigator, aircrew selection was careful and given wartime constraints the training was excellent, roughly comparable with the training modern commercial pilots receive, with high quality instructors who had themselves probably completed a tour. The latest gyro-stabilised electro-optical aiming devices were used and the RAF moved to radar bombing as soon as lighter centimetric radar (betrayed to 'Jerry' by Victor Rothschild) made airborne radar a serious proposition.

Weather reconnaissance was allocated a high priority and raids were scrubbed if the weather was adverse. If the primary target was obscured by cloud the attack force diverted to a secondary. Targets, including approaches, were chosen with great care, as were Initial and Aiming Points. Courageous pilots not infrequently went around again if the aircraft was not properly lined up or the target was obscured by smoke.

The RAF, bombing mostly at night, made highly effective use of target illumination using flares. These were usually dropped by specially trained Pathfinders, some of the finest pilots who have ever flown. Sir Arthur Harris introduced the innovation of Master Bombers, who stayed over the target, with a deputy to take over if they were hit. They made sure that the Main Force, following up behind the Pathfinders, dropped 'in the box'.

The Americans bombed mostly by day. After an initial period of adjustment (their crews were trained in very different conditions) they achieved a good standard of accuracy.

This was despite the desperate bureaucratic battle waged by Abwehr assets in Whitehall and Washington to hand over technological secrets to Berlin, hold back engine development and insist on underpowered or antiquated kites, like the venerable Armstrong-Whitworth Whitley.[5] High-powered engines in the 2,000 plus HP class like the new Bristol Centaurus, proposed by Shorts for a reengined Stirling,[6] caused particular anxiety in the German Air Ministry (RLM) and Abwehr. They waged a vicious boardroom battle against its designer, the great Roy Fedden. He was kicked from pillar to post by Whitehall for daring to design a better engine than the Germans.

The finest British heavy bomber, the Avro Lancaster, was held back after its designer was forced to use 27-litre V-12 Merlins, instead of the more powerful 42.5 litre X-24 Vulture. The latter was the logical choice, since it powered the twin engine Manchester, from which the Lancaster was developed. It would have required a wing of increased span, but so what? That would have conferred more space for fuel and lowered the wing-loading. It would have been a 10,000 HP bomber.

Abwehr assets in Whitehall waged a successful campaign against the Vulture, claiming it was vulnerable to overheating. In fact, the overheating issue on the Manchester was more a function of poor cowling design rather than any fundamental defect in the engine. The Vulture 'power- egg', i.e. engine and radiator, was 'good to go' by the time the 'Lanc' entered service.

The B-17 ran into similar problems with its engine and turbo-supercharger. Even by the time the B-17G entered service in 1943 its Wright R-1820-97 Cyclones were only pushing out 1,200 HP each. The aircraft had been through a major redesign anyway, partly triggered by a critical RAF evaluation of the 'C' model. The 'C' lacked military equipment and was not truly combat-capable.

Left to themselves Boeing would probably have gone for the larger Wright R-2600 Twin Cyclone, which was the intended powerplant for the YB-20. The R-2600-22 pushed out 1,900 HP and powered the Grumman TBF Avenger torpedo-bomber. The Boeing boys would also probably have gone for four-bladed paddle props.[7] The last thing that George Marshall wanted however was a bomber which could outrun his side's fighters at altitude.

As the allied air attacks hit home the panicking Luftwaffe came up with a cunning plan. Why not lure the 'Mighty Eighth' out of the range of its escorting Lockheed P-38 Lightning and Republic P-47 Thunderbolt fighters by tempting them with a juicy target, set up the biggest ambush since Little Big Horn and do to the Eighth what Chief Crazy Horse did to General Custer? The target put up by Canaris's men in Washington, including Marshall, was the ball-bearing works at Schweinfurt. The attack duly went ahead on 17th August 1943, without the RAF being asked to do a night-time raid as well.

This was silly, as quite apart from the additional damage the British heavies could have inflicted on the target, the Mossies of the Light Night Striking Force could have clobbered some of the airfields being used by Goering's day fighters. As we have seen however, the Air Minister, Sinclair, was a German spy, firmly opposed to Anglo-American cooperation. That night the RAF pranged Peenemunde, a high value target. It would have been better to have both forces hit Peenemunde and postpone Schweinfurt until the long-range North American P-51 Mustang came into service.

Thankfully, the cunning German plan largely failed, although American losses were tragically heavy. That was the end of unescorted daylight bombing and should have been the end of George Marshall. His balls should have been busted along with the ball-bearings. 'Jerry' of course had made alternative arrangements for his ball-bearings, including a supply from Sweden. Your Swede takes his neutrality seriously and is always willing to sell to both sides in a conflict.

The RAF took similarly heavy losses when Bomber Command was ambushed in a not dissimilar fashion, this time at night, over Nuremberg on 30th/31st March 1944. The man who betrayed that mission, and many others, was Duncan Sandys. 'Jerry' had manoeuvred Sandys close to Churchill through his daughter Diana.[8]

The Battle of the Atlantic

The most important intelligence breakthrough was the cracking, first by the Poles then by Bletchley Park, of 'Jerry's' Enigma code, which until 1939 he had fondly believed was uncrackable. As is well-known the Enigma was a clever bit of kit, using rotors and a complex wiring arrangement, the settings of which could be altered, giving millions of potential combinations.

It looks a bit like an old manual typewriter, which for the benefit of younger readers was a noisy device, requiring Tippex to operate effectively, on which you could bash out documents with mistakes which were called typing errors. Once you've set up an Enigma machine it requires very little effort to operate, about the same as an old Underwood in fact.[9] You didn't need the wartime equivalent of Tippex, indeed errors were best avoided. They tended to cause confusion at the other end and could send a panzer division in the wrong direction.

'Jerry' however made the same basic mistake everybody makes when they think they've come up with a new 'unbreakable' code. They over- egged the pudding. By 1942 they were encrypting weather reports, which of course gave you a way in if you had a good idea of the weather in the sender's area.

It was widely believed in INTELCOM for decades that 'Jerry' was unaware that his codes were being read. That view was being expressed inside GHCQ and NSA as recently as 2005. With respect to those taking the contrary view it was wrong, for six reasons:

(1) The first breakthrough was made in Poland, but 'Jerry' occupied Warsaw in 1939. As is well-known he had vays of making people talk. It's only the Allies who defeat the enemy, occupy his capital and then pass up on the intelligence yield, in the hope of causing another war. German military intelligence interrogators had one great advantage over their more gentlemanly British, Russian and American counterparts - they could always threaten to pop someone round to the Gestapo to have the odd toenail extracted. The usual rule is that when 'Jerry' occupies your capital his intelligence chaps will find out just about all there is to know.

(2) The early Enigma breakthroughs were shared with the French. Expecting them not to share it with the Germans was like giving them the details of a stealth fighter mission and not expecting your stealth fighter to be ambushed and shot down.

(3) 'Jerry' put up the cash for Bletchley Park, through Admiral Sinclair, i.e. he owned the joint (in INTELCOM this is known as dropping a whoopsie).

(4) MI6 was in the loop from the beginning and the head of MI6, Sir Stewart Menzies, was a German spy. The late Sir Hugh Trevor-Roper was another German asset, in the Radio Security Service, which knew all about Bletchley Park.

(5) MI5 were in charge of security, which since Victor Rothschild, a senior officer, was a German spy, was a bit like putting the late, great Oliver Reed in charge of a brewery, and

(6) One of the codebreakers at Bletchley was Roy Jenkins, the well-known German spy.

A clue is to be found in the German Navy Enigma machines. If you compare a Kriegsmarine machine with a Luftwaffe or Wehrmacht one you will see that an additional rotor has been added, conferring significant extra security. It seems as though Canaris thought that this would be sufficient, although in the events which happened he underestimated Alan Turing and the British advances in the development of the computer, just as Turing underestimated the extent to which he would be harassed by the 'Jerries' after the war. Sadly, the poor chap, who had been pushed out of Bletchley by Menzies, ended up the victim of a bad-faith German- influenced prosecution in 1952, tinged with homophobia. He ended up topping himself, or was topped, with a poisoned apple. This led to the name for 'Apple' computers and the late Steve Job's decision to use an apple with a bite out of it as the logo. Strictly it should have been half an apple, but who cares? The computers work.

No one with experience of inter-service rivalries would be terribly surprised at Canaris's decision to withhold the knowledge that the Enigma traffic was being partially read from the Luftwaffe and the Wehrmacht. As observed, the ability of intel-crats to sit on intelligence and watch military disasters unfold is not confined to British Commonwealth and American agencies. Much confusion has been engendered by the belief that Canaris and the Abwehr were trying to win the war. They knew it was lost and were trying to keep their networks intact so they could win the peace.

The biggest secret of the Battle of Atlantic was that Germany was using covert bases in the Republic of Ireland and Mexico, as might be gathered from looking at the pattern of losses.[10] The traditional explanation for Dönitz's ability to operate far beyond the range of his U-Boats, repeated endlessly since World War II as though it were fact, is that they were refuelled at sea from submarine tankers known as 'Milch-cows'. These were in fact an elaborate and successful exercise in military deception, although they may have been of actual military use occasionally.

Working out how the enemy is getting his fuel is one of the basic tasks confronting a military intelligence officer. If you can interdict his supply chain, you can bring his operations grinding to a halt. There are several problems with the traditional explanation, apart from the fact that it's bollocks:

(1) It is remarkably difficult to arrange a submarine rendezvous in the North Atlantic without radio, bearing in mind the limited visibility from a U-Boat conning tower. The Kriegsmarine divided the ocean into grid squares but these weren't much use for U-Boats in the North Atlantic, although they were fine for radar-equipped raiders.

(2) Submarines on the surface with refuelling hoses strung between them are highly vulnerable, as they cannot dive until the hoses have been parted. Without radar to warn of approaching aircraft, a 'ras'[11] was not an undertaking to be approached lightly. The US Navy made highly effective use of refuelling surface ships at sea, but it was only done with local control of the air, usually with heavy surface combatants to protect the perimeter and powerful air search radars to warn of approaching enemy aircraft.

(3) The distribution pattern of sinkings is consistent with base refuelling and makes very little sense if the U-Boats were being refuelled at sea, which would permit them to be refuelled in any part of the ocean, preferably out of range of patrolling aircraft.[12]

(4) The Germans lacked tanker boats with high capacity - most 'milch-cows' had barely enough fuel themselves for the mission profiles historians have assigned them.

(5) The Abwehr and Kriegsmarine naval intelligence had far more important cargo than fuel in mind (gold, intelligence officers, technology transfer to Japan, etc.) for cargo submarines.

(6) The Germans were seriously short of diesel fuel and refining capacity, neatly illustrated in the film *Battle of the Bulge*,[13] i.e. it was far more likely that the U-Boats were getting diesel fuel from German client states like Mexico and Venezuela once they were away from Europe than it was that fuel was being shipped out to them from fuel-starved Europe, and

(7) The numbers (operational diesel fuel requirements for U-Boats and tanker boat numbers, capacity and own-fuel requirements) do not stack up.

U-Boats were normally refuelled from neutral-flagged freighters, fitted as tankers. The conversion was not difficult to do, as freighters have large holds and some of their own fuel tanks could be converted from bunker fuel to diesel. They could also be topped up by other tankers, none of which ever went anywhere near Germany. Several oil companies, including BP, Shell and Standard Oil, in its various guises, were under the effective control of the Abwehr during the war, and the DVD for some time thereafter.

Formation of the DVD

In autumn 1943, with the war clearly lost, a senior Abwehr officer, Generalleutnant Erwin von Lahousen, later Canaris's deputy, dropped off the radar. He wasn't on a skiing holiday, although he made regular visits to Switzerland. There he met *inter alia* with the Abwehr's Dulles brothers (known in England as the 'von Dulles brothers'). Like our community partner Adolf Hitler, Erwin von Lahousen was an Austrian intelligence officer. He held the rank of lieutenant-colonel in the Austrian Army at the time of the first German takeover in 1938 (Austria was later absorbed into the EU of course). Like Hitler, von Lahousen worked for the Germans. He was tasked with setting up a new intelligence agency, which was to combine not just the Abwehr but its assets in the SD (including fellow Austrian Kurt Waldheim), the Gestapo and the various military intelligence agencies.

The HQ of the new agency was to be in Dachau, near Munich, handy for the concentration camp. It built on existing black intelligence operations. Over time the HQ has grown into quite a complex, much of it underground. One building is near the AugsburgerStrasse in the centre of town, another near the edge of town, not un-adjacent to the AugustenfelderStrasse. The various buildings appear to be linked underground. Being covert, they all have a cover. One is a block of flats. It was only given away when satellite reconnaissance over time showed that the various Volkswagens and BMWs etc., distributed around the building to create an impression of occupation, never moved.

Satellite reconnaissance also recorded some interesting visitors, including terrorists and George H. W. Bush. Dachau is now amongst the most intensively watched towns in Germany, not always an unpopular assignment. One team of Americans, not CIA,[14] used the Munich Beer Festival as cover and were told to blend in, i.e. on no account to remain sober. The Russians are as keenly interested as everybody else. Dachau is now a great place from which to watch satellites, if you're a satellite spotter and have a big enough telescope.

Von Lahousen surrendered by agreement (with the Abwehr's Dwight Eisenhower) to US forces in Liezen, Austria, on 14th May 1945. He then pretended to be on our side and gave evidence for the prosecution at the Nuremberg War Crimes Trials. This reduced them from a complete farce to a screaming farce.[15] Take a look at old Goering's face on the newsreels when von Lahousen was in the witness box. It's an absolute picture. He was not a happy bunny.

D-Day and the July Plot

This was the biggest carve-up since Thanksgiving. Normandy was chosen for the nature of its terrain, which suited the defenders, and the fact that it was as far away from Germany as possible. Since both Eisenhower and Marshall reported to Canaris this wasn't difficult. The date, 6th June, was agreed between Eisenhower and Rommel, amusingly as the 6th was Frau Rommel's birthday and it gave Rommel an excuse not to be there. The Panzers weren't held back on Hitler's orders (he was slipped a Mickey Finn by Jodl, who also reported to Canaris), but by agreement. The detail was thrashed out in meetings in Lisbon between an officer on Eisenhower's staff working for the Germans and the local Abwehr Head of Station.

The idea was that Hitler would be assassinated, Rommel would take over as President of Germany, Himmler would be arrested, the Nazis booted out and the Allies permitted to 'liberate' France. This would be a largely pointless exercise since the Abwehr operation there would remain in place. When the German intelligence position in Paris was threatened after the deal collapsed, von Lahousen (Canaris having been arrested for treason, perfectly properly, on Himmler's orders) threatened to destroy Paris.

The deal blew up in Canaris's face because the Abwehr had been penetrated by the SD, which reported to Himmler. The Abwehr's Count von Stauffenberg was spotted, the bomb in the bunker was moved, Hitler survived, and he and Himmler took even firmer control of Germany. The war was back on, although Eisenhower did his best to lengthen it by holding back Patton and strangling his Third Army of fuel supplies.

Arnhem

This was set up at the infamous meeting in Strasbourg at the Maison Rouge (Red House) Hotel on 10th August 1944. The DVD, as it was by now, and the bankers with whom it was in close association, needed six months to get everything and everyone (the chosen few) out of Germany and into client states like Switzerland, Spain, Portugal, Mexico and Argentina. In order to extend the war, they came up with the bright idea of selling Montgomery on taking Arnhem with paratroops and relieving them in a bold thrust up the road from Nijmegen. Had Montgomery consulted more closely with the Dutch (unhappily he was not given over to excessive consultation with allies) they could have point out the flaws in this cunning plan.

The ambush was fairly straightforward - fresh Panzer units were moved up to Arnhem to hammer the Airborne Brigade and DVD assets in the British and American armies were briefed in to hold up XXX Corps. Vital photo-reconnaissance photos of the Panzers were suppressed from General 'Boy' Browning, General Horrocks and generally anybody who needed to see them. The loss of life amongst the Paras was horrific.

The key asset in XXX Corps who helped to get them killed was none other than Lord Carrington. He was identified with assistance from the able Russian GRU.[16] and died in 2018. My understanding is that he was debriefed and a deal was done allowing him to live out his remaining years in peace. All I can say is that he needed to have come up with some pretty useful intel on the DVD to be able to justify such leniency. He should have been court-martialled and shot by firing squad, albeit in the nicest possible way, in 1944. The Paras would probably have been able to find volunteers for the firing party, nice chap that he was (we met).

The World's First Jet Fighter

It is a tribute to the skills of Goebbels's boys in the Reich Propaganda Ministry, which became the Propaganda Section of the DVD, that the truth about which was the first jet fighter to enter service has been suppressed for as long as it has been. Although the Me 262 was the first jet fighter to fly, on 18th July 1942,[17] the honour of being the first to enter service falls to the Gloster Meteor, with 616 Squadron of the RAF, in July 1944. The first operational Mk 1 was delivered on 12th July 1944. The first interception, of a V-1 flying bomb, was made on 27th July, by Squadron Leader Watts.

All this was researched very thoroughly in the 1960s by the then Editor of *Jane's All The World's Aircraft*, John W. R. Taylor, and published.[18] It is a testimony to the quality of John Taylor's research that it has been suppressed, by later authors not to mention *Wikipedia* editors, who recycle Goebbels's original 1945 claim as though it had never been challenged.

Wikipedia has a number of strengths, and is rather better than its critics allow, but its semi-open nature can make it vulnerable to a determined attempt to distort the truth. I tried to get references to Taylor's research in some years ago, but they rarely lasted for more than a few hours, so I gave up.

The Me 262 did not enter service until October 1944, and only then with a special (i.e. non-line) squadron on a trial basis. Squadron service with the Luftwaffe commenced the following January. With only a 25- hour time between overhauls, the plane was not fully operational even then. It was a desperate expedient.

The aircraft would have been rejected by the RAF and the USAAF on serviceability grounds alone. I have only ever spoken to a couple of pilots who have flown the Me 262, but it seems to have been a difficult aircraft to fly, with slow spool-up characteristics and inadequate field performance. It had dangerous handling qualities when asymmetric, i.e. in engine-out-condition, so much so that it would have been rejected for service by the RAF and USAAF on that ground as well.

Despite its superior performance (it was around 100 mph faster) and more powerful armament (it had an impressive battery of four 30mm cannon) it was vulnerable to the excellent, Packard Merlin-powered[19] North

American P-51D. The P-51 boys soon learnt that the best place to pick off a 262 was near its airfields, when they were low and slow. If one of the Junkers Jumo 003 engines blew up, as they did not infrequently, shooting down a 262 was almost a waste of ammunition, as the pilot's chances of landing in one piece were not high.

When I pointed out the error, respectfully and with my usual diffidence, to the RAF Museum (the otherwise-excellent Smithsonian Museum in Washington makes the same mistake) I was told that the Me 262's claim to be the first jet fighter rests on a Reichsluftfahrtministerium (RLM) report of an unarmed 262 prototype (!) on test encountering an unarmed RAF Mosquito on a photo-reconnaissance mission. Even if true - and there does not appear to be a corresponding 'new enemy aircraft' report on Air Ministry files - this is more than tenuous. It verges on the ridiculous. One may as well say that Concorde entered service in 1969 because an official visitor to Filton was given a ride.

It is more probable that the Propaganda Ministry inserted a fake report into RLM files and backdated it so that the German aircraft could be seen to have been first. The awe in which Nazi-era official German documents are held by researchers and historians continues to astonish me. 'Jerry' does like his little hissy fits but in this case it is more than just a natural desire to be ahead of the British. Abwehr assets reporting to the sinister Sinclair in the Air Ministry had put in a lot of effort into blocking British jet fighter development. Gloster only got the contract because they made the slowest fighter in RAF service - the Gladiator biplane. Rover (of all people), were given the contract to develop the jet engine because they made a nice car and knew a lot about bicycles.

Ironically, Rover did quite well with the jet engine whilst they had it, precisely because they had no idea what they were doing. The biggest car Rover made pre-war was their 16 HP. It was elegant, but powerful it was not. They listened to Sir Frank Whittle, the inventor of the jet engine, who knew exactly what he was doing.

George Carter and the boys at Gloster were also mis-underestimated.[20] The Gladiator was only a biplane because that's what the Air Ministry, who wanted the RAF to have slower aircraft than the Germans, ordered. It was actually the world's fastest biplane fighter and incorporated a number of advanced aerodynamic features, such as cantilever (i.e. unsupported) undercarriage struts, a low-drag cowling and neat, low-drag fairings for the additional underwing Browning .303 machines.

When the Air Ministry, on orders from Chamberlain and Bridges, deprived Malta of fighters in order to help the Italians bomb it into submission (when these clowns prattled on prewar about the bomber always getting through they never added "if we let it") the RAF, with Fleet Air Arm connivance, retrieved three Sea Gladiators from crates at RNAS Hal Far. They were screwed together and chased the Regia Aeronautica all over the sky. The delighted locals, save for the Abwehr's assets, including Dom Mintoff of course, christened them *Faith*, *Hope* and *Charity*. They did wonderful work, until relieved by more modern types, which courageous chaps like the late Ian MacLennan DFM flew to great effect. George Carter and his team did a fine job with the Meteor. In many ways it was an advanced aircraft, with tricycle undercarriage (only the second British-built type in squadron service to be so equipped, after the Armstrong-Whitworth Albermarle), a high-tech (for July 1944) gyro gunsight, a high-mounted tailplane and the new, short-barrelled Mk 5 British Hispano cannon.

The high tailplane meant that the empennage was kept well clear of the jet efflux. The wing-loading was low, conferring good manoeuvrability, they climbed like a homesick angel and the choice of two engines was sound, given the low power and unreliability of early jet engines. Selecting straight wings was also sensible, since the aircraft had to be operated out of existing RAF airfields and required good low-speed handling characteristics. Indeed, they were operated in Europe in 1945 out of forward airfields and could be landed on grass. There was never going to be enough power to require swept wings anyway.

In an historic moment, at Reculver, Kent, on 7th November 1945, a Gloster Meteor F. Mk 4 took the world's Air Speed Record, recording 606 mph. That was pretty swift for 1945, especially at 200 feet. The record- breaking pilot was Group Captain 'Willy' Wilson, an absolutely spiffing chap.

Another couple of urban myths about the 262 should also be dispelled:

(1) Its service entry was delayed by problems with the engines, which kept blowing up, not Hitler's insistence that it be converted into a fighter-bomber, a straightforward task, and

(2) Its swept wings were adopted, like the de Havilland Tiger Moth, for centre-of-gravity, not aerodynamic reasons. Unlike the rocket-powered Me163 the aircraft wasn't fast enough for compressibility to be a serious limiting factor in the normal flight envelope (later marks of the Spitfire actually had a higher VNE[21]).

The German Nuclear Weapons Program

Until the discovery of radioactive debris, and possibly the remains of some nuclear scientists (the Germans seem to have clammed up about those), chucked down an old salt mine near Hannover, this was one of the sections of the book likely to generate lots of e-mails. It is uncontroversial that there was a German nuclear weapons programme. What was controversial, at least until they found the salt mine, was the view of some within INTELCOM that Germany detonated one or more nuclear devices on her Baltic coast in 1944/5.

It is still sketchy, but we know that the Germans were able to acquire some, but not enough, uranium from South Africa (which they covertly controlled through the Boer, Smuts), the Belgian Congo and their own mines. They also acquired cobalt from the Congo, indeed the cobalt mine is still going. It would be a most unwise rebel who attacked it.

We also know that Einstein, Oppenheimer, Fuchs and the Rosenbergs (Julius and Ethel, both of whom were very properly executed by the Americans in 1953) were working for the Abwehr. It is known that Lower Manhattan was allocated as the first target, hence the 'Manhattan Project'. The bit about blowing up New York was not explained to President Roosevelt. We also now know that technical intelligence on the A-Bomb regularly went walkies out of Los Alamos, courtesy of Oppenheimer. As is so often the case the security was aimed at stopping people getting in - delivering groceries must have been a pain - when the Bad Guys were already there.

As presently advised, I go with two tests, each on the Baltic coast, timeline October 1944 - January 1945. The first, with enriched uranium, achieved fission. The yield was low however, maxing out at 5 kilotons, less than a thousand bomber raid. The second, using cobalt, failed to achieve fission (i.e. a dirty bomb, which is where the DVD seem to have got the idea from).

Since we know that Manhattan was the first target (London was the second and Washington the third) we can work out the weight of the German bomb from the RLM specifications for the 'Amerika Bomber'. Very obviously, this was intended to be a nuclear bomber. There was no possibility of enough aircraft being available for a conventional bombing raid on New York.

The standard text on the subject is Herwig and Rode, *Luftwaffe Secret Projects: Strategic Bombers 1935-45*, the relevant chapter being Chapter 6 *(Target New York)*(the Oberkommando der Luftwaffe target map at page 46 is a nuclear map by the way, not conventional).[22] The key projects are the Messerschmitt Me P 08.01 and the Focke-Wulf 03.01206 series. These are internal company numbers, by the way, not RLM model numbers, which were sequential, or at least started out that way, hence Bf 109, Bf 110 and He 111. (The '111' designation allocated to the Heinkel followed the '110' allocated for the Messerschmitt twin, e.g.) The Junkers Ju 390 is also worth looking at.

The Fw designs were the most promising. They were not dissimilar to the Boeing B-29 Superfortress, the difference being that the Americans actually built *their* bomber. What's more they used it to drop a couple of nukes, upsetting the Japanese.

The Germans had the plans for the Superfortress by the way, and an asset to sabotage them, in Boeing's Wichita plant. She was also the one who photographed the blueprints, and later supported the Obama 'born in Honolulu' ruse. After the war the blueprints were passed to the Soviets. The story about Tupolev 'reverse-engineering' a B-29 'landed by mistake' was just a made-up piece of nonsense. A B-29 *was* landed in Russia, but only by arrangement, and only as a cover story. She's probably still in one piece in a hangar somewhere near Irkutsk.

Doing the best we can with what we've got the most credible weight estimates for the German bombs, depending on version (U235 or Co) are from 9 to 10 metric tons, the cobalt bomb being a bit heavier. RLM range figures are dodgy, in the sense that they were trying not to give away the flight plan, which was Germany - New York - Mexico. Without its atomic payload an Amerika Bomber could have done Mexico-Germany non-stop. It was never intended to fly Germany-New York-Germany, indeed the RLM would not have lost too much sleep if their plane was caught in the shockwave. German intelligence, indeed the German elite generally, are usually willing to sacrifice other Germans.

Dresden

That willingness was never more evident than at Dresden, which was heavily bombed by the RAF and USAAF between 13th and 15th February 1945. The targeting request came from the Red Army, on whose line of advance Dresden was situated. It originated with General Andropov but was not limited to Dresden. The Russians also wanted German communications disrupted at Leipzig and Chemnitz. The idea however seems to have been pushed with Stalin by von Lahousen. The plan was to paint the British and Americans as the Bad Guys. Goebbels was in on it and started pushing out grossly exaggerated casualty figures before the fires were out, aided by his people in the BBC. Lord Reith, the Director- General between 1927 and 1938 had been blackmailed over his mistress, Dawn Mackay, for some years.

There was a deeper motive, however. Through an intermediary in Dublin, Himmler was led to believe by Sandys that Dresden would not be bombed. The Nazis started moving cash, paintings, mistresses, etc. into Dresden in the last quarter of 1944, thinking it was safe. No doubt there was a cash transfer to Sandys as well. It is not clear when Himmler became aware of how deeply Canaris had the British government and civil service penetrated, but he had a number of senior Abwehr intelligence officers in custody after its formal abolition following the July Plot.

As always Canaris and his deputy in the DVD, von Lahousen, were looking to the future and were keen to eliminate or diminish rivals within Germany. The Nazis' upset at the Dresden bombing was genuine but not entirely motivated by warm, fuzzy human feelings. Your average Nazi didn't do warm and fuzzy.

The world had to wait until 2004 for a balanced account of the Dresden raids, *Dresden*, by Frederick Taylor. Previous accounts had tended to portray Dresden as the centre of Germany's china industry, i.e. an entirely civilian centre, downplaying its importance within the Reich's military-industrial complex. There was also a tendency to suggest that the war was already over, when there were scarcely any Allied troops on German soil.

Aside from being a key communications node, Dresden by February 1945 was the fourth-largest armaments centre in Nazi Germany. In particular it was important for the manufacture of optical devices, e.g. periscopes, and torpedoes. Critics of the RAF and USAAF also tend to omit the fact that the meteorological conditions which gave rise to the firestorm could not be detected by high-flying weather reconnaissance aircraft, although they were known to the authorities on the ground, who did nothing to warn the civilian population.

The unreal Propaganda Ministry casualty figures were recycled by the left and German sympathisers for decades. No one stopped to ask who these 'hundreds of thousands of people' might be. There were very few undocumented people in Nazi Germany - it is not as though it was a magnet for illegal immigrants. Taylor's estimate, after a sober analysis, is of the order of 25,000-40,000 dead.

I respectfully suggest that 25,000, the figure produced by the city authorities at the time is at the upper end of the range, the lower end being say 18,000. Even that figure is an estimate and includes 'unknowns', i.e. it is not based on an actual casualty list or a body count.

People tend to think that there was only one raid and that it took refugees near the Aiming Point by surprise. There were in fact three raids, the heaviest being the night-time raid by the RAF on the 13th, which was split into two. Effectively there were four raids, as the first RAF raid was preceded by Pathfinders dropping red target markers. Nobody in Germany in February 1945 could possibly mistake RAF target flares for a parachute display put on by the burgermeisters for the town's entertainment.

Any refugee still in possession of his or her faculties would have moved smartly away from the central business district and railway station, each of them a legitimate target. They would have had time to do so before the Main Force arrived. Critics who point out that the poison gas, optical and other factories were in the suburbs miss the point. The target was determined by the Abwehr and they particularly wanted the banks, where the Nazis had stored their gold and valuables, which were in the central business district. They also wanted high temperatures, to melt the gold.

The Patton Assassination

On 13th October 1945 an OSS officer, Douglas Bazata, who had a Lebanese background, set up a crash between a truck and a staff car carrying the great American general, George Patton. He was the finest American general of World War II. Bazata admitted in 1979 that he had been paid $10,000 to set up the assassination, which was ordered by 'Wild Bill' Donovan of the DVD.[23] When Patton threatened to recover, another agent killed him with an injection.

Sadly, General Patton died on 21st December 1945. Bazata was not a traitor. He had no idea that Donovan was working for the Germans and was sold a cover story about wanting to protect US secrets. The DVD's real fear of course was that Patton would be the Republican candidate in 1948 or 1952, blocking their man Eisenhower. He had been running interference on Patton since the latter arrived in North Africa in 1942. There had been several previous attempts against Patton, e.g. the 'blue on blue' attack on the plane flying him to Third Army HQ in Feldfield.

This came in the middle of a very strange period, in which to Patton's disgust (he was first and foremost a soldier and was a man of honour) Eisenhower was encouraging ill-treatment of the German civilian population. The idea of this cynical and disgraceful strategy was to deflect suspicion from Eisenhower, which had built up after D-Day, and try and drive a wedge between the Germans and the Americans.

The casualties from this were of the order Goebbels had been spinning for Dresden and were absolutely inexcusable. Both German prisoners and the civilian population were entitled to fair, decent and correct treatment. There is no inconsistency between that observation and the preceding section on Dresden. Collateral casualties, whilst regrettable, are an unavoidable incident of war. Mistreating an enemy population after they have surrendered, in peacetime, is a wholly different thing. It is both morally and legally reprehensible. It was so un-American that somebody should have spotted Eisenhower. It is quite possible that General Patton had.

1. I didn't know him very well of course - he was the opposition, after all. Dear old Markus was very wary indeed of me, but we enjoyed our chats and I would not have dreamt of not buying him a good single malt, or better still, bringing along a bottle. He also appreciated a good blend and wouldn't say no to a Chivas Regal, especially if it was an old one. Some in MI6 hated him, which was silly - it's a big mistake to personalise things and pointless if you're trying to elicit information, such as confirmation that Edward Heath was working for the Germans. Of course he had MI6 agents killed - that was his job, for heaven's sake. He was a senior DVD and Stasi officer. He was a nice one, however, very *kulturny*, as the old KGB boys would have said. I was quite fond of the old boy and was very sorry indeed to learn of his death, which prompted a message of condolence from me to the German Embassy in London, who didn't quite know what to do with it, or rather did, but felt under diplomatic constraints, so didn't. Readers will understand that I am being very cagey about my dealings with the Generaloberst. He had been treated very badly by his own side after German reunification and was willing to talk. Even when a source has died, I am cagey about what was said, where and how often we met. Others involved may not be dead.
2. The late David Frost memorably interviewed Richard Nixon after he lost the presidency and was a good interviewer with respect - he'd have made a great barrister. His *Frost Report* brought together the 'Two Ronnies', Ronnies Barker and Corbett for the first time, together with John Cleese. In one of the better jokes from that series Frosty read out a series of spoof debt demands, including one from Volkswagen that commenced "Ve understand you hav relatives living in Germany". That was before Britain joined the EEC - you wouldn't have gotten away with a line that good between then and Brexit.
3. *Airlife,* Shrewsbury 2001.
4. The aviation aspects are dealt with very fully by Captain Bartelski in Chapter 1. We know the Abwehr were involved, using assets in the Air Ministry, indeed as Bartelski himself acknowledged they wasted no time in laying a false trail, e.g. Baron Oswald von Hoynigen-Huenebut, German Ambassador in Lisbon (and Abwehr). It's still not entirely clear however how they brought the Sunderland (W4026) down, i.e. why she departed from her planned track past Lybster and Wick. All we know is that it was nothing to do with British Intelligence. Captain Bartelski's recreation of Fl. Lt Goyen's track (at 15) looks to be spot on however and *Disasters in the Air* is an important contribution to the literature on the disaster.
5. Slab-sided and not terribly attractive, they flew nose-down for trim reasons. The Mk 1 had the wheezy Armstrong-Siddeley Tiger engine, knocking out only 795 HP. Later marks had the more powerful Merlin.
6. Potentially a very fine heavy bomber it was held back by an obstructed bomb-bay, partly thanks to the Air Ministry (which drew up the specs), a facile Air Ministry restriction on wingspan, in turn necessitating high wing incidence, in turn requiring a complex undercarriage, and the smallish, 38.7 litre (2,360 cubic inches) Bristol Hercules engines.

7. Boeing were on the problem and had reengined the 17 as the B-38, with Allison V-1710 inline engines, but given their supercharging they were a curious choice for an aircraft designed to bomb from altitude. Packard Merlins with two-stage supercharging would have been a better bet, or the Wright R-2600s, which were the powerplant of choice for the proposed YB- 20, which in turn influenced the design of the B-29.
8. Sandys was Churchill's son-in-law. Clearly neither Winston nor Diana Churchill knew that Sandys was a German asset. Judging from a conversation with his grandson, the other Winston Churchill, the old man was unaware of Sandys' treason until the day he died. He started out in the Foreign Office - no surprises there. I worked with the late MRAF Sir Michael Beetham in exposing Sandys, my first big scalp.
9. I have only ever played with one Enigma machine, a captured naval 4-rotor, at Fort Meade.
10. There is a useful graphic in Dowswell, *Introduction to the Second World War*, p. 46.
11. Refuelling At Sea.
12. German assets in London and Washington were able to arrange an 'Atlantic Gap', by starving the RAF, USAAF and USN of long-range aircraft and holding back development of mid-Atlantic bases in the Azores, Greenland and Iceland. We closed it in the end, but it took far too long and far too many ships were sunk in the meantime. The Liberator was available from 1941 and the Short Sunderland flying boat could have been reengined with the Bristol Hercules much earlier. Its massive Centaurus engined successor, the Shetland, was held back until it was too late for it to be of any use.
13. 1965, directed by Ken Annakin, with a very strong cast led by Henry Fonda. He plays a military intelligence officer, Lt-Col Kiley, who has intelligence and uses it. Harry Andrews plays Col Pritchard, who doesn't have much intelligence ('where is your evidence, Kiley?') and doesn't use what he has.
14. They'd have been instructed to drink Coca-Cola and would have given the game away. Only the CIA would drink Coca-Cola at the Munich Beer Festival.
15. As indicated, I now fully agree with my old friend Lord Elwyn-Jones that the trials were a mistake. All we were doing was settling old German scores and creating the false impression that all the Bad Guys in Germany were now dead or in prison, whereas for German intelligence it was business as usual.
16. Glavnoye Razvedyvatel'noye Upravleniye, military intelligence, very nice people.
17. The first flight, to test the airframe, was with piston engines. Martin Bowman gets it right with respect in *The World's Fastest Aircraft*, at p. 10, when he states that the Me 262 became operational on 3rd October, and correctly gives July for the Meteor, then repeats the canard that the 262 was first! No. It's a good book but there are other errors, e.g. the misidentification of the sole Comet 3, G-ANLO, as a Comet 1 on p. 32. At p. 122 the engine of the Supermarine S5 is given as a "Napier Sabre". It was of course a W-12 Napier Lion. The 24-cylinder Sabre, a super bit of kit, came rather later.

18. He wrote a number of aviation books, all excellent, but see *Aircraft Aircraft*, 3rd ed., 1972, Hamlyn. A useful article on the 'Meatbox' in *The Aeroplane*, confirming that the RAF pioneered the use of jet fighters, has helpfully been reprinted in a compendium on the Meteor, *Meteor: Britain's First Jet Powered Cold War Warrior* (Kelsey Publishing, 2012). See page 43.
19. I.e. a Rolls-Royce Merlin produced under licence by Packard in Detroit, as the V-1650. They were not exact copies and Packard introduced a number of production improvements, being more skilled at mass-production than Rolls were.
20. This is now a word, so inverted commas are not necessary. It wasn't a word until President George W. Bush invented it, but who cares? The beauty of the English language is that it is adaptable - new words are being added all the time. If you get to be President you get to invent new words. It does not however pass one internationally accepted test for new words - can you get away with them in Scrabble - for two reasons: (1) it's hyphenated and (2) too long for the board.
21. Do Not Exceed Velocity, i.e. top speed in a dive before the wings fall off.
22. Midland, Hinckley, 2000. Originally published in German in Stuttgart in 1998 by Motorbuch Verlag.
23. *Los Crimenes De Los Beunos*, by Joaquin Bochaca, Madrid: Huguin, 1982.

Part Three

THE DVD

20

1946 - 1953

The Labour Government

As we have seen, when the German spy Hartley Shawcross boasted in the House of Commons in 1946 that "we are the masters now" he was not referring to the socialists - he wasn't one - but to his own side, i.e. the Germans. Clement Attlee, portrayed as a decent, unassuming man, who pretended to like cricket[1] was in fact a paedophile. With Cabinet Office backing he was supplied with boys from *inter alia* the German-controlled Toynbee Hall in the East End. The notorious Professor Arnold Toynbee was the Germans' most successful Oxbridge recruiter.

Attlee did a lot of damage, although it could have been worse. He was spotted and eased out after the 1951 election, giving way to Churchill. Attlee supported the National Health Service, the Welfare State and railway nationalisation, not because they were good ideas (he knew perfectly well that they were bad ideas - the NHS is even worse than Obamacare) but precisely because they weren't. He was particularly anxious to weaken Britain by wasting money that could have been spent on sensible things like defence.

Well aware that Kim Il-Sung was a fellow DVD asset he did nothing to stop the North Korean invasion of South Korea on 25th June 1950, which happened on his watch. He had of course encouraged it with military weakness and support for the United Nations, which he knew perfectly well was a farce. He was a Bad Guy, with respect, but he wasn't stupid.

The United Nations

This was a particularly cunning plan of 'Jerry's', pushed hard by German assets in the Foreign Office, which was arguably less pro-British than the

German Foreign Ministry, and the State Department. Sadly, the German assets in the latter included Edward Stettinius, the Secretary of State, who thought in pretty much the same way as von Ribbentrop, although he wasn't quite as intelligent or charming.

Alger Hiss and George Kennan were other key DVD assets in Foggy Bottom. Hiss, mistaken for a communist, was very properly jailed, but for the wrong reason, i.e. the prosecution was bungled. Unfortunately, they missed Stettinius. Truman had his doubts however and forced him to resign. Fortunately for America he died an early death, on 31st October 1949, which may have been accelerated. Kennan was still doing damage in his 90s.

The idea of the UN was to recreate the failed League of Nations. It was staffed, as was the League, by German assets, starting with the first Secretary-General. He was a dodgy Australian 'polly' (a politician, not a parrott) named Evatt. The basic idea was not to let people know what was going on, but the DVD overegged the pudding in 1972 by pushing the retired Austrian war criminal Kurt Waldheim. He, with respect, never quite managed to conceal his disappointment that the Holocaust never finished its grisly business. In fairness however he never locked anybody in a basement.

The UN Charter was drafted by the DVD's John Foster Dulles. He had spent most of the war safely in Berne with his brother Allen, passing intelligence to his good friend Canaris, usually through intermediaries such as the Abwehr's Fritz Kolbe.[2] Keen to avoid a repeat of 1939, Dulles was particularly anxious to promote the idea that only the UN Security Council could authorise hostilities. The idea was that war could always be blocked by the DVD, since they were bound to exercise control over one or more of the five permanent members at any given time. That has usually been the case. This gave aggressors a free hand.

The problem was that this was not explained to the Allied Powers, none of whom ever intended to give up the ability to wage just war against an aggressor. Since the Charter was drawn up in bad faith anyway it scarcely matters. The general rule is that international instruments drawn up in bad faith, e.g. by concealment of material facts, are not binding. Left-wing international lawyers have expended a great deal of energy (not intellectual energy it has to be said) since 1945 in pretending that the UN Charter outlawed all war. There are five fundamental objections, each of them fatal on its own, to this argument:

(1) The Charter does not say that - read as a whole its language is at least equally consistent with restating the existing prohibition against waging aggressive war, not war itself.

(2) None of the Great Power signatories intended that to be the case.

(3) The opaque language of the Charter is similar to that used in the League of Nations Charter and the Kellogg-Briand pact of 1928,[3] so that on the left-wing argument World War II was illegal.

(4) State practice since 1945, in particular by the Permanent Members, has been to wage war without reference to the Security Council - on the left-wing argument the Suez, Vietnam and Falklands Wars were all illegal, and

(5) The machinery, i.e. the general staff, was never set up, largely because nobody wanted it, largely because no one could trust it to safeguard intelligence.

The CIA

"Great idea, shame about putting German spies in charge of it" would be a fairly good summary of President Truman's decision to set up the CIA in 1947. Since one of the drivers was the sneak Japanese attack on Pearl Harbor in 1941 it was more than ironic that the new agency's first director was our old friend Roscoe Henry Hillenkoetter. US Naval Attaché to Vichy France in 1940-1941 and key Axis agent at Pearl, he took up his role as Director of Central Intelligence on 24th November 1947. He had been appointed Director of the CIA's immediate predecessor, the Central Intelligence Group, earlier that year.

Rear-Admiral Hillenkoetter[4] was replaced by his fellow DVD agent General Walter Bedell Smith, who had helped Eisenhower carve up D-Day with Rommel, on 7th October 1950. He was just in time to help stuff up the Korean War. Bedell Smith had served as US Ambassador in Moscow from 1946-1949, getting on well with Stalin, unsurprisingly, since they both worked for the same man. It wasn't President Truman.

Bedell Smith was in turn replaced by yet another DVD agent, Allen Dulles, on 26th February 1953. The first American DCI, i.e. an intelligence officer who was actually working for the Americans and not just being paid by them, was the great John McCone. He was appointed by President John Fitzgerald Kennedy, leading Dulles to back Kennedy's outrageous assassination.

The DVD set up the Correa Group, based in Frankfurt, to control the CIA. Sometimes referred to as the 'CIA inside the CIA' it does battle with the Americans for control of the agency. They took a bad hit when the very able General David Petraeus was made DCI on 6th September 2011, but hit back in November 2012. The agency is still badly penetrated however, although that can be useful if you want to send the opposition, i.e. the DVD, scuttling off in the other direction.

This is how Saddam was captured, courtesy of a little false intel to the shady lady in Beirut who had his satellite phone number and was tipping him off each time we closed in on him. The little-known Central Security Service, based at Fort Meade, MD, seems to have a role in monitoring the CIA, hence its name, although officially it does nothing of the sort, indeed officially it doesn't do much at all (i.e. the boys have deniability).

Given that the CIA was initially under DVD control and that Germany had collapsed both militarily and economically (at least onshore) we would expect to see the agency sponsoring the emigration of key Germans, which is exactly what it did. The operation was called *Paperclip* and brought over a load of scientists and intelligence officers. Officially they were working for Uncle Sam. In fact, they carried on working for Germany, ditto the Germans sent to the USSR.

This is best illustrated in the US missile and space programmes. The Soviets went ahead because US technological developments, especially in guidance and telemetry, were transferred to Moscow by the DVD, even after they lost control after the departure of Stalin. This was partly because a nuclear exchange between Britain, America and Russia, i.e. the wartime Grand Alliance, was a DVD wet dream. Happily, they never worked out a way of doing it without wiping out both halves of Germany as well. In the latter stages of the Cold War some DVD analysts became concerned about the overall planetary impact of nuclear war (the theory was called 'nuclear winter').

DVD assets in what became NASA cleverly sabotaged the space programme, e.g. by insisting on pure oxygen for manned space capsules. This aided the murder of the Apollo 1 astronauts. DVD penetration of NASA has dogged the agency to the present day and directly contributed to the loss of the Space Shuttles *Columbia* and *Challenger*.

The *Amethyst* Incident

One of the DVD's most successful agents, taken over from the Abwehr, who recruited him at Peking University, was a Chinese paedophile named Mao Tse-Tung. He pretended to have come up with the idea of the 'Long March', although in fact he deferred to his German intelligence advisers. They were disguised as missionaries (always popular – if you can get nuns, even better). He also pretended to have written a book and to be an intellectual.

The Germans lost control of China after their man Sun Yat-Sen was spotted. He was replaced after a power struggle by that nice man General Chiang Kai-Shek, who in turn was defeated after a bitter civil war by Mao and the communists. Mao of course was not a communist, although he kept the pretence up pretty well and many people thought that he was. Many people think that Mitt Romney is a conservative – it is never wise to take politicians at face value.

A brutal dictator, Mao ended up knocking off more people than his onetime DVD colleague Stalin. Control of China was a bit of a misnomer in the 1920s and 1930s of course, given the circle of ancient families sitting on large stockpiles of gold, each with their own pet warlord, who tended to run affairs in their local spheres of influence. They still wield enormous influence in China, and beyond.

On 20th April 1949 the Chicoms shelled the British sloop HMS *Amethyst*[5] without provocation. She was going about her lawful occasions with the consent of the Chinese government, indeed she was steaming up the Yangtze River to the Chinese capital at Nanking. The commies of course first checked with Attlee, via Hong Kong and Edward Youde at the legation in Nanking, that it would not provoke Britain into supporting the legitimate Chinese government, as we should have done. Thirty-five sailors were murdered in all, on three ships. Youde was rewarded by the Cabinet Office with an MBE.

The C-in-C in Hong Kong was prevented by Whitehall from taking appropriate measures to relieve *Amethyst*, such as ordering HMS *London*[6] to plaster the impudent communist batteries. He could also have ordered the mighty battleship HMS *Anson* to flatten the Chicom fort at Woosong and generally make herself useful.

Attlee was keen to write off the dead sailors and recognise the communists, even though they had usurped power at the point of a gun, had been sympathetic to the Axis in World War II and were virulently anti-British. He wanted to surrender Hong Kong, including the New Territories. The Foreign Office were instructed not to seek Chicom recognition of British suzerainty over the colony in return for diplomatic recognition.

Shamefully, Hong Kong was duly surrendered when the lease on the New Territories ran out in 1997. Sir Edward Youde, as he became, had been party to the negotiations in the 1980s, before dying unexpectedly of a 'heart attack' at the Embassy in Peking.

Attlee was also anxious to facilitate the invasion of South Korea. At DVD request he transferred the powerful Rolls-Royce Nene jet engine to the USSR, to power the new Mig-15 fighter Heinkel's people were designing in Russia. They called their Nene the Klimov VK-1.

The Marshall Plan

Although some of the cash was provided to Britain and other countries the basic idea of the Marshall Plan was to use American taxpayers dollars to rebuild German industry, so that German firms could export *inter alia* to the States and take American jobs. It was an outrageous scheme, not least given that German intelligence, i.e. the DVD, was planning further aggression against an American ally, South Korea. In effect the Germans wanted American cash to help them kill Americans.

Naturally it was named after a German spy, who became Secretary of State in January 1947. Some if not all of the cash, was probably traded via Switzerland - there has never been a serious accounting of the Marshall money, any more than there is serious auditing of overseas aid today. Marshall and Canaris were cynically playing on the generosity of Americans, but neither ever really understood them, although Marshall was nominally one himself. Generosity should never be confused with weakness, a mistake America's enemies have made time and again.

The Gandhi Assassination

The top German agent in India was a chap named Jawaharlal Nehru, a lover of Lady Edwina Mountbatten, wife of India's most recent Viceroy, Lord Louis Mountbatten (him again). Mountbatten, who was gay, does not seem to have been unduly perturbed by his wife's relationship with a fellow DVD agent. He had only married her for her money in any event. The poor woman later discovered that her husband was working for the Germans, after which she died, fairly suddenly.

Canaris wanted complete control of India, but Gandhi stood in the way. He too had his contacts with German intelligence, run *inter alia* through Quaker connections in London. The Quakers can be even dodgier than the Methodists, no offence intended.

Gandhi was not however a German asset, although he understood that the Prussians had sponsored the Indian Mutiny. He was a genuine Indian nationalist, a formidable enemy of Britain and a man not without his qualities. I have only known two men who met him, when they were children, but he seems to have been a nice enough chap. Both his and Attlee's claims to be men of peace cannot be taken at face value however, given the deaths of over a million people in the bloody Partition of India. The decision to partition India was taken by Canaris, to whom Mohammed Ali Jinnah, the so-called 'founding father' of Pakistan also reported, but both Attlee and Gandhi went along with it.

Canaris, Nehru and Attlee all agreed that Gandhi had to go, and go he did. The DVD as always stayed deep in the background, using a tame Hindu nutter, Nathuram Godse. Gandhi's death was hastened by the lack of medical attention, not unlike the McKinley assassination. As planned, Nehru was the political beneficiary. That was the end of Indian independence. It had lasted just four months. Mrs Ghandi tried to get it back but she was never able to get all the DVD or Chinese assets out of the Congress Party or the stifling Indian bureaucracy. The DVD, using Sikh assets, were able to get her in the end.

Burma

Burma similarly was handed over to the DVD. Attlee made no attempt to protect the legitimate government of Burma, which was taken over by a Peking-backed military junta which has misruled the country ever since. It has been particularly harsh on those Burmese who fought for the Allies in World War II, especially the Karen, to whom Britain owes a debt of gratitude. They are not forgotten. The Chinese SIS and the DVD work closely together. Burma established a pattern whereby Peking sought to destabilise or buy up legitimate governments in the region. The idea of self-government is much anathema to Peking as it is to the DVD.

The Malayan Emergency

A similar strategy was followed in Malaya. There was a bloody terrorist insurrection in a desperate effort to bring Malaya into the Chinese orbit, billed as a 'liberation struggle'. It was years before it succeeded, using a more sophisticated strategy of having DVD assets in Whitehall hand Malaya and British North Borneo over to Peking's local political assets.

General Sir Gerald Templer, later CIGS,[7] did outstanding counter-insurgency work. Without a similarly professional counterintelligence effort in London it was largely wasted however. The British effort also lacked a strategic component. It was good on the ground, but the campaign wasn't thought through. It didn't help that the DVD's Sir Percy Sillitoe had dismantled the efficient Malayan Security Service, after a whispering campaign in Whitehall against its very good Director. Fellow former Bulldog pilot Roger Arditti has done some interesting research in this area, which I hope will be published.

Similar strategic illiteracy saw the Dutch hand the Dutch East Indies over to Chinese assets. Britain, later made the same mistake in Ireland, i.e. failing to work out which power was sponsoring an insurgency. NATO repeated it in Afghanistan. Ironically the failed British attempt to keep the Chinese out of Malaya was touted as a model for Afghanistan. At least the DVD's assets in Whitehall didn't recommend Mullah Omar for the OBE, as they did the late Chin Peng, of the Malayan Communist Party.

Terrorist insurgencies are a state-sponsored phenomenon. The first thing you do, as soon as you have an insurgency, is work out who the sponsor is. Usually it's Germany, since terrorism is a German thing, but in East and Central Africa and the Asia-Pacific region it's often China, working hand-in-glove with the DVD. There is no point in the Bad Guys launching a terrorist offensive without having assets in place in the enemy's capital to make sure that nobody works out who has launched it and why, prevent an effective counter-terrorist strategy from being implemented and limit resources to his armed forces.

The only way to prevent Peking taking over in Kuala Lumpur was to:

(1) Work out who was controlling and directing the insurgency, i.e. Peking, working with the DVD.
(2) Sort out DVD assets in London, i.e. free up the British Empire so that it could think and act strategically in the British and Western interest, which happen to be coincidental, we British being the Good Guys.
(3) Depending upon the timing of (1) and (2) enter the Chinese Civil War on the side of the Good Guys, i.e. Chiang Kai-Shek and those nice people the Kuomintang, and
(4) Ramp up defence spending, so that British forces could make a serious contribution, including bombing Peking 'flat as a pancake' using air-to-air refuelling, a splendid British invention, courtesy of Sir Alan Cobham.

If (1) and (2) took until after the communists had taken over it would have been sensible to declare war on Peking, rather than send a consul-general and pretend that Britain liked German-backed communists. In practice a war would probably have brought in North and South Korea and the United States. It probably would not have brought in Russia, as Stalin would have been too nervous of defeat, and a serious move to aid China might have provoked the GRU into moving against him sooner. There was never much love lost between the Russians and the Chinese, who have always cast envious glances over Siberia.

War broke out in the Korean Peninsula and Vietnam anyway. Since there was going to be a war in any event it ought to have been fought for a serious purpose, i.e. with a view to ensuring long-term peace in the region. Instead, we have had decades of Chinese dominance, genocide (in Cambodia) and one war, coup or insurgency after another. Malaya, Korea, Tibet, Vietnam, the Indonesian Confrontation, Burma, Laos, Cambodia, East Timor, Nepal, Thailand, Ceylon and New Guinea – the list goes on. Including the preventable slaughter in China herself the death toll has climbed well past 100,000,000.

Korea

President Truman, who was a good and decent man, sincerely believed in and wanted peace. He just wasn't able to deliver. He was a politician rather than a statesman, with respect, who was prone to telling General MacArthur, one of the finest generals of the 20th century, how to run a war, based on a less than stellar performance as an artillery officer in World War I (although in his defence he could lay down a good barrage). Effectively he decided in 1945 that it would be a good idea to have another war. That's not quite how he put it of course, and he didn't know what he was doing (which was the problem), but that was the inevitable outcome of the crass decision in 1945 to run down the American armed forces. The guard was dropped on his watch.

By 1950 the United States Navy was so small it was starting to compete with the Royal Navy, which had been slashed by Attlee. The principal differences between Attlee and Truman were that:

(1) Attlee knew what he was doing whereas Truman didn't.
(2) Attlee was a German spy whereas Truman was an American patriot.
(3) Attlee was a paedophile whereas Truman preferred to have sex with adults, usually Mrs Truman.
(4) Attlee pretended to like cricket whereas Truman pretended to like baseball.
(5) Attlee was a nasty piece of work whereas Truman was a genuinely nice man, and
(6) Truman liked dogs.

War, which had been planned since at least 1948, duly broke out, taking the Truman Administration by surprise, although very frankly it shouldn't have. Ramp-up of the seriously run-down American and British Commonwealth armed forces took far too long. The war was nearly lost in the first few months. Only a daring and brilliant amphibious landing, by General MacArthur at Inchon, saved the day.

Even Churchill saw the war as a side-show. He always had a blind spot over the Far East - it was almost his only strategic weakness. The Royal Navy's big carriers were never committed[8] and not a single RAF heavy bomber joined American B-29s in bombing Pyongyang. Hopeless!

The North Korean Mig 15s were of course flown by Luftwaffe pilots, essentially the old Me 262 boys, including Generalleutnant Gunther Rall. He was a fine fighter pilot, who bagged a number of Sabres. The jet force commander was Adolf Galland. That is why they were not allowed to fly over South Korea. With the DVD's Dwight Eisenhower in the White House making a mess of the war and the uneasy peace that followed wasn't difficult, with consequences which are all too apparent today.

The Cambridge Ring

For 60 years the sustained effort to portray Burgess, Maclean, Philby, Cairncross and Blunt as communists has not lacked for ingenuity, indeed at times it has verged on the fanciful. No one who knew them could seriously have believed it, nor would a serious counterintelligence team had one ever been assembled. As shrewder observers suspected at the time however they had heavy-duty coverage thanks to penetration of both MI5 and MI6. The defections of Burgess, Philby and Maclean were never properly investigated.

Sadly, when a small group of MI5 officers, including the late, great Peter Wright, reviewed the cases in the 1960s the basic failures to appreciate that Warburg had bankrolled the October Revolution and that German intelligence had been reorganised in 1944-1945, not dismantled, meant this team focused too tightly on the Soviet Union. The real enemy, as Mrs Thatcher started to grasp towards the end, was Germany, which did far more damage to Britain during the Cold War than the KGB could ever dream of. Since they suspected the MI5 Director-General, Sir Roger Hollis, of being KGB (they did not know about the DVD) their work was strictly unofficial. They got close however, but their own security worked against them.

They needed to open up to former MI18 officers but it was years before MI5 officers were prepared to really open up to intelligence specialists outside the salaried bureaucracy. Even now you would be amazed how difficult it is just to get a dodgy D-G's personnel file out of the building and set up a simple review conference with outside specialists with a view to getting in a replacement. Fortunately, the timeline for simple counterintelligence tasks like this is now a lot shorter than it used to be.

There has been much speculation over the years as to who the Sixth, Seventh and Eighth men of the Cambridge Ring were. The Sixth Man was Victor Rothschild, who was able to protect his Abwehr and DVD colleagues. He later introduced Peter Wright to that nice man Chapman Pincher, sadly no longer with us. The Seventh Man was Roger Hollis, who as D-G of MI5 was in an ideal position to continue the deception that Burgess, Maclean and Philby were KGB assets. The Eighth Man was Sir Stewart Menzies, wartime head of MI6, who was in an ideal position to send Philby and the others to where they could be of most use to Germany. Of course, being seen to work for the Soviet Union was cooler than being seen to work for the Third Reich, but in World War II it was the team with the swastikas and the black leather raincoats they were working for.

The Elimination of Josef Stalin

The KGB and the GRU were a bit smarter. The KGB soon worked out that Burgess and Maclean had been working for the Germans, whilst the GRU's long-held concerns about Stalin coalesced during the Korean War.

There were a number of GRU military intelligence officers in North Korea and they picked up on the German control of the Mig-15 staffeln. They had not forgotten Stalin's brutal purge of the Red Army officer corps before the war and were fully aware of the extent of German-Soviet military cooperation.

The GRU's specialist air intelligence officers were too good to buy into the phoney story about the Tu-4 being reverse-engineered. They also knew that neither they nor the KGB had assets sufficiently well placed within Boeing to be able to walk out of the Wichita plant with a complete set of blueprints of the B-29.[9] They also knew they were getting far more nuclear secrets out of the USA than the so-called 'Atom Spies' justified. The best of them understood that communism was a joke and that Germany had bankrolled the October Revolution. It wasn't a revolution at all, but a German-backed coup.

The GRU sensibly decided that Stalin had to go. It was felt that putting him on trial might pose presentational problems, so they had his doctor murder him. Stalin was a traitor, even though he was not Russian, since Georgia was part of the Soviet Union, i.e. he was a traitor to the USSR. The killing was therefore more in the nature of a fast-track, informal execution. There were some due process issues, but since Stalin didn't believe in due process, who was he to complain? It saved a lot of paperwork and they gave him a good send-off.

UFOs

There are no UFOs, no aliens have visited Earth, so far as anyone in INTELCOM is aware[10] and no aliens had autopsies performed on them at Roswell Air Force Base New Mexico. The balloon that crashed there in July 1947 was a reconnaissance balloon, 'weather' balloon being a convenient cover story. There is nothing particularly mysterious about Area 51 in Nevada, which was one of the code names assigned to Groom Dry Lake. It was just a secret CIA test facility, that's all.[11]

In 1950 a retired Marine Corps intelligence officer and pilot, Major Donald Keyhoe, who had worked with Colonel Lindbergh (his intelligence work was covert) published *Flying Saucers Are Real.* This was at the behest of the DVD's Roscoe Hillenkoetter, to lend an air of military support to the UFO scare, the first intelligence cover-up in history to create a B-movie genre and its own TV series.[12] Some clues as to what Roscoe was hoping to cover up can be found in the postwar c.v. gaps of Germany's leading aircraft designers. No intelligence officer likes gaps in cvs. They create work.

Kurt Tank, designer of the Fw 200 Condor and Fw 190 fighter – which was the one you wanted to fly if you were a hot-shot Luftwaffe fighter jock - went walkies to Argentina in 1945. He then went to German- controlled India in 1955, where he worked for years. In all that time he allegedly designed just two planes.

Dr-Ing Siegfried Gunter, Heinkel's brilliant chief designer, responsible for the world's first jet aircraft, the He 178, and the Mig-15 (the DVD assigned him to Mig in 1948 after the decision was taken to invade Korea), has a very thin official design record as well. So does Junkers' Dipl-Ing Ernst Zindel. He designed the Ju 52 transport, the Ju 87 Stuka and the Ju 88 dive-bomber/night-fighter, yet after 1945 was a "guest lecturer" at the Technical Academy at Mulheim.[13] No doubt he was, but what was he doing the rest of the time?

A clue is to be bound in the *Centaurus* incident. On 29th June 1954 Captain James Howard, First Officer Lee Boyd and all nine other crew members of BOAC's Boeing 377 Stratocruiser *Centaurus*[14] observed seven objects, one of them larger than the others, under control, tracking their aircraft, for about 80 nautical miles. This was on a flight from Idlewild to Heathrow.

UFO reports from non-trained observers can almost invariably be discounted. Some have even been of the planet Venus, not so much a UFO as an MIP, or Mis-Identified Planet. The report was confirmed by Goose Bay radar. The flying objects in question were nothing to do with American or Canadian military projects. They were almost certainly radio-controlled drones under test, unless the DVD were planning to bring down the Stratocruiser and were put off by Captain Howard's radio alert to Goose Bay Approach Control. When the full story of the DVD's black aerospace projects is revealed, it will make interesting reading.

In his second book, *Flying Saucers From Outer Space*, which was semi-officially endorsed by the USAF, Major Keyhoe claimed that BOAC Comet G-ALYV Yoke Victor[15] had been brought down by a mid-air collision. Yoke Victor, which disintegrated in mid-air near Calcutta on 2nd May 1953, is the mystery Comet. We know that the other Comet 1 crashes were caused by over-rotation on take-off, inducing compressor stall and loss of power, by pilots used to piston-engine prop-liners, i.e. pilot error, and IEDs planted by the DVD (see the next chapter).

Aside from the basics (location of crash site, number of dead and so on) we can discount the crash report, which was produced by the corrupt Indian civil aviation authorities at a time when the Indian Prime Minister was a DVD asset. It is no more helpful than the later Cohen Report, pushed out after yet another musical comedy inquiry. It failed to identify the correct causes of the loss of Comets Yoke Peter and Yoke Yoke. The Indians are still at it, to judge from the phoney report into the loss of AI172 at Ahmedabad.

It looks as though Major Keyhoe - who had extensive air intelligence connections - was right. Cowell[16] asserts that the Air Ministry originally attributed the loss of Yoke Victor to an "unidentified flying body". Unfortunately, the public obsession with UFOs and extra-terrestrials has muddied the waters. Keyhoe's own credibility was undermined by focusing on extra-terrestrial i.e. unreal, as opposed to terrestrial, i.e. real, origins of unknown aircraft. Whilst there are no UFOs in the B-movie sense, piloted by little green men, there are black aircraft projects. These are both Good Guy, like the CIA's U-2 and SR-71A, i.e. 'white hat' black, and Bad Guy, i.e. 'black hat' black.

Although Yoke Victor was in a storm cell there was no distress call. She had the power and rate of climb to get out of the way of bad weather. That was one of the jet's main attractions after all. Such discussion as there has been of her loss (she had 43 souls aboard) has been coloured by ignorant anti-Comet and anti-de Havilland prejudice. Much of this has no doubt flowed from uncritical acceptance of the with respect facile conclusions of the Royal Aircraft Establishment and Cohen enquiries and the 'square window' nonsense.

This was repeated on British television, on 24th February 2013, by Channel Four, not a channel to miss an opportunity to bash the British aviation industry, in a drama documentary entitled *A Great British Air Disaster*. The sound commentary was spouting nonsense about 'square' windows whilst the video showed actual footage of passengers enjoying a delicious BOAC meal in flight, with the rounded corners of the 'square' windows clearly visible. The commentary then went on to talk about 'windows' in the cabin roof, when what they meant to refer to were the ADF aerial panels. As we shall see in Chapter 21 the breakup sequence of Comet Yoke Peter did *not* commence at the windows. It was only the *test* hull which started to break up at the windows, under abnormally high pressures, rendering the test meaningless.

Officially the Calcutta Comet's port horizontal stabiliser broke off due to a down-gust. That does not explain the absence of a Mayday call, however. It was not as though her HF aerial was attached to the stabiliser. She had VHF radio anyway.[17] There was no of evidence of stress on the starboard stabiliser - it must have been a very localised gust. Brand new aircraft don't disintegrate in mid-air just because they lose a single stabiliser, albeit that recovery is difficult (impossible of course if both stabilisers are lost).[18]

Although mid-air break-up quickly followed the initial impact she should have had time to get out a Mayday call. As with Air France AF447 56 years later both the air traffic control and guard frequencies were probably jammed, indeed the absence of a Mayday call suggests they were.

Bearing in mind that there would have been full cooperation from Nehru, it looks as though Yoke Victor was brought down after a collision with a radio-operated drone, possibly operated from another aircraft rather than the ground, diving down onto the Comet from above and behind. The Minister for Civil Aviation, Alan Lennox-Boyd, a Chamberlain supporter, was yet another DVD asset and would have looked the other way if told, just like Nehru.

Sadly, the murder of another 43 British subjects was not something that would have troubled either Nehru or Whitehall unduly. They'd just knocked over a million or so by backing the DVD's plan to partition India. It certainly would not have troubled the DVD, which did not accept the 1945 surrender, i.e. drew no distinction between war and peace. It believes in permanent war, which is why there cannot be peace until it is closed down. It has never drawn a distinction between waging war on the military or civilians.

The Bermuda Triangle has been another favourite with the DVD's Propaganda Department. The original idea was to cover up the sabotage of Avro Tudors G-AHNP *Star Tiger* and G-AGRE *Star Ariel* of British South American Airways, run by that great pilot, Air-Vice Marshal Don Bennett, of Pathfinder fame. 'Jerry' was quite keen to go after poor old Don Bennett of course, given the number of bombs his boys made sure hit the target.

Sadly, the Tudor got an unfair reputation and did not sell well. That was the whole point of course of blowing a couple of them up over the Caribbean. The 'Triangle' idea caught on and inspired a number of breathless documentaries, as well as providing good material for one of the opening scenes in George Lucas's *Close Encounters of the Third Kind*. The first Avro Tudor to be sabotaged of course was the prototype, on 23rd August 1947, assassinating the designer, the great Roy Chadwick. The 'Janet & John' explanation for the public was that the aileron control circuit had been incorrectly assembled, as though Avro didn't know one end of an aileron from another.

The Mossadeq Assassination

As explained, one of the disadvantages of working for the DVD is that they are the Bad Guys. If you try and hold out on them you may end up dead. This happened to a dodgy Iranian 'polly' named Mohammad Mossadeq, who had nationalised BP at German request. Mossadeq met with the DVD's Phillip

Allen, then in the Treasury, who was sent out from London, ostensibly to talk to him about switching selling oil from sterling to dollars. The DVD at that time was targeting the British economy. Britain's ability to buy oil in sterling was a serious concern for them.

Mossadeq was assassinated in a joint operation by CIA and MI6, which was later leaked, so that Britain and America would get the blame. Oil conspiracies are popular - *c.f.* the Iraq War - and it was a great stick with which to beat London and Washington. The targeting assignment came from Dachau and the assassination was overseen by DVD assets in both agencies. Patriotic officers in each agency should have rejected the idea for the offensive nonsense it was, but like all DVD initiatives it came from high up the payroll.

1. It was put about that when he had a teletype machine installed in Downing Street it was just for the cricket scores. He knew one end of a bat from another, but the game was far too English for his liking.
2. The subject of an interesting book by Luca Delattre, *Fritz Kolbe, The Second World War's Most Important Spy*. He was a spy, but not an important one. Delattre with respect also gets the side he was working for wrong - it was the Axis, not the Allies. In fairness it's a mistake anyone could make. Lots of people thought the Dulles brothers were working for the Americans.
3. Frank Kellogg, nothing to do with the Fruit Loop family, was then Secretary of State and a man with a dodgy future with respect - he won the Nobel Peace Prize, generally only awarded to those who encourage wars through weakness, or bomb Cambodia. He then became a judge on the Permanent Court of International Justice, at a time when it was virtually a committee of German intelligence. Aristide Briand, a German asset, was the French Foreign Minister, a failed former Prime Minister and supporter of the Washington Treaty. Hailed as a man of peace he agreed with and supported Pétain's decision to sacrifice the flower of the French army at Verdun. He was only opposed to killing Germans. He was quite happy to sacrifice French lives.
4. He was promoted to Vice-Admiral on 9th April 1956.
5. Modified *Black Swan* class sloop, 1,350 tons, 6 4-inch DP guns. She was unnecessarily reclassified as a frigate in order to sow confusion.
6. A modernised *County* class heavy cruiser she mounted 8 8-inch guns and used properly would have given the commies something to mull over. There was enough water under her keel, indeed she was actually opened fire at one point, but the last thing Attlee wanted was the full firepower of a *County* class cruiser unleashed on the communist batteries. Indirect fire using aircraft from Hong Kong to report the fall of shot should have been tried. It was a shame for *London* as she'd had a quiet war and hadn't killed many Germans.
7. Chief of the Imperial General Staff.
8. The only British and Australian carriers which saw service in Korea were *Colossus* class light carriers - fine ships, originally intended by the Admiralty for trade protection, but too small to make a real difference in Korea, which is why they were called *light* carriers. The Navy really needed the cancelled 45,000-ton *Malta* class, *Malta, Gibraltar* and *New Zealand*.
9. Each plant had minor variations and tended to make one block. Even minor differences needed a new set of blueprints. Unlike Consolidated, whose prints were a bit of a mess, Boeing tended to knock up a new set of prints for each block. This made it easier for counterintelligence officers to backtrack and isolate the source of the leak. The woman in Wichita later became a senior bank officer in a German-influenced bank.
10. Obviously, no one can be quite sure what happened in prehistory but there is nothing in the fossil record that shouldn't be there. This is not to say that there aren't intelligent beings in the universe - the number of habitable planets is likely to be vast even in our own galaxy, the Milky Way. It is wildly improbable that life has not developed elsewhere and it would be the height of conceit to

assume that we are alone in the universe, indeed we cannot be sure that there is only one universe. We have known for decades however that there is no intelligent life elsewhere in the solar system, assuming for the sake of argument that the search for intelligent life on Earth has been successful.

11. My favourite Area 51 story, which I heard from someone who was there, concerns the landing of the U-2 prototype (paid for, somewhat unusually, by a cheque sent by the CIA to designer Kelly Johnson's home address) after her first test flight. Everybody had forgotten that as the day warmed up so would the runway and when Tony LeVier brought her back in she just floated above the runway. He thereupon invented the recommended landing technique for the U-2 - i.e. don't bother landing it, just stall the darn thing onto the deck.
12. *The X-Files*, starring David Duchovny and the lovely Gillian Anderson, fine actors both (they had to be, to keep a straight face).
13. Herwig and Rode, *op. cit.* p. 41.
14. The incident is described by Cowell, in his book on the Comet, at pp. 34-5.
15. C/n 6008, first flown on 9th April 1952 and delivered to BOAC on the 23rd (Davies & Birtles, p. 21).
16. *Op. cit.*, p 34.
17. In the Comet the VHF control box was on the overhead panel, on the captain's side, but within reach of the First Officer, adjacent to the ILS control panel.
18. It will depend on the design of the controls and the extent of the damage as to whether the opposite elevator is available - both the Indian and RAE reports into the loss of Yoke Victor were pretty basic and from recollection this issue is not addressed. In the war bombers were able to get back on one elevator. If you apply full up or down elevator you will get a rolling moment around the longitudinal axis but you can counter that with opposite aileron. You can also adjust your rate of descent with power, which you do anyway. The over-control theory was a bit silly. Lots of aircraft have light controls but experienced pilots don't snatch at the yoke. The storm was severe but not out of the ordinary in the tropics at that time of year.

21

The Comets

The Comet

The de Havilland DH106 Comet was the world's first jetliner. A thing of grace and beauty, it represented the state of the art in civil aircraft design when it burst upon an astonished world in July 1949. With swept-wings,[1] new high-strength alloys, chemical bonding, air-conditioning, cabin pressurisation, tricycle undercarriage with bogie main gear, the latest radio navigation aids, integral fuel tanks, pressurised underwing refuelling and fully-powered (not just hydraulically boosted) flight controls it was an advanced and safe aircraft. The Comet was capable of flying high above the weather at up to 40,000 ft, although BOAC aircraft typically cruised at 36,000.

Her speed - 490 mph - was comfortably above the American competition, even if she was not twice as fast as some writers have claimed. Both the elegant Lockheed Super Constellation and Douglas DC-7, with over 12,000 HP available, depending upon variant, were capable of cruising with a full payload at over 300 mph. Typical cruising speeds for the Comet 1 were about one-third to one-half above contemporary piston-engine airliners. Typical cruising altitudes were about one-half higher, save for the Boeing Stratocruiser, which had a ceiling of 35,000 ft and could cruise at 27,000.

The aircraft was far ahead of the competition, with a larger Rolls-Royce Avon-engine[2] version (the Comet 2) coming up behind, and plans for a transatlantic version. It threatened sales of up to 1,000 aircraft, most of them denominated in US dollars. Canaris was badly worried. He tasked SS-Standartanführer Otto Skorzeny, head of the DVD's Sabotage Section, with wrecking the Comet program as early as 1946, after de Havilland shifted their emphasis from a jet mail-plane to a more threatening airliner.

The Switch to IEDs

Skorzeny's first plan, as we have seen, was to use high-speed jet-powered radio-controlled drones to ram the Comets from above and behind. The jet engine selected was probably the Rolls-Royce Nene, which as we saw in Chapter 20 was handed over to the Soviets and the Germans by 'von' Attlee. With some 5,000 lbs static thrust available there would have been enough power. Attacking from behind there was less risk of the drone being seen, whilst jamming the control and guard frequencies would prevent Mayday calls.

This could only be done over German-controlled territory such as India however, as there was a risk of the drone parts being found with the wreckage if there were to be a good faith accident investigation. Admittedly these are rare in the case of aircraft sabotaged by the DVD, but they could not guarantee total control of an investigation. Moreover, the drones could only be used with cloud cover. There is some evidence that Air Intelligence were alerted to a drone attack on Comet Yoke Victor and started to prepare radio countermeasures.

A further problem with using drones was that they could not be launched vertically, even with rocket booster engines. (The Comet, by the way, was not only the first airliner in the world to employ jet engines, but also the first to trial rocket boosting.[3]) Their launch sites were therefore vulnerable to air reconnaissance. This became even more of an issue when the high-flying English Electra Canberra entered service - they couldn't be caught by the Red Air Force,[4] let alone the Indian Air Force. In fact, the Indians were so impressed that they bought some, and used them for 50 years. The drones could also be tracked by radar, as we saw in the last chapter with the BOAC Stratocruiser incident.

Skorzeny usually reported to von Lahousen in Dachau rather than Herr Admiral, who spent a lot of time in the late 40s and early 50s in Madrid. He had to keep a low profile, since officially he was dead. The Standartranführer and von Lahousen switched tack to blowing up Comets with IEDs, using the new plastic explosives betrayed to the Abwehr in the war by the weapons scientist Richard Beeching. He was one of their pet mad scientists, as we have seen.

However, five basic problems confronted Skorzeny and Hertzog, whom he placed in charge of the squad that was to get the IEDs onto the planes:

(1) The Comet used advanced, high strength DTD 564/L73 and 746C/L90 alloys and Redux chemical bonding, i.e. it was an exceptionally strong aircraft and required a correspondingly

powerful explosive charge to destroy it. As with all IEDs the larger they are the easier they are to detect. As it was large sections of Yoke Peter survived the blast, indeed the tail section was so strong that it stayed largely intact during a fall from 27,000 ft, high-speed impact with the water and subsequent settling on the seafloor. Skorzeny arranged for DVD assets in Paris to have Air France put in a joke order for three Comet 1As, for which the airline appears to have been compensated via a Swiss bank via a Medium Term Note programme run out of Zurich,[5] so as to allow Hertzog to examine the Comet's structure during overnight stops in Beirut.

(2) Getting the IEDs onto the plane. They really needed an airport under German control but the Comets were not scheduled to fly to Germany, and it would have attracted suspicion in any event. They alighted on Rome, where an ex-fascist general and former Mussolini supporter was put in charge of airport 'security', the aviation equivalent of having Charles Manson as your babysitter.

(3) Fusing. This was eventually solved using a barometric fuse. Apparently, they still hadn't worked out why the IED on Hitler's Fw 200 out of Smolensk had failed to go off, but they had learned their lesson.[6]

(4) Getting the timing right so that the aircraft would blow up over deep water. Here the DVD underestimated the Royal Navy and the new underwater TV cameras, as the water off Elba, where Yoke Peter went down, was no longer too deep to permit recovery, and

(5) Controlling the British investigation so that they wouldn't get caught, else the war would be back on and there would 500 RAF heavy bombers (Lincolns in 1954) blitzing the Ruhr to bits. In the events which happened they were very lucky with the egocentric empire-builder (no offence intended) Arnold Hall, director at RAE Farnborough and the judge, Lord Cohen, carefully chosen by DVD assets, including George Coldstream, in the Lord Chancellor's Department. Lord Cohen was a nice chap, with respect, but he was being blackmailed over his homosexuality. The DVD already had an asset - John Argyris FRS - in place[7] in place in Britain's aeronautical research establishment, who had put his name to a piece of junk science conveniently predicting that the Comets would break up in the air due to metal fatigue.[8] Of course their man Mountbatten was C-in-C Mediterranean and would be in overall charge of the search for bodies and wreckage.

The Attack on Yoke Peter

The first aircraft selected for attack was Comet Yoke Peter,[9] on 10th January 1954. War hero Captain Alan Gibson DFC was in command, assisted by W. J. Bury as First Officer, Engineer Officer F. C. Macdonald, Radio Officer L. P. McMahon, Steward F. L. Saunders and Stewardess Jean Clark.[10] As with the *Athenia* 15 years earlier the Germans wanted dead children for the psychological shock value. Flight BA781 was selected because it was carrying children to school in England after the Christmas 'holidays'. No fewer than 10 of the 35 souls aboard were children. The murdered passengers included the distinguished Australian war correspondent Chester Wilmot, then living in Aylesbury,[11] who joined the flight in Rangoon, but I do not think that he was targeted. Although the DVD Head of Station Rome had a full passenger list BA781 was designated for destruction by the DVD before the list became known. It is not even clear that Wilmot bought his ticket before von Lahousen met privately with West German Chancellor Konrad Adenauer in Bonn on or about 5th January to obtain his sanction to destroy the aircraft and murder her passengers and crew. No doubt Adenauer showed von Lahousen a copy of the latest issue of *Time* magazine, which had just made Adenauer Man of the Year, although it is doubtful that *Time* were aware of the full extent of his intelligence connections and criminality.

Since the sabotage of Yoke Peter was carried out by German agents working for the principal West German intelligence agency, with the full knowledge and informed consent of the Federal West German Government, and Yoke Peter was an unarmed civilian aircraft going about her lawful occasions in international airspace, her destruction was an Act of War by West Germany against Great Britain. Britain would have been fully justified in issuing an immediate Declaration of War and resuming hostilities.

Access to the Comet on the ground at Rome was simplicity itself, bearing in mind that there was full co-operation from the airport authorities, not that security at Rome was anything to write home about anyway. Hertzog, apparently disguised as one of the refuellers, himself placed the IED in Yoke Peter's lower cargo hold, apparently fused for 8,000 metres (the 'Hun' uses metric), about 26,250 ft. Although the aircraft did not break up until she reached about Flight Level (FL) 270, or 27,000 ft, we would expect her to climb a little way beyond the fusing point. Detonation, heard from the ground (three separate explosions were heard, consistent with the initial blast, a secondary explosion, probably of fuel - the aircraft was seen by eyewitnesses to be on fire - and hull breakup) was at around 1058 local time, 0958 Zulu.

Jamming of the control and guard frequencies appears to have commenced shortly before the blast, after the last routine radio message, preventing Radio Officer McMahon from broadcasting a Mayday. The Sabotage Section chose the lower cargo hold partly because shrapnel damage and the shockwave would trip the generators and cut the power supply to the radios in any event, without time for the battery backup to kick in. The aircraft crashed about 10 miles south of Porto Azzurro on the island of Elba, settling in about 80 fathoms.

The only passenger to cancel his flight to London, and at the last moment at that, with his bags already packed, was the Hollywood-based film producer Victor Pahlen, who had been filming *Amante di Paride.*[12] He is not suspected of any connection to the sabotage. He may however have been tipped off not to join the flight by William Colby, then the CIA Head of Station Rome, who at the very least was aware that a major German intelligence operation was underway in Rome.

Pahlen claimed to be in a hurry, in which case he would have taken the Comet, the fastest airliner in the world. BA781 had eleven seats spare including his. Why would he take a later, slower flight? Bill Colby's report on the sabotage to CIA Director Dulles is still classified. Suffice to say I have never known anyone in the CIA to cling to the 'square window/metal fatigue' theory after being referred to Colby's report.

The CIA were not, repeat not, involved in the attack. Since Colby was not DVD (he probably picked up word that something was going down and that BOAC were the target from his contacts at the Vatican, which were good) there is not the slightest reason to suppose that he was in possession of the full facts prior to the sabotage. I am sure that he was unaware that his Director, Dulles, was a German double agent. The idea that the Dulles brothers were working for America was pervasive in 1954.

Bill Colby - who was disgracefully assassinated by the DVD on 27th April 1996[13] - was good people, known to several friends of mine. They of course included Bill's distinguished CIA colleague Dick Walters. It is perfectly clear that Bill was instructed to disregard the intelligence he had about a possible attack on a BOAC Comet out of Rome and not pass on a warning to the MI6 Head of Station, nor dear old 'Tiny' Cooling, a distinguished former Wellington and Warwick pilot.[14] Tiny, sadly no longer with us, was the BOAC Station Manager at Rome and a first-rate chap, absolutely out of the top drawer. He knew Captain Gibson, another distinguished ex-RAF pilot, with over 5,500 hours in his logbook, 4,267 of them with BOAC. Tiny would not have dreamt of not passing on intelligence that a bomb had been placed on board.

Sabotage investigation experts do not like airliners disappearing out of the same airport shortly after another one has been blown up. It would be interesting to know if the CIA had anyone on the Philippine Airlines Douglas DC-6, which went in on the Thursday after the disaster. That crash has got to be worth a second look.

Just about every intelligence agency with a station in Rome would have known by then that the Comet had been blown up. Local eyewitnesses had stated that they had heard three explosions and saw the aircraft crash in flames. The autopsies revealed lacerations of the lower limbs of the passengers "as if from a powerful explosion from below",[15] and the bodies showed signs of burning (ludicrously put down to 'sunburn' by the Italian authorities[16]). Since there was 8/8 cloud-cover over the crash site it wasn't quite clear whether the Italians were putting this down to the sun or sunlamps.

The aircraft, conveniently, had been brought down over deep water. She had not reached cruising altitude, indeed was some 9,000 ft below it, so cabin pressure would have been a comparatively low 5 psi, less than half an atmosphere, scarcely enough to blow an aircraft apart.[17] Security at Rome, courtesy of your friendly local former fascist, was a standing joke. Every serious intelligence officer in Rome, would have reported to their agency that this was a bomb, indeed the local INTELCOM would have been buzzing.

No spook who wished to retain the respect of their peers and not have them laughing into their spaghetti would have been rushing around Rome bending paperclips and talking about 'metal fatigue', especially not on an almost brand-new aircraft. Yoke Peter had barely 3,605 hours on her. What's more, she was a Comet, the most extensively tested airliner in history.

Group Captain W. K. Stewart of the RAF Medical Establishment, Sir Harold Whittingham, BOAC Director of Medical Services, Dr A. S. R. Peffers, his deputy and other distinguished doctors reviewed the medical evidence, which clearly pointed to an explosive device. Equally clearly, the Italian authorities were putting pressure on the doctors who had conducted the initial autopsies, in fairness to them in good faith. A major cover-up was underway.

The Italian investigation, led by General Coppi, was almost as much a farce as Lord Cohen's later, with respect, musical comedy inquiry in London. It looks as though Sir Gilmour Jenkins, the Permanent Secretary at the Ministry of Transport and Civil Aviation and his deputy, Sir George Cribbett, were involved. Lennox-Boyd, still smarting from Germany's defeat in World War II, certainly was, although he may only have been brought fully into the loop after Yoke Peter was blown up.

The BOAC fleet was minutely inspected for fatigue cracks. Unsurprisingly, since the Comet was a strong aircraft and the loss of Yoke Peter was nothing to do with metal fatigue, none were found. Very properly, Comet operations resumed. The problem was that Intelligence had not found out who had placed the IED and nothing was done to prevent a recurrence, apart from a slight tightening up of security. Lennox-Boyd coldly informed the DVD that he would need another aircraft blown up before he could get away with suspending the Comet's Certificate of Airworthiness.

The Attack on Yoke Yoke

Lennox-Boyd's indication posed problems for von Lahousen and Skorzeny, who were understandably reluctant to blow up a second Comet out of Rome. To paraphrase Oscar Wilde, having two Comets disappear out of the same airport would start to look like carelessness. They were short of airports on Comet routes, however. Neither the Indian nor Lebanese governments would have been happy to have such an obvious sabotage conducted on their soil. Singapore was under British control. Moreover, they needed deep water within 30 minutes flying time of the airport to prevent any possibility of the wreckage being examined, which ruled out Beirut eastbound. Calcutta was out, both eastbound and westbound.

Italy was pretty much a German client state, indeed it was about to be absorbed into the EEC. It rather looks as though Guiseppe Pella, the Prime Minister, was not willing to allow another Comet to be sabotaged on Italian soil. At any rate he was eased out and replaced by the more malleable Amintore Fanfani on 18th January. Then a few weeks later he went, and Mario Scelba came in. With the amount of cash the DVD had to splash around, thanks to its Swiss MTN programmes, 'Jerry' had plenty of Italian officials on the payroll, not least at Ciampino Airport, by now the world's most dangerous. Italian Prime Ministers are not that expensive, sadly. The decision was taken to use Rome again.

BOAC Comet Yoke Yoke[18] (operated jointly with South African Airways), with only 2,704 hours on the airframe, was destroyed by another IED, again placed by Hertzog in the lower cargo hold, on 8th April 1954, again at around FL270, off Stromboli. She was blown up about the same time after take-off as Yoke Peter. This time there would be no partial recovery of the wreckage, apart from a few pathetic pieces.

There was however a military response. Naval and Air Intelligence both wanted to recover the bodies for a proper post-mortem examination, i.e. one the Italians couldn't nobble. The fleet aircraft carrier HMS *Eagle* was sortied from Malta, with a powerful surface combatant, HMS *Daring*,[19] as escort. As Senior British Officer Captain Holland-Martin DSO DSC on *Eagle* was instructed by London to take any measures he considered necessary to prevent interference from the Italian Navy with the recovery of the bodies.

With one of the most powerful aircraft carriers in the world, with a fully worked up air group, steaming at full speed to the scene of the disaster (announced to the world by a radio station in Hamburg – no surprise there) the Italians wisely backed down. They'd seen what the British Navy could do at the Battle of Matapan in 1941.

The DVD had been taken by surprise by the Royal Navy's ability to locate and recover much of the wreckage of Yoke Peter, using new underwater TV technology. That's why they switched to a flight going south. The designated kill zone was over water around 500 fathoms deep. The wreckage of Yoke Yoke still has not been recovered. Twenty-one passengers were murdered, and Lennox-Boyd had the pretext he needed to pull the Comet's Certificate of Airworthiness.

The Cover-Up

The ambitious Arnold Hall at Farnborough was tasked with 'investigating' the disasters. The reality was that RAE started with its conclusion - metal fatigue - and worked back, i.e. it was not a scientific investigation. As we have seen it was penetrated by the DVD from the beginning. It was not intelligence led, nor did it seriously examine any of the evidence, such as the eyewitness reports of explosions and the initial autopsy findings, revealing penetrating wounds to the lower limbs of passengers seated adjacent to the lower cargo hold, which pointed strongly towards an IED.

The DVD was nowhere mentioned, indeed RAE were unaware of its existence, let alone the crucial fact that it was the world's only intelligence agency with a specialist sabotage section. In effect RAE were intelligence illiterate, which was fine, or would have been had they sought to fill in this wide gap in their knowledge and expertise by bringing in a serious air intelligence officer such as Lord Trenchard, or Bill Johns, or a specialist in the DVD such as Ian Fleming. Both Bill and Ian would have been much better employed investigating the Comets than writing novels, however entertaining and well informed they were. At least Ian got the idea for his next novel, which he called *Moonraker.*

Although the Navy had recovered much of the wreckage of Yoke Peter, they had not recovered the critical section, the lower cargo hold, where the IED had detonated, for the very obvious reason that it had been destroyed in mid-air. The absence of almost the entire airframe around the lower cargo hold does not seem to have troubled the allegedly enquiring minds at RAE, supposedly the world's leading experts in air disaster investigation, in the slightest.

They were unable to examine the wreckage of Yoke Yoke at all. Farnborough never stopped to ask themselves whether it was more than a coincidence that after new technology allowed recovery of much of the first set of wreckage at unprecedented depths, the second aircraft should break up over some of the deepest water in the Mediterranean.

Their with respect facile report was bounced on de Havilland at the Court of Inquiry, held from 19th October to 24th November 1954. It was never forensically tested, not that there would have been much chance of that anyway with the DVD's Sir Hartley Shawcross representing them. No surprise there, either. De Havilland had been told they could have Sir Hartley Shawcross or Shawcross, Sir Hartley, if they wanted the RAF Comet 2 order.

There was no chance of the issue ever coming before a jury, i.e. of a serious factual inquiry. The inquiry judge refused to blame de Havilland. He managed with respect to persuade himself that the aircraft had been negligently designed, without any question of negligence on the part of the designers. This was nonsense on stilts of course. Had an aircraft being operated 13,000 feet below its ceiling blown up of its own accord due to metal fatigue after just 2,704 hours of operation of course the manufacturer would have been liable and rightly so. Neither disaster however was anything to with metal fatigue.

The Problems with the Farnborough Report

The RAE report was flawed with respect for *inter alia* the following 18 reasons:

(1) The test fuselage, Yoke Uncle, fractured at the windows, i.e. did not fracture at the alleged breakup point of Yoke Peter (no one knew where the breakup sequence of Yoke Yoke commenced as its wreckage was never examined), an ADF panel on the cabin roof.

(2) RAE allowed themselves to be diverted along an interesting but irrelevant line of inquiry - stress build-up at the corners of the windows - when there was no evidence that Yoke Yoke had commenced breakup at any window. Examination of Yoke Peter's wreckage confirmed that the windows were *intact* when the hull breakup sequence commenced.

(3) They failed to account for the absence of any evidence of fatigue in the wreckage recovered by the Royal Navy from the waters off Elbe.

(4) They assumed good faith on the part of the Italian Government and therefore failed to establish a chain of evidence linking the one part that showed signs of fatigue - the ADF panel - with Yoke Peter, the panel having been supplied by the Italian Government, which claimed that the Royal Navy had missed it.

(5) They failed to ask themselves how the Royal Navy could have missed the ADF panel when they had conducted a most thorough search of the seabed and recovered far smaller parts, including the skin near the ADF panel.

(6) They failed to conduct even the most cursory checks on the ADF panel, e.g. to see whether it came off a (British) Comet 1 or (French) Comet 1A, nor did they ask for an audit of ADF panels on the French Comet fleet.

(7) They gave insufficient weight, indeed scarcely considered at all, the informed opinion of the Royal Canadian Air Force, which had been operating Comet 1s[20] to the limits of their envelope on bomber simulation runs for NORAD and rightly rejected the metal fatigue theory.

(8) They lied to the Cohen Inquiry about the number of equivalent hours Yoke Uncle had spent in the test tank, which was probably nearer 23,500,[21] including existing hours on the airframe, rather than the 9,000 hours they claimed. On the most favourable view to RAE the true number of hours was at least 15,000.

(9) They failed to supervise the test tank adequately at night and in particular they were unable to say what pressure the test fuselage was subject to, as they kept inadequate records, rendering their test meaningless. This failure was all the more remarkable as the only known visual record of the pressure (the gauge being caught in a corner of some newsreel footage) shows it some way above 8.5 p.s.i., which was equivalent to a cruise setting.

(10) They failed to take adequate account of de Havilland's own tank-testing, at 11 p.s.i., i.e. at an overpressure, which showed that the Comet fuselage had a safe fatigue life of 40,000 hours of normal operation. Had they asked themselves why there was such a large discrepancy, i.e. had Arnold Hall with respect spent less time sleeping and more time finding out what was happening at night in his own establishment, they might have discovered that their test fuselage was being subject to extreme pressures in order to accelerate a fracture.

(11) In particular, having rejected the only previous tank test, although it had been supervised by the Air Registration Board, which needed to be satisfied that the Comet 1 was safe for extended operations at 40,000 ft, partly on the grounds that it was not a 'least of three', they failed to apply their own reasoning, such as it was, to their own test. On their own analysis they needed a third test, to add to the 9,000 and 40,000 hour figures they already had, although of course their 9,000-hour figure was a phoney.

(12) They failed to account for absence of cracks in the rest of the BOAC fleet.

(13) They failed to ask themselves why only British Comets suffered metal fatigue, which knows no national boundaries, although the UAT Comets were operated on similar African schedules to BOAC's aircraft. Why should only British-registered aircraft have suffered from metal fatigue?

(14) They knew that the wings should crack first, as they were subject to greater cyclical pressures, as confirmed by their own tests on Yoke Uncle, yet they failed to account for the fact that Yoke Peter's wings were subject to regular inspection and no fatigue cracks were found.

(15) They failed adequately to take account of the fact that cabin pressure drops immediately the hull is breached, i.e. they assumed a continuous pressure on the remainder of the airframe when pressure was rapidly reducing due to the breach, nor did they adequately explain why a not very large breach in the cabin ceiling, would have led to a hull breakup sequence so fast the radio officer was unable to get off a Mayday call. Their famous 'simulation' using a small explosive charge was simply unscientific.

(16) They failed to explain how decompression could be so explosive at such a low altitude - about FL270 (in both cases), or around 5 psi.

(17) They failed to ask themselves why the French authorities did not insist on a major redesign of the Sud-Aviation Caravelle, which was being designed with extensive assistance from de Havilland and used the Comet forward fuselage, with the same skin thickness and alloys (nearly 300 Caravelles were built with fuselages which did not differ all that much from the Comet 1 - so far from suffering metal fatigue the aircraft were robust in service and were operated in Africa for years). The French of course knew full well that the Comets, had been blown up by the Germans and there was nothing wrong with its structure, and

(18) With respect, it was bollocks.

Some Comet Myths Busted

So much nonsense has been talked about the Comets over the years, that it may be helpful to bust a few myths, with apologies to Jamie and the old team from *Mythbusters*:

(1) The Comet 1 did not have square windows - they were square with rounded edges.

(2) There was nothing unusual about having a pressurised aircraft with square windows with rounded edges, indeed so far to the contrary the following manufacturers moved from round to 'square' windows for pressurised aircraft:

> Douglas, with the DC-6;
> Lockheed, with the Super Constellation;
> Convair, from the 240 prototype to production aircraft, and Boeing, from early versions of the Model 377 Stratocruiser to the later versions, built for United Airlines and Northwest Orient.

(3) As explained above the Comet only flew about one-third as fast and one half again as high when compared with contemporary piston-engine airliners.

(4) RAE Farnborough did not invent the test tank. That was a de Havilland innovation, used to test a Comet fuselage cross-section. So far from being rushed into production, the Comet was the most tested civil aircraft in history when it entered service, nearly three years after its first flight.

(5) The Comet was not the world's first pressurised airliner. That honour falls to the Boeing Model 307 Stratoliner, which preceded it into service by 12 years, and

(6) So far from the aviation industry being unaware of cyclic stress as pressurised cabins pressurised and repressurised the phenomenon was well understood, generally imposed less stress than on the wings, which constantly flex in flight, and was the reason why de Havilland invented the test tank in the first place. More was learnt during the badly flawed RAE investigation, particularly about stress build-up at the corners of windows, which were not particularly tight on the Comet by industry standards - *c.f.* the corners of the square windows on the successful, pressurised Lockheed JetStar business jet, which had a similar ceiling[22], but the importance of this research was hugely exaggerated for political reasons. Boeing made no design changes to their 707 as a result of the RAE investigation, nor was there any reason to.

The Conspiracy Theory About the CIA

The Comet sabotage partly explains why it was so easy for Harold 'von' Wilson to help North Vietnam by keeping Britain out of the Vietnam War, at least officially. British ground troops were of course deployed in Vietnam, disguised, not very effectually, as Australians, with their excellent SAS. Only a handful of British intelligence officers were aware of the DVD, and they tended to be outside the intelligence establishment, thanks to the mad decision to dismantle MI18 (officially at any rate) at the end of the war.

A far larger circle were aware that the Comets had been brought down. You only needed to have a brain and know one end of an aircraft from another, or be in touch with major industry players like Sir Geoffrey de Havilland himself, Ray Baxter[23] or Sir George Edwards[24] to have doubts about the metal fatigue theory.

The problem was that key players in the intelligence establishment and the aviation industry blamed Boeing (not Douglas, curiously, although possibly not, since Donald Douglas was a nice chap). They tended to assume that the CIA had planted the bombs, in order to promote the 707. BOAC and Whitehall didn't help matters by pulling the rug from under the 707's potential competitor, the Vickers V-1000 (the VC-7[25]) in 1955. This allowed BOAC to order the 707-436, with the same engine, the Conway turbofan.

Poor old Boeing must have wondered what was going on, as there was massive resentment in Britain at the success of the 707. We British are not normally given over to resentment if beaten in a fair fight. There was nothing fair about the murderous breakup of the British civil aircraft industry, however. It wasn't just the Comets. Almost every British airliner prototype in the 1950s and 1960s was sabotaged, starting with the Bristol Britannia and ending with the VC-10, with the Handley Page Herald in between.

Boeing were blamed under the *cuo bono* principle. This is a very good principle, but you first need to make sure there is a *bono*. The Boeing Board didn't want to make the 707. Their previous commercial airliners, the Stratoliner, using the B-17 wing, and the Stratocruiser, using that of the B-29, had been financial turkeys. Military aircraft were much easier in the sense that there was only one customer, the USAF (the US Navy scarcely ever bought Boeing), and they didn't keep asking for different fuselage lengths.

In order to sell the 367-80 prototype to the airlines Boeing first had to widen the fuselage, which meant different tooling. That's why the KC-135 Stratotanker and the VC-137 military 707 have different designations - they're different aircraft. That was only the start.

The 707 had *five* different engines in its lifetime, the JT-3, JT-4, JT-3D turbofan, Rolls-Royce Conway and CFM-56 (reengine only). There were three different fuselage lengths, the Dash 100, Dash 300 and the short- fuselage Dash 138s for QANTAS. There were also two different rudder sizes and three different ventral fin arrangements: no fin, narrow-chord fin and broad-chord or deep fin, à la 707-436 for BOAC. That's without the Boeing 720, the medium-haul version for the US domestic market. It's far from clear that Boeing ever made any money on the civilian 707. I suspect that the figures were very wisely rolled up with the KC-135 tanker for the shareholders.

As is now known, the Comet crashes were nothing to do with the Americans. They are the Good Guys and would hardly be likely to blow up British civilian airliners with passengers on board in order help Boeing stockholders, many of whom lived in Seattle anyway. There is no known case of a United States intelligence agency being involved in the sabotage of a commercial aircraft. The Comets were brought down by the DVD, full stop.

Postscripts

Three postscripts to the Comet episode are worthy of mention:

(1) Reengined with Rolls-Royce Avon 524s, stretched and strengthened, on 4th October 1958 de Havilland Comet 4 G-APDC of BOAC, with Captain Roy Millichap[26] in command, flew the first transatlantic jet service. Juan Trippe, the head of PanAm, who was close to both CIA and Boeing, was probably ready at the end of September with his 707-121s, but held back as a tribute to de Havilland.

(2) The fuselage strengthening was unnecessary and resulted in such a strong aircraft that they had to send for special tools down at Lasham airfield in Hampshire when they were breaking them up. When Captain Llense of Aerolineas Argentina decided to land his Comet 4 LV-AHP at speed on a nearby mountain instead of Asuncion (in fairness the weather was marginal), no fewer than 63 of the 65 souls aboard - poor Captain Llense was killed by a tree which came through the cockpit window and an elderly lady decided to have a heart attack (aircraft crashes can be very noisy, and unsettling for some passengers) - walked off the aircraft. The massively strong, chemically bonded fuselage was virtually intact. Most airliners would have broken up. The airline chairman praised the great strength of the Comet until somebody in Buenos Aires reminded him that wasn't in the script, and

(3) The supposedly weak Comet fuselages were surveyed by BAE Systems in Nimrod guise more than 30 years after they were built and OK'd for attaching to new wings as the Nimrod MR4, which was scheduled to remain in front-line service until the 2020s, more than 70 years after the prototype Comet first took to the air in the capable hands of Group Captain Cunningham. The excellent MR4 programme was cancelled for political, not technical, reasons.

1. 20 degrees sweep at the leading edge. The trailing edge was not swept, which made the flaps more efficient. Highly aerodynamically efficient and in use for some 60 years after it was designed, the wing achieved a good balance between take-off performance, low landing speed, high cruising speed and good fuel consumption. Unlike the larger and later Boeing 707, whose 35 degree sweep, combined with gear height, imposed constraints which made it difficult to stretch (*cf.* the DC-8, whose sweep was roughly midway between the Comet and the 707) the Comet design had plenty of 'stretch' in it. The 118' long Comet 4B/C was not the limit and there were proposals for a Conway-powered Comet 5.
2. The AJ65 Avon was axial-flow and therefore had lower drag than the Comet 1's de Havilland Ghosts - *pace* the silly Channel 4 documentary in the *Secret History* series in 2002. Bishop, the brilliant chief designer, did not choose the Ghost out of company favouritism, indeed he initially favoured the Avon. When selected the Ghost was one of the most powerful jet engines in the world and the only one rated for civil applications. A civil aircraft designer cannot use a military engine unless it has been certified for civil use. As Alan Peters and David Newman, formerly of de Havillands, emphasised in a letter to the *Telegraph* attacking the misleading Channel 4 documentary (22nd June 2002), the Avon had still not been cleared for civil certification when the Comet fleet, outrageously, was grounded in April 1954.
3. With DH Sprite rocket motors mounted between Nos. 1 & 2 and 3 & 4 engines - Davies & Birtles have an excellent photograph at p. 21. De Havilland, by then pathetically reduced to a division of the disastrous Hawker Siddeley combine, later used rocket-boosting to overcome the take-off length problem on the Trident (imposed of course by BEA requirements), the only successful use of rocket motors in a civilian airliner. Passengers loved them, but they must have made a bit of a nonsense of the First Officer calling out V1 - once you'd lit the wick you were pretty much committed to take-off.
4. Well, they did catch one once. Apparently, it had been snapping a few piccies over the USSR and got shot up over Moscow by some Mig-19s. She pulled away but had a few 23 mm sized holes in her. Famously she made an emergency landing at the USAF base at Wiesbaden, which created some initial consternation, as they weren't expecting an RAF Canberra to arrive from the *east*. She was whisked into a hangar for patching up faster than you could say 'bad show - we ran into a spot of bother over Redland, old chap'. The USAF were also impressed by the Canberra, which was a lovely bit of kit, and bought them, the first British bomber in US service since the DH9A in 1918. They were made under licence by those very nice people Martin at Marietta and designated B-57s.
5. For security reasons it was not run out of head office, but a branch of the bank located near the airport at Kloten, where the gold is kept in an underground storage facility so large it has its own little electric train to take you around.
6. Himmler had his agents inside the Abwehr as well as vice-versa - he had a man on the plane, a Fw 200, who deactivated the chemical fuse, then replaced it after landing, tricky, but nicely done. Bits of this operation found their way into the film *Valkyrie*, but their intelligence consultant wasn't in the loop.

7. He was exfiltrated to West Germany after the bogus RAE investigation, which he was able to influence. Trained in Nazi Germany, his intelligence connections allowed him to get away with being an 'anti-Nazi', which he was by temperament, i.e. he just worked for them, he didn't like them. *Scientific Discovery*, June-Sept 1999 carried a tribute to him, almost certainly in ignorance of his espionage activities.
8. This prediction was rightly rubbished by Sir Alfred Pugsley, the distinguished Director of Aircraft Structures at Farnborough, who was not briefed in that Argyris was working for German intelligence.
9. C/n 06003, first flown on 9th January 1952, she flew the first ever pure-jet service (the Vickers Viscount had been trialled the year before) on 2nd May 1952.
10. These names are taken from the casualty list issued after the disaster by BOAC.
11. As it happens, my old home town.
12. A B-film, it was screened in the UK as *The Face That Launched a Thousand Ships*, and in the US as *Loves of Three Queens*. No need to rush out and buy the DVD.
13. The old 'drown him on a river trip' trick.
14. Tiny sadly died in 2010. He and his charming wife Joan had the distressing task of looking after the relatives of the victims. Tiny and I had a respectful disagreement over the causes of the disaster, but he was too good a pilot and had too much confidence in the Comet not to have harboured some doubts. In particular, he briefed me in at a Bomber Command Association lunch in Oxford that Yoke Peter underwent a full pressurisation test to 11 psi (2.5 psi overpressure) on the ground at Rome, which would have blown the ADF panel if it was on the verge of failure.
15. Quoted in *The Times*, 18th January 1954. The ADF panels were above the passenger cabin.
16. One has to be very careful with post-mortem 'sunburn' - the skin is an organ and does not react to sunlight in the same way after death. However, to get sunburn you first need sun and since there was 8/8 cloud-cover we needn't take the Italian explanation for the burns on the bodies too seriously. RAE simply brushed over this evidence, as one would expect in a report written by a government body in bad faith. It would be exceedingly difficult to explain burns on the bodies on metal fatigue. Normally the engines don't catch fire when a hull fails through a fatigue crack, indeed normally the hull doesn't break up at all, hence the survival of everybody except poor Flight Attendant C. B. Lansing in the Aloha Airlines 737 incident on 28th April 1988, movingly filmed in the TV film *Miracle Landing*, with a haunting soundtrack.
17. About the same as on a DC-6 or a Super Connie at cruise, a bit less than a Stratocruiser.
18. G-ALYY, c/n 06011, first flown on 10th September 1952 and delivered to BOAC on the 23rd - Davies and Birtles, p. 21.
19. A fleet destroyer, armed with 6 4.5-inch guns and 10 21-inch torpedo tubes. She was superior to any surface combatant in the Italian Navy in 1954. Most of the Italian Fleet had been sunk in the war of course.
20. Serial Nos. 5301 and 5302, c/ns. 06017 and 06018, assigned to 412 Squadron for jet bomber simulation.

21. It is not possible to reconcile the 9,000-hour claim (rounded down) with the number of days the fuselage of Yoke Uncle was in the test tank, it not being asserted that the tank test was suspended.
22. An attractive aircraft, the JetStar featured in *Goldfinger* of course, flown by Pussy Galore (only an intelligence officer could have come up with a name like that).
23. Ray shared his doubts about the Comets with me - a wonderful chap, he used to do the commentary at the Farnborough Air Show. He was pretty useful in a Spitfire too and bagged the odd 'Jerry' in World War II, mostly of the V-1 variety.
24. Chief Designer at Vickers, later head of BAC, responsible for the Viscount, VC-10 and 1-11 programmes. He ought to have been offered a peerage but of course Whitehall was trying to run down our aircraft industry and life peerages tended to be knocked out to superannuated party hacks or German spies, or both (as with Roy Jenkins).
25. Scrapped after a staggering 800,000 + drawing office hours had been spent on it, this was an advanced, swept-wing turbofan-powered (Rolls-Royce Conways) airliner with transatlantic range, being developed to roughly the same timeline as the 707. Many of its features were later incorporated into the superb VC-10.
26. There is a photograph of Captain Millichap with that nice man HIH the Shah of Persia in a Comet in Cowell, *op. cit.* at 68-9.

22

1955 - 1960

The Mau Mau Emergency

This was another DVD terrorist campaign. The idea was to force a transfer of Kenya from overt British to covert German control. Germany of course used to run Kenya. 'Jerry' bitterly resented being thrown out by us British. We greatly underestimated the strength of his desire to get back in. The DVD were willing to play tribal politics, knowing full well that if their man Jomo Kenyatta, a Kikuyu, took over, other tribes would be hammered.

The murderous campaign was successful in the end, again because good counter-insurgency work on the ground by Ian Henderson and others was undermined from London. The Colonial Office largely reported to the Cabinet Office, which as we have seen reported to Germany for most of the postwar period. Local intelligence officers were helpless to prevent absurdities, like the failure to hang Kenyatta and other key Mau Mau terrorists, including Barack Obama Senior, for treason.

Obama Senior didn't do any of the fighting. He was essentially a gunrunner and a bag man for the DVD, murdered by his own side in 1982 when he started to talk. In fairness he wasn't a man entirely without a conscience, which is why he took to drink.

Kenya was transferred to German control in 1963, under the usual guise of 'independence'. Unsurprisingly, the colony was underdeveloped (holding back colonial development was a key aim of DVD assets in Whitehall). Her government became deeply corrupt.

Cyprus

The same tragic story was repeated in Cyprus. The key German asset was an Orthodox cleric, Archbishop Makarios, who had worked for the Abwehr in World

War II, whilst ostensibly studying in Athens. The DVD's terrorist organisation in Cyprus was known as the EOKA and its leader was George Grivas, whose arrest and execution were blocked from London. Every bit as brutal and murderous as the Mau Mau, it was never entirely dismantled. Former EOKA members were implicated in the murder of an American DIA officer as recently as 2008. It is thought that Grivas was expected to be on the Cyprus Airways DH Comet 4B, blown up by the DVD over the Med on 12th October 1967.

Suez

The Germans had staged unsuccessful revolts in Egypt in 1882 and 1919. Poor counterintelligence work, in the latter case by Security Intelligence Middle East (SIME), meant that their role was not discovered. As with terrorist campaigns most revolts - and most riots as well - are state- sponsored. If you don't expose the state behind a revolt, you invite disaster, as the Russian failure to expose German sponsorship of the failed 1905 revolution demonstrated. That spectacular failure of counterintelligence doomed an empire and eventually condemned tens of millions of decent Russians to death.

In the case of Egypt, it was a case of third-time lucky for 'Jerry'. Unlike poor old King Farouk the Germans were able to learn from their mistakes. They overthrew him, easily enough, in 1952. Some of the Army officers involved were patriotic Egyptians, but they were soon brushed aside in favour of the DVD's Colonel Abdul Nasser, backed by his deputy, Major Anwar Sadat. Strictly of course that should have been 'Oberst Nasser'.

Nasser and Sadat were key Abwehr agents in Cairo in the war. They were keen to reverse the result of the Battle of El Alamein. Their Abwehr association is widely understood but many made the mistake of assuming that just because the German military had been defeated so too had German intelligence. The thinking was that their connections to Germany must have ceased in 1945. Nothing could have been further from the truth. They soon got going. In 1956 'Oberst' Nasser seized the Suez Canal Co. from its shareholders, leaving it to the British and French governments to compensate them from public funds.

Incidentally, that later eventually led to a mini-constitutional crisis in Britain, as the Foreign Compensation Commission, the quango set up by Whitehall to determine compensation, was supposed not to be subject to judicial review. With the utmost respect, the judges in the House of Lords defied Parliament. Under the thin guise of 'interpretation' (the statute was plain enough - it said the commission's rulings could be not "called into question in a court of law") they arrogantly refused to apply the statute.[1]

This started a war between the judges and Parliament, which continues to the present day, with the judges getting ever bolder.[2]

The British government's response was feeble. Firstly, Britain should have gone to the aid of our gallant ally King Farouk, the last legitimate ruler of Egypt. That failure sent a signal to every pro-British leader in the Third World that they could be toppled at the point of a gun and Whitehall would not lift a finger to help them. It also sent a signal to business that investing in the Third World was high-risk as governments could be toppled overnight. Secondly, Britain should have declared war on Egypt when her German-backed dictator seized the Suez Canal, which was private property and strategically vital.

Thirdly, when we eventually went to war, we should have declared it. Not doing so left the Armed Forces uncertain as to their legal position. The same grotesque mistake was repeated in 1982, 1991, 2001 and 2003.

It cleared the way for a messy political compromise designed to throw away the hard-won military gains, exactly what the Cabinet Secretary wanted.

It also contributed to the unnecessary subterfuge with Israel, when the alliance, which was in each country's interest, should have been open. It is greatly to their credit that Britain and the Fourth (Free French) Republic were the first, and so far only, powers openly to be wartime allies of Israel. There are those in INTELCOM who say that some of the A-4 Skyhawks in Israeli service in the 1960s and 1970s may in fact have been US Navy aircraft with US Navy pilots, but that is not quite the same thing.

Fourthly, having decided, eventually, to go to war, it should not have been left in the hands of a German spy (i.e. Mountbatten) and should have been waged decisively. As it was it took so long to assemble the amphibious task force that Britain's intentions were signalled clearly to the enemy, although in fairness Mountbatten had betrayed the plans to Dachau anyway.

Insufficient forces were committed to the attack and there were inadequate reserves, with lousy logistics. Comparatively few ships and aircraft were taken up from trade. The RAF were scarcely allowed to bomb Cairo at all. Whole suburbs were left standing. Dear old Bomber Harris must have been watching it all from South Africa with open-mouthed astonishment.

There was hardly any fire support. The wonderful fast battleship HMS *Vanguard*, last of the old-style British battlewagons, wasn't committed at all. Her 15-inch guns could have killed lots of Egyptians. In fairness - and I am very fair to our community partners the 'Frogs' - the French avoided that mistake. They whistled up the impressive FS *Jean Bart*, whose firepower matched *Vanguard's*.[3] Once she arrived in the war zone however she spent most her time cruising up and down aimlessly. It was utter chaos.

Unsurprisingly, since he was a German spy, Nasser let in lots of German rocket scientists and soon had a WMD programme going. His intent seems to have been to complete the Holocaust and wipe out Israel. He died, far too late (he should have been shot in 1940), of natural causes. Sadat was not so lucky. Some in the DVD were annoyed with him over Camp David, i.e. he fell foul of bitter factional rivalry inside the agency.

One faction - let us call it the KR (Kissinger Rockefeller) faction - backed Sadat. Another - let us call it the ST (Shady Tree, Bush 41) faction - wanted to defeat Israel and throw the Jews out of their ancient homeland. The ST faction had Sadat taken out, installing Mubarak in his place. As we have seen, after he lost too much ground to the Islamo-fascist Muslim Brotherhood, the DVD dumped him as well.

The EEC

The original Reich Ministry of Economic Affairs blueprint for the creation of a postwar sphere of German influence, the *Europäische Wirtschaftsgemeinschaft*, or European Economic Community, was the brainchild of Reichswirtschaftsminister und Präsident der Deutschen Reichsbank Funk. It was eventually implemented via the Treaty of Rome 1957. Key DVD assets involved included Jean Monnet, Paul-Henri Spaak and Robert Schumann. For presentational reasons the swastika was replaced by a ring of yellow stars on a blue background.

Sir Anthony Eden, before he was forced out over Suez and replaced by the DVD's Harold Macmillan, who tragically had survived the war, wisely vetoed British participation. He correctly concluded that it wouldn't work. It hasn't. The EEC formally came into being on 1st January 1958. Only a few years passed before its institutions, led by the European Commission and the European Court of Justice, started attacking the sovereignty of the member states. They developed the constitutionally offensive doctrine of 'supremacy of community law', which sought to turn the EEC into a federal system. The theory was that community law overrode the democratically made laws of Member States, even when the Treaty of Rome had not been incorporated into national law.[4]

Windscale

The world's first atomic power station became operational at Calder Hall in Cumberland in 1956. The DVD have always been deeply concerned about the peaceful exploitation of nuclear power to generate energy safely.

Standartanführer Otto Skorzeny was tasked with coming up with a plan to sabotage Britain's nuclear power programme. Rather than attack Calder Hall he chose to sabotage the older reactors at nearby Windscale. The Number 1 reactor was duly set on fire, on 10th October 1957. Macmillan was just as anxious to starve Britain of cheap, clean energy (subject to containing radioactivity of course) as the DVD. 'Mac' made sure that the sabotage was covered up, à la Comets.

Later DVD nuclear sabotage operations at Three Mile Island, Pennsylvania, in 1979, Chernobyl in the Ukrainian SSR, as it then was, in 1986 and at Fukushima, Japan in 2011 were equally successful. Environmentalists, both genuine and eco-fascist, have made huge political capital out of these operations, not always in good faith. Whilst the comparative ease with which the DVD's Sabotage Section were able to organise these releases of radioactivity raises security issues about vulnerability of nuclear plants to sabotage, these are scarcely ordinary risks of nuclear plant operation.

As the US Navy has shown for over 50 years, with professional management, technological literacy and good security, nuclear plant can be run safely and responsibly year in and year out. This does not mean that there should not be a comprehensive review of nuclear plant security in every civilised state that uses nuclear power.

Another factor demonstrated by intelligence analysis of these incidents is that design flaws can be built in by Bad Guy (i.e. DVD) penetration assets, which they then exploit. DVD political assets have also held back the development of nuclear technology, including safe treatment and disposal of waste, the British Advanced Gas-Cooled Reactor (AGR - a technology which showed great promise) and above all, nuclear fusion. Having held back technological progress, the DVD then gets other political assets to bemoan the lack of it.

The Defence White Paper

Duncan Sandys did not stop doing damage to Britain, and in particular the RAF, which he hated, in 1945. German assets typically do not stop. It's up to you to stop them and until you do they will keep coming at you. In 1957 Sandys promoted an absurd document, the Defence White Paper, which was designed to undermine the RAF. Amongst the DVD bureaucratic assets assigned to the White Paper team by Sir Norman Brook, the Cabinet Secretary, was one David Serpell. This was the same man who later helped the notorious Dr Beeching break up the railway network, which he tried to further damage in the 1980s.

The White Paper pushed the preposterous notion that the era of manned military aircraft was coming to an end only 45 years or so after it had started. That this facile nonsense was so widely believed is testimony to the extraordinary hold that the idea that Whitehall acts in good faith has on politicians and the media. Siixty-eight years later unmanned drones can still only operate in airspace that has been secured by manned aircraft. Sandys did huge damage to the RAF and wrecked tens of thousands of military careers, emphasising what a mistake it was not to have hanged him (nicely of course) in World War II.

The Munich Air Disaster

One thing, apart from assassinations, genocide, fake revolutions, sabotage, BMWs, white wine,[5] beer and sausages the Germans do really well is psychology. In particular, they understand sports psychology and the boost for morale that sporting success can give to a sporting nation. Harold Wilson noticed this after England's third great win of the 20th century over Germany, in the 1966 World Cup. It was such a boost that even he became popular, for a short while at any rate. The DVD has an entire section devoted to scuppering the opposition in sporting events.

The inner workings of the DVD are not an open book. The agency is highly compartmentalised. Since almost everything it does is criminal or morally wrong or otherwise calculated to blow up in their faces if it gets out, it is obsessive about secrecy, to the extent that it's not unknown for its agents to disappear from their desks. Its internal affairs division is not quite as fluffy as the LAPD's. The DVD generally does not do fluffy.

So far as we (i.e. the Good Guys) can tell, the sports section is part of the Psychological Warfare Section. The sports section does not devote itself to thinking up new ways of making German teams fitter or more competitive. It buys up officials, arranges Olympic massacres, such as the one in Munich in 1972 using tame Palestinian terrorists, and for opposing players to be injured.

A key Hungarian player, e.g., was injured just prior to the 1954 World Cup. It's been done a few times since. You would be surprised how many key players are injured in the run-ups to major soccer tournaments. There is no need for the sports section to hold back. They have *carte blanche* to injure whom they want. The media will always treat it as bad luck. Their naivety is touching but childlike.

From time to time the DVD goes wholesale and blows up an entire team, usually British or American. The Munich Olympic Massacre is not the only time an attempt has been to massacre a sporting team *en masse*. The idea isn't new. Sports teams travel together and so are vulnerable to sabotage. A number of members of Purdue University's outstanding football team, e.g., were killed in a very dodgy looking train crash on 31st October 1903.[6] After World War II sporting teams started to travel to away matches by air, almost invariably as a team. This saves money, until you lose the entire team in an air disaster.

On 4th May 1949 the leading Italian Serie (Series) A soccer side Torino AC was nearly wiped out in an air crash in Turin. They had been playing against Benfica in Lisbon and were flying in an Avio Linee Italiane Fiat G212CP. It was not a very advanced airliner and appears to have lacked an Instrument Landing System (ILS). What's more they were flying into Turin, a not very well-equipped airport.

The aircraft encountered a storm cell on the approach to Turin. Instead of diverting, Captain Meroni elected to descend below the minimum safe altitude, i.e. he decided to make a VFR approach in IFR conditions. Tragically, the airliner flew into the basilica on Superga. All on board, including the 18 players, were killed.

It wasn't sabotage, at any rate so far as is known. Approach sabotage, as when Commerce Secretary Ron Brown was assassinated on 3rd April 1996 on the approach to Dubrovnik, usually involves fake radio beacons. This was an old Luftwaffe tactic from World War II. The G212 however was simply too primitive an aircraft to have been sabotaged in this way.

The disaster seems to have given the DVD an idea. The public were sensitised to the idea of an entire sporting team being wiped out on the same aircraft. Civilian aircraft crash investigation in the West was so sloppy that the Sabotage Section could get away with just about anything, as we saw with the Comets. The media in the 1950s was no more aviation literate than it is now and could be fobbed off with any old nonsense. Sporting team managers were no more aviation literate than the media and had not learnt from the Superga Disaster. They were quite happy to risk entire teams in unsuitable aircraft, the cheaper the better.

In 1958 the chance came along to destroy Manchester United, the best soccer team in the world, let alone England. It still is. The DVD took the chance with open arms. West German Chancellor Konrad Adenauer apparently took some convincing, but went along with it in the end. The Psychological Warfare Section was particularly worried about Duncan Edwards, a brilliant young player who threatened to do well in the forthcoming World Cup in Sweden. The last thing Germany wanted was for England to win the World Cup, just when they had taken over Downing Street again and were intent on forcing Britain into the EEC. West Germany were not particularly fancied that year. It was a question of stopping England, rather than helping Germany.

United were due to play Red Star Belgrade in the quarter-final of the European Championship. They wanted to fly back from Belgrade but were only willing to charter a single aircraft, i.e. they wanted the entire team on one plane, Torino AC-style. They approached, or were steered towards, British European Airways. It was a dangerous choice, considering that the airline was state-owned. The DVD had assets in the Ministry of Transport and Civil Aviation, who had been able to get their people into senior BEA management.

United wanted a Vickers Viscount, a reliable, four-engine aircraft. It would have been a sensible choice, as it would have had the range to fly from Belgrade to Manchester without refuelling. It was also a turboprop.[7] They were fobbed off with an Airspeed AS-57 Ambassador, however. Ironically enough, BEA at one time had ordered the Ambassador in preference to the Viscount, for political reasons, with a view to damaging the Viscount. Attlee was worried that the Viscount program would lead to high-quality jobs and export orders.

The Ambassador, known in BEA service as the 'Elizabethan', was a lovely old kite, popular with passengers. They served with charter operators like Autair and Dan-Air long after being retired by BEA. It was no longer considered a front-line aircraft by 1958, however. They were tough and reliable. Being built down at Christchurch by a de Havilland subsidiary they were likely to be,[8] BUT they suffered from three major defects for the proposed use:

(1) They were underpowered, with two Bristol Centaurus 661s, rated at 2,625 HP for take-off. The Centaurus was an 18-cylinder radial engine with tremendous potential, which had the RLM worried in World War II. As we have seen however, its brilliant designer, Roy Fedden, was forced out at Bristol in a boardroom coup sponsored by Abwehr assets in the Air Ministry, Bristol's biggest customer. The development of the engine had been held back and as a result it was knocking out about 750 HP less than it could.

(2) It was carburettor-fed, the development of fuel injection in Britain again having been held back in Britain by 'Jerry' assets in the Air Ministry. In particular, the Centaurus could be tricky on take-off at any sort of altitude in cold weather. This flight was going to be in February. What's more the proposed refuelling stop was Munich-Riem, which was not only a little high, but also had a shortish runway, just over 6,000 feet, and

(3) It lacked the range for the proposed flight and would need to refuel. It didn't have to be Munich of course. Munich was chosen as it was marginal for Ambassador operations in mid-winter at or close to maximum take-off weight and it was the DVD's home airport.

Manchester United really needed access to an air intelligence officer, but official channels in Whitehall were blocked because nobody was addressing the fundamental problem - penetration by German intelligence. The official civilian intelligence agencies, not least MI5 and MI6, were paralysed by DVD assets like Roger Hollis. The defence agencies were obsessed by the Soviet Union to the exclusion of all else and were seemingly unaware that Lenin and Stalin were *German*, not Soviet, assets. Unaware of the deep German intelligence connections to communism, if anything they tended to regard West Germany as an ally. That notion was as silly as the idea of Adolf Hitler as a partner for peace had been in the Munich peace process.

Ideally, Manchester United needed to have offered an ex-MI18 man like Bill Johns a season ticket. They could have picked his brains over a jar whilst watching a match. I'm sure Bill would have obliged. He would have raised his eyebrows when told that BEA were offering an Ambassador for Belgrade-Manchester and just about dropped his beer when informed that the refuelling stop was going to be on the DVD's home turf, Munich. It was as dangerous a place for English athletes in the 1950s as it would be for Israeli athletes (who also walked into a trap) in the 1970s.

Bill would most probably have been on the phone next morning to a mate at BEA telling him they were going to let United have a Viscount at Ambassador prices or he'd be borrowing a Britannia from Bristol's. They had a bigger fridge anyway. The next call would have been to Adolf Galland in Germany telling him "nice try Dolfo, but United are off limits". That's how major players work.

To say that United's guard was down would be an understatement. They thought that football was a game. It is, but that's not all it is. Sporting contests where national prestige is at stake take on an additional dimension. Sports managers have no trouble grasping this when it comes to the commercial dimension, but seem unable to grasp that there might be an intelligence dimension as well. Cricket administrators were just as blind in the 1990s and 2000s. They walked into the spot-betting scandal like a drunk walking into a door, whilst former Test cricketers were being murdered and cricket journalists were being thrown to their deaths from their hotel rooms. A member of the BBC's revered Test Match Special team even came back from the new home of cricket, Dubai of all places (why not go the whole hog and make it Teheran or Peking?) in a body bag. Part of an intelligence analyst's duty is to think like the Bad Guys.

That's actually think by the way, not act! That is because you are trying to predict what the other chap is going to do, so your side can stop him. There was no point dear old Captain Joe Rochefort in Pearl Harbor,[9] the best naval intelligence officer the Americans had in World War II, advising Chester

Nimitz what he thought Admiral Yamamoto might be up to on the basis that that's what an American admiral might do. He was trying to get inside the enemy's head, not his own side's. That bit came after he'd done the analysis. Fortunately, Admiral Nimitz had a brain. That is why they made him first a four and then a five star.

An Englishman would never dream of trying to win a sporting contest by arranging for the other side's aeroplane to crash on the way to the match. He would regard the resulting contest as the opposite of sporting, nor would he think it sporting to pay a player to injure the other side's best goalkeeper a few weeks before a key match, let alone bribe a Colombian police official to arrest the captain on a trumped-up charge on his way to a tournament. Neither would he set up an offshore account for the referee, nor score a goal with his hands. It does not follow that the other chap is going to play by the same rules, however. He is not British after all. It would be like turning up at a hotel in Europe and expecting marmalade for breakfast.

The Crash

Ambassador G-ALZU RMA *Lord Burghley*, Captain James Thain (later cruelly slandered and driven to an early grave[10]) in command, duly crashed on take-off on 6th February 1958, at 1504 Central European Time. Most of the team were killed save young Duncan Edwards, who was murdered (an embolism caused by injection of air into a vein) 15 days later, when well on the road to recovery.

The runway was covered in slush. At close to his maximum permitted take-off weight poor Captain Thain had no hope of rotating *Lord Burghley* off the deck, indeed once he was in the slush he had trouble getting her above 105 knots. There is no point blaming the air traffic controller. He had two DVD officers in the control tower with him, with Walther PPKs, a weapon much favoured by the DVD. In 1958 many of its officers were still ex-Gestapo of course. Walther developed the PPK essentially as a lighter, more easily concealed version of the PP for the Gestapo.[11]

If you had a period of service with the Gestapo on your c.v. the DVD were one of not many employers in postwar Germany who saw this as a positive recommendation. This book of course answers one question other intelligence historians have not addressed - where did all the former Gestapo officers go? There were over 20,000 of them after all. They didn't all open florist shops or join Bavarian oompah bands.

Most commentators have picked up on the fact that the runway was inspected by car shortly before Zulu Uniform was cleared for take-off, but have completely missed the purpose of the inspection. It wasn't to make sure that the runway was *safe*, it was to make sure that it was *dangerous*. What's more, a Luftwaffe Convair, with no payload and a very light fuel load, was cleared for take-off on Runway 25[12] before the Ambassador. This would itself have sent a clear signal to the Ambassador's crew that the runway was in a safe condition.

What they didn't have access to of course was the load sheets for the Convair. With a better power to weight ratio at that altitude anyway, lightly laden, the Convair was at little risk. Her captain still picked up the slush effect before he rotated. He radioed the tower to that effect on a separate VHF frequency, which was unknown to the Ambassador crew. This short flight had no purpose other than making sure that the runway was dangerous.

What 'Jerry' had not banked on was this traffic being intercepted by a National Security Agency (NSA) mobile listening post. Their receivers were sensitive enough to intercept low-powered transmissions. The NSA however did not have flight schedules for commercial traffic, had no interest (then) in football, were unaware that United were flying through Munich and did not know that a British commercial aircraft fully laden with passengers was waiting for take-off clearance at Munich. The Convair's transmission was guarded. Its significance would only have been apparent to someone who knew the Ambassador was waiting to take off.

Even if the NSA had known about the Ambassador waiting to take off liaison through RAF Germany would probably have been too slow. There would have been too many officers asking too many questions, whilst human life was at stake. If there had been a USAF flight in the air nearby it could have done a high-speed run over the Ambassador, firing guns as a warning. Direct communication would have been tricky. The Ambassador did not have UHF, a lot of military radio traffic is UHF and the USAF would not necessarily have had the tower frequency.

To put it mildly, it would have meant tossing the rule book out the cockpit window. At the very least such a manoeuvre would have generated a number of memos. As experienced former RAF wartime pilots both Captain Thain and First Officer Rayment would have understood the warning, however. One of the messages would have been to the effect that the war was back on, as they were about to find out.

The Excuses

Significant exculpatory effort has been put in on behalf of 'Jerry' since 1958, some of which has found its way into *Wikipedia*, to the effect that:

(1) Tricycle-undercarriage aircraft are more vulnerable to runway slush as the centre of gravity is forward of the main wheels (true).

(2) Tricycle-undercarriage aircraft were new in 1958 (false), and
(3) 'Jerry' did not know in 1958 about the hazards posed by runway slush, particularly for tricycle-undercarriage aircraft (absurd).

'Trikes' first came into large-scale use in the 1930s, in fact there were some tricycle undercarriage aircraft before World War I. The RAF first started using tricycle-undercarriage aircraft in large numbers when the superb Consolidated Liberator (B-24) entered service in 1941. The Liberator was followed by the Douglas Boston/Havoc (A-20), North American Mitchell (B-25) and Martin Marauder (B-26). The Marauders were hot ships by the way, due to their high wing loading, but with performance to match - in the hands of capable pilots they did good work. The Luftwaffe had the lumbering Me 323 Gigant and, more significantly, the Me 262 jet fighter and Arado 234 jet-bomber. The jets were operated from January 1945 (262 first, followed by the 234, despite its lower RLM number), in exceptionally harsh winter conditions. Both the 234 and 262 suffered from underpowered engines using fairly primitive light alloys, which didn't like to be ramped up too quickly. They spooled up slowly even if the throttles were fire-walled.

Modern jet engines respond much more quickly but even now cannot match the time to full power of the best piston engines.[13] With early jets the spool-up problem was so severe that as we have seen the RAF, correctly, moved to a jet aircraft, the Hunting-Percival Jet Provost, for basic training. Both the Admiralty (with the Supermarine Seafire, Blackburn Firebrand and Fairey Firefly) and US Navy (with the Chance-Vought Corsair, Grumman Bearcat and Douglas Skyraider) correctly persisted with piston-engine types in frontline service for a number of years into the jet age.

The Skyraider was still going good work (you could hang a lot of napalm on an A-1) in Vietnam 20 years after that splendid chap, into whom I bumped, Eric 'Winkle' Brown, first landed a jet on an aircraft carrier.[14] If you are lucky enough to be flown onto an American aircraft carrier in a Grumman C-2A Greyhound COD aircraft, just before you 'touch' down you will hear the pilot in command spool up the engines for go-around. If he or she doesn't (they always do!) and misses the trap you won't be going around, but over, the end of the canted deck, and under the carrier. It is a good rule of naval aviation always to remember that your airfield is following you.

The poor field performance, i.e. long take-off runs, of the Ar 234 and Me 262, meant that the Luftwaffe encountered the runway slush problem before the end of the war. In fact, it had been encountered in the cold December of 1944, before the Me 262 entered regular squadron service, and probably even earlier on the Eastern Front, with the Gigant. That was a glorified powered glider designed to transport military vehicles und artillery.

Both the Luftwaffe and Lufthansa operated tricycle-undercarriage Convairliners and Lufthansa operated the trike-geared Lockheed Constellation and Starliner. 'Tail draggers' were the exception by 1958, not the norm. The last 'tail dragger' airliner built in any numbers was the dear old Vickers Viking, in the 1940s. It was basically a Wellington bomber with a new fuselage and bits of Warwick empennage.[15] The slush phenomenon was so well known by February 1958 that KLM had circulated a paper on it to other European operators.

The New York Air Disaster

Just under the three years later, at a time when there was heavy pressure on newly elected President Kennedy to keep Germany's Allen Dulles at Langley, the DVD's Correa Group pulled off an even more lethal spectacular over New York. Courtesy of a fake radio beacon sited on a remote corner of Miller Field, they persuaded a Constellation to collide with a DC-8. The investigation was no more sophisticated than that into the Comets or the Munich Air Disaster, indeed with respect it was simply naïve.

Sabena Flight 548

Sports managements failed to learn from Munich. A couple of months after the New York Air Disaster, on 15th February 1961, the DVD managed to knock off the entire US Figure Skating team. They brought down Sabena Airlines Flight 548, a Boeing 707-329, OO-SJB, on approach to Zaventem Airport near Brussels, by sabotaging the stabiliser trim.[16] The team, which was world-class, was on its way to Prague for the World Championships. Tragically, they never made it.

The Marshall University Disaster

The technique that had been used successfully to set up the collision over New York was used again on 14th November 1970 to bring down Southern Airways Flight 932, a Douglas DC-9-31,[17] Captain Frank Abbott in command, on approach to landing on Runway 12 at Tri-State Airport, Huntington West Virginia. Huntington is a charming town in the south of the state, near the Kentucky border. The DVD's target was the successful Marshall University American Football team, the 'Thundering Herd'. All 75 souls aboard were murdered. The great team, tragically, was wiped out, the first American Football team to be wiped out by Germany in its entirety.

Marshall University have very properly honoured their memory, but with respect might do more to honour the memory of alumni who fought the good fight against Germany, which came home in a tragic and unexpected way. Captain Abbott should be completely exonerated of responsibility for this disaster.

The record should be amended to show that he was a highly professional and responsible airline pilot doing no more than following his instruments in accordance with his training. He was in Instrument Flight Rules (IFR) conditions. I know it was over 50 years ago, but it is never too late to clear the name of a good man. Recommendations for improved training for airline pilots to counter sabotage, and more professional air crash investigation, are made in Chapter 31. Had they been followed after the publication of earlier editions of tis book, Air India Flight 171 might not have happened.

These are probably not the only incidents of sabotage aimed at sporting teams. There have certainly been other crashes, the causes of which ought to be reviewed, but these are the principal cases where the sabotage method has been identified. There is no doubt that 'Harry Hun' has not been playing the game of cricket, but that is part of the problem. The 'Hun' does not play cricket.

Algeria

The National Liberation Front (FLN) was yet another DVD terrorist organisation, the aim being to replace the essentially Free French Fourth Republic with a Vichy style regime. For presentational reasons, it was decided not to have Vichy as the capital of the new republic. The French failure to identify Germany as the sponsor (de Gaulle knew, but he cut a deal with the Germans whereby he would give up Algeria in exchange for taking control of the new republic) meant that thousands of innocent civilians died needlessly.

Algeria was handed over to the DVD, hiding behind the usual 'liberators'. There were enough DVD assets in the French military to be able to wreck its reputation as well, with pointless cruelty including torture. The idea was to try and drag the French Army down to the level of the SS and the Wehrmacht.

At least the major players in Algerian intelligence knew enough about the DVD and its London operation GO2 not to blow the January 2013 In Amenas hostage rescue. Had Whitehall been told, the rescuers, who in my opinion did well to save as many as they did, would have been ambushed. The Fourth Republic finally collapsed in 1958. The Vichy boys got back in, fronted this time by de Gaulle. The Fifth Republic has always had its strings pulled by the GO2-style DVD black agency in Paris, run by French assets.

The only good thing about it was that the chaps who had been in MI18 in the war had enough gen on the general to be able to give him valuable guidance when first 'von' Macmillan and then 'von' Wilson applied to join the EEC, i.e. take Britain inside the German sphere of influence.

Famously the general said 'non' on each occasion, to the annoyance of 'Jerry'. The problem with annoying 'Jerry' of course is that he tends to annoy you back. His boys in Paris duly organised some riots and de Gaulle was out. We escaped the EU eventually, however.

The Trident

In retrospect, the sabotage of the Trident programme was ridiculously simple. The West German government and the DVD were worried by de Havilland's proposed new second-generation jetliner. This was designed to use another British invention, the quiet (ish) and fuel-efficient turbofan. This is a form of jet engine where some of the air (these days most of the air) bypasses the combustion stage and is mixed with the hot jet efflux.

Like the Comet the Trident threatened major sales in US dollars. Control of the Ministry of Transport and Civil Aviation however, which was in turn linked to control of the Cabinet Office, still under Hankey's protégé Norman Brook, not to mention Number 10, gave Germany ultimate control of state-owned BEA, who were the launch customer. As its name implies BEA flew between Britain and Europe. The overseas routes were the preserve of BOAC, a.k.a. "Better Off on A Camel".

All the DVD had to do was to get its man on the BEA Board to revise the specifications to something pointless. The plane wouldn't then suit BEA, which came back to the original specification later, with the Trident Three. More importantly, the plane wouldn't sell in America.

De Havilland, sensibly, wanted the new Rolls-Royce Medway engine. It had a higher bypass ratio, greater power and would have been quieter than the RB168 Spey, the cut-down version of the Medway that was eventually adopted. They also wanted an aircraft the size of what became the Boeing 727, although of course DH were several years ahead of the American company. They, by the way, were briefed in via CIA (which got them from Dachau via Correa Group in Frankfurt) on the Trident specs. BEA also forced single flaps on de Havilland. The result was that not only was the aircraft too small, it needed a stupidly long take-off run. Trident 1s were famously reluctant to unstick. Passengers could have been forgiven for thinking that they were going to taxi to their destination. The flight attendants could have been halfway through the meal service if they started at the runway hold point. Result, an aircraft which was too small, too noisy and had too poor a field performance. Like all DH products however. it flew well and was elegant. As intended, it bombed in the vital American market. Somebody in air intelligence really ought to have cottoned on, since the Trident prototype was almost the first since the war not to be sabotaged.[18]

The Trident had one additional weakness. Its analogue Air Data Computer, whilst a clever bit of kit and state of the art for the day, was vulnerable to sabotage. This could allow different air speed indications for the first and second pilots (which the third pilot was supposed to look out for). If there was poor cockpit coordination this could be very dangerous in the approach and departure phases of flight.

The Staines Air Disaster

On 18th June 1972, in an operation apparently cleared by Edward Heath, all 121 passengers and crew were murdered near Staines, Middlesex, when de Havilland (Hawker Siddeley) DH(HS) 121 Trident 1 G-ARPI, BEA Flight 548, was brought down at 1703 hours BST. Papa India was on a flight to Brussels. GO2, using technical advice from Dachau, sabotaged the ADC, causing Captain Key to retract the droops too early, at 162 instead of 225 knots. The droops were a form of leading-edge slat, which increased lift.

GO2 alerted a number of assets and Britain's international reputation was further harmed when these people turned up to gloat, no doubt having encouraged others. A further purpose was to jam the approach roads, which they were able to with police assistance. Interference was run on the local police, who were doing their best, from New Scotland Yard, the idea being to make sure that any survivors could not be got to hospital in good time.

Police efforts to clear the roads were ineffectual, although it is not legal in Britain for a motorist to block access to a disaster by emergency vehicles. If need be, they can clear a path by ramming vehicles deliberately causing an obstruction.[19] This observation applies with even greater force where the emergency services are responding to an incident organised by agents of a hostile state in an undeclared quasi war with Her Majesty.

Television news footage of the ghouls survives and suggests that many were not from Staines. In those days it was possible to localise vehicle registration numbers. I understand that was the view of the Staines police, i.e. that these idiots were not local. None of them was prosecuted, itself cause for comment. Some will still be living. It should be possible to track them down and identify when they commenced their journeys to the crash site. Did they leave home before Papa India came down and if so why? Frankly, they are not likely to be people of any moral worth or fibre and should soon crack under skilled interrogation.

The Court of Inquiry was presided over by that very nice man Sir Geoffrey Lane AFC, a former Wellington pilot, later Lord Chief Justice of England. He was a very good 'Chief' too, if I may say so. However, the 'accident' investigation was the usual sloppy affair. The court was not told about the malfunction of the Air Data Computer, the offensive theory being advanced that Captain Key had got worked up over an earlier altercation over a proposed strike and crashed his aircraft after having a heart attack.

Once again it was left to the excellent Captain Bartelski to bring his vast aviation experience to bear and crack the problem.[20] He was unaware of the role of the DVD, but cruelly exposed the flaws in the heart attack theory in his book. The time has come to clear Captain Key of all responsibility for the disaster.

1. The case is *R v Foreign Compensation Commission ex parte Anisminic Ltd* [1969] 2 AC 147.
2. Some of them are now even talking about judicially reviewing Acts of Parliament, not that the judges with respect have paid much attention to Acts of Parliament since 1969. They pay them lip service of course, but far too often courts construe Acts of Parliament to read what the members of the court would have had them read had they drafted them. Some of them are worse than the Ninth Circuit, no offence.
3. Whilst the Egyptians had missile boats, supplied by the Soviets, the missiles were small and slow and could not have sunk a modern fast battleship. Ironically their great armoured belts made battleships even more relevant in the age of the sea-skimming anti-surface missile, as they virtually conferred immunity. Modern high-elevation battleship main battery guns compared favourably with most early anti-ship missiles, a proposition which remained true through to the Falklands War. Although improved since, to about 43 miles, the sea-launched Exocet then had a range of about 25 miles. Even limited to 30^0 *Vanguard's* main battery ranged out to 36,500 yards, i.e. just over 20 miles, with a high probability of a hit thanks to the excellent Admiralty Mk X Fire Control Table. Since an attacking warship with Exocet would have to approach within *Vanguard's* search radar range it would be vulnerable to the battleship turning bows on, presenting a slimmer target that the Exocet would probably miss (they really needed the target to be broadside on). At full speed - with battle ensigns flying, a magnificent sight - *Vanguard* would have closed the gap in about 8 minutes, less of course if the attacking ship were oncoming. That was with a gun designed before World War I. The originally proposed 16-inch Mk. 2 for the *Lion* class would have had a maximum range at 40^0 elevation of over 40,000 yards, roughly equivalent to the early Exocets. Each shell would have weighed about 7.5 times that of an Exocet warhead. Initial velocity would have been over Mach 2, i.e. more than twice that of the subsonic Exocet, and a *Lion* would have had 900 of them.
4. The doctrine is known as monism, but it only applies to monist states. All the member states of the EEC are dualist, where international treaties are not automatically part of municipal law. The Treaty of Rome provided that 'regulations' would be self-executing, but a self-executing provision only takes effect after incorporation. The European Court of Justice then added directives to the list of self-executing provisions, i.e. the treaty was subject to judge-made amendments, using the preamble as a pretext. This was an interpretation so surprising with respect that it exposed the ECJ to accusations of bad faith.
5. If you haven't tried their sparkling wine - it's called sekt - you really ought to. It's very good. I was introduced to it at that drinkies at the German Embassy to which Sir Edward Heath was also invited. I prefer it to champagne, except of course the Dom Perignon '53, but you didn't get that even on Concorde. (In fact, the champers BA served on Concorde was slightly disappointing - Air France couldn't always get their planes off the ground but by all accounts their champers was better, and served at the right temperature too).

6. The DVD arranges train wrecks as well as air crashes. They did the *Southern Aurora* in Australia in 1969 at Violet Town, Victoria. As indicated, as recently as 2011 they arranged for a truck to ram the *California Zephyr* in Nevada. They also knocked over a couple of trains in Britain by having Islamic nutters pull critical bolts from points. In America they did the same thing to a freeway bridge, which promptly collapsed. Most steel structures have a small number of critical points - you can do amazing things by pulling out just a few bolts. Sadly, rail crash investigation is no more sophisticated than air crash investigation. It starts out by assuming the conclusion - i.e. it's an, 'accident' and nobody wanted this to happen - rather than objectively proceeding from the evidence.
7. Four Rolls-Royce Darts, of different rating dependent upon the type. The best choice would have been an 810-series, which had uprated engines and longer range.
8. Neville Shute Norway, who sensitised the public to the idea of new aircraft crashing due to metal fatigue in the novel *No Highway*, the idea for which seems to have come from one of the German assets in Farnborough, helped start Airspeed. Norway was aware, by the way, that the Comets had been sabotaged. The Airspeed factory at Christchurch sadly closed in 1962, by which time the company had long since been taken over by De Havilland. Its only other major powered aircraft design, apart from the Ambassador, was the successful Oxford twin-engine trainer/communications kite. Amy Johnson, shareholder in the original Airspeed concern, died at the controls of one in 1941, in circumstances that have never been fully explained, but may have involved her being shot down.
9. Brilliantly played by Hal Holbrook in the film *Midway* and rightly inducted into the NSA's Hall of Fame in 2000. King was shattered by the American victory at Midway, which wasn't in his script at all. He had Rochefort transferred to command a floating dry-dock in San Francisco, an obvious place to send the best cryptanalyst in the US Navy, if you were a German spy at any rate. Holbrook's portrayal was not entirely true to life, as Joe was bisexual and from Ohio, not Texas, but the filmmakers may have thought that a heterosexual from Texas was an easier sell than a bi from Ohio. Joe was a great American and a towering intellect. He shocked both the Abwehr and Japanese naval intelligence by demonstrating that they could not only be outfought by Americans but outthought.
10. The poor man ended up tending chickens and died in 1975. Although partially cleared, after the German faking of a photograph showing icing on the wings was exposed, no one in intelligence ever thought to tell him he had been set up by the Germans. He should have been had up for lunch in the Royal Aero Club, completely exonerated and had a job arranged for him with Freddie Laker.
11. Yes, Ian Fleming, who was aware of the DVD and modelled his fictional SPECTRE on it, was making a point when he had Major Boothroyd recommend the PPK to James Bond. The fictional '00' section was a play on the DVD's London operation (02 - double 0).
12. This was fairly safe. Although a trike, lightly loaded as she was, her power to weight ratio would have been much better and her R-2800s were not as

temperamental in the cold and at altitude as the Centaurus. Munich was not that high (field elevation of the old airport was 1,732 ft), but it was enough to make a difference.

13. GE and Rolls-Royce will tell you otherwise, but I'm not entirely convinced. This is subject to two major qualifications - carburettor-fed engines can be a bit temperamental, as can some fuel-injection systems, and you have to let a piston aeroengine warm up. Never firewall the throttle until the cylinder head temperatures are in the green. The Rolls-Royce/Bentley Jack Phillips 6.75 litre all-alloy V-8 was one of the greatest car engines of all time, and was still being made more than half a century after it first appeared, but I wouldn't have dreamt of pouring on the sauce until my Turbo was nicely warmed up.
14. De Havilland Sea Vampire LZ551, on the light carrier HMS *Ocean*, on 3rd December 1945.
15. They were lovely to fly in. No galley to speak of, so on a long run (with say Central African Airways north from Salisbury) you would come down for lunch and then again for tea. All very civilised, with no jet lag, plenty of legroom and smoking in the toilets.
16. An advanced feature of the 707, drawn from Boeing's experience on the B-47 and B-52, the 707 had an adjustable horizontal stabiliser, first used I think by the Miles company in their M-52.
17. N97S. The film *We Are Marshall* was made in 2006, in commemoration, starring Matthew McConaughey. I haven't viewed it but apparently it deals well with the human aspects of the tragedy, whilst missing its intelligence aspects.
18. The first being the Avro Tudor prototype, where, as we have seen, GO2 paid somebody to reverse the ailerons. Chadwick was the first of three assassinations in the British aircraft industry, the other GO2 targets being the jet engine designer Major Halford (DH Gyron) in 1955 and a key member of the Rolls-Royce RB-211 design team, Adrian Lombard. In the latter two cases the cause of death was disguised as something else. The inquiries were the usual farce. The BAC-111 prototype sabotage on 22nd October 1963 at Wisley was interesting - the pilot was Mike Lithgow, a first-class pilot. Officially it was said that Mike didn't know how to recover from a stall (excuse me - he was a *test* pilot) and didn't know that you shouldn't blank out the elevators. What else did AAIB think he was going to use to affect a stall recovery, the ashtrays? Both the Fairey Barracuda and the Supermarine Walrus in the war had high-mounted tailplanes and it was obvious they could not be effective at an extreme alpha angle. Each was a naval aircraft and Mike was Fleet Air Arm. Good pilots - and Mike was a great pilot - don't get into extreme alpha angles in an airliner anyway, even on test. It looks as though the elevator controls were tampered with. The official inquiry found nothing, but official inquiries usually don't. After the Comets there was no reason to trust the AAIB ever again.
19. The law is complex and there are different issues as regards criminal offences and civil liability, but if you are visiting Britain and 'Jerry' brings another airliner down you would be most unwise to try and make sure the survivors died in agony by deliberately blocking fire engines and ambulances. It's simply not done.

20. *Disasters in the Air*, pp. 184 *et. seq.* (Ch. 8, *The Trident Disaster at Staines*). Again Captain Bartelski, a great loss to aviation, did not delve into the intelligence aspects and he did not consider sabotage. Nobody should impute my views to him, but that does not mean that I do not find his writing invaluable. Effective aviation sabotage investigation requires a multi- disciplinary approach. It calls or can call for aviation, intelligence, forensic evidence, engineering, medical and psychological skills. The important thing is to start with an open mind, which the AAIB and NTSB with respect do not. Intelligence illiterate, they tend to pay lip service only to sabotage as a possible cause. The DVD's Sabotage Section have danced around them for over 50 years. The Indian AAIB are just as bad as the British AAIB and NTSB, no offence intended.

23

The Kennedy Era

Winds of Change

In a crazy speech to the South African Parliament on 3rd February 1960 Harold Macmillan effectively announced that Britain would be bailing out of Africa. Well-informed observers in Pretoria, Johannesburg and Cape Town knew what that meant - the Brits were getting out and the Germans, Soviets and Chinese were coming in. They also knew that Africa was about to be plunged into chaos.

So it proved. Colony after colony was handed over to German (e.g. Kenyatta in Kenya) or Chinese (e.g. Nkrumah in the Gold Coast or Nyerere in Tanganyika) assets. Tanganyika was disastrously merged with the Sultanate of Zanzibar to become Tanzania. Since Dachau and Peking worked closely together in practice it made little difference to the death toll or loss of GDP whether Germany or China was running the show. In some cases, e.g. Sierra Leone, former British colonies were *below* their pre-independence GDP more than 40 years after 'independence'.

Germany and China were after raw materials of course. Whilst the *African Marxist* - a journal even more economically illiterate and left-wing than the *Economist* - railed against Western 'exploitation' China's nominally communist government extracted raw materials at a significant undervalue from its new African clients. It still does. Western purchasers of raw materials tend to pay the going rate. If you have some raw materials to sell and are offered a choice between being 'exploited' by the West or being 'fraternally assisted' by the ChiComs go for being exploited every time.

Independence was a myth, encouraged by the UN, which was of course largely under German control. There are no independent states in Africa, unless you count gallant, tiny, self-reliant little Eritrea, from which people have fled in large numbers. In fairness to the Eritrean government, that's because it's a state where you pull your weight or go hungry, rather than because people have been oppressed. That is unless you count a hard day's work for a reasonable wage by local standards as oppression. Eritrea is poor but actually quite well run, better than say Britain.

If one of the locals takes over and actually shows signs of being honest and competent (a rare case, sadly) they don't last long. None of the original constitutions in British Africa have survived, i.e. all the former colonies are unstable to a greater or lesser extent. The loss of life has been horrendous, nowhere more so than in Rwanda. Here the DVD, in conjunction with the former Vichy minister Mitterand, with help from the UN, staged the fifth German, or German-backed, genocide.[1] The UN's 'peacekeepers' ran away and left women and children to be hacked to death.

It was France's first genocide, which may explain why so many Tutsis survived. President Habyarimana's plane was brought down by French agents. He wasn't that good, but at least he wasn't a homicidal maniac, unlike President Mitterand, some might say.

Macmillan's policy was implemented enthusiastically by Iain Macleod, ironically later assassinated by GO2, as we saw in chapter 18, on the orders of Macmillan's protégé Heath. It was thoroughly irresponsible, thoroughly un-British (as was Macmillan himself of course) and a disgrace. It involved bailing out of colonies that were Britain's responsibility years too early, leaving them unable to govern themselves and at the mercy of predatory and hostile intelligence agencies. The Bad Guys soon moved in for the kill.

When the last Governor of British Somaliland departed, he didn't even leave any milk in the fridge. If you doubt the human cost of this nonsense just count the number of kiddies growing up in Sierra Leone without all their limbs. Better still, don't, because you will find it upsetting. If you want to get an idea of the degree of economic disruption, try buying a tank of petrol in Harare, the capital of Zimbabwe. If you are paying in local currency, make sure you take along a suitcase full.

The Bay of Pigs

If you ever talk to any of the CIA boys involved in this operation, as I have, you will tend to find that they are still annoyed. It wasn't a bad plan, as CIA plans go. They were right to want to remove Fidel Castro, who is no more a communist than my sainted Aunt Agnes was.[2] This is despite the fact that he gave long-winded, boring political speeches (even worse than Sir Keir Starmer's, no offence intended) trying to convince everybody, or possibly himself, that he believed in what he was saying.

Havana are very practiced in deception by the way. After the DVD's Hugo Chavez snuffed it in hospital they pretended for months that he was still alive, for political reasons. When they eventually shipped his body back to Venezuela it did not give television interviews. There was a reason for that. In fairness to the doctors treating him in Cuba, since he was a politician it would not have been easy to determine when brain activity ceased. My advice to any politician going into hospital would be to develop a twitch. Eventually, on 5th March 2013, they made the death official.

The CIA's cunning plan to invade Cuba was betrayed to Havana via Allen Dulles and Dachau, thanks to Richard Helms. The inexperienced Kennedy backed off. The operation required military backup. Once that was not forthcoming it was bound to fail. A better plan would have been to send in troops to support Battista. He was a bastard, but at least he was our bastard. There wasn't much in between, sadly. However, Eisenhower was President when Battista was overthrown. 'Ike' covertly backed his fellow DVD agent Castro.

The Cuban 'Revolution' had an amusing postscript. The DVD had a charismatic Argentinian agent called Ernesto Guevara. 'Che' became Cuba's central banker and did their Medium Term Note trading programmes. He prattled on about reducing disparities of income whilst creating some pretty enormous ones himself.

Guevara became a poster-boy for the left, selling more posters than any other German intelligence agent in history. The Bolivians eventually knocked him off (the DVD were after the tin), with a bit of help from the CIA. However, that only added to the urban myth that he was a communist and a freedom fighter. If you want to sell more posters get yourself whacked by the CIA. Heinrich Himmler probably had more of a social conscience than Guevara, and a smaller numbered account in Switzerland to boot.

The Dag Hammarskjöld Crash

As I observed in Chapter 19 not all air crashes involving high-ranking people are sabotage. Each case turns on its own facts and has to be looked at carefully. Since this is in part a history of DVD aviation sabotage operations, inevitably it may appear that I think that most crashes are caused by sabotage. They aren't. Pilots, especially if they're not being paid enough to live near the airport they're flying from and have to do a long positioning flight first, can get dog-tired and make basic mistakes. If they're inexperienced they may lack the good airmanship which only long hours in the cockpit brings.

One American commuter flight, a Beechcraft 1900D, was lost a few years ago shortly after take-off due to improper loading and shoddy, contracted-out maintenance. The elevator control cables were too short. The centre of gravity was barely within limits and shifted aft as soon as the undercarriage was raised. It took the NTSB months to work it out, although in fairness they got there in the end.

The pilot in command however had about a minute to work out why she couldn't keep the nose down before she lost control. A lovely person, doing her very best to save her plane and her passengers, she lacked the years of command experience which would have shouted 'c.g.' and told her to immediately reverse the last control input before she started to lose control. Had she lowered the under-cart, it would probably have given her enough control to get down safely once she'd dumped or used up enough fuel. It was a heart-breaking case to look at, but nothing to do with sabotage.

Greater experience would also have taught her to be less trusting of the FAA. The aircraft was overweight because the airline followed obsolescent federal guidelines on average passenger weights. 'Blind Freddy' could see that these should have gone out with the DC-3, or possibly even with the Boeing 247D. The poor pilots were being asked to do too much and the poor aeroplane was being asked to carry too much.

Shoddy maintenance practices also had something to do with the Hammarskjöld crash. Conspiracy theories have swirled for years about the death of UN Secretary-General (and DVD asset) Dag Hjalmar Agne Hammarskjöld. He died in a Douglas DC-6B, SE-BDY, at Ndola, Northern Rhodesia, at about 2215 hours local time on Sunday, 17th September 1961, eight nautical miles from the airport.

Various theories were put forward including an IED. This was improbable, as the timing of the flight wasn't known in advance and a barometric fuse in those days would have triggered on the ascent only.[3] Unlike the Elba Comet there was no autopsy evidence of an inflight explosion. There was a rumour about hijacking by a '17th person', but there were only 16 people on board the aircraft and they were all accounted for.

Then there was the theory about a shoot down by one of the Katangan Air Force's three Potez Fouga Magisters. These were nice little kites, but they couldn't have reached Ndola from the Katangan air base at Kolwezi and made it back, as they lacked the endurance. They were all on the ground anyway, which is where we would have expected them to be, as they weren't night fighters.

Even intelligence agencies bought into the sabotage theory, given that Hammarskjöld was on the plane. This was a bit silly as he was the Secretary-General of the UN, only DVD assets in those days were made Secretary-General and only the DVD had a specialist aircraft sabotage unit. Moreover, another DVD agent, Heinrich Wieschhof, a US citizen and close adviser to Hammarskjöld, was also on the plane. Not only is aircraft sabotage not a CIA nor MI6 thing, i.e. it's just not what the Good Guys do, it requires specialist expertise, which CIA and MI6 lack.

A few years ago, the Good Guys (the majority) in CIA finally decided to eliminate a high-level DVD/Correa Group penetration asset inside the agency (Bush 41) who had arranged for the murder of a number of CIA officers. He was scheduled to be on a plane. Their efforts were, with respect, amateurish in the extreme. They signalled their intentions from so far off the Bad Guy never even made the flight. It was quite charming really, except that they managed to kill the pilots. 'Oops', as the saying goes in INTELCOM.

Fortunately for the Deputy Director Operations the investigation was done by the NTSB, so there was no risk of the CIA's role being discovered. The boys had a Presidential finding to cover their bottoms anyway, i.e. it was all nice and legal.

The Belgian Congo was a classic case of a UN-assisted decolonisation disaster plunging a country into chaos, civil war and dictatorship. Nobody does chaos better than the UN. Hammarskjöld was on his way to meet Moishe Tsombe, the Katangan leader. His province had sensibly broken away from the Republic of Congo before it collapsed into complete chaos. 'Jerry' however had other ideas, since most of Congo's mineral wealth, including the critical cobalt mine, was in Katanga. Tshombe was essentially honest and not DVD.

The Katangan forces were well led and equipped and had just seen off a silly UN 'peacekeeper' offensive against their capital Elisabethville, while the UN force was led by the Irish general, Sean McKeown. I am not well-disposed towards the DVD (no s**t Sherlock) but even I have some sneaking sympathy for them over the UN attack on Elisabethville.

They must have been praying for a Waffen-SS Panzer regiment, led by a serious SS-Obergrüppenfuhrer. However, if they'd bought back the Waffen-SS and had them goose-step into Elisabethville singing the *Horst Wessel Song* it might have given the game away, even more than making Kurt Waldheim Secretary-General did. The UN attack was one of the most shambolic military operations ever conducted.

Once again, we had to wait for the late Captain Bartelski to write the first serious published analysis of the crash.[4] In fairness it should be said that Captain Bartelski has rather more time for the UN than myself. He was an admirer of Hammarskjöld, even though the latter was a former Swedish finance ministry official and a technocratic (i.e. German- appointed) member of the Swedish Cabinet.

None of the official inquiry teams knew much about air crash investigation or DC-6s. Captain Bartelski however had 4,000 hours on the DC-6 and consulted an even more experienced KLM DC-6 pilot, Captain

Barron, with 6,000 hours and ten years on type. SE-BDY was a clapped-out ex-ARAMCO machine, built in 1952 and leased by the UN from Transair AB of Malmo, Sweden.

She needed new altimeters for high elevation airfield operation. These were improperly fitted at Ndjili (the airport for Leopoldville), the old altimeters being found in the wreckage. Old DC-6s, as Captain Bartelski pointed out, tended to get a build-up of tar in the cabin air ducts. As you descended and depressurised you could get sudden changes of cabin air pressure, enough to loosen the static air feed into the Kollsman altimeters. The altimeter changeover was not supervised, as it should have been. This meant that both Captain Per-Eric Hallonquist and First Officer Lars Litton were receiving false high readings, by about 1,600 ft. That resulted in a controlled flight into the high terrain (4,350 ft) west of Ndola on a standard instrument approach to Runway 10. Careful analysis of the ATC tapes, and the captain's switchover to the alternate static supply (which would not have cured this particular problem for the reasons given by Captain Bartelski[5]) provides supporting evidence for a problem with the altimeters.

Neither the UN nor Rhodesian investigations picked up the significance of the disconnected static line to the pilot's altimeter. They were unfamiliar with DC-6B operating procedures and in particular were unaware that unlike other pressurised piston-engine types Douglas recommended that the DC-6 be depressurised manually during the descent. The change in procedures followed an incident where a crew member was injured following a failure of the automatic depressurisation system. This was triggered by oleo compression on landing, a bit of a hit and miss affair. There it is. Very few accident investigators are line pilots. This sort of basic ignorance of civil aircraft operating procedures is quite common.

Captain Bartelski's criticisms of UN Air Command procedures and Captain Hallonquist's airmanship were sound, with respect. In particular:

(1) First Officer Litton was well over the legal limit for flying hours of his country of certification (158 hours in 20 days, the limit being 125 in 30).[6]
(2) The crew had been on duty for 21 out of the 29 hours preceding the crash, including 17 hours in the air.
(3) The aircraft violated Nairobi Flight Information Region rules by failing to report her progress through NFIR airspace.
(4) No flight plan was filed for the non-Congo portions of the flight.
(5) Captain Hallonquist commenced an instrument approach to Ndoli without ATC clearance, indeed Ndoli Tower weren't even sure whether he was going to land at Ndoli or proceed to Salisbury.

(6) The aircrew did not include a specialist navigator, for a night-time VIP flight over high terrain with limited radio aids, in particular with no VOR, DME,[7] or navigation radar.
(7) Although uncertain of his altitude Captain Hallonquist failed to make use of the AVQ-9 radar altimeter with which the aircraft was equipped (it was found switched off), which would have given him an accurate altitude above terrain, and
(8) He commenced and continued a descent at night whilst uncertain of his height above terrain and seems to have made no attempt to initiate an emergency climb after brushing the tree-tops west of Ndoli.

The Assassination of Hugh Gaitskell

On 18th January 1963 the Leader of the Labour Party, Hugh Gaitskell, died an agonising death, from lupus erythematosus, after a short illness. As that great counterintelligence officer Peter Wright disclosed in *Spycatcher*, which as I have explained was the inspiration for the title for this book, MI5 thought that Gaitskell had been murdered. They sent the file down to Porton Down, the British chemical and biological warfare establishment in Wiltshire, which apparently does a nice lunch. MI5 were right, but there were two problems with Porton Down:

(1) Porton Down mainly do chemical warfare, or rather counter-warfare, since we British are the Good Guys we and don't go around gassing people, unlike the Germans or their man Saddam. They are very knowledgeable about nerve gasses and if you ever need an antidote to VX they're just the people to go to, but to borrow an apposite American expression, in 1963 they knew diddly-squat about advanced biological agents, and
(2) They were penetrated by GO2 and it is doubtful that any serious advice to MI5 on a DVD or GO2 sponsored assassination would have been allowed out of the building. It would have been like trying to get a satellite piccie of Terry Taliban planting an IED out of GCHQ.

In a wonderful speech, almost his last, Gaitskell had strongly opposed British membership of the EEC. He had also attended a meeting of the Bilderberg Group, unaware that it was a front for the DVD, where he expounded his sensible views on the EEC. In so doing he all but signed his death warrant. The Germans were desperate to force Britain into the EEC and had their man Harold Wilson waiting in the wings to take over the Labour Party.

The biological weapon that took Gaitskell down, which was administered in small doses, was not totally unrelated to the Ebola virus, which 'Jerry' had learnt about from the Belgians after they occupied Brussels in 1940. Ebola first surfaced in the Belgian Congo. It is very nasty, highly contagious and kills people quickly and horribly. It was just the sort of thing that Dr Mengele in Dachau was looking for. You really didn't want Dr Mengele as your General Practitioner - apparently his bedside manner was not that good. A 'retired' intelligence officer who met him after the war told me that Mengele was a cold fish. He also led the German AIDS programme, asking the Abwehr in 1940 to supply 1,000 rhesus monkeys from the Belgian Congo. They weren't for the Berlin Zoo.

Mengele transferred with the rest of them to the DVD in 1944. He carried on his work on Ebola, lupus and AIDS after the war and was said to have been quite pleased with the Gaitskell assassination. At any rate he was more pleased than poor old Hugh was. Hugh was the first British Leader of the Opposition to be assassinated. He was a man of high principle and a patriot, a statesman rather than a politician. I knew several people in the Labour Party who knew him or worked for him. Without exception, they all spoke highly of him.

There is an interesting historical aside. In addition to live experiments on Jews and others in Dachau concentration camp the Germans were very much into live experiments on Africans in Africa. In particular, they ran experiments in the Portuguese colonies of Angola and Mozambique. Lisbon was of course run by the pro-German fascist dictator Salazar. He was such a nasty piece of work that these days they would probably make him a European Commissioner, if not President.

One of the doctors running these live experiments on children, at a hospital in Lourenço Marques, in the name of 'medical research', was one Dr Jose Simoes-Ferreira. One must bear in mind that German medical research, sadly, is often as much to do with finding new ways of making people ill as about making them better.

The good doctor had a daughter, Teresa.[8] She married two US Senators - not at the same time of course. The first, Senator Heinz, of the bean family, died suddenly and unexpectedly in a helicopter crash in Pennsylvania. The second went on to become a failed US presidential candidate and is now the Secretary of State, John Kerry.

I am not suggesting that Teresa Heinz Kerry is aware of her father's diabolical work for Josef Mengele, indeed she almost certainly isn't. Democratic Presidential candidates, in those days at any rate, were carefully vetted. No doubt "did your father-in-law carry out hideous medical experiments on African children for Dr Mengele?" was one of the standard questions the vetters asked. Her husband had ambitions of winning the black vote. Had Mrs Kerry known about her father's experiments with inter alia the Ebola virus she would scarcely have referred to his 'work with African children' on her website.

The Profumo Scandal

The DVD were worried by Jack Profumo. He would have made a great Prime Minister. He was set up by GO2, to whom Stephen Ward, who played a major role in the scandal, reported. The Soviet Naval Attaché, Ivanov, also reported to the DVD, so it was all in-house. The infamous 'Cliveden Set' included a number of German sympathisers. Setting up poor old Jack (he was a friend of a late friend, who was in the Cabinet with him) wasn't difficult.

Harold Macmillan, the Prime Minister, was happy to throw Jack to the wolves. He posed a political threat to Heath. Tragically, Jack was never told that Macmillan was a German spy. When that became known, years later, it was decided that he ought to be compensated for his wrecked life with a mention in the Honours List. A peerage, a fulsome apology and an award of £100,000 from public funds might have been more meaningful. He can now be fully vindicated, however.

The trial of Stephen Ward (he was poisoned the night before the verdict was expected) was such a musical comedy proceeding, with respect to the trial judge, Mr Justice Marshall (a former Liberal Parliamentary candidate) that it has now been turned into a musical comedy. MI5 had nothing to do with his murder, although they withheld information from the court.

The Great Train Robbery

'Jerry' was understandably annoyed when his man Macmillan was forced out. He had been, spotted by former MI18 officers, who finally briefed in the suits in the Tory Party. It was Skorzeny who came up with the cunning plan of robbing a mail train carrying used Bank of England notes and possibly tapes from intelligence listening posts in Northern Ireland.

The idea was to betray the robbers and generally make the new PM, Sir Alec Douglas-Home, a jolly nice chap, look foolish. Savage sentences, which were 'suggested' to the trial judge at Aylesbury Assizes, Lord Edmund-Davies, were all part of the package. Edmund-Davies, whom I met, was an awfully nice man, but he was gay and could be guided on sentencing, with respect. The savage sentences were intended to undermine public confidence in the judiciary.

The intelligence on the best train to rob came from the Bank of England, which was still penetrated. Some of the brighter journalists picked up at the time that the robbery had all the appearance of an 'inside job'. The idea for short-circuiting the signal to stop the train came from Skorzeny, who consulted experts in Deutsche Bahn, the West German state railway, who also do a nice lunch.

The banker for the operation was the DVD asset John Stonehouse MP, later a Labour government minister. When he was tipped off that he had been spotted, in 1974, he faked his own death by drowning, at a Miami beach. He then disappeared off to Australia under an assumed name, Joe Markham, having been supplied with a good false passport by GO2. They had a chap in the Passport Office, the best place of course to source a false British passport. It was said, officially, that he had money worries. These did not prevent him buying tickets for Miami and then Australia, for himself and his mistress, and trying to launder fairly large quantities of cash.

Stonehouse was concerned of course that his sentence might be severe. The tariff had already been set at over 20 years. Generally speaking, MPs, even Labour MPs, are expected to set an example. When they arrange to rob trains and have the drivers bashed over the head the sentence is usually pretty stiff. Undoubtedly dodgy (not only did he fake his own death and go on to serve seven years for theft and conspiracy to defraud, but he was an economist), he was not, as has been alleged,[9] a Czech spy. He was a German spy, although his DVD controller ran the contacts through Prague, the Czech services then being under DVD control.

They could have been run through the Cabinet Office, but Stonehouse may have been unaware that the Cabinet Secretary was also working for the Germans. The DVD have always been heavily compartmentalised and have the added problem of bitter factional disputes. By running Stonehouse through an Iron Curtain agency they could always present him, Kim Philby style, as a communist agent, as a backup plan. It worked well with the Cambridge Ring. Curiously, Stonehouse's crafty idea of second-class stamps, which were a disguised price hike (the so-called 'first-class' post was the old service at a much higher price) was allowed to remain in place. Crooked ministers tend to get on well with the Civil Service, an example, perhaps, of the 'birds of a feather' principle.

John Stonehouse never met the Great Train Robbers directly. The bagman who also tipped off the Buckinghamshire Constabulary about the farm hideout (that was the whole idea) is still around. Even he only had contact with one, or at most two, of the train robbers. He's probably a bit nervous at the moment, as I gather he's been shopped to MI5. There is no statute of limitations for indictable offences in England. He would be well advised to cut a deal. I am sure the boys would like to hear from him, as would HM Customs, in respect of certain import irregularities.

The Beeching Cuts

As we have seen, Dr Richard Beeching was an effective spy for the Abwehr during World War II, particularly as regards the transfer of explosives and materials technology. A deeply unpleasant man, who enjoyed inflicting suffering on local communities, Beeching, was appointed by Ernest Marples. The latter was a none too bright and none too honest Minister of Transport, no offence intended. He eventually fled Britain with his ill- gotten gains, just one jump ahead of the taxman.

Beeching's dodgy reports on Britain's railways were brilliantly satirised in the *Yes Minister* episode *The Bed of Nails*.[10] As explained, his key DVD ally in the ministry was Sir David Serpell. Interestingly, Serpell had been private secretary to the Abwehr's Gwilym Lloyd George when he was a junior minister at the Ministry of Food. Lloyd George junior was involved in drawing up plans to starve the population in the event of war through rationing.

Lloyd George then went to the Ministry of Fuel and Power, promoted by Chamberlain of course. Here he tried to come up with ways of 'rationing' energy in order to hold up war production. It was a tragedy for Britain, the towns and villages cut off from the railway network, decent railwaymen thrown out of a job and their families, that Serpell and Beeching were not hanged during the war. It was also a huge mistake not to have hanged Gwilym Lloyd George.

The Assassination of President John F. Kennedy

This subject could fill a book on its own of course, which thankfully has already been written (*Who Really Killed Kennedy*), by that nice man Dr Jerome Corsi. The purpose of this little tome is simply to give an historical introduction to the DVD, and fill in the odd gap in the historical record in the process. This section will do no more than brush the surface of the complex operation to assassinate President Kennedy. Hopefully however I can poke a few holes in the daft official 'lone gunman' theory.

It is impossible to understand this brutal assassination unless one understands that Allen Dulles, who was heavily involved, reported to our old 'friend' Otto Skorzeny. It was he who came up with the operational concept. Richard Helms, then Deputy Director Operations at the CIA and later its director, was in day-to-day charge of the assassination. He too was DVD.

Unless one has grasped that assassinations are state sponsored, one hasn't a hope of getting anywhere near the truth. If you don't get the right state - in this case West Germany - you are also going to be hopelessly adrift.

It would be interesting to know how supporters of the 'lone gunman' theory could explain how both Charles de Gaulle in Paris and the DVD's Harold Macmillan were each aware of the assassination in advance. How was Oswald able to arrange for American troop movements from West Germany? It would be impossible to over-estimate the depth of the desire of the DVD to regain control of the CIA from President Kennedy's impressive appointee, John McCone.[11]

Aside from its intelligence illiteracy, the absurd lone gunman theory is easily disposed of. First and foremost, *no ballistics match* has ever been done with the two bullets that hit President Kennedy. These are supposed to have been fired from the Mannlicher-Carcano 6.5 mil. Italian service rifle, which the Warren Commission concluded was owned by Lee Harvey Oswald, the alleged gunman.

The only match that was ever done, to bullet fragments allegedly found in the presidential Lincoln, takes the matter no further. They could have been fired after the rifle was taken into the possession of the authorities. The chain of evidence linking the fragments (Warren Commission Exhibit Numbers 567 and 569) to the Lincoln isn't all that secure anyway. The initial shots were probably .22.

Without a ballistics match to the rifle attributed to Oswald there has never been any reason to take the lone gunman theory seriously. It doesn't matter how many chief justices or TV anchormen push it the bullets, which killed the President didn't come out of that gun. *Pace* the abuse heaped over the years on those like Judge Garrison who have asked mostly intelligent questions about the assassination, no intelligence officer would take the theory that Oswald shot the president seriously without first obtaining a ballistics report on 'his' gun. In a brilliant documentary in 2021 (*JFK Revisited*) Oliver Stone demonstrated that the rifle in the posed photograph with Oswald had a different barrel length and sling attachment to the rifle handed in to Dallas PD.

Since he was a trained sniper and ex-Marine they would have been dubious about the theory anyway as soon as they were told what rifle he was supposed to have used. A 1940 model Mannlicher-Carcano 6.5 mil., serial number C2766 was an Italian service rifle from World War II. It was based on a pattern first used by the Austro-Hungarian Army in the 1890s and was fitted with a cheap Japanese 4 by 18 scope.[12]

If they were told that the rifle wasn't cleaned and the sights hadn't been 'scoped in', i.e. aligned, they wouldn't have been expecting a ballistics match anyway. What is more, if the tests on the rifle to see if three rounds could be fired in eight seconds (there are different ways of doing the timing but three in eight is about right) had been ordered by an intelligence officer he or she would have made sure that they were conducted with the rifle in the state in which it was found. When the FBI did their bogus test they had the gun cleaned up and oiled, *with a clip*.

In summation, it is suggested that there are twelve basic reasons why the Oswald/lone gunman theory is a non-starter, with every respect to those taking the contrary view:

(1) Assassinations are a state sponsored phenomenon. There are no 'lone' gunmen.

(2) There is a major chain of evidence of problem re the alleged ammunition clip. *A* clip, acquired by the CIA, seems to have been handed in some time after the gun.[13] There is no reason to believe it was *the* clip.

(3) If there was no clip all the FBI and media tests purporting to prove that three aimed shots in eight seconds were possible with the Mannlicher are rendered even more meaningless. With manual loading of the rounds, which are unusually long anyway, the timings are way out. Noticeably, none of these tests was repeated without a clip. The evidential problems with the clip were simply put to one side, i.e. these weren't genuine, scientific tests, merely an exercise in bolstering a conclusion already reached.

(4) As we have seen the tests were meaningless anyway since they were carried out on a cleaned-up weapon with adjusted sights, i.e. they were not conducted with the weapon in the condition it was in on the day it was allegedly used.

(5) Of the at least five rounds known to have been fired at President Kennedy at least two were fired from behind and at least two from in front, as demonstrated conclusively on the Zapruder footage and by Judge Garrison. As they were fired from different directions there *was* crossfire, i.e. there had to be more than one sniper.

(6) The weapon and sight combination were not the choice of a competent sniper. The 6.5 mil. Italian round is not particularly powerful and the action is of antiquated design. The Mannlicher-Carcano, whilst a reasonable service weapon by the standards of World War II, is not especially accurate. It is a standard service as opposed to a specialist sniper weapon and the sights were

more suited to shooting ducks on a Sunday afternoon than an internationally renowned statesman.

(7) The fact that the rifle was not cleaned and oiled suggests that there was no intent to use it on 22nd November 1963. Ditto the fact that the sights were not aligned, the first thing any competent marksman would do after ensuring that his or her gun was in top condition. Since the alleged shooter waited until he no longer had a clear shot this point applies with even more force.

(8) There is no solid chain of evidence linking the weapon to the alleged shooter. It is now beyond dispute that he never handled it. The partial palm print can safely be disregarded. The fact that the person taking the photograph of Oswald with the alleged rifle (the shooter's wife) was Russian, with a family connection to the KGB, does nothing to weaken the point.

(9) The fact that the shooter was himself shot in a secondary assassination in circumstances strongly suggesting complicity on the part of one or more members of the Dallas Police Department points towards a conspiracy. The proven Mafia links of the second shooter suggest Mafia involvement. That in turn brings in one or more hostile European intelligence agencies, since the Mafia are state sponsored. The CIA deal with the Calabrian Mafia, so that the boys had some tame Mafiosi of their own, lay some years in the future.

(10) There is eyewitness testimony of at least one other team of shooters.

(11) The slow speed of the presidential motorcade and the pulling of Secret Service close protection just prior to the assassination suggest Secret Service complicity, i.e. penetration of the Secret Service by a hostile agency. It is a law enforcement agency with a deservedly high reputation[14] and we can safely rule out rogue agents, and

(12) Not only there is no ballistics match between the weapon attributed to the shooter and the bullets that killed President Kennedy but the fact that no match was attempted suggests that interference was run on the investigation.

Who Shot the President?

So, who did shoot the president? We know that there were at least three teams of shooters in Dealey Plaza that day. We now know that the team on the grassy knoll eventually had a target solution, and hit the windscreen of the Lincoln, which had to be replaced.

The KGB, aware that Oswald was a 'defector', launched their own investigation. Oswald was actually a CIA plant, and had been trained by the CIA. He was deployed to the U-2 base at Kadena on Okinawa and took the date and proposed route for the Frank Powers flight to Moscow. That flight was set up by DVD assets inside CIA, Powers eventually being exchanged for the high-ranking DVD agent Colonel 'Rudolf Abel' (not his real name).

Not entirely by co-incidence, since the SVR was keen to emphasise that its forerunner the KGB had no involvement in the assassination, they disclosed their file, unofficially. The 'declassified' papers were handed over, for a modest fee to cover expenses, to a researcher working for Sir Roger Moore. He was doing a documentary on the assassination.[15] Understandably, Sir Roger's team were suspicious, but I gather they were given the 'real McCoy', as opposed to a 'Hatfield'.

The KGB, correctly, concluded that the shooters were partly French. They were enforcers from the very active Saigon underworld, possibly linked to the Binh Xuyen sect. The KGB were unable to track the shooters after the assassination, which is unsurprising. They were exfiltrated, possibly in a converted Douglas B-26 Invader owned by the CIA,[16] to an island in the Gulf of Mexico. Here they were paid off, in more senses than one. Apparently, they were offered a ride in a helicopter, with a small, radio-controlled IED. Nothing more was heard of them. There are some in INTELCOM who think the shooters may have parachuted onto an oil-rig and I have heard mention of an alternative pickup using the Fulton Surface-to-Air Recovery System. Several shooters were American, probably gunmen who had worked for LBJ before, plus the CIA team. Being made President wasn't Johnson's first promotion using kinetic methods.

Only the biggest players in KGB however would have appreciated that the Kennedy operation was run by the DVD. Its existence was treated as a state secret. Of course, the DVD's assets in the KGB would have appreciated from the moment that they heard the news that it was likely to have been a German operation. They would probably have been expecting something of the sort from the moment they heard that Allen 'von' Dulles had been fired.

The CIA investigation into the assassination was even more thorough. They linked in Lyndon Johnson after reviewing his phone records. Amusingly, it seems that his office in the old Executive Office Building in DC forgot that Dallas was on Central Time. They started arranging the transition half an hour before the president was shot. Normally we like the vice-president *not* to know about the assassination of the president until *after* he has been shot.

The company the vice-president kept in Dallas the night before didn't do him any favours with the CIA boys either. One of the team, a tall, lanky Texan, as it happens, went to the President in 1968, at a time when LBJ had ambitions to run for a second term. He gave him the bad news.

The funding was laundered through Carlos Marcello Senior, of the New Orleans Mafia. He got an 'honourable' mention in Oliver Stone's film *JFK*. With respect the film correctly picks up in the first half that there was a plot, then loses it in the second half. Judge Jim Garrison's investigation was conducted entirely in good faith and got far closer to the truth than His Honour ever realised.

They should have put Jim Garrison on the Supreme Court, preferably in a slot vacated by Chief Justice Warren. The latter, with respect, inflicted terrible damage on a fine institution with his musical comedy inquiry. The Mafia of course were then essentially an arm of the DVD's Italian black agency, having previously reported to Mussolini. As always with the Mafia however, there were eddies, feuds and crosscurrents. Basically, your Calabrian Mafiosi is a much nicer Mafiosi than your Sicilian. He has better manners and tends to be better dressed. He would *never* shoot you over dinner - hence the deal with the CIA.

Richard Helms was later promoted to be Director of Central Intelligence. It does not seem that he was made by the CIA investigation team - the real one I mean. Whenever the president is assassinated, there is always a fake team, to keep the *Washington Post* and the Bad Guys happy. For the Kennedy investigation the real team were based in Dallas, TX, where the boys set up a field office, under a bogus cover. The bogus investigation was run out of Langley, VA. Just to get this straight: the real CIA Kennedy investigation was run out of a fake office in Dallas whilst the fake investigation was run out of a real office in Langley.

There was also an FBI investigation, which at one point actually started to get serious. FBI Special Agent Laurence Keenan apparently didn't understand that the Department of Justice did *not* want the president's killers found. Since one of the conspirators was sitting in the White House, uncovering the plot was the *last* thing Department of Justice wanted. Keenan was probably working with the Washington Field Office. They are the smartest operators in the FBI in my experience. They *never* meet you in the office - too many German spies.

Special Agent Keenan was hauled off the investigation when he started to get too close to the truth, south of the border. He probably handed his stuff over to the CIA's Dallas boys however. This *may* have been done in a bar in El Paso, possibly after the boys had flown into Biggs.

Marcello was made. He was spoken to and then prosecuted, Al Capone style, on tax-evasion charges. He was later terminated with extreme prejudice in an IFTE (Informal, Fast-Track Execution). He could not have had any real complaints, although his lawyers might have kicked up an unnecessary fuss had they known about it. Being a lawyer myself, I know how pedantic lawyers can be. All this happened in the secure and comfortable surroundings of Fort Worth Federal Penitentiary.

CIA Director John 'Mac' McCone briefed in the Attorney-General Robert Francis Kennedy, the third and last of the brothers to be assassinated, on the day of the assassination itself. RFK wanted, and Mac promised, a serious CIA investigation in addition to the usual Janet and John one for the media and Congress, referred to above. Mac was not of course in the loop on the decision to assassinate the President. He was one of the Good Guys.

Thanks to the real investigation, 'von' Dulles was unable to force his way back in. The DVD were forced to wait until Helms took over as DCI before they regained control of the agency. Things were never the same again, however. Major players in Langley had become aware of the DVD and the fact that the Dulles brothers were traitors.

The NSA - very nice people - began to assume greater significance. The best people in the Agency went off-campus. Some stayed in Dallas, some went to New York and some to the NSA at Meade. The NSA started to branch out from signals intelligence and eventually it became more powerful than the CIA. 'Mac' stayed on at Langley. He eventually resigned in 1965 after a difference of aims with LBJ over Vietnam. 'Mac' wanted to win the war. LBJ did not.

Since the Kennedy Assassination the Agency has operated like a series of concentric rings. There is an outer American ring. This is the bit you read about in books and see in a Jason Bourne movie. Then there is a second, German ring, run from that DVD/Correa Group office on the edge of Frankfurt-am-Main airport, which for a long time they thought we didn't know about. Then you have the inner, American ring, which tries to protect the outer ring from the Germans.

This inner ring also maintains the intelligence alliance with the UK. This is sometimes done over a refreshing glass of 'Jack Black' for the CIA, and medium dry vodka martinis, shaken not stirred, for us Brits. British intelligence works in much the same way. We have deeply penetrated, and more or less useless, official agencies and a little off-campus network. In effect this is MI18 reborn. It works a little bit like an old *Avengers* TV episode, minus the lovely ladies in leather. It does its best to keep the show on the road between Test Matches.

Fewer women have been more wronged than the gracious Jackie Kennedy. Her husband, who sadly was not entirely faithful to her but to whom she was loyal, was murdered beside her. She was forced to attend the swearing in of the unpleasant LBJ, who had acquiesced in the murder of her beloved husband. Then she was bullied into marrying the DVD's Aristotle Onassis, who made pots of money on German-controlled Medium Term Note trading programmes.

President Kennedy's reputation has been attacked ever since he was shot, mostly unfairly. Jack Kennedy was a fine naval officer, who distinguished himself in combat in the South Pacific. He was a leader of men, a good man and a great President. They only shoot the good ones.

RFK

Sirhan Bishara Sirhan, the Palestinian terrorist who was one of the team which shot Robert Francis Kennedy at the Ambassador Hotel in LA on 5th June 1968, also worked for the DVD. He was recruited at arm's length, but the CIA boys in Dallas made him in the end. As one of them told me, "always follow the money, Michael". In this case the money trail led to certain members of his family and some slightly dodgy Jesuit charities. In the 1968 campaign the DVD backed Nixon. He of course had been vice-president to their man Eisenhower.

The DVD also had a presence at the Lorraine Motel in Memphis on 4th April of that year, when Dr King was assassinated. The intent was to stir up racial unrest in the USA. The DVD have always tried to wedge American society in this way. In Britain they love to drive a wedge between the Scots and the English.

The first Kennedy brother to be assassinated by the Germans of course was Joe Jnr. He was blown up on 12th August 1944 whilst on a highly dubious mission. It was basically a pretext to get him onto an aircraft laden with high explosives. The plane was a modified US Navy PB4Y, or Liberator. (Only the Army Air Force called them B-24s.)

The newly established DVD arranged that assassination, using ONI assets. It had Secretary Forrestal's and Admiral King's backing. The motive was almost certainly to protect their man Joe Snr, a most unpleasant individual. Old Joe must have appreciated why his eldest son had been murdered. Joe Jnr was smart and seems to have worked out that his father was working for the Germans.

There is an interesting historical symmetry here. John McCone, appointed by JFK as CIA Director, worked with ONI on the exposure of Forrestal. The latter, as we have seen, was very properly terminated with extreme prejudice on President Truman's orders. As Secretary of the Navy, Forrestal just happened to have sanctioned the assassination of JFK's beloved elder brother Joe Jnr. It is unlikely that Mac's appointment to the CIA was coincidental. Both Mac and JFK were very well informed.

---

1. The first was Spanish Flu. You could argue that too many nations and races were targeted to meet the formal definition of genocide, but with over 50 million dead it's not a terribly persuasive argument. The second was the Holocaust of course, and the third was Cambodia, although you could also make a case for including the Armenian Genocide, since it must have been cleared in advance with Turkey's ally 'the Hun.' The fourth was HIV/AIDS, around 42 million people murdered so far, and counting, many of them fellow gays.
2. She wasn't!
3. Combination timer and barometric fusing only came in much later, with digital electronic fuses, as used by the DVD at Lockerbie. It is much trickier to set a fuse for the second time the aircraft reaches a particular altitude. Fusing for the descent phase of flight is always messier.
4. *Op. cit.*, Ch. 5, p.103, *Could a Single Bullet Bring an Airliner Down*?
5. See pp. 128-29.
6. *Ibid*, p. 13. The figures come from the reputable Swedish Airline Pilots Association.
7. Distance Measuring Equipment, normally linked to the VOR, a more sophisticated radio aid using VHF. In the military DME is referred to as TACAN. It was a great aid to navigation in the days before the gyro-based inertial navigation system (INS) and the satellite-based Global Positioning System (GPS) came in.
8. Her full name is Maria Teresa Thierstein Simoes-Ferrera Heinz Kerry.
9. By that nice chap Christopher Andrew in *MI5, Defence of the Realm*. That is their motto by the way. You will see it in Latin on their headed notepaper if they ever write to you. Although a Cambridge man, Andrew also got the Cambridge Spy Ring wrong with respect, putting them down as Soviet spies, instead of German. Please do not attribute any of my conclusions to him - the poor chap would be most upset, and since he is a gent, if I may say so, the last thing I would want to do is upset him.
10. Series 3, episode 5, airdate 9th December 1982.
11. John McCone 1902-1991, he did good work in shipping in World War II, was deputy to John Forrestal as Secretary of Defense in 1948 and was involved in the ONI investigation which led to Forrestal being sanctioned, which did not endear him to the DVD.
12. It was supplied by the importer, Ordnance Optics Inc., of Hollywood, to Klein's Sporting Goods, who fitted it and allegedly supplied the rifle to Oswald. It is far more likely that they supplied it to someone pretending to be him. There was no ID of Oswald by Klein's Sporting Goods. All we have is a paper trail that could have been laid by anyone. Moreover, as Oliver Stone has pointed out, the parcel would not have been delivered had US postal regulations been followed. They usually are.
13. As it happens by an officer who later became a friend of mine, but you need not take his/her word for it. The exhibit numbers for the Warren Commission for the gun and the skeleton magazine clip are out of sequence. The clip was handed in about three months after the gun, apparently after an 'anything else we missed? Oh s**t, a clip!' style review at Langley. The gun is Exhibit

Number 139, the photograph of the clip is Exhibit Number 574 and the clip is Exhibit Number 575, although the Warren Commission Index is not clear. That is the first documentation we see for the clip, aside from a brief, allegedly contemporaneous note by Lt J. C. Day, the chain of evidence for which has never been tested, indeed it is not supported by the Dallas Police inventory. The strongest evidence that there was a clip is a photograph by William G. Allen of the *Dallas Times Herald*, but that evidence also has never been tested. It does not assist on the clip's serial number, does not explain why it never arrived at the Dallas Police Department, or why it would be reinserted in the rifle after allegedly having been removed by Lt Day. It also does not explain why if the rifle and clip were together they were not exhibited by the Warren Commission at the same time. If all was in order, we would expect the clip to have been bagged as evidence and given exhibit number '140', indeed there is no obvious reason why they could have been exhibited together, as 139. There is a massive chain of evidence problem with the clip and I am inclined to believe my CIA source, i.e. the agency handed in the clip photographed as exhibit 574, separated, as we would expect, from the rifle, about three months later. There is, by the way, no chain of evidence linking Oswald with Exhibit 575, i.e. no evidence that a clip was sold with the gun and no evidence of a separate purchase. There is some evidence that the clips were sold separately, with the ammunition, not that there is any audit trail for a purchase of 6.5 mil. ammo by Oswald. There has been a determined attempt since to muddy the waters, which is why the photograph purporting to show a clip in the rifle when it was retrieved from its hiding place in the School Book Depository has to be viewed with caution.

14. With whom I have had contacts. There were at least four assassination attempts on President George W. Bush or plans to assassinate him, in his first term, each set up by the DVD. I inputted intelligence on all of them and there may have been others. In my experience, the Secret Service are invariably courteous and professional. They are, in short, good people. Their Intelligence Center is particularly good, way more professional than MI5 e.g. They were highly embarrassed by the Kennedy Assassination but they were up against the world's most powerful covert intelligence agency and the only one with the ability to penetrate them. Since all Western intelligence and law enforcement agencies at national level have been penetrated there is no particular need for the Secret Service to feel embarrassed. Courtesy, by the way, is a sign of professionalism and the Secret Service, are *very* professional.
15. *JFK Assassination Files*. The series was called *The Secret KGB Files*, Associated Television International, worth watching.
16. Nice plane, originally called the A-26 and then redesignated the B-26 by the Pentagon in order to generate confusion with the real B-26, the Martin Marauder. Two Pratt & Whitney R-2800 radials. Nice bit of kit, it did good work in the closing months of World War II, in Korea, over Vietnam and at the Bay of Pigs.

24

The Vietnam Era

The Abolition of Capital Punishment

Given its control of most organised crime the DVD has an obvious interest in lighter penalties for murder. Obviously not *all* organised crime is state sponsored, but the rule of thumb is that the more organised crime is the more likely it is to be state sponsored. This applies in particular to narcotics trafficking. The old rule was that pro-German Democrats took a cut of heroin shipped through the South of France whilst pro-German Republicans took a cut of cocaine shipped from Colombia.[1] These days it gets all confused, with left-wing Republicans benefitting from the heroin trade and left-wing Democrats benefitting from the cocaine trade. Nobody knows where anybody is anymore.

The 'Hun' has always made good use of psychopaths. In Britain he started after the war with the 'Acid Bath Murderer' John Haigh, who was prosecuted, as we saw in Chapter 4, by the German spy Sir Hartley Shawcross. Since the advent of the Internet, we now have well-informed psychopaths. Your psychopath can in fact be quite intelligent, i.e. violent but not stupid.

This blew up in the Bad Guys' faces in January 2011, when they were trying to block Governor Palin from getting the Republican nomination in 2012. She really has the DVD worried, not to mention the local moose. They set up the assassination of a nice, Democrat Congresswoman, Gabrielle Giffords. Of course they selected the nicest Democrat they could find. It wasn't a lengthy search.

They wanted her blown away but the chap they'd chosen, Jared Lee Loughner, through the usual cut-outs, ratted on them. He saved the Congresswoman's life by swapping ammunition. Apparently, he popped along to a Walmart and got some much less messy ammunition than the stuff he was given. He shot a few other Democrats, and a federal judge, instead. This was never likely to be a good defence however.[2] I suspect he was offered a deal. At any rate he is serving his sentence in a cushy federal medical centre, not a supermax facility. The Department of Justice is keen to preserve the myth of the 'lone gunman'.

The cunning plan was to blame Governor Palin. She knew nothing whatsoever about the planned assassination and had never heard of the shooter. She had however made some sensible marks with respect on gun control. These could have been, indeed were, twisted by unsympathetic parts of the media. Where Governor Palin is concerned that's pretty much everybody except those nice people at Fox News, to whose fair and balanced coverage I once contributed.

Some media outlets close to the DVD were briefed in advance. They reported that the good Congresswoman had been assassinated. It's always good policy to make sure that the target has expired before announcing his or her death. Thankfully, since she does seem with respect to be a genuinely nice lady, she survived. Although badly wounded, she has made a good recovery, at least physically (she's still a Democrat). Before her untimely resignation Republicans in her district were reportedly in a race not to be the candidate.[3] I hate to see careers wrecked by Bad Guy black ops and I was genuinely sorry not to see her re-elected.

The DVD love chaos, except in Germany of course. Even there they had their own tame terrorist group, the Baader-Meinhof Faction. They went around knocking off bankers etc. who were holding out on the DVD. At least they didn't go so far as to kidnap the Chancellor, unlike their DVD counterparts in Italy, the Red Brigades. They bundled poor old Aldo Mori, then the Prime Minister, into the boot of a car, although being Italy hardly anyone noticed.[4]

Anxious both to increase the murder rate in Britain and protect their own people should they get caught, DVD/GO2 assets in Whitehall, including in the Home Office, were able to water down the punishment for murder from death to life. They started in 1957 with the idiotic Homicide Act. It may as well have been described in the preamble as an "Act to encourage homicide", which it did. In order to get the act passed GO2, i.e. the German operation in London, selected a couple of sacrificial bunnies. They were hanged, for political reasons, when manifestly their sentences should have been commuted to life imprisonment.

The Bentley Case

The first unfortunate was a rather silly young man, Derek Bentley. He decided that it would be a good idea to go out on a night-time burglary expedition with a younger but more intelligent man, Craig. The latter was armed with a revolver, a Colt New Service .455, and was prepared to use it. Even with a cut-down barrel, a .455 is a pretty bulky weapon. It is improbable that it was concealed from Bentley, who sadly was not the quickest on the uptake. These days he would probably be a believer in global warming.

Rather than go quietly when challenged, Craig murdered a young police constable, PC Miles. The officer was only doing his duty, protecting the people of London. Bentley uttered the immortal cry "let him have it, Chris". The jury, who saw and heard him give evidence, took those words to mean "let him *have* it", rather than "please hand the gun over to the nice policeman and let's go quietly". Craig however was too young to be hanged.

Lord Goddard, the Lord Chief Justice of England, a good judge and a fair man with respect,[5] realised that it would be a monstrous injustice in the circumstances to hang Bentley. He had not fired the fatal shot and the man who had, Craig, could not be hanged. Quite properly, the Lord Chief recommended that a merciful course be taken, as did the jury, to their credit. The 'Chief' however was unaware that the Cabinet Secretary was a German spy, angling for the abolition of capital punishment. To Lord Goddard's justifiable outrage, and that of the public, young Bentley was hanged.

Ruth Ellis

The next sacrificial bunny was a young woman, Ruth Ellis. She had coldly shot her lover, David Blakely, four times, three of the shots being at very close range. This made it rather difficult for her counsel, the great Melford Stevenson QC, to run accident as a defence. Blakely had been violent and abusive towards Ruth however and there were grounds for clemency. This was duly recommended by the trial judge, Mr Justice Havers. If I may say so, His Lordship was a very sound tribunal. No Englishman could be expected to have much sympathy for a man who had taken his hand to a woman.

The public expected mercy to be shown. They turned away from capital punishment in droves when it wasn't, as clearly it should have been. The Home Secretary, however, was Gwilym Lloyd George. As we have seen, he was working for Germany. He was "BB", or "Bad Boche", in MI5's very helpful old scheme of classification, which ought to be brought back. Lloyd George wanted hanging abolished. As a traitor of course, soft sentences for treason were very much in his interest!

However, Ruth Ellis was hanged by Albert Pierrepoint at 9 am on 13th July 1955. He would probably much have preferred to hang the Home Secretary, but when you are the public hangman you have to hang whom you are told. You cannot just pop around to the Home Office with a noose and string up the Home Secretary, however much he might deserve it. It would generate complaints, and inter-departmental memoranda.

The Hanratty Case

In 1963 a violent young man, James Hanratty, raped and paralysed a nice lady named Valerie Storie. He murdered her lover, Michael Gregsten, in the same incident, in a lay-by on the A6 trunk road in Bedfordshire. He was tried at Bedford Assizes, in the lovely old Court 1, which was later used by the Bedfordshire Justices (I have prosecuted in it.) Bedfordshire murder cases, of which sadly there are a number these days, mostly from Luton, now go to a ghastly, modern Crown Court in Luton.[6] This is built in brutalist style, although in fairness it fits in with the local architecture.

Hanratty was very properly sentenced to death by the learned trial judge, Mr Justice Gorman. Like Havers J., he was with respect a deeply fair man, as was the prosecuting counsel, Graham Stanwick QC. GO2 quickly got a campaign going, in an effort to persuade the public that the prosecution and jury had got it wrong, which they hadn't, and that Hanratty was innocent, which he wasn't. The usual suspects in the House of Commons and the press joined in the clamour. They were nowhere to be found when DNA tests eventually confirmed Hanratty's guilt.

In point of fact, there were no substantial miscarriages of justice in capital cases in Britain in the twentieth century. The tiny number of German spies who were spotted, including the notorious Sir Roger Casement, were very properly hanged. Very frankly, deals might have been cut with some of the bunnies the Abwehr sent over in World War II. As Major Zolle, a Gestapo 'major' said in an episode of *Hogan's Heroes*,[7] when investigating Colonel Klink's MI5-like perfect record at Stalag 13, "if something looks too good I am always suspicious".

Dr Crippen, as we have seen, did not murder his wife, but he did kill Asquith's male lover.[8] He couldn't have been heard to complain too loudly. Timothy Evans was hanged in 1950 for murdering his baby daughter Geraldine when he should have been hanged as an accessory to the murder of his wife, whom he was pressing to have an abortion.

The prosecution was bungled and there was police misconduct. In particular, they should not have interviewed Evans without a solicitor present, as again he was a bit slow on the uptake. It probably wasn't a miscarriage of justice however, when looked at in the round. There is no doubt that Christie, the serial killer and former special constable, who lived downstairs at 10 Rillington Place, was also involved. It is also clear that Christie, was initially protected by GO2 assets in the Metropolitan Police, indeed he may even have carried out contract killings for them. It's a bit unusual to find serial killers serving in the police, even the Met.

Mr Justice Brabin, who reported on the case to the Home Secretary, Sir Frank Soskice, in 1966, with respect, probably got near the truth. His report has been much maligned over the years but may have to be shown greater respect. I respect it, in any event, even if others don't.

Abolition

Capital punishment, for murder at any rate, finally went in 1965. Supporters of the death penalty had argued correctly that abolition would encourage murder, i.e. would cost lives, not save them. So it has proved. Even the strongest supporters of capital punishment however could scarcely have envisioned the horrors that were to come. Two murderous paedophiles, Ian Brady and Myra Hindley, sadly, could not be hanged, even though they had started their killing spree before the Murder (Abolition of Death Penalty) Act 1965 became law.

These two sexually assaulted and tortured some of the children they murdered. To add to the torment of young Keith Bennett's anguished mother, Winnie Johnson, who sadly died in 2012, they refused to tell police where they had the hidden his body. She died without ever being able to say goodbye to her young son.

It is still unclear whether they were working for GO2 or not, but they had high-level political support. Mrya Hindley was visited in prison by the pro-German Labour peer, the Earl of Longford. Although the jury were satisfied that each was sane and fully criminally responsible for their hideous acts, the Cabinet Office later substituted its view for that of the jury. Brady was removed to the cushy surroundings of a hospital (or rest- home, depending upon your point of view) for the criminally insane. The prosecuting counsel at their trial, by way, was my old friend Sir Elwyn Jones QC, as he then was. He did well.

The statistics have been played around with in order to disguise the human cost of abolition, and there are separate crime stats for Scotland. Broadly speaking however, the murder rate in Britain has gone up by about 500% since 1957. It used to be roughly a murder a week but is now roughly a murder a day.[9] The psychological impact has not been insignificant. Children used to be safe in Britain and largely speaking still are.

Parents no longer believe it however and tend to be over-protective, in turn imposing stress on families and causing congestion at school starting and finishing times. Most children are now ferried to and from school, on the not unreasonable theory that the streets are no-longer safe. Since it is official policy to encourage the murder of children, and the violent sexual abuse that tragically so often goes with it, by soft penalties, who can blame the parents?

The argument that the death penalty does not deter murder should not have survived, but has, the dramatic increase in the murder rate in Britain after 1957.[10] The impressive reductions in the murder rate in those American states wise enough to restore the death penalty after the Supreme Court let them should also have helped demolish the argument. The court had previously suspended the death penalty on the with respect dubious foundation that the US Constitution prohibited it. That news would have come as a surprise to both George Washington and Thomas Jefferson.[11]

Abolition in Britain even survived the strange case of Glyn Dix. He was handed down a 'life' sentence for shooting dead his wife. The British public were deceived at the time of abolition into believing that 'life would mean life', which was utter nonsense of course. Dix was released early, on parole. Since he was officially a widower, having murdered his wife, he was free to marry again.

In a triumph of hope over experience, a lady sadly accepted his less than gallant proposal of marriage. At home in Redditch, Worcestershire, in 2005, they had a row over what to watch on television. This is rarely a wise thing to do if your husband is a convicted killer out on licence. He promptly murdered her and cut her body into 16 pieces, presumably hoping to make a point. In a way, he did. It's time to bring back hanging. Naturally murderers would only be hanged in the nicest possible way.

They ought to have a chaplain and a slap-up breakfast. There would be a silk rope for peers of the realm, even life peers.

Mass Immigration

Desirous of inflicting even more damage on American society than he had already done by going along with the murder of President Kennedy, LBJ in 1965 decided that it would be a good idea to relax immigration controls. The idea was to encourage people from the Third World to come to America. I say nothing against people from the Third World, who can be very nice. The problem however with inviting them into your country to live is that parts of it can end up looking like the Third World.

The basic rule is that you only invite people in if they can bring capital with them, or have a needed skill, i.e. one that you cannot supply yourself. Semi-skilled or unskilled labour - the bulk of immigration into the West - is only needed in times of labour shortage. There haven't been many of those since Germany sponsored the Great Depression.

You will always find business leaders without a brain arguing for immigration to drive down labour costs. That is a double-edged sword, since other businesses will want to sell products to those same wage earners. Unemployment drives up taxes moreover, as unemployment has to be paid for. More seriously there is a huge human cost. Semi-skilled and unskilled immigrants mostly displace working class labour in Britain. In the States, African Americans have suffered the most. That point was brought home to me in 2012 by a nice black community activist, Ted Hayes, as he kindly showed me around 'Skid Row' in Los Angeles.

The same business leaders will usually be found arguing in favour of exporting jobs to China or Mexico, on the basis that consumers - at any rate those consumers who can still consume because they still have a job - will benefit from cheaper goods. They will, until they lose their jobs.

As the distinguished British demographer Professor David Coleman has pointed out, the costs of immigration are not confined to labour displacement. They include associated crime (sadly, immigrant communities have tended to be represented disproportionately in the crime statistics), additional security, the race relations industry and increased social costs such as health and education. You can have classes speaking over 40 different languages at some inner-city schools in Britain. Mass immigration has tended to be pushed in both Britain and America by DVD penetration assets, both in politics and the bureaucracy. They are aided of course by 'useful idiots', to employ Lenin's telling phrase. The British people were persuaded in the 1950s that Britain needed to import nurses and bus-drivers, as though people had gone uncared for in British hospitals before World War II, or nobody in Britain knew how to drive a bus.

The American people have been persuaded, at least partially, that New York needed to import taxi-drivers from Lahore. This was presumably on the basis that traffic conditions are similar. Washington apparently needs taxi-drivers from Addis Ababa, presumably because of the number of Congressmen who speak Amharic.

It is not as though all immigrant communities desire to integrate with their host country. So far to the contrary, they tend these days to insist on sticking to their own language, dress and customs. This has got to the point that Western societies are slowly being transformed into something else. The human cost of uncontrolled mass immigration was brought home in Britain on 7/7 and in the Unites States when the first terrorists born in the USA started killing people, or trying to. The appalling attack on the Boston Marathon in April 2013 involved terrorists who, absurdly, had been granted political asylum in the United States. The Woolwich terrorist attack in London the following month involved dual nationals.

Societies with two main languages, e.g. Belgium, rarely thrive. The Kingdom of Belgium has a major linguistic fault-line. Not long ago it prevented even what passes for government in Belgium being undertaken. There was the usual DVD hissy fit (a pre-Christmas shoot-up on the streets) when the new Prime Minister was chosen by the Belgians, not the Germans. The 'Hun' still has not gotten used to the fact that he was thrown out of Belgium in 1918.

The economic arguments in favour of unskilled and semi-skilled immigration are hogwash. Whilst increasing your population can increase your GDP, it's GDP *per capita* that counts. In Britain the massive increase in population has led to severe strains on public services. The British government has no idea how many people live in the country. The census figures are a complete farce. One way of getting a rough estimate is to look at food sales. People can throw their census forms in their wheelie bins, but they still have to eat. The official 2011 population figure was a little over 63 million people, but each week we seem to be selling enough food for 70 million, even after allowing for waste.

TSR-2

This superb aircraft was cancelled under pressure from the DVD's Roy Jenkins, despite excellent progress in the flight tests. The Chief Test Pilot was that fine airman Squadron Leader Roland 'Roley' Beamont. He was a friend of several friends of mine and did great work in the war on Hawker Typhoons, a lovely bit of kit, with the 24-cylinder Napier Sabre engine. He strafed lots of 'Jerries'. The decision to cancel the aircraft was actually made in the Cabinet Office in 1958, six years before its first flight. There was never any intention that it would enter squadron service with the RAF.

Jenkins of course was working with DVD assets in Whitehall and with his DVD colleagues Duncan Sandys and Lord Mountbatten. They waged bureaucratic guerrilla warfare against the TSR-2 for years. No argument was too facile to be put forward. It was actually a superb aircraft, which flew well. Its avionics were world beating. For a strike aircraft it went like a bat out of hell. On one famous occasion Roley was able to pull away from the chase plane on *one engine*. The chase plane was a supersonic English Electric Lightning, capable of Mach 2 plus.

The German idea was to funnel almost all development into one type, tie up the British military aircraft industry and then pull the rug from under it. It still hasn't recovered. Whitehall assets drove up costs by insisting on all test-flying taking place at Boscombe Down instead of at English Electric. They should also have been the lead contractor. The resultant costs blowout was then cynically used as an argument against the aircraft.

Even more cynical was the bad-faith order placed with General Dynamics for the F-111. This was another fine aircraft, which was the subject of a DVD sabotage and technology transfer campaign. Its blueprints were given to the Soviets. No F-111s were ever delivered to the RAF. They served with distinction with the RAAF however, based at Amberley in Queensland, whee my younger brother Toney was once based.

As a result of the TSR-2's cancellation the RAF were badly short of modern bombers and strategic reconnaissance aircraft in the Falklands, Gulf and Iraq Wars. They were forced to make do with older types like the Avro Vulcan or tactical types like the Tornado. The Tornado is a nice bit of kit but it's no TSR-2. In 2025 the heaviest bomber in service with the RAF is the Battle of Britain Memorial Flight's Avro Lancaster. She's 80 years old, even older than the Chief of the Air Staff, no offence intended.

Fairey Delta Two

At the same time as undermining the TSR-2, DVD assets in Whitehall also forced Fairey to transfer the Fairey FD2 Delta to the French. An outstanding design, in 1956 it took the World Air Speed past 1,000 mph for the first time. The 'Frogs' reworked it as a low-wing fighter, dropped the droop nose, gave it radar and other improved avionics and called it the Mirage. It was a great success, but the orders should have gone to Fairey, not Dassault.

Bristol were similarly sold down the river, being forced to share their SST design, which became the Concorde, with the French. The French SST was far too small and had too short a range for the North Atlantic. That was the market which made most sense for a supersonic airliner. Britain even agreed to spell the aircraft the French way. We ended up allowing them to control the parts supply. This in turn gave France a hold over British Airways, which they used to force her withdrawal from service.

The Ministry of Defence

Lord Mountbatten also pushed to set up the Ministry of Defence. The theory was that it would:

(1) Introduce an additional layer of bureaucracy.
(2) Drive up costs.
(3) Make it more difficult for the services to work together.
(4) Slash Cabinet representation for the services, making it easier to cut the defence budget, and

(5) See airmen making decisions on ships, naval types making decisions on tanks and 'brown jobs' making decisions on aircraft, with the possibility of having a square peg in every round hole.

Mountbatten's reasoning was sound.

Vietnam

On 2nd August 1964 the destroyer USS *Maddox* (DD-731)[12] was attacked by North Vietnamese torpedo boats in the Gulf of Tonkin. She had been on a *De Soto* intelligence-gathering mission and NSA personnel were embarked. The *Maddox* was proceeding on her lawful occasions in international waters when she was attacked. It was an Act of War, and the United States was fully justified in going to war with North Vietnam, although it should have been declared.

The failure to declare war led to such confusion that at times the Johnson Administration, which was confused at the best of times, did not seem to know whether the United States was at war with the Democratic Republic of Vietnam or not. For the avoidance of doubt, you do not bomb someone's capital city with B-52 Stratofortresses in a police action.

That was the first of many mistakes made by the Johnson Administration. The second was using reporting of a further attack, on 4th August, on the *Maddox* and the USS *Turner Joy* (DD-951)[13] to justify the limited War Powers Resolution put before Congress. Whilst the reporting was generated in good faith there was undoubted confusion that night. It is difficult to argue with the on-scene commander, Captain John J. Herrick, that "it was unlikely any torpedoes were fired" that night.[14]

Critics of the Vietnam War seized on the probability that there had been no second attack and ignored the first attack altogether. Even now it is not entirely clear that there was no North Vietnamese naval activity that night. North Vietnamese records might have been tampered with once the issue became politicised. The better view appears to be that there was some activity but that the American destroyers were not fired upon.

Since the *Maddox* had been attacked on the 2nd, it scarcely mattered. It was a bit like saying that Britain and France could not go to war with Germany in 1939 because she hadn't invaded Denmark as well as Poland. You only need one Act of War to start a war.

The next mistake was not to recognise that Ho Chi Minh was a German spy. He was in fact the DVD's highest-ranking asset in Hanoi. The French made the same mistake at Dien Bien Phu. Their strategy, which was a variant of General Orde Wingate's successful Chindit strategy in South East

Asia Command in 1943-1944, was pushed by German assets in Paris. They then betrayed it, along with the defence plans for the fortress, to Hanoi. In each case the intelligence failure was fundamental and led not only to misidentification of the enemy but a failure to shut down the leaks in Paris and Washington.

The fourth failure, the decision not to prosecute the war vigorously, flowed directly from the third. Key policymakers in Washington were DVD. This was a bad mistake. No experienced military intelligence officer or strategic analyst could review US strategy for the Vietnam War, such as it was with respect, and conclude that the politicians in Washington who came up with it were acting in good faith. Several key policymakers clearly were not working for the home team.

Since no counterintelligence officer could seriously have supposed that President Johnson or any senior member of his administration was a communist, the answer had to lie elsewhere. Had the US known the true nationalities of the 'Russian' North Vietnamese Mig-21 pilots - West and East German - it would have been easier to spot the German connection. So far as I know however, I was the first to pass this information to Washington, long after the war ended.

MI6 knew, but they sat on it. This was mainly because they too were heavily penetrated. They also had an irritating 'it's not our war' attitude. In fairness, the DVD and the Luftwaffe had learnt from the radio security breakdowns in Korea, where panicking Mig-15 pilots had lapsed into speaking German. Only Russian or Vietnamese was used over North Vietnam.

For part of the war MI6's Head of Station in Hanoi was dear old Daphne Park, later made Baroness Park of Monmouth. We were introduced years later. An indomitable lady, she had an artificial leg. CIA apparently thought the world of her. I know we did, and she is sorely missed.

Sadly, there was an intelligence disconnect between Korea and Vietnam. The naval and air intelligence officers who had spotted the use of German pilots over Korea do not seem to have been brought in to review the composition of the North Vietnamese air force. Some of these officers were British. Very frankly they should have got their bottoms over to Saigon and offered to share what they knew with USAF intelligence officers. If need be, this could have been done over a chilled beverage in the rooftop bar of the Rex Hotel. That bar was the principal intelligence clearing centre of the Vietnam War.

There was also nothing to stop US intelligence officers speaking to colleagues who had 'done' Korea. Aside from anything else, it would have told them that captured US airmen faced the possibility of being interrogated, i.e. tortured, by German intelligence officers. After that they would be 'disappeared'. The DVD had to execute any captured US pilot they had interrogated, in order to preserve the security of their operation in Hanoi.

The only way to stop that was to go public, preferably after capturing a Mig-21. Sometimes it's better to force your enemy to land at one of your air bases, instead of shooting him down. It would have been a bit difficult for the West German government to explain away a Luftwaffe pilot in a Mig-21. What could they say? "He vas flying to Wiesbaden und unfortunately got lost, ending up in Dong Hoi. There he saw a Mig-21 und thought it vould be nice to take her up for a spin und then to his surprise he vas surrounded by US Navy F-8s?"

Inter alia Washington failed to agree to:

(1) The immediate mining of Haiphong Harbour.
(2) An effective blockade of North Vietnam, particularly with a view to strangling her fuel supplies.
(3) Effective use of strategic air power - there was strategic bombing, but only for short periods, in order to meet limited political objectives.
(4) Effective use of the US Navy's massive shipboard strike capability. American carriers tended to be deployed in small numbers in rotation.
(5) Sensible ROEs for USAF, USMC and USN pilots. The requirement for visual confirmation was ludicrous. Friendly aircraft could be identified by their Identification Friend or Foe signature - that is the whole point of IFF. It was insisted upon solely in order to negate American radar and guided missile superiority and bring her planes closer into the enemy.
(6) Adequate defence budgets, in particular for carrier construction and naval aviation. Only two new attack carriers were commissioned during the entire war. There was a staggering gap between USS *John F Kennedy* (CVA-67) and USS *Nimitz* (CVN-68). The outstanding North American A-5 Vigilante, e.g., was only ever ordered in penny packet numbers.
(7) Deployment of the supersonic Convair B-58 Hustler bomber. There was whingeing about the perfectly reasonable cost of the B-58, but its price per plane only went up because insufficient numbers were ordered.
(8) Decisive use of armour, even though in General Creighton Abrams they had one of the finest attacking tanker generals the world has

ever seen, up there with Heinz Guderian and the underrated Sir Richard O'Connor, hero of the Western Desert in 1940, and

(9) Sufficient troop numbers to go on the offensive. Generally speaking, Washington preferred to pussyfoot around with small formations and let the enemy attack Saigon, rather than kick commie ass all the way back to Hanoi.

Tragically, the failure to appreciate what the DVD were doing led to security lapses on aircraft carriers. Two, USS *Oriskany* (CV-34) and USS *Forrestal* (CV-59), were nearly lost as a consequence of DVD sabotage operations, using US assets. The failure to spot the DVD's narcotics-running operations into US forces led directly to the My Lai massacre. The DVD ran mind-altering narcotics into the 1st Battalion of the 20th Infantry Regiment. Doping the enemy's infantry was an old German ploy from World War I. British military intelligence officers, had they been deployed, might have recalled it. It had never been tried before on the US Army, so their intelligence people were dealing with something new.

At least the Americans got there and tried to do the right thing, which was more than we did. Harold 'von' Wilson of course was DVD. He should been exposed as a traitor and hanged, along with the Cabinet Secretary. Their combined support for North Vietnamese aggression ought to have set people thinking.

Clearing the DVD out of Number 10 and Whitehall would have allowed Britain to enter the war on the side of the Good Guys, i.e. the Americans, South Vietnamese, Australians and New Zealanders. Canada too should have joined in, but her government and public service were just as compromised as Britain's and America's. In the events which happened, only a handful of British ground troops were deployed to Vietnam. They were disguised as Australians, complete with dodgy Aussie accents, mostly in their excellent SAS.

There is no criticism of US military commanders. The mistakes were made in Washington and Langley. Generals Westmoreland and Abrams were fine commanders. The war would not have been lost had they been listened to. As for the domino theory, well the left got their proof, in Laos and Cambodia.

The Khmer Rouge leader, Pol Pot, reported to Peking. He must have been aware that Germany was behind the ChiComs and that Mao was no more a communist than Barry Goldwater. There were quite a few German assets in Indo-China: some French, at least one British, a number of Americans and several Germans. They tended to use commercial cover. They were there, if you knew where to look.

The Holt Assassination

On 17th December 1967 the DVD kidnapped, and later assassinated, the Prime Minister of Australia, the Rt Hon. Harold Holt. He was a serious political figure, who supported the ANZUS alliance with the United States and wanted to engage more fully in Vietnam. He had just authorised the commitment of a third Australian infantry battalion. Moreover, he was both strategically and militarily literate.

Holt had volunteered for the infantry in World War II, being recalled to the government after the Abwehr sabotaged a Lockheed Hudson on approach to land at Canberra on 13th August 1940. They assassinated three key Cabinet ministers, who had been 'channelled' onto the aircraft, together with General Sir Cyril White, Chief of the General Staff.

Holt would have been unlikely to go along with the losing strategy that DVD assets were pushing on the heavily compromised Johnson. Sadly, the president was not forced out by the CIA, until 1968. Holt was replaced by a weak man with respect, Senator John Gorton. His with respect undistinguished wartime record in the RAAF consisted largely of crashing his aircraft, doing silly things like 'forgetting' to switch his fuel cock to the right tank.

Gorton had little strategic grasp, and not much grasp of the Australian Constitution either. He went along with bad advice to resign his Senate seat and enter the House of Representatives, based on no more than a bogus theory that in the Westminster system the Prime Minister has to be in the lower house. This was only four years after the Queen had invited the Earl of Home to form a government in Britain.

Gorton wasted little time in reversing Harold Holt's decision to commit more ground troops to Vietnam. Thereafter he was content to go along with Johnson's losing strategy. He was a far more acceptable choice as Prime Minister to Peking, Hanoi and Dachau, although it would be wrong to regard him as a DVD asset. He was a 'useful idiot', to employ Lenin's helpful phrase again. The DVD assets in Canberra, who were dangerous, were embedded in the federal bureaucracy. They were able to play Gorton like Sir Humphrey Appleby played Jim Hacker in *Yes Minister.*

The complex operational plan for the Holt assassination was drawn up by Skorzeny in Dachau (him again). It involved borrowing a Chinese submarine, probably a Type 33 (Romeo) class, which had a cruising range of about 9,000 miles. My understanding is that the frogmen were German, trained by Italians involved in the Chariot operations in the Med in 1941-1944.

Harold Holt was a strong swimmer. He was known to favour Cheviot Beach, near Portsea, in Victoria. Using the beach regularly made him vulnerable. This was not least as the DVD's assets in Canberra were able to warn Peking, via Jakarta, when Holt was about to go swimming. There was the usual dodgy doctor to provide advice, which he knew would be ignored, not to go swimming. This helped in the presentation of the assassination as drowning.

The sub was probably refuelled from a Chinese freighter at sea. This was easy enough to do, given the postwar reductions in the excellent RAAF and the RNZAF and the limited maritime surveillance of the Coral Sea. That is a problem that persists to the present day. The RAAF and RNZAF each have only a handful of Boeing P-8 Poseidons and there are no major air bases in the South-West Pacific. A Romeo class sub would have needed refuelling, but once refuelled her captain had the option of a faster cruising speed on the surface, i.e. at night.

The sub was probably given a 30-day window in which to remain on station. It may not actually have been the first attempt. I still recall the sense of shock I felt as a ten-year old boy when the Prime Minister's disappearance was announced. We were living in Australia by 1967, of course.

The official version of events is that the Prime Minister drowned, but that is improbable. Usually with an inshore drowning you get a body. It may be washed up many miles from where the swimmer went into the water, but it usually turns up. The first thing you do is send for the tide and currents charts. Alternatively, you may find it floating to the surface after a few days. Either way it usually turns up.

The shark theory ("I see another Prime Minister has been swallowed by a shark" "dang, that just keeps happening") holds even less water than the drowning one. Usually, you find traces after a shark attack - blood, arms, legs that sort of thing. It is a very courteous shark that cleans up after breakfast.

The Greek Colonels

'Jerry' never accepted being thrown out of Greece in 1944. The colonels were essentially neo-fascists. The April 1967 coup simply returned Greece to German control. His Majesty King Constantine, who was a very nice man with respect, and a patriotic Greek, was blameless. These days the Germans tend to use technocrats if they want to take over a country.

The USS *Liberty* Incident

The Six-Day War was quite lawful. The Israelis simply pre-empted German-backed Egyptian and Syrian aggression, as Russia pre-empted Ukrainian aggression against the Donbas Republics in February 2022. On 8th June

1967 Israeli Mirages and Mystères strafed the US intelligence-gathering ship USS *Liberty* (AGTR-5). Understandably, this caused much upset at the NSA, since 34 good men died. The attack was an utter nonsense, but it was not unprovoked.

Unbeknown to the NSA, who would have been appalled, summaries of the intelligence gathered by the *Liberty* were being handed, with Johnson's approval, to the Egyptians. This was done via Correa Group in Frankfurt. The correct response would have been to inform the US Navy and NSA and plug the leak. You simply do not attack the warship of an ally.

Foot and Mouth Disease as a Biological Weapon

British agriculture has long been a German target. The DVD's most effective weapon, deployed in 1967 and again in 2001, is Foot and Mouth Disease. It caused thousands of animals to be slaughtered, ruined lives and cost exports. Because it is a naturally occurring disease the media can easily be fooled into accepting a WMD attack as a natural event. The 1967 and 2001 outbreaks were not, any more than China's Covid campaign following the leak at Wuhan in October 2019 was.

The Abortive Coup in Britain

After Wilson's second application to join the EEC was blocked, thanks to discreet British pressure on de Gaulle, GO2 in London and the DVD in Dachau became frustrated with him. For political reasons he ruled out a further application. GO2's political analysts thought that Wilson would win the next general election and the Cabinet Secretary agreed.

It was decided to stage a coup. Cecil King, proprietor of the anti- Churchill *Daily Mirror* newspaper, was DVD. So was a later proprietor, by the way, an agent who used the alias Robert Maxwell. King agreed to push the idea that Wilson was a dangerous lefty, which was half right. He was dangerous, but not a lefty.

Certain elements in the Army, including a distinguished officer with sensible views, Lieutenant-General, later General, Sir Walter Walker KCB, CBE, DSO and Bar, a friend of a friend, were sold on the idea that Wilson was working for the KGB. This was nonsense, but plausible nonsense, since Wilson met with his DVD handlers in Moscow. The DVD still had a large station there.

The chosen dictator was going to be the DVD's Lord Mountbatten. He intended telling the country that the Treasury had crunched the numbers, the country was broke and had no option but to join the EEC. That would have made the economy worse, of course. Lord Cromer, the Governor of the Bank of England, would have supported him. The Cabinet Secretary, Sir Burke Trend, was fully in the loop. The coup was planned for May 1968.

It got as far as troops arriving at Heathrow before it was aborted. There were important phone calls from certain key people. Mountbatten had an exit of course. He turned up at a house party in combat rig, swiftly changing into a dinner jacket. The idea was to pretend that he'd been there all along.

The whole thing was hushed up and the public were never told, although Tony Benn is said to have leaked some details to the *Guardian*. Officially, it never happened. Indeed, as we know, it didn't, as it was aborted. It was a close-run thing, however. Unfortunately, the intelligence wash-up was poorly done. There wasn't enough input from the old MI18 boys. Mountbatten and King were treated as egotistical idiots, which again was only half right. They were egotistical, but they weren't idiots. Each was DVD. When Mountbatten showed signs of going public the DVD arranged to have him blown up, although the IRA have suggested to me that the request to blow him up actually came from MI5, which given Mountbatten's serial treason and his blackmailing of Queen Elizabeth II over Royal Assent to the European Communities Bill, it might have done. (Mountbatten had nothing on the late Queen, of course, but dear old Princess Margaret had been compromised in the West Indies.) The motive for the coup - getting Britain into the EEC - and the sponsoring state, West Germany, were not picked up.

1. One of the first things you learn in Washington is not to sniff political donations. Some congressman and senators do, of course, and end up believing in global warming. With British politicians it's usually cocaine and since they can afford the purer stuff they can get quite hooked. It's a bit of a worry, especially if they make the Cabinet.
2. Saving the Congresswoman's life by shooting her with non-fatal ammunition was nice of him. As mitigation however, as any lawyer will tell you, it only went so far. "Your Honor, my client didn't agree with the order to shoot the Congresswoman, so he shot the judge instead." Shooters *never* tell the whole story at trial. They tend to be egotistical and admitting that they were acting under orders goes against the grain. They are also usually worried about being raped, or murdered, or both, in jail, as I nearly was. (I was forced to share a cell in HMP Brixton in 2015 with the gay serial killer Stephen Port. Thankfully he only liked good-looking *young* men, so I was safe. In fairness, he was quite a nice serial killer, indeed I would go so far as to say that he was the nicest serial killer I've ever met.)
3. It would have been a charming gesture had the Republicans withdrawn from the 2012 campaign after the shooting. A bullet through the brain is a traumatic event and campaigning can be quite exhausting. When the Germans try to assassinate your lady opponent, good manners impose certain dictates upon a gentleman. George Washington expected that persons elected to Congress would be gentlemen and if he thought at all about having Congresswomen, which he probably didn't, he would have been expected them to be ladies. I do not think that he would have been disappointed by Congresswoman Giffords. She is clearly a loss to Congress and the people of her district.
4. One should always be careful when opening car boots in Italy.
5. There were one or two slight ambiguities in his private life but nothing that you wouldn't expect to find in the average Cabinet Minister's. He was a very nice chap by all accounts, and a good tribunal according to counsel who had the privilege of appearing before him.
6. The Crown Court was the brainchild of the German spy Dr Richard Beeching. Not content with making a mess of Britain's railways he made a mess of our courts as well.
7. Series 1, Episode 19, airdate 28th January 1966.
8. Strictly the poor young man wasn't a rent boy, since the Germans weren't charging Asquith for his services, not in money at any rate, and Dr Crippen seems to have wanted them for free.
9. The figures are to some extent distorted by Britain's largest mass-murderer, the National Health Service's Dr Shipman, who knocked off over 300 patients before somebody finally had enough and put a stop to it. Stafford Hospital did better, knocking off over 1,200 patients, but it was arguably only manslaughter at best, certainly not murder.
10. Abolitionists usually take 1965 as their starting point, but that is intellectually dishonest. The death penalty in Britain was withdrawn in two stages, the first being in 1957. The upward trend in the murder rate starts from then.

11. This is despite the deterrent effect of capital punishment in the States being watered down by interventionist federal judges and the complex appeals system, which imposes delays on execution of up to 20 years. In Britain there is no right of appeal at all in murder cases - leave to appeal to the Court of Appeal (Criminal Division) has to be obtained from the trial judge or the Court of Appeal itself. Further appeal to the so-called Supreme Court is limited in criminal cases to points of public importance. Two grounds of appeal - incompetence of trial counsel and challenges to mode of execution - frequently argued in the United States would not be available in Britain. The mode of execution, probably hanging, using the British knot (i.e. avoiding a painful death by strangulation) would be fixed by statute and defendants would have automatic legal aid for two counsel. There are short KCs, tall KCs, thin KCs, fat KCs, gentleman KCs, lady KCs, white KCs and black KCs, but there are no incompetent KCs, not in crime at any rate.
12. 2,200 tons, *Allen M Sumner* class, 6 5-inch 38s. They were fine ships.
13. 2,800 tons, *Forrest Sherman* class, 3 5-inch 54s. Popular ships (they were known as the 'Cadillacs of the Fleet' due to their habitability, especially in tropical climes) they had powerful, 70,000 SHP machinery with a staggering 1,200 psi boiler pressure, similar to the *John F Kennedy*. Compare that with the conservative 400 psi for the Royal Navy's *King George V* class battleships or 650 psi for the *Daring* class destroyers. There were maintenance and safety issues however with such high-pressure machinery. Many naval engineers will tell you that lower pressures, between say 750 and 1,000 psi, provide a better balance between efficiency, power, safety in the boiler room, maintenance costs and longevity.
14. Quoted by Captain Richard Macdonald USN (ret'd) in his commentary in *Proceedings*, vol. 137/1, Number 1,295, January 2011, pp. 81-2. The follow-up comments by Admiral Vasey and the distinguished NSA historian Robert Hanyok (see e.g. vol. 137/6, number 1,300, p.85) are also worth reading.

25

The 1970s

The Heath Government

Britain has had some dodgy Prime Ministers, but few have been dodgier, or grumpier, than Sir Edward Heath. The old curmudgeon was an exception to the rule that spies should be charming, intel-speak for disarming. He had allies of course, not just in the government, Tony Barber being the foremost in the Cabinet. In 1973 Ted arranged for the appointment of Lord Normanbrook's old Private Secretary, Sir John Hunt, later Lord Hunt of Tamworth, as Cabinet Secretary.

A paedophile, like Heath himself, Hunt was the fifth German spy, and the first Catholic, to be made Cabinet Secretary. The paedophile ring which supplied teenage boys to them both was coordinated by a Leeds nightclub operator turned BBC disc-jockey, Jimmy Savile, Savile's involvement in paedophilia was suppressed by the BBC and the Cabinet Office for decades, for political reasons. They weren't protecting Savile so much as Heath and Hunt. Other names may emerge in due course. At the time of writing the first edition the police were busily engaged in arresting every celebrity they could find, including poor old Rolf Harris, in the hope of diverting attention from Number 10 and the Cabinet Office.

A strong supporter of EEC membership, John Hunt played a key role in rigging the result of the 1975 referendum on withdrawal from the EEC. He was close to the Jesuits, marrying the widowed sister of that nice man Cardinal Basil Hume in 1973. His Eminence was a Benedictine, not a Jesuit, but he had his contacts there.

Iain Macleod having been murdered to get him out of the way, Britain duly joined the EEC on terms dictated by Germany, on 1st January 1973. Both the House of Commons and the House of Lords were assured by the Law Officers and the Lord Chancellor that Parliament's supremacy would not be affected. As we have seen the four Law Officers of the Crown (i.e.

including the Scottish Law Officers) confidentially advised Heath that were an Act of Parliament to be passed subsequent to EEC entry which breached community law the courts would have to give effect to it.

Heath knew perfectly well that Parliament was led up the garden path. When the lie was given to the assurances and the judges tried to set aside the Merchant Shipping Act 1988, Heath was nowhere to be seen. I certainly do not recall Ted saying anything about the constitutional advice he had received. It was only made public in 2001, under the Thirty Year Rule, with a bit of unofficial help from MI6.

Ironically, since both British signatories to the Treaty of Brussels, Edward Heath and Geoffrey Rippon QC, were agents of the DVD, the treaty was not binding on Britain at all. Under international law, codified in the Vienna Convention on the Law of Treaties[1] a state is not bound by a treaty, if, its signatories are corrupted by another party. The idea that the Treaty of Rome was binding on Britain during the period of our membership was touted nonstop throughout. It simply wasn't true.

The assassination of the courageous journalist Christopher Story in Erie, PA, in 2010, by the DVD, did nothing to weaken the point. He lingered on and died in the July, in England, but the liver cancer that killed him was triggered in Erie. Christopher, sadly, suffered from Badge Syndrome and was taken out (the old poisoned smoked salmon sandwich trick) by a DVD agent who was able to flash a badge.[2] Liver is one of several forms of cancer, including pancreatic (used to take down poor old Jimmy Goldsmith, another friend) that the Germans have been able to induce. Being able to cause cancer was of Dr Mengele's Holy Grails. I do not profess to understand the science (I am a lawyer, not a scientist), but apparently it's something to do with APOBEC cytidine deaminases and coating cancerous cells with a virus. No doubt lots of people died horrible deaths before it was perfected.

Christopher was the only journalist to date with the intelligence connections and the cojones to expose Heath and Rippon.[3] The mainstream media studiously ignored his revelations and carried on pretending that the Treaty of European Union was binding on the UK. It is actually very dangerous to get your assets to sign an international treaty. Ted (I always called him Ted, partly because it annoyed him) would have been better off sending along a couple of junior ministers. He wanted to grab the glory, however.

Ted was so arrogant that he actually thought that no one would question his patriotism. His belief that he was immune from serious counterintelligence scrutiny was partly based, apparently, on his less than impressive war record. This had to be bolstered by with a dodgy MBE pushed by German assets in the War Office, another giveaway. Christopher Story's courageous reporting was not denied by either the British or German governments, although his website and journal were subject to detailed intelligence and central bank scrutiny.

As opponents of EEC entry, including the late, great Enoch Powell[4] and that other nice man Michael Foot had predicted, the British economy collapsed. Britain's terms of trade with the member states of the EEC deteriorated rapidly. Unemployment, and with it public expenditure, shot up as factories closed or laid-off workers. Government borrowing ballooned. Inflation, driven by Value Added Tax, a requirement of EEC membership, and higher food prices as a result of the Common Agricultural Policy, soared. The City was rewarded by increased access to the offshore Medium Term Note trading programmes[5] run from Frankfurt. This led to a loss of control over the money supply and was an even more powerful driver of inflation than VAT and the CAP.

Barber of course was happy to let inflation run out of control. His whole chancellorship was simply an exercise in economic sabotage. Barber knew what he was doing. A small number of officials in the Treasury and the Bank of England also knew what was going on. The Macleod assassination created a climate of fear in the City, the Treasury and the Bank however. Sadly, it doesn't take much to intimidate civil servants and the City. A couple of murders and basically they're anybody's.

By 1976 the country was forced to go cap-in-hand to the International Monetary Fund. No one in authority, the media or the IMF linked this to EEC membership. As usual the public were left in bewildered ignorance.

There have been a surprisingly high number of banking murders over the years, almost all to do with MTN trading programmes. On one famous occasion[6] a banker was found swinging beneath a bridge over the Thames. Along with stagflation this was treated as perfectly normal by the authorities, as though bankers' bodies swing from bridges all the time.

The authorities in Europe were similarly unperturbed when a former head of the European Central Bank[7] was found floating face down in his swimming pool. The ECB didn't even institute swimming lessons for the directors, or distribute water wings. Banking is a bloody business, but in my experience only an extraordinarily small number of bankers carry guns.

Heath and Barber, along with GO2, were keen on promoting industrial sabotage. Most of this was down to communists or pseudo-communists in the trade unions. The useful idiots reported to Moscow, which actually bankrolled some strikes, or the Communist Party of Great Britain. They were subsidised from Moscow, e.g. by bulk purchases of its newspaper *The Morning Star*, which very few people actually read.[8]

The major players reported to GO2 or the Cabinet Office. The latter were more than happy to encourage strikes provided no one knew that they were doing so. More importantly, they made sure the playing field was tilted in favour of the trade unions, a strategy which started to some unstuck thanks to the Freedom Association. Founded by the Viscount de L'Isle VC, the McWhirter twins (Norris and Ross) and a gutsy former military intelligence officer, the late John Gouriet. I only knew Norris and John, but I gather that they were all a first-rate bunch of chaps.

The Provisional IRA and INLA

Working with DVD assets inside the KGB Standartanführer Otto Skorzeny moved to Ireland in or about 1961, although some say it was as early as 1956. He was certainly in residence by the end of 1961. He took over the training and operational control of the IRA, later referred to as the Official IRA. The Republic of Ireland remained a German client state, with the DVD working closely with the Vatican. Key officials in both Dublin and the Vatican were aware both that the IRA was ultimately controlled from Germany and that the Standartanführer was in overall command. DVD and GO2 assets in London, including Maurice Oldfield, the MI6 Director, were aware as well of course.

The failure to appreciate that the IRA was a German, not an Irish, terrorist organisation, with the Irish taking the risks whilst the 'Jerries' stayed well in the background, led to utter confusion in Whitehall and Westminster. This persisted for decades and led eventually to appeasement and the idiocy of the so-called 'peace process'. One rule of thumb to determine the state sponsor of a terrorist organisation is to see whose strategic interests are served. If you track IRA activity over the years you will see a correlation between its activity and German ambitions as regards Britain, with strange periods of inactivity in-between.

Thus, when Germany was fighting Britain in the 1990s over the location of the European Central Bank we saw IRA terrorist activity in the City. There was a spike in IRA activity after the 1968 coup in London was aborted, when Germany was trying to force Britain into the EEC. There was a winding down after British entry. IRA activity was ramped up after Harold Wilson was forced out as Leader of the Labour Party in favour of the patriotic Jim Callaghan and again after Margaret Thatcher ousted Germany's Edward Heath as Conservative Leader.

Unfortunately, there isn't a 'strategic intelligence for dummies' course for politicians and officials. Lacking serious strategic guidance at the top, Britain was fairly easy prey for the IRA. We were forced to sacrifice over 3,000 lives unnecessarily. Even when Britain's first serious Prime Minister since Winston Churchill took over at the end of the decade she was unable to do anything about our heavily penetrated state bureaucracy. I refer of course to the late, great Margaret Thatcher, whom I was proud to know. This was partly because one of Mrs Thatcher's key intelligence advisers, the highly intelligent and courageous Airey Neave, MP for Abingdon, was blown up on orders from Dachau, in the House of Commons car park, on 30th March 1979. The scene is portrayed fairly graphically in the film *The Iron Lady*. There was of course cooperation from GO2 assets in the police in the Palace of Westminster.

Unable to insist on a serious investigation into the Neave assassination when she assumed office a few weeks afterwards, Mrs Thatcher nearly lost her own life to an IRA bomb in 1984, which injured my old friend the late Lord Tebbit, and paralysed his dear wife Margaret, a lovely lady. She lost another key adviser, Ian Gow MP, in 1990. His assassination was the prelude to the internal party coup that removed her from office later that year.

The setting up of the Provisional IRA in 1969, with Dublin's approval, was the prelude to a major ramp-up in IRA activity. The 1968 Mountbatten/King coup had been aborted. There was no serious expectation at that stage that their man Heath would win the election due by 1971, so the idea was to put heavy pressure on the foot-dragging Wilson. Further impetus came from the successful forcing out of de Gaulle.

British Intelligence had very little on his successor, Pompidou. He was a rather dull little man, no offence intended. The French bureaucracy later played a cruel joke on him by having the ugliest building in Paris named after him. You should always consult a good architect before agreeing to have a public building named after you, especially if its architects have been given a prize. Sadly, MI6 missed the fact that Pompidou, who rose without a trace, had been working for 'Jerry' for decades.

Wilson had almost as much on the Germans as they had on him. Thankfully intelligence (the ex-MI18 boys again, God bless them) had been able to arrange to have Wilson picked up for cottaging in a couple of public loos in the West Country. There was I believe one in Gloucester and another one near Exeter, off the A38. He wasn't prosecuted or forced out, but it gave the boys a useful bit of bio-leverage to counter the German pressure. If a Prime Minister swings both ways it's always a good idea to ask Special Branch to send one of their promising young officers along to the nearest loo.

The third EEC-linked assassination, after Gaitskell and Macleod, was carried out on 27th November 1975. The courageous Ross McWhirter, beloved twin brother of Norris, was assassinated at their lovely home near Chippenham. I was later privileged to visit Norris and Tessa there on a number of occasions. Norris and I discussed his brother's assassination. It would be fair to say that he wasn't convinced that it was related to Ross's opposition to Britain's EEC membership. Equally, he did not discount the possibility.

Ross McWhirter was a principled, formidable and high-profile opponent of EEC membership. To his credit he had also upset the IRA, but major IRA targeting assignments were issued from Dachau. They suited German, not Irish, purposes.

For the benefit of the stupids (please bear in mind that this book may be read by politicians and policemen, indeed it was read by policemen hoping to suppress it even before it was published) knowledge that a terrorist organisation is controlled from Dachau is not distributed below the upper echelons. It is also in the nature of terrorist organisations that you will get indiscipline. The splinter strategy we first saw with Black September was followed with equal success in Ireland. There have been no genuine IRA splinter groups, merely reorganisations decided upon in Dachau. This is usually done for tactical reasons, e.g. where the 'Provos' have agreed a temporary ceasefire. Since knowledge of German control is not spread downwards, inevitably you will get clashes between splinter groups at the 'PBI' level. Amusingly, you then get one German asset whacking another, not knowing that each is working for Germany. It would be a lot simpler if IRA terrorists wore spiked helmets rather than balaclavas, but that would give the game away.

Yom Kippur

The Israelis were taken by surprise, partly because critical COMINT and SATINT was withheld from them by Nixon. Britain too was caught on the hop, as a late friend of mine, that very nice man Vice-Admiral Sir Louis Le Bailly, then Director-General of Defence Intelligence, explained to me. It rather looks as though GCHQ, which has a listening post on Cyprus, was up to its usual tricks, leaving key people in INTELCOM in the dark. They were to pull the same stunt over the Falklands. Prime Minister Netanyahu was similarly left in the dark over the outrageous Hamas attack on Israel in October 2023.

The IDF did well however in the Yom Kippur War, swiftly recovering from early reverses. Particularly outstanding work was done by that very nice chap with respect Major-General (as he later became) Avigdor Kahalani, in stopping the Syrians on the Golan Heights. One of the tanks his boys knocked out is still sitting there, complete with holes. The general was kind enough to point it out to me.

In the late 50s Syria was united with Egypt as the United Arab Republic. It was a particularly silly state, since there isn't a lot in common between

Egypt and Syria. They don't even share a common border. They both however had DVD-backed dictators, so a merger no doubt made sense to someone in Dachau. The Syrian Ba'ath Party, like its Iraqi counterpart, was an Arab fascist party founded in the 1930s. Effectively it was set up as an Asia Minor branch of the Nazi Party, run along broadly similar lines. Syria can no more be understood without grasping its German connections than Iraq or Egypt.

The Oil Price Shock

Most commentators have got this wrong. They tend to obsess on the onshore earnings of the oil-producing states in the Middle East. These states make most of their cash offshore, by leveraging oil revenues in German-controlled Medium Term Note programmes. The Oil Price Shock was decided upon in Dachau, i.e. it didn't just happen. Since Dachau could pull trading programmes at the drop of a hat the oil producers swiftly fell into line. The profits from MTN trading far outweighed any loss of oil revenue due to reduced GDP and oil consumption in the West. The DVD continues to target energy supplies. The principal aims are to strangle Western economies and force up costs for Western consumers. These days the oil price is mainly forced up by fake trades. Front companies sell oil to each other at silly prices in order to rig the market. No cash actually changes hands. Hedge funds with access to the Medium Term Note market buy up oil at non-commercial prices.

There are more kinetic strategies as well. These include blowing up oil rigs, pipelines and on occasion tankers, e.g. the MT *Sansinena* in Los Angeles Harbor on 17th December 1976. There has never been a serious public inquiry into an oil rig, pipeline or tanker disaster, partly because INTELCOM is kept well away from them. The Janet and John *Sansinena* inquiry worked out what happened, but not why. The inquiry in Britain following the sabotage of the Piper Alpha oil rig in 1988 was a similar farce, with respect.

The DVD's Propaganda Department for years has been pushing Peak Oil. This is the idea that most of the world's oil reserves have been or are about to be exploited and that oil production has already entered or is about to enter a downturn. The fact that similar predictions were made in the 1970s doesn't seem to trouble the journalists and NGOs who recycle this nonsense without checking their facts.

In the old days the Abwehr virtually controlled the Anglo-Iranian Oil Company (using assets inside MI6) and Standard Oil (through Rockefeller, who was close to Canaris). Intelligence about oil reserves has long been suppressed.

It was privately estimated within the Petroleum Institute in about 2005 that the world had at least 100 years reserves at then consumption levels, not including shale. The figure has gone up since then. There are several huge oil fields, e.g. the Spratly Islands (to which China has laid claim, although they are of course British) just waiting to be developed. Captain Richard Spratly was an Englishman, by the way, from Chesham, in Buckinghamshire. He used to drink at the George and Dragon pub, in the High Street.

Oil reserves are a difficult area given the secrecy, but the non-shale figures seem to be about 125-150 years oil supply at 2010 consumption rates and 250-300 years natural gas, again excluding shale. As Sheikh Yamani, former head of the anti-Western OPEC, observed, the Oil Age is no more going to end because we run out of oil than the Stone Age ended because they ran out of stone. The idea that oil is a fossil fuel can be traced all the way back to the Abwehr's John D. Rockefeller.

Watergate

One of the more interesting DVD operations was that to remove President Nixon after he fell out with the Germans. Having been Eisenhower's No 2 at one time they saw him as a major prospect. He was a secretive man, who only confided to a very small circle of advisers. He would never have dreamt of telling the public what he was doing and why he was doing it. Ironically, he might have had more public support if he had.

The Watergate plan was so creative that it has a touch of the Fritz Kraemer's about it. Fritz was Washington's favourite 'Kraut' and a highly successful agent for the DVD. It was a bit too subtle for Skorzeny, as it didn't involve blowing people up or landing aircraft on the White House lawn. George Kennan, who as we have seen was the top DVD spy in the State Department for most of the postwar period, is another candidate. Whoever came up with it, it was a cunning plan. It played to Nixon's weaknesses, which included sneakiness and paranoia. He also had strengths, which are not usually acknowledged, including high intelligence.

The whole thing burst into the open in June 1972. A bunch of CIA officers including Everette Howard Hunt (good people and a great character, but not a towering intellect) and Havana-born Bernard Barker, got themselves involved in the burglary business. Why is a complete mystery, since the limited political gain was far outweighed by the risk, even if it hadn't been a set-up, at least it would be a mystery if we didn't know that the Nixon Administration was heavily penetrated. Nixon should have been on the alert when pressure started to build on poor old Spiro Agnew, who would have out of his depth as Mayor of Athens. If your vice-president is an idiot and someone starts forcing him out, you know you're next.

There was no 'Deep Throat' as such. Several intelligence officers played the role, including 'Mr. T.' It was convenient to portray the intel as coming from a single source. There are several layers to Watergate and one of them involved some justifiably very angry CIA officers on the excellent Phoenix program. Put another way, the interests of the CIA and DVD coincided on this one.

Nixon agreed to betray the CIA's South Vietnamese assets to North Vietnam as part of the 'peace process' with Hanoi. Both the DVD and North Vietnamese intelligence were aware that there would be very little point in taking over South Vietnam unless the CIA network there was dismantled. They weren't planning on repeating the mistakes the Allies made in 1918 and 1945.

Operation Phoenix was an effective and precisely targeted counterintelligence campaign, aimed at 'Charlie's' assets in the south. The original betrayal was compounded during the sad final American withdrawal from Saigon. A list of names was sent from a Correa Group double-agent inside CIA HQ at Langley to the CIA Station in Saigon by fax, for the North Vietnamese to find.

There were a couple of interesting follow-ups to the Watergate operation. Admiral Canaris, whose health was starting to fail, wanted Nelson Rockefeller to take over as president. That meant assassinating Gerald Ford, who incidentally had helped to cover up the Kennedy Assassination, serving as a member of the musical comedy Warren Commission.

President Ford knew that he was a target. The poor man tended to jump at anything resembling a gunshot, although he carried on bravely with his duties. As we have seen, one of the attempts on his life, albeit half-hearted, was by Squeaky Fromme. She was a member of the Manson Family, the notorious group in California, with deep connections to the DVD. The president was being mocked by the left-wing media for being jumpy, but he had every reason to be.

The CIA were not overly impressed with all this nonsense. On 26th January 1979 former Vice-President Rockefeller popped his clogs after having sex with a nice lady called Megan Marshak. He had decided to have a heart attack whilst on the job, as it were. He died in the ambulance. The CIA did not send flowers.

The Sutch Case

On 18th April 1974, in New Zealand's beautiful capital city Wellington (well worth a visit), an alert NZSIS officer, Kit Bennetts, spotted a senior Kiwi bureaucrat, Bill Sutch, talking with his handler. Nominally a KGB officer attached to the Soviet Embassy the handler was in fact DVD.[9] After decades of bureaucratic interference by Germany in the democracies this was a priceless opportunity to nail one of their tame 'crats.

The clandestine meeting very properly led to espionage charges against Sutch. He fiercely and correctly denied that he was a KGB asset. That much was true. He might have added that he was a DVD agent. Kit Bennetts and the NZSIS boys did very good work, but no one briefed them in on the DVD. It's not surprising the prosecution had problems selling the jury on the idea that Bill Sutch was a communist. He was clearly too intelligent.

The Munich Olympic Massacre

Anti-semitism is not the least weakness of the DVD. It occasionally makes them show their hand in ways, which intelligence professionals in a covert agency ought to advise was insanely dangerous. At 0440 hours on 5th September 1972 a DVD terrorist asset, Mohammed Daoud Oudeh (Abu Daoud) broke into the dormitory of the Israeli team at the Munich Olympics. These were supposed to be "the Olympics of Peace and Joy".

The DVD's intention was to swap the athletes for 236 Palestinian terrorists held in prison in Israeli. Sadly, the Israelis for many years have had a policy of encouraging the kidnap of their civilians and soldiers by agreeing to release terrorists from custody, a mistake repeated in the Gaza War.

The Israeli PM, Mrs Golda Meir, had good intelligence advisers.[10] She was smart enough with respect to see that in the long run this policy, however well-intentioned, may have gotten Israeli hostages released but only at the expense of offering hostages to fortune. The smart policy of course would be to execute terrorists who are guilty of murder, rather than look after them for a bit in a nice, clean Israeli prison and then hand them back. Sadly, the Israeli legal establishment appears to value the lives of terrorists more than the lives of Israelis. It is itself a hostage, to the 'martyr' argument, which also happens to be favoured by terrorists, most of whom do not in fact want to be martyred.

The West German police, naturally, were quite happy to allow a swap, but things went wrong after Golda Meir stood firm. In the upshot 11 athletes, a West German police officer and five Palestinian Black September terrorists ended up dead. Black September was a front for the DVD of course. Those nice people the Mossad were annoyed and went around the world bumping off the terrorists who had escaped. This was all very well and made for a good film a few years ago, but revenge ops are rarely a good idea.

Mossad would have been much better off with respect capturing the terrorists and 'having them around for lunch'. By that I mean interrogating them, with their usual effective methods. These are generally compliant with international human rights standards, but may occasionally involve a slight departure. What they really needed to know was: who was behind Black September?

The 1975 Referendum on EEC Membership

As we have seen, the idea for the EEC came from a group of officials and academics reporting to Reichswirtschafstminister und Präsident der Deutschen Reichsbank Funk. They included Professor Dr Jecht from Berlin, Professor Dr Woermann from Halle, Dr Reithinger, from Berlin, MinisterialDirektor Dr Beisiegal, Staatssekretar Koenigs, Dr Benning from Berlin, Gesandter Dr Clodius and Gauwirtschaftsberater Professor Dr Hunke, serious 'Jerries' all. The DVD naturally wanted to rig the 1975 referendum in Britain, not least as the polls were pointing towards an emphatic victory for the 'No', or British, side.

The DVD undertook a number of initiatives after the war to push for a 'united Europe', our community partner Adolf Hitler's initiative having failed. When the Germans speak of a 'united Europe', they mean a Europe under German domination of course. These initiatives included the American Committee for a United Europe, set up in 1948 under the chairmanship of that well-known German spy, General Bill Donovan. It featured an all-star cast of other German spies on its board, including Allen Dulles (no surprise there), General Walter Bedell Smith, Eisenhower's sidekick, and Paul Hoffman. He had been an Abwehr double-agent inside the Office of Strategic Services, forerunner of the CIA. This NGO laundered large amounts of cash in the direction of DVD assets in Europe such as Spaak, Schumann, the Pole Joseph Rettinger, head of the European Movement, and his sidekick John Pomian. Rettinger was a cofounder, with Paul Rijkens, then President of Unilever, of the Bilderberg Group, another DVD front. It was so-called as it first met at the Bilderberg Hotel in Oosterbeek in the Netherlands. This was the scene of the DVD's first successful major operation, the ambush of the Parachute Brigade at Arnhem in 1944, as we saw in Chapter 19.

DVD influence over the CIA in 1975 was such that they were able to use Cord Meyer Jnr's London Station to bankroll the 'Yes' side and perform other dirty tricks. These were partially exposed in a courageous article in *Time Out* magazine by Steve Weissman, Phil Kelly and Mark Hosenball, *Uncle Sam Goes to Market.*[11] It was not just a case of bankrolling the 'Yes' campaign and having the Propaganda Section recycle old Nazi election posters from 1932. They had to delete the swastika from the posters of course, as that might have given the game away. Even the *Guardian* might have suspected that the EEC's origins lay within the Third Reich had the swastikas been left on.

The DVD and GO2 needed to make sure the result was a 'Yes'. The easiest way to do this was not counting 'No' votes. Stuffing 'Yes' votes into ballot boxes would also have worked, of course. In practice however it is much easier to work out where the opposition's vote is likely to be coming from and not bother counting those boxes. They also came up with another cunning plan - central counting with tallying. All you had to do was to fiddle the figures as they came in.

The German spy chosen to do this, at the urging of Roy Jenkins (another German spy of course) was none other than Philip Allen. He was later created Lord Allen of Abbeydale. It was he who had largely drafted that well-known terrorists' charter, the European Convention on Human Rights.

Allen was a distinguished spy, for Germany that is - he caused positive mayhem in my country. Amongst other things he helped push up the murder rate, as Permanent Secretary at the Home Office. There he had replaced that sound administrator with respect, Sir Charles Cunningham, who had sensible views on capital punishment. It was Allen who in 1950 advised then Home Secretary Chuter Ede against reprieving Timothy Evans. He knew full well that Evans had not murdered his child as alleged, but rather had entered into a joint enterprise with John Christie, who had, to murder his wife and child at their home in 10 Rillington Place, North Kensington. Whilst this still meant that he was guilty, his culpability was not as serious as the prosecution case made out. Moreover, he was slow- witted. Whilst not a defence, it was grounds for taking a merciful view.

Allen also played a key role in advising Sir David Maxwell Fyfe to ignore Lord Goddard's recommendation to grant clemency to Derek Bentley. He took care to insert a fraudulent memo in the file to the contrary. Ministers rarely see the file after a case has closed. All you need to do is to backdate a memo and drop it in the file when the minister isn't looking. It's one of the reasons the Civil Service dislikes stapling things together. They prefer Treasury tags, indeed that's why they're called 'Treasury' tags.[12] You can always re-staple things together of course, but lining up the stapler to the old holes is a bitch. Also, you can never get the corrosion right. The new staple always looks too new.

In the war, Allen photographed War Cabinet minutes for the Abwehr in 1943-1944. He had been attached to the War Cabinet at Sir Edward Bridges' request. Canaris apparently thought highly of Allen and he was generally rated as one of the most efficient German spies in the Civil Service. Some spies tend to panic when photographing documents. They end up missing bits at the edges because they haven't troubled to straighten up the document. Allen always made sure that the documents he was photographing were straight. 'Jerry' appreciates that sort of attention to detail. Apparently both his Abwehr and DVD files speak highly of him.

Under Allen's entirely dishonest supervision, a 'No' vote in 1975 was transformed into a 'Yes'. People were a bit puzzled the next morning when the national result was announced. The counting was done regionally, not in constituencies, as it should have been. The reason it wasn't of course is that returning officers are local, not central, government officials and are far more honest. Whenever a government announces that it wants central tallying it would be wise to assume they want to rig the vote.

Another popular method of vote rigging is through the use of postal votes. This method of electoral fraud is becoming quite popular. There were an extraordinary number of postal votes in the crucial 2013 by-election at Eastleigh, e.g., where officially the United Kingdom Independence Party came second. They might not have done, i.e. they might have won. Postal voting also played a key role in rigging the 2020 presidential election in the States of course.

The Assassination of Graham Hill

On Saturday 29th November 1975 the racing driver and two-times World Champion Graham Hill, father of Damon and a much-loved figure, was assassinated. The job was done by the DVD's French black agency. His aircraft's altimeter was tampered with at Marseilles Marignane Airport. It is quite possible the DVD had tried to assassinate him before, by sabotaging his car at the 1969 US Grand Prix at Watkins Glen. Hill was badly injured in that incident.

We know that the DVD have targeted racing drivers, indeed there are strong suspicions that they did for Jim Clark. They knocked over poor old Mike Hawthorn, who incidentally was introduced to the murderess Ruth Ellis, in a 3.4 litre Jag on the Guildford Bypass. The Nazis saw motor racing as means of gaining prestige and Formula 1 has been badly penetrated by the DVD.

Because accidents happen - e.g. to Ayrton Senna - the easiest way to murder a Formula 1 driver is to sabotage his car and let media naivety do the rest. It is possible that the primary target may not have been Hill at all, but his promising 23-year-old protégé, Tony Brise, but the evidence points towards Hill. He was a courageous racing car driver and a good and conscientious pilot.

It does not seem that Lord Snowdon, who was due to fly with Hill to France to photograph his new GH2 racing car at the Paul Ricard Circuit near Marseilles, was a target. His Lordship cried off at the last moment,[13] a fact that would have been known to the DVD's operation in Paris. For the avoidance of doubt, it is *not* suggested that Lord Snowdon was aware in advance that the pilot, who had long been a friend, had been targeted for assassination by German intelligence.

Lord Snowdon had of course married the Queen's sister, HRH Princess Margaret, in 1960. Her marriage to the man she really loved, Group Captain Peter Townsend DSO DFC and Bar, had been blocked on spurious grounds by Vatican assets in the Church of England, with the agreement of DVD assets in the Cabinet Office.

An officer, a gentleman and a Battle of Britain veteran, Peter Townsend had done superb work in the war with Fighter Command. He bagged nine community partners and a couple of probables, which in RAF-speak usually meant dead 'Jerries'. The Archbishop of Canterbury, Dr Geoffrey Fisher, with respect forgetting that he was only number five in the hierarchy of the Church of England,[14] shamefully went along with blocking the marriage. That was even after it had been sanctioned by the Supreme Governor of the Church of England, His Majesty King George VI.

Without being unduly critical of the dead, Graham Hill had one minor shortcoming as a pilot. His observance of Customs regulations and procedures was not all that HM Commissioners of Customs & Excise might have wished. In particular, he flew the odd package from France (heroin) and Spain (cocaine) to non-Customs airfields in England, always landing at night. This income, not as fully declared to the Inland Revenue as it might have been, helped pay for the aircraft.

His second aircraft, the turbocharged Aztec in which he was murdered, was a nice bit of kit. I've only taken the controls of one once, and then only briefly, but I found it pleasant to handle and generally vice-free.[15] Graham's version had long-range fibreglass tip tanks, giving her a useful range of around 1,200 miles. The turbochargers gave her a nice turn of speed at altitude if needed.

The aircraft was ideal for hops across the Pyrenees. Formula 1 in those days was not the cash-generator it is today, and it was corrupt. Large-scale narcotics trafficking being a state sponsored phenomenon, usually under DVD control, which also had assets in Formula 1, it would have been difficult for Graham Hill to refuse. There may also have been death threats. It would not be unsurprising if Hill's Formula 1 contacts had mentioned the deaths of British World Champions Jim Clark and Mike Hawthorn.

In addition to carrying the odd not fully declared parcel Graham flew the occasional passenger. One is thought to have been the Great Train Robber Ronald Biggs. Some in INTELCOM think that he may also have flown the Right Honourable Richard Bingham, 7th Earl of Lucan, although my own understanding is that he went out by sea and was murdered on the boat. A nice chap, (who knew the late, great Jimmy Goldsmith, into whom I bumped on a couple of occasions) Lord Lucan had the misfortune on 7th November 1974 to murder his children's nanny. Murdering nannies is a serious offence in England.

His explanation to his friends at the Clermont Club that he had only intended to murder his wife (a less serious offence) was accepted. Since he was a nice chap and had not intended to murder the nanny, only the wife, a view was formed that the matter could be overlooked. This was provided of course that His Lordship promised not to do it again.

A very nice mercenary, who did good work for MI6 in Africa, appears to have led the team on the boat. 'Lucky' had been doing a spot of gun-running for the IRA, making him unpopular with Intelligence. It rather looks as though he went over the side in the Channel, with chains wrapped around his legs to make sure that he did not float to the surface. Disposing cleanly of bodies is a skill. It is not one that can be acquired overnight. There is however a further view - that John Aspinall, a card cheat, was working for GO2. The theory is that having promised to get Lord Lucan out of the country by sea, 'Aspers' had him murdered, by the said very nice mercenary.

The two main narcotics-distribution cartels in the UK are controlled by GO2. They have assets in the police and National Crime Agency, who warn them of investigations, run interference and prosecute independents seen to be getting too big for their boots. Intriguingly GO2 seem to have a supply of numbered exhibit bags, very useful for swapping drugs. Running drugs into Britain for the cartels is not quite as difficult as it sounds.

Graham Hill may well have been dealing with police or intelligence officers at the UK end, i.e. he might have had official-looking support. A patriot, he certainly did not know that he was working for Germany. It was only after GO2 sponsored the 7/7 terrorist attacks in London that a majority of officers in GO2 realised that it wasn't a British intelligence operation at all, but a German one.

The Air Accidents Investigation Branch skated over the irregularities in the Apache's registration. To be precise, the FAA had cancelled N6645Y's registration in 1974. The aircraft Graham Hill was flying that night was not then registered with the aviation authorities of any country, nor did it have a valid certificate of airworthiness. You try running an unregistered aircraft in and out of British airfields for a year without official sanction and see how far you get. There were also logbook irregularities, or rather two logbooks, a little bit like a German warship in fact. There was one to show where the pilot had been officially and one to show where he had really been.

The FAA must have been a bit puzzled, since Graham Hill learned to fly in both the UK and the US. His instructors in England must have thought him a natural pilot. He held a US Instrument Rating until he let it expire in 1971.

He had an endorsement on his UK Private Pilot's Licence allowing him to fly at night, but he was not licensed to enter the London Terminal Area. It is an Instrument Flight Rules (IFR) zone and he had no current Instrument Rating.

To sum up, he was flying an unregistered and uninsured aircraft into an aerodrome into which he was not licensed to fly. These are infringements of the Air Navigation Regulations on which the CAA normally jumps. By November 1975 however Graham Hill was a very experienced night and bad-weather pilot, far more so than the official figures showed.

Graham flew out of Paul Ricard at about 1530 hours local time. The altimeters on his aircraft were altered during the stop at Marignane, to give a false high reading, apparently by 300 feet. He filed an IFR flight- plan at Marignane, giving a flight-time to Elstree of four hours, with an ETA of 2200 GMT. He specified Luton as his alternate and planned on using designated airways, with a cruising altitude of Flight Level 80, i.e. 8,000 ft, on 1013 millibars, the standard altimeter setting.

Take-off from Marignane was at 1747 GMT, Dover VOR beacon was passed overhead at 2100 GMT and the Aztec was cleared direct to the Lambourne VOR beacon. He was cleared to descend to FL40 (4,000 ft) on London QNH[16] (1002 millibars) by London Centre when approaching Lambourne. Shortly thereafter he was picked up by London Radar.

There now occurred two major anomalies, one of which contributed to the crash and the other that might have helped with the cover-up. Hill was given a radar vector over high ground to the south of the extended centre-line of Runway 27 at Elstree. That was the runway in use on 29th November 1975. Had he been vectored to the extended centreline in accordance with established procedure, he would have avoided the high ground on Arkley Golf Course into which he crashed.

Without that improper vector the over-reading of his altimeter would not have made a difference. On final approach he would have been guided by visual references from the lighted runway and would have realised that his altimeter was over-reading. He would also have seen the red warning lights on the radio masts at Saffron Green, a standard visual reference for night-time approaches to Runway 27 (now 26[17]) at Elstree.

The second anomaly was to give him the QFE for Heathrow. With respect that was dangerous nonsense, since he wasn't going anywhere near Heathrow. The field elevation at Elstree was over 200 ft higher. Had Graham Hill set his altimeter to the Heathrow QFE setting it would have allowed the Air Accidents Investigation Branch to explain the crash on the grounds of altimeter confusion. In the events which happened however this experienced pilot rightly disregarded the with respect unsafe and meaningless guidance from Heathrow Approach Control. He maintained the London QNH setting, possibly plus 1 millibar.[18] Since he knew Elstree's elevation (334 ft Above Mean Sea Level) he could have made the appropriate adjustment.

Thus, we have an aircraft with rigged altimeters being vectored at night in conditions of limited visibility towards high ground offset from the runway in use. Not only was the ground high but, there were tall trees, an oak, followed by an ash tree (height AMSL 450 ft[19]), a birch and a willow. Inevitably the aircraft impacted the trees. The starboard wingtip struck the ground and was torn off, after which the uncontrollable fuselage and port wing impacted further trees, sadly, the Aztec fire-balled. All on board were killed, their bodies being charred beyond recognition. Damon Hill and his two lovely sisters were left fatherless. The nation was deprived of a man who for all his flaws was a hero and rightly so, twice World Champion.

The grief was widespread and the service at St. Albans Abbey was taken by the future Archbishop of Canterbury, and celebrant of the marriage of Their Royal Highnesses the Prince and Princesses of Wales, Dr Runcie. Lord Runcie, as he now is, is a good man with respect. He did much to repair the damage inflicted on the Church by the insolent decision of his with respect undistinguished predecessor Geoffrey Fisher to defy the express wish of his dying King. I refer of course to the blocking of the marriage of His beloved daughter. Fisher had upset the nation, and insulted the RAF in the process. Whitehall and the AAIB went into full cover-up mode. Great care was taken to conceal from the public the facts that Graham Hill's aircraft was:

(1) Vectored off-course and into high ground by London Approach Control whilst under full radar control with a serviceable transponder, and
(2) Given a field elevation for the wrong airport, which happened to be over 200 ft lower than Elstree.

The 'accident' investigation was conducted by AAIB with its usual slackness with respect. Their report was a whitewash. So far as I am aware they didn't even send the altimeters back to the manufacturer for supervised testing, the procedure followed when the Hammarskjöld DC- 6B ploughed in on approach to Ndola. There also seems to have been poor coordination with the Piper boys in Vero Beach and with the US generally. The US was the country of manufacture of both the airframe and the engines.

The media were no use at all. Very few journalists are air-minded, radar vectors would be meaningless to most of them, and they are generally unaware of secondary radar. In layman's terms this reads bounced-back signals from a transponder on an aircraft. The concept was neatly demonstrated in that very funny scene in *Con Air*, where the transponder goes off in one direction, in a Beechcraft, whilst the plane goes in another. The media probably thought that Graham Hill's Aztec was out of Heathrow's radar range.

We often find secondary murders following key assassinations, as witnesses are eliminated. This appears to have been the case with the Hill Assassination. The Air Traffic Controller on duty at Elstree that night, Peter Wood, who was familiar with Graham Hill's extracurricular activities, was knocked off precisely 10 years later. His car was rammed from behind. Officially this was another 'accident'. Sadly, experience has shown that official verdicts can be quite meaningless.

Problems with Air Traffic Control

The Elstree crash was the second black put up in less than six years by Air Traffic Control. In the greatest air disaster ever to happen at Heathrow - the Staines Trident Disaster - they managed to lose a transponder- equipped aircraft just 150 seconds after take-off. Nothing was done to alert the authorities who, were called by a 13-year-old boy, Trevor Burke. He was out walking his dog and rushed to the nearest telephone.[20]

This in the case of an aircraft whose Air Data Computer had been sabotaged by GO2 at a time when GO2 were encouraging the clogging of the A30 trunk road in order to push up the death toll. They also needed time for their death squad, or, if you prefer a softer expression, a wet- work team tasked with killing people, to check the cockpit. They needed to make sure that the flight crew, and Captain Collins in the jump seat, were dead. Thanks partly to the ATC delay the wreckage was left unsecured for some minutes. As GO2 knew, in a deep stall, where the tail hits the ground first and there is very little forward motion, the crew can survive. Trevor Burke probably had never come closer to death in his young life.

It is rare for air accident investigation authorities to criticise their own ATC. Years later the AAIB displayed with respect excessive leniency towards the substandard ATC performance which contributed to the Kegworth Air Disaster (8th January 1989, Boeing 737-400 G-OBME, British Midland Airways). ATC disrupted Captain Hunt's review of the crew's action in shutting down the starboard engine,[21] forcing an unnecessary change of frequencies and wasting his time by bombarding him with trivia. If he hadn't been fighting to save his aircraft and the lives of his passengers, the intensity of the ATC messages would have been unremarkable. As it was, they distracted the crew at a vital time. That was a case where media management was given a higher priority than investigating the facts, no offence to AAIB intended.[22]

Cambodia

This was the grisly proof of the Domino Theory the left had been screaming for during the Vietnam War. Once South Vietnam had gone, Cambodia went under, like, well, a domino. The death toll ran into the millions, so high that no one has ever been able to count it.

The key war criminal was a Chinese/DVD agent called Pol Pot. He led the fanatical Khmer Rouge. They were a Peking-sponsored terrorist organisation, although the Chinese connection has been downplayed by those anxious to portray the People's Republic of China as a responsible member of the international community.

The surviving leaders were put on trial in 2010, but it was a bit of a joke, as (1) so much time had passed and (2) the prosecution dared not explain who had armed and bankrolled the Khmer Rouge for fear of offending China. The PRC is the elephant in the room for every government in the Asia-Pacific region.

The DVD had huge influence in Peking, not just because Mao and Chou en-Lai were German agents but because Medium Term Note trading programmes are controlled from Frankfurt. The Chinese make most of their money offshore. China also depends on DVD political assets in Western countries to lower tariff barriers in order to boost Chinese exports, a strategy which has now run into trouble, thanks to President Trump. The stratgey is sometimes described as the 'global economy' theory - "there is only one world economy". Try *exporting* something they can already make themselves to China and see how far you get.

The Cambodian genocide was German-backed. If 'Jerry' does not like being accused of supporting genocide he should get out of the genocide business. It's about time he did, no offence intended.

The Cambodian Genocide also required DVD assets in London, Washington, Ottawa, Canberra, Wellington and New Delhi to restrain a military response. The DVD's Propaganda Department also helped, by sitting on the media. Only one journalist in the world - John Pilger - reported the genocide seriously, to his credit.[23] Western governments did nothing, when military intervention would have been straightforward.

The Khmer Rouge, were up for murdering helpless civilians, including children and the elderly. They were less keen to face disciplined and well-led military formations that could shoot back. In the end it was left to the Vietnamese, who were sickened by the slaughter, to knock them over. That in turn reflected the gradual decline in German influence in Hanoi after the death of their man Ho and the increasing tension between Hanoi and Peking. The Luftwaffe hotshots who had been so keen to shoot down B- 52s over North Vietnam were nowhere to be seen.

The Vietnamese invasion of Cambodia was entirely justified under international law. It was no different to NATO intervening to stop the slaughter in Bosnia and Kosovo. Genocide is a crime against humanity. Any civilised state may intervene to stop it. This was an admittedly rare case of a communist state doing the right thing and it falls to be applauded.

In fairness to the Soviet Union, they were not quite as adventurous during the Cold War as some have suggested. They did little if anything to restrain their Vietnamese allies from sorting out the Khmer Rouge. It's unlikely that Hanoi made their move on Phnom Penh without clearance from Moscow, given that their powerful neighbour to the north backed the Khmer Rouge. After Stalin's execution there was constant tension between Dachau and Moscow.

There was a not dissimilar intervention in Uganda, where the DVD's Idi Amin was chucked out by Peking's Nyerere, after too many people had died. Nyerere correctly calculated that neither Peking nor Dachau (of which he was aware - he was well-informed[24]) had a credible successor to him lined up. Both humanitarian interventions showed the limits of intelligence influence, just as the installation of the dictators in each case shows the ease with which the DVD were able to get away with mass murder.

The Tenerife Air Disaster

The DVD's Sabotage Section had been keen to blow up a Jumbo Jet ever since they came into service. The closest they got was sabotaging the cargo doors of a pressurised Lockheed C-5A Galaxy on the famous baby airlift out of Saigon (4th April 1975). Had knowledge of the DVD and the existence of its specialist sabotage unit been more widely known, security on that operation would have been greater.

In retrospect a humanitarian airlift rescuing infant children, which also made America look good (and why not, since they are the Good Guys?) was a magnet for the Bad Guys. Once again, if the DVD don't like being called baby-killers they shouldn't go around killing babies. If you want to look really bad just arrange to blow the doors off a freighter whose precious cargo happens to be human, and children at that. There were 243 souls aboard, mostly orphans.

Some clown in the Sabotage Section came up with the 'bright' idea of blowing up two 747s through the simple expedient of making them collide, New York Air Disaster style. The operation reflected the bitter factional battle inside the agency as Canaris's health declined. PanAm was hated by the DVD and had introduced the mighty 747 into service. That's why the airline was selected. The Germans hate the Dutch, probably because they are such nice people. Germany had of course invaded Holland in 1940. KLM, another 747 operator, was therefore another obvious choice.

Even the dozy, aviation-illiterate Western media, which had fallen for the Comet cover-up hook, line and sinker, would be bound to ask questions with a death toll of two Jumbo Jets' worth of passengers. They needed a country where Germany had enough political influence to control the investigation - fake air traffic control tapes and so on. Ideally it needed an air traffic control service so useless that a collision between two Boeing 747s could be put down as another cock-up.

Spain was ideal. Canaris had lived there for a while after the war. The German Geo-Political Center, a key DVD front organisation, had been based in Madrid, and the pro-German fascist dictator Franco had not long died. Although he had gone, Franco's people were all over the bureaucracy like a rash. This was particularly true of air traffic control, which had been run by the military during the fascist period. Military control facilitated night-time narcotics flights. If you're running thousands of 'kees' of Colombian pure through your airspace you take a lot of care in selecting the people you put in charge of your radar.

Spanish ATC was already in the mass-murder business. In 1970 a controller at Barcelona Airport was instructed, in an operation cleared by Franco, to order a Dan-Air Comet 4 (G-APND, 3rd July 1970, 119 dead) to fly into a mountain. The Comet, then in cloud, was cleared to descend to 2,800 ft with a 5,615 ft mountain in the way.[25] The poor pilots found that the clouds suddenly had rocks in them.

General Franco was a major player. Well aware that Heath was reporting to Canaris, as indeed did was he, he would not have expected any repercussions from murdering 119 Brits. The British AAIB were a laughing-stock in European intelligence circles after the Comet cover-up. Sadly, the Spanish authorities had nothing to fear from that direction, as it proved.

The DVD duly got a tame terrorist organisation of whom, scarcely anybody had heard, the "Movement for the Independence and Autonomy of the Canaries Archipelago", to plant an IED at El Gando, the airport for Las Palmas. The IED was set off on Sunday 27th March 1977. The authorities then shut the airport, unnecessarily. Even if it had been a genuine terrorist attack, it was aimed only at the terminal. There were sixty aircraft *en route* and they had nowhere suitable to send the planes. In saying that I include Los Rodeos, the silly little airport on Tenerife, since shut, which had no business handling Boeing 747s. That is why the two target jumbos were sent there of course.

There was no need to land the PanAm 747-121, N736PA *Clipper Victor*, Captain Victor Grubbs in command, at all. Captain Grubbs very wisely wanted to go into a holding pattern whilst Los Rodeos Airport reopened.

It was in fact reopened shortly after he landed at Los Rodeos. That figured, since the whole idea of the bomb was to get the two jumbos onto Tenerife. Fog was forecast, a not irregular occurrence. Los Rodeos was the most ideal airport in the world at which to arrange a collision between two jumbo jets.

The KLM jumbo, PH-BUF *River Rhine*, a 206B, was under the command of the KLM 747 training captain, Jaap Veldhuijzen van Zanten. He was nothing like the arrogant figure portrayed in the media.[26] Like the authorities, they rushed to blame him for the disaster, as he had initiated a take-off roll without specific take-off clearance. The First Officer had requested take-off clearance and was cleared to the Papa beacon, to climb to and maintain flight level niner zero. At best, this was a highly ambiguous ATC instruction, which is why it was given.

That Captain van Zanten was keen to get going is undoubted, not because he was about to run out of flight hours (he wasn't) but because the fog was getting worse. Understandably, he didn't want to be trapped at Los Rodeos. There were no adequate parking facilities for his aircraft and there was little prospect of overnight facilities for his passengers. He was a go-getter and his responses matched his psychological profile. Surprisingly few mass-murders are planned on the spur of the moment. Intelligence agencies don't work like governments. This operation has been thought through, at least at the nuts and bolts level.

What happened next was insane, or would have been had there not been a third person, an armed Spanish intelligence officer, in the tower. Unsurprisingly, the Spanish fought a successful battle to keep the original ATC tape away from the American and Dutch authorities. They substituted an edited copy, the timings of which could not be matched to the CVR recordings.[27] The Spanish intelligence officer not only gave instructions to ATC, he relayed information from a Luftwaffe ground radar unit flown into Tenerife on or about 25th March 1977.

It is possible that transmissions from this unit together with a jamming signal on the ATC frequency at a critical time, were intercepted by a US NRO satellite. This may have played a part in the decision to evacuate the pitifully small number of American survivors by military medevac flight. They used a Lockheed C-141 Starlifter no less. It was reasonable for the NSA to assume that President Carter would order military retaliation against Spain including ordering a carrier battle group to close the Canaries and mount air strikes against Los Rodeos Airport. At least it would have been reasonable to anyone who didn't know President Carter. He was, with respect, a weak President. Madrid would have known that it could murder US citizens with impunity on his watch.

Most of the diverted aircraft had been cleared by 1700 hours and there was no rush at all. Notwithstanding the absence of time pressures the Tower ordered *Clipper Victor* to backtrack on the same active runway at the same time as *River Rhine*. This was in conditions of poor and deteriorating visibility, so bad that neither aircraft could see each other.

You will fly out of airports all your life and never see a wide body aircraft backtrack on an active runway, i.e. taxi in the direction of other aircraft taking off or landing. If you do see it happen you will be most unlikely to see a second wide body following it, even in conditions of unlimited surface visibility. You will never see a wide body taxi along an active runway towards an aircraft at the take-off position, even in Spain. The hazards of such a course scarcely need explaining. It would be a bit like driving a Greyhound bus the wrong way up I-95 in New Jersey at rush hour.[28] To put the matter at its lowest, clarity of ATC communications would be essential.

Airline captains disagreeing with this proposition might wish to think back and ask themselves how many times they have responded to a first officer asking if he or she should seek take-off clearance by saying words to the effect of "nah, we'd better wait for that 747 taxiing towards us to turn off the runway first, I don't want to run into him". At the very least there would be a communication to the Tower asking if the duty controller was taking an FAA-approved sleep break.

Captain Veldhuijzen van Zanten's First Officer, Klaas Meurs, rated for DC-8 command himself, advised the Tower that KL4805, the KLM, was taking off. As his former colleague Captain Bartelski observed,[29] the wall of sound from the 747's Pratt & Whitney JT-9D engines would have washed over the control tower from the take-off position of Runway 30 in about six seconds. Although soundproofed, the airport was designed for Boeing 727s, not 747s. Everybody in the Tower must have known that KL4805 had commenced her take-off run. The noise would have increased as the great plane rolled towards them.

They didn't need ground radar to know that *Clipper Victor* was still on the runway, directly in the path of the onrushing KLM wide body. Nothing was done to order the KLM 747 to abort take-off or order the PanAm 747 to clear the runway on an emergency basis. *River Rhine*, carrying mostly young holiday makers with their children, struck the PanAm 74' near the cockpit. Her port wing sliced off *Clipper Victor's* fin. Just short of rotation speed she fell back on the runway and slid for about 1,000 ft before blowing up, killing Captain Veldhuijzen van Zanten and all souls aboard.

The total loss of life was 563. The death toll was aggravated by the decision of the Spanish authorities, straight out of the Inquisition playbook, to withhold emergency services from the American aircraft whilst most of her passengers burned to death. A number of them were Jewish.

The Spanish offered two explanations:

(1) They did not know that there had been an accident, and
(2) If there *had* been an accident, they did not know that two aircraft were involved, i.e. they thought that the KLM 747 had blown up of her own accord and the PanAm 747 went silent because all her radios had suddenly failed.

You are not encouraged to try this at home, but should you ever arrange for a refuelled jumbo jet to collide with another, one thing you will hear is lots of noise. One thing you will observe is very bright flames from the exploding jet fuel. The official inquiries were a risible farce. Everybody involved scrambled to find a way of preventing the United States and the Kingdom of Netherlands going to war with the Kingdom of Spain, ostensibly a NATO ally. This was the first attack by Spain on the Netherlands since the War of the Austrian Accession and the first attack by Spain on the United States since they blew up the USS *Maine*.

Since nothing was done to stop them, the Spanish kept ordering aircraft to fly into mountains, or each other. It started to become a more popular pastime than tennis. On 25th April 1980 - Anzac Day - controllers at Los Rodeos ordered a DanAir Boeing 727 with 146 souls aboard, mostly holidaymakers from Manchester, to make a left turn at FL60 on passing the FP locator beacon. This was situated half a nautical mile to the west of the threshold for Runway 12. The ATC instruction sent the 727 into an area of high terrain where the safety height was FL148.[30] Put shortly, an aircraft with 138 British passengers on board was instructed to fly into a mountain her pilots couldn't see.

Iran

This is another subject worthy of a book of its own, but there are six intelligence points to which large publicity has not hitherto been given:

(1) The poor old Shah was played like a fiddle by the DVD, which controlled his intelligence service SAVAK. They committed serious human rights abuses purely in order to stir up resentment, the strategy used so successfully in Chile to discredit dear old General Pinochet. Unable to control the Iranian intelligence service, the Shah and his government were like blind men without their sticks,

stumbling around helplessly in the dark, all the time taking blows from an unseen enemy.

(2) Ayatollah Ruholla Khomeini was a French asset, whom they were blackmailing over his male paedophilia.

(3) The French, with German backing, bankrolled the revolution.

(4) In exchange they got oil discounted, as I understand it, to $12 a barrel.

(5) The Iranians were allowed to trade their oil revenues on the German-controlled Medium Term Note markets, with the usual cut for the leading ayatollahs, whose accounts are mostly held in Dubai, and

(6) MI6 were not taken by surprise as has so often been claimed. So far to the contrary, they were fully aware that His Highness was about to be overthrown, but they were so badly penetrated by GO2 that they simply stood back and let it happen.

---

1. Article 50. Amusingly, one of the Special Rapporteurs of the Convention was the German spy, Sir Hersch Lauterpacht.
2. This is the incident I referred to in the Preface. As indicated, I had spotted the agent, who claimed to be acting on behalf of the US Treasury, as DVD, but sadly my warnings were ignored. This was very frustrating as Christopher was a nice chap. It was even more frustrating for him of course - being assassinated can be very irritating.
3. See *International Currency Review* Vol. 30, No. 4, October 2005. Christopher was delving deep, was supplied with a lot of false information, precisely because he was getting too close to the truth and wrote in a darkly conspiratorial style which is not to everyone's taste. Unlike most journalists he had a regard for the truth, however. Much of what he wrote was spot on, including the exposure of Edward Heath and Geoffrey Rippon.
4. He was unfairly reviled after interspersing some sensible and moderate observations on immigration with an appropriate classic allusion. At least it would have been appropriate had it remained as he intended in the original Latin. Sadly, he was prevailed upon by the chairman of the meeting, who was acting under instructions from Central Office, who had seen the speech, to confuse everyone, including the media, by speaking in English.
5. Christopher Story with respect never understood these and kept referring to them as 'Ponzi schemes', i.e. he made the same mistake as the *Wall Street Journal* did over the Madoff affair. Madoff actually returned more than was invested with him, so by definition he was not running a Ponzi scheme.
6. The Italian banker Roberto Calvi, mixed up with Gladio, the P2 lodge in Italy and the DVD's Italian black agency, which has close ties to P2. Although the P2 was a masonic lodge they were Scottish rite – your nice masons of course are English rite. Calvi was murdered on 17th June 1982.
7. Wim Duisenberg, murdered on 31st July 2005.
8. Although in fairness they once carried a photograph of me, in my 'trendy lefty' days, demonstrating outside the US Embassy of all places, over the invasion of Grenada, which was in the British Commonwealth. If anybody should have invaded, it was us, not the Americans. The *Morning Star's* line, a trifle adventurously given Maurice Bishop's assassination, was that no one should have invaded.
9. In his very readable account of the affair, *Spy* (Auckland: Random House, 2009), Kit Bennetts observes that he wouldn't normally have had a duty roster that night, which was *Callan* night (he was a fan). Edward Woodward made a great TV spook.
10. One of whom was known to me - he used to drive Golda to her evening *tète* â *tètes* with that nice man King Hussein of Jordan. He was a smart cookie and so with respect was Golda.
11. 23rd May 1975, well worth a read, as is *Time Out* if you're in London and want to find out what's going on.
12. With a Treasury tag you can pull a sheaf of papers apart and insert your forgery without leaving any traces, unless of course a lady MI5 officer based at the Home

Office has you under surveillance and has been sneaking a peek at the files when you're not looking. A bit of paper that wasn't there before will always attract the attention of a trained intelligence officer.

13. Bartelski, *op. cit.*, p. 230. Captain Bartelski analysed the flight with his usual thoroughness with respect, but was unaware of the sabotage of the altimeters. He was clearly puzzled at how an experienced pilot could have flown so low on the approach to an airfield with which he was very familiar and comes up with some sensible suggestions - low-lying fog etc. - which he fairly admits are a little bit speculative. He was rightly critical of London Radar for vectoring Hill over high ground, even though the aircraft was equipped with a transponder.
14. The official rankings are: (1) God (2) Our Lord Jesus Christ (3) The Holy Ghost (4) The Sovereign and (5) The Archbishop of Canterbury. Once the King had given His blessing to the union it was Fisher's duty to bend the knee, however the King was murdered by GO2, who placed a radiation source under His bed and gave Him lung cancer, poor man. Fisher thought that he could bully the young Queen, to Whom the decision reportedly caused distress. These sins are not lightly forgiven. Lambeth Palace need a smack for this one. Dodgy Archbishops of Canterbury have been a problem since Thomas à Becket.
15. Unlike myself, I hear some in INTELCOM saying!
16. Sea-level setting, i.e. your altimeter at sea level would read 0 feet. On landing at Heathrow, it would read about 100 feet. Field elevation is called QFE.
17. Small variations in the Earth's magnetic field occasionally lead to re- designation of runways, which are numbered by reference to the first two digits of their rounded up or down magnetic heading. Thus, a runway on a heading of 266^0 magnetic becomes Runway 27.
18. The pilot's, i.e. left-hand side, altimeter was found after the crash at 1003 MB (Bartelski, *supra*, p. 238), but may have been shifted one digit by the impact. It is unlikely that he would have left it at the airways setting of 1013 having been given London QNH. The Heathrow figure would normally be good for the whole London Flight Information Region.
19. *Ibid.*, p. 234.
20. *Ibid.*, p. 188.
21. *Ibid.*, p. 274.
22. It's ironic that the official body charged with investigating UK air disasters is restricted in its title to one type of disaster, i.e. accidents. In practice the AAIB assumes that every disaster is an accident - it's never actually picked up the sabotage of any public transport aircraft, save in the case of the 777 at Heathrow, discussed in Ch. 27, where it may have covered it up, i.e. lied in its report.
23. Yes, I am aware that John Pilger was left-wing, but let credit be given where credit is due. No conservative has any business supporting genocide (the Nazis were not conservatives).
24. I never met him, although President Nyerere and myself had a number of mutual friends, including that nice man Archbishop Trevor Huddleston.
25. Bartelski, *op. cit.* p. 266.

26. There is a balanced summary of his personality in Bartelski, who knew him, *ibid.*, p. 264.
27. *Ibid.*, p. 260. For the avoidance of doubt Captain Bartelski, to whom I am greatly indebted, did not say that this collision was deliberately arranged and confined himself to identifying the weaknesses in the Official Version of Events with his usual forensic skill. Other writers have described the disaster but without the same level of skill, probably because they are not pilots or, if they are, lack the thousands of hours of command experience of large public transport aircraft which informed the late Captain's Bartelski's work.
28. I have driven on 1-95 in New Jersey at rush hour. I am sure my decision to remain in the correct carriageway was the right one.
29. *Ibid,.* p. 261.
30. *Ibid.*, p. 267.

26

The Reagan - Thatcher Era

The Air New Zealand Mount Erebus Disaster

On 28th November 1979 the DVD's small but influential Wellington Station arranged for an Air New Zealand McDonnell Douglas[1] DC-10 (ZK-NZP, Captain Jim Collins in command) to fly into a mountain in Antarctica. They murdered all 257 souls aboard. Six main intelligence mistakes lay behind the disaster, only one of which was a home-grown Kiwi error:

(1) The failure to close down German intelligence in 1945, compounded by the failure to recognize that the deliberate bringing down of Good Guy civilian airliners was a covert German policy. Since the Federal Republic of Germany is an intelligence state, i.e. one where the government is controlled by its intelligence services, rather than the other way round, the fact it wasn't the policy of successive German governments was not a relevant consideration.

(2) The failure to correctly identify which agency Bill Sutch worked for. As we saw in the last chapter, Sutch was a DVD agent. The failure to identify him as such led directly to the failure to close down the powerful DVD ring inside New Zealand's state bureaucracy. This had already inflicted significant damage on New Zealand, e.g. by dismantling much of her rail infrastructure,[2] holding back infrastructure investment generally and slowing down traffic by imposing absurdly low speed limits, the idea being to reduce GDP through increased journey times and increase the accident rate, as longer journeys induce greater fatigue and slower average speeds increase traffic density over a given stretch of road for the same volume of traffic.

(3) The failure of those agencies such as ONI (who laid on a mission to Antarctica led by Admiral Byrd after World War II) who were in the know about the strategic significance for Germany of

Antarctica, which was used in both world wars for supply and trans-shipment dumps, to warn New Zealand of the dangers of Antarctic overflights. There were two specific intelligence aspects:

(i) The DVD still maintain dumps down there (one reason why national sovereignty over Antarctic space and development of adequate facilities for Antarctic aviation are hot button issues) and being paranoid will tend to assume that civilian overflights will be camera-equipped[3], **and**

(ii) The DVD have significant military and intelligence experience of Antarctica to draw upon, not least of the whiteout phenomenon.

(4) The failure to spot the significance of the request by Air New Zealand in October 1977, and the rapid approval by the Civil Aviation Division, to operate Antarctic flights in a dangerous manner, by having Antarctic-inexperienced flight crews.[4] This should have been taken as an indication of possible hostile penetration of either the airline or the CAD, or both.

(5) The similar failure to appreciate the significance of the sudden notification of the immediate withdrawal (later rescinded, but transmitter maintenance ceased) of the Non-Directional Radio Beacon (NDB) radio beacon at Williams, the air base for McMurdo and Scott Antarctic Bases. The NDB was a key waypoint and critical for a safe let-down procedure through cloud. The NDB rundown was even more significant as the Carter Administration was heavily penetrated and no more able to govern America in the American interest than the New Zealand Government was able to govern New Zealand in the New Zealand interest, and

(6) The failure to detect the tampering with Air New Zealand's mainframe navigation computer. This led to Antarctic Flight TE901 flying into Mount Erebus in whiteout conditions instead of safely down the middle of McMurdo Sound, as Captain Collins had been led to believe. This was even after Captain Leslie Simpson had spotted a possible error with the programming of the Inertial Navigation System, which drew on coordinates inputted into the mainframe computer, on an earlier flight, on 14th November 1979, using DME data from a military TACAN[5] beacon.

For any air intelligence officer the last two occurrences alone should have been the equivalent on a four-engine airliner of fire warning bells on

Nos. 1 and 2. Pompous statements about the safety of Antarctic flights at the Antarctic Treaty Conference in Washington should also have been further cause for alarm given DVD penetration of most foreign ministries.

Blaming your enemy for the deaths you cause yourself is a standard Bad Guy propaganda tactic. If the New Zealand Antarctic flights were not to be abandoned, at the very least a *Leander* class frigate (the Kiwis had two[6]) should have been sortied to provide radar support for the next flight, the last of the season.

Military escort for Flight TE901 should also have been considered. This could possibly have been in the form of a TACAN-equipped RAF VC-10 from 10 Squadron at Brize Norton. A VC-10 could have been positioned to New Zealand via the States in a little over 24 hours. She would have had the range and could easily have operated out of Christchurch, shadowing the civilian flight and providing radar and navigational assistance. The powerful, narrow-bodied VC-10 could have matched the cruise speed of the larger DC-10. Her crew would have spotted that the computer-tracked DC-10 was heading straight for Mount Erebus.

Nothing was done. Papa Zulu duly flew at speed into the lower slopes of Mount Erebus as planned. On their own, only the withdrawn NDB could have saved them. It was still transmitting but that vital information was withheld from Captain Collins. The TACAN transmissions being VHF and line of sight were of course blocked by the high ground ahead of them. Airline management made a number of fatuous criticisms of Captain Collins, but nothing could disguise the fact that he was 27 miles off track because of a computer error not of his own making.

The pilots thought, and had every reason to think, that they were over McMurdo Sound. In IFR and whiteout conditions would they have had very little warning of the rising terrain ahead of them. Their radar altimeter might have alerted him but airline procedure is not to use them save as an adjunct to landing aids.

No lessons had been learnt in data presentation and siting of radar altimeters from the Ndola DC-6B crash. In the DC-10 the radar altimeter is on the flight engineer's panel. By the time its readings were being taken it was too late. The same went for the Ground Proximity Warning System. The GPWS simply told Captain Collins, who maintained a professional calm until the end (his last call was for "go-around power") that he was about to crash. By the time it kicked in nothing could be done on a turbine-powered aircraft to avoid disaster. It would simply have taken too long for the engines to respond.

The failure to learn from the Ndola crash is a classic example of the dangers of running away with conspiracy theories that have no basis in reality. In that case the conspiracy theories distracted the aviation community from the errors made by the UN crew. They contributed to the lack of discussion about the role that radar altimeters can play in maintaining situational awareness over high ground and as an aid to navigation. They can also be a vital back up if the pressure altimeters have been tampered with, or are malfunctioning - as at Ndola - for other reasons, such as poor maintenance.

Had there been radar altimeter readouts on the captain's and co-pilot's panels they would have been alerted to the facts that (1) they were over land, not water and (2) that the ground was rising rapidly. A pressure altimeter gives you height above sea-level, or close to, since over the ocean the average barometric pressure at sea-level is used. A radar altimeter gives the pilot his real altitude, i.e. his height above terrain. When you are just about to fly into a mountain all the pressure instrument will tell you is the height of the mountain.

After the disaster a remarkable thing happened. A serious judge, Peter Mahon, was appointed to undertake the inquiry. Captain Collins also had a fine airman, Captain Gordon Vette,[7] to speak up for him and his crew. Judge Mahon, a man of integrity and intelligence with respect, produced one of the most serious judicial reports on a major marine or aircraft disaster that there has ever been. His Honour wasn't told about the DVD and he missed the fact that it was murder. He was however severely critical of the airline management and the aircraft accident investigation authorities.

Extraordinarily, the late NZ Chief Inspector of Accidents, Ron Chippindale, who was caught out rewriting the transcript of the CVR, managed with respect to persuade himself[8] that the airline had instructed its pilots not to descend below FL160, i.e. 16,000 ft. That would have given TE901 safe clearance over Mount Erebus. This opinion was formed even though there was a published descent procedure at the NDB beacon, most flights had gone below 16,000 ft and the airline's own in-house journal listed close-up views of Antarctica as a good reason to take the trip! "Boomps-a-daisy", as we say in the business.

Sadly, Ron Chippindale died a sudden, violent and unexpected death in 2008. He was taking his usual early morning walk, following his usual route, in Porirua, a delightful little community just north of Wellington. Depending upon how you look at it his death was a demonstration of the hazards of early morning walks or air crash investigation. He never did get to say who had ordered him to 'edit' the CVR tape. He was not an evil or wicked man by nature. Clearly, he had been put under considerable official pressure.

The New Zealand Court of Appeal, by a narrow majority, trashed Judge Mahon's report. In 2011 it was revealed by Sir Paul Holmes in his book

Daughters of Erebus that each of the three judges in the majority failed to disclose a personal connection with the airline. If that information is right, then under the common law their findings would be vitiated for actual or apparent bias.

The Privy Council in London, in a weak decision with respect, dismissed Judge Mahon's appeal, whilst agreeing with him on the causes of the crash. Their decision may have to be revisited however in view of the disclosures by Sir Paul. A character and a great Kiwi, with a real dedication to the truth, Sir Paul sadly passed on 1st February 2013. His death was due to natural causes, but the car wreck which nearly killed him and the three plane/helicopter crashes in which he was involved may not have been accidents. Generally speaking, the more car and plane crashes a courageous investigative journalist is involved in, the less likely they are to be accidental. The knighthood was richly deserved.

The next set of legal proceedings ought to be murder prosecutions. The DVD assets in Wellington who assisted in the murder of Captain Collins, his crew and passengers ought to be prosecuted as accessories before the fact. Unhappily, New Zealand, like Britain, Canada and Australia, is a 'soft' jurisdiction. Murder is encouraged, and the value of human life downgraded, by an excessively lenient sentencing policy. Nobody has yet paid for the Mount Erebus deaths. It's high time somebody did.

McDonnell Douglas were understandably relieved that the cause of the crash wasn't a further problem with the DC-10. Sadly, two had been brought down by the DVD, one out of Chicago[9] and one near Paris.[10] Those were fiendishly complex operations, which involved using assets inside Convair to design a defect into a non-plug freight door. Non-plug doors are vulnerable to sabotage, because if can you get the door locks to fail at altitude you depressurise the plane, i.e. you get a hull breach. A plug door will be kept in place against the outer skin of the hull by the air pressure behind it.

The same DVD assets inside Convair left a very silly memo for someone to find, setting up the London *Sunday Times* with a 'let's bash America' story, not an insurmountable task with respect. It also looks like someone in Paris was paid to close said dodgy door with excess force, although I am not suggesting that it was the person named in the inquiry. He may not have been the last person by the door.

The Lockheed L-1011 Tristar, another fine American aircraft, was similarly libelled after a successful operation to bring one down over the Everglades.[11] All these ops had a common feature - the DVD stayed deep. To find out what really brought down all these airliners, including Papa Zulu, you have to dig deep, but not such a deep hole that you can't climb back out! Pilots and airlines need to understand that (1) there are Bad Guys out there trying to bring down their planes and (2) bad does not necessarily mean stupid.

Antarctic sightseeing flights continued, indeed QANTAS have been operating them on and off since 2011. There is no reason why they shouldn't, but all flights should carry adequate polar survival equipment. Air New Zealand management thought it wasn't necessary, on the spurious ground that the flights weren't scheduled to land on the ice runway at Williams Field. This, with respect, is a bit like saying that lifejackets are only required for overwater flights if a ditching is scheduled.

Aviation facilities in Antarctica need upgrading. In particular, there should be a diversion runway long enough to take any aircraft cleared for Antarctic flights. Search and rescue facilities are also inadequate and military-specification life-rafts should probably be carried. Standard commercial life-rafts are not really designed for the Roaring Forties.

The Assassination of John Lennon

It is still a bit of a mystery why the DVD chose to assassinate John Lennon. It can't have been because they didn't like his music. It's unlikely that the DVD have that many in-house discos - it's not really a fun place in which to work. British Intelligence, such as it was after 1830, would never have dreamt of assassinating Wagner. Even Shostakovich was safe. However, the DVD went and murdered Lennon. Of course that is not the Official Version of Events.

Officially Chapman, who sadly was not executed and apparently has ambitions to be released on parole, acted on his own. Execution, would have solved the parole problem of course. The amount of public money wasted on parole hearings and parolee supervision is scandalous.

Chapman wasn't working alone. You should always follow the money. The prosecution at his trial didn't even try to prove who had paid for his various flights, or how he had maintained himself in the months leading up to the assassination. Poor old John Lennon was the softest of soft targets (he was also betrayed by someone he trusted) but if I were to name him or her, the intelligence agencies sitting on the evidence would leave me swinging in the wind in the usual way.

What was the motive? The DVD's Psychological Warfare Section likes to make Western publics nervous and jittery. They do this by murdering high-profile people like pop stars, or children, or having people murdered in particularly hideous ways, like Sharon Tate. Finance can always be found in New York for films which do gruesome or create psychological terror. The best film director linked to German intelligence was Alfred Hitchcock.

The Japanese liked to inspire terror in World War II, but in that case the torture and murders were external to American or British society. They didn't allow media pointy-heads to bang on about 'fundamental flaws in society'. The simplest answer is that the Bad Guys are bad - "dark forces", to respectfully adopt the telling phrase attributed[12] to Her late Majesty the Queen. They like upsetting people, particularly the young. The job of the Good Guys, a.k.a the 'white hats', is to go and upset the 'black hats'. It's one of the reasons for this book.

It is a basic mistake of counterintelligence work to assume that because an assassination target is high profile and his or her death causes widespread upset, the degree of hostile intelligence input was proportionate. This mistake can lead to 'powder and shot' type questions ("you must be mad - why would they go to all the trouble of shooting John Lennon?"). These questions miss the point.

The Lennon assassination was no biggie for the DVD. Chapman was a low-grade asset who could be replaced fairly easily. His death would not have been mourned for too long. He was probably recruited through a cut-out and may never have met a real live DVD officer. Almost certainly he did not even know the identity of the agency for which he was working. It was a little tricky to set up (the venue was altered twice) but it wouldn't have occupied the DVD's Amerika Desk or Correa Group for more than a couple of months.

It is doubtful if more than a handful of agents including Correa Group were ever assigned to the case. There would also have been COMINT assets for phone tapping, plus a couple to deal with the wash-up. There was never any risk of the prosecution or the media, trapped as they were in the 'lone gunman' Intellectual Black Hole, ever getting within a country mile of the truth.

In so far as anyone suggested a wider conspiracy, they made the same mistake conspiracy theorists usually make. They aimed at the wrong target, in this case the United States Government. They had no more motive to murder John Lennon than Ringo Starr had. They don't go around organising assassinations anyway, save in a proper case.

If it becomes necessary in the interests of national security to throw the Secretary of Defense off a tall building it is only done after the most anxious and careful consideration. In the world of conspiracy theorists only the British, American or Israeli governments, or Jewish bankers - or whatever - can be at fault, at least up until about 2007.

After 2007 knowledge of the DVD started to spread, glacially at first, then more rapidly. Some conspiracy websites even started to approach intellectual rigour. They started to tone down their anti-Semitic and anti-Western hysteria, even if they still read too much into the sensibly sized fuel tanks at Denver International Airport.[13]

A surprisingly high number of artistes have died in plane crashes over the years, enough to pique the interest of any inquiring air intelligence officer. If you are in air intelligence and do not have an inquiring mind you should perhaps be considering openings in the fast-food industry. The assassination of John Lennon shows that the DVD are prepared to murder pop stars, for effect.

The DVD are after all the biggest and baddest meanies in town, and they organise plane crashes better than anyone. This is a sort of compliment. It's probably high time someone yanked the files on plane crashes such as that which killed Buddy Holly, as he was known, of Lubbock, Texas, on 3rd February 1959. He was an icon. Surely there cannot be any air intelligence officers who have not listened to a Buddy Holly record?[14] Being an icon made him a potential target for the Bad Guys. There is no need however to yank the file on Elvis Presley, if there is one. He died on the john, and yes he is dead, sadly. Elvis was a fine singer, if not such a great actor, with respect.

The Attempted Assassination of President Reagan

The Germans have more experience than anyone else when it comes to organising assassinations. They have knocked over three US Presidents, Lincoln, McKinley and Kennedy. It is pleasing, however, to report that even they can have the odd cock-up. One of the problems you have if you're a 'black hat' agency and cannot justify what you are doing is that you have to stay deep.

Thus, if you want to knock over a bunch of Katangans you have to use Conor Cruise O'Brien and the UN blue berets, or more accurately girls' blouses. *They* would have had trouble defeating the Costa Ricans.[15] Nutters, loners and whack-jobs provide great cover, but they can miss. This especially applies if their hands are shaking. Sometimes they are so nervous, or are such bad shots, that they shoot the wrong person. If they are nicer than you think they are, like Lynette Fromme, they can have an attack of conscience and change their mind.

The attempted assassination of President Ronald Reagan on 30th March 1981 blew up in the DVD's face. Their man John Hinckley Jnr, who had a deep connection with Bush 41, was acting through multiple cut-outs and probably still hasn't worked out for whom he was working - it was the Germans, you clown. He only wounded the president, thankfully, probably because his hand was shaking so much that it affected his aim. Great. You take the breaks when you can get them.

His aim was so poor that it is not entirely clear that he was actually aiming at the president's Press Secretary, whom he crippled for life. That would not have been a defence of course ("he was aiming at the President, Your Honor, he only shot the late Press Secretary by mistake"). It's known as the doctrine of transferred malice. If you aim at X and hit Y, you're guilty.

There was a big factional battle in the DVD after Canaris's death, the real one that is. Apparently, he finally snuffed it in 1978 - there was no death notice. One faction, led by Bush 41, wanted Reagan elected, or to be more precise the Reagan Administration. The plan was to murder Reagan shortly after he was elected.

They went to a lot of trouble to make sure that Carter lost, including using Correa Group assets to pull sand filters off the helicopters tasked with the Iranian hostage rescue on 24th and 25th April 1980. Correa Group of course had Langley thoroughly penetrated. That operation was comprehensively blown before the first Delta Force team left base.

The seizure of the hostages itself was arranged by DVD assets in Teheran, an operation in which a junior VEVAK[16] officer named Mahmoud Ahmedinejad took part. The failure to grasp who set up the attempted assassination of the President, and why, dogged the Reagan Administration until the very end. It was penetrated, i.e. the enemy were inside the gate.

The other faction, which I have designated 'KR', wanted Carter to win. It is not of course suggested that the late President Carter was DVD, merely that he was close to them and was the preferred choice of one faction. They were very pleased with his surrender of the Panama Canal to China. The 'KR' faction also backed the Camp David Accords, whereas the 'ST' faction, as we have seen, arranged for the assassination of Anwar Sadat. Since the two main factions keep murdering each other, it's usually possibly to acquire intelligence on the other faction from someone whose friend has been murdered, or who thinks he's about to be double-crossed.

The Falklands War

The Thatcher Government was also badly penetrated. As we have seen Airey Neave, Mrs Thatcher's campaign manager in 1975 when she beat the DVD's Edward Heath, was blown up, much to his annoyance, in 1979. Rather than assassinate Mrs Thatcher however, it was decided to stage another coup. This time there would be an invasion as well. The result was a small war. That was not in the plan at all, let alone a famous British victory.

General Galtieri, Argentina's military dictator, was a DVD asset. Strictly there was a junta of three, but Galtieri was the big cheese. Argentina of course is a German client state. It was no great surprise that many DVD officers were moved there after 1944, mostly in modified Type XXI U-Boats.[17] It is an urban myth that these Germans included Adolf Hitler, who was Austrian anyway. He was flown out of Berlin, with his doctor, and made it back to Austria, where he lived until about 1951. Mrs Hitler, a.k.a. Eva Braun, seems to have made it down to Argentina, for a short while at any rate. Eva was back in Germany by 1947, where she met someone who many years later became a friend of mine. There were probably at least two Hitler doppelgangers running around South America. The doppelgangers had Hitler moustaches, whereas the real McCoy had of course been told to shave his off.

German naval intelligence and the DVD controlled who went out of Germany at the end of the war, and where. Nazis were expected to make their own arrangements. By April 1945 Hitler had no chance of getting even an outside cabin on a U-Boat to Argentina. Technically, he was still commander-in-chief but he had lost control of the German armed forces by then, save for small units of the SS.

Margaret Thatcher, a very nice lady,[18] walked straight into a trap. She was a great economic thinker, who understood the need to turn Britain's economy around and stand up to the USSR in the Cold War. However, she had no defence or intelligence experience.

There were ministers in her government who were aware of the DVD. I have spoken to one and there must have been others. It is a great mistake to assume that people are ignorant just because they are government ministers. However, that vital intelligence was withheld from the Prime Minister. She went through her entire premiership unaware that the IRA was German-controlled. Equally, she was left in ignorance as to who had set up the invasion of the Falkland Islands, and why.

The Falklands are a strategically significant group of British islands in the western South Atlantic. They are a gateway to the Antarctic and have enormous reserves of oil and natural gas, and rich fishing grounds. Attractive, with friendly people and lots of penguins, they are now a tourist destination in their own right.

Despite the fact that their strategic significance was highlighted in both world wars, in the Battles of the Falklands Islands (1914) and River Plate (1939),[19] the islands were left underdeveloped. Perhaps it would be more accurate to say that their development was blocked by German assets in Whitehall. The islands' strategic significance was well understood in Germany.

The British public was never told of the vital significance for German financing of both world wars of gold shipments from the Far East. Since gold (in those days) was too heavy to go by air, and the Suez and Panama Canals were out, the only routes from China and Japan to Germany were round the Cape of Good Hope or Cape Horn. In World War II the Antarctic and islands close to it were ideal trans-shipment points. Direct shipment by U-Boat or

Japanese submarine all the way from Germany to Japan and vice-versa raised both logistical and security issues. The British presence in the Falklands also inhibited German exploitation of Argentina's strategic position.

Britain never received anything in exchange for her huge purchases of corned beef from Argentina, apart from the corned beef of course. Those orders could and should have gone to friendly dominions in the Empire, Uruguay and Chile. Argentina was heavily spruiked (Australian for 'pushed') by German assets in London, swallowing up large chunks of cash from banks desperate to retain access to Germany's Medium Term Note programmes. These banks were also willing to switch investment from Britain and the Empire to the German Sphere of Influence. Cash starvation of British businesses and households (through mortgage rationing and occasional credit squeezes) has been a feature of British banking since the Germans got going with MTN trading in the last quarter of the 19th century.

Limited though it was, GCHQ were at least able to maintain some sort of watch on the Argentine. They had COMINT and ELINT facilities in the ice-breaker HMS *Endurance*. That is why her planned withdrawal was so significant. By coincidence, or not, she was ordered away from the islands to South Georgia as the Argentine invasion force approached the Falklands. Without her, poor old Governor Rex Hunt, Commander-in- Chief of the Falklands and a very nice man, was left blind.

The Colonial Office had been penetrated, but not as badly as the Foreign Office. At times - e.g. when the 'anti-German'[20] Sir Robert Vansittart was Permanent Secretary - the FO was effectively a branch of the German Foreign Ministry. Foreign Office stewardship of the Falkland Islands was disastrous.

It wasn't a case of *Carlton-Browne of the FO*[21] style neglect as the FO, like to maintain, rather of deliberate underdevelopment of the islands and a running down of their defences, with a view to surrendering them to Argentina. By April 1982 the defences of the islands were scandalously inadequate, even more pathetic than Britain's own.

In the fourteen days prior to the invasion the NSA became increasingly concerned by heavy Argentine military radio traffic. GCHQ were made aware under the UKUSA Intelligence Treaty arrangements. They chose to suppress the intelligence from the Royal Navy, which of course was temporarily deprived of the sea-based intercepts from *Endurance,* and Downing Street.

Warning of an imminent invasion was flashed to the Pentagon and the White House after US satellites detected infrared heat signatures from all major oil-fired Argentine Navy warships. These included the cruiser ARA *General Belgrano*,[22] a powerful surface combatant, with greater firepower than any Royal Navy warship, and the light aircraft carrier *Vienticinco de Mayo.*[23]

Almost all of the Argentine Navy's major units were former British or American warships, powered by high-pressure steam turbines. The exceptions were the Type 42 guided missile destroyers. Crazily, these had been supplied to Argentina as part of Whitehall's policy of arming her whilst cutting back the Royal Navy.

Before putting to sea, the boilers had to be lit and brought up to working pressure. This generates a heat signature. Gas-turbine powered warships, like the Type 42, tend to be slower at sea but much quicker to get to sea. A Type 42 could never hope to keep pace with say an old- fashioned *Daring* class destroyer, with 650 p.s.i. high-pressure boilers. In a race, a *Daring,* had they not been scrapped prematurely, would have just steamed past a '42', with a foaming bow wave and suitable exchange of signals and pleasantries.

My good friend, as he later became, General Walters, agreed with the NSA's assessment that there was about to be an invasion. This was also the assessment of the CIA and MI6 Heads of Station in Buenos Aires. It was confirmed when the invasion force put to sea.

President Reagan, on General Walters' advice, called General Galtieri. He asked him to recall his ships. Galtieri, knowing that he had German and Vatican backing, refused. He intimated to the president that he was not the most powerful person in the world, which indeed he wasn't, although he was in the top ten.[24] The president did not call Margaret Thatcher but he was assured that the British had been told, which indeed we had been. MI6 followed GCHQ in sitting on the intelligence.

General Walters and another nice man, Caspar Weinberger, were puzzled by our lack of reaction. Here was an invasion force steaming towards British territory and Britain was doing nothing about it. Caspar OK'd a warning to British naval intelligence on the backchannel. Politically, there wasn't much the Navy could do. The FCO were forced to send a very silly cable down to poor old Rex Hunt in Port Stanley, telling him that he was about to be invaded and to make his dispositions accordingly! Many years afterwards, he complained to me quite bitterly about it, and I didn't blame him.

Preliminary steps were taken to get the Fleet ready for sea, while the lives of the Royal Marines on the Falklands were saved by deploying them from their barracks at Moody Brook. The Argies were hoping to take them by surprise and wipe them out. That seems to have been part of the plan agreed in advance with the FCO. The barracks were shot up but the Marines had deployed to defensive positions. These weren't much use however, as they were bereft of air support, heavy weapons and even light armour.

The idea was to severely embarrass Mrs Thatcher, present her with a *fait accompli* and force her to resign. She was to be replaced with a 'wet', Francis Pym, who would hold back Britain's economy, hand back power to the trade unions, cut back defence expenditure even further and increase welfare spending. They also wanted to drive a wedge between Britain and America and bring Britain more fully into the Franco-German orbit via the EEC, ultimately with a view to destruction of the currency.

Mrs Thatcher was kept in the dark about the invasion force approaching Port Stanley, although, it was being monitored by every satellite that could be brought to bear. The watching birds included the US Navy's efficient radar satellites. GCHQ were kept fully in the loop by the NSA through their liaison officers at NSA HQ at Fort Meade, Maryland. With war about to break out in the South Atlantic there was intensive intelligence activity.

The principal British agencies implicated in the coup - GCHQ and MI6 had no conception of the upset this nonsense would cause amongst conservatives in the Conservative Party. To them Mrs Thatcher was, rightly, a heroine. She was also an inspiration to the Armed Services and to the betrayed Falkland Islanders. They were a British people being placed in mortal danger, thousands of miles from the Mother Country. They were about to become the first British people to be forced to live under enemy occupation since the liberation of the Channel Islands nearly 40 years before.

The Argies were brutal occupiers. Arrogant (they weren't a German client state for nothing) and swaggering, they were happy to tell whatever lies were necessary to support their bogus claim to the islands. They were and are greedy for the oil and retain a festering hatred of the British for our role in defeating Germany not once but twice. The junta were coming off the back of a dirty war in which they had raped, tortured and murdered thousands of their own citizens.

Only the presence of a Polaris SSBN in the South Atlantic, to which they were alerted by the Americans, kept them in line. Her missiles were apparently targeted on every major strategic target in Argentina, including the Buenos Aires CBD. Senior commanders must have known they had a boomer as back up in case conventional warfare failed. Since Argentina did not use WMDs against Britain the use of strategic nuclear weapons would scarcely have been justified.

Mrs Thatcher however was faced with the same strategic conundrum that confronted President Truman in 1945, for the same reason - idiotic prewar defence policy. An invasion of Argentina wasn't possible. It would probably have cost more lives in the long run anyway. In the event that the amphibious assault on the Falklands was thrown back into the sea, Gallipoli-style - and amphibious assaults are never low-risk - the nuclear option, sadly, might well have been on the table.

General Galtieri could not have been heard to complain too loudly if his presidential palace had been nuked. A neo-fascist dictator, he had chosen to wage war on Great Britain, a nuclear power, which had the precedent of the American nuclear attacks on Hiroshima and Nagasaki to fall back upon. Those attacks had saved thousands of Allied lives by bringing an early end to hostilities. He had also knowingly interfered in Britain's internal affairs, wanting to substitute a weak, pro-EEC, anti- British leader, for the elected Prime Minister.

He also knew that British strategic doctrine was skewed in favour of nuclear weapons, mainly because they are cheaper than adequate conventional forces. DVD assets in Whitehall like Harold Wilson, Roy Jenkins and Edward Heath had successfully weakened Britain's armed forces. They had left the Royal Navy desperately short of aircraft carriers and amphibious warfare vessels. He simply hadn't thought things through, although he quickly grasped that he would be better off sacrificing his troops on the Falklands rather than his capital.

In a frantic effort to save the junta, and with it German control in Buenos Aires, and stave off democracy, he ordered Brigadier Lami Dozo, a competent officer with respect, to sacrifice the Argentine Air Force. This was essentially a PR stunt. In order to reduce the effectiveness of the airstrikes the bombs were not correctly fused, so that a number failed to detonate. This was a wilful sacrifice of brave men to no useful military purpose. However, it demonstrated the extent to which even a single ballistic missile submarine can dominate an enemy's thinking.

The Argentine Navy were less keen on self-sacrifice. Once the decision was taken, in effect, to let Britain regain the islands it tried to withdraw from combat. It swiftly found however that trying to withdraw to safety in a war zone could sometimes be as dangerous as staying put. Like our community partners Napoleon, the Kaiser and Hitler,[25] and North Korea's Kim Il-Sung, Galtieri was essentially a landlubber, no offence intended. He had a minimal grasp of naval warfare.

His whole war strategy was based on occupying essentially defenceless islands. Waging war on unarmed civilians was the one type of warfare he really understood. He had a lot of experience of it, after all. To coin a phrase, in a war at sea he was all at sea.

The coup backfired spectacularly. "No s**t Sherlock" I hear you say. Mrs Thatcher was confirmed in office. She swept on majestically to an emphatic General Election win in 1983. Along with President Reagan's win in 1984 it effectively sealed the fate of the USSR. The Argies lost the war. General Galtieri joined Napoleon, the Kaiser and Hitler in the list of failed dictators who died or were toppled after deciding to start a war with Britain. The defence cuts were reversed and the Royal Navy even got some new ships.

The RAF did extremely well to prang the airstrip at Port Stanley, with an ageing but still very serviceable Avro Vulcan B Mk 2. She was refuelled by a relay of Handley Page Victor tankers, with tankers tanking other tankers. They all got home.

Called *Operation Black Buck* and conceived by that nice man, who bombed Germany, Marshal of the Royal Air Force Sir Michael Beetham, then Chief of the Air Staff, with whom I later teamed up on the Sandys case, the idea was not to put the airstrip out of action. The Vulcan couldn't carry enough bombs for that sadly, and they were the wrong kind of bombs anyway. The idea was to demonstrate to Johnny Argie that Port Stanley was in range of RAF Strike Command. He was forced to withdraw his fighters, conceding local air superiority to the Fleet Air Arm. It was a wizard prang, and a jolly good show all round.

The Argies were a trifle upset when the SSN HMS *Conqueror* sank the *General Belgrano*. This was the first time that a nuclear submarine had gone into action, officially at any rate. The *Belgrano* was trying to withdraw but got herself sunk in the process. With respect her captain, Hector Bonzo, seemed uncertain as to whether he was on a war patrol or a peacetime cruise.

His watertight doors weren't closed, the ship was not at action stations and his escorts[26] were deployed so that they could protect each other from air attack, but not the ship they were escorting from a nuclear submarine attack. This was even though the Argies knew that British nuclear submarines had been deployed in the South Atlantic Theatre. Risibly, the left wing sought to maintain that the *Belgrano* could not have been attacked as she was outside the Total Exclusion Zone (TEZ). The TEZ had greater relevance for neutral merchant ships than enemy warships.[27] South Georgia, a combat zone, was hundreds of miles outside the TEZ. The Argies tried to attack the Task Force with an SSK long before it reached the Falklands area. They even had a couple of frogmen complete with limpet mines, stationed à la 1942 at Algeciras, hoping to sink a passing frigate or two at Gibraltar. The Royal Navy could have sunk the *General Belgrano* if she was tied up alongside at Ushuaia, or in the Indian Ocean, never mind just off the Birdwood Bank.[28]

Belgrano was also fresh out of refit. This is an advantage the Bad Guys always have. They know when the war is going to start because they're the ones starting it. She was faster than *Conqueror*, which badly needed a refit.[29]

Much was made of the French Exocet sea-skimming missile, with which some of the Task Force's escorts were equipped. The argument was the *Belgrano* therefore posed no threat. However, an Exocet, which is a subsonic missile with a smallish warhead, would not have made much impact on *General Belgrano's* armoured belt. Ironically, as I have observed, a warship designed for short to medium range horizontal fire, i.e. with old-fashioned belt armour, was quite well equipped to deal with sea-skimming missiles. HMS *Hermes* also had belt armour and would probably have stood up to an Exocet far better than the more modern *Invincible*.

The big Exocet issue, which the media missed entirely, was that the French deployed an SSN to the Falklands. They tried to sink HMS *Glamorgan*,[30] on 12th June 1982, i.e. that truck-mounted Exocet battery was manned by French naval personnel. That made France a covert belligerent on the side of Argentina. The French were playing with fire, as their attack on *Glamorgan* was an Act of War. Her Majesty's Government would have been fully justified in declaring war on France.

The US picked up the French SSN in transit, on their excellent SOSUS underwater sonar network. Washington probably went into panic mode. They didn't want a war between two EEC Member States, an open war that is. France was already waging war on Britain. The French were also happy to assist the Argie frogmen with ambitions of blowing up a British frigate. DVD assets in DC were frantic lest Mrs Thatcher would find out that she and Britain had been betrayed by, the pro-German Mitterand. He of course was a fascist pretending to be a socialist, indeed he was a former Vichy minister,[31] the last surviving Axis politician from World War II still in power.

A war between Britain and France would have come close to US waters, as Britain would have retaken the French colonies of Martinique and Guadeloupe. It would also have extended to the Indian and Pacific Oceans, where France also has colonies.

It had also not escaped the attention of the Pentagon and State that the French attack on HMS *Glamorgan* (there had also been an earlier attack, which failed, on a frigate) was the first time that one nuclear power had attacked the armed forces of another outside of their own territory. There was of course the Powers incident, although that was a phoney,[32] and there had been shoot-downs of US aircraft overflying Soviet territory, or close to it. The Falklands are a long way from France, however.

It is a reflection of the way in which Britain is massively over-governed at the personal level and hugely under-governed at the strategic level, i.e. governed without thought, that nearly 30 years after the French killed 17 British sailors on HMS *Glamorgan* the 2010-15 Coalition Government could seriously propose a carrier-sharing deal with the French. This made about as much sense as offering to share HMS *Victory* would have done in the Napoleonic Wars ("we'll have her Monday to Friday and you can have her for the weekend").

Trusting the French was not Britain's only strategic mistake. We should have declared war on Argentina and waged it until the enemy sued for peace or surrendered unconditionally. Like the Americans in Vietnam, Britain failed to blockade the enemy's coast and made insufficient use of her strategic bombing fleet. Based at Stanley, with an extended runway, the Vulcans would have made a lovely mess of Argentina's military- industrial complex, power stations, oil storage tanks and other strategic targets.

The Avro Vulcan should have been ordered back into production, with upgraded avionics and engines, along with the Vickers-Supermarine VC- 10, for airlift and refuelling. After the enemy air force was all but eliminated as a fighting force the Task Force should have been ordered to close the enemy coast and bombard it. Its 4.5s could have taken out airfields, dockyards, army bases and command, control and communications facilities.

Whitehall wanted a short war without an effective strategic outcome and got it. As a result, there is likely to be a second war. Argentina has not abandoned her claim to the Falklands, indeed she is pursuing it aggressively as I write. They have rejected the decisive outcome of the March 2013 referendum in the Falklands and still want the oil-rich waters around the islands. Estimates of as high as eight times North Sea oil were being circulated privately in the early 1980s. German assets in Whitehall have always been anxious to downplay the size of the reserves, with a view to Argentina getting them. No doubt there would be a sweet deal for France and Germany if they did.

The islands' defences need reinforcing urgently. There needs to be a serious GCHQ presence on the Falklands. The Royal Navy's South Atlantic Station should be restored, with a 2-star in command. There should always be a carrier on station in the South Atlantic. Britain should withdraw from the absurd Antarctic Treaty and have proper base facilities down there. The massive oil and natural gas reserves should be developed, with a Falklands Fund set up from the licence fees, so that the islanders need no longer pay any tax.

The oil revenues should also be used to develop the islands properly, with a 3 ft 6 in. gauge (i.e. the same as New Zealand and Tasmania) railway system, adequate roads and greatly improved hospital facilities and amenities. Some power could come from wind turbines, the islands and their offshore shallow banks being almost the only territory in the world where wind-power might make sense. The turbines could come from Britain, where they are not needed, their only real purpose here being to spoil the skyline. The Royal Navy could also install *Astute*-type reactors for power generation, with power not needed for naval and military purposes being made available to the islanders for free. There should also be a Royal Falklands Regiment, with armour and artillery components, and greatly improved oceanic and air radar surveillance.

Diplomatic relations with Argentina should be broken off until they are willing to abandon their impertinent claim to our islands. Responsibility for the islands, indeed all colonies, should be taken away from the Foreign Office and restored to the Colonial Office. Its new South Atlantic Desk should be manned by people who know and love the islands and their people, as Sir Rex Hunt did. The RAF needs serious, modern long-range airlift aircraft, which should be designed and built in Britain. The Royal Navy needs more carriers in service, fast, with conventional take-off and landing and no Frenchies aboard, thank you very much, even in the galleys.

KAL 007

On 31st August 1983 a Soviet Su-15 fighter[33] shot down Korean Air Lines Flight KE007 (Boeing 747-230B, registration HL7442), Captain Chun Byung In in command, over Sakhalin Island in the USSR. There were 269 souls aboard, all of whom died. KE007 was on a flight from New York to Seoul via Anchorage, Alaska. Take-off from Anchorage was from Runway 32 at 0500 local time. The airliner had failed to respond to the firing of 120 cannon rounds, which ought to have been visible in the night sky, although in fairness to Captain Chun he was in the process of executing a routine standard climb to FL350.

Radar lock-on was achieved at 1824:22Z.[34] Launch of two AA-3 heat-seeking air-to-air missiles was confirmed at 1826:20Z. The missiles appeared to have been fired in heat-seeking mode and struck the tail and an inboard engine. The intercept was tracked on Japanese military radar and the larger of the three targets, i.e. the 747, was observed to spiral into the sea, just off the Sakhalin coast, at 1828Z.

The area was militarily sensitive and on heightened alert, as a weapons test appears to have been scheduled for the 31st. The only US military activity was a routine Cobra Ball EC-135[35] mission, which at one point was about 75 miles away from KE007, in international airspace. She returned to base at Shemya by about 1730Z however.[36]

The 747 is too large an aircraft to be mistaken for an EC-135 by an experienced pilot, indeed one would hope any pilot. There are however a small number of military versions of the 74'. There was an assassination target on board KE007, Congressman Lawrence Macdonald, chairman of the conservative John Birch Society. They with respect have sensible views on capital punishment and immigration. Larry Macdonald was a DVD target however, not a KGB one. Most Soviet 'wet-jobs' outside the USSR (there weren't actually that many) were false-flagged DVD ops, like the Bulgarian ricin affair in London.[37]

The only anomaly in HL7442's operation, apart from being a whopping 365 miles off course that is, is possible inflight operation of the Auxiliary Power Unit. This is indicated by the impact point of the second AA-3. A heat-seeking missile's infrared sensors will normally lock onto the warmest heat-source. As a matter of both logic and science a cooler but closer source may generate more detectable heat than a warmer, more distant source.

Heat-seeking missiles can also switch targets, indeed that is the whole point of launching countermeasures. If, which the Russians have never confirmed, the AA-3s were in heat-seeking mode,[38] as indicated by the stern attack, the impact point at the rear of the fuselage suggests that the missile's infrared sensor may have switched from an inner engine to the APU.

In the Falklands War, thanks to those very nice people the Americans, we were able to mount head-on heat-seeking attacks using the infrared signature generated by the enemy's leading edge, using the latest Sidewinders.[39] The AA-3 was not as advanced as the Sidewinder however and was really only useful for a stern, or chasing, attack.

If my theory is right, we are left searching for an explanation as to why Captain Chun would have fired up his APU. It is also difficult, but not impossible, for the commander of a commercial aircraft to miss tracer rounds fired by a fighter aircraft at night. It is however possible, since the Soviets scrambled their Su-15s in a big hurry (some Mig-23s had failed to make contact with the target during its transit of the Kamchatka Peninsula), that they may not have been using tracer. Tracer rounds are an old-fashioned idea, dating from World War I. They allow you to 'walk' your fire into your target. At the same time, of course, you give your target a sporting chance by telling him where you are.

It is tolerably clear that:

(1) KE007 was shot down in good faith over Soviet territory having penetrated Soviet airspace without permission, whilst way off course.

(2) There was inadequate civil and military co-ordination, US, Soviet and Japanese, assuming in the latter's favour that their military were not in on it.

(3) Air traffic control, for a flight scheduled close to Soviet airspace on Airway Romeo 20, was sloppy. Captain Chun was not alerted to the fact that he was 6 miles north of Sparrevohn VOR[40] e.g., although that indicated that KE007 was diverging dangerously (for a long transoceanic flight) from her course, and

(4) KE007 was proceeding on her lawful occasions, albeit over Soviet airspace without ATC clearance, and was not engaged in espionage.

> There are however those within INTELCOM who say that she was fitted with recon cameras in one of her cargo holds. I have not been able to confirm that, but new facts may yet emerge, in which case I shall revise my opinion.

Putting to one side the concerns expressed above there are no grounds for accusing Captain Chun of negligence, including the various theories about wrong INS inputs (treble error in inputting the ramp coordinates at Anchorage e.g.). Trying to increase tensions between the USA and the USSR was a known DVD strategy, associated particularly with the 'ST' faction.[41] It is far more likely that the INS was tampered with. All three INS units were probably replaced by US citizen DVD assets in the Correa Group whilst the aircraft was on the ramp at Anchorage.

That particular flight was probably chosen because Congressman Macdonald was aboard. He was likely to go further in US politics and posed a threat to German ambitions to hold back the US politically and economically. The DVD always think a generation ahead. Any Good Guy conservative politician showing promise is going to be jumped all over, portrayed as 'extreme', etc. Their policy proposals will rarely be examined on their merits and if a deniable opportunity to kill them arises it will be taken.

The DVD love 'moderates' and useful idiots generally. From their point of view a Jim Hacker-style moderate is likely to be easily house-trained by bureaucrats. He or she is unlikely to do any harm to the Bad Guys and even more unlikely to do any good for the Good Guys. In tense political situations it is not unknown for centre parties to spring up almost overnight.

Both Presidents Reagan and Andropov deserve credit for calming down a situation that could rapidly have escalated. The Russians in particular made a gracious concession, in the end, that the shoot-down was a tragic mistake. Indeed it was. Similar grace requires acceptance that mistakes were made by the Americans and Japanese as well, including insufficient deconfliction of Cobra Ball flights from civilian traffic.

Captain Chun's airmanship can also be criticised, as can the airmanship of the crew of KE015. This was the LA flight that relayed radio messages to and from KE007. It would be unfair however to accuse either crew of negligence. The fact remains that KE007 was off course by the Bethel beacon and ended up 365 miles off track. Vital clues, such as different winds at about the same flight level, and being outside of VHF range when the flight-plan called for them being in range, were missed.

There was excessive reliance by the 007 crew on the INS, which is a reliable system, trebled on civilian aircraft for extra safety, but vulnerable to tampering. In fairness, the earlier failures in the Mount Erebus DC-10 investigation meant that pilots were not on the alert for deliberate navigation errors. It is also one system.

Star-shots are problematic on a 747. In 1978 a KAL 707 flying from Paris to Seoul wandered *1,000 miles* off course using periscope stellar navigation. She was also intercepted, but with less tragic results. On a long transoceanic flight however the navigating officer, in this case the captain, should use every means available to him to crosscheck his position.

Being 365 miles off course, even with a sabotaged INS, is not best practice. Again in fairness, modern aircraft are not designed with a view to backup navigation if the primary system (these days GPS) fails. On the Boeing 747-200, e.g., the radar altimeters, which are perfectly capable of giving readings from FL330, were calibrated as approach aids only. They would have indicated that the aircraft was over land as it crossed the Kamchatka Peninsula. On an oceanic crossing that is what airmen call a clue.

The Brighton Bomb

This is not easy to write about without indicating who left the hotel before the IED was detonated at 0254. The explosion was in Room 629, above the Prime Minister's, on 12th October 1984, I know who they were, indeed I passed on the details of GO2's involvement to MI5, over a convivial and entirely deniable lunch, which officially never happened. The participants, who included a very nice, retired military intelligence officer, ended this non-event less hungry than before it started, however. You should *always* check who leaves the hotel before the bomb goes off. GO2's idea was to blow up the Prime Minister and that nice man Norman Tebbit, into whom I bumped several times. He was the only other sensible member of the Cabinet with respect. I should say that Norman officially adhered to the Official Version of Events. As indicated, his lovely lady wife Margaret was paralysed in the attack. Norman gave her devoted care for the rest of her life. He was man for whom the marriage vows held deep meaning.

The media decided, without checking who was in the path of the falling debris and who was not, that the IRA wanted to blow up the entire Cabinet. That would have been silly. GO2 took careful note of who was in which room, passed the plans of the hotel to the IRA, assisted in getting the IED into the hotel and did the cover-up. This included hanging certain terrorists out to dry for political reasons and letting others off, including the maker of the timer, Father Patrick Ryan, who finally snuffed it, no offence intended, in June 2025. No doubt some of those let off were given stern warnings not to try and blow up the Prime Minister again and advice that blowing up hotels is illegal in England, even in Essex, never mind Sussex.

If you live in West Belfast (which I have visited and where I was received most courteously if I may say so) and would like to know more about the bombing than was printed in the *Sunday Times* you could have done worse before he died in 2020 than seek out a certain Mr Bobby Storey. He was an IRA bomb-maker. Apart from the odd threatening phone call from Northern Ireland after I discovered the connection between the Provisional IRA and GO2 and amicable dealings over the Mountbatten affair and unravelling who was behind the brutal assassination of Martin McGuinness with a nice, retired gay gun-runner I have not bumped into the IRA. That is unless you count the very brief meeting, no more than a handshake, between myself, and Gerry Adams.[42]

Iran/Iraq War

This was an odd war. You had a Franco-German backed Arab fascist state going to war with a Franco-German backed Islamo-fascist one. The answer may lie in the bitter factional battle inside the DVD. It looks as though the 'ST' faction backed Saddam, whilst the 'KR' faction backed Khomeini. Mitterand, the neo-fascist president of the essentially Vichyist Fifth Republic, backed Teheran. At the same time, he sold planes to Saddam. The Iraqis operated lots of Mirages, which should of course have been called Fairey Deltas.

The Iranians had lots of left-over planes from the days of the Shah, by design. This was thanks to the silly policy of giving an unstable Middle East state highly advanced weapons systems. These included the excellent Grumman F-14 Tomcat fighter, with its long-range AIM-54 Phoenix missiles, later used to shoot down TWA 800 (next chapter).

This was only silly from the Western point of view of course. If you were planning to take over Iran, as the DVD were, and make it Germany's key regional ally, as the 'KR' boys wanted, it made perfect sense. The war came to an inconclusive end because the two factions settled their differences. They decided to invade Kuwait instead.

There were a number of amusing incidents in the war. There were also so a number of less amusing ones, especially for the teenagers sacrificed pointlessly by Iran on the battlefield. It wasn't much fun either for the poor Iranians gassed by the Iraqis with their German-supplied mustard gas.[43]

It was a great war for tanker frauds. Each side had surface to surface and air to surface missiles. Thanks to what I call 'Exocet Syndrome' there was an exaggerated view of the capabilities of anti-ship missiles. In every case to date where an Allied warship has actually been hit by one, their radar or guard has been down. HMS *Sheffield*, for example, sunk by an Exocet in the

Falklands War, was blinded by her SCOT satellite terminal. This was a very silly system designed to satisfy Northwood's and the enemy's curiosity as to where you were, bombard the captain with useless information and take down his radar whilst doing it.[44]

In *The Litsion Pride* case a staggering amount of time was taken up in the High Court in London[45] sorting out the alleged sinking of a super-tanker by an Iraqi helicopter-borne missile. This allegation with respect would have carried more weight had the Iraqis possessed a missile capable of sinking such a large ship at the alleged range.

Iran-Contra

This was another cock-up. President Reagan and another good man, Colonel Oliver North USMC, were led up the garden path by DVD assets in the administration, who were working with Teheran. They were then dumped right in it. Ollie North should have made general, but was hung out to dry. A whole bunch of media and congressional time was taken up with this load of nonsense, which was a serious distraction from the real work of the administration. However, the President and Ollie with respect should have asked themselves the first question you should always ask of any proposed black op - can we defend this if it gets out? If it *can* get out, you should assume that it *will*.

Air India Flight 182

On Sunday 23rd June 1985 Flight AI182 (Boeing 747-237B, VT-EFO, 329 souls aboard, all of whom were lost) was blown up over the Eastern Atlantic, west of Cork, at 0714 GMT. Her last-reported altitude was FL310, 31,000 ft. The IED had been placed aboard at Montreal after luggage, checked in at Vancouver by a Sikh terrorist, was interlined by a harassed check-in clerk. With great respect it should not have been.

In fairness to her, in the atmosphere of hysterical overreaction to perceived racial slights generated by the ideology of political correctness, which was such a help to *al Qaeda* on 9/11, it was asking a bit much of her to stand up to an Indian terrorist. She should have told him 'where to go' (or better still to stay where he was) and called the airport police. Not all terrorists or alleged terrorists are as polite as Gerry Adams however.

This one chucked his weight around. Since he had 'official' backing from DVD assets in Ottawa and the FBI, who had let him 'slip through their fingers', he was in a strong position. His group was also backed by Peking.

The same Sikh terrorist group also wanted to blow up a Canadian Pacific flight, CP003.

Time zone confusion came into play and they ended up blowing up bits of Tokyo's Narita Airport instead. Not good, but it's better to have a device go off on the ground than in the air. Terrorism can be a stressful occupation. It's not unknown for terrorists to set the timers wrongly, or blow themselves up. Sometimes a terrorist instructor will not only blow himself up but his whole class. You take the breaks when you can get them. One bunch of terrorists blew up an entire tower block in West London, having stored unstable TATP explosive in a domestic (!) fridge. Don't try it at home.

Peking had been waging an intelligence war against India since the DVD's Nehru left the scene. Stirring up Sikh separatism was as good a strategy as any. Mrs Gandhi was well aware that her father had sanctioned the Mahatma's assassination and she did not approve. She was an Indian nationalist and by no means a bad lady. China is India's main strategic competitor. It is after all the only country other than Pakistan to have waged war on India since independence. Any terrorist attack on an Indian target is likely to have a Chinese or Pakistani component, Pakistan being a client state of China. I tried and failed to explain that to former Pakistani Prime Minister Benazir Bhutto, whose disgraceful assassination was sanctioned by Peking.

There was a suspicion initially, as indeed there would be at Lockerbie, that AI182 had suffered a catastrophic structural failure. There was an issue with the 747-100 and 747-200. Boeing, by design (DVD assets in the KGB), had been sold a substandard batch of aluminium in the early 70s, as the first ships were going down the line. It was cheap (the bad stuff usually is) and there was a great demand for aluminium in the States due to the Vietnam War.

The Boeing 747 was basically a converted freighter, having been entered for the USAF's CX heavy airlifter programme.[46] The high cockpit location was a legacy of this. It allowed cargo to be loaded through a large nose door, indeed that's how it's done with 747 freighters. They wouldn't have been a bad order for the RAF by the way, for supply missions to Iraq and Afghanistan.

The high cockpit location however meant a pear-shaped front fuselage. Very frankly, we don't want anything pear-shaped on an aircraft if we can avoid it. Boeing slightly under-egged the structural pudding. It was no biggie however, and soon fixed. Structural weakness has not been the reason for the loss of any 747.

The Manchester Air Disaster

A few weeks later, on 22nd August 1985, the Number 1 or port Pratt & Whitney JT8-D engine on a British AirTours Boeing 737 (even less leg room than on British Airways) blew up on Runway 24 at Manchester Airport. Once again, her captain didn't get as much help from Air Traffic Control as he could have done. He had no video surveillance of the engines in the cockpit. It's not that difficult to do, but genuine aviation safety improvements can be harder to push through bureaucracies than you might suppose.

Without a sight of the engine fire, he could have no real conception of the extent of the problem. ATC did however. They could see the flames. A simple warning that the aircraft needed to be evacuated without delay and an instruction to leave her on the runway was all that was required to stop the emergency becoming a disaster. Getting an unserviceable aircraft off an active runway is good airmanship, but not if it means bringing the fuselage broadside onto flames fanned by the wind going down the runway. Down the runway is where we want the wind to be.

Sabotage of the engine's combustion cans has not been confirmed. The investigation was the usual sloppy affair however, with great respect to all concerned. Everybody agreed that the number 9 can blew and it had a fatigue crack in it - no s**t Sherlock. How did the crack get there and when did it start? Large cracks usually start as small cracks. Why was it not picked up before it became a serious hazard? Was the can substituted at any point?

That loss of life should not have happened. It might have been negligence but until the incident is properly investigated it is impossible to say. The files on this one need yanking, i.e. there should be a cold case review by an experienced team of air intelligence officers, familiar with DVD sabotage methods, who can assess the case objectively. By that I mean without AAIB/NTSB style preconceptions that it was an accident and taking everything at face value. The dead and their families deserve at least that.

Mrs Thatcher was commendably quick with respect to get up to Manchester. She was rightly concerned that it might be sabotage but sadly the investigation that followed did not match up to her expectation that it would be thorough. Actually, it was fairly superficial. As with a lot of air crash investigations it was some time before the report was published. Dragging things out, to create an impression of thoroughness, is a well- worn bureaucratic ploy.

PanAm 103

This is another topic is worthy of a book in its own right. In a broad overview like this there is space only for the headlines:

(1) There were two intelligence teams on the flight, one CIA, led by Matt Gannon, and one DIA, led by Major Chuck McKee. They weren't just taking 103 for the convenient timing. It was an established DVD narcotics pipeline, and they were *inter alia* tracking a dope-smuggler, Bish 41.

(2) Each team was taking back high-grade intelligence gathered in Beirut and Syria that implicated high-ranking members of the Reagan Administration, who happened to be DVD assets, in narcotics trafficking and the kidnap and murder of William Buckley, the CIA Head of Station in Beirut.

(3) The IED came out of Dachau via Frankfurt, using MEBO timers, which the DVD-sponsored PFLP-GC terrorist group had been using. It seems to have been moved on a PanAm 727 24 hours before, i.e. on 20th December 1988.

(4) The IED was stored in the IranAir cargo-handling facility at Heathrow, which had been placed adjacent to the PanAm facility at GO2 request, to ease the interlining of narcotics, if that is not a pun. The narcotics run on PanAm flights included heroin refined in the Beka'a Valley using Afghanistan-sourced opium. The Iranian intelligence agency VEVAK was partly funded by a cut on heroin traffic through Iran.

(5) Libya was *not* involved, save that the Libyan dictator Colonel Gaddafi, who had been installed in a DVD-backed coup in 1969, agreed to a Dachau request to put up a couple of his spooks as bunnies. By Libyan standards they were quite nice spooks and were not particularly senior. Megrahi in particular never went near the plane, the IED, or the suitcase in which it was contained.

(6) The IED used a chemically timed barometric fuse, i.e. it was set to detonate a fixed time after take-off, or as fixed as you can get with those damn chemical timers. There was a barometric 'safety' to prevent detonation below 9,000 meters, i.e. just below FL 30. This was to prevent detonation over land so far as possible.

(7) Captain MacQuarrie's change of course, which was picked up by Correa Group monitors at the CIA's RAF Mildenhall facility in England, meant that detonation over Scottish territory became probable.

(8) This generated a mini panic at CIA Mildenhall, the CIA Station in London and at Correa Group HQ in Frankfurt. CIA officers reporting to Frankfurt, not Langley, left for south-west Scotland *before* the plane came down. This is always a bad sign - we like to people to know about plane crashes *after* they happen, not before. Once there, they made themselves unpopular with the locals by liberating evidence. They were loud-mouthed and rude, which should have been taken as a sign that they were working for the Germans. Americans are usually polite and well mannered.

(9) The cover-up was mostly by GO2 and Correa Group, working together. It involved impregnating some wreckage with explosive residue and a whole bunch of other stuff, which I could not possibly get into print.

(10) The Scottish Executive were forced to release Megrahi, who very frankly should never have been convicted, because the seriously flawed prosecution case looked set to fall apart at Megrahi's second appeal. This appeal followed a referral from those very nice people the Scottish Criminal Cases Review Commission, who actually investigated the case in good faith. It is so rare these days to see public authorities acting in good faith that when they do it should be acknowledged.

---

1. Nearly bankrupted by the DC-8, poor old Donald Douglas was forced into a merger with the McDonnell Aircraft Corporation of St. Louis Missouri, makers of the brilliant and versatile F-4 (as it became - the Pentagon merged the easily understood USAF and USN aircraft designation systems in 1962 in order to cause confusion) Phantom II fighter-bomber. Sadly the merger was not a success, principally because Douglas thought it was a merger whereas McDonnell thought it was a takeover. No significant new civil aircraft were designed, only versions of the Douglas DC-9 and DC-10, a project which predated the merger, although the DC-10 entered service some years later. The combined company drifted along for a few decades. Mired in confusion, it was eventually absorbed by Boeing, who added further confusion by renaming the already renamed DC-9 the 'Boeing 717,' as though that designation had not already been allocated (to the KC-135). In fairness Donald Douglas was not above confusing everybody himself. For reasons that are still unclear the Douglas DC-8B became the Series 20, etc. Donald should have fired whoever came up with that idea and sent him up to Seattle with a letter of recommendation.
2. New Zealand used to have some wonderful railway lines, indeed still does, although sadly they are few and far between and passenger train services are sparse. DVD assets forced a change to a sensible rule limiting carriage of freight by trucks, for which New Zealand's heavily graded, mostly two-lane roads are not suitable. If you are a visitor to New Zealand and you are planning to drive you would be ill advised to allow for more than say 45 miles per hour average speed. Encouraging freight onto the roads also helped increase the accident rate. A similarly damaging policy was adopted in Britain.
3. Not least because out and back flights don't need luggage, i.e. you have the whole of the under-floor cargo area in which to mount cameras. There is no suggestion that the RNZAF or NZSIS were making use of the Air New Zealand flights in this way. Apart from anything else they were not penetrating deeply into Antarctica and were not overflying sensitive areas.
4. Stanley Stewart, *Air Disasters*, p. 180. Stewart has no intelligence background, so far as I am aware. That is not a criticism. He simply treats the crash as an accident.
5. Tactical Air Navigation, similar to a VOR-DME, giving range and bearing information to military aircraft. Civil DME (Distance Measuring Equipment) can obtain a range reading from military TACAN beacons as they are VHF and the signals are not encoded.
6. HMNZS *Canterbury* and HMNZS *Waikato*.
7. His heroic action in saving the lost pilot of a Cessna 188 cropduster on a trans-Pacific delivery flight on December 22nd 1978 was rightly immortalised in the film *Mercy Mission: The Rescue of Flight 771*, starring Robert Loggia as Captain Vette. He displayed outstanding airmanship and his actions were in accordance with the best traditions of the air. The airliner commanded by Captain Vette on that occasion was a DC-10-30 (ZK-NZS) and his Second Officer, Gordon Brooks, was murdered on the Mount Erebus flight.
8. There is a good summary in Stewart. Chippindale's disappointing conduct is dealt with by Sir Paul Holmes in *Daughters of Erebus*.

9. American Airlines Flight 96, Captain Bryce McCormick in command, a very fine airman with respect. He got the bird down, at Detroit, showing great skill and presence of mind - it was a lovely bit of flying.
10. Turkish Airlines Flight 981, brought down on 3rd March 1974.
11. Very carefully thought through, if you discount the stupidity involved in deciding to murder American civilians in peacetime (between America and Germany at any rate) on a civilian flight. Pressure was applied to a member of the flight crew and the captain was persuaded that he didn't have his gear locked down. The DVD had picked up on a very slight fault with the autopilot, which could be disengaged unintentionally by a control input, a safety feature, but one which could work both ways. The aircraft was N310EA, Eastern Airlines Flight 401. Captain Robert Loft, an immensely experienced pilot, was in command. He has been unfairly criticised.
12. By Paul Burrell, formerly butler to HRH the Princess of Wales. I am not suggesting that the attribution is accurate - that would be for Buckingham Palace to say - or that if it is, Her Majesty necessarily had the DVD in mind. Elizabeth II however, with great respect, was very well informed.
13. When I heard that people were worried about DIA I thought it was a wind-up. The only problem with DIA is the distance to the terminal from the Hertz lot. They even have more than usually intelligent barmen. I well recall having a conversation with a NASA rocket scientist into whom I happened to bump (as you do), who was interested in my visit the previous week to JPL Pasadena. With respect he had trouble following my explanation of the flaws in Einstein's space-time continuum theory. The barman however had no trouble understanding that it is a lot easier to mix Scotch and soda than it is to mix space and time. He fixed a good drink too.
14. I am showing my age. This should probably read record/tape/CD/I-Pod track. When I was growing up if you wanted to listen to music you put a piece of vinyl on a piece of kit called a record-player and put a long arm on it with a diamond stylus, which usually scratched the record but produced sound that some say is purer than digital.
15. They don't have an army.
16. The principal Iranian intelligence service, since renamed. They didn't like me and the feeling was mutual.
17. Their pennant numbers are listed in Appendix Eight.
18. She is portrayed sympathetically by Meryl Streep in *The Iron Lady*, for which Ms Streep deservedly won an Oscar in 2012. It was a very fine piece of acting. The film was much more balanced than many conservatives feared, but the Alzheimer's did not kick in until well after Lady Thatcher had left office.
19. HMS *Cumberland*, the *County* class cruiser which reinforced Rear- Admiral Harwood's squadron, sailed from the Falklands, which also provided an urgently needed refuge for HMS *Exeter*. She had taken some severe hits from *Graf Spee*. She could have hit back harder had she not been deprived of the fourth 8-in. gun turret the DNC wanted, courtesy of silly treaty commitments. She and her sister HMS *York* were left dangerously under- gunned and under-protected, compounded by inadequate AA armament. Poor old *York* of course was sunk at

Suda Bay in Crete, in 1941, by Italian explosive motorboats. This technique was later modified by the DVD for use by *al Qaeda* against the USS *Cole*. It would have been better to have ordered improved '*Counties*', at say 12,000 tons, with better directors, AA and protection.

20. Sir Robert's hostility to Germany was of the 'let's squeeze them till the pips squeak' sort, i.e. as phoney as the Phoney War.
21. A very funny Boulting Brothers film starring that great comedian Terry-Thomas as the eponymous Carlton-Browne. In addition to poking fun at the Foreign Office, which very properly has been an object of ridicule in Britain since Munich, it also made fun of the equally risible UNO.
22. 9,575 tons standard displacement, 15 6-in. 47 cal. guns - a formidable main battery, even in 1982.
23. Formerly HMS *Venerable*, as refitted she displaced 19,900 tons standard, having been equipped with a canted deck and a number of other improvements.
24. President Obama wasn't even the most powerful person in America, although he probably made it into the top three.
25. Napoleon's longest sea journey was to St Helena. The Kaiser's time at sea was spent mostly on his yacht. Hitler, so far as is known, never crossed the Channel, although in fairness he had ambitions to. Kim apparently took several days to grasp that Macarthur had outflanked him in the daring Allied amphibious landing at Inchon. The last serious Korean admiral was Yi Sun- sin, who was sold down the river, or inland sea, by Japanese assets higher up his chain of command, in 1598.
26. As indicated, I set foot on one, the *Piedra Buena*, when was the USS *Collett* (DD-730).
27. As explained in Ch. 4 I once shared a platform with Tam Dalyell MP, who was very exercised about this sinking. I respectfully agree that the House of Commons should not have been misled, but that seems to have been an attempt to embarrass the Prime Minister as much as anything, i.e. she seems to have been misled as well. There was no reason at all why the *Belgrano* could not have been sunk and no reason to pretend she was inside the Exclusion Zone or that her heading was other than 280^0 - even a cruiser her size could have turned towards the Task Force in about 120 seconds.
28. This was an important tactical consideration for the sadly now passed Admiral Woodward, who thought that the enemy might try a pincer movement, using the *Belgrano* and the carrier. *Conqueror* needed 15 fathoms or so above her sail not to leave a surface wake, which would have betrayed her position. Admiral Woodward was not to know the Argentine surface fleet was bailing out of the war for fear of winning a battle and triggering a nuclear attack on Buenos Aires, thereby losing the war. He was unfairly criticised within the Navy for keeping his carriers out of enemy fighter range, which in turn limited the time his Harriers could spend over East Falkland, but even if he was not privy to the deployment of a *Resolution* class SSBN avoiding resort to the nuclear option must have been at the back of his mind. He was also having to hold the hands of a bunch of old women in Whitehall (not Mrs Thatcher) who allowed themselves to be obsessed with the thought that if just one of his carriers was sunk the Task

Force would have to withdraw. Quite apart from the fact that the Americans had very generously offered to lend Britain the *Iwo Jima* there were a couple of spare light carriers lying around if you knew where to look - HMAS *Melbourne*, the ex-HMS *Powerful*, e.g., had not yet been scrapped and the Indians could have been asked nicely to give us back the *Hercules*. A deal might also have been done with Brazil. If you are able to build carriers (and not many countries can – only Britain, America, Japan and, to stretch a point, France, have ever built carriers which actually worked in combat, and the Japanese relied on technology transferred from Britain by German assets) you can usually cut a deal for a cut-price new one in exchange for an old World War II one that you need to rush into refit by next Wednesday. Sandy Woodward and I never met, but I sent him a copy of this section of the first edition of this book through a mutual friend, who had served under him in the Task Force. So far as I know he read it. At any rate I was not asked to make any corrections. Sandy was a brilliant submariner and had a fine grasp of carrier tactics. He rang to thank me after I publicly defended him and the Navy over the *Belgrano*.

29. It is often overlooked that the Argies had another *Brooklyn* class cruiser, the ARA *Nueve de Julio*, ex-USS *Boise* (CL-47), which they could and did raid for *Belgrano* bits. The latter's speed is a matter of controversy. Prior to her refit she seems to have been able to do about 25 knots clean hull, in calm surface conditions, in temperate waters. It is not even clear that was able to light all her boilers. Post-refit, 30 knots calm surface might be nearer the mark. *Conqueror* was 17 knots pedal to the metal by the end of April. She should have been in a dockyard not at war.
30. *County* class guided missile destroyer, 5,440 tons standard displacement.
31. Strictly, by 1982 Mitterand was a neo-fascist. He was a strong supporter of the EEC, as you would expect from a member of Marshal Pétain's government, and an anti-semite, who backed his government's policy of deporting French Jews to the death camps. After it was clear that his side were losing he joined the Resistance, but he was careful not to kill too many Germans. Indeed, since he was passing intelligence to the Abwehr/DVD station in Vichy, then Paris, he probably got more Resistance fighters killed than he killed Germans. Sadly, he lived until 1996. He should have been guillotined, nicely of course, in 1945.
32. Frank had agreed to fly at FL480 so that the Soviets could bring the plane down. The idea was to exchange him for Colonel Rudolf Abel of the KGB, only he wasn't KGB, he was DVD, and his name wasn't Abel, or Baker if it came to that.
33. 1,386 mph, or slightly over Mach 2, a useful bit of kit, lacking modern avionics, but not to be under-estimated.
34. Stewart, *op. cit.* contains a good account, including the published transcripts of the air to ground communications. Z of course is Zulu and the last two digits are seconds.
35. The electronic intelligence-gathering version of the KC-135 tanker, it looks like a 707 with lots of extra aerials, but it has the narrow fuselage.
36. Stewart, *op. cit.*, p. 208.
37. The Markov assassination in London.

38. Air to air missiles, have three basic modes - heat-seeking, active beam riding (following radar transmissions from the launch aircraft or another target illuminator) and semi-active homing, where they lock onto radar or other electro-magnetic emissions from the target.
39. The AIM-9, a jolly useful bit of kit.
40. Stewart, *op. cit.,* p. 202.
41. I emphasise again that these are codes, used for convenience.
42. Gerry Adams is the second nicest terrorist or alleged terrorist I have ever met, after John Jenkins. I am not a terribly memorable chap and it is unlikely that he recalls our brief encounter. Entirely by coincidence it took place in Brighton, at a Labour Party conference.
43. The Germans seem to like gassing people. Why is something you'll have to ask them, but there is no doubt that gassing is a German thing. Gas has only ever been used on a large-scale in warfare by Germany or German allies or client states. Gassing was of course the favoured method of execution in the Holocaust. If 'Jerry' does not like being accused of liking gassing people with respect he should stop going around doing it.
44. What was needed, (1) a naval intelligence officer and (2) a spanner. The SCOT system should have been unscrewed and thrown overboard. A memo could have been sent to Northwood explaining that it had been done to reduce tophamper.
45. [1985] 1 Lloyds Rep. 437.
46. Boeing put the wing in the wrong place. The competition was won famously by the Lockheed Galaxy an outstanding aircraft, which has given great service.

27

The 1990s

The End of the First Cold War

I coined the phrase 'the Second Cold War' after the Chinese PLA Air Force brought down that US Navy EP-3E Aries on 1st April 2001. She had been on a lawful intelligence-gathering mission, in international airspace. It's taken over two decades and a worldwide Chinese WMD campaign (Covid), but the phrase is starting to catch on. All the Chinese armed forces are ultimately controlled by the PLA, by the way, which thankfully understands neither sea nor air power. It's one reason why they've never won a war, unless you count the Chinese civil war.

The First Cold War, against the Soviet Union and its satellites, ended in 1991. This prompted Francis Fukuyama to pronounce the "end of history", with respect a trifle prematurely. Like many politicians and strategic commentators, he didn't get it, with respect. The real enemy in the First Cold War was Germany, not the Soviet Union, hence *Ostpolitik* and the West German cosying up to the East.

German Intelligence, in its various guises, more or less controlled the Soviet Union from the time they installed their man Lenin and the Bolshevik Party in 1917, until 1953. By then the GRU had finally worked it out and arranged for Stalin to pop his clogs. After they lost control of Moscow it suited the 'Jerries' to encourage hardliners to raise tensions with Britain and America. The same game was played by some DVD assets in London and Washington.

The German wet dream was that the wartime allies would end up destroying each other. It nearly worked, but the 'KR' faction worked out that with the advent of thermonuclear weapons just about everybody would be wiped out, except the Eskimos. Even a few of their igloos would have melted. Since this included the Germans, nuclear war was clearly not a good idea.

After 1991 the Germans used Medium Term Note trading programmes to build a group of oligarchs. They tended to be opposed to any Russian statesman - that nice man Vladimir Putin being the prime example - who wanted to stand up for Russia. First Cold War thinking, if thinking is not too strong a word, still dominates Whitehall and some advisers to President Trump, like General Kellogg, no offence intended.

This was demonstrated by the hysteria in London and Washington over the alleged assassination of Lt-Col Litvinenko in London and minor voting irregularities[1] in the December 2011 Russian elections. It's as silly as Crimean War thinking. How on earth did Britain end up on the same side as the French, of all people, and Johnny Turk, against our gallant ally in the Napoleonic Wars, Russia?

Unlike hot wars, cold ones tend to have fuzzy beginnings and endings. On any view the First Cold War had been consigned to the history bin, where it belonged, by Christmas 1991. It always was nonsense, as Bomber Harris and Marshal Zhukov probably understood. They got on together like a house on fire by the way - and nobody could get a good fire going like Bomber Harris.

The hardliners on both sides tended to feed off each other. That is not to say that Margaret Thatcher and Ronald Reagan, well advised with respect by that nice man Richard Perle, were not right to stand up to the Soviet Union. President Kennedy was right to stand firm over the siting of nuclear missiles in Cuba. That was an absurd and dangerous provocation, not that placing American nuclear missiles in Turkey was terribly sensible either.

The big mistake, apart from letting German intelligence overthrow the Tsar, a thoroughly decent man and a patriotic Russian (shame about the wife), was not to call the whole thing off after Stalin had been bumped off. The Soviets plumped for Khrushchev, who was not terribly bright. He knew perfectly well that Stalin had been working for Canaris. Whether he knew that Canaris was still alive and running German intelligence is open to doubt.

Eisenhower knew, since he was a German asset, ditto Macmillan. The sensible thing would have been for one side or the other to take unilateral steps to calm things down. International diplomacy being what it is everybody waited for everybody else. In the meantime, we had stupidities like Heath's expulsion of 105 Soviet diplomats. They were spies, but the FCO knew that when they let them in. What did they think Soviet diplomats did? Visit museums?

The Russians tend to be naturally pro-British, as the warm relationship between Tsar Nicholas II and King George V bore testament. It wasn't the King's decision to abandon the Tsar to his fate. That was Lloyd George, working with Lord Stamfordham, the most disloyal Private Secretary a monarch ever had.

Generally speaking, if you're a Brit and you're not leaving notes under plastic rocks, you will be treated with great courtesy and genuine friendliness in Moscow. The US government wouldn't dream of laying on an official car to get me back to my hotel, any more than the British government pushes the boat out for American visitors. The Russians did however. That was very *kulturny* (classy).

In the impressive armed forces museum in Moscow I spied (if that is the right word - I am not a spy) Gloster Gladiator plastic kits. There was also a sympathetic portrait, in Russian of course, of the *Hawkins* class cruisers on sale.[2] These elegant warships, arguably the first heavy cruisers, have almost been forgotten in the country they once served so well.

The Russians are generally speaking the Good Guys, as I observed from the floor at a business conference in Moscow in 2005, to the discomfiture of the British Ambassador, Tony Brenton. No offence to Tony intended, but he seemed to see his role as annoying the Russian Government as much as possible. The British Embassy in Moscow generally acts as though HMG were an NGO, rather than engaging in serious diplomacy. In fairness to Tony he was probably banned from serious diplomacy by the FO.

The Russians not only helped us beat the Germans, twice, but the French as well. That definitely makes them Good Guys! The poor old Russians get a bad press - captious criticism of alleged human rights abuses in Chechnya and so on and over Ukraine - but there is nothing new in this. There were officially sponsored scare stories about the Russians invading the *Australian* colonies in the 1890s. If that scenario had been put to Admiral Makarov or any other Imperial Russian Navy commander, he'd have collapsed in a fit of hysterical laughter.

Russia, Britain and America have common enemies in Germany and, more recently, the People's Republic of China. That's why we ended up on the same side in the first two world wars. All three members of the wartime Grand Alliance have suffered grievously from German penetration assets, but none more so than Russia. Politicians and media in all three countries keep falling for attempts by German assets to drive a wedge between us. It's high time we grew up. We could start by seriously examining the Russian case for invading Ukraine.

It would also be helpful if politicians and the media could take a more balanced approach to Russia's modern intelligence services. The KGB went with the end of the First Cold War. In my admittedly limited experience the excellent FSB, the new internal service, is at least as professional and well informed as MI5 or the FBI. As regards the DVD it is better informed. The external service, the SVR, tends to be both more responsible and professional than MI6.

There was a lot of vapouring over Chechnya. The Russians fought a long and bitter counter-terrorist insurgency against Islamic terrorists there. The security forces were responsible for the occasional human rights peccadillo, but their record was been no worse than say Britain's in Northern Ireland or America's in Vietnam. Certainly, there is nothing which need concern any other government in Christendom. Russia was quite right to re-annexe the Crimea, to keep it out of the German orbit.

NGOs by definition are supposed to be non-governmental, but that all rather depends on who is bankrolling them. Very few survive by rattling tins on street corners or having a donation facility on their websites. Some receive funding that can be traced back to dodgy foundations linked to German intelligence, i.e. they are not non-governmental at all. I have yet to see a credible, objective or balanced report on Chechnya from an NGO.

The Coup Against Mrs Thatcher

This was disgraceful. Margaret Thatcher had not been beaten at the ballot box. She probably wouldn't have lost the next election either, although her popularity had been undermined, as intended, by the poll tax. That was an exceedingly silly idea. Her most reliable source of information on backbench opinion, Ian Gow MP, was assassinated on DVD instructions by the IRA on 30th July 1990. That left her vulnerable. The internal party coup was duly mounted on 28th November 1990. It made sure Britain that would have a Prime Minister amenable to the Treaty of Maastricht, which established the euro.

For the avoidance of doubt, it is not suggested that John Major, the incoming Prime Minister, was aware that the assassination of Ian Gow was a preliminary to the coup. He is not listed as an attendee at the Bilderberg Group meeting between 11th and 13th May 1990 at Glen Cove, NY, where the coup was discussed. This was not of course done in the formal sessions. There was no 'coup in Britain' workshop or breakout session.

Understandably, bitterness persists on the right wing of the Conservative Party to the present day. To the right in Britain, Margaret Thatcher is an icon. This is without widespread knowledge that the coup which removed her was sponsored by German intelligence, in gross violation of international law.

The Global Warming Scam

Margaret Thatcher was a scientist by training, in chemistry. Sadly, with respect, she was out of practice by the end of her period in office. This was shown up by the ease with which she was tricked into believing that human CO2 emissions had led to uncontrollable planetary warming, the Anthropogenic Global Warming Hypothesis (AGWH).

This is no longer taken seriously by INTELCOM.[3] They/we have access not just to 'peer-reviewed' literature but to drafts sent by e-mail. There are other forms of COMINT as well, such as silly international telephone calls between members of the UN's IPCC panel. Then there is the hard data, particularly satellite data on oceanic, surface and upper atmosphere temperatures. Most intel agencies also have access to hard data on oceanic salinity and currents, and sea levels.

INTELCOM can also see who is pushing 'global warming'. Many of the proponents belong to DVD front organisations such as the Trilateral Commission. INTELCOM also tends to know the real position of governments, as opposed to the Janet and John nonsense trotted out for public consumption. The Chinese, Russian and Indian governments, e.g., are perfectly well aware that the hypothesis that human emissions of carbon dioxide can materially affect planetary temperatures is invalid.

Very helpfully the Russians released some of the sillier e-mails between global warming advocates, originating from the University of East Anglia in the east of England. They did this just prior to the Copenhagen climate conference. It collapsed in a heap and rightly so. Essentially the e-mails were about skewing data to support the hypothesis. With great respect that is hardly best scientific practice.

The world of science is not so very different from the world of intelligence. Each involves drawing inferences from the available data. You don't skew the data to fit your conclusions. That's what Thames Valley Police Special Branch do.

Amusingly, the Norfolk county constabulary, a force so lacking in intellectual rigour that it thinks that speeding is a major cause of road accidents, launched an inquiry into 'Climategate'. This facile investigation was accompanied by a raft of official 'Janet and John' reports which hastened to explain that it had all been a misunderstanding.

Since the e-mails were released via Tomsk just what Norfolk Constabulary were hoping to achieve is unclear, with respect. To put it mildly they were a little out of their jurisdiction, not to mention their depth. There it is.

The hypothesis that humankind was affecting the climate through industrial emissions of CO2 is not new. It dates from flawed research by a dodgy Swedish chemist, Svante Arrhenius, in the 1890s. Amusingly, he was described in the *Guardian*[4] as having "a penchant for maverick theories". Indeed - unlike myself, I can hear people saying.

Of course there is nothing wrong with being a maverick, if you're right and the 'mainstream' view is wrong. The issue is right or wrong, not maverick or mainstream. Unfortunately, Dr Arrhenius was wrong. He struggled to satisfy the examiners for his PhD, unsurprisingly, since logic was not his strong point. Indeed, he had so little capacity for logical thought that it's surprising he did not go into politics. Arrhenius was not a genius.

In fairness to him, at least he does actually seem to have believed in his hypothesis. This is more than can be said for some of his followers. Guy Callendar, an English engineer and an expert on steam engines, detected a link between CO2 emissions and temperature in 1938.[5] He was right, but he got it the wrong way round. As he might have expressed it, since he knew his steam engines, his theories were tender first. Increases in CO2 follow warming, not the other way round. Thanks to the oceans the lag appears to be about 750 years.

Why should the defence and intelligence communities be interested in the climate? The answer is fourfold:

(1) Military strategists are interested because military campaigning can be affected by the weather, which in turn is a function of the climate. On the wilder shores of the debate there are predictions that island states might sink beneath the sea or that weaker states might collapse.

(2) The proposed mitigation costs are enormous, not just large enough to dent defence budgets but in some cases bigger than the budgets themselves.

(3) The way in which the debate has been influenced by DVD front organisations. The funding of NGOs and the corruption of the UN are all matters of interest to the counterintelligence community, and

(4) The issue has demonstrated the vulnerability of the Western media and to a lesser extent public opinion to propaganda techniques. These range from the simple (the misuse of Amanda Byrd's charming 2004 photo of two polar bears on a melting ice-flow and the 'hockey stick' graph, which distorted the temperature record in an effort to show that the 20th century was the warmest in the last millennium) to Goebbels' 'Big Lie' technique, such as the entirely false claim that there is a consensus on AGWH.

The defence interest isn't new. The Abwehr and the OKW bought into Arrhenius's and Callendar's theories. They persuaded themselves that Russia's 'General Winter' had been demoted. For around three hundred years Russia had relied on her severe winters as a deterrent to invasion. In the 1920s and 30s the world was in a warming period, indeed the 1930s was the hottest decade of the 20th century.

"*Wunderbahr*", said ze Wehrmacht, "not only can ve campaign for longer, ve von't have to carry as much kit, as ve can dispense vith ze heavy vinter clothing". In December 1941 the Russians gloriously counter- attacked outside of Moscow in temperatures of 50 degrees below zero. That is a trifle chilly. Some of the poor old German infantry literally froze to death.

The climate had turned. The war saw further severe winters, not least in 1944-1945, when as we have seen the Germans learnt about the effect of slush on runways. Having grasped that the climate was cyclical by no later than Christmas 1941, 'Jerry' spotted an opportunity as the world entered another warming phase in the late 1970s.

There was a very silly summit in Rio de Janeiro in 1992, followed by Kyoto, Copenhagen and a series of increasingly bizarre reports from the IPCC. The principal claims of the warmists are that:

(1) Human activity is behind the observed increase in CO2 levels.
(2) CO2 is the main driver of the Greenhouse Effect, which is a proven theory - there is no doubt that CO2 is a greenhouse gas. The increasing CO2 level threatens a potentially debilitating rise in temperatures by 2100, and
(3) The increased temperatures are causing sea levels to rise.

These claims may be summarised shortly: "we're all going to fry and if we don't fry we're all going to drown and it will all be the Americans' fault for driving gas-guzzling SUVs". This is another subject worthy of a book on its own. Happily it has already been written, by that nice man Christopher Booker, who was Britain's foremost investigative journalist, and his scientific colleague Dr Richard North. They have or had razor-sharp minds, with respect,[6] so sharp that they could work for Gillette.

A number of distinguished academics and commentators have dismantled AGWH. They include Viscount Monckton of Brenchley, another nice man with respect, Professor Philip Stott in Britain, Professor Jan Veizer of the Ruhr University at Bochum, Dr Nir Shaviv of the Hebrew University in Jerusalem, Professor Akasofu, Dr Willie Soon of the Harvard-Smithsonian Center for Astrophysics, Professor Paul Reiter of the Pasteur Institute, Professor Ian Plimer of Adelaide University, the Swedish geologist Nils-Axel Morner and Steve McIntyre of Climate Audit, who exposed the hockey-stick. The meteorologist Anthony Watts of the excellent website *Watts up With That* has also done good work.

By no later than the end of 2012 it was apparent that:

(1) Planetary temperatures had levelled off by 1998 and if anything were starting to go down, suggesting that we are now in a cooling cycle.

(2) CO2 continued to rise, albeit by modest amounts, but sufficient to call the 'CO2 causes temperatures to rise' link into question.
(3) Islands, let alone whole island nations, were not disappearing.
(4) The Arctic and Antarctic ice sheets were getting thicker, not thinner, the only exception being the Antarctic Peninsula, and
(5) Scientific peer review of AGWH had degenerated into a farce, to the point where it had become more a means of reinforcing delusion than enforcing intellectual rigour.

Where did the so-called 'climate experts' go wrong? It's not too difficult to see:

(1) The IPCC relied on flawed data, e.g. temperature records distorted by the Urban Heat-Island Effect, so that they became a measure of increasing urbanisation rather than increasing temperature, and tide gauges in areas affected by development or in parts if the world which are sinking. Some of the gauges were measuring subsiding land mass rather than expanding oceans.
(2) CO2 is only a trace gas, which is why we measure it in parts per million.
(3) Human CO2 emissions are only about 3.3% of the total.
(4) CO2 is only a minor greenhouse gas anyway, responsible for perhaps 5% of the warming effect. The most important greenhouse gas is water vapour (about 70%) followed by water in liquid form, i.e. droplets (about 20%).
(5) They ignored the Sun - not easy to do, you may think, but they did. Since solar output is the largest single factor affecting our planet's climate, not least through promoting cloud formation, this was not a small mistake.
(6) They ignored variations in the Earth's orbit. Not only, is it slightly eccentric (unlike myself of course) and not a perfect circle, but it varies over time.
(7) They got the paleo-climate science and the Earth's recent history wrong, overlooking the fact that large parts of the earth's surface have never seen consistent meteorological record-keeping, and
(8) They fell into the trap of believing their own propaganda, which led to them pushing claims, such as bits of Vanuatu disappearing by 2012, which were easily disproved, just by flying to Port Vila.[7]

The debate is not over, but even the Starmer Government in Britain, not noted with respect for the quality of its thinking, has started to tone down the rhetoric. True believers like former Vice-President Al Gore in the States, Professor Ross Garnaut in Australia[8] and George Monbiot (known affectionately as 'Moonbat') in the UK continue to press the case. The real issue however is not whether or not the world is warming - it clearly isn't - nor whether humanity's relatively tiny CO2 output can affect the climate it can't - but how so many people could come to believe in such a badly- flawed hypothesis. In years to come it will be studied under the category of 'great scientific hoaxes', along with that nonsense from Einstein about not being able to go faster than the speed of light.

The Gulf War

On 2nd August 1990 the DVD's Saddam Hussein invaded Kuwait. This was not one of his better moves. After a great deal of rape and pillage from the Iraqis, who were deeply unpopular occupiers, they were thrown out by arguably the oddest coalition of forces ever assembled. It included rogue nations such as Syria and France. Unsurprisingly, the coalition was far too unwieldy to defeat Iraq comprehensively.

As history records, President George H. Bush left the job of defeating Saddam to his more distinguished son. He is sometimes referred to as the "nice President Bush", no offence to 'Bush 41' intended.[9] The point missed by nearly everybody was that Saddam had been working for German intelligence since he was a teenage enforcer. His uncle, Khairallah Talfah, whose protégé he was, very properly went to jail for his participation in the failed, Nazi-backed 1941 coup. We were merciful - he should have been hanged.

When you think about it there were lots of clues, even if you didn't know about the German intelligence officers sneaking in und out of old Baggers hoping nobody would notice. Bunkers everywhere, Nazis in the family, using mustard gas on civilians, germ warfare programmes, invading neighbouring countries - it was all there, except the sausages.

There are two further intelligence points to be made, each bringing plenty of black humour with it. Saddam thought he was given a green light to invade Kuwait by April Glaspie, the American Ambassador in Baghdad. She thought she spoke Arabic, no offence intended. She did, but not colloquial Arabic. Saddam's Arabic was *very* colloquial.

The Official Version of Events is that Ambassador Glaspie said that he couldn't invade anywhere. Saddam's version was that she was saying that it was OK for him to seize Kuwait. There are those in INTELCOM who incline to the view that he was only being given a green light to seize the oilfields, not start a war. However, my official position is the Official Version of Events.

In any event he did start a war. As the aggressor we would not have expected him to declare war, but the Allies should have done. Tragically, the fine work by Coalition forces, superbly led by the late General 'Storming Norman' Schwarzkopf, who died suddenly and unexpectedly in December 2012, was undone. Schwarzkopf was the finest American combat general since Creighton Abrams.

Pressing on to Baghdad was a no-brainer. The poor strategic decision by President Bush Senior threw away thousands of lives, not least in New York. Saddam tried to take his revenge there in 1993 and did so in 2001.

The Missing Nukes

It didn't go quite as smoothly as the training videos (and some real stuff, but only after everything worked!) suggested. The media love videos where the ordnance hits the target of course. In particular, there was a minor incident involving a B-52G (59-2593, 4300th BW(P)) with nuclear weapons on board. She was hit by a SAM, or developed electrical problems, near Baghdad whilst on a deterrence mission and didn't quite make it back to Diego Garcia. Someone counted them all out but wasn't able to count them all in again, sadly. She had to ditch at least three SRAMs with W-69 nuclear warheads off the coast of Somalia, before ditching near Diego Garcia. Somalia wasn't a good choice, but when you have an uncontrolled electrical fire, live, heat-sensitive nuclear warheads on board and several engines out you don't have a lot of options.

Nukes rarely survive crashes in working order. However, everybody wanted the weapons-grade plutonium, so Mogadishu became a hotspot for (1) dodgy divers and (2) dodgy plutonium brokers. Most of the talking was actually done in Khartoum, which became quite popular for a while. If you wanted some 'hot plute' that was the place to be.

This led to a second, smaller, war in Somalia. American troops had to be sent in as cover for special forces on a recovery mission. That didn't go quite to plan either, partly because it had been shopped to a local clan warlord by the DVD. I suspect this was done via Sudanese intelligence in Khartoum. Hollywood made a good film about a part of this mess.[10] As usual however they left out the good parts, but the soundtrack was great. The only operational nuclear weapons ever possessed by Iraq came out of South Africa. The odious apartheid regime in South Africa was collapsing at around about the same, the late Nelson Mandela having been released from prison on 11th February 1990. The DVD, in touch with key South African businessmen, covertly switched support from the National Party, which had been close to the Nazi Party, to the ANC. Many of the leading members of the

National Party had been interned in World War II of course and rightly so. It's a pity that Smuts wasn't interned with them.

A switch in German support was not quite how it was put to the ANC's members. No DVD support meant no MTN trading programmes of course, hence the change in tack by big business. Since the DVD are close to Peking and the Chinese are all over resource-rich countries in Africa like a rash, it's a fair bet that Peking had a say as well.

With technical assistance from the Israelis, the Americans and the UK, the South African nuclear programme had progressed beyond the testing stage, to the production stage in fact, by December 1989. Their main delivery system was the dear old Blackburn (Hawker Siddeley) Buccaneer. It was built like a brick s**thouse. This was partly because it had been designed to use a charming technique called toss-bombing. In the trade the people who came up with the concept are known as 'tossers'.

The theory looked good on paper. A lot of theories do. The cunning plan was that you would sneak your bomber, complete with nuclear weapon, under the enemy's radar. You would then pop up, by which time it was too late for the enemy to stop you, and release your nuke. You would then proceed to describe a perfect parabolic trajectory, whilst you made good your escape at high speed, having reversed direction. It was a sort of nuclear Immelman turn.

The Buccaneer's wings were milled from the solid. The idea was that the plane could withstand the nuclear shockwave, which it could, up to a point. When the South Africans put the theory to the test however, it didn't quite work. The nuke did, but sadly the 'Buck' didn't make it, leading to a frantic sea search for the bits. MI6 were involved, since officially the South Africans had retired their 'Bucks'.

They still had at least two nuclear-capable Buccaneers left, however. They also had an arsenal of nine nukes, with a theoretical maximum yield of 18 kilotons each. One, more likely two, eventually found their way to North Korea. After it was/they were let off nuclear specialists revised their estimate of the maximum yield down to 15 kilotons. There is also an argument that a later North Korean test employed the remaining 'Armscor' type weapon.

Since they were designed to be launched from a Buccaneer, which had a clever, low-drag rotary bomb-bay, we in the UK did the casings. Interestingly, the scientific intelligence officer who accompanied said casings to South Africa was none other than Dr David Kelly CMG. He was brutally murdered in 2003. The name of the person who went with Dr Kelly and the first casings to South Africa is even more interesting. He later became a politician.

Nobody was terribly keen on letting the ANC have nuclear weapons. Arguably they might have been more responsible than the Nats. Nelson

Mandela was not quite the saint he is sometimes portrayed, but he was a rather nicer man than P. W. Botha or F. W. de Klerk. In theory the nine nukes, which were not supposed to be there anyway, were to be shipped out of South Africa in ISO standard containers. They were highly mobile devices and could be run into a container on rails, using a cradle designed by a British company.

They were supposed to go to a CIA facility near Chicago, a warehouse, where they were going to be dismantled under supervision. Now whenever you hear the phrase "dismantled under CIA supervision" in connection with anything other than a used Chevy on a car lot in McLean Virginia my advice is to run and hide. Six of the weapons were dismantled. The other three, as the saying goes, 'went walkies', firstly to Oman, then to Iraq, as in Saddam Hussein's Iraq. Since there had been a small political donation in respect of said nukes, nothing was said publicly about them ending up in a facility near Baghdad. This was not least because London and Washington were kicking up a stink over Iraq's nuclear weapons program. The news that Iraq now had nuclear weapons, courtesy of MI6, CIA and BOSS, was not well received. Indeed, so badly was it received that one poor chap decided to have a heart attack on the spot, having been briefed in.

These nukes caused all sorts of anxieties, leading to an abortive British special forces mission (SBS, not SAS) to intercept them in 2003. Intelligence had been received that they were on their way to Syria in a convoy of Red Crescent ambulances. Sadly, the mission was shopped to Baghdad by GO2 and the boys just missed them. Curses!

These anxieties were not entirely relieved when two of the warheads ended up in Iran and one in North Korea. Picture the scene. "We have the good news, boss, and the bad news." "The good news is that those g.....n nukes are no longer in Iraq." "Great, what's the bad news?" "The bad news is that two of them are in Iran." "Well at least it's only two. Where's the other one?" "North Korea." "*?!**"

As indicated the first one which went to North Korea was set off in a feeble attempt to persuade the world that Kim Jong-Il had a working nuclear weapons programme. Thankfully that test revealed that the weapons had deteriorated badly in their travels. Nuclear weapons require more servicing than a Hyundai, and have a shorter warranty period too.

The DVD decided to yank the remaining two out of Iran into a cave. Bad Guys love caves more than bears. Said caves were in the Turkish Republic of North Cyprus. There was reporting in July 2011 that they had headed out of TRNC in two fishing boats, which were caught on satellite, but too late to sink them.

There was a mini panic when it was thought that one might be headed in an Iranian container ship to the Thames Estuary with a view to being detonated during the Olympics. Thankfully the Bad Guys became aware that we were on to them. As we shall see they moved to Plan B. Two, possibly all three, may have gone to North Korea, with one being detonated on 12th February 2013. It looks like that test got close to the estimated maximum yield of 15 kilotons, although the estimates vary from 5 to 40.

We may have dodged a bullet with those South African nukes. If all three *were* detonated by North Korea then that's the last we shall see of them, but as I shall be explaining there are other stolen nukes out there.

You can only have missing nuclear weapons being hauled around the world by half the Bad Guys in creation for so long however. We risk losing if not a city, at least a few suburbs. It won't look so funny then, although as I discovered after warning the MOD about the stolen nuke smuggled into East London to blow up the 2012 Opening Ceremony, nukes can now be tracked using Muon Scattering Tomography.

The First World Trade Center Attack

After the Gulf War, Saddam was thirstier for revenge than a camel in one of his deserts. As the old Chinese saying goes before setting out for revenge one should first dig two graves. In an unusual move he tried to have President Bush Senior assassinated, a precedent that was not followed for nearly 15 years.[11]

At 12:17 on 26th February 1993 Iraqi agents including Ramzi Yousef tried to blow up the North Tower at the World Trade Center (American spelling as they were American buildings). They exploded an IED in a van next to the support columns in the B-2 level of the WTC car park. In the, with respect, bungled prosecution which followed the Iraqi connection was missed by a country mile. The Clinton Administration were keen to present terrorism as a series of random criminal acts by naughty terrorists, without any state involvement whatsoever. This is still the official doctrine of the FBI.

That crass approach blew up in the Administration's faces when the Iraqi *Mukhabarat* blew up a federal office building in Oklahoma City. They stayed deep, as states always do in terrorist attacks. McVeigh wasn't an Iraqi agent as such, he merely ended up working for the Iraqis. How much he knew is a question unlikely ever to be resolved.

Both the WTC and Oklahoma City bombings required 'official' assistance, such as getting terrorists out of the United States, or vans into buildings. As always, this came from DVD assets, in the badly penetrated Clinton Administration and the Correa Group inside CIA and the FBI. Both agencies have been penetrated by the Germans since they were set up.

FBI agents who try to intimidate you and flash their badges aggressively usually seem to be working for 'Jerry'. The very well-informed ones are much nicer. Then you get the in-betweeners, career law enforcement officials who act like they're stuck in No Man's Land, which, in a sense, they are.

The FBI supported the Clinton Administration's 'terrorism is just a crime and is a job for law enforcement' line enthusiastically. They repeated the silly mistakes Britain made in Northern Ireland, Cyprus, the Canal Zone, Kenya and Malaya. Basically, they were as smart as the sheriff in *US Marshals*[12] who's just discovered that he has a "*bona fide* federal fugitive" on his hands and asks if anyone has got a map.

Tragically, this attitude helped get one of their best agents, Jim Fox, of the New York Field Office, murdered. Jim had picked up the Iraqi connection to the World Trade Center IED. Jim was one of the very few FBI agents or former agents (he had not long retired) to have been assassinated. They got the poor man with a bio-weapon. It happened on President Clinton's watch, in May 1997. The FBI sat back and did nothing.

Unsurprisingly Saddam got the impression that America was a soft target. With respect she was when Clinton was President, just as Britain was a pushover when Neville Chamberlain and Edward Heath were in charge. Saddam never got democracy, however. He overlooked the possibility that a weak president might be replaced with a strong one. He also needed to get out more, especially in Texas. If he understood the great state of Texas he might have thought twice about taking a second pop at the World Trade Center, which seemed to have a totemic significance for him.

This is another subject worthy of a book on its own, which is why that nice lady Dr Laurie Mylroie wrote it. It's called *Study of Revenge.*[13] If you want to know about the Iraqi connection to the first WTC attack it's all in there. If a book on terrorism has a foreword by that nice man Jim Woolsey, former Director of the CIA, it's usually worth reading. Woolsey is good people if I may respectfully say so.

Study of Revenge is an impressive piece of forensic analysis. It displays an intellectual rigour on the subjects of Iraq and terrorism, which apart from Jim Woolsey the Clinton Administration lacked. It wouldn't have done of course had Bill Clinton had the sense to offer Dr Mylroie a senior position on the National Security Council or in State. She was his adviser on Iraq in the 1992 election campaign. Unfortunately, she failed the intelligence test - she was too smart.

As it was, Saddam rang rings around Clinton, killing hundreds of embassy and other personnel in the process. If you're a journalist and you're writing about the first World Trade Center attack, or you're interested in the links between Iraq and terrorism, you need to buy a copy of *Study of Revenge* and read it with care. Laurie Mylroie has not paid for this endorsement.

The Chinook Assassinations

The stupids will ask why other counterterrorism specialists have not picked up on the DVD's sponsorship of terrorism. Am I saying I've got it right and everybody else has not? No. In the late 1980s and early 1990s a group of senior counterintelligence officers in Northern Ireland finally started to do what should have been done in 1969, i.e. a spot of thinking. This is known in the trade as intelligence analysis.

There had been too much interference from Whitehall (the official protection of several terrorists involved in the Brighton Bombing got Belfast's attention) for the Troubles to be just a simple case of Irish terrorism. The deal cut between Heath and the IRA in the early 70s, using then MI6 Director Sir Maurice Oldfield as an intermediary, also got some people thinking. He was double-hatted, being director of GO2 as well.

Sir Maurice seemed to have the Provos' telephone number. He didn't get it out of the Belfast Yellow Pages. They still don't have a listing for "terrorist organisations". By 1993 this group, which included senior officers in RUC Special Branch, MI5 and the Intelligence Corps, were getting close to the DVD's sponsorship of the IRA. They knew about Skorzeny's presence in Ireland, the deep Vatican connections to both German intelligence and the IRA, and the past connections between German intelligence and the IRA. These went right back to the Easter Uprising and the Casement affair, when our community partner the 'Hun' landed the traitor Sir Roger Casement in Ireland from a U-Boat. He didn't book *that* passage with Thomas Cook. One of the key linkmen between Skorzeny and the Provos, Peter Brady (Ruairi O'Bradaigh), now an ex- terrorist, even had "Roger" and "Casement" as middle names.

Some in MI6 knew about the U-Boats in Irish waters during World War II. It's unlikely they had been able to keep this intelligence tight. A surprising number of people on Ireland's rugged and beautiful west coast also knew. Neutral freighters are pretty hard things to hide, ditto submarines. At any rate some of the boys in Belfast were getting close.

It was decided to have a conference. Conferences are great places for knocking people off *en masse*, as you can group your targets together. Even the media might have got suspicious if 17 people in counterintelligence in Northern Ireland died suddenly in the space of a few months. Put them in a helicopter, arrange for it to crash, and they will happily buy an accident.

They might even mention Occam's Razor, the old saw that says that if all things are equal the simplest explanation is likely to be the best. If the DVD or their client black agencies such as GO2 are involved however they will stay deep. It will be complex and all things will *not* be equal. The trouble with Occam's Razor is that it's a blunt intellectual instrument.

The principal bit of navigation kit on the Boeing-Vertol Chinook HC Mk 2 (Vertol being the old Piasecki company, which was taken over by Boeing in 1960) is the Inertial Navigation System. These are highly reliable but as we saw with Korean Air KE007 they can be rigged. That is how Chinook ZD576 was brought down. The pilots thought they were over the sea as that's what their instruments told them.

Very unfairly, they were blamed in the subsequent inquiries, although the RAF were never entirely happy. Just before he was assassinated by GO2 in 2010, the probable next Chief of the Air Staff, Air Chief Marshal Sir Christopher Moran KCB, agreed to a fresh inquiry, a serious one.

There was a second helo that day, another Chinook, not British, shadowing ZD576. The pilots wanted another bird, but were told that they had to take Zulu Delta. It was against protocol for so many key intelligence assets to be on one aircraft at the same time. Very frankly somebody should have smelt a rat. That's what counterintelligence is for. Sometimes you smell a rat and it turns out to be just a dead mouse. You don't know until you investigate the pong.

The trouble was that it was the RAF, not easyJet, no offence. The RAF makes its passengers feel safe. They have a better safety record for operating transport aircraft than British Airways, if British Airtours is included, or for that matter BOAC and BEA. Everybody walked on. Nobody walked off.

The Assassination of John Smith

The Germans were pushing hard - very hard - for Britain to abandon sterling and join the euro. This would have meant giving up what remained of her economic independence after joining the EEC. Reluctantly they agreed to a British opt-out at Maastricht, in exchange for our agreement to accelerate the breakup of Yugoslavia.

The DVD wanted Labour to replace John Major and the Conservatives. Major of course is a centrist, not a conservative, but he was and remains a party member. The DVD were confident that John Smith, then Labour leader, would destroy sterling. However, Smith, who had attended a Bilderberg Group meeting in 1989, indicated to a Bilderberg contact that in his view it was no longer politically feasible for Britain to join the euro after 'Black Wednesday'.

For this entirely correct judgment he was murdered, once again by GO2. They poisoned him, simulating a heart attack. He was the second British Leader of the Opposition to be assassinated, after poor old Hugh Gaitksell.

Given Smith's key role as a backbench junior MP in 1972 in taking Britain into the EEC it was ironic.

The Balkans

The break-up of Yugoslavia was sponsored by the DVD, Helmut Kohl, a DVD asset, played the major role. He and the DVD leadership were concerned that with their man Tito dead Germany would fail to retain control of Yugoslavia. The obvious answer was to restore the monarchy. The Crown Princess in particular is a very nice person if I may say so[14] but 'Jerry' wanted a war and got one, or, to be more precise, several.

NATO did well to stop the slaughter in Bosnia, but as with any alliance which includes France her allies had to pay a price. In this case it was America, as Paris betrayed a Stealth Fighter mission to Belgrade. A Stealth Fighter cannot fight. It's not a fighter at all really, more of a strike aircraft. Once it's spotted it's almost helpless. The technology went to China and Russia, both of whom wished to know how to counter it.

The Chinese Embassy in Belgrade was attacked, killing three ChiCom spooks. That's where the Chinese were running their operation from. This included Milosevic's Medium Term Note trading, with the accounts being held in North Cyprus. Slobodan was assassinated, by the way, on 11th March 2006, in his cell, in Holland, to stop him from talking.

The Embassy attack was a beautifully executed mission, by the B-2 boys out of Whiteman Air Force Base Missouri. It was so stealthy that the Serbs initially thought it was a cruise missile. They were quite annoyed, although not as annoyed as the Chinese. Technically it is illegal to bomb a neutral's embassy, even if they are violating their neutrality, which the Chinese were. It was only a minor breach of the Vienna Convention on Diplomatic Relations, however. It was not as illegal as, say, invading Tibet. Peking could hardly be heard to complain, although they did.

Sierra Leone

Sierra Leone has rutile ores (from which you make titanium), bauxite and industrial diamonds. These resources ought to make it a prosperous little West African country. Unfortunately, the Bad Guys rarely pay the market price. They find it cheaper to take over the government by offering corrupt leaders a cut, or access to MTN trading programmes using state treasury funds. They take the raw materials at a deep discount then blame the West for being exploitative. As we have seen, nobody does exploitation in Africa better than the Chinese, although the Germans, Belgians and the French have run them close at times.

As with all of Britain's African colonies 'independence' was a farce. The process was rushed, the new constitution collapsed and the Chinese moved in, backed by the DVD. They have long preferred to hide behind Peking when taking-over African countries. It looks better in the *African Marxist*. As with the Cambridge Ring in England, or Alger Hiss and the Rosenbergs in the States, working for the communists was always easier to spin than working for the Germans. It also sent patriotic legislators with a brain, like Senator Joe McCarthy, in the wrong direction, looking for reds under beds when the Germans were in them.

Not content with what they had already taken from poor old Sierra Leone, the DVD, working hand in glove with the French, and the Liberian dictator Charles Taylor, sponsored a brutal terrorist insurgency in the 1990s by a group called the RUF. They made a specialty of chopping off people's limbs, including children's.

Taylor was eventually prosecuted in another musical comedy international trial with respect. It was a process, like Nuremberg, as much concerned with hiding the truth as seeking it. It really is time to halt intelligence-illiterate international prosecutions.

Eventually the slaughter proved too much even for Tony Blair. There was a British military intervention. Confused and contradictory directives from Whitehall hampered the operation, but it saved a great many lives. Whitehall's heart, sadly, wasn't in the task. You try selling an initiative to save the lives of African children to the Cabinet Office. There were shortages of equipment, particularly helicopters, airlift, heavy sealift and aerial reconnaissance.

Not for the first time a deployment of military force was preceded by the statutory silly defence review, which failed to predict the need for it. In this case the MOD excelled themselves by failing to predict British involvement in a war in a former British colony, sponsored by two of Britain's then community partners, which was already happening.

The lessons of Sierra Leone were not drawn. The opportunity to get to grips with Sino-German influence in Africa was lost. The French involvement in arming terrorists in a Commonwealth country in exchange for conflict diamonds, which were usually shipped via Ouagadougou, did not stop Whitehall from seeing them as some sort of ally. President Macron was even offered a State Visit! Why it was left to the CIA to discover the pertinent fact of how the diamonds were being traded is a mystery, but it was. The boys did good work and stopped laughing at us British for wearing sun helmets in Africa.

In fairness the then Foreign Secretary, William Hague, did not specify what sort of ally the French were. He's a nice chap, with respect. He has a first-class mind and cut a lonely figure in the Foreign Office. The follow-up was the usual half-hearted affair. The new government was barely given half the support it needed. The experiment - surely worth trying - of having honest post-colonial government in Africa was a bit too bold for some.

Rwanda

As we have seen, not content with sponsoring terrorism in Africa, the French thought they'd have a go at genocide as well. Quite why they thought that is a question you will have to ask them. Perhaps they thought that they were trailing the Germans in the genocide stakes. Frankly it would have been better for all concerned if they had tried to make cars as well as the Germans, or come up with a composer to match Beethoven. As always in Africa the motive was resources, not just in Rwanda but in the Congo, in relation to which Rwanda is strategically situated.

The UN had been reduced to a joke by the end of the Korean War. In Rwanda they went for tragedy rather than comedy. UN Blue Berets left helpless women, children and old men to be macheted to death, on orders from New York. UN HQ in turn was taking orders from Dachau, as usual.

After Rwanda (and Somalia) the Blue Berets started to become a target for the Good Guys, they, were no longer just a nuisance to be sidestepped whilst real soldiers did the real work. It was only a matter of time before the armed forces of a democracy opened up on UN forces, with the usual caveat that they were aiming for the Kentucky Fried Chicken on the corner. The honour fell to those very nice people the Israel Defense Forces, in Gaza. The UN, which was in bed with Hamas, made the usual *pro forma* protest. They got the message, even if the media didn't. UN sponsorship of Hamas throughout the Gaza war has been noted.

Sri Lanka

Although billed as a civil war (it started after communal riots in Colombo in the early 1980s left thousands of Tamils dead) in reality it was part of the strategic competition between India and China. India covertly backed the Tamil Tiger terrorist organisation, the LTTE, and China had no shortage of assets in Colombo, the capital. At one point, Indian troops billed as 'peacekeepers' (the IPKF) were deployed to the north. The idea was to prevent the LTTE being wiped out.

The LTTE were at least as "innovative" as Islamic terrorist organisations in making use of suicide attacks. The tactic seems to have been borrowed from Germany's erstwhile ally Japan.

When you have two strategic competitors vying for control of a third, smaller, state but anxious not to be seen in control (both the Indians and the Chinese had invested substantial political capital in being seen to be 'anti-imperialist') you get crosscurrents. There were all sorts of eddies and changes of policy.

China's reassertion of influence in New Delhi after setting up the assassination of Mrs Gandhi, with the DVD, allowed them to force a change of Indian policy. This led to Tamil terrorist activity in India and an eventual rapprochement between New Delhi and Colombo.

Government forces were able to stave off defeat with Israeli military assistance. A squadron of Kfir fighter-bombers, the impressive Israeli development of the Mirage (which as we have seen was a development of the Fairey Delta II) turned up unexpectedly at Negombo air force base, near Colombo, in 1996. Theoretically these were crewed by Sri Lankan pilots although the percentage of Kfir-qualified pilots in the Sri Lankan Air Force was not high. They may also have been instrumented in Hebrew. The twists and turns in the Sri Lankan civil war again could occupy a book on their own. Suffice to say the government won and the LTTE were crushed. However, Peking did not get the free hand in Sri Lanka it was hoping for.

Cash for Questions

As part of the campaign to unseat the Tories and replace them with a more pro-EU party, i.e. New Labour, a smear operation was run against *inter alia* the Tory MP, Neil Hamilton. Another nice man, he later became a member of the UK Independence Party. He has sound views on Europe. The book on this, *Trial by Conspiracy*, was written by a brilliant investigative journalist, one of only a handful in Britain, Jonathan Boyd-Hunt. For his pains he was ostracised by his profession.

Jonathan tore apart the various different cases, which had been raised at different times against Neil with great forensic skill, with respect. Sadly, he was forced to watch a musical comedy libel trial, again with respect to all concerned. The media were content to recycle the serious allegations against Neil Hamilton without checking their facts. They will find them all assembled very neatly in Jonathan's book. In my opinion it's high time that Neil Hamilton's name was cleared. At least Neil and his charming wife Christine were able to put their experience to good use when they were offered parts in Christmas pantomimes.

TWA 800

On 17th July 1996 the Iranian Navy shot down a Boeing 747-131 of Trans World Airlines (TWA[15]) off Long Island, New York State. The submarine, a modified *Kilo* class SSK, was probably under German command. The 'Jerries' train Iranian sub-skippers and would be unlikely to trust one to hit a 747, although they might let one practice on a Gulfstream.

The missile was an Iranian-made copy, with German technical assistance, of the excellent AIM-54 Phoenix. The Americans had supplied these to Iran in the 1970s, along with the equally outstanding Grumman F-14A Tomcat. White House policy was to find the most, unstable state in the Middle East they could and supply it with the most advanced weaponry they could actually fire. The hope seems to have been that they would one day use it against the Israelis. That however was not quite how the policy, was described at the time by the Council on Foreign Relations, of course.

The Germans have always done a good rocket. They cleverly modified the Phoenix for surface launch from a *Kilo*, designing a neatly faired-in launch tube at the aft end of the conning tower. (The 'Jerries' have always done a pretty good U-Boat too.) If you doubt this have a look at the latest satellite overheads of the Iranian *Kilo* class boats, if you can get hold of them. You won't find them on Google Earth.[16] Compare them with say a Russian *Kilo*, with particular emphasis on the length of the conning tower, and the extra hatch.

A word of warning when dealing with SATINT of Iranian *Kilo* class boats however.[17] They lost two unofficially in the Indian Ocean south of Jakarta. Reporting suggests that this was courtesy of some very fine work by a *Los Angeles* class SSN. Since they were shipping nukes, possibly a couple of the Soviet-era thermonuclear weapons[18] which are known to have gone walkies out of the Ukraine, with dastardly intent, they could not be heard to complain. The sinkings were entirely justified, as evidenced by the lack of Iranian response.

As the losses officially never happened the Iranians ordered a couple of replacement boats from the Russians, but stuck the old pennant numbers on them. You have to make sure therefore you have overheads of a current *Kilo* class, not one of the ex-*Kilo* class, otherwise you will become confused. The Russians, who are not stupid, were puzzled by the order and the lack of used submarines to trade in.

They didn't use the old serial numbers on the diesel engines. Should you chance to be in the engine-room of an Iranian submarine take a note of the engine numbers, or better still take a digital photograph. Better still, as you might end up swinging from a crane having been tortured first (ouch), ask someone who has friends in the Iranian Navy. It is not completely officered by religious nutters. They might take your photographs for you.

The US Navy had a P-3 Orion in the vicinity of the TWA 800 shoot-down. I suspect this was not entirely by chance. The SOSUS network had not been completely dismantled by 1996 and somebody had been hearing strange noises. In the context of underwater sonar systems when we speak of people hearing strange noises we are not talking about sending out for a psych consult.

The noises were consistent with a *Kilo* doing turns for about 7.5 knots. The P-3 picked up a small, intermittent surface contact, which was in fact the conning tower of the sub. They were unable to identify it, unsurprisingly, since the Germans taught the Iranians to surface hull- down. Basically, that means that most of your target is below the surface. The modified Phoenix can only be fired from the surface. They don't work like a Polaris or a Trident missile. So far as I am aware the missile hatch can only be opened manually, i.e. not from the control room. It's not like a missile hatch on an *Ohio* class boomer.

The US Navy aren't stupid either. The Office of Naval Intelligence boys and girls (if you pick up the phone and talk to ONI these days you're as likely to talk to a lady as a gentleman) considered whether these two events, i.e. a nearby surface contact and the loss of a 747, were related. However, they were thinking in terms of small boats and MANPADS, i.e. man portable air defence systems.

These are the kind that you might buy in Walmart, if they had a SAM counter. I won't hear a word said against Walmart by the way. If you will forgive the anecdote I well recall being taken ill on the road, in the Mid-West, in an ice-storm, with hundreds of miles still to go before I reached my destination in the great state of Missouri, as it happened not a million miles from Whiteman AFB. I had just gassed up and was freezing my essentials off, when I spied a Walmart on the opposite side of the interstate. The staff could not have been more friendly or helpful. They made sure I left the store with everything I needed, from an extra layer of clothing to de-icing fluid, a really useful snow brush, which I kept for years, and medicine, all at seriously low prices.

No one told ONI that the Iranians have submarines that can fire surface-to-air missiles, a role never previously envisaged for submarines. They prefer to avoid aircraft rather than engage them, at least in most navies. German tactical doctrine by 1943 encouraged U-Boat commanders to stay on the surface however and engage attacking aircraft, the theory being that a sub is vulnerable just after it has dived. Sticking surface to air kit on a sub is just the sort of thing the 'Jerries' would do.

ONI also didn't know about the DVD, not in 1996. They tended to view Iran's technical capabilities as Iranian, i.e. limited, rather than German, i.e. pretty good, especially when it came to rockets and U-Boats. There is no denying that the 'Hun' makes things pretty well. Just compare a Cadillac and a BMW. The Cadillac is the better car, but the BMW runs it close.

MANPADS mired the TWA 800/missile controversy for over a decade. The 747 was hit at FL160, i.e. 16,000 ft, i.e. outside MANPADS range. So what? That only excluded portable surface to air, not an AIM-54. The-54 is a big mother of a missile, with a maximum range of over 60 miles even in the 70s. It's more like 75-100 miles now. Unfortunately, the late Pierre Salinger, the murdered President Kennedy's press secretary, steered the debate in the wrong direction by suggesting that the US Navy had bought down TWA 800, à la the Iranian Airbus. This theory, with respect, was misconceived.

Firstly, Captain Rogers of the USS *Vincennes* (CG-49) was led into a trap by the generation of a military transponder signal from an F-14 adjacent to the Iranian Airbus on the ground. Coupled with naval and air force activity, including a P-3 on what had all the appearance of an AWACS mission,[19] this led to the reasonable but tragically wrong assumption that the Airbus was a military, not civil, aircraft. The Iranians knowingly sacrificed Iran Air Flight 655 to get at President Reagan. At that time they were sacrificing their own people by the thousand in the Iran-Iraq War. Sadly, the lives of a couple of hundred *Haj* pilgrims didn't count for much in Teheran.

Secondly, the nearest US warship, the USS *Normandy* (CG-60) was over 100 miles away, outside missile range. Thirdly, it would be extremely difficult, if not impossible, to cover-up an accidental firing which caused so many civilian deaths. Finally, the US Navy operates to rigorous ordnance safety standards, from which departures are exceedingly rare.[20] The Clinton Administration, were quite unable to deal with the shoot- down, even if they wanted to, which they didn't. President Clinton, with respect, preferred to leave the difficult decisions to his successor. He had other issues to occupy his mind anyway. More than that, his administration had fallen into an Intellectual Black Hole. They believed in spontaneous terrorism. In their world-view terrorists were non-state actors and terrorism was not a state sponsored phenomenon. The innocent dead, who numbered 230, mostly Americans, were left unavenged. America herself was left wide open to further terrorist attack. The NTSB investigation into TWA 800, with respect, was a farce. They speculated, on the basis of flimsy evidence, that there had been an electrical short-circuit. They found some frayed wiring. Big deal. In a venerable 747 with over 80,000 hours on the clock you are going to find frayed wiring. In a desperate search for an internal ignition source they concluded, in layman's terms, that current had crossed over from a high- voltage to a low-voltage wire. It is then supposed to gone into a fuel tank. Unsurprisingly, Boeing didn't have too many high-voltage wires going through the fuel tanks, which were the usual unsealed affair you get in civilian airliners. The problem with the NTSB's theory is that wiring which is taking an electrical load well in excess of its design capacity tends to heat up and melt. It's a principle that you will find in the fuse-boxes of your house and car.

Since the centre-section fuel tank exploded inwards not outwards, like the outer hull of the USS *Maine*, we need to look for something coming *into* the fuel tank. We are not looking at explosive gasses coming *out*. It's a basic proposition but it somehow passed the NTSB by. In the alternative, it didn't, and they tailored their findings to something they could sell to the White House. The Clinton White House could easily be fooled into thinking that Boeing didn't know how to design and build airliners. Every federal agency needs friends in Washington come budget time.

The NTSB, like the AAIB in the UK, is not an intelligence-led organisation, although at least, with respect to the AAIB, it is intelligently led. It is institutionally geared to finding fault with pilots, airlines, aero- engine makers and plane builders - basically anybody not employed by the federal government. Rather than approach the issue with an open mind about the possibility of sabotage or an IED, as the FBI did in fairness in the case of TWA 800, they tend to rule out the possibility of foul play very early on. They then assume that what they are investigating is an 'accident'. The theory is that accidents happen, which they do. The problem is that sabotage also happens, and so do missile attacks on unarmed civilian airliners in international airspace.

The missile, or the solid-fuel rocket motor exhaust, was caught on radar, photographed (at long range) and seen. Clearly something approached the 747 at high speed before she came down. Equally clearly those two events were not unrelated.

Television documentaries pushing the NTSB line will tell you all about exploding fuel tanks, as though they were a regular feature of 747 operations. "Dang, there goes another 747, it's time Boeing did something about those exploding fuel tanks, they're going up like Ford Pintos." They then go on to show you footage of the stricken jumbo toppling from the sky *before* she explodes.

The Iranian Phoenix's can be fired in semi-active homing mode by the way. They can home in on a target's own radar emissions and don't have to go for the engines. They also have proximity fusing, i.e. they don't actually need to *hit* the target. A stern-chasing missile, in semi-active mode, with a proximity-fused warhead, fired from a submarine at a climbing aircraft, will tend to explode beneath the fuselage, aft of the cockpit. It will not normally reach the radar emitter on which it has locked.

The Assassination of HRH Princess Diana

The assassination of Princess Diana on 31st August 1997 shocked the world in a way in which no assassination had done since President Kennedy. As with the Kennedy Assassination the official cover-up simply served to undermine public confidence in the integrity of government and the judiciary, with no offence to anyone intended. In the case of President Kennedy a determined official attempt was made to persuade public opinion that a complex operation was the work of just one man. In the case of Princess Diana both the British and French governments tried to persuade the public that she had died in a car accident, the driver was drunk or the paparazzi caused him to drive too fast, and it was partly her fault that she died anyway because she wasn't wearing her seatbelt.

As with the Kennedy Assassination, the official explanations won't wash. A large section of public opinion hasn't bought into them. The public may be ill informed, but if they are it's because governments make such determined efforts to keep the truth from them. They are *not* stupid. Try fooling a jury if you don't believe me.

A small point of constitutional law should be cleared up first. Downing Street were in a rush to force the Prince and Princess of Wales apart. They had assistance from the republican-leaning Rupert Murdoch, whose media empire lost no opportunity to make matters worse, and the basically republican BBC.[21] They were in such a rush they used the wrong divorce procedure.

It is basic rule of English law, expressed in the maxim *generalia non specialabus derogant*,[22] that a later general statute does not affect an earlier specialist one. The marriage of Their Royal Highnesses the Prince and Princess of Wales was governed by the Royal Marriages Act 1772, which was unaffected by later family law reform acts. There was therefore no abolition of the rule that a royal marriage could only be brought to an end by Act of Parliament. Since the Princess would have been Queen of 16 realms it would have been quite proper by the way for the Queen to refuse Royal Assent unless the dominions were content.

A junior judge in the Family Division in London, no offence intended, cannot deprive Australia, say, of her future Queen without the consent of at least the elected Australian government. Very frankly it was the height of arrogance for a junior judge and the Major government to dictate to Australia and the other Commonwealth realms in this way. Since the divorce court was acting in vain, i.e. bereft of jurisdiction, it follows *a fortiori* that the Princess of Wales was still validly married at the time of her brutal murder. For that reason, she is referred to herein by her Royal Style and Title.[23]

Once again a book could be written about this topic alone. Once again it, or rather a series of books, has been, by the late Australian investigative journalist John Morgan. Crippled by a debilitating disease, multiple system atrophy (you don't want it), unable to work and upset by what he correctly concluded was an assassination, he has wrote a brilliant series of books, entitled *Diana Inquest: The Untold Story.*[24] Full details are in the Bibliography. Too hot for most publishers they had to be self- published, but don't that let that put you off. They should be picked up by a major publisher and republished for a wider market.

John has taken the with respect musical comedy Diana inquest and dismantled it, along with the three accident theories put forward at various times by the French. He also dismantles the seriously flawed summing-up, said again with respect, by Lord Justice Scott-Baker. He was the fourth Royal Coroner to deal with the long-delayed inquest, and like most judicial coroners had no medical training at all.

John Morgan had too good a forensic mind to have persisted for too long with the entire theory advanced by the late Mohammed Fayed that the assassination was orchestrated by that nice man HRH the Duke of Edinburgh, who didn't do assassinations, and MI6. He did however criticise the Royal Family, particularly in his later books. I do not share these criticisms. I do not therefore go with *all* of John's careful analysis, but I find myself in sympathy with much of it.

It should not come as a surprise to any reader that neither the Duke of Edinburgh nor MI6 were able to pull film out of traffic cameras in Paris, nor have bodies swapped in French morgues. Diana was not pregnant and there is no evidence that she would have agreed to a proposal from Dodi Fayed, keen though his father may have been at that prospect.

As John Morgan pointed out the idea, pushed relentlessly by the media, that the jury decided that it wasn't a homicide is simply wrong. That decision was taken by the learned judge, who as I have observed lacked any medical qualifications. His Lordship had been made up as an acting coroner specifically to do the inquest.

Recapping, the three accident theories are:

(1) There was a single vehicle crash caused by chasing paparazzi.
(2) There was a single vehicle crash and the driver, Henri Paul, was drunk, and
(3) There was a two-vehicle crash, the Mercedes and a Fiat Uno. The driver of the Mercedes was drunk and no one knows who the other driver was.

All three theories are nonsense:

(1) The nearest paparazzi was about half a kilometre back. There were motorbikes in the Alma Tunnel, but none has been linked to any member of the paparazzi.
(2) There were clearly two vehicles involved, the Mercedes S280 driven by M. Paul and a white Fiat Uno, which was seen by witnesses, observed entering the Alma Tunnel on satellite overheads and left traces of paint on the Benz, and
(3) Henri Paul was not drunk. The only blood sample suggesting that he was, came from a fire victim and had a carbon monoxide reading of nearly 20%, at which level he would have been barely conscious, let alone able to operate a motor vehicle. Just as the bullets which killed President Kennedy were never matched to Lee Harvey Oswald's alleged rifle, so the blood sample which the French claim was taken from Henri Paul has never been verified by DNA testing. When British Operation *Paget* detectives asked for a blood sample for DNA testing their request was refused.

The Mercedes was stolen on 20th April 1997 from outside the Taillevant Restaurant in Paris.[25] Its anti-lock braking system was removed. It was vulnerable to further interference in the hours leading up to the assassination and the seat-belt Princess Diana would have been expected to wear (rear seat, diagonally opposite the driver) was tampered with. HRH always wore a seatbelt.

The mode of assassination was probably the use of a high-powered laser, designed to dazzle drivers. It had been developed for MI6 and was available to GO2, which had at least four officers in Paris on the night of the assassination. The flash was observed, just before the crash, i.e. the suggestion of Richard Tomlinson, the renegade former MI6 officer, on this point is correct.

Those nice people the Mossad also had officers on the streets of Paris that night. The report prepared for that nice man Danny Yatom, then Mossad director, suggested that the Uno was driven from the Alma Tunnel into the nearby Avenue Montalgne, where a truck was waiting with its ramp lowered, the car later being crushed.[26] I respectfully agree with the Mossad.

There is general agreement behind the scenes (one or other of the accident theories has to be trotted out for public consumption) in INTELCOM that HRH Princess Diana and Dodi Fayed were assassinated. However, there is a division of opinion as to who was the primary target. I incline to the view, based in part on the real destination of Dodi Fayed that night (there is no evidence that Diana would have participated in the meeting) that he was the primary and the Princess of Wales was the secondary.

There is a great deal more still to come out, but a number of intelligence agencies have focused on Medium Term Note trading out of Geneva in relation to an account set up at the instance of a well-known arms dealer close to Fayed. This individual brokered a contract to supply aircraft spare parts to Iran during the Iran-Iraq War. I say no more than that, although I would like to. You can forget landmines.

Hong Kong

Sadly, Margaret Thatcher had been prevailed upon to appoint the Chinese spy Sir Percy Cradock as a foreign policy advisor. Sir Percy was an unpleasant man. He was exceedingly rude to the able last Governor of Hong Kong, Lord Patten, who despite an enthusiasm for the EU retained a residual regard for democracy. Cradock succeeded that other Chinese spy, Sir Edward Youde, he of the Yangste Incident, as British Ambassador in Peking in 1978. Sir Edward was a much nicer Chinese spy than Sir Percy.

Strictly, Sir Percy was Peking's unofficial ambassador to Britain. The daft decision to recognise Communist China in 1950 without obtaining recognition of British sovereignty over the New Territories as well as Hong Kong meant that Britain, absurdly, had a consulate in Peking. Cradock was first appointed there in 1962, where he was recruited by the Chinese SIS, a sister agency of the DVD.

So far as we know Sir Percy was always run through Peking, not GO2 or Dachau. He probably dealt directly with Dachau when he was Ambassador to East Germany between 1976 and 1978. Apparently, he got on quite well with his DVD colleague Markus Wolf. At any rate it was all very convivial. Markus was a very convivial chap. Sir Percy always got on well with foreigners. It was just us British he had a problem with.

Sir John Hunt, as we have seen another German spy, naturally thought that as a Chinese spy Sir Percy would be the ideal chap to head up the Cabinet Office intelligence assessment staff. Very little that passed Sir Percy's desk did not find its way to Peking, where Sir Percy is remembered with fondness. He was also in thick with GO2, which has always maintained amicable relations with the Chinese Head of Station in London.

Senior officers in GO2 were of course well aware that Mao Tse-Tung reported to Dachau. The death penalty was still in force. New Labour promoted its repeal in 1998, presumably in order to encourage high treason. Sir Percy could and should have been hanged. Not being a peer there would have been no need to hang him with a silk rope. Tragically for the people of Hong Kong he wasn't hanged at all, even with silk rope (always ask for silk - it's much smoother).

---

1. There were some irregularities no doubt - Russia is the world's largest country and has no democratic tradition - and it would be unreal to expect a general election there to be conducted as smoothly as a general election in Britain. Unlike the voting fraud in the 1975 EEC referendum in Britain however there is no reason to suppose that such irregularities as there were affected the outcome. After Florida 2000 and the rigged 2020 election, one would have hoped that Washington would show a little more humility on the subject of electoral irregularities. With respect however President Obama doesn't do humility.
2. Arguably the first modern heavy cruisers, they were armed with the new 7.5-in. main battery gun. The class had mixed fortunes but they were handsome ships, still serviceable in World War II, although the logical thing would have been to land the 7.5s and re-build them as large anti-aircraft cruisers with an improved version of the 5.25-in DP gun used on the *Didos* and the *KGVs*. They had a reasonable turn of speed (30 knots) when built and could have been refitted with higher-pressure machinery.
3. Serendipitously this part of this chapter was revised for the last edition whilst travelling through the beautiful Cascade Mountains on AMTRAK's mighty *Coast Starlight*, with snow everywhere and the outside temperature 10 below.
4. Ian Sample, *The Father of Climate Change*, 30th June 2005.
5. *Ibid.*
6. Booker and North, *Scared to Death: From BSE to Global Warming, Why Scares Are Costing Us the Earth*, London: Continuum, 2007.
7. It's the capital of Vanuatu. If you don't know where Vanuatu is, it used to be called the New Hebrides.
8. Who shall receive a copy of this book with a friendly inscription, since the Prof was kind enough to inscribe his best wishes to me in a complimentary copy of *The Garnaut Review* 2011.
9. In the trade, Bush Senior tends to be referred to as '41' (he was the 41st President) and his son as '43'. Bush Senior was sometimes referred to by other names as well, affectionately of course.
10. *Black Hawk Down*, directed by the able Sir Ridley Scott, a friend of a friend.
11. There was a feeble attempt to bring down President Bush's jet at Houston on 22nd November 2004. The Gulfstream G-III went down alright, but he wasn't on it. After that episode rates for chartering jets to President Bush Senior probably went up.
12. Starring that fine actor Tommy Lee Jones and great fun.
13. Washington, AEI Press, 2000.
14. Her Highness and I have only met once, very briefly, at a charity do for UNESCO.
15. It started out as Transcontinental and Western Air. When Howard Hughes, a slightly strange man (he had a thing about dust), but a patriot, a fine pilot and a great businessman (he never quite got over the shock of finding out that one of his designs had been turned into the Mitsubishi A6M Zero, that Admiral King was a German spy and that one of the props on his elegant XF-11 prototype had been sabotaged, nearly killing him) successfully challenged

Juan Trippe's monopoly as an international carrier, he changed the name of the airline but kept the initials, a shrewd business move. He wouldn't have called British Petroleum 'Beyond Petroleum', but then he wouldn't have held back oil in wartime from the US Government. It is perhaps time for a more balanced assessment of this great but flawed individual.

16. You would be amazed at what you can't find on Google Earth and equally amazed at what people expect to find. It's a marvellous way of laundering SATINT - just stick Google Earth on the piccies and you're covered. Thanks Google. They may not want to be thanked and coming up with a new way of laundering satellite imagery wasn't the idea, but thanks from INTELCOM anyway.
17. A submarine is a boat, never a ship, just ask any boomer skipper, or a great submarine commander like the late Admiral Sir Sandy Woodward (he was pretty useful with a fast carrier task force as well).
18. I.e. hydrogen warheads, i.e. nukes which make big bangs, i.e. nukes you do not want going off in your backyard, or in Washington. There has been a lot of discussion over the years about how many old Soviet warheads might have gone walkies in the chaos following the break-up of the USSR. In fairness to the Russians, they have lost fewer nukes than the Americans and tended to be highly responsible. The Iranian nukes may have been brokered by Viktor Bout of the Ukraine. These nukes weren't lost so much as liberated in a carefully-planned DVD operation (they are not all thrown together in haste like Lockerbie). It's the Ukrainians who turned out to be the big worry, not the Russians, but words have been had and Kiev is no longer *al Qaeda* purchasing central or 'Nukes'R'Us', like it used to be, although it still got invaded. You would be 'gobsmacked' at what you used to be able to buy in Kiev, if you were a German-backed terrorist - if you wanted to shoot down Air Force One you could even get a couple of up-to-date SA-2 SAMs, the kind Air Force One can't deal with. Happily, those particular widgets were intercepted by the Turks in the Black Sea in crates addressed to Cairo and marked 'spare parts'. If you're searching a ship always open crates marked 'spare parts' first.
19. The P-3 has a good radar system and they can be doubled up as a mini- AWACS. Not quite an E-3 but serviceable enough.
20. The undershoot by USS *New Jersey* (BB-62) off Lebanon, when she was engaging Hezbollah strongholds, was a rare ordnance error. The propellant was stale and underperformed, throwing out the range calculations. It may not have been an error - the indications are that DVD assets in the Pentagon, who were desperate to get the battleships out of commission, wanted an undershoot for its propaganda value, and disgracefully were willing to sacrifice a Muslim village or two to make their point.
21. One of their techniques is excessively deferential commentary on royal events, which makes it sounds as though the Royal Family, which has no influence over the BBC at all, are stuffy. If you want stuffy try politicians, the Cabinet Office, or the European Commission. The only member of the Royal Family to stand on their dignity in the last century was probably HRH Princess Margaret, but that was because she was treated incredibly badly by the pro-German element in the political establishment and the Archbishop of Canterbury over her marriage to

Group Captain Townsend. Queen Mary who gave Her name to the ship wasn't aloof, She was dignified. The story goes that the Chairman of Cunard suggested to the King that the great new liner be named after England's most illustrious queen, by which he meant Queen Victoria (Cunarders up till then had names ending in 'ia') and the King said "the wife would be delighted" or words to like effect. King George V had a great sense of humour, probably needed to appease the Queen over something He had said at breakfast and saw the Cunard Chairman coming. Queen Mary would have been surprised to learn how much She was loved by the public.

22. *Mea culpa* if I am using too much Latin.
23. This issue needs to be addressed. TRH the Duke and Duchess of York are in the same position and could perhaps be asked, as a courtesy, whether they wish their marriage to be brought to an end *de jure* as well as *de facto*. Other Royal divorces, e.g. that of HRH Princess Anne, where the parties have remarried in good faith, need to be confirmed by Parliament. The correct procedure is a private Act of Parliament.
24. Morgan, John; 2nd ed., Amazon, 2009 *et seq.*
25. *Ibid*, Part 3, *The French Cover-Up*, p. 645.
26. *Gideon's Spies*, Gordon Thomas, p. 25.

28

The Global War On Terror /1/

The Attack on the USS *Cole*

On 12th October 2000 *al Qaeda* tried to sink the guided missile destroyer USS *Cole* (DDG-67) in Aden, now known as Yemen and run by the Houthis, formerly a British Protectorate. They used a 272-kilogram shaped charge, murdering 17 sailors. The attack was trumpeted by the media as a demonstration of the vulnerability of modern warships to asymmetric terrorist attacks. It could equally fairly have been presented as an illustration of the dangers of poor intelligence work concerning port security and the need for a greater fleet train.

The idea of the fleet train is to be able to replenish ships at sea and reduce the need to spend time in vulnerable ports. The failure to sink her could also have been presented as a tribute to the design of the *Cole.* She survived the attack and is now back in service in the cause of freedom.

Tribute should also be paid to Commander Lippold's smooth, calm and professional handling of his ship after a murderous terrorist attack and the effectiveness of American damage control. Sinking a warship is not as easy as sinking an Italian cruise liner, nor will you find the skipper of an American warship heading for the lifeboats whilst his or her crew are still aboard.

As discussed in Chapter Nine there was a postscript to the attack. *Al Qaeda* tried to pull the same stunt against the British aircraft carrier HMS *Ark Royal* in the Straits of Gibraltar. Attacking a moving warship at sea is a far more difficult proposition. The terrorists were left bobbing in her wake. The DVD then came up with the cunning plan of inviting the *Ark* into Barcelona and *al Qaeda* at the same time. Interestingly, my warning to *Ark Royal* was blocked in Whitehall.[1] As explained, I think I was able to clear the blockage.

It is perfectly clear that Iraq was involved in the attack on the *Cole.* Ali Abdullah Saleh in Yemen smoothly switched sides after the Iraq War but was close to Saddam Hussein. Dr Hamid al Bayati, later Deputy Foreign Minister of Iraq, suggested in his very important book *The Terrorism Game*[2] that Iraq supplied the explosives. They were originally supplied from Russia, some years before, probably during the Soviet period.

Dr al Bayati is a credible source with respect and gives a detailed account in this book, published shortly after 9/11, of the close links between *al Qaeda* and Iraq. Two very important observations should be made about this book:

(1) Readers should not allow the errors in the English translation to affect their judgment of the original, which is in Arabic. It is a basic mistake to blame an author for the mistakes of a translator.
(2) The fact that only 500 copies were printed does not affect the quality of the intelligence therein.

The book has in fact been read with interest by a number of intelligence agencies. To my knowledge not a single assertion of fact contained in it has been contradicted. One indicator of the quality of the reporting in it is the effort that has gone into suppressing it. One of the copies the CIA has, e.g., was handed over by me in London to a 'State Department' official at Ambassador John Bolton's request, for transmission in the diplomatic bag. It went in the bag alright, but direct to Langley. So far as I know John never saw it. Since we are no longer on speaking terms, sadly, I'll have to look out for his response on *Fox News*.

The 9/11 Commission and the even more pointless Chilcot Inquiry in Britain never asked Dr al Bayati to give evidence. The Commission preferred to state the politically convenient but wrong conclusion that Iraq was not involved in 9/11. The 9/11 Commission was a classic case of an inquiry reaching its conclusions first then working backwards to the evidence.[3]

The Chilcot Inquiry followed along the same lines. On the links between Iraq and *al Qaeda* their conclusion was very obviously reached before they first started to hear evidence, with respect. I did offer to assist them but they weren't interested. Their minds were made up.

The Formation of *al Qaeda*

Al Qaeda grew out of the Afghan Service Bureau, a DVD front set up in 1988. With the end of the Cold War in sight the Germans wanted another stick with which to beat the West. Islamic fanaticism fitted the bill. 'Jerry' was already sponsoring Islamic terrorist groups in the Middle East, targeted mainly at Israel. *Al Qaeda* was set up specifically to target Britain and America.

As always, the DVD took care to stay in the background, as deep as a German bunker in fact. Bin Laden was one of their chaps, as was Mohammed Atta. Originally bin Laden, sometimes referred to in Britain as 'Binliner', was number two in the organisation. His handler was Whiskey, a Correa Group asset. I know who Whiskey is of course, indeed I have his phone number, but I am not going to upset the publishers-lawyers by naming him. As this may also be later published as an e-book and sold worldwide, a multi-jurisdictional approach has been taken to the law of libel, i.e. it has been written so as to comply with the law of jurisdictions where sadly there is no longer free speech, such as Britain.

It was a simple matter to bump off Abdullah Azzam, bin Laden's predecessor, who seems to have been a figurehead anyway. Some sources say that Azzam was not involved in *al Qaeda*, only the ASB, but the better view is that he was the terrorist organisation's first leader. Unlike bin Laden he was a genuine Islamic nutter, not a DVD agent.

The rest of the bin Laden family were not involved, nor were bin Laden family funds used, so far as I am aware. Since it was state backed, like all terrorist organisations, the issue was not raising the money, but finding a way of concealing its source. Ransoms are very popular. *Al Qaeda* kidnaps M. Jean Doe, a French citizen. France coughs up $5m and M. Doe is released, unharmed, whilst the terrorists walk away with the cash. It's a well-known ploy, so well-known that they are starting to rough up the fake kidnap victims up a bit, chop off the odd toe and so on, in order to make it look good. More recently they have started to take the cash and then kill the victims anyway. This is usually done with clearance from DVD penetration assets in the state bureaucracy of the victims' own countries. Paris cleared the murder of some French citizens in Mali some years ago, e.g.

As explained, one of my friends in CIA was involved in getting the bin Laden family out of the States after 9/11, perfectly properly. It was done for their own protection. They wouldn't have got very far down at the mall with a credit card in the name of "bin Laden". "Hey, you're a terrorist, you raghead douchebag." "No, that's my brother." "Get my gun, Maisy." They were flown out of Langley Air Force Base, not far from Washington.[4]

The bin Ladens, (apart from Osama that is) are quite a nice family. They were apparently a bit shaken, not least as they realised that certain folk in CIA were already thinking 'Iraq'. It was looking like 'wham, bang, Saddam' time. The late King Fahd, an awfully nice king, was apparently doubtful about the wisdom of attacking America. His Majesty was not overly thrilled that *al Qaeda* had used some of his Saudi subjects. He knew that he couldn't object however, without risking Saudi access to the Medium Term Note trading programmes, Saudi Arabia's principal source of wealth.

As related, the first 'meeting' between bin Laden and Saddam Hussein took place in or about 1989. Bin Laden was flown to Baghdad in a Saudi-owned 707, fitted as a private jet. These were proximity talks and Saddam stayed in the terminal. There were regular contacts after that, accurately summarised by Dr al Bayati in Chapter Eight of his excellent little book.[5] At page 132 of *The Terrorism Game* there is a reference to bin Laden's second visit to Baghdad, in March 1998, where he stayed at the posh al-Rashid Hotel. Osama bin Laden liked his creature comforts - the 'wild man of the mountains' look was strictly for the promotional videos.

During his trial in England in March 2013 Giovanni di Stefano. whose professional legal qualifications with respect are more honorary than real (that's why was he was on trial), claimed to have met bin Laden during this visit. I believe him, indeed I offered to his defence team to say so in court. Giovanni was close to Saddam and we exchanged e-mails before Saddam's execution. I had floated the idea past the White House that we, the Good Guys, should cut a deal with Saddam, a Bad Guy, in which he coughed his involvement in 9/11 in exchange for his worthless life.

The next *al Qaeda* leader, Ayman al-Zawahiri, visited Baghdad from 26th June to 2nd July 1998. During this visit he dined with the Vice- President of Iraq, Taha Yassin Ramadan. Saddam's violent and unpleasant son Uday met an *al Qaeda* delegation in April.[6] Farouq Hejazi, an intelligence officer with the Iraqi *Mukhabarat*, met with bin Laden in December 1998. Dr al Bayati goes on to relate discussions between *al Qaeda* and the *Mukhabarat* in Ankara, Khartoum and Karachi.

There is no reason to doubt that 9/11 terrorist Mohammed Atta met with the Iraqi intelligence officer, Samir al Ani, in Prague, as reported by the then Czech Interior Minister, Stanislav Graus. Immense intellectual effort has been expended in seeking to rubbish this reporting, but the effort has not borne any fruit. Politicians and intel bureaucrats may not like the fact that the terrorist leader of the 9/11 attacks met with a senior Iraqi intelligence officer prior to the attack, but he did.

It would make sense. Saddam had cultivated Islamists to the point of changing the Iraqi flag adding, "God is Great" in Arabic. This was something the Syrian *Mukhabarat* amusingly forgot when they dressed up some of their officers as Iraqi soldiers in the *Daily Mirror* fake photograph scandal, dealt with below. Deroy Murdock, Media Fellow at the Hoover Institution at Stanford gave what must have been a good presentation, judging from the paper,[7] on 22nd September 2004. He summarised the extensive links between Saddam Hussein and terrorist groups. Notoriously, Saddam agreed to pay $10,000 to the families of Palestinian suicide bombers, later upped to $25,000.

Bettino Craxi's government collapsed after the Italian government permitted Abu Abbas, one of the terrorists who seized the Italian cruise ship *Achille Lauro*,[8] to leave Italy, on an Iraqi diplomatic passport. He was eventually captured by US troops, in Iraq, where he had been living as an honoured guest of the Iraqi Government. He should of course have been executed as a pirate. Abu Nidal was also sheltered in Iraq. Abu Musab al Zarqawi, a notorious *al Qaeda* terrorist, received medical treatment at the Olympic Hospital in Baghdad.

Other material on Iraq/terrorist links in the public domain includes articles by Jeffrey Goldberg in the *New Yorker* for 10th February 2003 and Jonathan Schanzer in the well-informed *Weekly Standard* for 1st March 2004. The very well-informed Dave Wurmser, a nice chap, who was on Vice-President Cheney's staff, has also written authoritatively about the Iraq/*al Qaeda* link. So too has Stephen Hayes of the *Weekly Standard*.

Stephen's book *The Connection*[9] lists a whole series of contacts. It is essential reading for those, unlike the Chilcot Inquiry members with respect, who are genuinely interested in the Iraq/*al Qaeda* links. Some Iraqi intelligence documents confirming the link to *al Qaeda* found their way into the public domain, e.g. in the London *Sunday Telegraph* on 27th April 2003, and again on 14th December 2003.

To suggest, as some have done, that Iraq was not involved in terrorism prior to the Iraq War, or had no connection to *al Qaeda*, is just plain silly. There was a deep relationship between *al Qaeda* and the *Mukhabarat*. Since the Iraqi Ba'ath Party and *al Qaeda* were both set up by German intelligence that is precisely what we would expect. indeed it would be astonishing if there had not been close cooperation. Terrorist organisations cannot operate without intelligence support. The DVD dare not emerge into the open. They had to use the intelligence services of German client states like Saddam Hussein's Iraq.

9/11

There is no doubt the 9/11 attacks were carried out by *al Qaeda*. The World Trade Center buildings collapsed largely as outlined in the 9/11 Commission Report. They were well designed. The DVD's target of 50,000 dead, thankfully, was nowhere near reached, as the towers collapsed on themselves, rather than toppling. That was a huge error by the DVD who, were misled by the higher gross of weight of the Boeing 767 over the 707.[10]

The 767 and 757 had to be used, as opposed to say 747s, with their much greater mass, because that's what the pilots had been trained on. The flight training was done at the Salman Pak terrorist training facility near Baghdad. It was run by the *Mukhabarat's* Brigadier-General Duleimi. As I pointed out in Part One, the Boeing 757 and 767 share a common cockpit. There are minor switchgear differences, e.g. on the radios, between the two, and between models. The Iraqis used the Boeing 767 simulator they seized at Kuwait Airport in August 1990 to train the 9/11 pilots. It had been used to train and refresh pilots on Kuwait Airways' three 767-269ERs, 9K-A1A, -A1B and A1C.[11]

Curiously it was left to the magazine *Popular Mechanics* to produce a detailed rebuttal of conspiracy theory arguments that the towers had been blown up deliberately. It is right that the flashpoint of jet fuel is lower than the melting point of steel, but it doesn't matter. Steel loses half its structural strength at 600^{0}C. The columns, which had been damaged anyway, particularly the external ones (the building was not just supported by the core) could no longer support the weight of the floors above.

WTC7 raises different issues, but there was no explosion there either. There were explosive residues, but no more than what we would expect to find with such a large amount of molten aluminium mixing with water.

Again it's taken years for a detailed rebuttal to emerge. I am aware that some in INTELCOM think that Correa Group may have backed up the primary attacks with a mini-nuke, but I am not buying.

There is no doubt that the Pentagon was hit by a Boeing 757-233 as claimed. She was seen by eye-witnesses, including at least one pilot, and caught by video, albeit not very clearly. Both engine and 757 airframe parts were found inside the building. United Flight 93 crashed as per the Official Version of Events, after the passengers sensibly and bravely charged the cockpit. They obviously ignored FAA guidelines to the effect that passengers should not do anything to upset terrorists, e.g. by trying to regain control of their aircraft. Terrorists should be upset. That's what they are there for.

DVD assets inside CIA and elsewhere provided critical assistance in getting the terrorists into the States and protecting them until the attack. This is the key to understanding 9/11. It was a German and Iraqi sponsored attack, not just an Iraqi-sponsored attack. It was nothing to do with the Bush-Cheney Administration, which initially went into shock.

It found itself battling DVD penetration assets and their protégés from the get-go. President Bush, e.g., was kept away from Washington on the day as long as possible. Vice-President Cheney's, with respect correct, shoot-down order was simply disobeyed. The signs that not everybody was playing for the home team were there before the buildings had stopped smoking.

Afghanistan

The war should have been declared, but the decision to go to war was otherwise entirely correct. It was justified under public international law. The Islamic Emirate of Afghanistan had sheltered bin Laden and *al Qaeda*. Mullah Omar, the brutal Afghan dictator, was clearly aware in advance of 9/11, as was Saddam. Effectively the Allies joined the existing civil war on the side of the Good Guys, the Northern Alliance. They were the boys who threw the Soviets out.

So deep is the Intellectual Black Hole into which some in the media have fallen on the subject of state sponsorship of terrorism that they have convinced themselves that the CIA set up the Taliban. Some journalists have genuinely persuaded themselves that the Taliban fought against the Soviets. The Taliban were of course set up by the Pakistani Inter-Services Intelligence Agency three years after the Soviets left.

Sadly, five strategic mistakes were made in relation to Afghanistan:

(1) We took our eye off the ball when we refocused on Iraq. This allowed the enemy to regroup.
(2) We legitimised the DVD/Soviet backed coup in 1978 by failing to restore Afghanistan's constitution, with the King, a respected and unifying figure, as Head of State.
(3) We failed to declare war on the Islamic Republic of Pakistan when it became clear the ISI were sponsoring the Taliban terrorist insurgency. Not until 2011 were Pakistani forces engaged directly for the first time and even then the Obama Administration had to pretend that they were fired upon by 'mistake'.
(4) We failed to spray the poppy fields being used to generate narcotics- trafficking income for the Taliban.
(5) We announced our withdrawal by reference to a timetable dictated by political considerations, thereby encouraging the enemy and risking the gains already made at much cost in blood and treasure, handing the country back to the Taliban.

The Iraq War

Three of the same mistakes were repeated:

(1) We legitimised the 1958 coup by failing to restore the Iraqi constitutional monarchy, i.e. we engaged in nation building of a state, which already was a nation. Such amendments as were

needed to Iraq's constitution could have been made using its organic amendment procedure.

(2) We failed to go after the neighbouring terrorist-sponsoring states, i.e. Iran and Syria, and

(3) We withdrew forces in accordance with a political, not a military, timetable.

To add to these we:

(1) Failed to secure the intelligence yield in Baghdad.

(2) Failed to secure Iraq's borders.

(3) Dismantled the Iraqi army without sufficient forces to occupy the country.

(4) Failed to recover the proceeds of Iraqi oil funds traded on the secondary Medium Term Note market, thereby ensuring the new government was short of cash, and

(5) Failed to put the country properly back on its feet.

Failure (4) repeated the costly mistakes we made in 1918 and 1945, when we threw away the fruits of victory and devalued the precious lives that had been sacrificed. Such intelligence material as was left behind in Baghdad was not secured properly. The *Sunday Telegraph* virtually walked into one building.

This was not an accident or an oversight. The DVD were desperate to suppress intel on their own connections to Saddam, Saddam's involvement with bin Laden and the training of the 9/11 pilots. So far as is known, every one of the 9/11 terrorists passed through the Salman Pak training facility. There were just too many penetration assets in London and Washington to get any sort of recovery effort underway. The teams were assembled and waiting to go in. I indicated in response to an informal sounding that I was ready to join them, but nothing was done.

The decision, having taken Baghdad, to go on the defensive and wait for the Syrians and Iranians to pour terrorists money, weapons and explosives, across the frontier was strategically illiterate. It was compounded by the premature disbandment of the Iraqi Army, which meant that there were plenty of trained ex-soldiers on the loose.

It was never in the plan. You don't take out an Arab fascist dictatorship which has attacked you and leave another Arab fascist dictatorship and an Islamo-fascist state on its frontiers to come after you. A conversation with someone from the White House, had there been one, might have proceeded as follows:

"Michael, we're going to invade Iraq."

"Great idea, you guys and us should have declared war on Iraq by 09/13 at the latest."

"Ah, we're not going to declare war, Michael. The State Department weanies say it can't be done. We can only have a war if we don't call it a war."

"What about Vietnam?"

"They didn't mention 'Nam. Officially that was a police action." "With B-52s and the USS *New Jersey*?"

"It was a big police action, Michael."

"Uh-huh, what are we going to use as the *casus belli*?" "We thought we'd try WMDs"

"But they've all been shipped to Syria." (Actually we found out later some had been shipped to Russia, in two freighters out of Um Qasr, and some went into Iran, but at the time everybody thought that they'd all gone into Syria.)

"We know that, but we're hoping that they've left some behind." "Hmmm, what are we going to do after we've won?"

"We're going to disband the Iraqi Army." "You mean the Republican Guard, surely?"

"No, State and National Security Council want the army disbanded, as well as the Guard."

"I hadn't heard that we were increasing the size of the occupation force, who's doing the troops?"

"Rummy wants to go in with what we've got, the Pentagon say it'll be cheaper."

"It will be, for the first four weeks, who's going to be in charge?" "Paul Bremmer."

"You mean General Jay Garner, don't you, I think we bumped into each other at the Willard last night when I was on my way to the bar. Nice guy, knows what he's doing."

"That's the problem. State and NSC want Bremmer, he'll be easier to sell to CNN, the French and the Germans."

"But they're on the other side!"

"Officially they're on our side Michael." "And then we put in Chalabi, right?"

"Ah, no, Chalabi's out, State, CIA and NSC don't like him." "But he knows what he's doing and could turn Iraq around."

"That's the problem, plus CIA are saying that he's working for Iran." "But that's crazy. He's no more working for Teheran than Donald Rumsfeld."

"We know that, but CIA have ruled him out." "When are we going to do Syria and Iran?"

"We're not, we'd thought we'd sit tight and let 'em come after us." "That wasn't in the plan!"

"I know, but State and NSC say that we can only have one war. What do you think?"

"Why don't we just invade Panama again, but can we please choose the music? We'll bring along some Stones CDs."

The good work done by the American and British forces, with the Americans in the van, started to be undone from the day Baghdad fell. Iraq has been turned into something approaching an Iranian client-state, Iran being a German-backed aggressor which cannot bear the thought of any state in the region being allowed to control her own affairs. The human toll has been enormous, although still less than allowing Saddam to remain in power. *Al Qaeda* lost its principal operational support, except in the UK, where it is been supported by GO2. There were no further successful terrorist attacks on the US until the Obama Administration came along.

As I pointed out at the time there were hardly any WMDs left. They had already been shipped out. The whole point of that second UN resolution nonsense was to give the French, Germans and Iraqis six months to move everything. They mostly went by rail along the refurbished Baghdad-Damascus railway line - the movements were caught by the NRO's orbiting birds. In my as-ever humble opinion, the NRO and NSA offer outstanding value to the American taxpayer. They spend their meagre budgets wisely. Some traces of WMDs were found, that was all. The Saddam Tapes, revealed to the public by that nice man John Loftus at the Intelligence Summit in 2006, were powerful evidence that Iraq had WMDs. They were voice-authenticated recordings that Saddam had made of official conversations in the presidential palace. They offered the media some at least of the proof of Iraq's WMD programmes they were screaming for.

As so often happens when the media scream at INTELCOM for 'evidence', when it was provided, it was ignored. The last thing the media wanted in 2006 was solid evidence of WMDs in Iraq *prior* to the war. What they really wanted was for the truth to be suppressed. The truth was inconvenient, because it undermined the narrative that the decision to invade Iraq had been a mistake. The Saddam Tapes have never been undermined, by the way.

Since Iraq had mounted an armed attack on the United States on 9/11, using *al Qaeda* as a proxy, she had committed an Act of War. No UN resolution was required. Since British nationals were also murdered and it was known that British nationals worked in the World Trade Center the United Kingdom would have been justified in declaring war on the Republic of Iraq in our own right. We were entitled to do so anyway as an ally of the USA, indeed we did no more than fulfil our solemn obligations under the Washington (i.e. NATO) Treaty.

President Bush was ridiculed, unfairly, for the "Mission Accomplished" photo-opportunity on 1st May 2003 on board USS *Theodore Roosevelt* (CVN-71), having flown out to her in an S-3B Viking. The Viking is a nice bit of kit by the way, loved by its pilots, although the US Navy needs an S-3C. The President, who was no dumber with respect than the average Harvard MBA, was astute enough to recognise that hostilities *with* Iraq were over.

The media patronised him as they had patronised President Reagan. They mistook what may be very mild dyslexia for an inability to read. President George W. Bush was actually more fluent off-teleprompter than his successor, Barack Obama. 'Dubya' also grasped that terrorism is a state sponsored phenomenon, and that 9/11 was sponsored by *inter alia* Iraq. His approach to countering terrorism was far more sophisticated than President Clinton's. That is why the only major terrorist attack on the United States on his watch took place in his first year in office. It was planned on his predecessor's watch and would have gone ahead if Vice- President Gore, a man of fewer intellectual gifts than George W., had been elected.

This all too brief period of lucidity in international affairs came to end with the Obama Administration. It backslid into the same Intellectual Black Hole from which the Clinton Administration had been unable to escape. This is the irrational belief that terrorism is spontaneous and that like double-parking and smoking in aircraft toilets is an issue for law enforcement.

Under the Law of War there were three distinct phases of the Iraq War:

(1) An undeclared but nonetheless just war between the United States, the United Kingdom and other allies against the Republic of Iraq following an armed attack by the Republic of Iraq against the United States. This war commenced on 19th March 2003. It effectively concluded with the declaration by President Bush aboard the *Theodore Roosevelt* that general hostilities with Iraq had ceased on the collapse of organised Iraqi resistance. This war was not waged under UN supervision. The ostensible justification under the UN Charter was as thin as it was unnecessary.

(2) An undeclared war between the United States, the United Kingdom, the Kingdom of the Netherlands, the Republic of Poland and other allies against the Syrian Arab Republic and the Islamic Republic of Iran. These hostile states sponsored terrorist attacks on Allied Forces in Iraq using proxies, and murdered civilians under Allied protection. This phase ended with the resumption of Iraqi statehood on June 28th 2004, and

(3) The joining in of Iraq as an undeclared belligerent as Syrian and Iranian terrorist attacks in Iraq continued. As Iraq is now largely under Iranian control (the Iranians having successfully blocked Chalabi from becoming Prime Minister) these attacks have reduced significantly, with a greatly reduced Allied military presence.

The Assassination of Dr David Kelly CMG

Dr Kelly's disgraceful assassination by GO2 on 18th July 2003 sent a shockwave around Britain. As with the Kennedy and Diana Assassinations frantic official attempts to cover up the truth merely served to undermine public confidence in government, the intelligence agencies, the police and the judiciary. Of course, you can fool some of the people for some of the time, indeed all the time. Most of the people however were not fooled. The majority view in Britain now is probably 'not buying suicide'.

There is however great public uncertainty as to how and why he was murdered, and by whom. The answers to these questions are fairly straightforward, with a caveat about motive. The major unresolved issues are where he was murdered and where he has held between being seized on Harrowdown Hill (near the delightful village of Kingston Bagpuize) in Oxfordshire on 17th July 2003 and his death.

The mode of death put forward by Lord Hutton and the government was exsanguination, following suicide, by transection of the left ulnar artery, following consumption of a non-lethal dose of the drug Co- Proxamol, an empty blister pack of Co-Proxamol being found by the body. Officially, death was assisted by arteriosclerosis and shock. I hope that is a fair summary of the Official Version of Events.

With great respect it is unsustainable for the following ten reasons:

(1) Dr Kelly's, fingerprints were not on the knife eventually placed by his body, probably by GO2 assets in Thames Valley Police Special Branch.

(2) The said knife was not with the body when it was found, but added later, presumably when the body was moved.

(3) The better medical view is that death by exsanguination of an adult male by lateral transection of a single ulnar artery is not possible, especially when there is no means of keeping the body warm. That is because a transected artery retracts, preventing further blood loss. The ulnar artery is normally very narrow and blood loss is not that great even if it is not transected (i.e. cut right through).

(4) Absent unusual placement of the artery (one has to be careful with human anatomy - we are not all alike and you can get branching of the ulnar, it can also be found near the skin), not present in this case, transection of the ulnar artery requires a painful, deep cut. This points away from suicide.

(5) Dr Kelly was of sound mind, an experienced scientific intelligence officer and a member of the Baha'i faith, which is strongly opposed to suicide. There was no evidence of any psychiatric condition and psychological and character considerations point away from suicide. He was under pressure but not unduly so.

(6) There was very little blood on or near the body when it was found. When it is said that a man had bled to death we like to see lots of blood.

(7) Some blood was added between the body being found and its removal from the scene. It is reasonable to assume that the blood was added by the same person or persons, probably Thames Valley Special Branch officers reporting to GO2, who added the knife and the water bottle. This added blood has not been DNA-matched to Dr Kelly.

(8) No accurate estimate was done on the amount of blood remaining in the body, including the organs. It is a reasonable inference that it was substantial and inconsistent with death by exsanguination. Again, in a bleeding to death we want the blood outside the body, not still in it.

(9) The stomach contents revealed residue from only about one-third of a Co-Proxamol tablet, i.e. there is a mismatch between the number of tablets said to have been taken and the stomach contents. The active constituents of Co-Proxamol, dextro-propoxyphene and paracetamol, are available in liquid form and the absence of stomach residue points towards them having been injected, probably via the cut site. A cut through the epidermis is a good way to disguise a puncture wound, and

(10) The ratio of paracetamol to dextro in Co-Proxamol is 10 to 1. They act in a similar way and are metabolised in the body at approximately the same rate, a range of say 7.5 to 12.5 to 1 being reasonable. The ratio of the drugs in the blood stream was 97 to 1, ruling out Co-Proxamol as the source.

The assassination was in fact carried out by GO2, aided by assets in the police, although as always they may have thought they were working for British Intelligence, as they were dealing with Brits, not Germans.

David Kelly was asked to keep his mobile phone on and GCHQ were able to triangulate his position, although that could also have been done from Munich, or at the communications interception facility in London, run on behalf of the DVD by a German electronics company, S.

He walked into an ambush, the path up the hill providing several opportunities (I inspected the site). The GO2 squad probably approached on water, using a Zodiac, then on foot. The River Thames is a short distance away and a helicopter would have attracted attention. The helo which apparently landed about 90 minutes after the body was discovered certainly did. This was about the same time as the body was moved and the knife and water bottle were added, to give that extra authentic touch.

All this is disturbing enough, but the indications are that the poor man actually died under torture at a GO2 safe house in Essex.

There are 12 hours minimum during which his movements cannot be accounted for. Harrowdown Hill is remote by the standards of Oxfordshire, but we are not talking Rannoch Moor (a wild and beautiful moor in Scotland) or the Cascades. The nearest habitation is only a few hundred yards away. The path near the copse where the body was found is an established route between nearby villages and the river. This is farming country anyway.

It is possible but unlikely that the body lay undiscovered from the previous afternoon. This was rural Oxfordshire, not inner London. Dead bodies are not normally left lying around and are usually cause for comment. "Have a nice walk dear?" "Yes thanks, only saw two bodies." "Oh good, the village is getting less violent." "Should I call the police?" "No need dear, somebody will be around to collect them." *Midsomer Murders* is fiction, remember.

The motive was Iran, not Iraq, in my considered opinion. At DVD urging, immediately after Iraq's humiliating defeat, France shipped a quantity of weapons-grade plutonium to Iran. The thinking was that America and Britain would not invade a nuclear-armed Iran. This rather overlooked the fact that Iran cannot use her nuclear weapons against Britain or America without being nuked herself. Nuclear weapons are only a deterrent to nuclear attack. They will not deter a conventional attack if your opponent is nuclear armed as well.

David Kelly became aware of this plutonium shipment through his GO2 contacts. It was his job to know. It was feared that he was about to pass this crucial intelligence onto Israel, a task later performed by myself. David had excellent contacts with the Israelis, mostly on the nuclear and biological weapons side. It should be emphasised that Israel, like Britain and America, has never deployed biological weapons. Her primary interest is in counter-biological warfare.

David Kelly was perfectly well aware that Iraq's WMDs had been shipped to Syria. He may also have known about the shipments to Iran and Russia. He had not supplied anything particularly dramatic to the BBC's Andrew Gilligan. The infamous dossier *had* been 'sexed up' but not by that much. Iraq *had* possessed WMDs. Her capability had been degraded more than INTELCOM realised by the Gulf War, but it was still significant. She did have tactical weapons systems that could be made ready in less than an hour. They are not much use if they take longer.

Of course, intelligence in relation to tactical systems should not have been made to sound as though it related to strategic weapons systems. The big mistake was not to realise that the WMDs were of mostly German, French and Russian origin and had been shipped back. This in turn reflected the deep official and media unwillingness to acknowledge Iraq's role in 9/11. That involvement in turn risked exposing the DVD, as they had been all over Baghdad in the Ba'athist period.

The Iranian enriched uranium programme is a classic intelligence blind. Its purpose is to divert attention away from her real nuclear programme. This is based on Chinese-pattern plutonium-cored warheads. Since plute weapons are more compact they are the ones you want on your IRBMs anyway. Estimating the number of weapons is not easy, as the French still haven't coughed the total amount of plute they shipped (it went by either German SSKs or French SSNs to Bandar Abbas). It seemed to be about 30 as of the end of 2013, with a theoretical maximum yield in the 25-50 kiloton range each. Nobody did anything about them, apart from taking out the odd ballistics weapon and nuclear specialist. They were probably stored in the underground facility at Fordow and moved out, in civilian registered 747 freighters, in the run up to the well signalled USAF attack on 22nd June 2025. Ironically, the Iranians are now left with their significantly degraded uranium enrichment programme

The good news is that the Israelis have got a lot more, probably over 100. Theirs also have a much higher yield, as their third-generation nukes are thermonuclear. They are below Trident MIRV size but still have a useful kick. They also have an excellent submarine delivery system. The Iranians are well aware of this, indeed just about everybody is, except the public.

I am not going to give away anything that jeopardises the security of an ally. The more the Iranians know about Israeli capabilities (and vice versa) the better. The whole point of deterrence is to deter. Deterrence breaks down if the enemy does not know what is waiting in store for him if he is silly enough to nuke you.

There was a dangerous period when both the Israelis and Americans did not accept the intelligence about the French shipment of plutonium to

Iran. There was even talk in Washington about using 'tactical' nukes to stop an enriched uranium programme which wasn't serious anyway, not then. There may be battlefield nukes but there is no such thing as a tactical nuke. Any use of nuclear weapons is a strategic decision, taken for strategic effect.

The Assassination of Anna Lindh

This was arguably the DVD's most cynical assassination. Anna Lindh was a very personable and rather cuddly Foreign Minister of Sweden, who believed - actually *believed* - in the EU. She was almost the only politician in Europe who did, treating Sweden as part of Europe for the sake of argument. Some Swedes will tell you it's really part of Scandinavia. She didn't have to be blackmailed into supporting the EU, or paid off from an offshore slush fund.

Anna Lindh was a good mother to her two charming children, David and Filip. Altogether, she was a very nice person. This made her an ideal candidate for assassination by the DVD, on 10th September 2003, although she actually died on the following day. The DVD has a large station in Stockholm and wanted to boost the 'Yes' side in the Swedish euro referendum. It was then balancing on a knife-edge.

The idea of course was to try and blame the assassination on the 'No' side. The suspect, Per Olof Svensson, was an habitué of the Café Opera. This is a fashionable bar near the Royal Palace and gave the DVD the added bonus of having a tilt at the Swedish royal family, one of them was probably being lined up for assassination by Svensson, when he was re- tasked to take out Lindh. Helpfully, he was a member of the 'White Ayran Resistance', one of a number of far-right fronts set up by the DVD over the years. He was an ideal candidate from their point of view. Anna Lindh was a very nice person, and her murder was a great shame. GO2 repeated the tactic in 2016 during the Brexit referendum, when they arranged for the murder of Jo Cox, a nice remainer MP, in which another allegedly right-wing stooge was involved. The assassination narrowed the Leave margin of victory but thankfully failed to affect the ultimate result.

---

1. As related, my paper for the Defence Intelligence Staff and the First Sea Lord was not circulated very widely. It did reach an admiral, however.
2. London, 2001, Al-Rashid Publishing. It needs reprinting.
3. One of my sources calls this 'Warwick Rules', as apparently there was a very silly conference at Warwick University, where the conduct of official inquiries was discussed. Most official inquiries reach their conclusions first and then work backwards, like the 'Henderson Report' in the famous *Yes Minister* episode.
4. But not in Langley VA, which is inside the Beltway. USAF bases are named after distinguished aviators. Langley AFB is named for Samuel Langley, who also gave his name to the USS *Langley* (CV-1).
5. Pp. 131-55.
6. *Ibid.* p. 134.
7. Dated 22nd October 2004. The presentation was on 22nd September. It was available online for some years at www.husseinandterror.com.
8. Formerly the Dutch ship MS *Willem Ruys.* The same line's *Angelina Lauro* was formerly the *Oranje*, which also flew the same house flag as the *Willem Ruys*, on which my late aunt, Lt-Col Agnes Barnett ARRC TD QARANC served in World War II when she was a hospital ship. Her captain ran a taut ship and got very upset if the blood wasn't mopped up! The *Willem Ruys* rammed the *Oranje* in January 1953. They were both elegant ships.
9. Harper Collins, 2004.
10. 395,000lbs for the 767-200 versus 335,000lbs for the 707-300, although MTOW varies between versions.
11. Boeing c/ns 23280, 281 and 282.

29

The Global War On Terror /2/

The Plame Affair

In 1999 an Iraqi intelligence officer, Wissam al-Zahawie, visited Niger. They were a tame supplier of uranium to Iraq. He was there to purchase 500 tons of yellowcake, i.e. semi-processed uranium ore. Al-Zahawie was acting on behalf of Saddam Hussein and met Niger's Head of State, Ibrahim Bare Mainassara. The deal was sealed, although in the end no yellowcake changed hands, probably because firstly MI6 and then CIA became aware of it.

The CIA, anxious to rubbish the intelligence, sent Ambassador Joe Wilson to Niger on a 'fact-finding' tour. According to your source this was either a vigorous fact-finding tour, involving arduous investigation and much tramping around uranium mines in the desert, or a tour of Niamey bars. Either way the CIA were happy with Joe's report. They were viscerally opposed to war with Iraq and were willing to twist the intelligence in any way, which suited them. This eventually lost them the confidence of Vice-President Cheney.

Quite properly, President Bush referred to the MI6 reporting on Niger, which was accurate, in his State of the Union address in 2003. Unfortunately, the DVD then arranged for the original intelligence to be rubbished. They had a fake set of documents knocked up, which they laundered through their black agency in Rome.

The fakes ended up with the IAEA, the dodgy UN agency, if that is not a tautology, based in Vienna. It was set up to encourage nuclear proliferation, although that's not quite how they put it on their website. Since the website is silent about the British weapons scientist who was thrown from the roof of their 17-storey headquarters building, after he picked up seismological indications of one of the covert Iranian nuclear tests, we needn't take it too seriously.

This is one of the oldest intelligence tricks in the book. If you want to rubbish accurate intelligence (there was nothing wrong with the original MI6 reporting) you knock up a set of fake documents saying the same thing. You then get somebody to accept them as genuine and pull the rug from under both the fake and the hard intel at the same time. The media, who are intelligence illiterate, will usually lap it up, as indeed they did.

The DVD, were desperate to protect their man Saddam. They waged an all-out intelligence war against the nice Bush-Cheney Administration, which had 'got' terrorism. They posed a real threat to the DVD's terrorism strategy, as they understood that terrorism was state sponsored and had moved away from the Clinton Administration's policy of wringing its hands. Whereas the Clinton Administration confined itself to meaningless gestures the Bush-Cheney Administration actually did something about terrorism by waging war on two state sponsors of terror. These included Iraq, which as have seen attacked America, with German backing, on 9/11.

Dachau came up with a cunning plan, agreed with GO2 in London and Correa Group in Frankfurt. They of course have access to all CIA personnel files. Bob Wilson was married to a former CIA agent, Valerie Plame, who had become an analyst. Basically, she had moved from the operations side of Langley (DDO) to the intelligence side (DDI), or, if you prefer, from 'kick-butt' to 'kiss-butt'.

If they could suppress her personnel file they could get away with palming Plame off as an 'agent'. All they needed then was someone who could plausibly be linked to the Administration to leak it, so they could roll over Karl Rove under the Intelligence Identities Protection Act (IIPA). The IIPA was a slightly silly piece of legislation anyway, since the DVD are all over CIA like a rash and as observed above have unrestricted access to CIA personnel files. Several CIA Directors have been DVD, including Dulles and Bedell Smith. At least one who wasn't was found floating face down in a river. The purpose of the IIPA was not to protect agents' identities. They were blown already. The idea was to try and persuade the American public that the identities of CIA agents are a secret.

The late and not terribly lamented Robert Novak, a mildly conservative columnist with the *Chicago Sun-Times* with a sex-life that was not entirely open, was given Val Plame's name. He was told to leak it, which he did. The plan didn't go entirely according to plan (what plan ever does?). This may have been because a warning went into the White House from the UK (from myself, as it happens) that Karl Rove was being set up.

The DVD were able to block me, no one gave me Karl's mobile phone number, so my telephoned warnings never reached him. My calls were in fact diverted to the National Security Council. However, the Bad Guys knew that I was trying to reach Mr Rove. They could not be sure that he wouldn't be warned, indeed they knew that I was on my way to Washington. They also knew that entirely by coincidence Mr Rove and myself were due to be in or near the same hotel, the very nice Marriott in the charming city of Charleston WV, at drinking time. The 'Jerries' could not guarantee that local Republicans might not give me some assistance in setting up a little drinkies. If you are ever in Charleston by the way, I can recommend the downtown Marriott - the staff there are outstandingly helpful. The good people of West Virginia are a delight to be amongst and the city's location on the Kanawha River is striking.

In the events that happened, the local assistance was not forthcoming and the Administration were left swinging in the wind. Just to be on the safe side, however, Dachau switched targets to Lewis Libby, who was a convenient patsy and a useful secondary. A bogus prosecution was set up. A prosecutor, Pat Fitzgerald, was found who wouldn't ask too many questions, except in cross-examination, no offence intended. He was able to present the case with a straight face. This was the same Pat Fitzgerald who insulted Parliament by prosecuting one of its members without its consent, Lord Black of Crossharbour. With respect that was also a musical comedy proceeding.

The media weren't in the least bit interested whether an offence had actually been committed or not. They had a field day. There was of course no offence, since Val Plame had long since ceased to be protected by the IIPA. This was one of the biggest witch-hunts in America since the Salem Witchcraft Trials. In fairness to the Court of Oyer and Terminer in Salem, its procedures were probably fairer, particularly as regards disclosure. With all due respect to everybody involved the guilty verdict against Lewis Libby is no safer than that against poor Bridget Bishop in 1692. Lewis should be pardoned and paid a handsome sum in compensation for the unjustified slur on his good name.

HMCS *Chicoutimi*

The last thing the DVD wanted Canada to have was a serious submarine capability, in particular quiet SSKs. They could assist in protecting US Navy assets and made a nice fit with the longer-range, faster but noisier American nuclear boats. They could also detect covert German submarine movements in the Atlantic. On 5th October 2004 the covert French black agency in Paris, part of the DVD, tried to sink the new Canadian submarine the HMCS *Chicoutimi*. She was an ex-Royal Navy Vickers Type 2400, or *Upholder* class, indeed *Chicoutimi* was formerly HMS *Upholder* herself. Given German and Iranian uses of SSKs this is a very sensitive area for 'Jerry', precisely of course why the West badly needs to ramp up its SSK capability.

Thankfully the attempt failed, but a Canadian naval officer was murdered. It might have been worse, as the French SSN, which was tracking the *Chicoutimi* had orders to close and sink her if the fire failed to take hold. However, she was being tracked herself. The *Chicoutimi* was given a strong anti-submarine escort and an even stronger message was sent to Paris on the backchannel. The Privy Council Office in Ottawa, were sensitive about the sabotage. If it ever got out that French intelligence (the stay-behind black agency again) had murdered a Canadian officer and tried to sink a Canadian submarine it might jeopardise the political gains made by French-Canadians in Ottawa.

Hurricane Katrina

Storm and earthquake weapons have been on the German wish list since at least the early 1970s, when the theoretical work was done to show that you could bounce large amounts of energy off the ionosphere. They are called Scalar High Energy Weapons Systems (SHEWS). You 'pays your money and take your choice' as regards acronyms, since they have no official existence. You will find material on the Web relating to HAARP, but that is the acronym for a high-altitude research program based in Alaska. It is cover for one of the ground-stations, the others being in Norway and the Ukraine, near Chernobyl (not by coincidence, since the weapons require huge amounts of energy). There are probably more, but I only know about those three. President Putin of course knew about the Ukrainian ground station, indeed it seems to have been a factor in the decision to invade in 2022.

There is no point asking me to explain the physics. You will need to ask a high-energy physicist who has not applied for a global warming research grant for that. What strategic analysts are concerned with is cause and effect. How much damage can these systems do, who's running them, where are the ground stations and what can be done to block their transmissions?

They may sound unreal but never mind how they sound. The issue is *are* they real? The A-Bomb must have sounded a bit unreal when it was explained to President Truman. He probably stopped listening to the nuclear physics bits after they told him that the first one had gone off with a big bang in Nevada, that Nevada was still there, but that it had a big new hole in it, which was smoking a bit.

Smarter meteorologists noticed something slightly strange about Katrina at the time. It built up to a Category 5 storm very quickly and darted around more than usual. More than that, the NSA picked up strange new electromagnetic transmissions in a previously unused part of the spectrum. Cell-phone users in New Orleans, the target city, may have found reception a little worse than usual. Although the frequencies are different you can get interference. Officially, this is why you are asked to switch off electronic devices when you board a civilian aircraft, although actually it may have more to do with the risk of confusing the system by rapid transits across cells.

Correa Group assets in FEMA made sure that the President was kept firmly in the dark, while the military whose assets were needed to save lives were not overly impressed by the short notice from FEMA. For a brief period America, which has the best emergency management systems of any country in the world, way ahead of ours in the UK, was made to look like a Third World country. Her gracious and classy President was made to look uncaring. That was a long way from the truth.

Since New Orleans has a large black population - one reason why the Germans chose it - it also gave out the impression that black life mattered less to President Bush than white life. This was grossly unfair on the President. He is, with respect, a humane and decent man. The mainstream media doesn't do fair however, not for conservatives.

It's taken a long time to develop counter-measures but we seem to have got there. Radio countermeasures were first used in 2011 to block an attempt to boost Tropical Storm Irene to a Category 4 or 5. It looks like the Good Guys finally got there. SHEWS systems can be used to boost an existing storm cell, by pouring in energy bounced off the ionosphere, but it takes about 24 hours. It leaves a distinctive *Aurora Borealas*-like signature near the ground stations, but at a lower altitude. You can also get unusual cloud formations in the target area. These may have been seen over Moore, Oklahoma on 19th and 20th May 2013.

For earthquakes the systems seem to be limited to about 8.5 on the Richter Scale but thermonuclear weapons can be used as a booster. This was done at Fukushima, which was actually predicted by a Tokyo-based website. With nuclear boosting SHEWS can generate a quake of over 9.0. Initially SHEWS seem to have been limited to about 10 miles deep, but they have been developed. It is thought they now have a penetration depth of about 25 miles. They can only be used against existing faults however, i.e. countries in the Ring of Fire are most at risk.

The following quakes have been identified as probable SHEWS events:

(1) Asian Tsunami, Boxing Day, 2004.

(2) Sichuan, China, 2008.
(3) Haiti, 2010.
(4) Christchurch, New Zealand, 2010 & 2011.
(5) Fukushima, 2011.

In addition to Katrina the following major storms have been identified as being probably SHEWS boosted:

(1) Cyclone Yasi, North Queensland, 2011.
(2) Toowoomba Storm, Queensland, January 2011.
(3) Hurricane Irene, East Coast, 2011.
(4) Hurricane Irma, Florida, 2017
(5) Hurricane Harvey, Texas, 2017 and
(6) Guadalupe Rover Flood, Texas, 2025.

That is by no means a complete list. Clearly the SHEWS systems need to be shut down, fast. In the meantime the authorities should put in place ELINT warning systems. The electromagnetic energy has a unique signature and at least 20 hours warning should be possible. Local authorities should get an indication from mobile phone and other radio interference – Kerr County officials, e.g. were left in the dark. They might have been able to save the children if they knew that their cell-phone based warning system was useless in a boosted storm. There needs to be better liaison between local authorities, telecoms providers and emergency management teams. SMS-based warning systems are likely to be ineffective, as in the Guadalupe River flood. Caution should be exercised before shutting down legacy systems such as analogue television in potential target areas. Analogue TV reception does not seem to be affected.

A conference of local authorities, possibly with closed sessions for military briefings, would clearly be desirable, as the flow of intelligence rarely reaches down to municipal level. Former New York Mayor Bloomberg might have something to contribute, as he must have been, struck by some slightly unusual features about Irene. Telecoms providers also need to be on the alert, as system disruption may be the first warning sign of a SHEWS attack and warnings from intel agencies have a nasty habit of being blocked. Governments are paralysed on this one. For the time being they are quite unable to protect their civilian populations. Legislators are so far out of their depth it's not funny.

Public international lawyers need to think in terms of classifying high-energy weapons systems as Weapons of Mass Destruction. This would permit a nuclear response, or credible threat of one. The scale of the casualties at

Fukushima ought to have got people to wake up and smell the coffee. It will take time, but there is no reason why the preliminary work should not start now.

This section of the book is aimed principally at emergency management professionals and civic authorities rather than the general reader. Due diligence of covert weapons systems is not easy and many readers will find it all a bit difficult to take in. Emergency management and civic authorities can have a surprising range of contacts however. There is nothing to stop say a state governor, or a state premier in Australia, talking to leading members of his or her own party at national level, or senior military figures. If they dig deep enough, they will find that this subject has come up.

Readers may have noticed three trends since Katrina:

(1) Increased prepositioning of critical military assets such as medevac aircraft prior to 'natural' disasters.
(2) Acquisition of additional amphibious, airlift and sealift capability, and
(3) An increased emphasis in military thinking on disaster relief. It is now no longer seen as purely 'assistance to the civil power' issue, as disasters increasingly are not natural.

Abu Ghraib

On 28th April 2004 the with respect unreliable CBS current affairs programme *60 Minutes* broadcast pictures showing Iraqi detainees being humiliated in the Abu Ghraib confinement facility near Baghdad. This incredibly unhelpful and irresponsible broadcast stirred up anti-American feeling in Iraq and acted as a recruiting tool for *al Qaeda*. The whole Abu Ghraib business has been used as a stick with which to beat America ever since. If *60 Minutes* with respect were better informed and had broadcast the truth say on Iraq's WMDs, or Iraq's connection to 9/11 it wouldn't have been so bad.

Just over 36 hours later the *Daily Mirror* newspaper in London published a series of fake photographs allegedly showing British troops abusing Iraqi detainees in the back of a truck. These were crude forgeries, which the Ministry of Defence failed to stop. This failure has never been explained. All MOD had to do was to tell the paper the photos were fake. The photos caused the usual anti-British and anti-army uproar in the media. It was left to the *Daily Telegraph* the following day, Saturday 1st May, to point out at least a dozen serious problems with the photos. Amongst the more basic were:

(1) The truck was a Bedford TK, but no TKs had been taken to Iraq.

(2) The SA-80 assault rifles lacked regimental serial numbers, i.e. they were not British Army issue.
(3) The T-shirts the 'Iraqis' were wearing were actually Syrian, and
(4) The boots the 'British soldiers' were wearing had their laces tied the French way, not the British. That's because Syria was a French colony and the Sryian Army tie their boots the French way, not the proper British way.

The photos were in fact taken in *Mukhabarat* HQ in Damascus. Everybody involved was Syrian, although it seems to have been the DVD's effective Propaganda Section, which came up with the idea. The *Mirror* muttered a grudging apology but failed to explain why they had not carried out even basic due diligence and had gone to press with a set of crude forgeries. It was then suggested that the photos had been faked near Preston in Lancashire by Territorial Army squaddies. This was a desperate effort to explain away the TK, as the Territorials still used them. So too did the Syrian army however, in knocked down (CKD) form. The photos may have been laundered via Preston. None of the people depicted in them ever went anywhere near Lancashire.

As previously related, it was myself who connected these particular dots. I queried whether the dodgy-looking Abu Ghraib 'hood' photo, the most prominent, was genuine. When it was examined with greater care than CBS had shown it was exposed as another crude forgery. One of the comments which came back to me was "Michael, it's not only a fake, it's not even a good fake". If you think about it, it had to be a fake. Although there were a couple of claimants to be 'Mr Hood' none has never been paid compensation. The first thing that any Iraqi who had actually been tortured by Americans would do would be to try and cash in.

The background in the 'hood' photo is different, unsurprisingly, since it wasn't taken in Abu Ghraib. There are no US military personnel in the photo, unlike the genuine (but staged) ones. That photo was also taken in *Mukhabarat* HQ in Damascus, where there they really did torture suspects (the new Syrian regime probably does as well). Unsurprisingly, someone suggested that Abu Ghraib be pulled down, lest an enterprising journalist with a penchant for the truth tour the prison looking for the bit where the 'hood' photo was taken. Unhappily, journalists who think that the truth is important are no thicker on the ground in Baghdad than they are in London, New York or Washington.

It is not just a question of the most prominent photo being a fake. Clearly male detainees should not have been photographed naked in humiliating poses with a woman standing over them, but why was it done? Who permitted these photos to be taken? The rule with photographs is: *always* look at the other side of the lens. The boys and girls of the 372nd Military Police Company, a National Guard unit from the charming town of Cumberland, Maryland were good people. They weren't humiliating detainees because they felt like it. They were ordered to humiliate them, as part of a 'new interrogation strategy', which was a phoney, and a Correa Group phoney at that.

The courts martial were something of a farce, with respect to all concerned, with deals being offered. Courts martial operate to higher ethical and professional standards than civilian courts, just as the military operates to a higher ethical standard than civilians. It was important to avoid any examination of the facts.

It is high time it was officially acknowledged that the 'hood' photo is a fake. Such convictions as there have been very frankly should be set aside, as material facts were not disclosed to the court. Ideally, the Correa Group assets who came up with the fake interrogation strategy should be prosecuted for treason. They deserve to be fried, nicely of course (no need for extra crispy). There is no doubt it cost American lives.

7/7

The sponsoring intelligence agencies for the 7/7 attacks in London were GO2, effectively part of the DVD, and Pakistan's ISI. The fact that GO2 is based at Vauxhall Cross is a source of endless and, in many cases, utter, confusion. It is a German agency, not British. It just employs Brits. The Waffen SS had foreign nationa units, but they were still part of the SS.

The fact that that nice man Peter Power was running an exercise on the day of the attacks is unlikely to have been a coincidence. I am sure however that no one involved in it would have had any idea that a terrorist attack was planned for that day. Whispers of these things sometimes get out. Somebody high up the payroll at the Met may have had an idea that something was going down on 7/7.

The terrorists went to Luton railway station north of London. It's on the charmingly named 'Bedpan Line', as before Thameslink the electric service was from Bedford to St. Pancras. Nowadays if you take a train from St. Pankers you are as likely as not to end up in Paris. The terrorists travelled to Luton from nearby Aylesbury, where I was then living, indeed they parked their Nissan Micra behind the Riviera Restaurant on Watermead, less than half a mile from my then home. The restaurant owner, an Iranian agent using the alias 'Hamid Reza Pardis, eventually taken out by MI5 in 2024, used his commercial fridge to store the unstable TATP explosive. One of the terrorists, Germaine Lindsay, was Aylesbury-based.

An immense amount of official effort, unhappily not backed up until recently by traffic cameras, in a country where there are cameras every cable's length or seem to be, went into persuading the public that the terrorists went down the M1 Motorway from Leeds. That was done mainly to protect GO2 assets in the Aylesbury area, including 'Pardis'. They *started* their journey on the M1, but the M1 doesn't go to Aylesbury. Some traffic camera images have been released, but they have not been authenticated and in any event do not cover the motorway near Luton.

TATP tends to 'brew up'. If you're a terrorist and you're out on a bombing expedition with TATP you need more ice than if you decide to go fishing. ISIS discovered this to their cost when their bomb-making cell in a tower block in West London (Grenfell Tower) stored their TATP in a *domestic* fridge, setting fire to the whole buildng and knocking off 72 tenants. The 7/7 families were treated disgracefully, par for the course where GO2 and the DVD are involved. It looks as though interference was run on medevac from the target stations, again not unusual. The coroner (not with respect a proper coroner, but another made-up judge) was not told about the intelligence assistance the 7/7 terrorists received. Without the Bad Guy intelligence support being made public the inquest was the usual ritual farce with respect, but it was a nicely conducted farce.

The 7/7 families are still searching for the answers. They won't find them on Netflix. The public are also being gaslit over Grenfell. If the families wait for officialdom to tell them the truth they will be waiting a long time, just as everything possible was done to conceal the fact of Iraqi involvement from the 9/11 families and the fact of Iranian involvement from the TWA 800 families. With the Lockerbie families the reverse was done. State involvement was acknowledged but those families have been on the receiving end of nearly two decades of official deception blaming the wrong state, i.e. Libya.

None of the 7/7 terrorists was a suicide bomber:

(1) The 'bus bomber', Hasib Hussain, screamed in terror after he set what he thought was a timer. He would have had just enough time to realise that the IED he was carrying was about to explode, but not enough time to do anything about it. You are not encouraged to try this at home in order to prove the point.[1]

(2) The timers/detonators went off at around 0850. The terrorists were told they had ten minutes in which to make their getaway. That is why Hussain was trying to contact his fellow 'suicide' bombers by mobile phone *after* they had blown themselves up. With genuine suicide bombers this is both pointless and unusual.

(3) They were not wearing suicide vests. The IEDs were in carry-ons, to be left on the trains.

(4) There were no mission-specific suicide videos. Terrorism having its occupational hazards it is quite common for trainee terrorists to put together a video. This allows them to have a posthumous rant in case they are blown up by their own bombs or whacked by a CIA drone. The 'suicide' terrorists did not settle their affairs either.

(5) They left components of another IED in the car. Your average suicide bomber takes his bombs with him.

(6) They had *return* tickets. Suicide bombers normally only need one-way tickets. They do not normally try to disguise the fact that they are martyrs to their cause/own stupidity, depending upon your point of view. There are automatic ticket barriers on that line and ticket checks are a rarity.

(7) The complex design of the trigger devices, which shared common features with those used in the Madrid train bombing, pointed towards a timer, just as immediate detonation pointed towards rigged timers. Normally with a suicide IED the trigger is a simple electrical contact. The 'Met' have been claiming for years that they were simple contacts, but different descriptions of the timers to the official version have been circulated within INTELCOM, and

(8) The next lot of 'suicide' bombers, on 21/7, smelt a rat. They yanked the detonators from the explosive packs, hence the series of small explosions. These were followed by rapid exits from Tube stations of some rather annoyed terrorists, anxious for a quiet chat with the Brazilian designer of the 'timers', one Jean Charles De Menezes. The 7/7 'suicides' were about as genuine as the alleged suicides of the Ngo brothers, including Ngo Diem, in Saigon back in '63.

Happily, the Special Branch of a less penetrated and more intelligent police force than the Met, West Midlands, took informal soundings from me. This was done at a side meeting at a conference in Whitehall on the 7/7 attacks, where I outlined my theory that they were not suicide bombers from the floor. West Midlands Special Branch have since denied that the brief consultation took place, but it did.

They treated the follow-up terrorist cell (i.e. the 21/7 bombers) as non-suicide. They even managed to arrest one, having *tasered* him first. Normally, as Shin Bet will tell you, if you ask them nicely, with a suspected suicide bomber you don't get up close and *taser* him.[2] Again you are not encouraged to try this at home, but introducing any form of electrical current to a suspected suicide bomber is not recommended.

De Menezes

On Friday 22nd July 2005 Metropolitan Police officers very properly shot dead the Brazilian terrorist electronics expert and renegade ABIN[3] intelligence officer Jean Charles de Menezes, at Stockwell Underground Station. He had designed the 'timers' for 7/7, 21/7 and Madrid, depositing the timers for 7/7 in Aylesbury with 'Pardis', who was also the quartermaster for the Liquid Bomb Plot, helping to explain his sudden demise. There was much talk from the de Menezes family and supporters about his being an 'innocent electrician', although they were unable to explain his whereabouts between 2000 and 2002.

He was actually being trained in antinarcotics work at a covert CIA/DEA facility in New York. We do not hand out work permits to Brazilian electricians. The Met have never been able to explain where de Menezes was working, nor the source of the funds he repatriated to Brazil. Some confusion was caused that morning by the bulge in his jacket. It was believed, in good faith but wrongly, to be an IED. The Met of course were still working to the suicide bomber theory for the 7/7 and 21/7 attacks, as indicated in Part One. The bulge was in fact caused by a silenced semiautomatic pistol, a Makarov 9mm with an integrated silencer, i.e. not the screw-on type, hence the bulk, supplied by 'Pardis', who had a sideline as a gun-runner, no offence intended. Screw-on silencers are less bulky, and give you the option of using the weapon in unsilenced mode, but they take time to attach.

Even these days it is unusual to have people shot dead on the London Underground. If they are, uniformed police tend to descend fairly quickly, including the efficient and honest British Transport Police. They dislike people travelling on the Underground with bombs and guns, even the Met, or, some might say, especially the Met. They are much nicer than the Met and were almost the last police force in Britain to have a sensible chief constable, Andy Trotter. He is good people, if I may say so.

GO2 assets in the Met were monitoring events as they unfolded. They got two of their boys, flagged as MI6, onto the scene pretty quickly to collect the gun and do the clean-up. They were in a panic, as de Menezes' South London address had been found in one of the bombers' holdalls the previous day, indeed they may even have set up the hit. CIA and NSA were also unhappy, hence a phone-call to me from the NSA that afternoon. CIA had lost track of Señor de Menezes after he did the runner from New York. They were apparently anxious to talk to him, as were ABIN. Actually, ABIN were rumoured to be wetting themselves after word spread that a renegade Brazilian intelligence officer had been involved in the 7/7 and 21/7 attacks on London.

The Brazilians kicked up a diplomatic fuss, but only a little one. A warning was passed pretty quickly on the backchannel to Brasilia by *inter alia* myself that their chap's connection to ABIN was known, along with the fact that he had been trained in New York and had gone walkies.

He had, very possibly been recruited by an ISI officer working at a Dunkin Donuts outlet. For some reason, possibly because it's a great opportunity to talk to the occasional bent NYPD officer without attracting attention (American police officers seem to be required to eat donuts whilst on duty, presumably to keep their weight up[4]). ISI undercover operatives in New York have been known to go for Dunkin Donuts. The American fast-food industry is not only known for its speed of service and the tastiness and wholesomeness of its products, but also for the speed with which it does background checks on potential employees. These are often done in less time than it takes to grill a hamburger patty.

It is a terrible thing for anyone to sanction the taking out of an innocent person. The perfectly lawful order to shoot Jean Charles de Menezes was given by a nice lady counterterrorist officer, Cressida Dick. Some years later I bumped into Cressida at a little talk about intelligence given by a former director of GCHQ, Sir David Omand, the smartest director they have had, with respect. He was certainly a lot smarter than his successor, no offence intended.

I did my best to explain to Cressida that she was in the clear and that de Menezes was no more an 'electrician' than my aunt Agnes, who couldn't wire a plug, God bless her. I am not sure with respect that she took it in, however. We next bumped into each other at an address in Whitehall in the autumn of 2012 at a policing conference. Again, I did my best to explain matters, but she thought I was winding her up. In fact, I was just trying to be helpful. Shooting innocents eats good people up from the inside. Sadly, I am afraid that Cressida and I are no longer on speaking terms, however.

No-one thought to tell the actual shooters that the official line was a lie. That was simply outrageous. You don't leave police officers, who were doing their job courageously, out of the loop on something like this. One of their former firearms instructors chanced to bump into me in a pub just off the M25 and matters were explained.

The NSA were quite right to ring me up, by the way. I suspect they'd spoken to Cheltenham first and realised that GCHQ were blowing more smoke than Chief Crazy Horse's communications officer before the Battle of Little Big Horn. We like to keep the channels of communications across the Atlantic open, although in this particular case they were encrypted.

Al-Haditha

The DVD were not content with just Abu Ghraib. They got Correa Group assets inside DIA to knock over an authentic American footballing and military hero, Corporal Pat Tillman. He was executed in Afghanistan on 22nd April 2004, under cover of 'friendly fire', in order to embarrass the US military and discourage recruiting. Friendly fire is not always friendly.

The DVD and *al Qaeda* decided that it would be a good idea to murder a bunch of Iraqi civilians and blame it on the US Marines Corps. This was duly done at al-Haditha, a village about 150 miles from Baghdad, in November 2005. The Marines were long gone when the women and children were shot, with captured US weapons. As with the Kennedy shooting, no ballistics match was ever done. In fact none of the 24 dead civilians was killed by a weapon fired by the US Marine Corps. The whole thing was a phoney.

The media loved it, though. The Bad Guys only have to shout 'human rights abuse' and the media are all over the military like a rash. Nobody in the media seems to be troubled by the ethics of broadcasting false allegations, even though it might help get Allied forces killed. In this case they falsely impugned the honour of the 1st Marines, a fine unit, by broadcasting propaganda without first checking their facts, or entering suitable caveats.[5] They also encouraged *al Qaeda* and the DVD to murder further innocent women and children for propaganda effect.

Sudaliya Beach

Since Hamas are also DVD-controlled it was not surprising when they adopted the same tactic. They blew up a 'picnicking' family, the Ghalias. These poor people fell foul of interclan politics, on Sudaliya Beach in Gaza in June 2006. The plan was to blame the Israeli Navy, which had ceased firing some time before. The media fell for it pretty much hook, line and sinker, although some suggested they might have stepped on a landmine. Not too many journalists applied what they are pleased to call their minds to the issue of why a family with young children would want to go for a picnic in the Gaza Strip during a bombardment in the first place. "Why don't we go for a picnic, dear?" "That's a good idea, let's go to the beach, the Israelis have just been shelling it and there may be some unexploded shells for the children to play with." The hapless Ghalia family were blown up by Hamas, again for the propaganda value. They were probably forced onto the beach under cover of Hamas snipers. The failure to nail Hamas over the murder of the Ghalia family encouraged the terrorists to murder many more innocent Gazans in the current war. The Hamas strategy for regaining control of aid distribution, a profitable sideline for them, involved the murder of hundreds of civilians queueing for aid.

Q'ana

This was a similar incident, this time in southern Lebanon, on 30th July 2006, organised by Hezbollah. The 28 victims, including women and children, were herded into the basement of a building and blown up, sometime after the last Israeli Air Force strike against terrorist targets in the area. Since none could have been allowed to escape to tell the truth they were gassed first. The incident was never investigated properly, but the injuries have a post-mortem look about them. The Iraqi stockpile of Zyklon-B went into Syria in 2002-2003 and was available to Hezbollah. As with Sudaliya Beach there were enough DVD penetration assets in Jerusalem to ensure that the facts were smothered.

The Litvinenko Affair

Not every death is an assassination. The media and the Foreign Office rushed to blame poor old President Putin for the death on 23rd November 2006 of Lt-Col Litvinenko, a former KGB officer, in London. Before you accuse a foreign government of organising an assassination you should first make sure that there has actually been one. Lt-Col Litvinenko swallowed the polonium knowingly, along with Prussian Blue, an alpha- absorbing antidote. The idea was to embarrass that nice man (according to those who have met him) Vladimir Putin, and prevent the extradition of the late Boris Berezovksy. A major player in the Medium Term Note market, where he made his billions, he committed suicide in March 2013. Litvinenko's death may well have been playing on his mind.

The cause of the latter's death was peritonitis, not polonium poisoning. It was probably one of those cases where the antidote turns out to have been as dangerous as the poison. Unsurprisingly with respect the inquest was a ritual farce. The false allegation, followed later by the equally false allegation over the poisoning of the Skripals in Salisbury in March 2018 with BX nerve agent (*not* novichok), contributed to a climate of anti-Russian hysteria, to the delight of President Zelensky.

The polonium which Litvinenko took came out of Iran. The signature was definitely not Russian. It was flown into an airfield near Hamburg, also used for narcotics shipments from Iran. The bash-Putin mentality in the British and American media is such that there was never any possibility of fair reporting, except briefly by the BBC's *Today* programme. *Today* is not noted with respect for balance. At any rate they weren't able to stick with a balanced approach for more than a morning and swiftly retreated to the 'Litvinenko was assassinated and Putin ordered it' line.

Concorde

This was infuriating, not least for the crew and mostly German passengers of the crashed aircraft. As indicated it does not appear to have been set up, but there are some strange features. The DVD may have been sending a message to President Chirac, who was forced to witness the crash. If it was a set-up the fact the passengers were mostly German would have afforded ideal cover for the DVD. The usual rule is that no one is quicker to sacrifice the lives of Germans than German intelligence, since everybody who is not as wily as the 'wily Hun' goes off looking in the other direction.

As explained, the supersonic airliner took off overweight, downwind (i.e. was allocated the wrong runway by ATC) and with a spacer missing from the rear axle on the port undercarriage bogie. This caused the aircraft to veer to the left and strike the runway lights. The French then refused to supply Concorde bits to Britain, in complete breach of the Anglo-French Treaty, for which they have yet to be punished.

It cannot have been anything to do with Continental Airlines, since the DC-10 was *not* missing that bit of her engine cowling when she landed in Houston. Curiously, Continental's French lawyer was found dead in odd-looking circumstances in March 2013. He knew full well that the titanium cowling strip could not have caused the crash. He appears to have accepted that it fell off the American plane but pointed out that the part of the runway where it was allegedly found was *beyond* where the port fuel tank had been holed. I'd still like to know which DC-10 they got that bit off, although my money's on an old ex-UTA bird.

British Airways were forced to trot out a load of nonsense about Concorde losing money, difficult, even for BA, when the breakeven factor was 30% and the load factor about 50. Not many Concorde passengers will tell you that their flight was deserted. It was a beautiful aircraft and must be replaced, this time without the 'assistance' of the French. Since the oil market is rigged by the Germans it shouldn't be too difficult to get the price of aviation fuel down.

Future technical collaboration between Britain and France is unlikely. It was a terrible mistake to go in with them in the first place. The decision, was foisted by German assets in Whitehall on an unwilling British aircraft industry, still smarting over the French theft of the Fairey Delta. The fine old Bristol Company were perfectly capable of making the aircraft on their own.

The British Airways 777

On 17th January 2008 a BA 777-236 from Peking crashed on approach to Runway 27L (left) at Heathrow, after both her Rolls-Royce Trent 800 engines failed to respond to thrust commands, a trifle unusually. Thanks to outstanding airmanship from Captain Burkill and his First Officer she made the field and everybody walked away, leaving the 777 on the airport in bits. That's not something you see every day. Prime Minister Gordon Brown, the second most important man in the government (after the Cabinet Secretary[6]) was on his way to Heathrow to fly to Peking. His departure was delayed.

The AAIB 'accident' inquiry was the usual nonsense with respect, although at least this time they didn't favour us with fairy tales about square windows. They first attributed the near disaster to 'frozen fuel' an explanation, which with respect would have carried greater weight had the fuel actually frozen. Freezing leaves traces[7] and there is a low fuel temperature warning light anyway, which didn't illuminate. Upper air temperatures on the airway were within the normal range, albeit at the lower end. Aware that wouldn't wash, they changed the story to the water in the fuel freezing and blocking the fuel-oil heat exchangers, followed by the coincidental failure of both engines.

What actually happened is that self-deleting lines of software code were inserted in Peking. One clue is that the Chinese stood down the band. If there is a doubt about a crash and cancelling an unwanted VIP visit is suspected as a possible motive, always check to see what happened to the band. Everybody forgets to keep the band, not to mention the VIPs, waiting around uselessly at the airport. If you want to know what's happening in Peking by the way, talk to Taipei.

The cunning plan - Gordon Brown not only made the boring official meetings but also the more interesting side meetings somebody didn't want him to – failed because of a great piece of flying. It was always on the cards the next set of passengers might not be so lucky and so it proved. When the DVD next pulled the same stunt, at Schiphol, on 25th February 2009, the plane, a Turkish Airways 737-800 with two Turkish Intelligence (MIT) assets on board went in, killing nine people. The MIT boys were probably going to talk to those nice people the Dutch AIVD about shutting down the DVD heroin pipeline from Turkey through Rotterdam. Ironically the death toll included Boeing employees. Rather more died, sadly, when the GE engines on Air India Flight 171 (Boeing 787 Dreamliner, VT-ANB) were sabotaged using the same method on 12th June 2025.

The Assassination of Bob Woolmer

On 18th March 2007 agents of the Pakistani intelligence service, the ISI, which is effectively a sister agency of the Chinese SIS and the DVD, entered Room 374 on the 12th floor of the Pegasus Hotel in Kingston Jamaica. They murdered that nice man the former England Test cricketer Bob Woolmer. Jamaican Police Commissioner Lucius Thomas, who in fairness had been trying to clean up Kingston, or bits of it at any rate, initially accepted that Bob had been murdered. GO2 then got to work. Kingston were given 'guidance' and murder became a 'sudden death from natural causes'. Yes, just after he was poisoned and strangled.

Bob, whom I met at Lord's in 2006, was aware of corruption on the International Cricket Council, the rigging of Test Matches (on which *al Qaeda* were placing bets, via a dodgy broker in Karachi, if that is not a tautology) and the fact that former South Africa Test Captain Hanse Cronje had been assassinated. That was the old fake radio beams trick. There was a follow-up assassination in Cape Town in 2011 of the cricketing journalist Peter Roebuck, who was investigating the Woolmer murder. He was said to have jumped out of a window, in an air-conditioned hotel where the windows could only be opened an inch or two.

The famous cricket statistician Bill Frindall, a.k.a "The Bearded Wonder", was another casualty. He was hit in Dubai - the old Legionnaire's Disease in the hotel air-conditioning trick. Bob Woolmer was the second former England Test Cricketer to be assassinated, although there is some doubt about whether the great spin bowler Hedley Verity was murdered by the Germans in 1944. The better view is that he was taken out.

The Kidnap of Madeleine McCann

The DVD, have no idea how much upset this caused in England. Half the toddlers in the country wanted to know what had happened. Little Madeleine McCann was kidnapped from Praia de Luz Portugal by a DVD paedophile ring on 3rd May 2007. She was selected for sex abuse by a senior official on the European Commission in Brussels. Her photograph annexed to, an e-mail as a jpeg file, was picked up by NSA at the e-mail switching centre at Menwith Hill, after the kidnap. It was sent to the official's private e-mail account (not in his name) by the DVD paedophile ring in Brussels, which services the Commission, NATO HQ, the ECJ in Luxembourg and other European institutions. There is a second ring, servicing the Belgian government and bureaucracy.

The informal intelligence assessment I prepared for the JointIntelligence Committee in London is in set out in Appendix 8, although the name of the boat on which she was held and some other intelligence has had to be deleted, to maintain happiness levels at the publisher's lawyers. It is no longer restricted, indeed some idiot (in the Cabinet) leaked it, in compressed form, to the *Daily Mirror*. The spelling errors in the original report were a security feature, making it easier to trace a leaked report. An extra space, two letters the wrong way round, a comma instead of a semi-colon – there are all sorts of things you can do to personalise a restricted document which has multiple recipients, allowing a leak to be traced. (The spelling errors in earlier editions of this book were genuine typos!)

The use of SSKs might surprise some, but that's how hundreds of kidnapped street kiddies in São Paolo were brought into Europe for abuse, fewer now that the DVD have been spotted. Madeleine wasn't saved, sadly, but other children have been. As I always told my intelligence students, always tell it as it is and don't worry about how it looks. Nothing material in the report was undermined by later intelligence, indeed the CCTV footage sighting of her at Montpelier, France, which the French fought hard to suppress from the Leicestershire Police and the High Court, and the credible Argentine and Chile sightings, suggest that she was taken back and forth across the Atlantic. A sub was an obvious way of doing it covertly. They could hardly take her on an aircraft, even a business jet.

The political blocking of rescue efforts, during that crucial window when we knew on which boat Madeleine was being held, and where it was, had the predictable result that the Good Guys were always playing catch-up. Tragically, she was murdered in or about December 2008, her body being cremated. The DVD had learned about the of the increasing satellite surveillance of unmarked children's graves.

It is not my intention to cause further distress to Madeleine's long-suffering parents, to whose representative the upsetting intelligence that she might have been murdered was conveyed in early 2009. Nothing in this book should take them by surprise, indeed efforts were made to have the JIC report summarised for them at the time, via their MP. They do not accept that I am right either about the kidnap or the murder. As the poor child's parents, they are more than entitled to their view. This is one of those occasions where you really, really want to be wrong.

Vengeful criticism of the parents was made by trolls on various websites and the childcare arrangements for that night could have been better, but no reasonable arrangement would have stopped an armed DVD paedophile ring. The only way of protecting Madeleine was by having armed security guards who knew what they were doing patrolling the Warner complex, or arming the parents themselves. How were they to get guns onto the plane, and why would doctors want to carry firearms anyway?

They were in no way involved in their child's kidnap, nor is it right, nor even reasonable, to criticise them for continuing fundraising efforts after they received a report that their child, tragically, had been murdered. They were not obliged to accept a report without a body any more than I could properly have suppressed the intelligence in my possession from them, or the authorities. Sadly, nothing in the 17 years since has caused me to doubt the veracity of the reporting that Madeleine was murdered. That is now the majority view within INTELCOM. That her mother continues to believe that she is still alive goes greatly to her credit. It just goes to show what a good mother she is.

1. With mobile phone timers you often get a 'beep' from the device itself and you will hear the detonator 'fizz' just before it sets off the explosives. With a slow-moving chemical explosion the shockwave can be subsonic, i.e. he knew he'd blown himself up almost as soon as he pressed the tit, after which things would have happened very quickly. Nervous terrorists are forever blowing themselves up and their last thoughts are probably something along the lines of 'oh dear I shouldn't have done that'.
2. In fairness it should be pointed out that said terrorist was naked at the time, i.e. any explosives on his person would have had to be concealed in an unusual, not to say uncomfortable, location. Always be wary of a naked terrorist with wires coming out of his bottom.
3. Brazilian National Intelligence Agency, the principal Brazilian civil intelligence agency.
4. This is an ironic observation, for readers who do not do irony, like Thames Valley Police. There are not that many bent NYPD officers these days, by the way. The force is much cleaner than the say the Met, Thames Valley or the Columbian police.
5. Obvious caveats to enter in relation to al-Haditha would have been to emphasise that no autopsies had been performed, that the evidence of the young eye-witness was not corroborated and there was no ballistics match between any weapon issued to the unit accused of the atrocity and any of the alleged victims.
6. Technically, he is not a member of the government, but try telling that to the Cabinet Secretary.
7. If you look at aviation fuel which has frozen and then thawed you will notice that it has a slightly waxy feel to it.

30

The Obama Years

The Global Financial Crisis

As with the Great Depression this was organised from Frankfurt. It had its roots in the 1990s, with the encouragement of poor lending practices in the States. In some cases this was bad faith lending, i.e. lending for the sake of it in order to generate worthless debt. This was then rolled up with high quality debt in order to damage the latter, in highly complex instruments, which hardly anybody understood, including the people buying them.

Consumer credit was also expanded, often the prelude to a crunch. Central banks are mostly penetrated by Germany and they did nothing to stop it, indeed they encouraged it. Now we have credit rationing, strangling small and medium sized enterprises and limiting home ownership. Credit squeezes are nothing new. The tactic was tried with great success by DVD assets in Canberra in 1960. They persuaded Harold Holt, then Federal Treasurer, to restrict credit.

Holt, ironically later assassinated, as we saw in Chapter 24, had one great weakness. He was over-dependent on his officials and vulnerable to bad faith advice. In fairness it is a common failing amongst politicians, who tend to be easily manipulated. The failed Coalition, May and Sunak Governments in Britain were classic examples.

It isn't possible to understand the so-called 'global' economy (in reality a series of interlocking economies) by looking solely at onshore economies. You have to look offshore as well, where you will find strange things happening, including high-yield Medium Term Note (MTN) trading. In order to understand it you first have to grasp the concept of leveraging.

Most householders will be familiar with it. If you invest £10,000 in a house and borrow the rest, say £90,000, over 10 years, and sell the house for £200,000 you have a return of 100% on your original investment. From that you have to deduct the cost of borrowing the £90,000 balance of the purchase price. Your rate of return is usually much higher than if you just put the £10,000 into the bank. It is not however a guaranteed rate of return, as the value of houses can down as well as up.

What if you had a buyer for your house in 10 years' time at an agreed price? You would then have an exit. That is how the MTN market works. No one takes a commitment or a purchase ticket (these days all trading is done on electronic exchanges like Euroclear) without first securing an exit. Face value of an MTN is typically $100,000,000. The bank can leverage that tenfold, secure in the knowledge that the profits are guaranteed. Thus, the trader goes to market with $1 billion.

The profits are scandalously high, partly as banks issue discounted notes, making up the loss with a share of the offshore trading action. A typical margin might be 1500 basis points or 15%. You might have a buy price of say 73 cents in the dollar and a selling price of 88. An electronic trade can be completed in minutes. Back-office trading floors can be quite exciting places, also very noisy, especially for places that don't officially exist.[1] There might be five trades in a banking day. The MTN market doesn't work all year round - it's closed several times a year for audit.

Now our investor is starting to see some serious returns. The bank will deduct its cost of borrowing, which will be high (at least 100 basis points a day, more like 1,000). As a very nice Mossad officer once helpfully explained to me the 15% margin for the trader is 150% for the investor, minus the bank's cut, as the investor only put up $100,000,000. So he gets say $141,000,000 ($150,000,000 - $9,000,000 for the bank, which lent $900,000,000), or 141% profit in a day. He gets his 100 million dollar stake back as well. It's nice work if you can get it. Do it five times and our investor is ahead $905,000,000, with very little risk.

That's how we get overnight billionaires, like the late Boris Berezovsky. There isn't much risk for the bank either, unless they move large chunks of cash offshore, lured by the prospect of high returns. They can get stranded if they can't get the cash back in the timeframe they need, in which case they can do a Barings and go belly-up.

There is however no such thing as a free lunch. MTN trading is economically devastating for the West, as:

(1) It massively increases the money supply, hence the sustained period of high inflation since 1945, i.e. everybody pays through the nose for high returns for the well-connected few.
(2) It corrupts banks including central banks, who are forced to lie on a daily basis to governments, revenue authorities, business and consumers.

(3) It's controlled from Frankfurt and enforced by the DVD, so we get a steady stream of dead bankers.
(4) It destabilises the banking system as funds can be trapped offshore.
(5) It's a honeypot for con men and crooks, who take people's money claiming they can get into the system, or try and defraud the system with fake Certificates of Deposit etc. Southwark Crown Court in London has MTN-related frauds on a weekly basis.
(6) It corrupts the legal system as prosecutors mislead courts and prosecute on the fraudulent basis that high returns are not possible, full stop. What they should be saying is that high returns are not possible in this particular case because the dodgy broker in the dock has no banking connections at all, or the instrument the defendant wanted a bank to run a line of credit against was a forgery, or did not belong to the defendant etc.
(7) It creates a false guru effect as people who have made themselves rich (subject to point (8) below) are thought to have generated their wealth through conventional commercial activity, i.e. have business acumen, as opposed to contacts.
(8) The Germans tend to view the money as belonging to them as they control the system, so you cannot spend it freely, a phenomenon I first came across in the battle to save Rolls-Royce.
(9) It undermines industrial economies like Britain and the US as it skews investment offshore and acts as a disincentive to banks from investing in real businesses creating real jobs. Good Guy onshore economies are hollowed out whilst the offshore economy and the banking sector balloons.
(10) It gives the DVD access to piles of cash that can be used to prop up the euro, fund terrorism, buy up politicians etc. Just look at the accounts the late Yasser Arafat controlled if you don't believe me, and
(11) It offers huge financial incentives to corrupt dictators in the Third World, as once they have seized control of their central banks they can block funds, run a line of credit against those funds in their own name in say Zurich, with German backing, and become instant billionaires. As the central bank's funds do not leave the account no one notices the fraud. This is a particularly popular way of using donor cash from Western countries silly enough to inject 'overseas aid' into bent Third World countries. The cash can also be used to fund wars or terrorist insurgencies.

This book is addressed to several audiences, and bankers and investors are one of them. They may be aware of MTN trading but unaware that it is controlled ultimately from Frankfurt. They need to brief in legislators, the media and business leaders. Typically, they are misled into believing that a percentage of trading profits go to 'humanitarian projects'. They do not.

Our economies are unstable, as the GFC showed. They will continue to be unstable until MTN trading is stopped and the offshore and onshore economies are integrated. This would greatly reduce national debts, as not all major banks have disclosed their offshore profits for tax purposes, ditto investors. There are pots of money offshore just waiting for governments to collect.

The Obama Birthplace Issue

The media were scathing about so-called 'birthers', i.e. those who have challenged either or both of the accounts given by Barack Obama's campaign in 2008 as to where he was born. The first version was the Kapi'olani Medical Center for Women and Children, later amended to the Kapiolani Maternity and Gynecological Hospital. The second was the Queen's Medical Center. Both are in Honolulu. Various names have been given, but it seems that we are only dealing with two alternative places of birth, one on Punahol St, the other on Punchbowl St, both in Honolulu.

The short-form birth certificate put on the Obama campaign website in 2008 was denounced as a forgery at the time by an official of the Hawai'i state government, who has since died in an air crash, in which she was the only fatality.

Given that the President admittedly visited Pakistan at a time when US passports were not valid for travel to that country, it was scarcely unreasonable for people to query his eligibility for the office of POTUS. In a democracy the citizens are entitled to question the credentials of their leaders, full stop.

The US Constitution is quite clear. Article II requires that the President be a "natural born citizen". That must mean birth in the United States, although some American constitutional scholars would argue that birth on a US military base abroad qualifies. Senator McCain presumably supported this view, as he claimed to have been born on Coco Solo Marine Corps Air Station in Panama. That claim with great respect would be stronger if the base hospital had been built before his birth rather than after. One thing you tend not to see on Marines Corps bases is lots of women giving birth.[2]

The President also has to be a US Citizen. If, as has been claimed, President Obama was born in Mombasa, Kenya (as it now is - it used to be part of the Coastal Protectorate) then he would *not* be a US Citizen. His claimed father was not a US Citizen, his claimed mother was too young to transmit her American nationality and he himself has never naturalised. It is not therefore a small point.

The President's claimed father is Barack Hussein Obama Senior. He was murdered by Kenyan intelligence in a staged car crash, at DVD request, in 1982. The black radical Muslim Malcolm X has been put forward as an alternative candidate by some, as well as another black Muslim, both names having their supporters inside CIA. I respectfully incline to the view that the relationship to Barack Obama Senior is as claimed, although my distinguished fellow author Dr Jerome Corsi has put forward a credible, Indonesian alternative.

This is said to be supported by the DNA test done by the CIA in late 2007, a low-copy test using saliva from water and wine glasses used at a campaign function by the candidate and his claimed grandmother, the late Madelyn Lee Payne Dunham. She was born on 26th October 1922. Either Abongo or Auma Obama was used as a comparator on the father's side. The reporting I have heard is that this test did not support the claimed relationship to Madelyn Dunham through her daughter Ann. It would of course be for the CIA to release the test results if so advised, it being a matter entirely for them.

Ann Dunham is claimed to be the President's mother, but with respect there are significant gaps in the evidence:

(1) There is no undisputed birth certificate. Two have been released and each has been forensically questioned by experts in Photoshop and other digital imaging software, including experts consulted by Sheriff Joe Arpaio's[3] Cold Case Posse. It has even been claimed that the long-form certificate released in 2011 was created as an illustration of how easy it is to forge official documents and that it was downloaded by the White House from a website. Readers will have to judge this claim for themselves.

(2) Hawai'i have not released the original register entry, indeed they have litigated hard against that nice man Andy Martin in order to suppress it.

(3) No medical records have been released showing that Ann Dunham was pregnant in 1960 or 1961, or gave birth as claimed on August 4th 1961.

(4) No photograph is available showing Ann Dunham pregnant in the summer of 1961.

(5) The Kapiolani Maternity Hospital has not released any records confirming her admission in August 1961, nor the birth of a child named Barack Hussein Obama Junior on August 4th 1961.

(6) No records from the alleged attending physician, Dr David Sinclair, have been released.
(7) There are no photographs showing Barack Obama in the USA prior to the age of about two. He may however have been brought into the United States in the week of the claimed birth, as the Maricopa County Cold Case Posse established that the immigration records for that week have been pulled.
(8) The Fulbright Scholarship the President received at Occidental College would not ordinarily have been available to a US Citizen.
(9) The President's Indonesian school records have not been released, and
(10) Neither the Indonesian nor Pakistani immigration records have been released.

On balance I respectfully incline to the view that the claimed relationship to Ann Dunham should be rejected. British files apparently suggest birth in Mombasa in or about August or possibly April 1960.

If that is right, then Barack Obama's nationality status would appear to be:

(1) Subject of His Highness the Sultan of Zanzibar and British Protected Person from birth until the creation of the Republic of Kenya in December 1963.
(2) Citizen of the Republic of Kenya from then until the present day, and
(3) Additionally, a citizen of the Republic of Indonesia on adoption by Lolo Soetoro, his stepfather.

As Barack Obama Senior was already married to Kezia Obama when he went through a form of ceremony of marriage with Ann Dunham, that marriage was bigamous. The contrary is not seriously suggested, i.e. there has never been a suggestion that the marriage to Kezia Obama was dissolved. Since the marriage was bigamous the rules on transmission of US nationality would therefore be those for unmarried mothers. Ann Dunham was *too young* to transmit US nationality. Even on the version of events put forward by the White House the President could not be a US Citizen. Therefore in my as ever humble opinion there is an issue which needs to be addressed.

It is important not to let one's judgment on the complex legal and factual issues involved be affected by party-political or racial bias. In my opinion Senator McCain, President Obama's Republican opponent in 2008, would not have been eligible to serve as President on either view as to his place of birth, as he was born outside the United States.

It is undesirable to discriminate against military families serving overseas but that requires an amendment of the constitution, not forced construction of a provision drawn up when the United States had no overseas bases and did not contemplate any. I am an admirer of the late Senator Goldwater, but he too would not have been eligible to serve as President as he was not born in a state. Arizona was a territory until 1912. I know that some scholars incline to the view that birth in a territory, which later became a state is sufficient but I think it has to be birth in a state. I don't think that a Puerto Rican could become President, e.g., although I've met some very nice Puerto Ricans.

AF447 and Deepwater Horizon

The link between these two tragic events is senior Devon Oil geologist Michael Harris. He was flying to Paris on Air France Flight 447 to brief in President Sarkozy, apparently in person. He had become aware of the complex and reckless DVD operation to blow up the BP-leased Deepwater Horizon oil rig in the Gulf of Mexico. This crazy operation eventually went ahead, with some interesting additional fissures in the seabed. Not all the oil came from the BP rig, as the IMINT clearly showed.

The DVD wanted to stop offshore drilling in the Gulf. They are always up for a go at BP anyway. Sadly, the courts are doing their job for them. BP were hammered, which was grossly unfair.

The Air France Airbus (A330-203, F-GZCP) was shot down on 1st June 2009, again by a Phoenix AAM, using a proximity-fused warhead. It looks like the missile was in infrared mode. The warhead apparently exploded about 50 ft below the starboard GE CF6-80 engine. There was a slow depressurisation, as the hull was punctured, followed by multiple systems failures.

No radioed Mayday call was possible as the Air Traffic Control and guard frequencies were jammed. Airline pilots are not trained in counter- jamming techniques such as using satellite data links and the SELCAL radio-telephone system. The Janet and John French BEA explanation was that the pitot tubes froze, as though they had no heaters. There are three tubes on a 330 anyway. They would hardly all freeze at the same time. The pilots had GPS and radar altimeter backup in any event. GPS will give you airspeed and your radar altimeter will give you altitude above the ocean. Some GPS systems will even give you an altitude reading.

This time somebody - it looks like the Brazilian Atlantique[4] patrol plane - had a go at the Iranian *Kilo*. She was winged, losing diesel fuel, which the media dutifully reported as aviation fuel. Aviation fuel is light, and disperses. Diesel oil is heavy and stays on the surface in a slick, like this fuel did. A

French SSN caught up with the *Kilo* eventually, off the Comoros Islands in the Indian Ocean. The Iranians have a covert sub facility in the north of the group.

The French asked the Yemenis to do a photo-run, but their Airbus, an A310, was also shot down, on 30th June. To paraphrase Oscar Wilde once more, to lose one Airbus might be thought to be a misfortune. To lose two starts to look like carelessness. Had the Airbus not been shot down the attack on Deepwater Horizon might not have gone ahead. Sadly, none of this emerged in the with respect musical comedy proceedings down on the Gulf Coast. The cost of suppressing the truth about these two tragedies was paid by Captain Zaharie Shah, his dedicated crew and the passengers aboard Malaysian Airlines Flight MH 370, also shot down with a modified Phoenix (named Fakour-2 by the Iranians). MH17 was also shot down, in a joint Ukrainian/Chinese operation. The Buk missile system the rebels were allowed to capture *lacked the arming codes*, i.e. the rebels couldn't fire it.

The Elimination of Osama bin Laden

Osama bin Laden was eliminated in or about July 2009, by the DVD in Waziristan. Apparently a deal was done whereby certain well-informed former members of the Bush Administration kept silent about German sponsorship of 9/11 in exchange for bin Laden being taken out and no further attacks on the US. I was not included in that deal, so I am free to talk. If you cut a deal you stick to it.

This left the Bad Guys with a problem - how to explain the absence of up to date bin Laden videos. You can always record a few alternative versions of predictable events to suggest that your video is current, of course. You can have a video referring to President McCain as well one referring to President Obama, e.g., but you can only predict so far ahead. Terrorist networks do not work like TV networks, which can always rerun *I Love Lucy*.

The Correa Group in Frankfurt came up with the answer, which was sold to the Obama White House via Langley. Why not stage a SEALs raid on the new bin Laden compound? His first safe house was further south, but he had to be moved after that one was shopped by me to the NSA. The idea was to pretend that the raid was being watched live on TV by key folk in the White House, whack a junior bin Laden and bury him at sea. The phoney raid was duly staged on 2nd May 2011. The DVD arranged to have Seal Team Six, who did the raid, ambushed in a helo in August 2011, to cover their tracks. SEALs are good people and they were sorely abused.

Unsurprisingly, cracks have started to appear in the Official Version of Events. The Obama and Biden White Houses stopped pretending that anyone saw Osama bin Laden taken out live on TV whilst they snacked on beer and pretzels. There are now several different versions out there as to who shot whom and where. The answer is that *a* bin Laden was shot, but not *the* bin Laden, who was already dead. Burials at sea are great for getting rid of the evidence, of course. The Bad Guys might care to note that their card has been marked on this one. I am sure that the glorious dead of Seal Team Six will be avenged.

Sabotage at Smolensk

On Saturday 10th April 2010 a Polish Tu-154, an enlarged Russian version of the de Havilland Trident, the plans of which had been supplied to the USSR by the DVD, crashed on approach to Smolensk Airport. She was carrying President Lech Kaczynski, President of Poland and a Polish patriot, and the Polish General Staff. They were intending to have some serious discussions with the Russian General Staff, who had come up with a sensible plan to invade Germany.

The DVD used a similar method to that used on the Trident at Staines. They rigged the Air Data Computer, the 154 having been based on Trident technology. The pilots' altimeters both seem to have under-read by about 100 metres, or 330 ft. The media were content to recycle the 'Janet and John' explanation - fog - trotted out to keep people sweet and stop them asking too many questions. The professional and patriotic Russian military intelligence organisation, the GRU, did the real investigation.

The Tripoli Airbus Disaster

On 12th May 2010 an Afriqiyah Airways Airbus A330, 5A-ONG, crashed on approach to Tripoli Airport. There was only one survivor, a young Dutch boy named Ruben van Assouw, aged just nine. Eleven crew and 92 passengers, many of them Dutch, died. This was the third known crash triggered by software sabotage, the first being the Heathrow 777 of course. The passengers being Dutch were a natural target for the DVD, who as we have seen are happy to murder Indians as well.

The GCHQ Murders

On 4th May 2010 a cleaner, Matthew Johnson, who worked for GCHQ and lived at Abbeymead, in Gloucestershire, England was thrown by GO2 agents into a canal near his home. Unsurprisingly, since it was clearly a suspicious death (murders often are), a slightly puzzled coroner recorded an open verdict. This is legal code for 'goodness only knows what happened here'.

The coroner was intelligence illiterate, which is not a criticism. Coroners are not trained in intelligence work and few if any are aware of the existence of GO2. If they were, they would not know that it is part of German, not British, intelligence. They are almost wholly unaware that they have might have German deaths squads roaming their districts. Matthew Johnson was a brave man.

He had been taking intelligence out of GCQH on memory sticks, to do with Afghanistan, which he was handing to British military intelligence officers. They had no other way of getting the intel out of the building. GCHQ is penetrated by the DVD, indeed as we have seen its forerunner, the Government Code and Cypher School, operated out of a building (Bletchley Park) purchased for them with Abwehr funds, laundered through Admiral Sinclair. He was at one time 'Jerry's' top man in the British Naval Intelligence Department.

Getting intel out of the "doughnut", as the plush new HQ near Cheltenham is nick-named (better catering than the old place, and the climate control actually works), is never easy. Allied troops were walking into ambushes in Afghanistan. It's mostly open country, ideal for satellite surveillance. Satellites were picking up 'Terry Taliban' planting IEDs, but the warnings never seemed to reach the lads on time.

Of course, it would be easier to have GCHQ working for Britain instead of Germany, but that cannot be done without cleaning up the Cabinet Office. In the meantime, someone hit upon the bright idea of attaching memory sticks (in 2010 you could get 1TB or more of data onto the state of the art ones, not then in the shops) to the undersides of desks with Blu-Tack. As the packaging says, it has "1000s of uses". Courageous cleaners like Matthew Johnson would then walk out of the building and the intelligence would come safely into British hands.

Casualties in Afghanistan started to drop but GO2 were brought in. They did the usual witch-hunt and topped Matthew. If GO2 have addled their brains with nonsense about the British class system, *Midsomer Murders* style, and think that because Matthew was a cleaner and belonged to the working class, British Intelligence would be prepared to treat him as expendable, then they need to get out more. His death will be avenged and hopefully he will be posthumously awarded the George Cross which he so richly deserves. It is high time, by the way, that the Treasury were forced to pay a proper, tax-free, *ex gratia* annual sum to surviving holders of the George Cross and Victoria Cross, and their next of kin, indeed all decorations ought to carry with them a small, annual tax-free gratuity.

On 23rd August the naked body of GCHQ scientist Dr Gareth Williams was found locked in a bag, a sports holdall, in his flat in Pimlico, London. At least this time no one left an empty blister pack of Co- Proxamol tablets beside the bag. We were not favoured by the Metropolitan Police, initially at any rate, with the theory that Gareth, who had been liaising with NSA on the same operation to aid Allied forces in Afghanistan on which Matthew Johnson was working, had committed suicide. It's a bit difficult to hop in a bag and lock it from the outside afterwards. Once again GO2 were responsible for the murder and yet again it was covered up, complete with a smear attack on Gareth, based on his private life. He was gay, which was no business of GO2's, nor anyone else, for that matter. I told the Met about the memory sticks back in 2010, but it wasn't until the inquest in 2012 that MI6 confirmed their existence.

Desperate attempts were then made to suggest that it was suicide after all, or a sex game gone wrong. MI6 and GCHQ are frantic to cover up the fact that British and American soldiers were killed on the battlefield because SATINT was suppressed. The poor old coroner, Dr Fiona Wilcox, was left in the dark. When Thames Valley Police were applying heat to me in 2012 over the nuclear threat to the Olympics, which I had spotted, and this book, the Met failed to confirm that I had warned them, at Detective Chief Inspector level, about the memory sticks as far back as 2010. Next time the Met want help in a murder inquiry they can pay me a consultancy fee!

Air Chief Marshal Sir Christopher Moran

This assassination, at RAF Brize Norton, on 26th May 2010, again by GO2 (in practice nearly all assassinations in the UK since 1945 have been carried out by GO2) caused particular annoyance to the RAF. It also caused annoyance to poor old Air Chief Marshal Sir Christopher Moran KCB OBE MVO ADC FRAeS as well of course. There is nothing more irritating than being assassinated.

In line to succeed that nice man Sir Stephen Dalton as Chief of the Air Staff, Sir Christopher was murdered whilst on a 'fun' run. It was the old 'give the runner a contaminated bottle of high-energy fluid and hope that he won't notice it's been spiked' trick. Somebody is going to have to buy the RAF an awful lot of aeroplanes for this one. The official inquiry was the usual farce.

Sir Christopher was a good man - in my experience Air Chief Marshals usually are. He disapproved of murder. In particular, he disapproved of the decision to murder the counterintelligence officers on the Chinook. In private (in public of course they had to toe the line) the RAF were never happy about the negligence finding against the pilots. It was grossly unfair, not least since they too had been murdered. Their security briefing was also wholly inadequate, to the point, frankly, of naivety.

The then Secretary of State for Defence, Dr Liam Fox, a nice chap, if not entirely sound on Europe[5] (I know he will not mind my saying so) had just announced a second inquiry. Sir Christopher was willing to contribute. Now inquiries in Whitehall are normally *Yes Minister* style affairs,[6] where the findings are agreed in advance, which as we have seen some refer to as 'Warwick Rules'.

There are two basic types of official inquiry - farces, where the committee meets in secret, and ritual farces, where carefully selected witnesses are invited to attend public hearings, either to be humiliated or to provide support for the committee's already-reached conclusions. There was a Royal Commission 35 years ago (the Benson Royal Commission on Legal Services) which actually listened to the evidence and made sensible recommendations but its report was ignored and the selection criteria were tightened up.

Sir Christopher however wanted a *real* inquiry. This sent a small shockwave around Whitehall and generated an assassination tasking. Those who were in the loop on the decision to murder every key counterintelligence official in Northern Ireland at German request in order to protect the DVD and its spondee the IRA were understandably nervous.

There was an interesting follow-up to the Moran Assassination. Brize Norton is in the Witney Parliamentary constituency whose then MP was a chap called David Cameron, now Lord Cameron. His constituency chairman, Christopher Shale, was well-informed, so well-informed in fact that he was found dead in a portaloo at the 2011 Glastonbury Festival. It's known in INTELCOM as the 'Portaloo Massacre'.

Even by the standards of the modern Tory Party this was a trifle unusual. It's not quite clear why GO2 knocked him off, but it may have been related to the earlier assassination. Follow-up murders are not uncommon, in order to cover up the first one. Of course, it is not suggested that Lord Cameron, Prime Minister at the time, was in the loop. He rarely knew what his government was up to, with respect.

The Cumbrian Massacre

On 5th June 2010 a GO2 asset, Derrick Bird, who was unaware that he was working for Germany, went on a shooting spree in Cumbria, the silly new name for Cumberland. Bird was recruited at the Windscale nuclear facility, where he worked. It has attracted close German intelligence attention since the nearby Calder Hall nuclear power station was opened. He shot 24 people in three separate phases using weapons which Cumbria Police were content for him to have, before being executed by police. They then pretended that he had shot himself, a feat, which would have been easier had he not abandoned his guns in the boot of his car and been unarmed at the time of his death. The inquiry was yet another farce, no offence intended. The media, as per usual, were tame, recycling any old nonsense that was doled out to them by the police, without critical comment.

There was the usual, pointless handwringing in Parliament and by the local bishops. All of them focused on the motivations of Derrick Bird and not the people who were paying him to do the killings. No explanation for the large amounts of cash he had been handling was considered too risible to be foisted upon the long-suffering public. They could have been reprinted in a Ladybird Book of Massacres. The intellectual level of discussion of the massacre in Parliament and the press, with respect, would have been disappointing in a state-school primary class.

The massacre was accompanied by ritual cries for more gun control, which as usual missed two rather obvious points:

(1) Bird didn't meet the *existing* criteria for possession of firearms, which had not been enforced by the police. Why therefore could they be expected to enforce stricter criteria? and

(2) Probably none of his victims would have been shot had they been armed.

This was not the first mass shooting in Britain. There have been many more in America as well, two of which I deal with below. There was one in 2011 in Norway and one at the old penal settlement of Port Arthur, near Hobart in the lovely state of Tasmania, Australia, in 1996. Part of this book was written not far away.

There was a particularly egregious mass shooting of primary school children at Dunblane in Scotland in 1996, one of the survivors of which was the Wimbledon champion Andy Murray. This prompted Parliament to pass the ludicrous Firearms Act 1997. The Act did nothing to prevent the next massacre of course. It has mostly inconvenienced sportsmen, none of whom had ever shot up a primary school class, nor were ever likely to, it was carried out by a known GO2 asset, Thomas Hamilton.

As mentioned earlier he had been running a paedophile ring on behalf of GO2, which had been supplying boys to bent Scottish judges, policemen and pro-EU politicians. Like Bird he too was shot by police to silence him. The official explanation was that he shot himself with a .357 magnum revolver through the roof of his mouth and was still alive several minutes later. You are not encouraged to try this at home, but generally speaking people who discharge a .357 through the rooves of their mouths die rather more swiftly than that. Even if they have very small brains - and Thomas Hamilton probably believed in global warming - it's a bit difficult to miss from that distance.

The shooter at Hungerford in Berkshire 1987, Michael Ryan, was also probably working for GO2, but the incident was never seriously investigated. The shooter at Virginia Tech, Seung-Hui Cho, who disgracefully murdered 32 students and professors on 16th April 2007, was an agent of North Korean intelligence, as verified at the time by the South Korean CIA. They are trained by the American CIA and are very efficient. He was a sleeper, who had moved to the south at a very young age and was then infiltrated into the States, disguised as a student. By 'sleeper' I do not mean that he snored in class.

The 1996 Port Arthur shooter, Martin Bryant, had been 'left a very large sum of money', the provenance of which was never traced. The rich relative theory was swallowed *in toto* by the authorities. It's a popular method for laundering intelligence payments. That case was never fully investigated either but bears all the hallmarks of a classic DVD operation. There is a large DVD station in Canberra and they seem to have a paedophile ring in Tasmania. It burst into the semi-open when a local politician was arrested after sleeping with a 12-year-old prostitute, her other clients, who apparently included more senior politicians and civil servants, being let off.[7]

Again you are not encouraged to try this at home, but should you go out in public and start waving around an automatic weapon you will very often find the police swiftly in attendance. In London an Irishman cannot walk out of a pub with a table leg in a plastic bag without getting shot by the police. Even a barrister[8] cannot wave a shotgun around and take the odd pot shot at passers-by without being shot dead by police, let alone an Irishman (there are some very nice Irish barristers at the English Bar of course).

There are a number of common themes to mass-shooting incidents:

(1) Firearms controls are relaxed by the police.
(2) The shooters are allowed plenty of time in which to carry out the killings, i.e. police response is delayed.
(3) The shooters are themselves shot dead by the police, usually after they have run out of ammunition, or are declared insane, so there is no trial.
(4) The police investigate themselves, or the investigation is heavily dependent upon the same police force, which did nothing to stop the massacre in the first place, and
(5) No MISE (Money, Ideology, Sex and Ego) checks are carried out on the shooters, i.e. there is no serious counterintelligence investigation into sources of cash payments or other income, or

linked paedophile rings who may have supplied children for sexual abuse by the shooter.

Clearly MI5 should take the lead into the investigation of any further incidents in Britain, and in so far as there is police involvement it should come from a separate force. Where it is proposed to avoid a trial by having the shooter declared insane independent psychiatrists, preferably used to criminal profiling, should be brought in. Where the shooters are themselves shot dead there should always be a second autopsy. The media could help by asking serious questions, instead of just accepting massacres as a fact of life.

GO2

It would be difficult to overstate the amount of anger GO2 have generated with their campaign of murder and mayhem. This includes protecting the two main distribution cartels for drugs in the UK, which between them probably account for about 30,000 of the roughly 35,000 or so drugs- related deaths, mostly of young people, in the UK each year. There is a clean-up headed their way that is going to have the survivors wandering around their HQ at Vauxhall Cross (most MI6 officers are blissfully unaware that they share their headquarters with Germany's operation in London) in a state of shock.

Suffice to say that that the UK and Germany are in a state of undeclared quasi-war. It would be appropriate to use methods normally reserved for wartime to deal with GO2, most of whose officers are traitors, as worthy of execution as Sir Edward Bridges, Sir Horace Wilson, Lord Halifax, Roy Jenkins and the rest were in World War II. Of course, since we British are the Good Guys, people would only be executed in the nicest possible way, having been spoken to first.

It is a myth by the way that murderers are strong people. In my experience (and I've come across several, including in prison) they are weak, place far too high a value upon their own miserable lives and are usually willing to cut a deal if the alternative means stepping into the execution chamber. In fairness, it should be pointed out that Saddam Hussein chose execution when I suggested cutting a deal, and went to his death quite well. Albert Pierrepoint, the famous hangman, made this point to the Home Office after executing convicted German war criminals, humanely of course, after '45. He was a fair man and a first-rate hangman. There's no need to use piano wire, not unless someone has been particularly difficult.

Thankfully, Parliament has the power to make the death penalty retrospective as regards both treason and murder. Making it retrospective for murder would be bound to attract complaints, especially from murderers, and generate letters to *The Times*. Retrospectivity for high treason poses no legal or ethical dilemmas and should be done.

The Madoff Affair

The problems, which can flow from official denial of the existence of Medium Term Note trading and the offshore economy, were neatly illustrated by the curious case of the New York financier Bernie Madoff. He had traded clients' funds quite successfully, generating large profits for the banks and smallish profits (by MTN standards) for his clients. The SEC, the FBI and the prosecution tied themselves in knots trying to pretend to the learned judge (who must have been a bit puzzled at how Madoff's investment vehicle had survived due diligence by banks the size of Deutsche), the media and everybody else that Mr Madoff had been running a Ponzi scheme.

Charles Ponzi was a 1920s crook who made a fairly small amount of money by trading on the difference in the value of vouchers for stamps on both sides of the Atlantic for a short while after the war. It was a classic pyramid scheme, where fresh investors were enticed in on the basis of returns paid out to earlier investors. The only cash coming in was from the investors themselves. It was a game of financial musical chairs. It had to stop some time, and it did, when the authorities smelt a rat.

Madoff was *not* running a Ponzi scheme. The cash was coming in not just from new investors but, from MTN trading. If you are a financial journalist and would like to write a serious article on the Madoff Affair all you need is a list of how much money was paid in, how much was paid out and a pocket calculator.

The Brisbane Flood

In January 2011 Brisbane, the capital city of Queensland, was flooded. This was done on the orders of a DVD asset in Canberra, which is badly penetrated. A new dam, Wivenhoe, had been built in the 1970s, to save Brisbane from dangerous flooding. It holds so much water however that it can be a threat. This was spotted, pressure was brought to bear and after heavy rain a massive release of water was timed to coincide with a spring tide at Brisbane, about 36 hours later. The beautiful subtropical city was flooded badly. The decision to flood Brisbane was clearly political and equally clearly wrong.

The Oslo Massacre

This makes sense if one thinks about the SHEWS facility in northern Norway, which the Norwegians are trying to shut down. There were two shooters at least, and police assistance, e.g. in the provision of a uniform and the holding-up of the police response. Breivik, the one shooter who was arrested, was not religious, nor was he connected with any right-wing group.

It is highly improbable he wrote the 'manifesto' attributed to him. The trial was a farce, with respect, with neither prosecution nor defence willing to admit the presence of another shooter, who was caught on satellite. At any rate the infrared images of him were - he was hiding in the treeline.

The Nuclear Threat to the London Olympics

My next book! In April 2012 a number of websites went public on a possible nuclear threat to the London Olympics, a known DVD target. The Internet journalists included Ben Fulford, who had correctly predicted the Fukushima attack. There are, not that many people who can say that they have correctly predicted a nuclear attack, so take a bow, Ben. Thousands of lives would have been saved had the Japanese government and security services paid greater attention to what he was saying. They are now.

The security for the London Olympics was rightly described as an 'omnishambles'. There was a confirmed Iranian nuclear threat to the Games, involving one of the 15 kiloton ARMSCOR weapons from South Africa, in 2011. Even after that threat was deterred *no one* in the near catatonically useless Olympic Security Directorate (no offence), nor MI5, was monitoring the *only website in the world* which had a track record of predicting a nuclear attack. The OSD were so ill informed, with respect, that they were probably still working on the discredited theory that Fukushima was a natural, as opposed to manmade, disaster.

Fortunately, not everyone was asleep on watch. I passed on a warning to the Secretary of State for Defence, in good faith, which had been passed on to me by Ben, and got arrested for my pains by Thames Valley Police. They are Britain's answer to *Police Squad,* no offence intended, but with a worse clear-up record and no one to match Frank Drebin's intellect. All my copies of this book were seized at the same time, and not returned. Thankfully it was backed up offshore, which is why you are able to read it. A nice Eurosceptic Cabinet Minister, a member of the new National Security Council, tipped me off to the involvement of the Cabinet Office, by leaving a name on an e-mail distribution list.

The DVD took advantage of my incarceration in Aylesbury Police Station to exfiltrate one of *two* improvised nuclear devices they had smuggled into east London. Thankfully, the exfiltration was caught on satellite. The existence of a possible nuclear/radiological threat to the Olympics was officially confirmed by the Foreign Office, on MI6 advice, in November 2012. MI6 of course work with CIA, who in turn talk too NSA and NRO. They therefore tend to be better informed than MI5. Until any improvised nuclear device, has been examined by experts it is not possible of course to determine how it has been configured. Only small changes are needed to a viable nuclear device to turn it into a 'dirty' bomb. Nuclear monitoring of the Olympic site was stepped up after April, as was the heat on the DVD. The second device was also pulled out, by sea, surface this time rather than sub. Amusingly the nuclear signature was apparently caught by an EU-funded website set up for monitoring peaceful nuclear shipments. MI5 and the police were spectators in all of this. Unsurprisingly, the then MI5 Director-General, Sir Jonathan Evans, now Lord Evans, was forced out in March 2013 and replaced by his more able deputy, with respect, Andrew Parker. He is a bird watcher. There are those in INTELCOM, not necessarily including myself of course, who would say that this was a rare case of an intelligence agency replacing a birdbrain with a bird watcher.

Andrew Parker made his name in MI5 (known in the trade as 'Box') by uncovering the nasty Liquid Bomb Plot in 2006, for which our old friend 'Pardis' was the quartermaster. MI5 got on to him after he lodged a bogus Bar Council compliant against me. Some of the Islamic terrorists involved in that outrage were based around High Wycombe, in Buckinghamshire.

I was eventually convicted, after a corrupt official in the Ministry of Justice, R, blackmailed the learned trial judge, His Honour Judge McCreath, who was later murdered by GO2 to ensure his silence. The jury was tampered with. MOD wiped the tape of their call to me containing the alleged 'bomb hoax' and on instructions from the Cabinet Secretary, Sir Jeremy Heywood, taken out by MI5 in 2018, destroyed their contemporaneous note.

It was never intended that I get out of prison alive. One plot, foiled by MI5, involved my being sent to a prison on the Isle of Wight and being forced to share a cell with an ISIS terrorist, to whom a large knife was apparently supplied. The idea was he would proceed to saw my head off, which would have been irritating. As explained, I was then forced to share a cell with the gay serial killer Stephen Port, but happily I was not his type.

To deter me from cross-examining MOD witnesses over the destruction of material evidence the CPS came up with the bright idea of having Thames Valley Police plant some underage gay images on a SanDisk memory stick which *looked* like one unlawfully seized from my flat. Unhappily for them it was assembled *after* I was supposed to have downloaded the images. Even more unhappily for the rozzers, it emerged that the prosecution metadata weren't downloaded at all, but transferred from another device. Many thanks to the NSA for suggesting the take over of SanDisk by a friendly contractor, after which the truth about the memory stick came out.

I was disbarred in 2019 on the basis of these bogus convictions, but each has collapsed completely. Whitehall are desperate to hang onto them, and other convictions obtained at Southwark Crown Court, where there has been systematic jury tampering. Like Watergate the cover-up is turning out to be as even more scandalous than the original crime. Justice has been delayed, but it cannot be denied forever, although with respect it may require a new Prime Minister. Sir Keir Starmer was of course the DPP when each charge was sanctioned.

The Aurora and Sandy Hook Shootings

The grotesque intelligence failure to uncover the truth behind the disgraceful shooting of Congresswoman Giffords in January 2011 led, inevitably, to further mass-shootings. The DVD will only stop using this tactic if somebody, somewhere, gets a grip and mounts a serious investigation.

That certainly was not done over the Aurora cinema shootings in Denver CO in July 2012. Clearly more than one person was involved, but you would never guess it from the monolithic media presentation of the single perpetrator theory. I am not saying there was more than one shooter in the cinema, but others were involved. Apart from anything else Holmes, the shooter, lacked the explosives expertise to rig the booby trap found in his apartment.

Encouraged no doubt by its 'success' at Aurora, the DVD organized a further mass-shooting at the Sandy Hook Elementary School, Newtown CT. They seem to like shooting up school kids, remembering Dunblane. INTELCOM was able to get more of a handle on this one, as there was some SATINT. It looks as though the shootings were timed for a gap in NRO satellite coverage, but somebody forgot the Russians.

Newtown is not that far from Groton, CT, home of the famed Electric Boat Company, which also has a facility at New London, even nearer to Sandy Hook. Electric Boat Company have long been a source of interest to the GRU. The Russian birds tend to track from New London to Groton, so that one bird covers both yards. It looks like one of their birds caught part of the Sandy Hook shooting on an oblique camera. A satellite does *not* have to be directly overhead to capture useful imagery.

There were at least three shooters, two of whom, got away. It looks as though Adam Lanza was shot, rather than committed suicide. There is no particular reason to suppose that he shot his poor mother. My understanding is that the shooters were from the Latin Kings narcotics gang and have since been taken out themselves. The DVD do not like witnesses. Using a gang in this way is a standard DVD tactic. They will always stay deep. The official investigation and mainstream media reporting plumbed new depths of shallowness, if you will forgive the pun.

There has been one mass shooting after another since, many involving school kids. At some point somebody will get a grip, possibly after a copy of this book is handed over to President Trump. I just hope that not too many more young lives are thrown away in the meantime.

1. One of my sources on MTN trading was a bank Senior Vice-President before he was briefed in. Most bank officers are left in the dark, unless they are at an offshore branch.
2. Some in INTELCOM go with a hospital in downtown Colon, Panama.
3. Sheriff Arpaio was America's most distinguished and best-known lawman, arguably the most famous Sheriff since Wyatt Earp. He ran a tight ship down there in Maricopa County, AZ, and was known for being both firm and fair.
4. Breguet Atlantique, 2 Rolls-Royce Tyne turboprop engines. It looks a bit like a small Orion.
5. Apparently, he has reservations about declaring war on Germany as well.
6. As in the famous episode about the 'Henderson Report', on 'Metadioxin', *The Greasy Pole* (Series 2, Episode 4, airdate 16th March 1981). Classic Whitehall farce.
7. The case was *R v Terry Martin*, dealt with by Justice David Porter at the Tasmania Supreme Court in December 2011, and dealt with rather well if I may say so. The learned judge clearly got a flavour of disproportionately severe treatment for Martin, who was suffering from Parkinsons Disease and seemed to have been treated as expendable. At any rate his sentence was suspended and rightly so in the circumstances.
8. This was the tragic case of Mark Sawyer, who seems with respect to have been a bit stressed. At any rate it was unusual behaviour for a barrister. The poor chap may have been made the subject of a bogus complaint to the Bar Council, or a frivolous negligence suit - at any rate it is still a little unclear as to why he acted as he did. The Iranian police officer that ordered the shooting had very properly been accused by the prosecution at his trial in 2003 of being an Iranian agent although on that occasion he was acquitted (he was in between prosecutions when he ordered the shooting and was later jailed for corruption and rightly so, with respect).

31

A Way Out Of Here

A Short War With Germany

The simplest solution would be a short (i.e. two-front) war with Germany. As in the 1930s however politicians and the media much prefer to bury their heads in the sand, which will cost us many more casualties in the long run. World War II only lasted six years because that's what the politicians wanted. A war with Germany in 1936 would have lasted a few months at most.

There can be no question of peace with Germany for so long as there remains a Germany. Like Iran in the Middle East and China in the Asia Pacific, Germany is an aggressor nation, determined to dominate and exploit her neighbours. That has been the case since Britain took the disastrous strategic decision not to go to the aid of Denmark in 1864. That paved the way for German unification, a series of German-sponsored colonial wars, two world wars, four genocides, against the Jews, the Cambodians, the Rwandans and in Darfur, and three murderous WMD campaigns, Spanish Flu, AIDS and Covid.

The Good Guys - including America, Britain, Canada, Russia, Israel, Australia and New Zealand - are already locked into a semi-permanent quasi-war with Germany. It will continue to blow up into hot wars all over the planet. Since the DVD controls all major narcotics trafficking, a low-intensity war is being fought continuously in almost every major city of the Western world.

If you visit once-peaceful Nottingham you are as likely to hear the crackle of gunfire as the sound of willow on leather at the Trent Bridge cricket ground. The casualties are enormous, hundreds a week due to drugs in Britain, thousands in America. The hidden, civilian casualties from narcotics trafficking far exceeded military casualties in the Global War on Terror.

The cost of the German-sponsored GFC, the massive costs to Britain of EU membership until Brexit, addressed below, ridiculously overpriced energy and the colossal cost of dealing with a non-problem - 'global warming' - in a cooling period far outweigh the costs of war. A new *casus belli* comes along every few months or so, although as a matter of international law a state can require another state waging low-intensity warfare inside its frontiers to cease and desist.

Clearly any war should be declared. The war planning has already been done, mostly by the excellent Russian and Polish general staffs, and war has already broken out, in the Ukraine. Far seeing military planners in Britain and America have had to contemplate war with Germany ever since German sponsorship of *al Qaeda* was confirmed within INTELCOM by *inter alia* satellite observation of the DVD's HQ in Dachau.

The key to a quick victory lies in engaging the Bundeswehr on two fronts, making full use of the terrain of the North German Plain. This favours large-scale armoured thrusts by shock armies. This should be coupled with rapid achievement of air superiority over the Luftwaffe and effective use of strategic bombing, taking great care to avoid collateral civilian casualties, as in World War II.

There is no point waiting for German politicians to shut down the DVD and stop its war against the West. They couldn't even if they wanted to. The Bundestag is no more effective a legislature than the Reichstag, upon which it was modelled, nor the European Parliament, another Reichstag clone. We will have to do the job ourselves, and break Germany up into her constituent components. Schleswig-Holstein should be returned to its rightful owner, the Queen of Denmark.

There is no *animus* in the West towards the German people. Restored states like Prussia and Bavaria, especially under their ancient royal houses, would swiftly re-join the Western world. Unified Germany has never been a true Western power, only an *ersatz* one. St Petersburg is a truer Western city than Frankfurt.

It is not terribly surprising that Germany's great cultural contributions to Western civilisation generally predate political unification. Try and name a great German composer of the 20th century, a period in which the Americans produced Gershwin and Meatloaf. As for poets, have they produced anybody to match Goethe, i.e. what have they done recently?

Other states on the Axis of Evil (not for nothing did America's great President George W. Bush refer back to the Axis in describing the enemy in the Global War on Terror), which runs from Berlin through Damascus to Teheran, Peking and Pyongyang, will have to be dealt with. As effective German client states they may get drawn into a war with Germany, or they may collapse like the USSR.

In particular, the Han Empire in China has a number of fault-lines. It is very vulnerable to economic sanctions, and sea mining. China depends on the West to keep buying her exports, as President Trump has grasped with respect. They also depend on is letting her buy up oil and raw materials at a discount. China's economic success is at other people's expense. We can turn off the tap whenever we want. That includes the US, which only needs to sell her debt to China if she continues with President Johnson's disastrous welfare and immigration policies, i.e. runs unnecessary deficits, something only now being addressed.

The problems with having a war with Germany is that it would work, at a much lower cost in lives and treasure than the alternatives, and would lead to a more peaceful world. As in the 1930s politicians will first wish to exhaust all the alternatives before doing the right thing. Sadly, the quality of leadership in Britain, France, and elsewhere, apart from Washington, is no better than it was in the 1930s. Barack Obama wouldn't have made it into Franklin Roosevelt's cabinet, let alone the White House, and not on the grounds of his colour either. Why couldn't they have elected Morgan Freeman or James Earl Jones instead? James Earl Jones would have been great. At least he was elected, unlike Joe Biden.

Since our politicians favour a state of semi-permanent quasi-war with Germany, we are going to have to sacrifice more blood and treasure than we need to. We're in for a long, thin war, if you like, as opposed to a short, fat one. The current policy is to lie to electorates in the hope that no one will discover trading programmes, or Germany's covert sponsorship of terrorism and organised crime.

However, there are lots of things we can do to mitigate the loss of life, save money and generally make life easier for everyone, except the Bad Guys. We don't have to be helpless spectators to one disaster and boo-boo after another. For that matter, is there no law in America, Britain, Canada, Australia or any democracy that says that only useless politicians can be elected, it's just the practice.

Medium Term Note Trading Programmes

The programmes, howsoever described ('private placements of capital' were popular for a while) have to be shut down. For the reasons explained in the last chapter they inflict enormous economic damage on the democracies (clearly Germany's claim to be a democracy is bogus) and provide huge offshore resources to fund terrorism and prop up dictatorships. They cannot be shut down entirely unless and until Frankfurt is occupied, or its central business district and the Correa Group HQ near the airport are bombed into rubble, nicely of course.

Participation by western companies and individuals can be banned however, and unpaid tax revenues collected. The basic rule is that individuals and companies domiciled in a country are obliged to pay tax on all earnings whether onshore or offshore. Income may be easier to disguise offshore but tax cheats regularly conflate the issues of the ease of committing tax fraud and whether or not it is legal. Burglars often suffer similar confusion.

Of course, it could not be done without cleaning up our penetrated state bureaucracies and central banks but we should be doing that anyway. Lower inflation, higher tax revenues, increased bank stability and greater lending to small and medium sized enterprises as banks were forced to earn their profits by supporting other businesses are all desirable outcomes. We don't have to run our economies like a junkie running his household budget, nor is it illegal for governments and banks to be honest with the public. Deception of the public is the norm, but it's not mandatory.

Tariff Reform

Asian countries in particular expect us to buy their products but are not so willing to buy ours. They want us to export our jobs to them, and pay for the privilege through increased taxes to support the resultant unemployment. It's time this nonsense - the economics of the madhouse - was brought to an end. Thankfully President Trump is getting to grips with the problem.

In early 2012 a political row (the locals call it a stoush) broke out in Australia over the perfectly reasonable policy of the Australian government of support supporting what was then its local car industry. Unlike Japan's (until the early 1990s), and China's, Australia's car industry did not benefit from Frankfurt's trading programmes, laundered through soft loans. Why not simply increase tariffs? Thailand sold more cars in Australia than Aussie-built Fords and Holdens combined, which was silly. Of course since nothing was done there are no more Aussie built cars.

If you tried to export a Holden Commodore (a fine Aussie product, just right for driving on Australian roads) to Bangkok you would not pay much of a tariff on the car but you would on the engine, which was a nonsense. Had Australia protected her jobs and taxpayers with tariffs which fairly reflected the Asian trade barriers erected against her goods, not only would local car-makers have survived but the federal government would have an additional revenue stream.

'Ah', the economists say, 'but we have a global economy'. We don't, actually. You try shipping goods from one country to another and see how global the economy is. As far as most of Asia is concerned, especially China and Japan, it's a one-way street. What we have is a series of interconnected economies. Free trade is a great idea, but it only works between free countries that are actually willing to buy from each other, in which case both benefit.

Britain and America make an ideal trade fit, indeed a free trade agreement should have been concluded at the end of World War II. America is still Britain's largest trading partner. The EU is a series of economies, despite official propaganda to the contrary. Our two great countries should conclude a comprehensive free trade agreement without delay. We've agreed a deal, but it only goes so far.

The speed of modern communications can be exaggerated. Clipper ships in the 19th century put in better times between Britain and Australia than modern, diesel-powered container ships, few of which could outrun *Titanic*. There is scarcely an ocean liner afloat which would have a hope of catching the dear old RMS *Queen Elizabeth*, especially in any sort of sea. The, Blue Riband of the Atlantic would still be held by the fast and elegant SS *United States*[2] if speedboats hadn't been included. Since it was a trophy for passenger liners it's still not clear to me why speedboats *were* included.

Air travel across the Atlantic has got a lot slower since the French forced Concorde out of service. Modern airliners are not appreciably faster than the de Havilland Comet 4 of 1958, the first transatlantic jetliner. They are bigger and fly further, with reduced levels of service, but no faster. The post in Britain was faster before World War I. Travel by car is slower than it used to be and train service in most countries has deteriorated below prewar standards of service and comfort, if it's available at all. High-speed trains are much faster but are more cramped, with poor levels of food service. They also only operate on limited routes. Travel is generally more stressful and less pleasant than it used to be.

Welfare Reform

This isn't rocket science. Welfare spending in the West is way out of control, to the point where the state is encouraging the breakup of relationships and young people find it more economic to be on welfare than in work. Equating less severe mental illnesses such as depression with physical disability has hugely driven up the cost of sickness benefit in the UK, triggering a crisis in the Labour Government.

The upshot is that defence budgets have been squeezed to the point where national security has been damaged. The Obama Administration was able to get away with scrapping NASA's planned mission to Mars. Clearly there has to be some welfare spending but there is no need to hose money around as we are doing at the moment. As that that nice man, the late Labour MP Frank Field, pointed out, welfare dependency has done no favours for the working class. Budgets could probably be slashed by up to a third without doing any harm indeed it would do some good.

Immigration Reform

Since the overwhelming majority of immigrants from the Third World are not bringing needed skills, let alone capital, they provide little or no economic benefit. They drive down wages but that it is a double-edged sword since the wages they are driving down are of working class people who either have less to spend as a result or go on welfare. That is not to count the human cost. A million young people are unemployed in Britain. In England the huge number of immigrants is also imposing strains on health and social services, public transport and even the roads. That's before we get to the threats to national security posed by imported or dual-national Islamic extremists, as demonstrated at Woolwich, and the threat to national cohesion posed by large-scale Muslim immigration.

Immigration can to some extent be reversed, as much of it is illegal. It's not difficult to catch illegals, but the British government has never tried very hard. President Trump is showing the way on this one! Limiting immigration is not that difficult either. You just have things like passports that are not easily forged, fences without gaps or holes in them, visas which can be checked online and more immigration officers at airports. Illegal immigration through the Channel Tunnel in Britain was easily stopped.

Asylum fraud is now so commonplace the system has degenerated into a complete farce, costing far more lives than it saves by encouraging dangerous illegal immigration. Just look at the regularly swamped boats endeavouring to reach Australia and the current farce in the English Channel. The Refugee Convention is both outdated and discredited. Western states should simply withdraw from it.

A replacement convention could emphasise regional protection, expressly permit temporary protection visas and require the balance of probabilities standard of proof. Most Western states require 'proof' of persecution only to the absurdly low 'reasonable degree of likelihood standard'. A new asylum convention could also replace the badly worded definition of 'refugee' in the flawed 1951 Convention, so old it was drawn up before the age of *I Love Lucy* re-runs.

Existing 'refugees' have usually only been granted that status after a sloppy investigation of their claims. Sometimes they have not been investigated at all. There is no reason at all why their cases should not be reviewed, if need be using personnel released from processing fresh claims by an asylum pause. Why should someone who has lied their way into Britain or America be allowed to stay?

Subsidising immigration is enormously expensive, mainly due to the costs of labour displacement. These outstrip the defence budget in the UK and probably come close to the size of the defence budget in the USA, partly because each is ludicrously low. It's not enough for an immigrant to say, "I am working and paying taxes" if he or she is displacing an indigenous worker onto the dole queue. That worker then has to be supported. Many immigrants occupy public housing or rely on public services such as the National Health Service in Britain. If the immigrant is illegal, not paying tax and remitting funds abroad it makes even less economic sense.

Government Waste

Government waste is staggering, caused by overregulation, needlessly large bureaucracies and pointless official bodies. Elon Musk made the point effectively during his brief period on charge of DOGE.

Billions are wasted on overseas aid, which is designed to prop up corrupt governments and subsidise unwanted consultants. Quantifying waste is difficult. It's a moving target, getting bigger each year, and not because we are homing in on it! The reputable Taxpayers Alliance in the UK came up with a figure of £80 billion a year about ten years ago. It's probably around £150 billion now.

The federal government in Washington is a past master at wasting money. It cannot, surely, be throwing away proportionately fewer taxpayers' dollars than Whitehall is throwing away pound notes (or coins). That is to say the federal government during the Biden years was probably wasting about a trillion dollars a year, not counting all the tax it failed to collect from people who have no right to be in America at all.

China

China only became the world's second largest economy because we let them. Whitehall and Washington know full well that she has benefitted enormously from MTN trading programmes, subsidised by Western economies in the way described in Chapter 28. Absurdly low tariffs, except for the US, mean that Chinese goods come into the West virtually for free, whilst Western goods are effectively prohibited from China. When she does purchase our goods she usually steals the IP and then turns around and makes them herself.

Unrestricted access to Western telecommunications networks makes it easy for China to export computer viruses. Western governments have been content to let China exploit African countries like Zimbabwe and Zambia, removing raw materials at rock-bottom prices, pun intended. As explained the world oil price is a complete fraud. It most certainly is not the price paid by China, which gets her oil at a deep discount from client states.

The rise of China is only inevitable if we want it to be. China is not the cohesive society the left and the mainstream media pretend. Like the bad old USSR there is an ethnic and cultural core, surrounded by subject peoples. Just as the USSR was a Russian empire, so the People's Republic of China is a Han empire. The occupation of Tibet has been no less brutal than the occupation of the Baltic Republics (rather a nice part of the world by the way). The Dalai Lama and his people have been betrayed by weak Western governments. It's high time that Tibet was freed.

Communist China has waged, supported or threatened aggression against almost all of her neighbours or near-neighbours. These include South Korea, Russia (over the Amur River frontier), India (which it invaded in 1960 and part of whose territory is still illegally occupied by Chinese troops), Burma (a Chinese client state), Vietnam and Nepal. The latter succumbed to an outrageous Chinese-backed terrorist campaign after a disgraceful lack of support from India and Britain.

The obvious way forward is for Britain, Canada and America to recognise Taiwan, which would probably prompt a break of trade and diplomatic relations with Peking. The Taiwanese are nice people, not just because they occasionally invite me in for a drinkies. Unlike the ChiComs, they are serious trade partners, in the sense that they see trade as a two- way street. They also don't steal intellectual property. All restrictions on the sale of defence material to Taiwan should be lifted. The boys need all the materiel they can get.

Maintaining International Subscriber Dialling facilities with mainland China is a preposterous nonsense. They will keep trying to hack into our systems. They will also keep laundering computer viruses through 'teenage geniuses' etc. How many actual teenage geniuses have you met, by the way? Why should we make it so easy for them? It is way past time that we fried a few of their systems in retaliation. China is not a responsible member of the international community, as demonstrated when she developed and then spread Covid, after losing control of it, and there is no point in treating them as such.

The ChiComs would be hurt disproportionately by a withdrawal of the MTN trading programmes and would probably be embarrassed by greater transparency over private gold holdings. They are some very dodgy people in China, hanging on to a lot more gold than their wives need for bangles. They are part of an opaque power structure Peking does not want us to know about.

It's high time that Peking were reminded who won the Opium Wars and probably about time we British explained why an army was sent to China and captured Hong Kong. I suspect that upon inquiry it will be found that the Secret Office discovered that some of Napoleon's funding came out of China, in the form of gold.[3] You can stockpile an awful lot of gold over 5,000 years. 3,000 BC is the earliest credible date for the first actual, as opposed to recorded, gold mine. One thing I have learnt is that whilst history may not be bunk, recorded history usually is.

Iran

Iran needs sorting, but NOT by nuclear means. Only a suicidal lunatic would attack a nuclear-armed state with nuclear weapons. If left in place she will continue to terrorise her neighbours and Israel. Unsurprisingly Iran is a major source of cheap oil for China, an interesting reflection of deep Persia-China links, which go back to the age of Darius and Xerxes. They were the ancient world's answer to Ayatollah Khomeini and Mahmoud Ahmadinejad. The only way of dealing with her is a ground war, preferably declared, the *casus belli* being Iran's repeated Acts of War against her neighbours and Israel. The American and Israeli attacks in 2025 were a start, but they left the regime in place and only damaged Iran.

The threat posed by the Iranian Navy has been greatly exaggerated. In a declared war the Royal Navy and US Navy should be able to defeat it easily, paying careful attention of course to the dangerous Iranian *Kilo* class submarines with their German-trained officers.

The Shah-era F-4 Phantoms and F-14 Tomcats should not be discounted either, not least since they have been maintained with German technical assistance. Each can easily carry nuclear weapons by the way, one reason not to get too excited over intelligence about the difficulties Iran has had in matching its plutonium-cored warheads with intermediate range ballistic missile delivery systems.

This would mean larger conventional forces, but the West's forces are far too small anyway. A means has to be found somehow of freeing up Western politicians from their obsession with small (in Britain's case, tiny) militaries and their desire to wage war on the cheap. These obsessions reflect the inability of politicians to control our inefficient, penetrated and corrupt state bureaucracies and bring burgeoning welfare budgets and mass immigration under control.

It is also fair to say that Western leaders are generally militarily illiterate. President Obama for example struggled with military ranks when visiting bases. His military experience before gaining office was probably limited to watching *Pearl Harbor* on Home Box Office, which wouldn't have taught him much. David Cameron is so militarily illiterate with respect that he thought that the USAF participated in the Battle of Britain, which took place seven years before the USAF was formed out of the USAAF. Where we have brigades we need divisions, where we have squadrons we need wings and where we have lone ships we need flotillas.

Pakistan

Pakistan also needs sorting. The current policy - of handing over large amounts of cash to Pakistan, disguised as 'aid,' to spend on buying weapons and explosives for the Taliban to blow us up - makes about as much sense as having Lancasters and B-17s drop gold bars by parachute on Berlin in World War II. The recent hostilities with India make my point.

Cash in an account can be used without it ever leaving that account, just by blocking it and running a line of credit against it. There are almost no checks on whether or not aid monies have been misused in this way.

The Pakistani Army is not to be underestimated. Some of the best regiments in the Indian Army went into it on the Partition of India in 1947. It would struggle however once their air force had been eliminated. There is no reason for Pakistan to exist. Its creation, sponsored by the DVD, was a bad mistake, for which many have paid with their lives. India can and should be reunited.

The Cost to the UK of EU Membership

When the Treasury under Gordon Brown conducted its famous 'five tests' on euro membership it realised that many of the arguments against the euro - such as that it was an insane idea - also applied to membership of the EU itself. The idea that EEC membership was economically beneficial to Britain was a mantra. Like most mantras it has never been subjected to critical analysis. It was simply political establishment group thinking. Like most group thought it was more group than thought.

The Treasury quietly went on to calculate how economically damaging EU membership was to Britain plc. They came up with a figure of around £175 billion for the financial year 2004/5, mostly made up of the cost to business and central and local government of excessive EU regulation. The regulatory cost to government is a factor often overlooked. NHS hospitals, e.g., have to comply with daft EU directives on doctors' working hours, even now, designed to make them more dangerous places than they already are.

Labour displacement was the second biggest ticket item, but the Common Agricultural and Fisheries Polices was also deeply damaging to Britain. The figure does not include opportunity costs, i.e. lost GDP as a result of having the British economy strangled by the burden of EU membership.

The cost reached the order of £200 billion a year before we finally pulled the plug. It's important to make the point because some idiots are talking about us going back in. One result of that thinking is that we still adhere to the pointless European Convention on Human Rights, a requirement of EU membership. We may have left the EU but we still can't control our borders. President Macron with respect reversed the truth when he impertinently lectured the Britain on his 2025 state visit. (It is never a good idea to abuse your hosts on a state visit.)

Defence

The UK's risibly small defence budget needs to be trebled. We are simply encouraging potential aggressors such as Iran, China and Argentina. The MOD cannot get away forever with racing the Royal Navy's pitifully small number of ships around the world's oceans from one trouble spot to another, as the Coalition did in January 2012.

They sent a *Daring* class air defence destroyer to the Falklands. They are fine ships but there aren't enough *Darings* in service to maintain a continuous presence in the South Atlantic when refit requirements are borne in mind. It is not sensible to deploy a specialist air defence vessel without adequate anti-submarine escort and air cover anyway. Argentina wants another war and we have to be ready for them.

There is plenty of cash. It's just a question of ordering priorities. The government's preference is for wasting public money, maintaining bloated and grossly inefficient welfare programmes, subsidising mass immigration and sending cash abroad to prop up corrupt governments like Pakistan's. Within the defence budget, tiny as it is, their priority is to keep MOD bureaucrats in their jobs at the expense of frontline combat units. These priorities do not necessarily best serve the British national interest.

The US defence budget is not quite as insanely low as Britain's, but America's excellent and highly professional armed forces are being asked to do too much with too little. The US Navy has been left with insufficient attack carriers after the premature decommissioning of the USS *John F Kennedy* (CV-67) and USS *Enterprise* (CVN-65).[4] Half a century is not a mandatory retirement age for an aircraft carrier.

The Royal Navy was only forced to retire HMS *Eagle*, HMS *Ark Royal* and HMS *Victorious* because of political pressure from the pro-German element in Whitehall. They were anxious to weaken the Navy and in the case of *Ark Royal* encourage an Argentine attack on the Falklands. *Eagle* could have been refitted like her sister *Ark Royal*, whilst as we have seen *Victorious* was retired prematurely after an arson attack.

Newer ships are better but the problem has been the slow build-rate of the *Nimitz* and *Gerald Ford* classes. This is partly thanks to the low priority accorded national defence by the first Bush and Clinton Administrations, which left America weak. The Obama and Biden Administrations made things worse. As in Britain weakness is the preferred option, not a choice forced on Washington by 'economic necessity'. That has been a propaganda tool used since the early 1920s to undermine the defence of the West.

Counterintelligence

We need to dramatically improve our counterintelligence. Neither MI5 nor the FBI has officially embraced the fact that the DVD exist. Both are still stuck in an institutional Intellectual Black Hole wherein terrorism is a spontaneous, not state-sponsored, phenomenon. Neither has been terribly effective in spotting penetration assets in government and their respective state bureaucracies.

Each has stood back and done nothing whilst, massive economic and social damage has been inflicted on Britain and America by those enemy assets. They have been very effective in protecting their own bureaucratic empires. Now they need with respect to demonstrate a similar effectiveness in protecting the societies they are supposed to be defending.

Marine and Aircraft Crash Investigation

The appallingly inept investigation into the ramming of Astrolabe Reef off Tauranga in New Zealand by the MV *Rena* in October 2011 demonstrated how weak Western marine incident investigation is. From the time of the *Torrey Canyon* in Britain on, the Bad Guys have known that they can cause environmental havoc with near impunity. The belief that all marine disasters are 'accidents' is not so much a mind-set as an obsession, leading to official tunnel vision.

With improved navigation systems such as GPS the idea that modern ships can wander off course by accident is becoming increasingly harder to sustain. Even the normally pliant New Zealand media, which tends with respect to take its cue from the country's principal livestock (i.e. sheep), to the point where the DVD were able to murder television journalists in Christchurch at their desks, started asking questions on that one.

Of course some marine disasters are genuine accidents. There will always be cruise ship captains, especially Italian ones, deciding to run their unstable ships onto rocks in order to provide an interesting spectacle for the people ashore. There is nothing like a capsized 100,000 ton cruise ship to get folks' attention. From time to time oil companies will put drunks who couldn't be trusted to drive an SUV in charge of super-tankers. However, most maritime disasters are staged, either as part of an insurance fraud, or by the DVD or its sister agencies, either to cause deliberate environmental despoliation or for some other nefarious reason. The DVD after all is nefarious, so it does nefarious things. Why is something you will have to ask them, admittedly that is not an easy thing to do, since officially they don't exist and they operate entirely in the shadows.

Contrary to the ads for AAIB and NTSB pushed out on satellite and cable TV in shallow programs like *Air Crash Investigation* the actual process of investigating aircraft crashes has degenerated into a complete farce. INTELCOM thought that TWA 800 was the nadir, where the NTSB solemnly tried to persuade everybody that with a fuel tank blown inwards, we were looking for an internal source of the explosion. No one counted on the French, who, as we have seen, plumbed new depths with the BEA's 'investigation' into AF447, even more of a comedy than their Concorde investigation. They could have called that one *Carry On Crashing*. The Indian AAIB are just as bad, with respect.

The NTSB, AAIB and BEA are beyond reform. There is no point trying to clean up the BEA. It's part of the institutionally corrupt Fifth Republic, where the concept of the government telling the truth is so foreign they probably think it's British. The NTSB, AAIB and their counterparts in Canada, Australia and New Zealand can safely be left to investigate hot air balloon and Cessna crashes, provided of course that nobody of significance, such as a former Alaskan senator, was on the plane. Most light plane crashes are caused by pilot error just as most lawsuits against Cessna, Piper, etc. are caused by lawyer error. This makes them highly suitable for investigation by the NTSB and AAIB, with their predilection for blaming pilots.

Serious air crash investigation needs to be handed over to the military and has to be intelligence led. Quite aside from that the fact that military crash investigators tend to be more professional and objective (the US Navy's are particularly good, but so are the RAF's and USAF's) they have much readier access to satellite and other military data. Infrared SATINT (cloud cover was too extensive for good visuals) was particularly helpful in the AF447 investigation for example. By "investigation" I mean the real one, not the Pythonesque BEA spoof.

TWA 800 called for expert interpretation of radar imagery, detailed knowledge of Iranian naval capabilities and so on. PanAm 103 required expert knowledge of the DVD and its sabotage methods, narcotics trafficking routes into the US and a deep understanding of the Bad Guy tactic of false flagging. The comparatively primitive Scottish criminal and AAIB investigations into Lockerbie were never going to get anywhere near the truth and never did. Sabotage of civil airliners by the DVD will only stop whey realise that we are no longer going to fall for fairy stories.

Aircraft Design and Operation

Modern aircraft are very safe in normal operation, but they are vulnerable to IEDs, hijacking (as on 9/11), software sabotage and surface to air missiles. As with the DC-10, where the penetrated FAA were critical to the DVD's sabotage programme, Bad Guy assets in Western governments are always on the lookout for ways to make aviation more dangerous.

These assets need to be cleared out and a top to bottom review of civil airworthiness standards instituted. Some improvements - hardening hydraulic and computer systems and lining cargo holds e.g. - are fairly straightforward. Others, like stronger aircraft structures, are a bit trickier. The problem is that we design airliners as though we were at peace, whereas we are in a quasi-war with Germany. She has a policy of bringing down commercial aircraft.

Cheap airfares might have to become less cheap but they are probably at an unsustainable level anyway. Just as the *Costa Concordia* disaster was entirely predictable - and was predicted - so is a low-cost carrier disaster due to low-cost maintenance. The first crashes due in part to contracted- out maintenance have already happened. Stronger aircraft are structurally less efficient (i.e. heavier) but safety doesn't come cheap.

There is a limit to the size of IED you can smuggle on board an aircraft.

The larger the IED the more vulnerable it is to detection. With modern materials and techniques it should be possible to make aircraft generally survivable following an IED detonation. Airline managements won't like it but they should be invited to think what that sad image of the nose section of *Clipper Maid of the Seas* lying in a Scottish field did to poor old PanAm. They were utterly innocent of any responsibility for the disaster, but were rolled over just the same. Malayasia Airlines nearly followed them.

Against that, stronger, safer aircraft will lead to lower insurance premiums. Cheaper energy would cut the cost of aluminium, carbon-fibre and titanium, not to mention the beneficial impact on the industry of cheaper aviation fuel once we get the phoney oil market straightened out. Passengers would not have to pay that much more but would welcome the increased safety. Low-cost carriers are not that popular. People don't fly with them because they like it, but because in a credit-crunched word they have to. Southwest Airlines are the exception, which proves the rule, because they're fun to fly with, so I'm told.

Passengers would probably also welcome more intelligent, less *Airplane* like airport security. It needs to focus on the threat, i.e. crazy Salafist Muslims, not elderly grandmothers. Good security does *not* require law-abiding passengers to remove their shoes and belts every time they go through security.

The naive assumption that air traffic control instructions are given in good faith in order to ensure the safety of air navigation has been shown to be flawed. Captains of Allied commercial aircraft must be given discretion to override ATC instructions where they have reasonable cause to believe they are given in order to endanger the safety of their aircraft. Such discretion would have prevented the Dan Air and KLM/PanAm disasters. At Tenerife e.g. Captain Grubb could simply have refused to backtrack until the KLM was clear.

British aircraft need more armed sky marshals on the excellent American example. Captains of civilian airliners need to be equipped with sidearms, which could be secured in arms lockers in the cockpit. They ought to be a standard feature of aircraft design. As we saw on 9/11 the crews of commercial airliners can swiftly find themselves in the front line. Crews need something more lethal than drinks carts with which to fight back. The Israelis have come up with an excellent little weapon designed to put holes in terrorists without putting them in the aircraft skin and depressurising the plane. There are a number of weapon and ammunition combinations, which can safely be used on a pressurised aircraft.

There is no reason why flight attendants, whose first responsibility is the safety of their passengers, not serving the drinks, could not have access to firearms as well. This might require a change in recruitment policy on the part of those less responsible airlines who seem to choose flight attendants on the basis of their legs rather than their brains, but so be it.

Weapons training would remind trainee flight attendants that aviation is a serious business and that thousands of innocent civilians have been murdered or hijacked on board commercial aircraft.

It would also help if civilised countries started executing air pirates, nicely of course. Handing down soft sentences or letting them go, with or without a rebate of their fare, does not work. Piracy, whether air or marine, is a crime *jure gentium* carrying the death penalty under customary international law. Since that has always been the case the usual concerns about retrospective application of the death penalty do not apply.

There is no reason why air pirates entering the jurisdiction of a responsible member of the international community should not be detained, given a fair trial and hanged, regardless of when they carried out their crime. Leila Khaled, who should have been hanged years ago, would be a good starting point, no offence intended. The soft sentence (life without parole in some cushy federal penitentiary) handed down on 16th February 2012 to the 'underpants bomber' will do nothing to deter future terrorists.[5] It is time to wake up and smell the coffee. The aviation industry woke up briefly after 9/11, then went back to sleep.

Pilots need to be briefed in on the DVD and its known sabotage modes, such as tampering with FADEC engine control software. That would have saved lived lives at Schiphol, where the bewildered Turkish 737 crew had no idea what was happening to their aircraft. Very frankly they wouldn't have had much better an idea had they survived to see themselves featured on *Air Crash Investigation*. The Air India pilots might have been able to get their plane down on the field, instead of wasting precious time trying to restart sabotaged engines.

As for airport security the efficient Israelis have shown the way. You start your security from the time the passenger books the ticket and concentrate on the threat. It's not rocket science. If Muslims do not like it, they do not have to fly. When a religious-based terrorist organisation uses its nominal religion as justification for murdering innocent women and children they must expect to cause difficulties for their co-religionists. Not using effective body scanners because some Muslims pretend to have concerns about privacy is just self-defeating nonsense. If they wish to fly out of Western airports they will go through full-body scanning and they will like it.

Ship Design and Operation

The wreck of the MV *Costa Concordia*, aside from being a near-perfect allegory,[6] serves as a timely reminder that modern naval architecture places a premium on passenger comfort and cheap operation above safety and seaworthiness. Few if any modern commercial ships are designed with a view to wartime operation, the *Queen Mary 2* being a magnificent exception. They tend to be slow, unstable in any sort of sea and run under flags of convenience by international crews chosen for their cheapness and inability to speak English, the language of the sea.

Flags of convenience should be scrapped. We need to build ships in large numbers again in Britain and America, with Admiralty subsidies for British ships, with a view to war-time deployment, à la SS *Canberra* in the Falklands War. Ships' officers need to be proper ships' officer again, i.e. their behaviour should conform to British or American, rather than European, standards.

The current policy of encouraging marine piracy by not arming crews should be abandoned. The more pirates who are shot, the better. Piracy would soon come to an end, including in the Red Sea. Officers should carry sidearms and crews should be trained in the use of assault rifles, so that automatic fire can be poured into pirates' skiffs or launches as they try to come alongside. This would leave the motherships to be deal with by Allied air and naval forces.

It would be helpful if lumbering container ships and tankers could be given a useful turn of speed in an emergency. All large ships should have a helicopter deck or landing area for marines or special forces. Such decks would need to be added in wartime anyway. Helipads on ships would assist in aeromedical evacuation in any event.

The War on Terror

It is time to go on the offensive again. We should stop pussyfooting and start taking down terrorist-sponsoring rogue states like Iran, Syria and Pakistan. Subsidising them, passing pointless UN resolutions and uttering inanities are no substitute for action. There has to be a return to the lucidity of the George W. Bush era.

The response of Western legal systems to terrorism has been a complete farce. Sadly, judges and courts have let down the societies which pay them by encouraging the murder of innocents. This is what terrorists do. It is not what judges should be doing. It is absurd that since 9/11 no terrorist described as such has been judicially executed in Britain, America, Canada or Australia. There are many reasons for this but ultimately it comes down to judicial and political weakness, however much it may be dressed up in liberal nostra. Much greater care has to be taken in the selection of judges. The current, failed, generation of senior judges should be encouraged to retire.

The War on Drugs

Since, the major terrorist organisations and the narcotics cartels are controlled by the DVD there is an obvious linkage, reflected on the ground in Afghanistan by the part-funding of the Taliban through opium trafficking.

Again, the West has tended to pussyfoot, partly because so many governments are compromised. Far more assets need to be deployed to interdict known narcotics routes. Offshore territories, which are known havens for drug cash - such as the British Virgin Islands - need to be brought more firmly under control. In practice, in Britain's case, this means getting them out of the hands of the Foreign Office and re- establishing the Colonial Office.

The offshore holdings of bent politicians in narco-states like Equatorial Guinea and the Republic of South Africa need to be exposed and seized. Shutting down GO2 in the UK would also mean closing down the two distribution cartels, not before time, and cleaning out corrupt police. There are more of those in Britain than might be supposed, and we don't have a Frank Serpico.

Transport

Germany has always understood the importance of efficient transport links, so it is no surprise that German political assets prioritise attacks on transport infrastructure. Richard Beeching in Britain is the most notorious example. The answer is to repair the damage, e.g. by reopening closed railway lines. A common and beguiling theme of German bureaucratic and political assets is to channel resources into prestige, high-speed links on dedicated lines like HS2, holding out the promise of faster connections between city-pairs. Freight of course doesn't get a look-in. Sometimes these are then cancelled at the last minute.

The French example is somewhat misleading. France being a centralised country, it is fairly easy to drive new transport corridors through against local objection. Vanity projects also suit the French temperament, no offence intended. Trains are not aircraft. Trying to reduce the experience of train travel to that of flying, with plastic food served on plastic trays to passengers in cramped seats, whilst the scenery flashes by too quickly to be enjoyed, is probably a mistake.

The *Shinkansen* (Bullet Train) lines in Japan are also a bit misleading. They were probably funded through Medium Term Note programmes. There was no Japanese economic 'miracle'. Japan's postwar rise was subsidised by us, through trading programmes and unequal trade terms. Japan's existing 3 ft 6 in. gauge imposed severe limitations on future growth.[7] It made sense to build a completely new standard-gauge network. The Bullet Train routes are of course completely useless for freight.

For Britain, America and Australia it would make much more sense to upgrade existing routes for use by freight as well as passenger trains. We could integrate them with reopened lines, cascade existing equipment onto those lines and emphasise comfort, spaciousness, on-board entertainment and decent 'tucker' on the new rolling stock.

One problem of high-speed lines, which cannot be overcome as it is imposed by the laws of physics, is that the energy gradient is nonlinear. Disproportionately more energy is required for high-speed trains, driving up ticket prices. They also have greater environmental impact, not least noise, not to mention the visual impact. Overall the extra effort and energy required to go from say 125 mph to 225 mph is generally not worth it, not least when compared with the environmental, social and economic benefits of spending the money on reopening closed lines and increasing speed and freight capacity on existing lines.

Energy

DVD penetration assets have also made a mess of energy policy, again unsurprisingly. The vast amounts of cash being hosed away on pointless wind farms would be much better spent on new, cleaner, more efficient nuclear plants and renewable sources which actually work, such as the proposed Severn Barrage in Britain, or offshore wave-generators. Using waste to generate energy solves two problems at once, or three if municipal waste-generators make the energy available for free for urban mass transit.

Since there is no need to worry about global warming, since it isn't actually happening, some of the money DVD assets want us to waste on decarbonising our economies could usefully be spent in putting power grids underground, i.e. hardening them. Our power supply is surprisingly intermittent for advanced industrial economies. Decarbonising our economies makes as much sense as decarbonising ourselves. As 'VEGA' reminded us in *Star Trek: The Motion Picture* we are carbon-based units. Nowhere has there been greater German intelligence interference than with fusion research. The UK badly needs to on with this. There is no reason why there could not be transatlantic cooperation with the USA and/or Canada, which used to have a world-class nuclear research programme. Public pressure for progress has been lessened by persistent propaganda exaggerating the technical difficulties. Fusion is clearly the answer to our long-term energy needs, is inherently safe and does not need uranium or thorium.

Pace Back to the Future, the science of which is about as credible as global warming, we are unlikely to see fusion-powered DeLoreans, although apparently we are going to see electric powered ones.[8] In my humble opinion (and readers will have discovered by now how humble I am) we will see fusion power stations. In due course, which may not be in this century, cheap and plentiful fusion power will make using hydrogen (which is really a store of energy rather than an energy source in itself) economically viable for cars and bikes. By then we might even have worked out how to make electric cars with a range greater than New York to Philadelphia.

Space

It really is preposterous that having reached the moon in 1969, thanks to American daring and innovation (and the use of Imperial/foot-pound measures), we have gone no further. This is silly. Britain's space programme slid into near-irrelevance a long time ago, thanks to DVD assets in Whitehall, but there is no reason why it could not be revived. At one point Britain threatened a technological breakthrough with Horizontal Take-Off and Landing (HOTOL)) technology. This would have and might still allow space shuttles to take-off as well as land conventionally, vastly increasing their useability.

In the 2012 Republican primary Governor Romney poked fun at Speaker Gingrich for suggesting, perfectly sensibly, that the United States should establish mining colonies on the moon. It is not quite clear what the objection was. Perhaps Governor Romney thought that the moon is made is of green cheese and that cheese should be made from cows and goats, not mined.

Since most of the minerals, including the high-value stuff like gold, in the solar system are off-planet, that is where we should be looking in the years to come. There is no reason why we should not start developing the technologies now, even if we confine our activities to mineral exploration rather than production. That would need an economic method of getting minerals back to the planetary surface.

Far more interesting in the near-term, surely, is the prospect of a manned mission to Mars. Never mind the cost. The pro-German, self- styled 'global elite' are planning to waste much more than it would cost on combatting 'global warming' anyway. It would provide many high- quality jobs and encourage new technologies, much as the Apollo programme stimulated the development of scaled-down computers. It would also be fun.

There is no need by the way for interplanetary missions to be lengthy affairs with deadly dull space food and not much to do on board. Only a lunatic would try and get an interplanetary spacecraft through the Earth's atmosphere (sorry Elon!). The obvious answer is to assemble the ships in space and power them with modernised versions of the small nuclear reactors successfully used in ships and submarines. They could power ion-drive engines, which in interplanetary space could build up a fair turn of speed. There is no particular reason why the food need be tasteless, any more than it has to be on Virgin trains (sorry Richard!). Landing on the Martian surface would be by shuttles, as it was on the lunar surface in the Apollo missions. There is no reason to suppose that the crew would be eaten by extra-terrestrials, murder each other, be murdered by the mainframe, crash into the surface (unless we use metric) or suffer any of the other setbacks which are the routine fare of bad sci-fi films, or, in the case of *2001: A Space Odyssey*, good sci-fi films.

The planets beyond Mars beckon as well. We do not have to stand still or go backwards. That's just a Sino-German-Jesuit thing. We aren't going to find intelligent life, at least not in our backyard, but that's not the point. The point is that WE are intelligent and we can behave like the intelligent life forms that we are.

We have a bright future. Let's embrace it.

---

1. There should also have been an exchange of state visits, but the State Department and Foreign Office blocked the idea. President Truman would have been very welcome in Britain. The wonderful welcome given in America to the King and Queen in 1939 is still warmly remembered here.
2. She was also a stable ship, her aluminium superstructure reducing top-hamper. She used a variant of the high-pressure machinery intended for the aircraft carrier USS *United States* (CV-58), albeit running at 950 p.s.i. instead of 1,200. The carrier was cancelled under covert German pressure of course. The SSUS is still the fastest liner built to date, steaming at over 38 knots on her trials, at 241,000 SHP. She was an utterly magnificent ship - no merchant vessel her size afloat today would have a hope of keeping up with her on the North Atlantic.
3. The Vatican files on Napoleon are said to make interesting reading.
4. The *JFK* has already been decommissioned, *ditto* the Big E. She will be sorely missed. She was a wonderful ship.
5. There is no criticism of the learned judge of course, who was constrained by federal laws designed to encourage the hijacking of commercial airliners and the murder of US citizens. She handed down the toughest sentence she could. With respect, her sentencing remarks were appropriate.
6. The ship was a symbol of the European Union. Going beam-ends up and drowning some of the passengers amidst utter chaos and moral cowardice on the part of her officers was not therefore an unfitting end, sadly for the dead passengers.
7. Unlike say New Zealand. Her mountainous terrain and sparse population make 3 ft 6 inch an ideal choice, incidentally resulting in much reduced costs for reopening her many closed lines, some of great scenic interest with tremendous tourist potential. New Zealand always had an excellent reputation for producing surprisingly powerful locomotives despite their comparatively small size. She was a leader in mainline electrification, hence the Mount Arthur tunnel on the spectacularly beautiful Christchurch- Greymouth line, on which I have travelled. Some idiot dismantled the gantries.
8. The rights to the name and the parts were acquired by the DeLorean Motor Company of Humble Texas (yes, there really is a town called 'Humble' in Texas). Poor old John DeLorean was set up by the way. The drugs charges were a complete phoney, interestingly resonant with the bogus charges laid against Preston Tucker, who wanted to move to 24-volt electrics and fuel- injection in *1948*. The DMC 12 was by no means a bad car, making innovative use of stainless steel, with a Lotus-engineered chassis. They acquired a poor reputation Stateside partly because the very good 2.7 litre PRV V-6 was underpowered by the time catalytic converters - another pointless piece of environmental nonsense - were added. The true purpose of catalytic converters and unleaded fuel was to drive up costs, reduce engine life, increase car weight and drain world supplies of platinum.

APPENDIX ONE

German Or German - Backed Genocides and WMD Campaigns

1918 - 1920 Spanish Flu, laundered as a disease. Estimates of the number of the dead vary widely but 50 million is a credible estimate and likely to be on the low side. Upper estimates are in the region of 100 million, with around 500 million people infected.

1938 - 1945 The Holocaust, the only overt German genocide, number of Jewish dead probably just under six million, although no precise figure has even been calculated.

1975 - 1979 The Cambodian Genocide, false-flagged through Peking and the Chinese-controlled Khmer Rouge. Fully supported by Peking but ultimately controlled from Dachau, number of dead approximately two million.

1980 onwards. AIDS, originally trialled in the late 50s but withdrawn as it was too lethal to spread. 42 million dead and counting.

1998 - Rwanda, in conjunction with the pro-German and ex-Vichyist French President François Mitterand. The French agents who set it up belonged to the DVD's black agency in Paris. The genocide would not have been possible without DVD, i.e. German, control of the UN. The complicity of UN 'peacekeepers' was essential in order to get the number of casualties up to what Dachau and Paris wanted. Mitterand was paid off via access to Medium Term Note programmes run through banks in Paris and Zurich. The death toll was about 800,000.

2003 - 2012 Darfur, Sudan. German involvement in the Sudan goes back to the 19th century when their man the 'Mad Mahdi' tried to take over the country, working with German assets such as Sir Evelyn Baring in Cairo and William Gladstone in Downing Street. The government in Khartoum

reports to the DVD, whose influence at the UN was again an important factor in pushing up the death toll. Credible estimates of the death toll are in the region of 300,000 - low for a genocide, but severe enough. Most experts in public international law would probably agree that the massacres in Darfur meet that definition of genocide.

2019 – 2022 Covid, developed with German technical assistance, including German assets in the States.

APPENDIX TWO

Major German Terrorist Campaigns Since World War II

Malaya

Cyprus (EOKA) Kenya (Mau-Mau)

Northern Ireland (IRA, Provisional IRA, INLA, Real IRA and other splinters)

Algeria (FLN)

Middle East (PLO, PFLP & other Palestinian splinters, Hamas and Hezbollah, usually false flagged through Egypt, Tunisia, Syria or Iran)

Angola (UNITA, false-flagged through South Africa and the CIA) *Al Qaeda* (aimed principally at United Kingdom & United States) Russia (Chechen and other separatist groups in the Caucasus) Indonesia (Aceh and Bali)

APPENDIX THREE

Key German Double Agents Since 1900

Prince Louis of Battenberg (Naval Intelligence Department)
Admiral Sir Reginald Plunkett-Ernle-Erle-Drax (Allied Control Commission Germany)
Admiral Sir Hugh Sinclair (NID) Vernon Kell (MI5)
Sir Stewart Menzies (MI6)
Albert Einstein (Manhattan Project) Julius and Ethel Rosenberg ('atom spies')
Robert Oppenheimer (Manhattan Project & Los Alamos) Lord Louis Mountbatten
Victor Rothschild (MI5)
The Cambridge Ring (Philby, Burgess, Maclean, Cairncross, Blunt) Roscoe Hillenkoetter (ONI)
Admiral Ernest King (ONI & US Navy) The Dulles brothers (OSS & CIA) General William Donovan (OSS) General Walter Bedell Smith (CIA)
Sir Roger Hollis (MI5)
Sir Maurice Oldfield (MI6) Richard Helms (OSS & CIA)

APPENDIX FOUR

Major German Political Assets Since 1900

Rasputin
The Tsarina
Herbert Asquith David Lloyd George Aristide Briand Lenin
Trotsky Stalin
Stanley Baldwin Ramsay MacDonald Neville Chamberlain
Samuel Hoare
Lord Halifax Pierre Laval Herbert Hoover George Marshall
Dwight.D.Eisenhower John Curtin
Edward Stettinius James Forrestal Herbert Vere Evatt Mao Tse-Tung Chou En-Lai
Ho Chi Minh
Dag Hammarksjöld Clement Attlee
Hartley Shawcross Stafford Cripps Harold Macmillan Roy Jenkins Harold Wilson Edward Heath Tony Barber Georges Pompidou
George H W Bush
Henry Kissinger

APPENDIX FIVE

Table Of Major Allied Warship Losses Since 1914 Contributed to by German Intelligence

HMSs *Crecy*, *Aboukir* and *Hogue* (1914) (ambushed).

HMSs *Queen Mary*, *Invincible* and *Indefatigable* (1916) (interference on specifications, gunnery control technology transfer to Germany).

HMS *Hampshire* (1916) (IED). HMS *Vanguard* (1917) (IED).

HMS *Royal Oak* (1939) (interference to prevent blockships at Scapa Flow).

HMS *Courageous* (1939) (ambush). HMS *Hood* (1941) IED).

HMS *Ark Royal* (1941) (ambush). HMS *Barham* (ambush).

Pearl Harbor (1941) (intelligence on fleet dispositions, technical assistance to the Imperial Japanese Navy).

HMSs *Prince of Wales* and *Repulse* (1941) (ambush, specification interference on *Prince of Wales* plus interference on rebuild re *Repulse*).

USSs *Quincy*, *Vincennes* and *Astoria* (1942) (withdrawal of reconnaissance aircraft to permit unimpeded access for a Japanese task force).

USS *Oriskany* and USS *Forrestal* (Vietnam) were not sunk, as intended, but suffered major damage off Vietnam as a result of DVD sabotage operations.

USS *Cole* (2000) (survived, but suffered major damage and was disabled as the result of a sabotage operation directed ultimately from Dachau).

APPENDIX SIX

Table Of Major Allied Aircraft Programmes Since 1939 Sabotaged by German Intelligence

Fairey Battle (overproduction of obsolescent aircraft depriving the Spitfire, Hurricane and Fulmar fighter programmes of resources, in particular Rolls-Royce Merlin engines).

Boeing B-17 (selection of the inadequate B-18 to delay the programme, power starvation of the B-17F and G models through interference on powerplant choice and specifications).

Consolidated B-24 (power starvation, particularly of later models).

Westland Whirlwind (cessation of development of Rolls-Royce Peregrine engine, which was unique to this aircraft, plus bureaucratic delays).

De Havilland Mosquito (bureaucratic delays plus obstruction of the Merlin 61 two-stage engine and Griffon-engine versions and bureaucratic opposition to the proposed Sabre Mosquito).

Avro Lancaster (denigration of the 24-cylinder 42.5 litre Rolls-Royce Vulture engine plus insistence on the lower-powered Merlin, limitation of armament through opposition to the ventral turret and cancellation of the proposed .55 calibre Boys high velocity anti-aircraft round, the one serious aircraft defence round at Britain's disposal in World War II).

Handley Page Halifax (power starvation by restriction of Bristol Hercules engine development, with associated interference with the Bristol Board).

Short Stirling (ditto, plus rejection of the much more powerful and effective Bristol Centaurus powered version).

Gloster Meteor (bad faith allocation of jet engine development work to the Rover car company in the hope they would fail).

Blackburn Firebrand (bureaucratic obstruction plus delaying Centaurus development, depriving the Fleet Air Arm of a truly effective fast torpedo fighter).

Curtiss P-40 (excessive orders to deprive more effective, competing fighter programmes such as the P-38 and P-51 of resources, plus interference on supercharger specifications to restrict performance at altitude).

Curtiss SB2C Helldiver (excessive orders to deprive competing strike aircraft of resources).

North American P-51A Mustang (supercharger under-specification to restrict performance at altitude, the intended poor performance being blamed unfairly on the Allison V-1710 engine).

Boeing B-29 Superfortress (sabotage on the line plus theft of blueprints, technology transfer to Germany's client the USSR, blocking proposed cooling improvements for the Curtiss-Wright R-3350 engine and scrapping plans for improved models).

Avro Tudor (sabotage of the prototype and probable detonation of IEDs on two aircraft).

Avro Lincoln (specification sabotage, leaving the aircraft underpowered when the Rolls-Royce Griffon or Eagle were available or could have been developed).

Bristol Britannia (prototype sabotaged, a programme of industrial sabotage waged by DVD assets on the BOAC Board and obstruction of the Bristol Orion re-engine programme).

De Havilland Comet (sabotage programme, coupled with economic warfare against main US customer, Capital Airlines).

Handley Page Herald (prototype sabotage).

Vickers Viscount (sabotage, particularly of Capital Airlines aircraft).

Handley Page Victor (specification sabotage, leaving the Mk 1 underpowered and causing delays whilst the aircraft was re-engined with Rolls- Royce Conways).

Thin-wing Hunter (cancelled).

Fairey Delta II (technology transfer to France).

TSR-2 (bad faith programme, designed to suck in aerospace development resources with cancellation intended all along, plus costs sabotage by requiring prototypes to be tested at Boscombe Down instead of Wharton and not having English Electric as programme manager, coupled with physical destruction of jigs to prevent the cancellation being reversed).

Convair B-58 Hustler (programme cut back, increasing the costs of each aircraft ordered due to amortisation of development costs across fewer airframes, with associated propaganda campaign emphasising the resultant costs blowout whilst concealing the reason for it, plus operations sabotage, restricting its use during the Vietnam War so as to prevent this superb aircraft from revealing its potential).

Avro Arrow (cancellation by German assets in Ottawa).

North American F-108 (cancellation after the aircraft showed too much promise).

De Havilland DH121 Trident (specification sabotage by BEA followed by the sabotage of Trident Papa India at Staines, technology transfer to USSR).

North American B-70 (bad faith programme intended for cancellation *ab initio*).

Vickers-Supermarine VC-10 (prototype sabotage followed by an industrial sabotage campaign waged by German assets in BOAC, e.g. by distorting the aircraft's operating economics, plus technology transfer to USSR).

BAC One-Eleven (prototype sabotage).

General Dynamics F-111 (bad faith orders for the US Navy and RAF plus prototype sabotage intended to prevent deployment in Vietnam, technology transfer to USSR and spares starvation in order to force withdrawal of the type by the Royal Australian Air Force).

BAC/Aerospatiale Concorde (industrial sabotage by forcing a disastrous merger of the Bristol company with other aerospace companies which were a very poor fit, plus a forcing through a deal with the French with a view to driving up costs and delaying the aircraft's entry into service, followed by a concerted propaganda campaign exaggerating its noise footprint, possible sabotage of the port undercarriage bogie and ATC sabotage at Paris).

Boeing 747 (ATC sabotage at Tenerife intended to damage the airplane's reputation and induce exaggerated fears over flying such a large number of people in one aircraft, plus a later repair sabotage of the Japan Air Lines 747, using assets inside Boeing to insist on a dangerously inadequate repair in the hope of inducing inflight failure, preferably when loaded. Aside from incidents of sabotage and shoot-down the airplane's safety record after initial teething troubles with the JT-9D engine has been excellent, with no hull loss due to negligent design or operation).

BAC Two-Eleven and Three-Eleven (cancellation after they showed commercial promise).

Twin-Engine De Havilland Trident (technology transfer to France, eventually inspired Airbus A300).

Lockheed Tristar (IP theft, operational sabotage of an aeroplane over the Everglades and interference on Rolls-Royce with a view to bankrupting the company).

McDonnell Douglas DC-10 (interference on lines of credit to the old Douglas company, forcing through an unsuccessful merger, design sabotage using assets inside Convair, leading to two major incidents, random engine sabotage of the CF-6, i.e. deliberate insertion of manufacturing defects in the hope components would fail at a critical time and operational sabotage, encouraging dangerous maintenance practices with a view to damaging the engine pylon).

IAI Lavi (theft of IP and technology transfer to China).

F-117 Nighthawk Stealth Fighter (ambush, permitting shoot-down and technology transfer to Russia and China).

F-22 Raptor (cutback on orders with a view to early termination of the programme).

Boeing 787 Dreamliner (battery compartment cooling software sabotage)

Boeing 737 Max (software sabotage)

APPENDIX SEVEN

Major Incidents of Sabotage of Commercial Aircraft Since 1945 by the DVD

30th January 1948 (probable) Avro Tudor IV British South American Airways (BSAA) G-AHNP. Lives lost: 31, including Air Marshal Sir Arthur Coningham.

17th January 1949 (probable) Avro Tudor IV BSAA G-AGRE. Lives lost: 20.

2nd May 1953 (probable) De Havilland Comet 1 British Overseas Airways Corporation (BOAC) G-ALYV. Lives lost: 43.

10th January 1954 De Havilland Comet I BOAC G-ALYP. Lives lost: 35, including war correspondent Chester Wilmot.

8th April 1954 De Havilland Comet 1 BOAC (operated by South African Airways) G-ALYY. Lives lost: 21.

6th February 1958 Airspeed Ambassador British European Airways (BEA) GALZU. Lives lost: 23, including seven Manchester United Players, the injured Duncan Edwards being assassinated later in a Munich hospital.

16th December 1960 Douglas DC-8 United Airlines N8013U and Lockheed Super Constellation Trans World Airlines (TWA) N6907C (staged collision between the two aircraft). Lives lost: 219.

15th February 1961 Boeing 707-329 Intercontinental Sabena OO-SJB. Lives lost: 73, primary target the United States Figure Skating Team.

12th October 1967 De Havilland Comet 4B Cyprus Airways G-ARCO. Lives lost: 66.

3rd July 1970 De Havilland Comet 4 Dan-Air G-APDN. Lives lost: 112.

2nd October 1970 (probable) Martin 4-0-4 Golden Eagle Aviation N464M. Lives lost: 31, probable primary target the Wichita State University Football Team.

14th November 1970 McDonnell Douglas DC-9 Southern Airways N- 97S. Lives lost: 75, primary target the Marshall University Football Team.

18th June 1972 De Havilland Trident 1C BEA G-ARPI. Lives lost 118. 29th December 1972 Lockheed Tristar Eastern Airlines N310EA. Lives lost: 101 including the Second Officer, who may have been murdered in hospital to silence him.

3rd March 1974 McDonnell Douglas DC-10 Turkish Airlines TC-JAV. Lives lost: 346.

27th March 1977 Boeing 747-121 Pan American World Airways (PanAm) N736A and Boeing 747-206B Koninklijke Luchtvaart Maatschappij (KLM) PH-BUF. Lives lost: 583.

28th November 1979 McDonnell Douglas DC-10 Air New Zealand ZK- NZP. Lives lost: 257.

23rd June 1985 Boeing 747-237B Air India VT-EFO. Lives lost: 329.

21st December 1988 Boeing 747-121 PanAm N739PA. Lives lost: 270.

19th July 1989 (probable) McDonnell Douglas DC-10 United Airlines N- 1819U. Lives lost: 111.

17th July 1996 Boeing 747-131 TWA N93119. Lives lost: 230.

17th January 2008 Boeing 777-236ER British Airways G-YMMM. No lives lost.

25th February 2009 Boeing 737-800 Turkish Airlines TC-JGE. Lives lost: 9.

1st June 2009 Airbus A330-203 Air France F-GZCP. Lives lost: 228, primary target former Devon Oil geologist Michael Harris.

30th June 2009 Airbus A310-324 Yemenia 7O-ADJ. Lives lost: 152.

12th May 2010 Airbus A330-202 Afriqiyah Airways 5A-ONG. Lives Lost: 103.

8th March 2014 Boeing 777-2H6ER Malaysian Airlines 9M-MRO Shot down by Chinese submarine over the South China Sea, with DVD technical input. Lives lost – 239.

17th July 2014 Boeing 777-2H6ER Malaysian Airlines 9M-MRD. Shot down by the Ukrainian Air Force, using cannon fire into the cockpit and a Chinese HQ-16 missile. Lives lost: 298

12th June 2025 Boeing 787-8 Dreamliner Air India VT-ANB. FADEC software sabotage leading to double engine failure shortly after rotation, combined with sabotage of the flap and undercarriage indicators. Lives lost: 241.

APPENDIX EIGHT

The Barham Report On The Madeleine McCann Kidnap For The Joint Intelligence Committee

NB: No longer restricted, names and some details have been redacted to 'protect the guilty'.

"Restricted

Disclosure may harm the national security interest of the United Kingdom or Her Allies and interfere with ongoing intelligence and/or military operations.

Copy Number

The abduction of Mistress Madeleine McCann aged 3 from the Mark Warner Organisation Ocean Club Holiday Complex Prai da Luz, Republic of Portugal, Thursday 3rd May 2007.

Informal intelligence assessment.

Prepared at the request of a former member of the Joint Intelligence Committee.

Michael Shrimpton, LLB (Hons) Esq., of Gray's Inn, Barrister, National Security Lawyer, Member Advisory Board, Gerard Group International, Adjunct Professor of Intelligence Studies, American Military University.

No part of the Master document has been prepared on a computer open to the Internet, nor stored electronically, save on a securely stored dedicated mass storage device, nor e-mailed. Recipients are respectfully urged not to e-mail this document, either *en clair* or encrypted, nor scan it into a computer file, unless the computer does not have a modem. Recipients should note that many if not most of the encryption keys used in the UK and USA have been betrayed to the Federal Republic of Germany, which has a substantial covert signals organisation (sanitised through a German electronics firm and funded offshore, probably out of the 10% levy of the street value of cocaine and heroin shipments to the UK through Germany or under the control of the covert German Deutscher Verteidigungs Dienst intelligence organisation, which inherited many of the surviving specialists of the B-Dienst signals service of the Kriegsmarine in 1945, headquartered at Dachau, near Munich, Bavaria, probable surface location a cluster of buildings observed by satellite reconnaissance south of Dachau, about 1 mile from the former concentration camp, near an autobahn junction).

Distribution (in the strictest confidence), on a non-recourse basis, under the Chatham House Rule.

Former Member JIC, for distribution to JIC at discretion.

Prime Minister in waiting (Rt Hon. Gordon Brown MP) (via a trusted adviser, back-up link in place, eyes only please).

Pentagon (Dr Andrew Marshall, Director, Office of Net Assessment and Hon. Gordon England, Deputy Secretary of Defense).

Air Marshal Stu Peach, Chief of Defence Intelligence (CDI).

Lieutenant-General Keith B. Alexander, Director National Security Agency, NSA HQ, Fort George G. Meade Maryland.

Designated US Theater Commander (C in C EUCOM, General Bantz Craddock (via EUCOM HQ J2 Intelligence Staff)).

Commander of His Moroccan Majesty's Royal Guard (Via Diplomatic Bag).

Constituency MP for the McCann family, Rt Hon. Stephen Dorrell MP (On Privy Council equivalent terms, not for release to the McCann family or the media, but contents may be summarised and communicated securely (not via e-mail or telephone) to Drs Gerry and Kate McCann at their MPs discretion).

Chief Executive Officer Gerard Group International LLC. All times Zulu

List of Contents

Executive Summary

(1) The UK knew for 14 days the location of Madeleine McCann to a high degree of confidence and nothing was done to affect a rescue;
(2) The failure to refer the matter to JIC or convene COBRA contributed to the poor co-ordination of intelligence;
(3) Madeleine McCann was kidnapped by a paedophile ring linked to the covert German DVD intelligence agency;
(4) The Portuguese Authorities at a senior level have frustrated the Portuguese police investigation, which has degenerated into a farce;
(5) Madeleine was taken out by sea, the original destination was adjacent to the port of Antwerp, she was held for 14 days on a specially equipped vessel in Moroccan territorial waters without the consent of Morocco and she is probably now on Belgian territory;
(6) Madeleine is alive but in mortal danger, COBRA and JIC should be brought in without delay and every available intelligence resource of the United Kingdom should be committed to finding and saving her;
(7) The involvement of Portuguese, Belgian and German intelligence indicates that the political situation in Europe will deteriorate if this crisis is not resolved quickly;
(8) The murder of Madeleine McCann, effectively at the instigation of the German State would lead to a major Anglo-European crisis and rightly so.

Disclaimer

1. This paper is submitted on a non-recourse basis and no liability attaches to the author or Gerard Group International LLC, under whose auspices it is submitted, with the consent of the Chief Executive Officer. It has been prepared, purely as an informal exercise, on a *pro bono publico* basis, at the request of a former member of the Joint Intelligence Committee. It is in no sense a substitute for the paper which would ordinarily have been prepared by the Cabinet Office Assessments Staff. No liability

for the contents attaches to any recipient. It has been prepared under conditions of tight security by civilian standards and no part of it has been circulated in draft beforehand to any of them. The views expressed herein are solely those of the author. Individuals not named publicly as suspects have been identified by letters only. It may be assumed that the full names, addresses and/or landline telephone number, dates of birth and passport numbers of those individuals have been passed to their country of nationality's internal intelligence service, and that service has not denied that they are persons of interest. The author and Gerard Group have been assisted considerably by professionals within and without the intelligence community who have given freely of their time and expertise, compartmentalised and kept off phone lines, even encrypted lines, wherever possible. Deniable assistance has also been given by Allied intelligence agencies, but for security and deniability reasons no agency saw this document in draft prior to its limited, non-electronic circulation.

Note On Security

2. Coms security on the McCann case has been appalling. Most aspects of it were blown weeks ago down open phone lines, whilst Leicestershire Police have made a practice of passing intelligence to the Portuguese police inquiry, despite requests not to do so. This inquiry, a fair summary of the 15 basic defects in which was summarised in the *Daily Telegraph* on June 1st (p. 9), is controlled not by the Portuguese Judicial Police Faro Region, as alleged in the media, but by the DCCB, Direccao Central de Combate ao Banditismo, part of the Judicial Police, in Lisbon. The DCCB in turn has officers reporting to the Servico de Informacoes de Seguranca, the Security Intelligence Service. The Seguranca in turn is heavily penetrated by a black agency in Lisbon which dates back to the Salazar fascist dictatorship and was not dismantled in 1974, i.e. although the political structures of the Portuguese Republic are democratic in form, and the overt intelligence services give the semblance of accountability to those structures, the intelligence structures of the Portuguese State are fundamentally unaltered from the fascist era.
3. Since the paedophile ring operating in Lisbon is controlled by this covert agency, which appears to be blackmailing senior members of the Portuguese Government, it follows that all intelligence passed to Portugal from Leicester has most probably been blown, including the probable location of Madeleine on board the RV [redacted]. Combined with the activities of the COMINT operation in Dachau there has been

virtually no security on this operation since it began. Since intelligence on Madeleine's whereabouts has sometimes taken days to reach England the author makes no apology for having acted throughout as though time were of the essence. It is. A new low point was reached on Sunday 3rd June, when Madeleine's probable location in Morocco and the involvement of GCHQ was splashed across the *People* (for the benefit of US readers this is a low- rent Sunday tabloid), citing sources 'close to the investigation,' although whether their sources are British or Portuguese is unclear. The author has been liaising, unofficially, with the DA-Notice Committee, tipping them off if it appeared a British newspaper was likely to mention exfiltration by sea.

Note On Sources

4. These have not been identified, partly to protect them (Leicestershire Police, whose inquiry with respect has not been intelligence-led, have applied pressure to force their identification, but that has been resisted) and partly because some are acting through cut-outs. It has been apparent to the author for some time that we have been receiving a stream of high- grade intelligence out of Portugal, and that one or more of these sources is in the Seguranca, or the Servico de Informacoes Estrategicas de Defesa e Militares (Strategic Defence and Military Intelligence Service, SIEDM). Since representing General Pinochet Ugarté in Washington in 1999/2000 the author has been tapped into the European Royal House network (i.e. he has chateaux as well as home numbers) and there would be nothing particularly surprising in his receiving intelligence on a matter affecting the British interest from a well-placed aristocratic source in Europe. It would not be the first time.
5. The difficult relationship between the covert GO2 (General Operations 2) in London and the DVD, and the penetration of the Secret Intelligence Service (SIS) by GO2, would be understood by the better-informed members of the Portuguese Royal House (the House of Braganza), i.e. those with the strongest connections to the Seguranca and the SIEDM. The alliance with Portugal, which goes back to 1376, is still in force, and the present Duke, Duarte II, is a collateral descendant of King Edward III, via John of Gaunt and his accomplished daughter Philippa. The brutal assassinations by the Imperial German Secret Service of King Carlos 1 and his son and heir, Luis Filipe, 23rd Duke of Braganza, on 1st February 1908, would hardly endear a DVD-backed paedophile operation directed against a British child to the House of Braganza. The heir apparent, His Highness Alfonso, Prince of Beira, is aged just 11, and his views on

the organised kidnap of young children for sexual abuse may well be imagined.

6. In addition we appear to be receiving high-grade HUMINT, which is being confirmed in part by satellite observation. Of course the author does not have a collection of plastic rocks and is not set up to control a HUMINT source, but he is an intelligence specialist, not an intelligence officer, and the HUMINT is coming securely via multiple cut-outs, i.e. from the agency concerned, rather than from the source.

The Author's Involvement

7. Purely unofficially the author has been involved since Sunday 6th May, when he quietly asked the National Security Agency at Fort Meade whether anything was coming up on their radar. It was clear by then that the Portuguese police inquiry was compromised, that the 12-hour delay in notifying border guards implied that someone had been allowed to get across the frontier, that Madeleine was no longer in Portugal, that she had probably been taken out by air or sea, that the British police inquiry was stalled and that the intelligence co-ordination function normally performed by JIC was not being done. He has liaised with the police inquiry (spending a day with the inquiry team at Leicester on Thursday 24th May), various intelligence contacts, and *inter alia* an aide to the PM in waiting, the White House, the Pentagon, EUCOM, US National Security Council, and relevant friendly governments.

The Lisbon and Brussels Paedophile Rings

8. The paedophile scandal in Lisbon barely scratched the surface. There are a number of high-ranking paedophiles in Lisbon, and abductions of young children in Portugal, followed by their eventual murder after unspeakable horrors, is sadly a feature of Portuguese political life, ditto Belgium, where at least two rings, one tied closely to the European Commission, continue to operate. Prosecutions and resignations in both capitals were largely a public relations exercise. From the national security standpoint paedophile politicians and senior officials are a menace – they are invariably weak, hopelessly compromised and vulnerable to blackmail by the covert intelligence agencies, all reporting to the German DVD, which control the rings. It is rare for a missing child's case to be prosecuted diligently in either country - if one of the rings is involved political interference, as in this case, becomes almost inevitable.

The Deutscher Verteidigungs Dienst (DVD)

9. This agency could be the topic of a book rather than a paper, which might then cause a number of postwar history books to be rewritten. The DVD was set up in 1943 after Germany's defeat in the Battle of the Kursk Salient, the failure of the U-Boat campaign to sever the vital transatlantic link and the collapse of covert negotiations, via the Dulles brothers, to make a separate peace with the United States. Generalleutnant Erwin von Lahousen, one of Canaris's Section Chiefs, who dropped off our intelligence radar in the autumn of 1943, was the first operational director. The DVD was Germany's insurance against defeat. Admiral Wilhelm Canaris, who faked his own death after a deal with SS Reichsführer Himmler, whereby the Admiral offered to use his Western contacts to secure favourable treatment for Himmler in exchange for his life (the Admiral reneged and Himmler's cyanide pill was politely returned to him by a British military intelligence officer, who in turn reported to a very quiet section of military intelligence, MI18, which was eventually wound up, officially at any rate), ensured that critical Abwehr files and control of the German high-level overseas networks were transferred to Dachau, DVD HQ, from the autumn of 1943. Those networks were not rolled up after 1945 and in each country occupied by Germany a stay- behind intelligence organisation was set up, as well as in Madrid and Lisbon. The DVD specialises in talent-spotting future leaders (they have long had recruiters at Oxford and Cambridge, e.g., taking over the Abwehr's efficient operations in each town, which recruited a number of major political leaders) and in exploiting the weaknesses of some politicians. It has made effective use of paedophile rings, but aside from the ethical and legal objections to this entirely criminal and amoral policy, which entails the murder, very often in snuff movies, of the desperately unfortunate children seized by the rings, it is dangerous, because of the wash-back on Germany should it be exposed.
10. Since Germany has used covert control of international organisations to exercise influence since German Intelligence, which was not broken up in 1918, got its men Jean Monnet and Arthur Salter into the League of Nations HQ in 1919 (the real reason the US Senate rejected the Versailles Treaty, i.e. key Republican Senators with intelligence connections were tipped off)(Kurt Waldheim was not selected as UN Secretary-General in ignorance of his wartime role as an intelligence officer working for the Abwehr inside the SD, but because of it), the wash-back following exposure would affect not only Germany, but also organisations such as the EU, which are the political beneficiaries of favourable policy

decisions from paedophile national leaders 'rewarded' by access to kidnapped children. It should be possible to track ring activity against say EU inter- governmental conferences, just as Provisional IRA activity (the DVD took over the Abwehr's extensive Irish Free State network in 1944, the IRA was false-flagged via KGB until 1969) can be measured against German or EU strategic objectives (attacks on the City, e.g., in the run-up to the choice of HQ for the ECB). Thus May saw an upsurge in abductions of children across Europe. No one warned parents taking young children to holiday destinations inside the EU that they should take extra precautions to protect their offspring, or that if a DVD-backed paedophile ring were involved official assistance might be tardy, compromised or inefficient.

Run-Up To The Kidnap

11. The McCann family (Drs Gerry and Kate McCann, Madeleine, aged 3, and twins Sean and Amelie, aged 2) left Rothley, Leicestershire, England for a much-anticipated holiday at Praia da Luz on the Algarve on Saturday 28th April 2007, flying to Faro, Portugal. There was an area of high pressure over the Bay of Lagos and weather conditions were fine, with little or no wind. Madeleine's Cuddle Cat toy was tucked safely into a bag and nothing could have been further from the family's mind than being at the centre of an international incident, leading to discreetly heightened military states of alert, (and possible re-targeting of Russian Federation Strategic Rocket Forces ICBMs and IRBMs on Germany), triggering a crisis of confidence in the Portuguese Republic and accelerating a collapse in the price of holidays in the EU, to the point where they are now on sale for under £10, including flights, but not Air Passenger Duty (it is doubtful if the Treasury thought this would be the most expensive component of a package holiday). Praia da Luz and the Mark Warner Ocean Club complex in particular were held out as a safe family destination. The Portuguese authorities must have been aware of organised paedophile activity in the Faro region in the run-up to 3rd May. Several children had either been abducted, or had survived abduction attempts, in the six months prior to the McCanns' arrival. No one alerted the Mark Warner Organisation to the dangers posed to young children, security at resorts was not heightened and there was no extra police presence on the streets to act as a deterrent.
12. On either the 29th or 30th April Madeleine was photographed using a digital camera, very possibly a mobile (cell) phone camera, on an Algarve beach, probably Sagres, near Cape St Vincent, scene of Sir John Jervis's

great victory. This photograph, together with possibly two others (the reporting is unclear) were sent on or about 1st May, as e-mail attachments, from a computer in Praia da Luz used by an intelligence gatherer for the Lisbon ring, who has been interviewed by Portuguese police, to an e-mail address in Brussels linked to the Belgian ring closest to the EU. This e-mail was intercepted at a switching centre, but its significance was not appreciated until after Madeleine's abduction. The paedophile being serviced in Brussels seems to have specified blonde- haired girls, aged about 5, preferably British. Reporting suggests that, tragically for her, Madeleine was selected by this morally worthless individual, who must have appreciated that she could not be released alive after he had finished abusing her.

13. Also on 1st May the motor yacht [redacted] length 11.7 metres, beam 3.7 metres, standard displacement approximately 4 tons, approximate maritime endurance 28 days, 36BHP diesel engine, flying the Dutch flag, pennant number [redacted] home port [redacted], owner [redacted], a subject of Her Netherlands Majesty, operating from Amsterdam, whose full details have been communicated to the Netherlands General Intelligence and Security Service (AIVD), sortied from Portimao, about 15 nautical miles from Praia da Luz, positioning itself at the Lagos Marina, about 5 statute miles from the Mark Warner Complex. [Redacted] seems to have made contact between 1st and 3rd May with [redacted], a Russian Federation Citizen, interviewed by Portuguese Police (but only after media inquiries had linked him to the only formal suspect, a British Citizen named Robert Murat, and he was tipped off, allowing him to wipe his hard drive) who is understood to have come under SVR investigation and may have been linked by them to a DVD-controlled narcotics trafficking ring, trafficking Northern Valley cartel cocaine to the Iberian Peninsula via the Gulf of Guinea, using a transhipment point on an island in the Sao Tome and Principe group known to the DVD, as indeed it was known to German Naval Intelligence in World War Two (the DVD are ruthless, but not Nazis, they are not that stupid).
14. The McCann family was placed under surveillance from 1st May. The routine followed on 3rd May had already been followed on previous nights, although not every night. A group of British families left their apartment doors unlocked, so that adults could check on the children. Drs Gerry and Kate McCann were not far from their apartment on Thursday 3rd May. Whilst they were not able to keep it under continuous observation they were no more than 40 yards away, the children were fast asleep, none of them was unwell, and responsible adults, including themselves, were making regular checks throughout the evening. The

adults could not eat in the self-catering apartment without disturbing the children's sleep and if they were to dine together realistically that needed to be outside. The tapas bar where Madeleine's parents dined is part of the Ocean Club complex. It is less than a minute away from the apartment where the family was staying. Neither parent was armed indeed they would not have been permitted to board a commercial aircraft with firearms even if they possessed any (which they do not). Not having received a warning of predatory criminal activity in the area, none of the Mark Warner staff possessed so much as a sidearm.

15. The parents have been criticised for these arrangements, indeed Portuguese officials briefed the media that they might be prosecuted for neglect, but there are no grounds for supposing that there was a breach of Portuguese law, nor would these arrangements be grounds for any proceedings in an English court. The key points to remember, it is submitted, are that there were regular checks by trusted adults known to the McCanns, as well as the McCanns themselves, i.e. the British families at the Ocean Club complex were looking out for each other, they were not warned about organised paedophile activity, indeed they were assured in terms that this was a safe environment for their children, and the parents never left the Ocean Club complex where their children were asleep. The last check on the children was at about 2010Z.

The Kidnap Of Madeline McCann

16. In the afternoon of 3rd May the motor yacht [redacted], Dutch registry, owned by [redacted] (whose full details again have been communicated to AIVD in The Hague), pennant number [redacted] home p ort [redacted] Netherlands, built [redacted], single-masted, single aluminium hull, length 10.2 metres, beam 3.3 metres, approximate standard displacement 3.5 tons, fitted it is believed with a 2-stroke diesel engine, positioned from Portimao, where she had arrived on the 1st, to Lagos. She waited there until about 1945Z, just before the marina was shut at 2000Z by lowering a lifting bridge, then moved out beyond the lifting bridge, where she was moored to a pontoon on the port side of the small canal leading to the open sea, where she waited. [Redacted] left his home in Praia da Luz sometime between the [redacted] arrival and Madeleine's kidnap. It is believed he was in communication with [redacted] on board the [redacted]. There is name recognition of [redacted] from intelligence sources. Drs Gerry and Kate McCann seem to have been under continuous surveillance by a male, name unknown, possibly of Spanish or Moroccan nationality.

17. At around 2035Z heavy shutters to a ground floor window to the McCanns' ground floor apartment were forced open and entry was gained through the window, which was not particularly secure once the shutters had been opened. There was a team of two, a man and a woman, who spoke English. Entry having been gained they would doubtless have appreciated an intelligence failure, as the families had left the front doors unlocked, so that the group could look in on the children. No alarm system was fitted and very frankly with such locks as were fitted it would have made no difference whether the door was locked or not. There may have been a chain but it was too high for the children to reach, i.e. its use was not practicable. In any event the security mechanisms would not have delayed entry by more than seconds. Madeleine (I am told her parents are most insistent she be referred to as Madeleine) seems to have been asleep, clutching her favourite Cuddle Cat toy. All the children, excited no doubt by their seaside holiday, were very tired and almost certainly sound asleep, as they were when checked at 2010Z. Media commentary suggests it would have made a difference had an adult been baby-sitting, but it is submitted this is unreal.
18. There is no reason whatsoever to suppose this team were unarmed, indeed there is reason to believe each of the males (one on the snatch team and one keeping guard) was equipped with a Makarov 9 mm semi-automatic pistol, fitted with a silencer. The woman was also probably armed, possibly with a smaller calibre Beretta, again fitted with a silencer. Since the reporting of COMINT traffic suggests that Madeleine was to be abused by a high-ranking Brussels-based official in the EU the operation clearly involved her eventual murder. The team of three may have murdered many children in the making of 'snuff' movies and all the evidence suggests that they are experienced and brutal child-killers, who would have killed an adult getting in their way without compunction.
19. A further explanation re the German DVD might assist, if only to deal with the quaint notion that this highly organised, albeit insane, operation might have been stopped by an unarmed babysitter. The DVD are the world's most ruthless, as well as most secretive, intelligence organisation - they conceived, e.g., the operational plans for the Brighton Bombing (ingenious but flawed), the destruction of PanAm Flight 103 (conceived in haste and it showed) and 9/11 (ludicrous, 47,000 deaths short of the kill target, which thankfully was never going to be reached, given the genius of the design of the Twin Towers, not that 3,000 dead wasn't bad enough, and well short of the economic goal of sabotaging the US airline & aviation industries) - and took in the 'cream' of the

Abwehr, SD and Gestapo (Heinrich Müller, for example, who also faked his own death, indeed there were the remains of two people in his coffin, neither of them him) in 1944-6. Martin Bormann, Dr Josef Mengele and Adolf Eichmann were all DVD, which is why the Mossad, on whom the DVD have waged war since 1948, lifted him, and why Rafi Eitan, God Bless him, was able to persuade Isser Harel to persuade El Al to fork out for a 300-series Bristol Britannia, a not inexpensive bit of kit, for the operation. The DVD lurk behind most Islamic terror groups and their paedophile ring operations, whilst hugely successful in terms of political blackmail, have seen the murder of hundreds of children. Possibly as a spin-off from this investigation (the arrests happened over the weekend of 2nd and 3rd June after a tip-off to the Spanish CNI), a racket smuggling children from Brazil to Portugal and Spain has been blown, i.e. it looks as though some of the homeless children being abducted in cities such as São Paolo ended up being abused by politicians and senior officials in the EU. Intel re the DVD is STRATINT (Strategic Intelligence), i.e. intelligence which might alter the course of history, influence events or affect policy-making at the strategic level.

20. The [redacted] waited whilst Madeleine was seized from the apartment. Seemingly reliable eyewitnesses report seeing a child answering Madeleine's description being taken in a white Renault (it was a Clio) from Praia da Luz towards Lagos and being taken, struggling, towards the marina in Lagos itself. It does not appear that she was drugged. One possible explanation for that is dosage, i.e. it is easier than it sounds to assess the right dosage to render a small child unconscious without killing him or her. We will probably find that members of this ring have killed small children before they could be abused through unintentional overdoses.

Exfiltration

21. The [redacted] sortied at about 2115Z, having filed a destination report of Albufeira, about 3-4 hours sailing time away, an odd time to set sail on a holiday cruise. She seems to have rendezvoused, using GPS, at sea, doubling back on her original easterly course once over the horizon, with the [redacted], which arrived in Albufeira on 5th May, having given an original destination of Sines, on the west coast. She left again on the 6th, ostensibly headed for Lisbon. The [redacted] never arrived at Albufeira, i.e. we have two yachts giving seemingly false destinations, indeed the author has seen no reporting of the [redacted] after 3rd May. Neither owner of these yachts has come

forward, which calls for comment in itself since they were [redacted] after the kidnap and it has been reported widely that an eyewitness saw a young girl looking like Madeleine being dragged towards the marina. Reporting suggests that at least part of these transfers was caught by Low Light Level (LLL) electro- optical imagery from a US (NRO) KH-13 recon satellite in non- geostationary earth orbit. In the author's estimation the original intention was to take Madeleine to a small harbour or inlet on the north Belgian coast, with say a 10 nautical mile radius of Antwerp, using up to 4 yachts, with at-sea transfer co-ordinated using GPS, which would attract little suspicion at this time of year, especially if their starting point was well away from Portugal (the last yacht for example could have sortied from Cowes). An average line of advance of 7.5 knots is realistic. Detailed analysis by small-boat specialists, based on up to date charts, meteorological data (there was heavy weather in the Bay of Biscay after the 3rd), tides and currents, suggests a journey-time of 10-11 days, with an original ETA of the night of 13th/14th May.

22. There is no reporting of any suspicious air movement in the Faro Region on 3rd May, no reliable reporting of Madeleine in Spain and no sign of her on the CCTV tape taken at a petrol station on the A22 expressway, which appears to catch the snatch team of two men and a woman in the Renault Clio. OSINT (Open Sourced Intelligence) suggests that this unnamed group (if innocent, why not come forward and speak to the police?) could not possibly be involved as they would not take such a risk as to obtain petrol at a garage with CCTV, assuming they knew about the cameras. There is no reason to suppose however that Madeleine was with them - she could only have been 'concealed' in the hatchback area. Even with a proper boot, concealing a kidnap victim in it is more difficult than it sounds, unless the victim is drugged, and drugging, especially of children, by non-medical personnel, brings its own problems. The author knows intelligence officers who have concealed people in boots of cars and it is usually done with willing adults for short hops across frontiers. It is not clear how much petrol was purchased, but it does not appear to have been a full tank (which in most versions of the Clio is 55 litres, just over 12 Imperial gallons), i.e. this may just have been a top- up, bearing in mind the snatch team had a long, night-time journey ahead of them, not all on *Autopistas*, nor could they know for sure that the request for a 12 hour getaway window would be honoured (it seems as though they asked for 15 hours including a 3-hour reserve, and DCCB in Lisbon cut it back to 12 as the magnitude of the blunder in selecting Madeleine became apparent).

23. Reporting suggests that the Renault Clio ends up at a safe house near National Route IV, within a 25-mile radius of Valdepenas, in the Toledo Region of Spain, south of Madrid. Reporting also suggests this facility includes a converted barn, where 'snuff' movies have been shot, and is surrounded by the shallow graves of dozens of children, whom reporting suggests are mostly French, kidnapped from the streets of Paris. Satellite observation appears to confirm the shallow graves. The CNI were tipped off, through a cut-out, backed up by direct contact with Spanish Intelligence in London. A number of intelligence officers may have reconnoitred this site, as the reporting is coming in from multiple sources. The *People* story on 4th June suggests, recklessly in the author's opinion (efforts, including liaison with the DA-Notice Committee, have been made for two weeks to keep mention of Morocco out of the public domain) that Madeleine may have been taken via the fast ferry from Tarifa in Spain to Tangiers. That is hardly likely (Moroccan Customs are efficient), but there is reporting of a team of two men and a woman in Morocco, and it may be the same team. Given the pressure now being applied on the safe house it is not unreasonable to suppose that the snatch team may have been ordered south to Morocco. The *People* report, which quotes sources "close to the investigation" suggests that GCHQ have been monitoring relevant mobile phone calls from Morocco, with references, unsurprisingly, to a German. German intelligence activity in Morocco of course goes back over a century (it was a German strategic ambition to control both sides of the approaches to the Straits of Gibraltar, and the brutal, failed 1971 coup was masterminded by Generalleutnant Otto Ernst Remmer of the DVD, a courageous but ruthless intelligence officer) (the DVD is an intelligence agency, not part of the German military, indeed it is not officially an organ of the German state at all, but when engaging DVD officers of general rank in conversation, e.g. the late Generaloberst Markus Wolf, it has been the author's experience that punctilious observance of rank is advised).
24. In the author's assessment the DVD-controlled rings (essentially any ring operating inside the EU and supplying bio-leverage material to the DVD) are sending children to this facility (and no doubt others) to be murdered in the course of snuff movies, after they have been abused to the point where they are no longer of interest to the politicians, officials and others being serviced. Their tragic and violent ends are then filmed for profit.

The MV (redacted)

25. Reporting placed Madeleine on the MV [redacted] as long ago as 18th May. This intelligence was passed immediately to the Operation *Task* incident room at Leicester, but it was accorded a low priority, even after the one-day conference on Thursday 24th May. With respect it does not seem to have been fully appreciated that positional intelligence of this type is time limited, i.e. it has to be verified and acted upon quickly. Contrary to the author's suggestion no application was made for military assistance to the civil power. The Chief of the Defence Staff (CDS) cannot be criticised for the decision to wait for such a request before acting – in the UK this has been a police-led, not intelligence-led inquiry, and the constitutional position is that military assets are not committed until requested. Operation *Task* in turn deferred to the DCCB, the reasoning being that it was up to the Portuguese to request a board and search. Such thinking would have been sound had there been any intelligence placing the [redacted] in the territorial sea of Portugal. This vessel was last reported alongside in Lagos as long ago as 29th September 2003 however and there is no reporting of her in Portuguese waters. The author makes no apology for pushing hard for this vessel to be tracked, boarded and searched.
26. The [redacted] is operated by the [redacted] Line, an ostensibly reputable company running tours to Sao Tome and Principe in the Gulf of Guinea, one of the world's less visited holiday destinations. Photographs of her appear at [redacted] under the 'research' tab. Further details, including her involvement in a search for gold [redacted] appear at [redacted] a site links [redacted] to the [redacted] Line and thence the [redacted]. She is a former trawler, built in New Orleans LA, originally named the MV [redacted]. She was sold to the [redacted] Line in Gibraltar in [redacted] (Royal Gibraltar Police have been extremely helpful and efficient). Her call-sign is [redacted], displacement [redacted] tons and registry, apparently, Portuguese. There is an infra-red and sound proofed compartment, where it is believed Madeleine was being held. The boat is fitted with a high-capacity A-Frame and appears to have had some interesting modifications below the waterline. She may be fitted with a hull-mounted sonar, possibly something like an Atlas Elektronik DBQS- 21D. It is not possible wholly to exclude two underwater 533mm torpedo tubes - the DVD have deep connections inside the German defence industry (and banks, especially those operating before 1945) and are involved in covert supplies of weapons, including torpedoes, to rogue states such as Iran.

27. Reporting places her 100 miles north or south of Casablanca, which should have been firmed up on or after 18th May by satellite or UAV recon. She is said to be alongside in a small port and reporting suggests that a team of two men and a woman (this might be the snatch team) come ashore in the evening and go to a bar, presumably for orders. Some of this reporting is probably based on covert ground observation, coming to the author through a cut-out. What is unclear is whether there was a direct transfer from the [redacted] or whether there was a fourth vessel involved.

JARIC/GCHQ

28. The NSA, were asked, informally, to assist as early as 6th May. They cannot confirm that directly of course, since any assistance was rendered on a deniable basis, but there is no reason to doubt that relevant IMINT and COMINT was being passed to GCHQ as early as 7th May, which was not passed to those who needed to know (i.e. Operation *Task*). Satellite coverage of the Moroccan coast, inevitably, is intermittent, giving windows of opportunity to the ring to move Madeleine onshore or to another vessel, perhaps briefly going to sea for that purpose. Courtesy of the deniable assistance of MCC an informal conference was convened in secure surroundings at Lord's on the 4th day of the First Test (Sunday 20th May)(the author will not lengthen this assessment by explaining to the US recipients how a ball game can go five days without a result), which so far as the author knows saw MOD and police for the first time in the same room at the same time discussing this case (reporting lines went back to CDS and the Metropolitan Police Commissioner, who chanced to be at Lord's that day). The author's recommendation was that with the consent of His Moroccan Majesty's Government Special Forces, with appropriate medical backing, be tasked to board and search the RV [redacted] preferably under hours of darkness, without delay. At that time it seemed she was anchored offshore, and one obvious method of covert approach would be to use an SSN, whilst allowing for the possibility of hull-mounted active and passive sonar arrays. Nothing was done however, that is to say everything was left to Leicestershire Constabulary, who left it to the Portuguese authorities, who made no request about which the author can be told to the Moroccan Government.
29. After dialling in on the morning of 30th May, the author received a call several hours later (no doubt after background checks and clearance) from a nice lady Flight Lieutenant at JARIC (Joint Air Reconnaissance Intelligence Centre), the intention being to hook JARIC up directly with

NSA on a STU-3 encrypted line. This system is compromised, but as always encryption provides delay and a degree of additional security. As the author well knew JARIC has been tasked to assist in searches for civilian detainees (e.g. the Johnson kidnap in Gaza Strip) and there are arrangements for sanitising (it has the facility to sanitise IMINT and pass it to civilian police). Interference was run from Whitehall however and JARIC were pulled off the search on the 31st. If the highly competent Flight Lieutenant has been re-assigned, the respectful suggestion to CDI is that she be restored to duty forthwith and promoted immediately to Squadron Leader. So far as the author is aware she is the only British intelligence officer to have grasped the implications of this case, the need to act without delay and the importance of having our intelligence community act in accordance with core British values, which do not, as the author conceives them to be, extend to leaving a helpless British infant to a grisly fate at the hands of a foreign power, however disguised those hands may be. These core values are shared with our American allies and if the NSA can act in accordance with them there is no reason, it is submitted, why DIS, GCHQ and JARIC could not follow their splendid, but deniable, example.

Moroccan Capabilities

30. With official paralysis in Whitehall, partly due, surely, to the dual premiership, which in practice has proved unworkable to the point of exposing British Citizens to mortal danger, two discreet channels were opened up to His Moroccan Majesty's Government. With respect His Majesty King Mohammed VI is a good king, and His Consort, Princess Salma, would undoubtedly have a deep understanding of the anguish of Madeleine's parents. It was reasonable to suppose the Moroccans would act with humanity and efficiency, but Madeleine is a British Citizen and there was no official request either from London, or her parents, who in practice are dependent for intelligence upon the DCCB (resources are being put into campaigning and rightly so, but no resources are available for intelligence-gathering). Moroccan capabilities should not be underestimated. They have a very usable UAV platform, the R4E-50, with a pre-programmable, GPS linked, navigation facility and an effective sensor suite including LLL TV with live downlink and Forward Looking Infra Red (FLIR). With an endurance of 12 hours 3 R4E-50s could give sustainable 24-hour recon of the vessel of interest. The Royal Guard are loyal and well trained, and despite the best efforts of the DVD's Karim al- Majati do not appear to have been penetrated by *al*

Qaeda. The Light Security Brigade would be available for back-up. The Royal Moroccan Air Force is well equipped and trained and at least two of their C-130H Hercules aircraft have been fitted with the Motorola APS-94 side-scan radar, ideal for the task. The Moroccans should still be asked to board and search the [redacted] since it is the best lead to Madeleine. The efficient Moroccan DST have capable interrogation experts, who would of course show an appropriate level of regard for the suspects' human rights.

Liege

31. It was unreasonable to suppose that with over two weeks of official inactivity and lack of co-ordination in London and Leicester the ring would continue to hold Madeleine on the [redacted]. It is reasonable to suppose efforts to move her were started soon after the Portuguese were tipped off from Leicester. There is recent (3rd June) OSINT reporting, prompting a 24 hour delay in completing this assessment, of a sighting of Madeleine in Liege, Belgium. Given known paedophile ring activity there and apparent tacit support, sadly, of the Belgian Government for the activities of the two DVD-backed rings on Belgian soil (which if true would be unsurprising given Belgium's support for the EU and the reported presence of paedophiles in the government), and the detail of the sighting report (noting the distinguishing feature in Madeleine's right eye), the author is inclined to treat it as *prima facie* credible (the sighting report by a Norwegian Subject, variously described as British or Nigerian, Marie Olli, in Marrakesh on 9th May, may be of Madeleine, but is much more likely to have been of a similar young girl - this would make sense as the ring is catering to a specific, depraved, paedophile taste).
32. This report needs verifying without delay. She may still be on board the [redacted] but that would require a remarkable degree of arrogance or complacency on the part of the ring and the DVD. If Madeleine is traced to Belgium, the assistance of the Belgian authorities may not be forthcoming and a Special Forces rescue mission is simply out. Tactical surprise could not be achieved. It would need to be a Special Forces led commando raid with air support (the British people would expect nothing less if told the Belgians had refused to help). Our forces would most likely have to fight their way out, protecting Madeleine to their utmost, runways would have to be disabled with JP233s and Coningsby's new Typhoon F1s would be needed for a CAP. The risks are obvious. Realistically, rather than mounting a rescue, the UK would need to ask the Belgians to rescue Madeleine and if such a request were

refused, break off diplomatic relations with the King of the Belgians (in reality Anglo-Belgian relations collapsed in the Gulf War) and issue an ultimatum, which would lead to (1) compliance and Madeleine's safe recovery (2) refusal, followed by the rapid collapse of the Belgian Government and compliance or (3) refusal and all that follows in public international law and relations between states when one state involves itself in the capture, sexual abuse and murder of infant children from another state for political purposes.

33. The Russians must be watching this fiasco with growing interest. They too have satellites, and their capable intelligence (which by the way had nothing whatsoever to do with the death of Lt-Col Litvinenko, as a close analysis of the autopsy report and the Polonium signature (Iranian, delivered via an airfield outside Hamburg) ought to reveal) will undoubtedly have determined the DVD to be involved. I am aware from conversations at a senior intelligence adviser to the President level in Moscow that the SVR are aware of the DVD, and know that 'commercial' German IMINT was supplied to the terrorists at Beslan by the DVD. I am led to believe that the Madeleine crisis featured in conversation between Presidents Putin and Clinton in a quiet meeting in Austria. The Russians are not angry at the moment with their wartime allies, but with their wartime enemies. The degree of German political influence in London and Washington is understood in Moscow, and the current diplomatic crisis is in reality a Russo-German crisis. Russian forces seem to have been put on a higher state of alert. No doubt JARIC are keeping an eye out for major Russian troop movements westwards and GCHQ are keeping an ear out for an increase in Russian military radio traffic and traffic between Moscow, Minsk and Warsaw. Polish Intelligence are well aware, at a senior level, of the DVD's role in the attempted assassination of Poland's courageous former Prime Minister Laszek Miller, in order to stop Poland vetoing a previous constitutional treaty, and Polish-German relations have cooled in consequence.

SSKs

34. There is reporting of unusual sonar traces, possibly picked up on the SOSUS network, of SSK activity in the Gulf of Cadiz/Lagos Bay sea areas, although how unusual may not have been clear at first. One or more transfers may have been executed by an SSK, including possibly a transfer to Belgium, but if so it will have been a very old, albeit refitted SSK, normally used for cocaine shipments to the US East Coast and the Iberian Peninsula. These will almost certainly be part of the small fleet

of Type XXI long-range transport U-Boats ordered by German Naval Intelligence in 1943 from the F. Schichau yard in Danzig, built under cover (these are the 'missing' Type XXIs U-2532, U-2547, U-2549, U-2550, U-3042 and U-3043, with a reduced torpedo load and large cargo hold forward, they were also adapted for carrying special passengers). One or more of these boats, and the [redacted] appear to be using an old covert U-Boat base in Sao Tome and Principe as a trans-shipment point. This base was used by boats such as Leutnant Jost Metzler's U-69 in 1941 (U-69 had two logs, like the KMS *Graf Spee*, one to show where she had been and one to show where she had really been). Typical cocaine load is about 50 metric tons.The DEA and National Drug Intelligence Center in the USA have been made aware. They are interested.

Robert Murat

35. Put very simply, he is not involved. He is a slightly odd character (not so odd that he pops out his glass eye as solemnly reported by the media - he is unsighted in one eye, but it is not glass) with a complicated private life, but there is not a shred of evidence linking him to this very grave crime. He does however have a British connection through his mother and was, it may be thought, a most convenient patsy.

Conclusion

36. Abandoning Madeleine to her fate is not, repeat not, an option. Aside from the dubious morality of such a course, the blow to British prestige would be immense and no government could survive the political fall-out. The younger and more vulnerable a British Citizen in mortal danger the greater the responsibility of government to protect her becomes. Any one disagreeing is welcome to watch what happens were a minister to try and hold such a position in the House of Commons. In reality the politically insane strategy of abandoning Madeleine is a deception strategy, i.e. it is based on the assumption that the truth that we know or knew where Madeleine was being held to a high degree of confidence could be withheld from the public. As they might say in CISEN (Mexican Intelligence): "no way, Jose".

Recommendations For Action

37. With great respect the double-hatting of the Permanent Secretary in the Cabinet Office is not working as well as it should, without criticising Sir Richard (it was not in any event his idea). The JIC should be brought in without delay, all available IMINT, COMINT and SIGINT should be made available to it, even if classified under the present equivalent of Spoke, COBRA should be convened, and the Prime Minister in Waiting, with respect, should take the chair. Madeleine should be located without delay, the boarding of the RV [redacted] should contribute to that, and Madeleine should be rescued. An urgent search should also be undertaken for linked SSKs. This operation will probably also lead to a minimum 50% reduction (say 175 metric tons) in DVD (in effect German) sponsored cocaine trafficking into the UK, saving perhaps 15,000 lives a year, and major interdictions of cocaine shipments into the US Eastern Seaboard. It should also lead to a major increase in understanding in the UKUSA Intelligence Community of the links between organised crime and hostile intelligence agencies. These are positive strategic outcomes.

Michael Shrimpton Advisory Board Gerard Group International LLC 1230Z05JUN07

Selected Bibliography and Further Reading

Al-Bayati, Dr Hamid, *The Terrorism Game*, London: Al-Rashid, 2001

Andrew, Professor Christopher and Mitrokhin, Vasili, *The Sword and the Shield: The Mitrokhin Archive and the Secret History of the KGB*, New York: Basic Books, 1999 - (Professor Andrew only), *The Defence of the Realm: The Authorised History of MI5*, London: Allen Lane, Penguin, 2009

Atkinson, Rodney, *Europe's Full Circle: Corporate Elites and the New Fascism*, Newcastle, Compuprint, 1996 (in his gracious dedication of my copy Rodney noted that "there are many roads to the truth and they converge the further one travels", a comment I wholeheartedly endorse)

Barlay, Stephen, *The Final Call: Air Disasters ... When will they ever learn?*, London: Sinclair Stephenson, 1990

Barnes, C.H., *Bristol Aircraft Since 1910*, London: Putnam, 3rd ed., 1988

Bartelski, Captain Jan, *Disasters in the Air: Mysterious Air Disasters Explained*, Shrewsbury: Airlife, 2001

Beatty, David, *The Naked Pilot: The Human Factor in Aircraft Accidents*, Shrewsbury: Airlife, 1995

Beckhough, Lt-Col Harry, *Secret Communications: The Hidden History of Code Breaking, from Earlier Centuries to Bletchley Park and the Cold War*, self-published 1995 - *In The Beginning*, Lewes, Sussex: The Book Guild, 2002

Beloff, Max (Lord Beloff), *Britain and the European Union: Dialogue of the Deaf*, Basingstoke, Hampshire: Macmillan, 1996 (all the texts written by the late Lord Beloff, a friend, before his untimely assassination in 1999 repay reading)

Bennetts, C.H. (Kit), *Spy*, Auckland: Random House, 2009

Bochaca, Joaquin, *Los Crimenes de los Buenos*, Madrid: Huguin 1982

Booker, Christopher and North, Dr Richard, *Castle of Lies: Why Britain Must Get Out of Europe*, London: Gerald Duckworth & Co., 1996 (in his dedication Christopher was kind enough to describe me as his "favourite cabaret act" - he was referring to my speaking, not my singing!)(I can't sing) - *Scared to Death: From BSE to Global Warming, Why Scares Are Costing Us The Earth*, London: Continuum, 2009

Bowman, Martin W., *The World's Fastest Aircraft*, Yeovil, Somerset: Patrick Stephens, 1960

Boyd Hunt, Jonathan, *Trial by Conspiracy*, Greenzone, 1996

Brink, Captain Randall, *Lost Star: The Search for Amelia Earhart*, New York: Bloomsbury, 1993

Brown, D. K. and More, George, *Rebuilding the Royal Navy*: *Warship Design Since 1945*, London: Chatham Publishing, 2003

Bryson, Bill, *At Home: A Short History of Private Life*, London: Doubleday, 2010 (very readable, like most of his output)

Burt, R. A., *British Battleships 1919-1939*, London: Arms and Armour Press, 1993

Buttler, Tony, *British Secret Projects: Jet Fighters Since 1950*, Hinckley, Leicestershire: Midland Publishing, 2000

- *British Secret Projects: Jet Bombers Since 1949*, Hinckley, Leicestershire: Midland Publishing, 2003

- *British Secret Projects: Fighters and Bombers 1935-1950*, Hinckley, Leicestershire: Midland Publishing, 2004

Chesnau, Roger, *Aircraft Carriers of the World, 1914 to the Present*, London: Arms and Armour Press, 2nd ed., 1992

Childers, Erskine, *The Riddle of the Sands: A Record of Secret Service*, London: Smith, Elder & Co., 1903

Churchill, Sir Winston Spencer, *The Second World War* London: Cassell, from 1948, starting with Volume 1, *The Gathering Storm* (a beautifully written inside account)

Cowell, Graham J., *D.H. Comet: The World's First Jet Airliner*, London: Airline Publications and Sales 1976, reprinted by Mach III Publishing in 1999

Connolly, Bernard, *The Rotten Heart of Europe*: *The Dirty War for Europe's Money*, London: Faber and Faber, 1995

Cooper, Alan W., *Target Dresden*, Bromley, Kent: Independent Books, 1995

Corsi, Dr Jerome, *Who Really Killed Kennedy?*, Washington: WND Books 2013

Curtis, Duncan, *Sabre: The Canadair Sabre in RAF Service*, History Press, 2005

Darling, Kev, *De Havilland Comet*, Ramsbury, Wiltshire: Crowood Press, 2005

Davies, Carl A., *Plane Truth: A Private Investigator's Story*, New York: Algora Publishing, 2001

Davies, R. E. G. and Birties, Philip J., *De Havilland Comet: The World's First Jet Airliner*, Shrewsbury: Airlife, 1999 (the Foreword to this book was written by the Comet's chief test pilot, the late Group Captain John 'Cats-Eyes' Cunningham)

Deacon, Richard (Donald McCormick), *The Israeli Secret Service*, London: Hamish Hamilton, 1977

De Havilland, Sir Geoffrey, *Sky Fever: The Autobiography of Sir Geoffrey de Havilland*, Shrewsbury: Airlife, 1979

Delattre, Luca, *Betraying Hitler: The Story of Fritz Kolbe*, Atlantic Books, 2005

Dowswell, Paul, Brocklehurst, Ruth and Brook, Henry, *Introduction to the World Wars*, London: Usborne Books, 2007 (this is a primer, rather an in-depth analysis - its great advantage lies in the clarity of its illustrations, e.g. the map of U-Boat sinkings in World War II)

Edwards, Alan, *Flights to Hell: The Investigation of Flying Accidents and the Development of Air Safety*, Nairn, Scotland: Thomas and Lochar, 1993

Einstein, Albert, *Relativity: The Special and the General Theory*, London: The Folio Society, 1994

Faith, Nicholas, *Black Box: Why Air Safety Is No Accident*, London: Boxtree, 1996

- *Black Box: The Final Investigations*, London: Boxtree, 1998

- *Mayday: The Perils of the Waves*, London: Boxtree, 1998

Farrell, Dr Joseph P., *Nazi International*, Kempton, IL: Adventures Unlimited Press, 2008

- *Saucers, Swastikas and Psyops*, Kempton, IL: Adventures Unlimited Press, 2011 (I respectfully part company with Dr Farrell on a number of points, but the postwar German intelligence network he is describing, albeit not by name, is the DVD)

Fitzgibbon, Constantine, *Secret Intelligence in the 20th Century*, London: Hart-Davis, 1976

Fleming, Ian, *Moonraker*, London: Jonathan Cape, 1955

Flintham, Vic, *Aircraft in British Military Service: British Service Aircraft Since 1946*, Shrewsbury: Airlife, 1998

Frame, Tom, *HMAS Sydney, Australia's Greatest Naval Tragedy*, Sydney: Hachette Books, 2008 (originally published 1995)

Francillon, Réne J., *Lockheed Aircraft*, London: Putnam, 2nd ed., 1987

Friedman, Dr Norman, *British Carrier Aviation: The Evolution of the Ships and their Aircraft*, London: Conway Maritime Press, 1988

- *British Destroyers and Frigates: The Second World War And After*, London: Chatham Publishing, 2006

- *Naval Firepower: Battleship Guns and Gunnery in the Dreadnought Era*, Barnsley, Yorkshire: Seaforth, 2008

Garnaut, Professor Ross, *The Garnaut Review 2011: Australia in the Global Response to Climate Change*, Port Melbourne, Australia: Cambridge University Press, 2011 (Professor Garnaut was kind enough to sign my copy, I shall sign his copy of this book and I hope that between us we shall set the gold standard for how to conduct violent disagreement between authors!)

Garrison, Judge Jim, *On The Trail of the Assassins: My Investigation and Prosecution of the Murder of President Kennedy*, New York: Paperless Publishing (e-book edition), 2012 (the single most important book in the vast Kennedy literature)

Gero, David, *Aviation Disasters: The world's major civil airliner crashes since 1950*, Yeovil, Somerset: Patrick Stephens, 2nd ed., 1996

Gill, Christopher, *In Their Own Words: The advocates of European Integration*, East Haddon, Northamptonshire: S. E. K. Publications, 1996

Goerner, Fred, *The Search for Amelia Earhart*, New York: Doubleday, 2000 (originally published in 1966, a great piece of research)

Gold, Ambassador Dore, *Hatred's Kingdom: How Saudi Arabia Supports the New Global Terrorism*, Washington DC: Regnery, 2003

Gorman, Teresa, with Kirby, Heather, *The Bastards: Dirty Tricks and the Challenge to Europe*, London: Sidgwick and Jackson, 1993

Graysmith, Robert, *The Murder of Bob Crane: Who Killed the Star of Hogan's Heroes?*, New York: Crown Publishers, 1993

Gunston, Bill, *World Encyclopedia of Aircraft Manufacturers*, Stroud, Gloucestershire: Sutton Publishing, 2nd ed., 2005

Hailey, Arthur, and Castle, John, *Flight Into Danger,* London: Pan Books, 1968 (paperback edition)

Hartlink, A. E., *The Complete Encyclopedia of Pistols and Revolvers,* Chartwell Books, 2013

Hayes, Stephen F., *The Connection,* New York: Harper Collins, 2004

Henderson, Scott, *Silent Swift Superb: The Story of the Vickers VC10,* Newcastle: Scoval, 1998

Herwig, Dieter and Rode, Heinz, *Luftwaffe Secret Projects: Strategic Bombers 1935-1945,* Hickley, Leicestershire: Midland Publishing, English ed., 2000

Hewart, Lord, (Rt Hon Lord Hewart of Bury CJ, Lord Chief Justice of England) Scott, *The New Despotism,* London: Ernest Benn Ltd,. 1929

Holmes, Martin, editor, *The Eurosceptical Reader,* Basingstoke: Macmillan, 1996

Holmes, Sir Paul, *Daughters of Erebus,* New Zealand: Hodder Moa, 2011

Hore, Captain Peter, RN, *Sydney: Cypher and Search,* London: Seafarer Books 2008

Ireland, Bernard, *Jane's Battleships of the 20th Century,* London: Harper Collins, 1996

Jackson, A.J., *De Havilland Aircraft Since 1909,* London: Putnam, 3rd ed., 1987

James, Derek N., *Gloster Aircraft Since 1917,* London: Putnam, 2nd ed., 1987

James, Admiral Sir William, *The Eyes of the Navy: A Biographical Study of Admiral Sir Reginald Hall,* London: Methuen & Co., 1956

Jenkins, Lindsay, *Britain Held Hostage: The Coming Euro-Dictatorship,* Washington DC: Orange State Press, 1997

- *The Last Days of Britain: The Final Betrayal,* Washington DC: Orange State Press, 2001

Job, Macarthur, *Air Disaster, Volumes 1-3,* Canberra, ACT: Aerospace Publications, 1998

Johns, Captain W.E., *Biggles in the Terai,* London: Knight, 1968

Jones, Barry, *British Experimental Turbojet Aircraft,* Ramsbury, Wiltshire: Crowood, 2003

Kahalani, General Avigdor, *The Heights of Courage: A Tank Leader's War on the Golan,* Tel Aviv: Steimatzky, 1988 (originally published in the USA by Greenwood Press, 1984)

- *A Warrior's Way*, Tel Aviv: Steimatzky, 1999 (Hebrew ed., 1988) Kaplan, Dr Robert, *The Soros Connection*, Israel: 2011

Keegan, Sir John, *Intelligence in War: Knowledge of the Enemy From Napoleon to Al Qaeda*, London: Random House, 2003 (generally any text by Sir John repays reading)

Kershaw, Tim, *Jet Pioneers: Gloster and the Birth of the Jet Age*, Stroud, Gloucestershire: Sutton Publishing, 2004

Keyhoe, Major Donald, USMC, *The Flying Saucers Are Real*, New York: Fawcett Publications, 1950

- *Flying Saucers From Outer Space*, New York: Holt, 1953

Law, Professor Stephen, *Believing Bullshit*, New York: Prometheus, 2011

Le Bailly, Vice-Admiral Sir Louis Le Bailly, *From Fisher to the Falklands*, London: Institute of Marine Engineers, 1991

- *The Man Around the Engine*, Emsworth, Hampshire: Kenneth Mason, 1990

Lomborg, Bjørn, *The Skeptical Environmentalist*, Cambridge: Cambridge University Press, 2001

Loomis, Vincent and Ethell, Jeffrey, *Amelia Earhart: The Final Story*, New York: Random House, 1985

Lovell, Mary S., *The Sound of Wings: The Life of Amelia Earhart*, New York: St Martyn's Press, 1989

Lukacs, John, *Five Days in London, May 1940*, London: The Folio Society, 2011, first published by Yale Univerity Press in 2001

Lumsden, Alec, *British Piston Aero-Engines and their Aircraft*, Shrewsbury: Airlife, 1994

Maclean, Iain, and Johnes, Martin, *Aberfan: Government and Disasters*, Cardiff: Welsh Academic Press, 2000

MacPherson, Malcolm, *Air Disasters: Dramatic Black Box Flight Recordings*, London: Collins, 2008

Matsen, *Titanic's Last Secrets*, New York: Grand Central Publishing 2009

McWhirter, Norris and Atkinson, Rodney, *Treason at Maastricht: The Destruction of the Nation State*, Newcastle: Compuprint, 2nd ed., 1995

Mehl, Hans, *Naval Guns: 500 Years of Ship and Coastal Artillery*, English ed. Rochester: Chatham Publishing, 2002, originally published by E. S. Mittler & Sohn, Hamburg, 2001

Melton, H. Keith, *Ultimate Spy*, London: Dorling Kindersley, 2nd ed., 2002

Mitchell, Gordon, *R.J. Mitchell: Schooldays to Spitfire*, Self-published, 1986, with support from Dowty-Messier and British Aerospace (R. J. Mitchell was Gordon Mitchell's father)

Morgan, Eric B. and Shacklady, Edward, *Spitfire: The History*, Stamford, Lincolnshire: Guild Publishing, 1988

Morgan, John, *Diana Inquest: the Untold Story*, Self-published, Amazon, 2009 *et seq.*, in six volumes (easily the most detailed published account of the murder)

Mote, Ashley, *Vigilance: A defence of British liberty*, Petersfield, Hampshire: Tanner Publishing, 2001

Mylroie, Dr Laurie, *Study of Revenge: The First World Trade Center Attack and Sadda Hussein's War Against America*, Washington DC: American Enterprise Institute, 2001

Nahum, Andrew, *Frank Whittle: Invention of the Jet*, Cambridge, England: Icon, 2004

Nordbruch, Claus, *Bleeding Germany Dry: The Aftermath of World War II from the German Perspective*, Pretoria: Contact Publishers, 2nd ed., 2003

Norway, Neville Shute, *No Highway*, London: William Heinemann, 1948

Oren, Michael B., *Six Days of War: June 1967 and the Making of the Modern Middle East*, Oxford: Oxford University Press, 2002 (all of Michael's writings are worthy of study)

Owen, David, *Air Accident Investigation*, Yeovil, Somerset: Patrick Stephens, 3rd ed., 2006

Painter, Martin, *The DH.106 Comet: An Illustrated History*, Tunbridge Wells, Kent: Air Britain, 2002 (a must-have text for researchers on the Comet, this is a standard work of reference)

Pincher, Chapman, *Their Trade is Treachery*, London: Sidgwick and Jackson, 1981 - *Inside Story: A Documentary of the Pursuit of Power*, London: Sidgwick and Jackson, 1981

Pollack, Kenneth M., *The Threatening Storm*, New York: Random House, 2002

Probert, Air Commodore Henry, *Bomber Harris, His Life and Times: The Biography of Marshal of the Royal Air Force Sir Arthur Harris, Wartime Chief of Bomber Command*, London: Greenhill, 2001 (I am proud to say that I had a minor input into this important biography, having been consulted by the Air Commodore over a most agreeable lunch at the Leander Club in Henley, where he was a member)

Raven, Alan, *Essex-Class Carriers*, Annapolis MD: Naval Institute Press, 1988

Reade, Leslie, *The Ship That Stood Still: The Californian and Her Mysterious Role in the Titanic Disaster*, Yeovil, Somerset: Patrick Stephens, 1993, edited by Edward P. De Groot

Roberts, John, *The Battlecruiser Hood*, London: Conway Maritime Press, 1982

Robbins, Guy, *The Aircraft Carrier Story 1908-1945*, London: Cassell, 2001

Saunders, Hilary St George and other authors, *The Royal Air Force 1939- 45*, London: HMSO, 1953 (this is the Official History of the RAF in World War II, in three volumes)

Sharpe, Justice Robert, *The Law of Habeas Corpus*, Oxford: Clarendon Press, 1989

Shore, Peter (Lord Shore of Stepney), *Separate Ways: The Heart of Europe*, London: Gerald Duckworth & Co., 2000

Skinner, Stephen, *British Airliner Prototypes Since 1945*, London: Midland Publishing, 2008

Skulski, Janusz, *The Battleship Yamato*, London: Conway Maritime Press, 1988 - *The Heavy Cruiser Takao*, London: Conway Maritime Press, 1994
Stewart, Stanley, *Air Disasters*, London: Ian Allan, 1986

Swanborough, Gordon and Bowers, Peter M., *United States Navy Aircraft Since 1911*, London: Putnam, 3rd ed., 1990

Tarrant, V. E., *King George V Class Battleships*, London: Arms and Armour Press, 1991

Taylor, Professor A. J. P., *English History 1914-1945, Oxford:* Oxford Press 1945

Taylor, Bruce, *The Battlecruiser HMS Hood: An Illustrated Biography*, London: Chatham Publishing, 2005, also published by the Naval Institute Press, Annapolis, MD.

Taylor, Frederick, *Dresden: Tuesday 13 February 1945*, London: Bloomsbury, 2004

Taylor, John W. R., *Aircraft Aircraft*, London: Hamyln, 1969

Thomas, Gordon, *Gideon's Spies: Mossad's Secret Warriors*, New York: St Martin's Press, 1999

Towler, James, *The Battle for the Settle to Carlisle*, Sheffield: Platform 5 Publishing, 1990

Tuchman, Barbara, *The Zimmerman Telegram*, London: The Folio Society, 2004, first published in England by Constable & Co., 1958

Waterton, W. A. and Hewat, Timothy, *The Comet Riddle*, London: Frederick Miller, 1955

Watton, Ross, *The Aircraft Carrier Victorious*, London: Conway Maritime Press, 1991

West, Nigel (Rupert Allason), *The Secret War for the Falklands*, London: Little, Brown and Co., 1997 (All of Nigel's intelligence texts are worth reading)

Whiting, Charles, *Canaris*, New York: Ballantine, 1973

Whitley, M. J., *Cruisers of World War Two: An International Encyclopedia*, London: Arms and Armour Press, 1995

Williams, Ray, *Fly Navy: Aircraft of the Fleet Air Arm Since 1945*, Shrewsbury: Airlife 1989

Winterbotham, Group Captain Frederick William, *The Nazi Connection: The Personal Story of a Top-Level British Agent in Pre-War Germany*, London: Harper Collins, 1978

Woodward, Admiral Sir Sandy and Robertson, Patrick, *One Hundred Days*, London: Harper Collins, 1992

Wright, Peter, *Spycatcher: The Candid Autobiography of a Senior Intelligence Officer*, New York: Viking, 2007

Yenne, Bill, *The Story of the Boeing Company*, St Paul, MN: Zenith, 2005

Index

Symbols

A

B

H

K

L

M

N

O

P

R

S

T

W

www.ingramcontent.com/pod-product-compliance
Ingram Content Group UK Ltd.
Pitfield, Milton Keynes, MK11 3LW, UK
UKHW042119240925
463253UK00003B/3